Welfare Benefits Handbook

Volume 2

1st edition

Carolyn George *et al*

Child Poverty Action Group

Published by CPAG
94 White Lion Street, London N1 9PF

© CPAG 1999

A CIP record for this book is available from the British Library

ISBN 1 901698 16 5

Design by Devious Designs 0114 275 5634
Typeset by Page Bros, Norwich
Printed by Clays Ltd, Bungay, Suffolk

Contents

Volume 2

Abbreviations used in the text

AA	Attendance allowance
AMA	Adjudicating medical authority
AO	Adjudication officer
BAMS	Benefits Agency Medical Service
CCB	Community charge benefit
CCG	Community care grant
CSA	Child Support Agency
CTB	Council tax benefit
DAT	Disability appeal tribunal
DEA	Disability employment adviser
DLA mobility	Disability living allowance – mobility component
DLA care	Disability living allowance – care component
DPTC	Disabled person's tax credit
DSS	Department of Social Security
DWA	Disability working allowance
EC	European Community
ECJ	European Court of Justice
EEA	European Economic Area
EEC	European Economic Community
EMO	Examining medical officer
EO	Employment officer
EOC	Equal Opportunities Commission
ES	Employment Service
ETF	Environment Task Force
ETU	Earnings top-up
EU	European Union
FC	Family credit
FEFC	Further Education Funding Council
GP	General practitioner
HB	Housing benefit
IB	Incapacity benefit
ICA	Invalid care allowance
IS	Income support
ITS	Industrial Tribunal Service

JSA	Jobseeker's allowance
LECs	Local Enterprise Companies
LMAO	Labour market adjudication officer
LMS	Labour Market System
MA	Maternity allowance
MAT	Medical appeal tribunal
MP	Member of Parliament
PAYE	Pay-as-you-earn
REA	Reduced earnings allowance
SDA	Severe disablement allowance
SERPS	State Earnings-Related Pension Scheme
SF	Social fund
SFI	Social fund inspector
SFO	Social fund officer
SHCU	Severe hardship claims unit
SHP	Severe hardship payment
SMP	Statutory maternity pay
SSAT	Social security appeal tribunal
SSP	Statutory sick pay
TECs	Training and Enterprise Councils
UB	Unemployment benefit
WFTC	Working families tax credit

Part 6

Work, incapacity for work and training schemes

Chapter 33

· ·

Work and incapacity for work

This chapter covers the rules about work and incapacity for work. It contains:
1. The full-time work rule (p2:5)
2. Incapacity for work (p2:14)
3. Appealing against a decision on your incapacity for work (p2:37)
4. Proposals for change (p2:42)

The full-time work rule (see p2:5) is relevant to your entitlement to:
- income support (IS);
- jobseeker's allowance (JSA);
- family credit (FC);
- disability working allowance (DWA); *and*
- earnings top up (ETU).

You should look at this chapter if you want to see if you count as in full-time paid work for the purpose of these benefits. (From October 1999 FC and DWA are due to be replaced by tax credits – see Chapter 23).

The full-time work rule is not relevant to your entitlement to other benefits although your entitlement to certain benefits may be affected by whether or not you work.

Your entitlement to some benefits may also be affected if your child works.

Your entitlement to **statutory sick pay** (SSP) and **statutory maternity pay** (SMP) is linked to your being employed – see pp1:16 and 1:92 for details of the rules relating to work for those benefits. You cannot qualify for SSP or SMP on the basis of self employment.

In order to qualify for **industrial injuries benefits** you must have been an employed earner (see p1:203 for details of this). Whether or not you are an **employed earner** or **self employed earner** is also relevant to your liability for national insurance contributions (see p2:256) and to the way your income from earnings is assessed for the purpose of mean's-tested benefits (see p2:387). However, the question of whether or not you are an employed or self employed earner is distinct from the full-time work rule.

You cannot qualify for **invalid care allowance** (ICA) if you are gainfully employed. Again this is distinct from the full-time work rule described in this Chapter. See p1:82 for the meaning of **gainful employment**.

The rules regarding **therapeutic work** which relate to your entitlement to benefits based on your incapacity for work are described later in this Chapter (see p2:16).

Lastly the rules relating to work for the purposes of your entitlement to maternity allowance are described on p1:101.

You can qualify for housing benefit (HB), council tax benefit (CTB), widow's benefits, disability living allowance, attendance allowance, child benefit, guardian's allowance and retirement pension whether or not you or your partner, if you have one, are working. However, your entitlement to an increase in your retirement pension for a dependant may be affected by the earnings of your adult dependant (see p2:96) and your entitlement to HB and CTB is affected by the level of income that you and your partner have.

You will not qualify for **child benefit, guardian's allowance**, or for an allowance within your **HB, CTB, IS** or **income-based JSA** for a child if the child is 16 or over and is working for 24 hours a week or more (see p2:124).[1] The work must be done for payment or in expectation of payment (see p2:7 for a discussion of what is meant by work done in expectation of payment).

Your entitlement to FC and DWA for a child aged 16 or over is dependant on her/him being in full-time non-advanced education (see p2:125).[2] Whether a child works does not affect your entitlement to FC or DWA but you will not be entitled to a credit within your FC, or an allowance within your DWA, for her/him if her/his income is over the amount of the credit or allowance (see p2:382).

You will only qualify for:
- SSP;
- IB;
- SDA;

if you are incapable of work. You may also qualify for:
- IS; *and*
- a disability premium within your IS, HB and CTB; *and*
- credited national insurance contributions.

This Chapter explains how the Benefits Agency assesses whether you are incapable of work for the purpose of IB, SDA, IS, national insurance credits and for the disability premium.

See p1:16 for how your incapacity for work is assessed for the purposes of SSP.

1. The full-time work rule

The full-time work rule (what the Benefits Agency calls '**remunerative work**') applies to the following benefits:

- income support (IS – see Chapter 20);
- jobseeker's allowance (JSA – see Chapter 14);
- family credit (FC – see Chapter 21);
- disability working allowance (DWA – see Chapter 22); *and*
- earnings top-up (ETU – see Chapter 24).

You will only qualify for **contribution-based JSA** if you are not in full-time work (your entitlement is not affected by whether or not your partner works).

You will only qualify for **IS** and **income-based JSA** if neither you nor your partner (if you have one) are in full-time work. However, the definition of full-time work differs for you and a partner (see below).

You will only qualify for **FC** if you or your partner are in full-time work (see p2:6)

You will only qualify for **DWA** and **ETU** if you are in full-time work.

See p2:4 if your child is working.

See pp2:387 and 2:396 for how your earnings affect your entitlement to means-tested benefits.

Full-time work

You will be considered to be in **full-time work** if you work for 16 hours or more each week (or 16 hours or more a week on average where your hours fluctuate) and you are paid or expect to be paid for the work (see p2:7).[3] If you are claiming IS or income-based JSA, your partner will be considered to be in full-time work if s/he works for 24 hours or more each week and is paid or expects to be paid for the work. Work includes self-employment and can also include work which is done from home (eg, writers) if you are paid or expect to be paid (see p2:7).[4] Paid lunch hours and breaks count towards the total hours you work, (and for DWA paid time off to attend a hospital or clinic in relation to your disability also counts),[5] as does overtime if you are paid for it or expect to be paid for it. Your total hours from more than one job are added together but, if you are claiming as a couple, you may not add your partner's hours to your own. See p2:7 for further information about how your hours are calculated.

In some circumstances a person who is actually working full-time may be treated as *not* working full-time (see p2:11). Also, there are some circumstances where people who are not actually working full-time may be treated as if they are (see p2:10).

In some circumstances you might be able to choose whether to claim IS/JSA or FC/DWA/ETU (see p2:13).

Income support and jobseeker's allowance

You cannot usually get IS or JSA if you are in full-time paid work (what the Benefits Agency calls 'remunerative' work). A partner's working hours do not affect your entitlement to *contribution-based* JSA, but you cannot usually get IS or *income-based* JSA if your partner works for 24 hours or more a week (or 24 hours a week on average where your partner's hours fluctuate). If you or your partner normally work over 16 to 24 hours, but are off sick or on maternity leave you can claim.[6]

Family credit, disability working allowance, or earnings top-up

To get FC, DWA or ETU, you or your partner must be in full-time paid work – what the Benefits Agency call 'remunerative work'. You or your partner must be employed at the date of claim (either as an employee or as someone who is self-employed – see p2:12). You are entitled if you or your partner work for 16 hours a week or more or, if your hours fluctuate, at least 16 hours a week, on average.[7] In addition, you must:[8]

- actually work for 16 hours or more in either the week in which you claim or one of the two preceding weeks; *or*
- be expected by your employers (or yourself if you are self-employed) to work for 16 hours or more in the week after the week you claim (this applies if you have just started work, for example); *or*
- if you are on holiday from work you must be expected to (or if you are self-employed, you expect to) work for 16 hours or more in the week after you return. You are not treated as on holiday if you are off sick or on maternity leave.[9]

The work must be your normal work and you must be likely to continue in that job for at least five weeks after your claim.[10] What is 'normal' depends on your individual circumstances[11] – eg, the likely future pattern of work, the past pattern and all other relevant circumstances.[12] If you have only just started work, but are likely to continue working, this should be sufficient to enable you to qualify.[13]

If you do not do at least 16 hours work the week in which you claim or one of the the two weeks preceding this, your claim is disallowed (unless you are expected to work in the week after the week in which you claim or you will be resuming work after a holiday and thus covered because you are *expected* to work more than 16 hours). This applies even if the reason you have not been working the necessary hours is because of sickness,[14] maternity leave, suspension, short-time working, lay-off or because you are only on call.[15] However, you should be treated as working if you are on duty and required to be available during a part of the day and/or night – eg, if you are a warden in sheltered housing.

What counts as paid work?

Paid work includes work for which you expect to be paid. This means you expect to get payment for work you are doing, now or at some date in the future.[16] You must have a real likelihood of getting payment for your work, not just a mere hope or desire to make money. A self-employed writer who has never sold a manuscript and has no agreement for publication may well be working with no real expectation of payment and so is not treated as being in full-time work even if s/he spends a lot of time writing.[17] However, to qualify for IS or JSA s/he would have to satisfy the other conditions of entitlement (see Chapters 20 and 14).

If you have set up a business and it is not yet making money but it is likely to do so in the future, you count as working in expectation of payment. Ultimately it depends on how viable your employment really is.[18]

Paid work includes work for which you receive payment in kind (such as free meals or accommodation[19] or free produce for farmworkers[20]). Note that payments in kind are generally not treated as 'earnings' (see p2:389) but as other income which may be disregarded (see p2:419).

Note that, for JSA, FC, DWA and ETU, all hours worked as a childminder are counted. For IS, the hours you work as a childminder are ignored, as long as the childminding is done in your own home.[21] Hours that you spend childminding in someone else's home are counted.

How your hours are calculated

In calculating your hours, include all the hours you actually work for which you are paid or which you do in expectation of payment. If you routinely need to work over your contractual hours, these extra hours also count. If you are self-employed, you count not only the hours spent on services for which you are paid, but also other time which is essential for your business – eg, preparation time.[22]

Where your hours fluctuate, your weekly hours are worked out as follows:
- If you have a regular pattern of work, the average hours worked throughout each work 'cycle' is used – eg, if you regularly work three weeks on and one week off, your hours are the average over the four week period.[23]
- If you work for part of a year only – for example, in a school or other educational establishment and your contract of employment continues throughout the year – your hours are averaged in a different way. The school holidays or similar vacations when you do no work are ignored, as are any periods not part of the school holidays when you are not required to work.[24] See p2:9 for more information about 'term-time only' workers.

- Where there is no recognisable pattern of work, the average over the five weeks immediately before the date of your claim is used, or over a longer or shorter period if this would be more accurate. The five-week period may not be appropriate when you have done a short period of overtime that is not typical or, for example, when there was a period of absence that distorts the average.[25]
- For **IS** and **JSA**, if you have just started work and no pattern of work is yet established or your working arrangements have changed and your previous work pattern no longer applies, the number of hours or average of hours you are expected to work each week is used.[26] This may happen if the change represents a new pattern of working or if there is a short-term change in your normal pattern. This may mean that you are no longer entitled to IS or JSA if your working hours increase or that you may qualify for IS or JSA if the number of hours you work each week goes down, for example, if temporary circumstances such as poor sales, bad weather or breakdown in equipment causes a reduction in hours. The decision may be reviewed when there is sufficient evidence to calculate the average of the actual hours you have been working.
- For **FC, DWA** and **ETU**, if you are employed and have not got a normal pattern of working hours (because you have just started a new job, or just changed your hours, or just returned to work after a break of more than four weeks – 13 for DWA), you qualify if it is expected that you will work 16 or more hours on average each week.[27] If you are self-employed and have not yet worked five weeks (or your hours have gone up to 16 or more over the past five weeks), you qualify if the average hours you expect to work amount to 16 or more.[28]

For **FC, DWA** and **ETU**, if you are unsure about whether you are working for 16 hours or more at the time of your claim, you should make a further claim in a week when you are more certain that you are working 16 hours or more. This is because it may take the Benefits Agency a long time to send you a decision on your first claim and, if the first claim is refused because you were working less than 16 hours a week, any second claim only runs from the date it is made unless you meet one of the specific reasons for having a claim backdated (see p2:489). Alternatively, if you are refused FC or DWA because you or your partner are not in full-time work and within 14 days of that decision you claim IS or JSA, your claim for IS or JSA can be backdated to the date you claimed FC or DWA.[29] Similarly, if you are refused IS or JSA because you or your partner are in full-time work and you claim FC or DWA within 14 days of that decision, your claim for FC or DWA can be backdated to the date you claimed IS or JSA.[30]

Appeal if you think your average hours have been calculated unfairly (see Chapter 56) if this means you cannot claim the benefit you want. You should work out first whether you are better off claiming IS/JSA or FC/ETU/DWA (see p2:13).

'Term-time only' workers

The rule for calculating average hours if you only work for part of a year means that it is the average of the hours of work during term-time which determine whether you are in full-time work throughout the year (see p2:7). If you work less than 16 hours a week during term-time you are eligible for IS or JSA. However, if you work 16 hours or more each week you are eligible for FC, ETU or DWA instead. If the average number of hours you work during term time is 16 or more, the Benefits Agency may say you are not entitled to IS or JSA during the school holiday, even if you are not paid any wages during the holidays. You may be able to challenge this if:

- Your contract of employment finishes at the end of school term.[31] Some non-teaching and teaching staff (eg, supply teachers) at schools or other educational establishments are not employed throughout the year; instead their contract terminates at the end of each term (for example, you may be employed as a sub-contractor rather than directly by the school or local authority). Where a term-time claim is made and the hours worked fluctuate, the average hours are calculated in the way described on p2:7 'How your hours are calculated'. If your claim is made after the contract has terminated – ie, during the school holiday – you should not be treated as in full-time work.

- Your contract continues over the school holidays you should only be treated as in full-time work for any part of the school holidays which is a 'recognised, customary or other holiday'.[32] If you are a school ancillary worker (such as a canteen assistant) rather than a teacher or lecturer, the school holidays are not necessarily recognised, customary, or other holidays in relation to you, but are often just periods of lay-off imposed by you employer and you should not be treated as in full-time work for such periods of lay-off.[33] If you are paid for some weeks of the school holiday you will normally be considered to be in full-time work during those weeks. However, the Benefits Agency has to determine the actual weeks that your holiday pay covers - if the holiday pay is not attributed to certain days the Benefits Agency has to consider which weeks you think of as your holiday, or if you have actually taken a holiday, when that was. It is important to remember that if you do not work full-time during term-time you should not be considered to work full-time during school holidays even if you are paid over those holidays.

If you are refused benefit in these circumstances seek advice.

If you are not considered to be in full-time work over the school holidays you may qualify for IS or JSA if you satisfy the qualifying conditions for those benefits. You will not qualify for JSA unless you can show that you are actively seeking work and available for work over the school holiday - in reality this may be difficult if you are only available for work for a short period. However, if you have a reasonable prospect of finding a full-time temporary job you should be considered to be available for work (see p1:297 for more details about availability for work and JSA).

You should always get advice before considering any changes to your contract of employment which might affect your employment rights.

People treated as being in full-time work

For the purposes of IS and JSA, you or your partner **are treated** as being in full-time work if:

- You or your partner normally work full-time, but you are off work because of a recognised, customary or other holiday.[34] If you do not get any holiday pay, you could try for a crisis loan (see p1:667) but you are not entitled to a JSA hardship payment (see p1:432).

  Whether you count as on holiday depends on the type of work you do. If you are a 'term-time only' worker (see p2:9), for example, a canteen assistant in a school or other educational establishment (as opposed to a teacher) and do not work in the school holidays, you can argue that you are not on holiday, nor are you in full-time work.[35] If your contract ends at the end of the school term, you do not count as being on holiday (see p2:9). You should always get advice before considering any changes to your contract of employment which might affect your employment rights.

- You or your partner are away from full-time work without a good reason ('good cause').[36] What constitutes 'good cause' for these purposes is not defined in the regulations but all of your circumstances should be taken into account in considering whether you have good cause for your absence. Whether or not your employer has authorised the absence is not conclusive, although if it is authorised it is likely that you have a good reason.

- You or your partner have stopped full-time work but you are still within the period covered by earnings received from your full-time work. You are treated as in full-time work during any period for which you receive:
  - pay in lieu of wages; *or*
  - pay in lieu of notice; *or*
  - holiday pay from your last job. However, unless you are involved in a trade dispute (see p2:187), you are not treated as in full-time work for any period for which you receive holiday pay if this is due to be paid more than four weeks after you left your job; *or*
  - an *ex gratia* payment in recognition of loss of employment[37]

  See p2:392 'Payments at the end of a job' for details of the periods covered by these payments.

- For JSA, your partner is treated as in full-time work if s/he is involved in a trade dispute and s/he would not be entitled to JSA in her/his own right because of this. Your partner is treated as in full-time work for the first seven days of the stoppage of work or withdrawal of labour, but this does not apply if you were receiving income-based JSA when the trade dispute started.[38] You cannot get JSA if you are the person involved in a trade dispute (see p2:191).

- For **IS**, you or your partner are involved in a trade dispute but only for the first seven days which fall after either the day the stoppage of work started or the day you withdrew your labour.[39]

People treated as not being in full-time work

For **FC, DWA, ETU, IS** and **JSA**, you or your partner **are treated** as not being in full-time work if:[40]

- you or your partner are working on a government training scheme and are being paid a training allowance;
- you or your partner are a volunteer or are working for a charity or voluntary organisation and are giving your services free (except for your expenses). Where you receive any nominal payment that is not just for your expenses you could be counted as in full-time work (but see p2:421 on 'notional income' rules), unless this is for a specific number of hours a week (under 16) and you are a volunteer for the remainder of the time;
- you or your partner are providing respite care for someone if the person requiring the care is staying with you and they are not normally a member of your household and you receive payments from a health authority, local authority or voluntary organisation for caring for them;
- for **IS** and **JSA**, you or your partner are disabled and because of this:
  - your earnings are 75 per cent or less of what a person without your disability would reasonably expect to earn, working the same hours in that job, or in a comparable one in the area; *or*
  - you work 75 per cent or less hours than those a person without your disability would reasonably be expected to work in that job or in a comparable job in the area;
- for **IS** and **JSA**, you or your partner are a foster parent receiving a payment for fostering a child from a local authority, voluntary organisation or a care authority (in Scotland);
- for **IS** and **JSA**, you or your partner work as a part-time firefighter, auxiliary coastguard, member of the territorial army or reserve forces, or a member of a lifeboat crew;
- for **IS** and **JSA**, you or your partner are performing duties as a local authority councillor;
- for **IS** and **JSA** you or your partner are working while living in a residential care or nursing home, or a local authority home.[41] This also applies during temporary absences from the home. It only covers people who are paid benefit at the special rates for people in homes;

- for **JSA**, your partner is involved in a trade dispute and it is more than seven days since it started.[42] In these circumstances s/he is not treated as being in full-time work. See p2:191 if you are the person involved in a trade dispute;
- for **IS**, you or your partner are involved in a trade dispute and it is more than seven days since the dispute started (see p2:188). This also applies for the first 15 days following your return to work after having been involved in a trade dispute. You can claim if you satisfy the other rules for getting IS described in Chapter 20;
- for **IS**, you are caring for someone (see p1:443). The Benefits Agency says that any hours of work you do are ignored, not just hours you spend caring;[43]
- for **JSA**, you are caring for someone, the hours that you spend caring for someone in the circumstances that allow you to claim IS as a carer (see p1:443) are ignored when deciding whether you are in full-time work unless you are employed and are being paid to act as a carer;[44]
- for **IS**, you are working as a childminder in your home;[45]
- for **FC** and **DWA**, the work you do is studying in connection with your course of education as a student.[46]

Although you or your partner are treated as not being in full-time work in these circumstances (although other work done at the same time is counted), to receive IS or JSA you must satisfy the other qualifying conditions. For JSA, you may be able to place restrictions on your availability for work because of your circumstances – for example, you are a carer or you have a disability (see pp1:296 and 1:297). If you are treated as not being in full-time work for the purpose of IS or JSA but are treated as being in full-time work for the purposes of FC, ETU or DWA you will be able to choose whether to claim IS/JSA or FC/DWA/ETU. In these circumstances you should work out which benefit you would be better off claiming (see p2:13 'In work or out of work benefits?').

Self-employed people

The full-time work rule applies to self-employed as well as employed earners. If you simply invest in a business and do not help to run it you are not treated as self-employed.[47]

A problem for some self-employed people is that they work long hours for little financial reward, sometimes even making a loss. Nevertheless, if you work for 16 hours a week or more and if the work is done in expectation of payment, it counts as full-time work. If you are in this position and you are considering reducing your hours to below 16 or abandoning your self-employment altogether you should first seek specialist advice. Alternatively, you may be entitled to FC, DWA or ETU (see Chapters 21, 22 and 24) to top-up your earnings from self-employment.

In calculating the number of hours that you work each week, the adjudication officer (AO) counts all the hours necessary to run your business, including time you spend visiting potential customers, advertising or canvassing, book-keeping and trips to wholesalers and retailers.[48] The AO should accept your statement about the hours you work unless there is a reason to doubt what you say.[49] The hours your partner spends helping you in your business do not affect your entitlement to *contribution-based* JSA, but if your partner works 24 hours a week or more you are not entitled to IS or *income-based* JSA. If your partner is working for you but not getting paid, s/he may be treated as receiving notional income (if you could afford to pay it) if s/he is an 'employee' (see p2:424).

Allowances which are paid under certain schemes to help you become self employed are not counted as payment for work.[50] However, if you work in your business for 16 hours or more each week and you reasonably expect to receive payment (other than your allowance), you are treated as being in full-time work. If you work less than 16 hours a week, you should check that you still qualify for the allowance from the scheme because this is usually paid to enable you to work full-time.

The Benefits Agency counts payments from your business to meet living expenses, whether in cash or in kind as payment for work unless the drawings are from the business capital.[51]

Like FC and DWA, ETU once awarded is normally paid for a fixed period of 26 weeks. If you are self employed you cannot qualify for an award of ETU if:

- your normal weekly earnings are calculated as £20 a week or less for the period of the award (see p2:396 for details of how earnings from self employment are calculated); *and*
- your earnings have been calculated as £20 a week or less for four previous awards of ETU.[52]

In-work or out-of-work benefits

Sometimes it is difficult to show that you normally work at least 16 hours a week and the distinction between **in-work benefits** (FC, ETU or DWA) and **out-of-work benefits** (IS or JSA) is not absolute. For example, you may fail to qualify for IS because you are found to be in full-time work, yet still fail to qualify for FC because the work is held not to be the work you normally do. You may also be refused both FC and IS because adjudication officers at the local Benefits Agency office and the Family Credit Unit interpret the rules, on the same facts, differently. If this happens, appeal against both decisions and ask for them to be heard together so a tribunal can decide which benefit is appropriate. In the meantime you could apply for interim payments (see p2:499). Note, however, that you are only eligible for an interim payment when you are appealing if it is clear that you are entitled to some benefit, and even then you may get turned down (see p2:499).

You could claim either in-work or out-of-work benefits if you have a partner and s/he works for 16 hours or more a week but less than 24 hours a week.[53] Alternatively, if you are a childminder working from home for 16 hours or more a week, you are not treated as in full-time work for the purposes of IS (see p2:12), and so may be entitled to claim either IS or FC, ETU, or DWA. In either case you may choose which benefit to claim. If you have to pay housing costs (see Chapter 46), in most cases it is better to claim IS or JSA. You may even claim both IS or JSA and FC, ETU or DWA at the same time. Although FC counts as income for IS and JSA purposes (see p2:405), it may still be worthwhile claiming FC if your circumstances are likely to improve in the foreseeable future as you may still keep your FC award for up to 26 weeks (see p1:468). Seek advice if this applies to you.

2. Incapacity for work

This section explains how the Benefits Agency assesses whether you are incapable of work for the purposes of qualifying for the following benefits:[54]
- incapacity benefit (IB);
- severe disablement allowance (SDA);
- income support (IS), if you are claiming this on the basis of being incapable of work;
- the disability premium within IS, housing benefit (HB) and council tax benefit (CTB) if your entitlement to the premium depends on you showing that you have been incapable of work;
- national insurance credits for incapacity.

A decision that you are capable or incapable of work in the context of a claim for one of these benefits is conclusive for the purpose of all the others.[55] A decision that you are capable of work is also conclusive for the purpose of a claim for jobseeker's allowance (JSA – see Chapter 14).[56]

The way your incapacity for work is assessed for the purpose of **statutory sick pay** (SSP) is explained in Chapter 2 – the rules described in this Chapter do not apply to SSP or to the assessment of your incapacity for work for the purpose of **industrial injuries benefits** (see Chapter 11).

If you are making a claim for a non-means tested benefit such as IB or SDA on the basis of your incapacity for work you should also consider applying for IS, HB and CTB. If you qualify for them, these benefits may be paid in addition to your non-means tested benefit although any IB or SDA you receive will be treated as income when calculating your entitlement to IS, HB, or CTB. As it may take the Benefits Agency some time to decide whether you qualify for a non-means tested benefit it is also worth claiming IS if you can, as your application for the other benefit may be refused.

If you are claiming IS or a disability premium within your IS, HB, or CTB and you are not receiving SSP, the Benefits Agency expects you to complete a claim form for IB (an SC1 or SSP1 form – see p1:50) and to send it to your local Benefits Agency with a medical certificate to allow them to assess whether you are incapable of work. You should do this even if you know that you will not qualify for IB.

'Incapable of work'

For all benefits except SSP and industrial injuries benefits, the question of whether you are incapable of work is assessed by way of one of two tests:
- the **own occupation test**, which applies for the first 28 weeks of your claim if you have a regular occupation when you fall ill (see p2:21); *or*
- the **'all-work' test**, which applies after 28 weeks, or from the start of your claim if you do not have a regular occupation when you fall ill (see p2:22).

Department of Social Security's Medical Service

The DSS has contracted a private company (referred to in this Handbook as the Medical Service) to provide advice to adjudication officers on medical questions relating to your incapacity for work. The Medical Service (MS) also carries out medical examinations of claimants. As a result of this you may be asked whether you agree to details of your medical condition and history being given to the Medical Service. It is not likely to be in your best interest to refuse to give your authorisation for this. The adjudication officer (AO) relies heavily on the MS doctor's assessment of your condition when making a decision on your incapacity for work, and the MS doctor's assessment may be incomplete if they have not been able to obtain information about your medical situation.

In addition, if you refuse to attend a medical examination by a MS doctor the AO can treat you as capable of work unless you have good cause for your refusal to attend (see p2:35). An unwillingness to be examined by a doctor from the MS would be unlikely, by itself, to be considered good cause for not attending.

The MS and the Benefits Agency must ensure that any information they obtain about you remains confidential.

Treated as incapable of work

In certain circumstances it is assumed that you are incapable of work without you having to satisfy the own occupation test or the 'all-work' test. In these circumstances you are treated as incapable of work whether or not you actually are. This is because:
- certain people do not have to satisfy the own occupation test or all-work test but are deemed to be incapable of work (see p2:18);
- when the all-work test applies, certain people are exempt from the test and are treated as incapable of work (see p2:24);

- certain people who fail the all-work test can be treated as incapable of work in 'exceptional circumstances'(see p2:28).

Work you may do while claiming

Even if it has been decided that you are incapable of work you are treated as capable of work for any week (starting on a Sunday) in which you actually do work. You are treated as capable of work for the whole week even if you do not work for the whole week. This applies whether or not you are paid for the work.[57]

However, you are only treated as capable of work on the actual days that you work, rather than for the whole week, if you work:
- during the first week of your claim; *or*
- during the last week that you were incapable of work; *or*
- during any week when you are undergoing treatment by way of plasmapheresis, parenteral chemotherapy, or radiotherapy, or regular weekly treatment by way of renal dialysis or total parenteral nutrition.

The following kinds of work are ignored, so you may undertake these kinds of work without being treated as capable of work:[58]
- the care of a spouse, a partner (if you live together as husband and wife), or relative (a relative is a parent, a son, a daughter, a parent-in-law, son or daughter-in-law, step-parent, step-son or daughter, brother, sister, or the partner or spouse of any of these relatives, a grandparent, grandchild, uncle, aunt, niece or nephew);
- domestic work (ie, cooking and cleaning, etc.) in your own home;
- work which is done only to protect someone or prevent serious damage to property or livestock during an emergency;
- work as a local councillor;
- work (for a maximum of one day a week) as a member of a disability appeal tribunal (see p2:627) or of the Disability Living Allowance Advisory Board;
- voluntary work if the work is not for a close relative and if the only payment you receive for the work is to cover your reasonable expenses. A close relative is a parent, a son, a daughter, a parent-in-law, son- or daughter-in-law, step-parent, step-son or daughter, brother, sister, or the partner or spouse of any of these relatives;[59]
- 'therapeutic' work which is work:[60]
  - which you do on the specific advice of your doctor; *and*
  - for which you do not earn more than £58.00 a week net; *and either*
  - you do for less than 16 hours a week, (but see p2:17), and which helps to improve, prevent, or delay the deterioration in the disease or disablement which causes your incapacity for work; *or*

- is part of a medically supervised treatment programme while you are an in-patient or a regular out-patient at a hospital or similar institution (see below for the meaning of similar institution); *or*
- is done as part of a sheltered work scheme for people with disabilities.

If you are considering doing 'therapeutic work' it may be advisable to consult the Benefits Agency first. This is because the rules are strict and it is important to ensure that you are not treated as capable of work.

In addition, if you work but the amount of work that you do is so minimal that it can be regarded as trivial or negligible you should not be treated as capable of work.[61] So, for example, a man who occasionally helped his florist wife to cut or pack a few flowers was not treated as capable of work as the work he did was considered negligible.[62]

If you are claiming IS, although you will not be considered to be capable of work as a result of doing any of these types of work, the hours that you work may affect your entitlement to benefit. If you work for 16 hours or more a week, and the work is done for payment or in expectation of payment, you will not qualify for IS (see p2:6), unless you can be treated as not being in full-time work (see p2:11).

The meaning of **'similar institution'** is not defined in the legislation. Guidance to AOs advises them to take account of the purpose of the institution, the type of treatment provided and the level of care offered when deciding whether someone is in a 'similar institution'.[63] The accommodation clearly must be an 'institution' and a Commissioner has stated that this means that there must be some sort of formal body or structure which controls all aspects of the care and treatment provided, including the premises where the treatment is carried out. So, for example, people renting accommodation from a private landlord where 24 hour nursing help and care was provided by the local health trust were considered not to be in a hospital or 'similar institution'.[64] The term 'similar institution' can include certain types of residential care homes and nursing homes.[65]

16-hour rule

'Therapeutic work', (which is done on the basis that it helps prevent or delay the deterioration in your condition – see p2:16), is only disregarded if you do such work for less than 16 hours a week.[66]

It is the average number of hours that you work which is important. Even if you work more than 16 hours in a week you are not treated as capable of work in that week if the average number of hours which you normally work is less than 16. Your average hours are calculated in the following way:
- if you have a normal work cycle, over the period of that cycle;
- otherwise, over the five weeks up to the end of the week which is at issue.

The rules on therapeutic work which applied before 13 April 1995 were more favourable, allowing claimants to do work for which there was 'good cause' (see pp49 and 50 of CPAG's *Rights Guide to Non-Means-Tested Benefits* 17th edition). If you were doing therapeutic work under these rules immediately before the new rules came into force, the old rules continue to apply to you even if you work for 16 hours a week or more until either:[67]

- you do no work for 57 continuous days; *or*
- your period of incapacity for work (see p1:40) comes to an end.

Deemed incapacity

You can be deemed to be incapable of work without having to satisfy the 'all-work' test or the own occupation test (see pp2:22 and 2:21):[68]

- if you are under medical observation as the possible carrier of an infectious or contagious disease, (or you have been in contact with a person with such a disease), and a medical officer for environmental health has given you a certificate excluding you from work; *or*
- if you are receiving in-patient treatment (including nursing) at a hospital or in a 'similar institution' (see p2:17); *or*
- on days when you are receiving treatment by way of plasmapheresis, parenteral chemotherapy, or radiotherapy or regular weekly treatment by way of renal dialysis or total parenteral nutrition; *or*
- on days when you are pregnant and there would be a serious risk to your health or your baby's health:
  - when the own occupation test applies to you, if you continue to work in your own occupation; *or*
  - when the 'all-work' test applies, if you work in any occupation;[69] *or*
- if you are pregnant or have recently had a baby; *and*
  - you would not be entitled to either maternity allowance or statutory maternity pay were you to make a claim; *and*
  - you are within the period beginning with the first day of the sixth week before the expected week of childbirth (see p1:106 or beginning with the actual day of your confinement if that is earlier), and ending on the 14th day after the date you had the baby; *and*
  - you have produced a certificate of your expected date of confinement or your actual date of confinement; *or*
- if you are a 'welfare to work beneficiary' (see p2:19 for the meaning of this), you can be treated as incapable of work without having to satisfy the own occupation test or all work test for up to 91 days if
  - in your last period of incapacity for work (see p2:19) you were either assessed under the all work test and found to be capable of work, or you were exempt from the all work test for one of the reasons described on p2:24 'People who are exempt from the all work test' (but not for the reasons given in the first two bullet points in that section); *and*
  - you submit a medical certificate confirming that you are incapable of work to the Benefits Agency; *and*

- you claim benefit for any day in your 52-week linking period (see p2:20); *and*
- the days fall within your 52-week linking period or within the first 13 weeks after the end of the 52-week linking period.

The 91 days do not need to be consecutive and so can be separated by days when you work or are not incapable of work. If you are incapable of work for more than 91 days within the above period you will have to satisfy the own occupation test or the all work test from the 92nd day of your incapacity for work (unless you can be treated as incapable of work for another reason).

Welfare to work beneficiary

You are a 'welfare to work beneficiary' if:

- you have stopped receiving a benefit (except SSP) which you were entitled to on the basis of being incapable of work (see p2:20) after being incapable of work for more than 196 days - known as your 'last period of incapacity for work' (you do not have to have been receiving benefit for all of the 196 days); *and*
- you are within the 52-week period which runs from the first day after the end of that period of incapacity for work (called the 52-week linking period); *and*
- your benefit stopped on or after 5 October 1998; *and*
- within a week of your entitlement to benefit stopping you start a training course for which you receive a training allowance, or you start work and you are paid for that work or you expect to be paid; *and either*
  - within a month of your entitlement to benefit stopping you notify the Benefits Agency that you have started work or training. You may notify the Benefits Agency either verbally or in writing. If you can, notify the Benefits Agency in writing, keeping a copy of your letter. If you notify them verbally be sure to make a note of the date you notify them and of the name of the person you told; *or*
  - you have successfully appealed against a decision that you were capable of work and as a result you have been incapable of work for more than 196 days. In this situation you do not have to notify the Benefits Agency of the fact you have started work or training and you only have to start work or training within one week of your entitlement to benefit ending not within a week of the decision that you were capable of work.

Even if you satisfy these conditions you will not be a welfare to work beneficiary if:

- your 'last period of incapacity for work' (see above) ended because you were found to be capable of work and either you did not appeal against this or you appealed but did not win your appeal; *or*
- you have previously had a 52-week linking period on the basis of being a welfare to work beneficiary and your most recent period of incapacity for work ended less than 28 weeks after the end of your last 52-week linking period;

- the work that you have started within a week of your benefit stopping is work that you can do while still being considered incapable of work (such as therapeutic work – see p2:16).

You will have been receiving benefit based on your incapacity for work if you were receiving IB, SDA, IS on the basis of your incapacity for work, national insurance credits for incapacity for work (see p2:267), or a disability premium within your IS, income based JSA, HB or CTB paid on the grounds that you are incapable of work.[70]

The 52-week linking period

You are only a 'welfare to work beneficiary' for a fixed 52-week period running from the day after the end of your 'last period of incapacity for work' (see p2:19). As this 52-week period is fixed it is not affected by whether you subsequently stop work or training or whether or not you have periods of incapacity for work within it.

If you are a welfare to work beneficiary as well as being treated as incapable of work for up to 91 days in the circumstances described on p2:18, you can immediately return to the same benefit and the same level of benefit that you were receiving before you started work or training, if you become incapable of work again within your 52-week linking period. Once your 52-week linking period ends you are no longer considered to be a welfare to work beneficiary. You can only become a welfare to work beneficiary again if at least 28 weeks have passed since the day your last 52-week linking period ended and you satisfy the other conditions described on p2:19. You will therefore have to have been incapable of work for a further 196 days. However, any days of incapacity for work which fall within your previous linking period can be counted when calculating whether you have been incapable of work for 196 days.

Example

Claudia has been incapable of work for over a year and has been receiving the long term rate of IB. She has been assessed as incapable of work under the all work test. She finds a job and stops claiming IB the day before her job starts. She notifies the Benefits Agency that she has started work on the day she starts her job. She works for four months but then becomes ill. Because she is considered to be a welfare to work beneficiary and is within her 52-week linking period she is not entitled to SSP from her employer (see p1:20) but she claims IB and is immediately entitled to the long term rate of IB. She is sick for two months and during those two months she is treated as incapable of work without having to satisfy the own occupation test or the all-work test. She then returns to work but seven months later becomes ill again. As she is by then outside her 52-week linking period she is no longer considered to be a welfare to work beneficiary. She therefore receives SSP from her employer.

The 'own occupation' test

If you cannot be deemed to be incapable of work your incapacity for work will be assessed by way of the own occupation test for the first 28 weeks of your incapacity for work if you have a regular occupation when you become ill or disabled (see below 'When the own occupation test applies'). The own occupation test is a test of:

whether [you are] incapable by reason of some specific disease or bodily or mental disablement of doing work which [you] could reasonably be expected to do in the course of the occupation in which [you were] engaged.[71]

Caselaw has helped to clarify what is meant by **'specific disease'**. Specific disease means a disease which has been identified by medical science.[72] This does not mean that you must have had a definite diagnosis before you are held to be incapable of work as, for example, the presence of symptoms may be sufficient to confirm that you are suffering from a disease. A disease is a departure from health capable of identification by its signs and symptoms.[73] If you do not have a specific disease, you may still satisfy the own occupation test if your incapacity for work arises from a bodily or mental disablement.

When the own occupation test applies

The own occupation test applies to you if you have a regular occupation when you become incapable of work. You are considered to have a regular occupation if, in the 21 weeks immediately before the start of your period of incapacity for work, you did paid work for more than eight weeks in one occupation for at least 16 hours a week.[74] Paid work includes work which is done in expectation of payment even if no payment is received.

All work done for the same employer counts as one occupation. If you have worked for more than one employer or have been self-employed during the period, you are still considered to have one occupation as long as all the jobs you did were of the same kind.[75] If you worked for at least 16 hours a week in two or more occupations for more than eight weeks during the 21-week period, the own occupation test applies to your last occupation. However, if you were working in more than one occupation during the last week in which you worked you must satisfy the own occupation test for each occupation.[76] If you normally work in an occupation for at least 16 hours a week, you are still treated as working in that occupation during any week when you are on paid or unpaid leave.[77]

The own occupation test applies for the first 196 days of your period of incapacity for work (see p2:22). When calculating this 196 day period you only count days:[78]

- when you were incapable of work; *or*
- when you are treated as incapable of work; *or*

- when you were entitled to SSP; *or*
- which fall within a maternity allowance period (see p1:101).

A **period of incapacity** for work in this context means four or more consecutive days of incapacity (unless you are undergoing certain forms of treatment such as renal dialysis – see p2:18 – when the period of incapacity means two or more days of incapacity in any seven consecutive days).

Any two periods of incapacity for work are joined together if they are separated by a period of eight weeks or less and your days of incapacity in your earlier period of sickness are added to those in your current period of sickness. This means that you do not start the 196-day period again if, having been sick, you go back to work for eight weeks or less but then go off work sick again. If you are a '**welfare to work beneficiary**' (see p2:19 for the meaning of this) any periods of incapacity for work can be linked in this way if they are separated by 52 weeks or less.

After the first 196 days of incapacity for work, the 'all-work' test applies (see below).

Evidence of incapacity for the own occupation test

For the first seven days of your incapacity for work the Benefits Agency should accept your self certification of your sickness. After seven days you are required to provide a medical certificate from your doctor. If it is unreasonable to expect you to provide a medical certificate the Benefits Agency should accept other evidence if this is sufficient to show that you should not work because of some specific disease or bodily or mental disablement.[79] The Secretary of State (see p2:565) also has the right to request additional information relating to your incapacity for work in your own occupation if this is reasonable.[80]

If the AO doubts your incapacity for work s/he may refer your case to the Department of Social Security's Medical Service (MS) for an opinion and you may be asked to attend a medical examination.[81] This would be unusual as a medical certificate is normally accepted as sufficient evidence of your incapacity for work. In practice, a referral to the MS is only likely if it is thought that you may be working, or if the AO is unsure of the diagnosis given on your certificate, or if you provide evidence of incapacity which is not in the form of a medical certificate. If you are asked to attend a medical and you do not do so, and you do not have good cause for not attending, you are treated as capable of work (see p2:35).

The 'all-work' test

You have to satisfy the 'all-work' test to show that you are incapable of work after 196 days of incapacity for work, or from the start of your claim if the own occupation test does not apply to you. The all-work test is a test of:

the extent of a person's incapacity by reason of some specific disease or bodily or mental disablement to perform such activities as may be prescribed.[82]

See p2:21 for the meaning of 'specific disease'.

The 'all-work' test is an 'objective' test of the extent to which your illness or disability impairs your performance of certain physical and mental activities. You are awarded points according to the level of difficulty you have in performing these activities and you are assessed as incapable of work if you score sufficient points in total. The test is carried out without reference to your last job, your usual job or indeed any job and does not take into account your education and training or any language or literacy problems. Although the test must be satisfied if benefit is to be paid, it is in reality a test, of disability rather than of incapacity for work.

Satisfying the 'all-work' test prior to your assessment

When the all-work test applies to you, you are treated as satisfying the test until you are assessed under it, if you continue to provide medical certificates.[83] However, there is an exception to this rule. If in the last six months you have been found to be capable of work under the own occupation test or the all-work test you are not treated as satisfying the all-work test while waiting for your assessment unless:

- you are suffering from a specific disease or bodily or mental disablement which you were not suffering from when it was decided that you were capable of work; *or*
- your condition has significantly worsened since you were found to be capable of work; *or*
- you were treated as capable of work because you failed to return the all-work test questionnaire (see p2:30) and you have since returned it.

If you cannot be treated as incapable of work while waiting for an all-work test assessment to be carried out, although you may claim benefit again on the basis of your incapacity for work, the Benefits Agency can delay payment of IB, SDA or IS until you have been assessed and found to be incapable of work. You may be sent another questionnaire to complete and you may be asked to attend another medical. However, the AO may carry out the all-work test assessment without asking you to complete a new questionnaire or asking you to attend a medical if s/he considers that there is already sufficient evidence to show that, on the balance of probabilities, you still do not satisfy the all-work test. It is therefore important that when you claim benefit again you provide any additional information that you can about your incapacity for work.

People who are exempt from the 'all-work' test

If you are in one of the categories listed below, you do not need to read the rest of this section: the all-work test should not be applied to you as you should be treated as incapable of work.[84]

You are exempt from the all-work test if:

- you were aged 58 or over on 13 April 1995; *and*
  - between 1 December 1993 and 13 April 1995 you had not been capable of work for more than eight continuous weeks; *and*
  - you continue to submit medical certificates to the Benefits Agency: *and either*
    - you were entitled to the old invalidity benefit on both 1 December 1993 and 12 April 1995; *or*
    - you were entitled to IS, HB or CTB on 1 December 1993 and had been incapable of work for at least 28 weeks prior to that date; and, on 12 April 1995, were getting a disability premium for one of those benefits on account of your own incapacity.

  (People in some of the above categories may also be entitled to receive transitional rather than ordinary IB see p1:47);

you were receiving SDA on 12 April 1995 and your spell of incapacity for work has continued since then and you continue to send medical certificates to the Benefits Agency;

- you are assessed as at least 80 per cent disabled for the purposes of SDA (see p1:64);
- you receive the highest rate of the care component of disability living allowance (DLA – see p1:170);
- you are terminally ill (see p1:167);
- you are registered as blind;
- you are suffering from tetraplegia, paraplegia (including uncontrollable involuntary movements or ataxia which render you functionally paraplegic), dementia or persistent vegetative state;
- you are getting disablement benefit (see p1:215) based on an assessment of at least 80 per cent disablement;
- you are getting constant attendance allowance paid at a rate which is higher than the 'lower weekly rate' (see p1:217);
- there is 'medical evidence' (see p2:25) to show that you are suffering from:
  - a severe learning disability involving severe impairment of intelligence and social functioning caused by the arrested or incomplete physical development of the brain or severe brain damage;
  - a severe and progressive neurological or muscle wasting disease;
  - an active and progressive form of inflammatory polyarthritis;
  - progressive impairment of cardio-respiratory function which severely and persistently limits effort tolerance;

- dense paralysis of the upper limb, trunk and lower limb on one side of the body;
- severe irreversible motor sensory and intellectual deficits from the multiple effects of impairment of function of the brain or nervous system;
- a severe and progressive immune deficiency state characterised by the occurrence of severe constitutional disease, opportunistic infections or tumour formation;
- a severe mental illness which severely and adversely affects your mood or behaviour and which severely restricts your social functioning or your awareness of your immediate environment.

The **'medical evidence'** required can be:
- evidence from an MS doctor (see p2:15); *or*
- evidence from any other doctor, a hospital or a similar institution (see p2:17 for the meaning of 'similar institution'); *or*
- parts of such evidence which is most reliable in the circumstances.[85]

See p2:18 'Deemed incapacity' for other circumstances in which you can be treated as satisfying the all work test.

Activities, descriptors and points – the 'all-work' test in detail

If you do not fall into one of the exempt groups listed above, and you cannot be deemed to be incapable of work in the circumstances detailed on p2:18, you have to satisfy the all-work test in order to be considered incapable of work. (Although some people who fail the all-work test can still be treated as incapable of work – see p2:28). The all-work test is a test of your ability to perform the activities set out in the regulations. There are two lists of activities, one physical and the other mental. The physical activities list includes such activities as 'walking up and down stairs', 'bending and kneeling', 'reaching' and 'continence'. The mental activities list includes activities such as 'daily living' and 'coping with pressure'. The lists are set out in full in Appendix 4.

In relation to each activity, there is a further list of what are called 'descriptors'. These are designed to measure the level of difficulty you have performing the activity they relate to, and each descriptor has a number of points allocated to it.

For example, for assessing your ability to walk up and down stairs, the descriptors are:

Descriptor	Points
Cannot walk up and down one stair	15
Cannot walk up and down a flight of 12 stairs	15
Cannot walk up and down a flight of 12 stairs without holding on and taking a rest	7
Cannot walk up and down a flight of 12 stairs without holding on	3
Can only walk up and down a flight of 12 stairs if you go sideways or one step at a time	3
No problem in walking up and down stairs	0

To be incapable of work under the all-work test you have to score either:[86]

- 15 points from the physical activities list; *or*
- 10 points from the mental activities list; *or*
- 15 points if you are combining scores from both the mental and physical activities lists (but see p2:27).

However, if more than one of the descriptors for any one activity in the **physical activities** list applies to you, the points for each of the descriptors are not added together. Instead, you receive the number of points attached to the descriptor which describes the highest level of disability which you experience in relation to that activity. The points you score for each separate activity are then added together. The exception is if you have difficulties in both activities 1 and 2 (ie, 'walking' and 'walking up and down stairs') when only the highest scoring descriptor which applies to you from either of these activities is counted.[87]

For the **mental activities** list, the points from all the relevant descriptors can be added together whether or not they relate to the same activity.[88] However, the mental health descriptors can only apply to you if your difficulty in performing the activities arises from a mental illness or disablement.[89]

Your ability to perform any of the activities is assessed as if you were wearing any prosthesis or other aid or appliance which you normally wear or use.[90] So, for example, if you are fitted with an artificial leg and have no problem climbing stairs when you are wearing it, you will score 0 for that activity even though without it you may not be able to climb stairs at all.

Example

Andreas suffers from angina and:
- cannot walk more than 400 metres (Activity 1, Descriptor (e));
- cannot walk up and down a flight of 12 stairs without holding on and taking a rest (Activity 2, Descriptor (c));
- cannot stand without the support of another person or the use of an aid (other than a walking stick) for more than 30 minutes without needing to sit down (Activity 4, Descriptor (d)).

Descriptor	Points
1(e)	3
2(c)	7
4(d)	7
Total score	14

Only the descriptor with the highest score from activities 1 and 2 is counted. In this case Andreas scores more for descriptor 2(c) than descriptor 1(e) so his total score would be 14. As his total is less than 15 he is assessed as not being incapable of work.

Combining scores from physical and mental activities lists

When descriptors from both the physical and mental activities lists apply to you, you can combine your points for these descriptors. However, when you are combining points in this way, the calculation of the points for mental activities is adjusted so that:

- a score of between 6 and 9 points (inclusive) from the mental activities list counts as 9;
- a score of less than 6 from the mental activities list is completely disregarded.[91]

Example

Carolyn suffers from arthritis in her hands and cannot turn a tap or control knobs on a cooker with one hand (Activity 7, Descriptor (f)). For this she scores 6 points.

In addition she suffers from a depressive mental illness which means that she:

- needs encouragement to get up and dress (Activity 16, Descriptor (a) – 2 points);
- does not care about her appearance and living conditions (Activity 16, Descriptor (d) – 1 point);
- avoids carrying out routine activities because she is convinced they will prove too tiring or stressful (Activity 17, Descriptor (c) – 1 point);
- is unable to cope with changes in daily routine (Activity 17, Descriptor (d) – 1 point).

Carolyn's total score for mental activities is 5. Because this is less than 6, and she is combining scores from both the physical and mental activities lists, her score from the mental activities list is ignored for the purposes of the test and her total score is the 6 points she scored for her physical disability. Carolyn is not incapable of work according to the test.

Suppose however, that in addition she feels too frightened to go out on her own (Activity 18, Descriptor (f) – 1 point). Her total score for mental activities is now 6 but, because it is to be added to her score from the physical activities list it counts as 9. Her total score is therefore 15 (9 for mental activities + 6 for physical activities). She is incapable of work.

Treated as satisfying the 'all-work' test

Even if you do not satisfy the all-work test because your score is not high enough, you can still be treated as incapable of work in certain 'exceptional circumstances'. You are treated as satisfying the all-work test if you are suffering from:[92]

- a severe uncontrolled or uncontrollable life-threatening disease, and you have medical evidence to show this. There must be a reasonable cause for it not to be controlled by a recognised therapeutic procedure; *or*
- a previously undiagnosed, potentially life-threatening condition (eg, cancer or ischaemic heart disease) which is discovered for the first time by the MS doctor; *or*
- you have 'medical evidence' stating that you are likely to undergo a major operation or other major therapeutic procedure within three months of the date of the medical examination carried out by an MS doctor for the purpose of the all-work test (see p2:33).

See p2:25 for the meaning of 'medical evidence'.

For more about the operation of the all-work test and practical advice on what to do if the Benefits Agency says you are capable of work, see p2:29.

Good and bad days, pain and tiredness

The most difficult word in the descriptors is 'cannot'. To take an extreme example, it might be said that someone 'can' walk up and down a flight of 12 stairs as long as they are physically capable of doing so even if they suffer a heart attack the moment they have got back to the bottom. Obviously the meaning of 'cannot' is not as strict as this but the regulations give no indication as to what else it may mean. This is a potential problem if your condition fluctuates so that on good days you 'can' perform an activity but on bad days you 'cannot'. It also affects you if you 'can' perform a task but only at the cost of experiencing pain or you can carry out an activity once or a few times but you would be tired, stiff or in pain if you carried it out repeatedly in the way which would be necessary if it formed part of your job.

If your condition fluctuates, in deciding whether a particular descriptor applies to you an AO (or a social security appeal tribunal (SSAT – see p2:630)) should adopt a broad approach rather than a literal one, considering your normal capacity to perform an activity. So, if you normally can't walk up and down a flight of 12 stairs when called to do so this descriptor applies to you even if you could on occasion manage to do so.

Case law has confirmed that:[93]

'The real issue is, whether taking an overall view of the individual's capacity to perform the activity in question, he should reasonably be considered to be incapable of performing it. The fact that he might occasionally manage to accomplish it would be of no consequence if, for most of the time, and in most circumstances, he could not do so.'

and that

'...the approach of [a] tribunal to the question of what a person is or is not capable of doing may include consideration of his ability to perform the various specified activities most of the time. To that extent "reasonable regularity" may properly be considered.'

Your ability to perform an activity should be considered in the light of your ability over a period of time that gives a true and fair picture of your condition[94] – the test should be applied on a broad and reasonable basis and not just on a day by day approach.[95]

In deciding whether you can normally perform an activity, matters such as pain, fatigue and the increasing difficulty you may have performing an activity on a repeated basis in comparison with someone in good health should be taken into account.[96] 'Pain' might include nausea and dizziness.[97] The AO or tribunal should consider whether you can perform the activity without too much discomfort and whether you can repeat the activity within a reasonable time.[98]

Any risk to your health in performing an activity should be considered, particularly if carrying out the activity is against medical advice. If the risk to your health is sufficiently serious you may be considered incapable of the activity.[99]

The descriptors may also be difficult to apply if you have an intermittent condition, rather than one in which the symptoms of your condition fluctuates day by day. An intermittent condition, such as Meniere's disease, is characterised by periods of ill health separated by periods of remission. In these circumstances commissioners have indicated that the AO or tribunal should consider your ability to perform the activities both during the periods when you are ill and the periods when you are 'well' to decide whether, and for what periods, you satisfy the all-work test.[100] Whether this is the correct approach may depend on the severity of your condition and the length of your periods of ill health. If your periods of remission are short you could argue that your ability to perform the activities of the all-work test should be considered across a period of time that is representative of your situation as a whole. However, whichever approach is taken it is your normal ability to perform the activities with reasonable regularity, taking account of limitations imposed by pain and fatigue, which is important.

The 'all-work' test assessment

The questionnaire

Unless you are exempt from the all-work test (see p2:24) or you can be deemed to be incapable of work (see p2:18), you are sent an incapacity for work questionnaire (an IB50 form) to complete. When the all-work test is first applied to you during your period of incapacity for work you are also asked to get a Form Med 4 from your GP which you should return with the questionnaire. Although it is advisable, returning the Med 4 form is not compulsory. Even if you do not return it the AO can still proceed with the all-work test.[101]

If the information on your original claim form suggests that you are suffering mental health problems, the Benefits Agency writes to your own doctor before sending you a questionnaire to try to assess whether those problems are severe – if they are, you should be exempt from the all-work test. If the AO decides that you are exempt, you are not sent a questionnaire. If your mental health problems are felt to be mild or moderate, a questionnaire is issued in the normal way.

The questionnaire is a long one but not all of the questions necessarily apply to you. The form refers to the various physical activities and 'descriptors' listed in Appendix 1 and asks you to assess which descriptors apply to you. The questionnaire also asks whether you have any mental health problems.

Completing and returning the questionnaire is very important. If you do not fill it in and send it back you are assessed as capable of work and your benefit stops unless you are considered to have good cause for not returning it (see below).

Failing to return the questionnaire

You have six weeks from the date when the questionnaire was sent to you to return it. If you have not returned it, a reminder must be sent to you at least four weeks after the questionnaire was sent. You must then be given a further two weeks from the date that the reminder was sent to return the questionnaire. If the Benefits Agency follows this procedure and you still have not returned the questionnaire in time you are treated as capable of work unless you can show that you had good cause for not returning it.[102] If you are treated as capable of work the Benefits Agency will review your entitlement to benefit, and your benefit will normally stop.

In deciding whether you have 'good cause' the AO must consider all of the circumstances including:[103]
* whether you were outside Great Britain at the relevant time;
* your state of health;
* the nature of your disability.

If you are treated as capable of work because you fail to return the questionnaire but you have a good reason for not having done so write to the Benefits Agency asking them to review their decision (see p2:570). If you haven't already done so, you should send the completed questionnaire and explain why you were unable to send it in time. In case the AO does not accept that you have good cause you should also make a fresh claim for benefit. If the AO decides that you did not have good cause you should consider appealing against this decision – see Chapter 56.

If you are exempt from the all-work test (see p2:24), or you are deemed to be incapable of work without having to satisfy the all-work test (see p2:18), you are not required to complete a questionnaire. In addition, if the Secretary of State has sufficient information to determine whether you are incapable of work then a questionnaire is not required.[104] Furthermore, the guidance issued to AOs (the Adjudication Officer's Guide) states that if you have been diagnosed as having mental health problems and you have not returned the questionnaire, it is not appropriate to decide that you are capable of work. Instead, the AO may refer your case directly to the MS (see p2:33) for a medical examination.[105]

Completing the questionnaire

When completing the questionnaire it is important that you include details of why you cannot perform particular activities to allow the AO to fully understand your condition and how it affects you. It is also crucial that you do not underestimate your difficulties even though it may be hard to dwell on and explain the negative impact your condition has on your ability to perform the various activities relevant to the test. Try to mention everything which may be relevant. Anything you forget to mention at this stage may make a difference to the decision and, if you then have to appeal, the SSAT may be less likely to believe you have symptoms which you have raised for the first time only after the AO's decision went against you. It may be worth letting someone who knows you well check your answers.

- Read the notes on the form before answering the questions. Always draft out your answers on a separate sheet of paper first.
- If you have 'good' and 'bad' days (see p2:28) you should answer the question on the basis of what you can do on your bad days and then qualify your answer in the space provided by saying that sometimes your condition is not as bad as that. If necessary, give a rough estimate of how often you would be able to perform the activity and how often you would not.
- Compare the draft of your answers with the list in Appendix 4 and work out what your score is. If your score suggests that you fail the test, you need to think again because it will be virtually impossible for you to persuade the MS doctor, the AO or an SSAT that you should pass it. Your answers should not be exaggerated but you should check that you have not underestimated any of your problems and that you have given all the detail you can in the space provided. If you can only perform the activities with pain or they would cause you tiredness or breathlessness you should explain this on the questionnaire. Similarly, if you would not be able to carry out the tasks repeatedly or would have to rest after performing them you should include these details.

- Although social security commissioners have decided that a person's ability to perform activities in a work context is not relevant to the all-work test,[106] your ability to perform an activity repeatedly or with reasonable regularity should be considered and this is relevant to your ability to perform the activities in a work environment. Therefore, it may be helpful to ask yourself whether you would be able to do a job which involved the activity you are considering. If you have tried to do jobs involving any of the activities in the past but have had to give them up for medical reasons, you should use the space provided to say so.

- If you have difficulties with English or with reading or writing it is vital that you get independent help (ie, from someone who is not connected to the Benefits Agency) before you submit the form.

- Some of the descriptors are relevant to your ability to complete the questionnaire. For example, the AO may be unwilling to accept that you 'cannot use a pen or pencil' if the questionnaire is completed in your own handwriting. This is not necessarily correct, if you do have difficulty in writing and have asked someone else to fill in your questionnaire, or have only been able to complete it slowly and with pain, you should explain this on the questionnaire.[107]

- Always make a copy of your answers before you return the original questionnaire to the Benefits Agency.

On receiving your completed questionnaire the AO considers whether your answers or the information on the Med 4 form which your doctor has completed (see p2:30) indicate that you are exempt from the all-work test (see p2:28). The Benefits Agency may request further information from your doctor about this. If you do not appear to be exempt the Benefits Agency provisionally assesses your score on the all-work test from the information you have given. If your score indicates that you would fail the all-work test, your case is referred to the MS (see p2:33) for a medical examination to be arranged. If your score indicates that you would pass the all-work test your case is referred to the MS for 'medical scrutiny'. If it appears that any of the mental health descriptors apply to you, you are asked to attend a medical examination.

Medical scrutiny

Medical scrutiny merely involves a doctor from the MS (see p2:15) considering the answers you have given on your questionnaire and any other medical evidence which is held. If the MS doctor decides that your answers are consistent with the medical evidence and that you score sufficient points to be considered incapable of work s/he can refer your case back to the AO without examining you. If your level of disability cannot be confirmed by the medical evidence you are asked to attend a medical examination.

Medical examinations

If you have to attend a medical examination you are sent an appointment to be examined by a doctor employed by the MS.

The MS is only required to send you notice of the examination seven days beforehand unless you have agreed to accept a shorter notice period, however in practise, you are normally given more notice of the examination than this. You should try to keep the appointment if at all possible. If you cannot do so, you should immediately contact the MS on the number at the top of your appointment letter to explain why you cannot make the appointment and to ask for another one. If the reason you cannot attend the examination is that you are too ill to travel, you should ask to be examined at home. In either case, it is a good idea to confirm in writing any arrangements which you make by telephone.

You can claim your expenses for going to the medical examination by completing Form FF 40B which is sent to you at the same time as the appointment letter. If you have to attend by taxi or minicab (eg, because you are too ill to travel in any other way or there is no public transport available) the Benefits Agency will not pay your fares unless you get permission before you travel.

If you fail to attend an examination without having good cause you are treated as capable of work (see p2:35).

For both physical and mental health assessments, the doctor asks you about your condition and assesses whether, in his or her opinion, you pass the all-work test, taking account of your degree of capacity in each of the specific areas of activity set out in Appendix 4. The doctor is supposed to consider all the information and reach his or her own judgement on the basis of:

- your answers to the questions on Form IB 50 (see p2:29);
- what you tell her/him;
- the results of the examination and any tests s/he may carry out;
- your appearance and behaviour during the assessment. This does not just mean during the examination itself. For example, when the doctor comes to greet you in the waiting area, s/he is also assessing your ability to walk and to rise from a chair, the doctor watches how you manage to put on or take off your clothes during the examination and considers the length of time that you have been sitting without apparent discomfort. How you interact with the doctor is relevant to her/his opinion of your ability to communicate with other people.

The doctor asks about your 'typical' day and uses the information you give to assess your ability to perform activities relevant to the all-work test. If you talk about doing your shopping the doctor may form an opinion on your ability to lift and carry, or if you discuss doing the cleaning this will be relevant to the doctor's assessment of your ability to bend and reach.[108] So, for example, if it is painful for you to do such tasks, or you have to use special equipment, you should explain this to the doctor.

The MS doctor has to complete a report choosing the appropriate descriptors, justifying the choice in everyday, non-technical, language. The report is then returned to the AO dealing with your claim.

MS doctors are told to carry out mental health assessments when:

- you have a mild or moderate mental health problem;
- you are taking medication which impairs your cognitive function;
- you have an alcohol or drug dependency problem which significantly impairs your mental function;
- you have certain physical or sensory disabilities which impair your cognition and/or your mental function (eg, tinnitus);
- you have mild or moderate learning difficulties;
- a previously unidentified mild or moderate mental health problem is discovered during the assessment.[109]

In relation to the mental health descriptors, MS doctors are advised to assess which descriptors apply and give reasons based on the evidence gathered from your questionnaire, medical reports, observation of you during the examination, and information that you have given.

At the medical examination be sure to tell the MS doctor in as much detail as possible exactly what is wrong with you and how it affects you. The doctor is unlikely to be able to tell how your condition affects you unless you explain this. If you just answer questions and allow yourself to be examined, there is a real chance that something important will be missed and if you have to appeal, the tribunal may be less willing to accept that you have symptoms which you did not mention to the doctor.

So for example:

- Be sure to take the medicines and other aids which you are taking or using. This may lead the doctor to ask questions which s/he would not otherwise have thought of.
- If you suffer from pain and you anticipate that attending the examination will increase that pain, you may be tempted to take additional painkillers to see you through. If possible it is better not to do this as it may mask your true condition and not allow the doctor to see you as you are when you are on your normal dosage of medication. If you have to take additional painkillers you should explain this to the doctor, and you should explain what you can and cannot do when on your normal dosage of medication.[110]
- The place where you are examined is likely to be a very artificial environment and doctors' tests are inevitably limited. For example, you may be able to bend over once or twice on the doctor's request without pain but you know that if you bend over for lengthy periods, you suffer intense discomfort and

could not possibly consider doing a job which involved repeated bending or lifting. If so, tell the doctor.

- Similarly, illness is not constant and you may have good and bad days. If the doctor is seeing you on a good day s/he will not necessarily know how bad things are on a bad day unless you explain.
- If you think there is a risk that you will become tongue-tied, make a note in advance of all the things you want the doctor to know. You could leave the note with the doctor to jog his or her memory when s/he is preparing the report to the AO, but if you decide to do this, make sure that you keep a copy first.
- When asked about the activities you perform on a 'typical day' be sure to explain how your condition affects your ability to carry out day-to-day activities such as going shopping, doing the chores, washing and dressing, sitting to watch the TV, etc.
- If you feel that you may need moral support ask a friend or adviser to come to the examination with you. This is useful if there is ever a dispute about what was said during the examination. Someone who knows you may be able to help by giving the doctor more details on the practical consequences of your illness.
- If you are not fluent in English, it is vital that someone with a good knowledge of English goes with you to see the doctor.

If, after you have seen the MS doctor, you are unhappy with the way the examination went, write down what the doctor said and did and what you are unhappy about before your memory fades. This may be helpful for your advisers if there has to be an appeal.

Failing to attend a medical examination

You must be sent notice of the date and time of your medical examination at least seven days beforehand, unless you have agreed to receive less notice than this. If, after being given such notice you fail to attend, you are treated as capable of work unless you can show that you had 'good cause' for not attending.

In deciding whether you have good cause the AO must consider all the circumstances including those detailed on p2:30. Good cause may also include having been too ill or distressed to be examined on that day, or wishing to be examined by a doctor of the same gender as you when none was available. You may also be able to show that you had good cause if your refusal to attend was based on a firm religious conviction.[111]

If you are treated as capable of work because you fail to attend the medical examination without good cause, your benefit is stopped. You should write to the Benefits Agency asking them to review their decision (see p2:570) explaining why you were unable to attend the examination. In case the AO does not accept that you had good cause you should also submit a fresh claim for benefit. If the AO does not accept that you had good cause you should consider appealing – see Chapter 56.

The adjudication officer's decision

The report prepared by the MS doctor is sent to the AO. It is important to remember that it is advisory only. It is the AO, and not the MS doctor, who takes the decision on whether you are incapable of work.[112] The AO is free to disagree with the MS doctor although it is rare for this to happen in practice and normally never happens where the MS doctor has advised that you pass the all-work test.

The AO considers the information in the report from the MS doctor, the information you have given on your questionnaire, the information given by your doctor, and any other related evidence. Using this information s/he assesses your score under the all-work test.

If you pass the 'all-work' test

If you pass the all-work test, you are notified that the Benefits Agency considers that you are incapable of work. You are informed that you do not need to send in further medical certificates from your doctor but you may be asked to undergo a further assessment under the all-work test at a later date. The MS doctor includes in her/his report a suggested date when your incapacity for work should be considered again.

If you fail the 'all-work' test

If your score is not sufficient for you to pass the all-work test the AO considers whether you can be treated as incapable of work (see p2:28). If not, you are notified that the Benefits Agency considers that you are capable of work and your entitlement to IB, SDA or IS will be reviewed and your benefit will stop. However, your IS should not be stopped if you can still qualify for it for a reason other than your incapacity for work (see p1:442).

If you have previously passed the all-work test and the Benefits Agency is now re-assessing you it is important to remember that IS, SDA and IB are normally awarded for an indefinite period, unless there is a good reason for limiting the award to a definite length of time (eg, because a change of circumstances is reasonably expected in the foreseeable future).[113] If the award is indefinite the AO can only stop your benefit by carrying out a review in the circumstances detailed on p2:572, and it is up to her/him to show that you no longer qualify for benefit: it is not up to you to prove that you are incapable of work.[114] If you have previously passed an all-work test, a different medical opinion, in itself, would not necessarily be a change of circumstances sufficient to justify that decision being reviewed. However, a different medical opinion may justify a review if it provides evidence of an actual change in your circumstances or of the fact that the earlier decision was made on the basis of a mistake about the facts of your case or was made in ignorance of the facts of your case.[115]

You should decide whether you think you are now well enough to work. If you think that you are but you do not have a job to return to you should sign on at your nearest JobCentre and claim JSA (see Chapter 14), unless you are entitled to IS (see Chapter 20). The disability employment adviser at the JobCentre may be able to help you to find a suitable job or training. Remember that the rules on linking periods of incapacity for work (see pp1:41 and 1:67) mean that if you try to go back to work but discover that your health does not permit it, you go straight back on to the same rate of IS, SDA or IB as you were previously getting, as long as you give up work within eight weeks and the Benefits Agency accepts that you are incapable of work again. If you are entitled to DWA (see Chapter 22) while you are working, this period is extended to two years (see pp1:41 and 1:67).[116]

If you think that you are *not* well enough to work you should consider appealing against the AO's decision (see below).

3. **Appealing against a decision on your incapacity for work**

If you do not agree with the adjudication officer (AO) that you are capable of work you should seek advice about appealing to a social security appeal tribunal (SSAT – see p2:630). See Appendix 2 for suggestions about which organisations may be able to help you. You should request a copy of the medical evidence that the Benefits Agency holds on your file, including a copy of the MS doctor's report because, if you fail the 'all-work' test, it normally means that the MS doctor's opinion was that you do not pass the test. Local Benefits Agency offices have been advised that they must provide a copy of the MS doctor's report as soon as possible after it has been requested. There is no rule that says the AO has to agree with the MS report if this conflicts with what you or your GP says. On the contrary, s/he is supposed to make a reasoned decision based on all the evidence – medical and non-medical. Despite this, it is likely in practice that the AO will prefer the MS doctor's evidence.

It is advisable to go and see your own doctor to discuss your capacity for work. In practice, it is very difficult to win an appeal if you cannot get your GP or consultant to support you. If your GP and consultant agree with the AO, you should seriously consider your position as your chance of winning the appeal is not good.

If your GP or consultant does not agree with the AO, you should appeal against the AO's decision. This is because if you are entitled to it, claiming benefit on the basis of incapacity for work is normally more advantageous than claiming alternative benefits. For example, if you are entitled to a disability premium within your income support (IS) the amount of IS you receive would normally be higher than any jobseeker's allowance (JSA) you would be entitled to. You would also not have to show that you are available for and actively seeking work. Similarly, once you qualify for the higher rate of short-term incapacity benefit (IB) or long-term IB you may receive more benefit than you would if you were claiming contribution-based JSA. Long term IB and severe disablement allowance (SDA) also entitle you to disability premiums for means-tested benefits (see p2:325).

The question for the tribunal is the same one which the AO had to decide, namely whether your score on the all-work test is sufficiently high for you to be assessed as incapable of work, but the tribunal is not restricted to considering only the evidence that the AO considered.[117] Any fresh evidence which you can provide which supports your appeal may increase your chances of success. Therefore all the advice given previously remains relevant at this stage.

If you appealed before 21 May 1998 the tribunal should consider your entitlement to benefit for the whole period from the date of the AO's decision to the date of your appeal hearing, so if there has been a deterioration in your condition since the AO's decision this should be considered by the tribunal.[118] However, if your appeal was made on or after 21 May 1998 the tribunal can only consider your circumstances at the date of the AO's decision.[119] If your condition deteriorates after the AO has made her/his decision this cannot be taken into account by the tribunal. Because of this it is important that you make a fresh claim for benefit on the basis of your incapacity for work each time your condition deteriorates and that you appeal if these claims are rejected. Doing so will ensure that you do not lose out if the tribunal decides that the original decision that you were capable of work was correct but that following a subsequent deterioration in your condition you are incapable of work. See p2:23, 'Satisfying the all-work test prior to your assessment', for details of how any fresh claim will be dealt with.

You may wish to consider the following points as well.

- Most disputes about incapacity for work concern the all-work test – if you do find yourself in a dispute about the own occupation test, you should refer to the advice on pp51-64 of the 17th edition of CPAG's *Rights Guide to Non-Means-Tested Benefits*, much of which will still apply to you.
- Although the tribunal makes up its own mind on the evidence before it, you are usually asking the tribunal to disagree with the professional opinion of the MS doctor. This raises a question of your credibility as a witness – the tribunal has to decide the case at least partially on its assessment of you. Your

appearance and behaviour are important, as is your record of claiming benefit. It is important to convince the tribunal that you are not exaggerating your situation.

- It is important that you get medical evidence to support your appeal either from your GP or your consultant if you have one, or from both of them. You should consider which descriptors you think apply to you and ask your doctor to refer in her/his letter to your ability in relation to these descriptors making the letter as detailed as possible. A background report commenting generally on your condition and on your doctor's views on your capacity for work is much less helpful. If your GP has been treating you on a regular basis for many years, then s/he should say so specifically, so that there can be no doubt that s/he is fully aware of your medical history.

- If you are getting IS or income-based JSA, or if your income is very low, you could ask a solicitor to obtain a consultant's report through the legal advice and assistance scheme. If your GP wishes to charge you for a letter your solicitor may be able to get money through the legal advice and assistance scheme to pay for this too.

- If you have not been able to obtain a medical report in any other way, you can ask the tribunal to obtain one free for you (through the AO).[120] This cannot be done in advance of the hearing, so there will have to be an adjournment if the tribunal agrees. Tribunals have been reminded by the commissioners of their power to obtain reports where claimants cannot afford them,[121] but they do not normally do so if your GP and the MS doctor agree on the diagnosis and disagree only on the effect of your condition on your capacity to work.

- Although the issue of whether or not you are suffering from a 'specific disease or bodily or mental disablement' is clearly a medical question, whether or not you can perform any of the activities in Appendix 4 is not. Doctors have no special expertise in assessing function as opposed to diagnosing and treating disease. At most, all a doctor might be able to say is that s/he would expect that someone suffering from the disease or condition which you have would usually have certain symptoms. Unless a doctor has actually observed you performing an activity there is no reason in principle why his or her view should be any more valid than your own view or the view of a relative, friend or colleague who has observed you trying to perform this task on a daily basis. If there is a dispute, the tribunal has to decide whose evidence it accepts. There is no rule which says that the tribunal has to agree with the doctor.

- It is often useful for a person who lives with you or who knows you well to attend the hearing to describe to the tribunal the day-to-day problems you suffer.

- You should bring a list of any medication you are taking with you to the tribunal hearing.

The medical assessor

When one of the issues which is to be considered by an SSAT is whether or not the claimant satisfies the 'all-work' test, it must sit with a medical assessor.[122] The assessor's role is to advise the members of the tribunal on medical issues. S/he does not examine you or take any part in making the decision.

Medical assessors are doctors who have been qualified for at least five years. They are selected from a panel maintained by the President of the Independent Tribunal Service (see p2:620).

The Independent Tribunal Service has issued guidance to SSAT chairs about the role of the medical assessor. This stresses that his/her job is to give impartial advice to the SSAT and that anything said by the assessor in the hearing should be in the presence of both parties who should be given an opportunity to comment.

The assessor can help the SSAT by:
- explaining the meaning of medical terms;
- explaining the significance of any medication the claimant is taking and advising on possible side-effects;
- explaining the normal progress of a medical condition and how it fluctuates;
- suggesting further medical evidence which the SSAT might decide to ask for.

The assessor should not:
- stay in the room with the SSAT after the hearing while the decision is being made or be present when the tribunal considers the case before the hearing;
- comment on the decision when it is given;
- give any assistance or opinion on whether any particular descriptor applies or whether the claimant is capable of work;[123]
- ask questions (although s/he may suggest questions which the Chair might ask).

Any evidence which the assessor gives which goes beyond her/his role – such as expressing an opinion on whether you are capable of performing an activity – should not be taken into account by the tribunal.[124]

Experience suggests that many medical assessors take a more active role than this, but that this is often in the claimant's favour. If this happens in your appeal, you will have to make a tactical decision on the spot about whether, on balance, it is in your interests to object.

When appeal tribunals are unified (see p2:648) it is intended that tribunals dealing with appeals on incapacity for work will be made up of two persons, one of whom will be a doctor. This may mean that tribunals will no longer be required to sit with a medical assessor when considering questions about incapacity for work. See p2:649 for details of when the provisions of the Social Security Act 1998 will be coming into force and CPAG's *Welfare Rights Bulletin* for updates on these changes.

Protecting your income and national insurance credits while waiting for an appeal

IB and SDA are not paid while your appeal is waiting to be heard. If you have appealed you can still qualify for IS but it may be paid at a reduced rate (see p1:443). For this reason, you may qualify for either IS or JSA (see Chapters 20 and 14) while waiting for your appeal to be decided and you will need to consider which benefit you would be better off claiming.

The advantage of claiming IS is that, as long as your appeal is waiting to be decided, you are not required to sign on as available for work.[125] However, if you only qualify for IS on the grounds of your incapacity for work, and you are appealing against a decision that you do not satisfy the 'all-work' test (see p2:22), your IS is paid at a reduced rate while you are waiting for your appeal to be heard (see p1:443). Your IS is reduced by 20 per cent of the personal allowance for a single claimant of your age. (Your IS is not reduced if this is the first time that the all-work test has been applied to you, and on 12 April 1995 you had been off work sick for 28 weeks or were entitled to invalidity benefit or SDA.)[126] If your appeal is successful, you receive arrears of benefit to make up for the difference between the reduced rate of IS you were receiving and the full rate of the benefit which you are claiming. You do not have to send in medical certificates while waiting for your appeal to be heard.

If you are appealing against a decision that you do not satisfy the own occupation test (see p2:21), your IS is not reduced but you have to send medical certificates until your appeal is decided.

Instead of claiming IS you may wish to sign on at the JobCentre and claim JSA. This may be preferable as your JSA is not reduced and a successful claim for JSA means that you receive Class 1 national insurance credits (see p2:267) while your appeal is waiting to be heard whatever the outcome. If you only claim IS, (then, except in the rare case that you qualify for credits on some other basis – see p2:266) you get credits for the period if you eventually win your appeal but not if you lose. A complete contribution record may be important to ensure that you get the maximum pension when you retire and, if you are a married man, to protect your wife's entitlement to a widow's pension should you die.

The following points are also relevant:
- the contribution conditions for contribution-based JSA are stricter than for IB. You are not necessarily entitled to the former just because you were getting the latter;
- similarly, you may not be entitled to IS (or income-based JSA) if you do not pass the means test (eg, if you have savings or other income) or if, for example, you have a partner who works for 16 or more hours a week (24 hours or more for income-based JSA). If so, you may have no alternative but to claim contribution-based JSA.

To be eligible for JSA you have to be capable of work (see p1:271).[127] Although, logically, it may seem that you would not qualify for JSA as you are saying in your appeal that you are incapable of work the AO's decision on capacity for work is binding on the JobCentre.[128]

However, to get JSA you must also convince the employment officer at the JobCentre that you are available for and actively seeking work (see pp1:291 and 1:308). To qualify for JSA you will need to be prepared to accept any reasonable work within your limitations. You will not qualify if you say that you are really too sick to work but have been told you have to sign on.

If your condition worsens

If your condition has significantly worsened since the AO's decision, or you are suffering from a specific disease or bodily or mental disablement which was not considered by the AO, you should make a fresh claim for IS, IB or SDA based on your incapacity for work. In such situations you should be assessed under the 'all-work' test again and should be treated as incapable of work until such an assessment is carried out (see p2:23).

---

4. Proposals for change

The Government is proposing to replace the all-work test with a personal capability assessment which will take account of what people are capable of doing as well as what they cannot do. The test will apply from earlier in the claim.

Notes

References are to statutes and regulations as amended up to 8 March 1999. All regulations are (General) Regulations unless otherwise stated. There is a full list of abbreviations in Appendix 13.

1 Regs 1(2), 7(3) and 7D(1)(b) CB Regs; reg 14 IS Regs; reg 76 JSA Regs; reg 13 HB Regs; reg 5 CTB Regs

2 Reg 6 FC Regs; reg 8 DWA Regs

1. The full-time work rule

3 Reg 5 IS Regs; reg 51 JSA Regs; reg 4 FC Regs; reg 6 DWA Regs; para 11(1), part II ETU(A&P) Rules

4 R(FIS) 6/83; R(FIS) 1/84; R(FIS) 1/86

5 Reg 5(7) IS Regs; reg 51(3)(a) JSA Regs; reg 4(4)(a) FC Regs; reg 6(4)(a) DWA Regs; para 11(4)(a), part II ETU(A&P) Rules

6 Reg 5(3A) IS Regs; reg 52(1) JSA Regs

7 Reg 4 FC Regs; reg 6 DWA Regs; para 11, part II ETU(A&P) Rules

8 Reg 4(5) FC Regs; reg 6(5) DWA Regs; para 11(6) and (7), part II ETU(A&P) Rules

9 Reg 4(6)(b) FC Regs; reg 6(6)(b) DWA Regs; para 11(7)(b), part II ETU(A&P) Rules

10 Reg 4(6) FC Regs; reg 6(6) DWA Regs; para 11(7), part II ETU(A&P) Rules

11 R(FIS) 2/83

12 R(FIS) 6/83; R(FIS) 1/84

13 R(FIS) 6/83

14 R(FIS) 1/85; *R v Ebbw Vale & Merthyr Tydfil SBAT ex parte Lewis* [1982] 1 WLR 420

15 R(FIS) 2/81; R(FIS) 1/84

16 R(IS) 5/95

17 R(IS) 1/93

18 CIS/434/1994

19 CFC/33/1993

20 R(FIS) 1/83

21 Reg 6(b) IS Regs

22 R(FIS) 6/85; para 50372 AOG

23 Reg 5(2)(b)(i) IS Regs; reg 51(2)(b)(i) JSA Regs; reg 4(4)(c)(i) FC Regs; reg 6(4)(c)(i) DWA Regs; para 11(4)(c)(i) part II ETU(A&P) Rules

24 Reg 5(3B) IS Regs; reg 51(2)(c) JSA Regs; reg 4(4A) FC Regs; reg 6(4A) DWA Regs; para 11(5) part II ETU(A&P) Rules

25 para 25145 AOG; reg 5(2)(b)(ii) IS Regs; reg 51(2)(b)(ii) JSA Regs; reg 4(4)(c)(ii)(aa) FC Regs; reg 6(4)(c)(ii) DWA Regs; para 11(4)(c)(ii) part II ETU(A&P) Rules

26 Reg 5(2)(a) IS Regs; reg 51(2)(a) JSA Regs; R(IS) 8/95

27 Reg 4(4)(b) FC Regs; reg 6(4)(b) DWA Regs; para 11(4)(b) part II ETU(A&P) Rules

28 Reg 4(4)(c)(ii)(bb) FC Regs; reg 6(4)(b) DWA Regs; para 11(4)(c)(ii) part II ETU(A&P) Rules

29 Reg 6(28) SS(C&P) Regs

30 Reg 6(27) SS(C&P) Regs

31 R(U) 2/87

32 Reg 5(3) IS Regs; reg 52(1) JSA Regs

33 CIS/14661/1996; CIS/521/1994; AOG memo JSA/IS 24

34 Reg 5(3) IS Regs; reg 52(1) JSA Regs

35 CIS/14661/1996

36 Reg 5(3) IS Regs; reg 52(1) JSA Regs

37 Reg 5(5) IS Regs; reg 52(3) JSA Regs

38 Reg 52(2) JSA Regs

39 Reg 5(4) IS Regs

40 Reg 6 IS Regs; reg 53 JSA Regs; reg 4(3) FC Regs; reg 6(3) DWA Regs; para 11(3) part II ETU(A&P) Rules

41 Reg 6(g) IS Regs; reg 53(c) JSA Regs

42 Reg 53(g) JSA Regs

43 para 25216 AOG

44 Reg 51(3)(c) JSA Regs

45 Reg 6(b) IS Regs

46 R(FIS) 1/86; CDWA/1/1992

47 CIS/649/1992

48 para 25117 AOG

49 para 25119 AOG
· 50 *Kevin Smith v CAO* (CA), 11 October 1994
51 para 25096 AOG
52 reg 7(5) Part II ETU(A&P) Rules
53 Reg 5(1A) IS Regs; reg 4(1) FC Regs

2. Incapacity for work

54 ss171A(1) and 171G(1) SSCBA 1992
55 s61A SSAA 1992; reg 19 SS(IFW) Regs
56 Sch 1 para 2 JSA 1995
57 s171D SSCBA 1992; reg 16 SS(IFW) Regs
58 ss171D and 171F SSCBA 1992; regs 16 and 17 SS(IFW) Regs
59 Reg 2(1) SS(IFW) Regs
60 Reg 17 SS(IFW) Regs
61 CIB/5298/1997
62 C.S. 5/54
63 para 67029 AOG
64 CDLA/7980/1995
65 *Botchett v CAO* (CA), *The Times*, 8 May 1996
66 Reg 17(2)(b) and (3) SS(IFW) Regs
67 Reg 7 SS(IB)(T) Regs
68 s171D SSCBA 1992; regs 11-14 SS(IFW) Regs
69 Reg 14(a) SS(IFW) Regs
70 Reg 13A(4) SS(IFW) Regs
71 s171B(2) SSCBA 1992
72 CS/57/1982
73 CS/221/1949
74 s171B(1) SSCBA 1992; reg 4(1) SS(IFW) Regs
75 Reg 4(2)(a) SS(IFW) Regs
76 Reg 5 SS(IFW) Regs
77 Reg 4(2)(b) SS(IFW) Regs
78 s171B(3) and (4) SSCBA 1992
79 Regs 2 and 5 SS(ME) Regs
80 Reg 6(1)(c) SS(IFW) Regs
81 Reg 8 SS(IFW) Regs
82 s171C(2)(a) SSCBA 1992
83 s171C(3) SSCBA 1992; reg 28 SS(IFW) Regs
84 Reg 31(3), (4) and (5) SS(IB)(T) Regs and reg 10 SS(IFW) Regs
85 Reg 2(1) SS(IFW) Regs
86 Reg 25(1) SS(IFW) Regs
87 Reg 26(2) SS(IFW) Regs; CIB/14516/1996
88 Reg 26(4) SS(IFW) Regs
89 Reg 25(3)(b) SS(IFW) Regs

90 Reg 25(2) SS(IFW) Regs
91 Reg 26(1) SS(IFW) Regs
92 Reg 27 SS(IFW) Regs
93 CI/95(IB); CSIB/17/1996
94 CIB/15231/1996
95 CSIB/684/1997; CSIB/597/1997
96 CIB/14587/1996; CIB/14722/1996; CIB/13161/1996; CIB/13508/1996
97 CIB/14722/1996
98 CIB/14587/1996
99 CSIB/12/1996
100 CSIB/459/1997; CIB/911/1997; CIB/6244/1997
101 CIB/15325/1996
102 Reg 7 SS(IFW) Regs
103 Reg 9 SS(IFW) Regs
104 Reg 6(2) and (3)(b) SS(IFW) Regs
105 para 18758 AOG
106 CSIB/17/1996; CIB/29/1997; CIB/14587/1996; CIB/14332/1996; CIB/14587/1996
107 CSIB/17/1996
108 paras 9-11, p94 and paras 31-35, pp80-81 *Incapacity Benefit Handbook for Medical Service Doctors* (see Appendix 3)
109 para 8, p159, *Incapacity Benefit Handbook for Medical Service Doctors* (see Appendix 3)
110 CIS/16182/1996
111 R(S) 9/51
112 Reg 20 SS(IFW) Regs
113 Reg 17 SS(C&P) Regs; R(S) 1/92
114 R(S) 3/90; R(S) 1/92
115 CIB/3899/1997
116 ss33(7) and 68(10) SSCBA 1992

3. Appealing against a decision on your incapacity for work

117 CSIB/9/1996
118 CIB/14430/1996; CIS/12015/1996; CS/12054/1996
119 s12(8) SSA 1998
120 s53 SSAA 1992; R(S) 3/84
121 R(S) 1/88
122 s61A(4) SSAA 1992; reg 21 SS(IFW) Regs
123 CSIB/101/1996
124 CSIB/72/1996
125 Reg 4ZA IS Regs
126 Reg 22A(3) IS Regs
127 s1 JSA 1995
128 Reg 19 SS(IFW) Regs; Sch 1 para 2 JSA 1995

Chapter 34

. . . .

The New Deal

This chapter covers:

The New Deal is a major Government initiative to help unemployed people find work or return to work. It is being funded by a one-off 'windfall levy' on the profits of privatised companies. The New Deal is targeted at specific groups of benefit claimants and is not restricted to people claiming jobseeker's allowance. There are four main New Deal programmes for:

- people aged 18-24 years old who have been unemployed for six months or more (see below);
- people aged 25 and over who have been unemployed for at least two years (see p2:73);
- lone parents (whose youngest child is at least 5 years old) (see p2:78); *and*
- people who are sick or disabled (see p2:81).

---

1. Summary of New Deal for 18–24-year-olds

The New Deal for young people is aimed at those aged 18-24 who have been claiming jobseeker's allowance (JSA) for six months or more. A person who enters New Deal and reaches the age of 25 is required to continue to take part (see p2:46).

The New Deal begins with a period of counselling, advice and guidance – the Gateway. This period will last for a maximum of four months. During, or at the end of the Gateway, if claimants have not been able to find work they will be referred to one of four options:

- a 'subsidised' job with an employer for a minimum of 26 weeks (including an option to get help to become self-employed); *or*
- full-time education or training for up to 52 weeks; *or*
- a job with a voluntary sector employer for up to 26 weeks; *or*
- a job with the Environment Task Force for up to 26 weeks.

From the start of the Gateway you are seen by a New Deal **personal adviser**. Contact with the personal adviser is maintained throughout and, if you remain unemployed, will continue after the option has been completed. If at the end of the option you reclaim JSA, you will remain on New Deal for up to 13 weeks during a period called 'follow through' (see p2:56).

Administration

The New Deal for 18–24-year-olds was introduced nationally in April 1998.

The Employment Service (ES) has overall responsibility for the New Deal, however, non-ES staff will be involved in the delivery of certain aspects – eg, providing training or support during the Gateway or delivering one of the New Deal options. Non-ES organisations are referred to as '**partners**' or '**providers**'.

2. Eligibility for New Deal for 18–24-year-olds

'Required entry'

You are *required* to take part in New Deal if you:[1]

- are aged between 18 and 24 inclusive; *and*
- have been claiming JSA continuously for six months (this includes people who are signing on to get national insurance credits only).

Time spent on other benefits – eg, incapacity benefit – or other training programmes do not count towards the six-month period.

The Employment Service (ES) says that taking part in the Gateway is not 'compulsory' – the compulsory element of New Deal is the requirement that you are expected to take up one of the options during or by the end of the Gateway period. Although guidance suggests you may be allowed to refuse one or more options in the early stages of the Gateway (see p2:52), this may be misleading (see p2:54). Also, if you refuse to take part in the Gateway you could be issued with a jobseeker's direction (see p1:384).

If you are required to enter New Deal you will be identified by the ES computer (see p1:353) as you approach your six-month Restart interview (see p1:373). The ES computer identifies people who have been unemployed for 24 weeks and checks how old they will be at 26 weeks of unemployment. If you are eligible for New Deal (ie, you are aged 18–24 at 26 weeks of unemployment), your Restart interview is replaced by an initial **New Deal interview** (see p2:50).

People reaching the age of 25

If you enter New Deal (from the start of the Gateway onwards) and reach the age of 25 you are required to continue to take part (unless you no longer need to claim JSA).

'Early entry'

You can choose to enter New Deal earlier than you are required to (ie, before you have been claiming JSA for six months). If you do so, a New Deal personal adviser must check your eligibility. You can enter New Deal 'early' if you:

- are within a *'special needs group'* (see below); *or*
- would otherwise be unemployed for six months but for short breaks in claiming JSA (breaks are allowed which, within a period of six months, add up to no more than 28 days).

It is important to emphasise that once you have entered New Deal you cannot 'opt out' at a later stage, even if you have chosen to enter early (ie, you were not *required* to participate at the time you entered the Gateway). If you do 'opt out', you may be 'sanctioned' (payment of benefit may be stopped or suspended – see pp2:68-73).

'Special needs groups'

The ES recognises that if you come within a 'special needs group' you are likely to have particular difficulties finding work and are therefore entitled to early entry. You come within a special needs group if:

- *You have a health condition or disability*: ES staff have been issued with guidance on the 'identification' of people with disabilities. If an adviser is unsure as to whether or not you have a qualifying health condition or disability s/he is advised to contact the local disability employment adviser (DEA) for advice.
- *You need help with basic skills (reading, writing, numeracy)*: The Basic Skills Agency have produced a 'screening pack' that can be used to provide an initial assessment of your level of competence in reading, writing and mathematics (the 'Basic Skills assessment test').

- *Your first language is not English, Welsh or Gaelic*: If you have language difficulties you are likely to be identified by ES staff (eg, by the new jobseeker interviewer when an initial claim for JSA is made – see p1:352) and invited to join early.

- *You are a lone parent*: Only lone parents who are claiming JSA can join New Deal for 18/24-year-olds early. If you are a lone parent receiving income support you may be eligible for the New Deal for lone parents (see p2:78).

- *You have been out of the labour market for at least two years for domestic reasons*: To be eligible, you must not have worked for more than 28 days in the past two years or if you are currently working part time it must not be for more than 10 hours a week.

- *You have left local authority residential care* within the previous three years.

- *You have been made redundant in a 'large scale redundancy'*: Training Enterprise Councils (TECs) or Local Enterprise Companies (LECs) will define this. Each ES district has its own agreement with the local TEC/LEC on the criteria that must be met – eg, a certain percentage of the workforce is made redundant, by an employer with a minimum number of employees.

- *You are an ex-regular in HM Forces*.

- *You are an ex-offender*: You count as an ex-offender if you have been in custody as a prisoner or on remand at any time within the United Kingdom.

- *You are 'severely disadvantaged in the labour market'*: For example, you are homeless or have a drug dependency or drink problem. If the personal adviser is of the opinion that you would benefit from early entry and you agree, the first New Deal interview (see p2:50) will be arranged.

Exemptions from New Deal

ES managers have a discretion to *exempt* you from New Deal – but this is described as a 'last resort'. People who may be exempted include potentially violent claimants and those with severe mental health problems. ES managers are advised that every effort should be taken to accept people onto New Deal and help them during the Gateway. After the Gateway, you may be excluded 'in very exceptional circumstances' if your problems are so severe that you do not know what is required of you and your presence would cause severe disruption to others.

If you are exempted, questions may arise about your entitlement to JSA – eg, are you actively seeking work or capable of work? You may be entitled to income support (see p1:441) or incapacity benefit on the grounds of incapacity for work (see p1:39).

3. **The Gateway**

The Gateway is the first stage of New Deal and lasts for a period of up to four calendar months. However, the length will vary depending on how soon you are ready and willing to be referred to a New Deal option.

Elements of the Gateway

The Gateway should provide 'a range of services to fit the needs of individual jobseekers within the locality'. It consists of a number of elements:
- an initial phase of 'intensive help' to find an 'unsubsidised' job;
- advice and guidance to identify the steps that may help you to find work – eg, training, and help with jobsearch skills;
- access to independent careers advice and guidance;
- help in preparing for New Deal options, including discussions with providers (see p2:46), short basic skills courses, 'tasters' of options (short spells on an option to see if it would be appropriate);
- if you have 'exceptional problems' – eg, homelessness or drug or drink dependency, help from specialist organisations. This help may continue while you are taking part in a New Deal option;
- if appropriate, access to support and help from a '**mentor**' – someone who will provide advice and guidance on a 'non-official' basis (see p2:52). A mentor is only available to a limited number of people taking part in New Deal;
- a 'New Deal Action Plan' (see p2:51) – this is kept by you and reviewed regularly;
- referral to New Deal options.

The pattern of the Gateway depends on your needs and any variation in local delivery arrangements. ES Guidance states that some of the elements will only be available 'according to need'.

New Deal personal adviser

While on New Deal you are provided with support from an ES New Deal personal adviser. The role of the adviser may vary locally. The ES adviser might provide most of the support you receive on New Deal (eg, advice and guidance to help you find work), referring you to 'partner organisations' as and when required. Alternatively, 'partner organisations' may deliver parts of the 'advisory function', including helping you through your New Deal Action Plan (see p2:51).

Whatever local arrangements are in place, the ES adviser must:
- check your eligibility for New Deal;
- carry out the initial New Deal interview (see below);
- help draw up a New Deal Action Plan;

- review the Action Plan and agree any changes to it and your jobseeker's agreement (see p1:364);
- maintain regular contact with you and any organisations providing services in the Gateway;
- carry out the pre-entry interview when you start a New Deal option (see p2:60).

Although 'partner organisations' may help you decide on an option, the ES adviser must confirm the start details. The ES adviser has responsibility for applying sanctions (ie, passing cases to the adjudication officer (AO – see p2:562) and issuing jobseekers' directions (see p1:384) – this cannot be delegated to a partner organisation.

During the Gateway, you will have regular interviews with the ES adviser. The number and frequency of the interviews will vary depending on the local arrangements for the Gateway, the stage of the Gateway you have reached and your needs, but four interviews over the full four-month Gateway period will usually be the minimum.

The first New Deal interview

The Gateway starts with the initial New Deal interview and is carried out by an ES New Deal personal adviser – this is the disability employment adviser (see p2:87) if you are disabled. The interview is normally arranged for your next 'signing-on' day. You should be interviewed on the date, or soon after, you have been unemployed for six months.

You are given a New Deal invitation letter and a New Deal leaflet. Because local arrangements for the New Deal can vary, the interview may not be held at the JobCentre. If the interview is on a day that you do not normally attend the JobCentre, you are able to claim travel expenses. You may be invited to a group information session before your interview. The interview normally lasts about one hour.

The personal adviser discusses your situation assessing any needs and problems you may have in finding work and identifying any special needs (eg, because of a health problem or disability you have). You may be given advice on looking for a job and your jobseeker's agreement may be amended to outline your 'responsibilities' under New Deal.

You will be asked what job you see yourself doing. The personal adviser will take into account your qualifications, work history, hobbies, salary expectations, any health issues, basic skills levels and your circumstances.

The adviser will be expected to:
- identify your skills, strengths and abilities;
- make sure your main goal is 'realistic';
- discuss any barriers to getting a job;
- carry out in-work benefit calculations;

- review your ability to look for work;
- consider 'motivational issues';
- encourage you to follow up any available opportunities.

Failing to attend the interview

The ES guidance is contradictory on whether attending the interview is compulsory. The ES has the general power to withhold JSA if you fail to attend an interview when required to do so (see p1:367). However, the ES may not immediately apply sanctions for failure to attend 'New Deal interviews'. The stated intention is to adopt a more 'flexible' approach to interviews under New Deal. ES guidance states that it should be explained to you that once the 'invitation letter' has been issued you have entered New Deal. When you have been formally notified of the interview, you will be recorded as a New Deal 'participant'. The ES guidance suggests that if you fail to attend an interview for a *third* time you may have your benefit stopped on the grounds of 'failing to attend' when required to do so. If you come off JSA after an invitation letter has been issued, you are required to rejoin New Deal if you reclaim JSA within 13 weeks. For more about New Deal and sanctions, see p2:68.

Subsequent interviews

You will be required to attend a number of interviews with your personal adviser while you are on the Gateway. Each interview will be used to:
- review your progress;
- consider unsubsidised jobs, particularly if you are what the ES describes as 'job ready';
- make sure your Action Plan is still relevant and make any changes that are needed;
- make any necessary changes to your jobseeker's agreement;
- consider, and, where appropriate, refer you to Gateway activities;
- consider, and, where appropriate, refer you to New Deal options;
- agree next steps.

The New Deal Action Plan

The information acquired from interviews with you is used to discuss and agree 'realistic and achievable job goals'. These, and the steps to achieve them, are recorded by our personal adviser in your New Deal Action Plan. Any restrictions on your availability (see p1:364) and any additional needs you may have are also recorded. You are given a copy of the Action Plan, which sets out the planned activities and the timescale. Your progress should be monitored and regularly reviewed. The Plan should be kept 'simple and short'.

Your jobseeker's agreement will be revised and brought into line with the Plan. Signing the Plan is not compulsory but if you refuse to agree to changes to the jobseeker's agreement which should reflect the Plan, your claim may be referred to the AO (see p1:320).

The Plan includes a Review Record section, which is completed each time you are interviewed. Partner organisations will have supplies of the record sheets and are required to send a copy to the JobCentre each time a record is made.

Services available during the Gateway

Services available during the Gateway include access to existing ES programmes (see p2:83), independent careers advice and help with job search.

ES advisers should encourage you to take up opportunities voluntarily. If you are reluctant, ES Guidance states that the adviser should 'make every effort to persuade the jobseeker to follow the action you have suggested if you still feel it is appropriate'. However, a jobseeker's direction can be used 'as a last resort' if you persistently refuse to follow advice (see p1:384).

Mentors and informal support

While you are on New Deal you may have access to a 'volunteer mentor'. The ES expects about 10 per cent of young people entering the Gateway to have mentoring support. Most mentors are independent, trained volunteers. The mentor's role is 'to help you find employment'. The relationship – although 'friendly and supportive' – should be 'job focused'. For example, a mentor will provide advice and support to you if you are nervous in interview situations or lack confidence.

The arrangement is voluntary, so you (or you mentor) can withdraw at any time, without fear of a penalty or sanction. The relationship should be confidential (for example, your mentor should not pass on what you say about your experience on New Deal without your permission).

Employers who provide subsidised employment will be asked to make support available to you via a 'buddy system' (access to a work colleague who will provide help and advice).

New Deal options

The clear aim is to get as many claimants as possible into unsubsidised employment during the Gateway – ie, a job not subsidised under the New Deal. If you do not find a job you will be able to consider four options:

• *Full-time education or training*: aimed at claimants without Scottish/National Vocational Qualification (S/NVQ) level 2 or equivalent qualifications (see p2:62).

- *A job with an employer who will be given a subsidy for up to six months*: The job should include the equivalent of at least one day a week in education or training to an approved level (see p2:57).
- *Work with a voluntary sector organisation*: Experience of work in the voluntary sector for up to six months, including the equivalent of one day a week education or training towards an approved qualification (see p2:66).
- *Work with the Environment Task Force (ETF)*: Experience of work for up to six months on tasks to improve the environment, also with one day a week education or training (see p2:66).

Timing of referrals

You are normally referred to the options at the following stages:

Option	Time on Gateway
Full-time education and training	after one month
Subsidised employment	after two months
Environment Task Force or voluntary sector	after three months

There should be flexibility as to when referrals are made – the appropriateness of the options will depend upon your needs. A referral should not be delayed if it is a clear option.

During the Gateway, referral to an option can be 'voluntary' in the early stages, but see p2:70. If you are uncertain whether to take an option you may be able to go on an 'option taster' – a short time with an option provider. You normally have a follow-up interview with your personal adviser after the 'taster' and your Action Plan may also be reviewed. If you are on a taster for less than three days you must remain available for and actively seeking work.

Combining different options

You are usually only able to participate in one option. In exceptional cases, however, more than one option is possible, subject to:
- no more than nine months in total being spent on New Deal options (not counting the period on the Gateway); *and*
- the second option usually being a subsidised job (eg, three months on the Environment Task Force and six months in a subsidised job).

Availability of options

Although the aim is to offer you as wide a choice of options as possible, a choice between all four options is not guaranteed. The ES says that 'in a minority of cases' the choice may be limited. For example, the education and training option may not be appropriate if you are already qualified to, or above, S/NVQ level 2 (but see p2:62). Where the full choice is not available, it may be possible (but again, not guaranteed) to offer choices within options.

When an option becomes 'compulsory'

When you have agreed to start an option you have a **pre-entry** interview with your personal adviser. As part of this, you will be given a formal notification confirming where, when and to whom you must report. If at this stage you are unsure whether to go ahead with an option, and it is not an employment option, your personal adviser should consider a 'taster'. If you then give up the taster option no sanctions should be applied.

If, by the end of the Gateway, you have not agreed to start a New Deal option and you are still receiving JSA you are required to attend the option the personal adviser considers the most appropriate. For more about the New Deal and sanctions, see pp2:68-73.

Only in 'exceptional cases' will your entry onto a New Deal option be delayed when you have come to the end of the Gateway, and usually only for up to three weeks. A reason for delay may be bereavement of a close member of your family or if you have a short illness.

Signing on

During the Gateway, you must continue to 'sign on' (ie, sign labour market declarations). You must continue to be available for and actively seeking work. If an activity you are taking part in on the Gateway clashes with the time that you are required to sign on, you should contact the ES who will arrange an alternative date or time.

Leaving the Gateway

If you come off JSA while on the Gateway – you go back on to it if you reclaim JSA within 13 weeks – you rejoin at the point you left. For example, if you spend a month on the Gateway, stop claiming JSA but then reclaim within two months, you have up to three months on Gateway on rejoining.

Financial support while on an option

You continue to receive JSA while you are on the Gateway – so long as you continue to satisfy the conditions for getting JSA. The payment you receive while on an option varies depending on the option you are on.

Linking rules

Time spent on a New Deal option is linked to your previous claim for JSA – if you reclaim JSA when your option comes to an end you are treated as being in the same 'jobseeking period' (see p1:274). This means that if you reclaim JSA you do not have to serve the JSA waiting days (see p1:277) and do not have to wait to requalify for help with housing costs (see p2:340).

If you leave your option early, you risk being sanctioned (see p2:70). However, the time you spent on the option is still linked to your previous claim for JSA (or your claim for national insurance credits).

Housing costs

While you are taking part in New Deal you continue to be treated as being entitled to income-based JSA for housing costs purposes, even when you are not actually receiving it. For example, you are not entitled to JSA while you are on the full-time employment option or when you receive a wage on the ETF or voluntary sector options. This does not mean that you continue to receive help with housing costs while you are on New Deal, but it does protect you for the purpose of the housing costs linking rules (see p2:359) and the housing costs waiting periods (see p2:358).

Example

Nigel has been unemployed for 18 months. He receives income-based JSA which includes mortgage interest on a loan taken out before October 1995. Nigel starts on the New Deal Gateway in April 1999. While on the Gateway he continues to receive JSA and help with his housing costs. In July 1999, Nigel starts on the full-time employment option. He receives a wage but he no longer gets JSA because he is in remunerative work. He does not get a job when the option comes to an end and so he claims JSA.

If Nigel was not treated as being entitled to JSA during the six months that he is on the employment option he would have to wait 26 weeks before getting full housing costs (see p2:358) when he reclaims JSA.

Unemployment insurance

While you are on a New Deal option you are treated as being in the same 'jobseeking period' (see above) for the purpose of the JSA linking rules (you are treated, for benefit purposes, as if you were unemployed and eligible for JSA). It is not always the case that you will be treated as 'unemployed' for the purpose of unemployment insurance payments (eg, for payment of housing costs). Your personal adviser will discuss whether you are likely to be eligible to receive payments, but you should always check with your insurance company or policy provider. Whether you will be eligible for payments will depend on the option you are on:

- **employment option**: insurance payments may be suspended while you are on the option. Your claim for unemployment protection insurance will be closed if you take up permanent unsubsidised employment;
- **Environmental Task Force/voluntary sector option**: if you receive an allowance, your insurance company or policy provider is likely to continue to

treat you as eligible for payments. This may not be the case if you receive a wage while on the option;

- **education and training option**: you may be required by your insurance company or policy provider to continue to actively seek employment even though you are not required to do so by the Employment Service. If you do not continue to actively seek work, you risk having your insurance claim suspended while you are on the option.

Absences

You may be allowed up to two week's sickness (if you have a medical certificate from your doctor) or six day's sickness (if you provide a self-certificate at any time and still remain on the option. Absences in excess of this may affect your continued participation on the option. However, if you have 'genuine and unavoidable reasons' for your absence, you should be allowed to continue, but repeated periods of absence will not be acceptable. If you are sick you must telephone on the first day of absence.

Holidays

You may take up to two weeks' holiday while receiving an allowance – the provider will consider what is reasonable in light of the length of the programme. You will be encouraged to take holidays during any educational establishment holidays (eg, vacations during the education and training option) or public holidays.

Confidential help line

There is a confidential 'hotline' available if you wanted to report any problems or concerns you have while you are on a New Deal option. The number is 0800 163339 (open 8am to 6pm Monday to Friday).

---

4. Support at the end of the option ('follow through')

While you are taking part in an option you continue to have access to your personal adviser.

The support available should increase during your last months on the option. Before the last month, you are interviewed for advice about finding work or other programmes that may be available. The aim is to improve your chances of moving from the option into a job – minimising the chances of you returning to JSA. You will continue to get support from your personal adviser for up to 13 weeks if you do not have an unsubsidised job after your option has ended. Support during this period is known as **'follow through'**. You will have access to independent careers advice and guidance if you want it.

Claiming jobseeker's allowance

If you return to JSA within 13 weeks of the end of your option your new jobseeker interview is carried out by an ES personal adviser, usually the same person you saw during the Gateway and while on the option. If you left your option early, you are re-referred to the option (see p2:72), and your claim is passed to the AO to decide whether you should be sanctioned (see p2:70).

Subsequent interviews

Interviews with your personal adviser continue for up to 13 weeks after your option has ended. During this time you receive 'intensive help' to find a job, including having access to independent careers advice and guidance. The number of interviews varies, but you may be interviewed up to six times over the 13 weeks.

If you continue to claim JSA at the end of the 13 weeks, you are taken off the personal adviser's caseload, unless you agree to continued support on a voluntary basis.

5. **Subsidised employment option**

The aim of the employment option is to help improve your chances of finding *permanent* (unsubsidised) employment by offering a period of subsidised work which includes at least one day a week, or equivalent, in education or training leading towards an approved qualification.

While you are on the subsidised employment option you are an *employee* and therefore receive a wage from your employer. Your employer determines the wage, but it must be equivalent to at least the amount of the weekly subsidy paid to the employer (see p2:58). From April 1999 you will be entitled to a wage at no less than the level of the minimum wage.

You have the right to be treated as an employee under the employer's procedures concerning:
* wage levels;
* health and safety;
* general terms and conditions;
* grievance procedures;
* equal opportunities policies; *and*
* compliance with all current legislation.

ES Guidance states that you should be recruited into 'Class 1 employment' – this means that you will have national insurance contributions deducted from you wage and you will be registered for tax purposes.

You should be treated like other employees and subject to the same terms and conditions if you are absent through sickness. For each complete week of absence you must be paid a wage at least equivalent to the employer's subsidy (see below). This should include any statutory sick pay which is due.

Because you are an employee you are eligible to receive a back to work bonus (see p1:588), child maintenance bonus (see p1:598), family credit (see p1:460) and disability working allowance (see p1:460) as appropriate.

Customary holidays

If you have a customary holiday while on the employment option, you cannot claim JSA (see pp1:291-293). Whether you are paid a wage by the employer during the holiday depends on the conditions of your employment. If you have not 'earned' enough leave to be paid for the period, you may not receive any wages. The employer only needs to make a payment to you for the customary holiday if they would otherwise make a profit from the subsidy averaged over a four-week period. You can apply for a crisis loan, although it could be difficult to get one in practice (see p1:667).

Payments to employers

Employers receive two payments from the ES. These are:
* a job subsidy; *and*
* a contribution towards the cost of training.

The amounts which can be paid to employers are:
* £60 a week for each person on the full-time employment option (average of 30 hours or more a week including training);
* £40 a week for each person on a part-time employment option (average of more than 24 hours a week, but less than 30 hours, including training);
* £40 a week for each person on a part-time option of less than 24 hours a week, if due to disability or caring responsibilities;
* £60 a week where a person on the option has placed restrictions on their availability because of a health problem or disability, regardless of the hours worked;
* up to £750 towards the cost of training where the employer arranges the training.

The New Deal subsidy to employers can be paid with some other funding particularly related to the employment of people with disabilities or people with special needs.

Employer's Agreement

The employer must sign an **Employer's Agreement** with the Employment Service (ES). The terms and conditions of the employment option include:

- As a New Deal employee you will receive high quality training, leading towards an approved qualification.
- Employers will aim, where you show 'the necessary aptitude, commitment' and will to work, to continue to employ you at the end of the subsidy period (ie, after six months).
- You will be offered access to a supporter in the workplace.
- Existing employees will not be dismissed or made redundant to make way for your subsidised New Deal job.
- Employers must not make a cash profit from the subsidy. You must be paid a wage *at least* as much as the subsidy (see p2:58) and no less than the minimum wage.

The employment option may be offered in conjunction with other ES programmes such as Work Trial and the Job Interview Guarantee scheme (see pp2:84-89).

Some employers have signed a national agreement with the ES.

After attracting interest from employers, the ES seeks to identify vacancies suitable for the employment option.

Vacancies

The JobCentre should only accept a vacancy as suitable for the employment option if the training content is agreed in advance. If prospective employers do not have their own arrangements for training, the ES can arrange this on their behalf or can refer them to a training provider.

A specified wage rate or range must be given for the vacancy (if not, the employer should not be accepted for New Deal). There must be a contract between you and the employer giving guaranteed minimum earnings that must be in accordance with the New Deal requirements. Commission only vacancies will not be included.

A vacancy which is expected to last only six months can be accepted, but the ES monitors such vacancies to ensure that the employment option is not being used to simply replace one New Deal worker with another. 'Wherever possible' vacancies should offer long-term or permanent employment.

Employment agencies

Employment agencies may employ New Deal jobseekers and receive subsidy payments. The agency must sign an employer's agreement and the rules about duration and part-time hours are the same as for other employers. A change of work location within the subsidy period is acceptable, as long as continuity in terms of hours, wages and training are maintained.

Discussing the option

The subsidised employment option will not normally be discussed with you during the first two months of the Gateway. The aim will be to try and get you an unsubsidised job. In 'exceptional circumstances' it may be obvious at an earlier stage that it is the most appropriate option for you, for example, if you are 'clearly disadvantaged and unlikely to gain sustainable unsubsidised employment'.

The factors to be taken into account in deciding whether the employment option is appropriate for you include:

- your suitability for jobs in the area;
- your determination to apply for jobs;
- your experience in job applications and interview techniques; *and*
- your training needs.

Starting the option

Where you and an employer have agreed a start date, the ES New Deal personal adviser may carry out a pre-entry interview. The purpose of the interview is to:

- formally notify you of the option start details;
- deal with payment issues;
- discuss other benefits you may be able to claim;
- explain the ongoing support you can expect from the personal adviser;
- issue a copy of the employer agreement; *and*
- discuss any concerns or issues you may have.

Monitoring

Employment Service staff and/or partner organisations visit your employer as part of monitoring and fraud prevention. The purpose of the visit is to ensure that your placement is running smoothly and that the conditions of the placement, for example, as set out in the employer's agreement, are being kept to. Your employer is asked about their expectations for the duration of the vacancy. If your job is not permanent, access to jobsearch advice and training should be encouraged. If your employer is unable to provide work for the full six months as expected, the ES will seek an urgent discussion with the employer about possible alternatives.

If it appears that the terms of the agreement are not being met by your employer, the ES will discuss the issues with you and your employer to try and resolve them. If there is non-compliance and this cannot be satisfactorily resolved, the agreement may be terminated – as a last resort.

Confidential help line

There is a confidential 'hotline' available if you wanted to report any problems or concerns you have while you are on your option. The telephone number is 0800 163339 or 0113 2858654 if you are deaf or hard of hearing.

Training

While you are on the employment option you are *guaranteed* quality off-the-job training leading towards an approved qualification. The aim is to help you to get an unsubsidised job and improve your long-term employability.

During the 26-week period, 26 days (minimum six hours a day) or equivalent hours agreed by the ES, of off-the-job training must be provided. The timing of the 26 days can be flexible (as blocks or day release) but must not be offered only at the end of the period. Off-the-job training should be a qualification approved under Schedule 2 of the Further and Higher Education Act 1992, and will normally take place away from an employee's usual paid duties. On the job training in support of an S/NVQ is accepted.

If you have 'pre-vocational' or basic skill requirements (ie, not qualified to S/NVQ Level 1) you should be given training to meet your needs.

As a New Deal employee you must be given an agreed **Individual Training Plan** customised to your needs and built on the New Deal Action Plan (see p2:51).

Self-employment as an option

If you are interested in becoming self-employed you may have the opportunity of taking part in the 'self-employment option' on the New Deal. While on the option you will be given advice, counselling and training and (if appropriate) you will have an opportunity to experience self-employment for an initial trial period ('test trading').

The aim of the self-employment 'option' is to improve your chances of finding independent self-employment or unsubsidised employment. The self-employment option will be discussed during the Gateway. If you pursue self-employment you must continue to be available for work (see p1:291). You can be treated as actively seeking work (for a maximum of eight weeks) in any week that you are taking steps to establish yourself as a self-employed person (see p1:312).

There are three stages in the self-employment route:

- **Stage 1**: during the Gateway you will be offered initial support and advice from your personal adviser and you will be offered an 'awareness session' provided by a provider. The aim at this stage is to discuss your self-employment idea and determine whether it is likely to lead to a sustainable business in the longer term.

- **Stage 2**: you will be offered one-to-one counselling by an adviser or the opportunity to attend a short course and also help to draw up a business plan. This stage will normally be completed within four weeks and will include advice and training on all aspects of self-employment, including, for example, marketing skills, sources of finance, sales forecasting techniques and book-keeping. You will be introduced to organisations that may provide support and funding (eg, providing development loans and grants).

- **Stage 3**: this final stage is a period of up to 26 weeks of 'test trading' if you have the potential to become self-employed but you are not able to do so immediately. The aim is to experience self-employment while still receiving support and guidance on the New Deal. You will be required to undertake training leading to an approved qualification. Before test trading you must have a business plan approved by the 'test trading' provider. You will be supported by a personal adviser or mentor while you are test trading and for up to two years afterwards while you are trading independently as a self-employed person.

Income while 'test trading'

You are paid an allowance by the ES equal to your JSA plus a £400 grant spread over the 26 weeks.

While you are taking part in test trading you cannot take wages from your self-employment nor use profit for personal use. Any profits you make are held in an account and only released to you when you leave New Deal. The intention is that you continue to receive a full training allowance as a form of guaranteed income during the early stages of self-employment. If you continue to trade independently after 'test trading' or if you get a full time unsubsidised job you will immediately receive any profits you made. If after test trading you return to JSA, any profits will be held for a further 13 weeks (and will not be counted as income or capital for JSA). After 13 weeks any money in the account will be treated as capital by the Benefits Agency.

6. The full-time education and training option

The aim is to improve your employability and skills for work by enabling you to reach S/NVQ level 2 or equivalent, or offer support if you have basic skills needs. In exceptional circumstances you may be able to work towards a higher level qualification, where this is likely 'to result in immediate employment'.

You will not normally start on the education and training option until you have spent one month on the Gateway. In 'exceptional cases' an earlier start may be appropriate, for example, if you have basic skills needs, a health condition or disability or you are an ex-offender.

You are *not* treated as being in relevant education while you are on this option.[2] This means, for example, that you continue to be eligible to receive housing benefit and council tax benefit even though your course will be 'full time'.

Suitability of the option

You should not normally be referred to the option before you have spent one month on the Gateway. ES staff are advised that people opting for the education and training option may need extra support before finally deciding on the option. You may have dropped out or failed in education and training in the past and may not see the option as appropriate for you. You may be referred for specialist advice from the Careers Service or a 'local adult guidance provider'.

Content and guarantees

As a participant on the full-time education and training option you are *guaranteed*:

- up to 52 weeks full-time education or training. Exceptionally, a further four weeks may be allowed, to complete the qualification;
- an approved qualification;
- help with jobsearch skills, depending on your needs;
- training within a 'realistic work environment' and a minimum of four weeks work experience. The aim, if possible, should be to use the work experience as a stepping stone to employment at the end of the programme;
- a period of induction to the programme;
- a personal tutor, who carries out a regular review of your progress;
- a 'record of achievement' (eg, a certificate at the end of the option);
- access to the facilities provided by the provider or establishment you are attending.

You are also supported by the ES personal adviser throughout the option and after completion if a job has not been found (see 'Follow through', p2:56).

You must be given a copy of a Training Plan (see p2:61) agreed between you and the provider within two weeks of starting the option.

Hours of attendance

While on the full-time education and training option you are required to attend on the days and hours agreed with your provider – this is a minimum of five full days for at least 30 hours. You are able to restrict your hours if you are a person with disabilities or a carer.

Transfers within the option

Only in 'exceptional cases' are you able to move onto an alternative course, and then only normally within the first month of starting the option. A transfer is allowed if you are 'clearly on the wrong course'. Although examples are not given in the ES guidance, this may be because the course is not suitable to achieving your agreed employment goals. The Training Plan will need to be amended if the new course is with the same provider. If the new course is with a different provider, a new Training Plan must be produced.

Part-time students

Part-time students receiving JSA enter the Gateway in the normal way. You may be able to continue with your study, whether in its existing format or by it becoming part of the New Deal:
* the study may be completed within the four-month Gateway period (but no New Deal funding will be provided during this period); *or*
* the study may be continued as part of the training (day release) provision on the employment, Environment Task Force (ETF) or voluntary sector options. The study must meet the quality requirements for the New Deal; *or*
* you may be able to transfer directly from a part-time course to the full-time education and training option.

ES guidance emphasises that your preferences must be considered: you should not be 'arbitrarily forced to completely abandon existing study areas' – except where it would not increase your long-term employability.

You cannot transfer directly from a part-time course to the full-time education and training option without approval. Participants may be required to end their course of study – although this should only be decided 'after careful consideration with the participant and the provider'.

Financial support

When on the option you are entitled to:
* an allowance;
* reimbursement of 'reasonable' daily travel costs;
* help with living costs if you have to live away from home;
* payments from a 'discretionary fund'.

The option provider should provide or meet the cost of any necessary training materials, any protective clothing, tools and equipment and books.

The allowance

The allowance is an amount equal to the JSA paid to you immediately before the start of the option. It can be paid to you by girocheque or Automated Credit Transfer (ACT) and is paid on the same day that you received JSA.

While you are on the option you are not treated as a 'full-time student' for benefit purposes, even though your course is technically 'full-time' (ie, a minimum of five full days for at least 30 hours a week). This means that you continue to be eligible to claim housing benefit and council tax benefit, even during term time.

Travel costs

Your 'necessary' and 'reasonable' daily travel costs are reimbursed by the course provider. The contract between the ES and the provider sets an upper limit for such costs. If the costs exceed the limit, an application needs to be made to the 'discretionary fund' (see below).

The 'discretionary fund'

The Employment Service meets some of the costs of attending the option through a 'discretionary fund'. The need for help from the discretionary fund should be identified when you are referred or once you have started on the option. The fund can cover:

- special equipment needs for people with special requirements, including people with disabilities;
- 'exceptionally high' costs of travel. Travel costs which exceed the limit agreed between the ES and the provider can be met, but the ES must be satisfied that the expenditure is 'cost effective' (eg, that you are using a weekly saver ticket instead of daily returns);
- a contributions towards living costs. If you have to live away from home in order to attend a course which is beyond daily travelling distance you will be paid a lodging allowance of £35 a day (including weekends where necessary).

ES guidance states that the discretionary fund can be used as a 'last resort' for childcare provision if alternative options for childcare are not available. You can be paid up to £12 a day for your first child and up to £20 a day if you have two or more children. The payments are made by your provider, but have to be authorised by the ES.

Claims for childcare can be made if you are:

- a lone parent; or
- one of a couple if *either* your partner is on the education and training option or other Government training *or* one of you receives attendance allowance, disability living allowance, incapacity benefit, severe disablement allowance or the disability or higher pensioner premium.

Each qualifying child must be less than 11 years old at the start of the course and care must be provided by a registered childminder or nursery or, if the child is aged 8-10 years, by an out of hours club run on school premises.

If your request for help from the discretionary fund is refused you are sent a letter outlining the reasons. You can challenge the decision by writing within 14 days of the date of the decision. The ES looks at the decision again, but you do not have the right to appeal to an independent tribunal.

7. **The environment task force and voluntary sector options**

You can take part in one of the following:
* the Environment Task Force (ETF); *or*
* the voluntary sector option.

As arrangements for the two options are very similar, they are discussed in the same section.

The aims of the ETF and voluntary sector options are to:
* improve your employability through high quality work placements and jobsearch help; *and*
* deliver benefits to local communities (voluntary sector option), or deliver 'environmental benefits' (ETF option); *and*
* provide training or education towards an approved qualification.

For both options you are *guaranteed*:
* 30 hours over five full days activity for up to six months, including a minimum of one full day, or equivalent, spent on training and time spent on jobsearch activities (this need not be directly related to the placement);
* quality work placements;
* a planned induction – this should make clear the aims of the option and placement and may last up to a week;
* a personal development plan – this is part of the *Action Plan*;
* regular reviews of your progress and performance – these involve the provider (see p2:46), personal adviser (see p2:46) and mentor (if you have one – see p2:52);
* help with your jobsearch. The amount of time you are given depends on your needs and may increase towards the end of your time on the option;
* a certificate and work reference.

You will also receive a Training Plan (see p2:61).

Work done on the ETF is intended to improve the local or regional environment. Projects could include forest and park management, reclamation of derelict or waste land, improving housing.

The projects in the voluntary sector option vary locally but could include work with young people, homeless people and local charities.

Suitability of the option

The ETF and voluntary sector options are generally considered appropriate during the latter stages of the Gateway. Employment Service (ES) guidance suggests that one of these options may be suitable for you when you:
- have received intensive help during Gateway and have not been able to find work or a place on the employment option (see p2:57);
- are not suited to undertake a subsidised job within the employment option and you need further help to become 'job ready';
- do not need full-time education or training;
- may have little or no work experience;
- need an opportunity to gain confidence in a working environment;
- are genuinely interested in working in the voluntary sector or in the environment (for example, to gain specialist work experience).

These options may also be suitable for you if you wish to enter a specialist employment field and need specific work experience. You may be highly qualified (eg, to degree level) and find one of these options more conducive to achieving long-term employability than other options.

Financial support

You are entitled to:
- an allowance or wage;
- help with travel costs;
- help with childcare costs.

Allowance or wage

When on one of the options, you receive either:
- an allowance of an amount equal to the JSA paid to you immediately before the start of the option, plus a grant of £400 paid in instalments over the six months of the option (the allowance will include an element of JSA); *or*
- a wage paid by the option provider. The amount is determined by the provider but must be at least as much as 'average' JSA plus the £400 grant. The wage is paid directly to you by the provider.

Where your provider offers a wage, you can choose to be paid either a wage or an allowance. Your allowance includes a small element of JSA – ie, 10p. If you choose an allowance, you continue to be 'passported' to other benefits (eg, free prescriptions and free school meals). You are likely to be better off choosing an allowance if you have mortgage interest costs or premiums included as part of your income-based JSA.

If you were having deductions made from your JSA (see p2:500) these continue if you receive an allowance. Deductions for overpayments of benefit (see p2:525) are suspended while you are on an option.

If you choose a wage, you must send in a form called an ES40 and your provider must return form ND9. ES guidance states that you can refuse an option, without being sanctioned, if it pays such a low wage that you would be worse-off financially.

New Deal participants who receive an allowance are given a copy of booklet ND40 'Rights and Responsibilities'. This gives information about New Deal options, allowance payments, what you must tell the ES and what to do if you leave the option.

If you accept a wage, you are entitled to in-work benefits (such as family credit and housing benefit). Time spent on a waged option counts for linking purposes for JSA (see p1:57). This means that if you claim JSA at the end of the option you do not have to serve waiting days (see p1:277) or re-qualify for help with mortgage interest.

Travel costs

You are expected to pay the first £4 a week in travel costs and the provider pays any additional costs.

Childcare

If you are eligible, the provider pays childcare costs of up to £12 a day for the first child and £20 a day if you have two children or more. The qualifying conditions are the same for the full-time education and training option – see p2:65.

8. **Sanctions and adjudication**

If you refuse or fail to take up activities or options in New Deal you risk losing your JSA (or your entitlement to credits – see p2:266). You can be sanctioned for refusing to take part in one of the New Deal options when you are required to do so (ie, when you receive a letter which explains that your JSA will be affected if you do not take up the option, leave the option without good cause or are dismissed for misconduct – see p2:72).

While you are taking part in New Deal the Employment Service (ES) can apply existing sanctions (eg, for refusing to carry out a jobseeker's direction) and powers to suspend or withhold benefit can be used (see p1:377). Existing powers to sanction jobseekers can also be used if you refuse to take part in New Deal. For example, if you refuse to attend an interview to discuss going on to the New Deal (ie, entering the Gateway) you can be treated as failing to attend for interview when required to do so and your benefit can be withheld (see p1:367).

Suspension during the Gateway

Before you are formally on Gateway your JSA may be affected (ie, payment of benefit suspended) if you:
- fail, without good cause, to attend an interview with an ES New Deal personal adviser when formally notified to do so.

While you are on Gateway your JSA may be suspended if you:
- fail, without good cause, to attend an interview with an ES New Deal personal adviser (or provider) when formally notified to do so. Once on the Gateway you are required to meet with your personal adviser on a regular basis (see p2:51) – at least once a month. You must also continue to sign on;
- fail to agree changes to your jobseeker's agreement. Your agreement may be amended to take account of any change in your circumstances or to reflect the content of your Action Plan (see p2:51). Agreeing an Action Plan is not a legal requirement for getting JSA but the ES should aim to make it consistent with the jobseeker's agreement (which is a requirement for getting JSA);
- fail or refuse to carry out a jobseeker's direction. Your personal adviser could issue you with a direction if you are refusing to co-operate during the Gateway (see p1:384);
- no longer satisfy the labour market conditions (eg, you are not available for or actively seeking work); but ES guidance states that 'there must be a balance between these activities and those undertaken during the Gateway'. While on a Gateway 'taster' (see p2:49) if it is for only three days or less you must remain available for and actively seeking work;
- fail, without good cause, to apply for a job notified to you by the ES;
- fail or refuse, without good cause, to start a New Deal option (see below).

Sanction period under New Deal

You will be treated as being sanctioned under New Deal if you:
- lose your place on a New Deal option through misconduct; *or*
- fail to apply for or accept a place on a New Deal option that has been notified to you without good cause; *or*
- fail to attend a place on a New Deal option without good cause; *or*
- give up a place on a New Deal option without good cause.

A sanction for one of these reasons is called a **'New Deal sanction'**. Any other sanction should be treated as a sanction under the JSA rules, even if the sanction is imposed while you are on New Deal. The distinction is important because the type of sanction determines the sanction period.

The sanction period is two or four weeks. The first 'New Deal sanction' imposed is usually two weeks. Any other sanctions incurred in the previous 12 months do not affect the period of the first 'New Deal sanction'. The sanction period is for four weeks if you have had a 'New Deal sanction' imposed within the past 12 months.

Example

Tony made a claim for JSA in March 1999. In May 1999 he is sanctioned for refusing to carry out a reasonable jobseeker's direction. In September 1999 (after he has been receiving JSA for 26 weeks) Tony enters New Deal. Before the end of Gateway he agrees to go on the Environment Task Force. After six weeks on the option he is dismissed for misconduct. When Tony reclaims JSA his case is passed to the AO. Although Tony has had a fixed period sanction within the previous 12 months, this is his first 'New Deal sanction' – the sanction period is therefore two weeks.

Sanctions relating to New Deal options

The New Deal options are 'compulsory' for the purpose of JSA. ES guidance states that in the early stages of the Gateway taking part in one of the options is 'voluntary' ie, you should not be forced on to an option by the threat of a sanction. However, although the emphasis is on not using compulsion, the guidance is misleading. The law allows the ES to sanction you if you refuse at any stage to go on an option. You could, for example, be sanctioned for failing to accept a place on an option after it has been notified to you.

ES guidance states that you will be formally notified of a place on an option even if it is 'voluntary' in the sense that you have chosen to go on it. There are two types of notification letter: for 'voluntary' referrals (ie, when you choose to go on an option) and 'compulsory' referrals (ie, you have not agreed or chosen to go on the option). In practice, because of the emphasis in the guidance on not using compulsion you should not be 'notified' of a place on an option which is 'voluntary' unless you have first agreed to go on it. However, once you have been notified, you risk being sanctioned if you then change your mind, even though your agreement was originally 'voluntary'. If you start an option, you also risk being sanctioned if you then:

- lose your place on the option through misconduct (see p2:72); *or*
- fail to attend the option without good cause (see p2:72); *or*
- you give up your place on the option without good cause (see p2:72).

A 'compulsory' referral will usually be made at the end of Gateway if you have not agreed to take part in an option. If you refuse to go on the option you risk being sanctioned. You also risk being sanctioned if you start the option but then fail to attend or give up your place without good cause, or if you lose your place through misconduct.

It is important to emphasise that if you are sanctioned in connection with a New Deal option (described by the ES as a 'New Deal sanction' – see below) you will not be eligible for hardship payments during the sanction period unless you are in a 'vulnerable group' (see p1:427). People who are not in a vulnerable group cannot get a hardship payment during the first two weeks of a sanction period (see p1:378). The sanction period for a first 'New Deal sanction' is two weeks. However, for a second 'New Deal sanction' the sanction period will be four weeks. You can be sanctioned every time you refuse to start an option. It is possible for the ES to make repeat referrals, each with a potential four-week sanction period. Your case must be passed to an AO.

Good cause

The meaning of good cause for sanction purposes is explained on pp1:408-413 and pp1:413-419. There is an additional good cause for the New Deal options: you are treated as having good cause if you fail to start, leave early or are dismissed for misconduct from any of the options if you have not had a formal notification – including a warning that your JSA may be withdrawn if any of these circumstances apply.

Attendance on a Gateway activity

The aim is to assess a New Deal option during the Gateway and for the option to be taken up 'voluntarily'. However, you can be required to take up a Gateway opportunity – eg, attending a 'taster' option or a careers advice interview.

Requiring attendance is only appropriate when you are judged 'to be wilfully and persistently' refusing an opportunity which the ES considers will be of benefit to you. When this stage is reached a jobseeker's direction is issued officially notifying you to attend. If you refuse or fail to carry out the direction, your case is passed to the AO. Any sanction imposed relating to a jobseeker's direction issued during the Gateway is treated as a sanction under the JSA rules, and *not* as a sanction under New Deal.

Referral process

Every referral to a New Deal option, whether 'voluntary' or 'compulsory', is formally notified to you by the personal adviser. There are two types of notification: when the 'referral' is 'voluntary' and when you are being required to attend (ie, when it is 'compulsory'). Because New Deal options are 'compulsory' programmes for JSA, even a 'voluntary' notification can result in you being sanctioned (see p2:70).

All notifications will tell you:
- where and when to attend; *and*
- that payment of JSA may be affected if you fail to start an option or if it ends early.

You are asked to sign the notification to acknowledge receipt – a copy is kept on computer in case of referral to adjudication. If you refuse to sign the notification or acknowledge receipt, it is posted to you. ES guidance suggests that no action be taken immediately if you say you will not attend: 'many people who say that they will not start, will actually start their option'. The ES will normally wait to see if you start the option before passing your case to an AO to decide whether a sanction should apply.

Failure to start an option

The ES will try and encourage you to start the option that you were notified of or an alternative. If you agree to start the same or a different option you are referred again ('re-referred'). If you do start an option your case is still passed to the AO but a sanction is not imposed. However, if you reclaim JSA within 13 weeks of the date of first failing to attend the option (for example, you lose your placement through misconduct), a sanction is imposed unless 'good cause' (see pp1:415-416) can be shown.

When you attend the JobCentre you are asked to give your reasons for failing to start (on form ND3). The form must be returned within seven days if you take it away for completion. If you refuse to complete the form, this is recorded on the papers that are sent to the AO.

Leaving an option early

If you leave an option early, your employer or the option provider is expected to inform the JobCentre immediately by telephone, confirming this in writing. The payment of an allowance or subsidy to the employer or provider stops as soon as written confirmation is received.

If you attend the JobCentre within 13 weeks of leaving the option you are asked to complete form ND3 giving your reasons for leaving. You will be encouraged to return to the option. If you agree, your case is still passed to the AO but a sanction is not imposed unless you reclaim JSA within 13 weeks of the date of leaving the option.

Dismissed for misconduct

If you are asked to leave an option, your employer or option provider should immediately inform the JobCentre. Payment of any allowance or subsidy to the employer or provider is stopped. If you return to the JobCentre within 13 weeks of the date of dismissal the case is passed to the AO. Details are entered onto computer and you are given form ES48S and leaflet ESL48. The JobCentre will not, at this stage, ask you for comments – this will be done by the AO if necessary. If, in the AO's opinion, there was misconduct the sanction is applied unless you have started an option or you have come off JSA. For more about the meaning of 'misconduct' see p1:388-395.

If you are still on JSA the AO should interview you straight away. At the interview, you are referred again to the option. The re-referral process and any subsequent adjudication action if you fail to start, 'must be undertaken quickly'. If you refuse to return to or begin an option – a series of sanctions can be imposed on you. The ES guidance states: 'Sanction periods should follow consecutively for people who persistently fail to accept offers of New Deal options'.

9. **Other New Deal programmes for people over 25, lone parents and disabled people**

The New Deal for young people is by far the largest New Deal programme. Other New Deal programmes include:
- a New Deal for the long-term unemployed;
- a New Deal for lone parents;
- a New Deal for disabled people.

New Deal for people aged 25 and over

This programme is very different from the New Deal for 18–24-year-olds; for example, there is no Gateway and the long-term unemployed over aged 25 do not have access to the same options.

Eligibility

To enter the New Deal for long-term unemployed people you must be aged 25 or over and claiming JSA. Entry can be 'automatic' or you may choose to enter 'early'.

You will be automatically referred to the New Deal if you have been claiming JSA or signing on for national insurance credits for two years. If you had been unemployed and claiming JSA for two years on 29 June 1998 (the date the New Deal was launched) you will be referred when you reach the next 'full year' of your claim. For example, if you had been claiming JSA for 27 months on 29 June 1998, you will go onto the New Deal after you have been claiming JSA for 36 months.

Early entry

You can choose to enter the New Deal 'early' if you:

- were unemployed for two years or more on 29 June 1998 and you opt to enter before you reach your next full year of unemployment;
- have been unemployed and claiming JSA for a year or more and your personal adviser agrees that you are likely to face 'severe disadvantages' when looking for work. For example, you have problems with literacy or numeracy, you are an ex-offender or homeless.

The advisory process

The New Deal begins with a series of interviews with a personal adviser – the 'advisory process'. The interviews are compulsory, you can be sanctioned if you fail to attend for interview without good cause. During the advisory process (which can last up to six months) you remain on JSA and will continue to have to show that you are available for and actively seeking work.

If you do not find an unsubsidised job, you may be referred to existing ES schemes, including:

- work-based training. This includes structured work experience with employers, or 'employed status' training;
- a Jobclub (see p2:84) or a Work Trial (see p2:88) for up to three weeks with an employer whilst remaining on JSA.

Two additional measures have been introduced as part of the New Deal for the long-term unemployed:

- a subsidised job for up to six months. An employer does not have to provide education and training as a condition for the subsidy (unless the employer is in a pilot area – see p2:75);
- an opportunity to study full-time for an employment-related qualification for up to 52 weeks whilst remaining on JSA (seep2:74).

Linking rule

Time spent in a subsidised job will *not* count as being in the same 'jobseeking period'. This means that if you are in a subsidised job for more than 12 weeks and claim JSA you will have to serve 'waiting days' (see p1:277) and requalify for mortgage interest payments (see p2:348);

Minimum wage

Wages under the New Deal will be covered by the minimum wage when it is introduced from April 1999. Employers offering education and training leading to a recognised qualification (see below) will be able to pay employees of any age at the 'development rate' of £3.20 per hour.

Pilot areas

There are variations to the New Deal for the long-term unemployed in a number of pilot areas. In some areas, the New Deal begins with a 13-week 'gateway' similar to the Gateway for 18–24-year-olds followed by a further 13 week 'intensive activity' period. The pilots will be for people who have been unemployed for a year or 18 months, depending on the location. Activities during the 'intensive activity' period could include:

- work experience with an employer or a community project;
- job focused training;
- advice and counselling leading to self-employment;
- arrangements for employment using the employment subsidy.

Full-time training and study

There is a concession to the general rule preventing you from getting JSA while you are on a full-time course (see p2:134 for meaning): if you are aged 25 or over you are able to take an approved full-time course and continue to receive JSA. **So long as you meet certain conditions, you are treated as satisfying the availability for work and actively seeking work requirements.**

The new rules are not formally part of the New Deal for people aged 25 and over but we have included them in this section as they are part of the package of measures for this group.

Eligibility

You are able to receive JSA as a 'full-time student' if:

- you are aged 25 or over; *and*
- you are attending a 'qualifying course' (see below); *and*
- you had been receiving JSA for a period of at least two years (including any linking periods – see p1:274) at the time the course started;[3] *and*
- you satisfy the conditions for being *treated* as available for and actively seeking work (see below).

A 'qualifying course' must:[4]

- be employment related; *and*
- last no more than 12 consecutive months; *and*
- be of a standard to at least that of a course or programme of learning described in Schedule 2 to the Further and Higher Education Act 1992 or s6 of the Further and Higher Education (Scotland) Act 1992.

The course must be approved by an employment officer (EO).[5] Once you have started the course you are treated as attending it until the last day of the course or at an earlier date if you abandon it or are dismissed from it. However, if you abandon the course without 'good cause' (see p1:416) or you are dismissed from the course for misconduct (see p1:415), you could be sanctioned.

Availability and actively seeking work

You are treated as available for and actively seeking work:[6]

- in any week or part week during term time so long as you provide written evidence, when requested by your EO, confirming:
  - that you are attending the course when you are required to do so; *and*
  - that you are making progress on the course.

  The evidence must be in the form of a document signed by you and on behalf of the college or establishment you are attending. You must provide the evidence within five days of it being requested;[7]
- in any week in which you are taking examinations relating to the qualifying course;
- in any week which falls entirely in a vacation, if you are willing and able to take up immediately any casual employment. You are treated as actively seeking work in any week if you take such steps as you can reasonably be expected to take in order to have the best prospects of securing casual employment.[8] 'Casual employment' means employment which you can leave without giving notice or, if you are required to give notice, you can leave before the end of the vacation.

While you are on the course you are not usually required to sign on, but the regulations require evidence of your attendance and progress to be provided 'as often as may be required' by an EO. The evidence must be in such form as the EO requires (in practice a standard form is likely to be used).

Employment officer approval

The factors an EO must take into account when determining whether the course is a 'qualifying course' are:[9]

- your skills, qualifications and abilities;
- whether the course will assist you to acquire new skills and qualifications;
- whether you would have to give up a course of study in order to undertake this course;
- any needs you may have because of your physical or mental condition;
- any time which has elapsed since you were last in employment (including self-employment);
- your work experience;
- the number of jobs in the labour market and, if relevant, the local labour market which require the skills and qualifications which you would acquire on the course; *and*
- any evidence whether the course, or type of course, has facilitated others to obtain work.

Good cause and sanctions

While you are attending the course you do not have to be available for and actively seeking work under the normal rules (see pp1:291 and 1:308) but other conditions for receiving JSA will still apply. For example, you must still have a valid jobseeker's agreement (see p1:315) and remain capable of work (see p1:292). You could be sanctioned for failing, without good cause, to apply for a notified job vacancy (see p1:404) or for failing to carry out a reasonable jobseeker's direction (see p1:384).

The course becomes 'compulsory' for the purpose of training-related sanctions (see p1:414) once you have started and been treated as available for work. The ES cannot require you to go on the course, but you can be sanctioned if you give up your place or fail to attend or lose the place through misconduct (see below). The sanction in these circumstances will be for two weeks (or four weeks if you have had a training related sanction in the previous 12 months).

Employment-related sanctions

For details of what is meant by 'good cause' see pp1:408-412, but you must also have good cause for:[10]
* failing or refusing to apply for or accept a notified job vacancy; *and*
* neglecting to avail yourself of a reasonable opportunity of employment.

In the situations given above you have good cause if:
* the act or omission took place in the four weeks before the end of your course or examinations; *or*
* the employment or vacancy was not for a casual job (which you have to be available for during vacations) or was not a permanent full-time job.

Training-related sanctions

Once you have started on the course, it becomes compulsory in the sense that you are sanctioned if, without good cause, you give up the course, fail to attend the course or lose your place on the course for misconduct.[11]

In addition to the circumstances described on pp1:416-419, you also have good cause if:[12]
* you give up or fail to attend the course within four weeks of the course starting; *and*
* the reason was because of your lack of ability; *or*
* because the course was not suitable for you.

The course is considered suitable if it is suitable 'in vocationally relevant respects', such as your personal capacity and aptitude, your preference, the level of qualification you are aiming at, the duration of the course and the proportion of time, if any, you have spent on training in relation to the length of the course.[13]

New Deal for lone parents

The New Deal for lone parents is a part of the Government's Welfare to Work initiative and is intended to help lone parents move from benefit into work.

The New Deal for lone parents is a *voluntary* programme for lone parents who are receiving **income support** (IS) whose youngest child is over five years and three months of age (referred to as the 'target group'). Lone parents who are receiving JSA have access to other schemes and programmes run by the Employment Service and are not invited to take part in the New Deal for lone parents.

The scheme is available to lone parents on IS with children under age five but they will not be specifically invited to take part.

The programme is being administered by both the Department of Social Security (DSS) and the Department for Education and Employment (DfEE). The DSS had lead responsibility for the first phase of the programme (see below) and will continue to be involved, but the programme will usually be delivered at JobCentres and the DfEE will have primary responsibility.

Implementation

The New Deal for lone parents has been implemented in three phases. Since October 1998, all lone parents whose youngest child is over five years and three months of age with a new or existing claim for IS will be contacted and invited to interview. Those with children under five years and three months will be able to participate.

Content of the programme

If you join the programme you have access to a New Deal adviser located at the local JobCentre. The adviser offers you a service 'tailored' to meet your needs.

The package of help provided includes advice on:
- job vacancies;
- in-work benefits;
- childcare arrangements;
- training (eg, to update skills and improve confidence);
- a Personal Plan to guide you to find work;
- in-work support to help ease the transition into employment.

Expenses

You can claim a full refund of reasonable fares incurred attending interviews with your adviser. There is also help with the cost of registered childcare if you attend 'approved activities' as part of the programme, including: interviews with your adviser, interviews with employers and attendance at

ES schemes or programmes. You need to obtain verification of the cost from your childminder and payments will usually be made in arrears.

The fee for some courses may be met (subject to a ceiling) if the course can be shown to improve your chances of finding work. Course fees will not usually be met if the organisation running the course is getting public funding (although the cost of registration fees or books may be met).

The initial interview

The New Deal for lone parents is not compulsory. If you are in the 'target group', you do not have to respond to the invitation to contact the JobCentre for an interview. If you do contact the JobCentre and agree to take part in the programme, you can leave at any time. Your IS cannot be stopped or suspended for refusing to take part in the New Deal for lone parents. You cannot be 'sanctioned' if you are on IS. This means, for example, that you can refuse to apply for job vacancies suggested by your adviser. You cannot be issued with a 'jobseeker's direction' (see p1:384).

When you contact the JobCentre you are offered an appointment to see a New Deal for lone parents adviser. During the interview the adviser actively encourages you to take part in the programme. If you are reluctant to make a commitment, you may be offered another interview in a few months time.

If you agree to take part in the programme you are given an Action Pack with information designed to help you in your preparation and search for work. Your adviser also completes an Action Plan setting out your main goals and the steps necessary to achieving them. The emphasis is on motivation and self-esteem, building confidence and identifying achievable work goals.

Looking for work

The sort of activities your adviser may help with include:
- job applications;
- help with CVs;
- preparation for interviews (eg, rehearsing interviews, questions to ask);
- compiling sample application forms and letters;
- providing information about ES programmes.

Your adviser should only help you to make job applications if s/he thinks that you are 'job ready'. Your adviser has access to JobCentre vacancies on the Labour Market System (see p1:353) but also encourages you to make speculative approaches to local employers.

In-work income calculations

Your adviser should be able to advise on the benefits you can claim when working. You should also be given an in-work or 'better-off' calculation, covering a specific wage or a range of wages. The calculations are usually made using specially-designed computer software. The computer better-off calculation should take account of any losses of benefit, your in-work expenses and the cost of childcare. This was not always the case on the first phase of the New Deal for lone parents. Although the calculations are usually accurate, you should always consider getting a second opinion on your financial situation if you take a job, particularly if you will be better off by only by a small amount. Ask for a copy of your adviser's calculation. You may want to get a second opinion from an independent advice centre.

There are a number of factors to bear in mind when doing a 'better off calculation' including:

* you will not be eligible for free school meals when you come off income support;
* you will not get help with housing costs (eg, mortgage interest) when you come off income support, although you will be eligible to claim housing benefit and council tax benefit (the amount will depend on your income);
* if you are getting help with your mortgage, you should get advice on the implications of the 'linking rules' (see p1:274) should you later need to reclaim IS (or income-based JSA). If you are not covered by the linking rule and you make a claim for income support (or income-based JSA) after a gap of more than 12 weeks you will need to re-qualify for help with mortgage interest payments;
* you could lose the higher (lone parent) rate of the family premium, if you break your claim for IS (or income-based JSA). You will remain entitled to the higher rate if the break in claim for IS or income-based JSA is 12 weeks or less (see p2:324).[14]

You should ask for detailed information about your liability for national insurance and income tax.

Your adviser is able to undertake 'fast track' family credit (FC) and, from October 1999, working families tax credit (WFTC) referrals. Your claim for FC (or WFTC) will be identified as a New Deal for lone parents claim which should guarantee a turnaround time of five working days. However, note that this means that your claim will be dealt with in five working days, not that you will receive benefit in five working days. Your adviser can act as a contact point with other agencies regarding other benefit issues, eg, IS and HB.

Childcare

One of the main barriers to work for lone parents is the cost of childcare. Your adviser can provide information about local child minding schemes and any help available as part of the New Deal programme. You should be realistic about the availability and cost of childcare before accepting any job offer.

Your adviser has access to contacts within the Child Support Agency (CSA) and can make representations to the Agency on your behalf if you need information or have a problem. Any effects on your maintenance and regularity of payments are matters to consider when deciding whether to take up an offer of work.

In-work support

Your adviser provides help to keep you in work. This may involve advice about in-work benefits and information about help with childcare.

New Deal for disabled people

Up to £195 million over four years is being allocated to a **New Deal for disabled people**. The aim is to help disabled people, or those with a long term illness, to move into paid work, and to provide access to training.

The focus is people with disabilities and those with a long-term illness who are getting incapacity benefit, income support with a disability premium or severe disablement allowance.

The programme includes the following measures:

- schemes to explore how best to help people move into work or stay in work. There will be access to work placements, work trials and training. Up to 20 schemes are planned in pilot areas;
- personal advisers who help with jobsearch, assess training needs and advise on 'in-work' financial support and benefits. They also offer advice to employers looking to employ or retain members of staff who are disabled. The personal adviser programme is intended to go nationwide in April 2000;
- an information campaign to publicise the existing help available to help people into work 'and to change the attitudes of benefit recipients, employers and the public';
- a programme of research and evaluation to determine the effect of the initiatives.

To encourage people with disabilities to take up opportunities to work, the Government introduced from October 1998 a one-year linking rule. People on incapacity benefit (IB), severe disablement allowance (SDA) or a disability premium (on grounds of incapacity) who work can receive the same rate of benefit if the job turns out to last less than a year.

Notes

• •

References are to statutes and regulations as amended up to 8 March 1999. All regulations are (General) Regulations unless otherwise stated. There is a full list of abbreviations in Appendix 13.

1. Eligibility for new deal for 18/24-year-olds
1 Reg 75(1)(a)(ii) and (b)(ii) JSA Regs

6. The full-time education and training option
2 Reg 54(5) JSA Regs

9. Other new deal programmes for people over 25, lone parents and disabled people
3 Reg 17A(2) JSA Regs
4 Reg 17A(7) and (8) JSA Regs
5 Reg 17A(3) and (5) JSA Regs
6 Regs 17A(3) and 21A JSA Regs
7 Reg 17A(3)(a) JSA Regs
8 Reg 21A(c) JSA Regs
9 Reg 17A(5) JSA Regs
10 Reg 72(3A) JSA Regs
11 Reg 75(1)(b)(iii) JSA Regs;
   s19(5)(b)(ii), (iii) and (c) JSA
   1995
12 Reg 73(2B) JSA Regs
13 Reg 73(4) JSA Regs
14 Sch 1 para 4 (5) JSA Regs

Chapter 35

Other help with getting into work

This chapter looks at some of the other help that you can get from the Employment Service and the Benefits Agency in order to get into work. It covers:

1. Job search programmes (p2:84)
2. Training (p2:85)
3. Extra help for jobseekers with disabilities (p2:87)
4. Other national schemes (p2:88)
5. Employment Zones (p2:89)
6. Single work focused gateway pilots (p2:90)

Not all people who would like to work are eligible for, or want to join, a New Deal programme. There are many other schemes available to help people find jobs, get the training they need to become employable and offset some short-term expenses involved in starting work. There is no automatic right to access any of these schemes; Employment Service staff will decide whether it is appropriate for you to join them. These schemes are separate to the New Deal programmes, but in some cases you could be referred to them by a New Deal adviser (see p2:49).

Only the Jobplan scheme (see p2:85) and most work based training for young people (see p2:85) are compulsory schemes, therefore you should be able to leave the other schemes at any time without losing benefit. However, if you have been sent on a scheme by a jobseeker's direction and you leave early or do not complete the programme satisfactorily you could be breaking a jobseeker's direction and, therefore, you could be sanctioned (see p1:384).

Both JSA and the New Deal legislation allow for pilot schemes to be set up, therefore there may be other help available in your area; ask at your JobCentre or personal adviser interview.

1. **Job search programmes**

Programme Centres

Programme Centres are an alternative to JobClubs (see below). They offer a different way for the Employment Service to deliver help with jobsearch and jobseeking skills to unemployed people. Following a series of successful pilots, 83 per cent of Employment Service Districts have moved to Programme Centre provision, some of these areas have kept some of their JobClubs as well.

You can be referred to a programme centre once you have been unemployed for 13 weeks, priority is given to those unemployed for longer. They are generally aimed at jobseekers aged 25 or over, but in some cases claimants on a New Deal programme may be referred by their advisers.

The centres deliver a series of 'modules' that can be tailored to meet the individual needs of the jobseeker. Modules cover various aspects of job search and guidance such as: setting job goals, CV preparation, telephone techniques and 'coping with setback'. Employment Service advisers aim to agree with the jobseeker a set of modules which best meet her/his needs.

Each programme centre has a 'resource area' where eligible participants attend regularly for an agreed period to apply for jobs and other employment or training opportunities. Access to phones, stationery, stamps and office equipment such as word processors, photocopiers, etc. is provided.

JobClub

You usually have to be unemployed for six months before you can be referred to a JobClub. However, flexibility has been introduced so that some claimants can be referred after 13 weeks unemployment, to bring JobClubs more in line with programme centres.

Most people referred to a JobClub will be 25 or over, but in some cases claimants on New Deal programmes can be referred.

This scheme normally involves attending for four half-days a week for a maximum of four to six months, the average duration is 12 weeks. You are helped to make speculative approaches to employers (the emphasis is on applying for 'hidden vacancies'). Telephones, directories, stationery and stamps are provided to help you carry out an intensive search for work. Your fares to and from the JobClub are reimbursed. In some areas there are specialist JobClubs for people with literacy or language problems or disabilities or who have been disadvantaged by very long periods of unemployment. There are also Executive JobClubs for people looking for executive or managerial jobs in areas where there is high executive unemployment.

For further details ask for leaflets CLUB1 and CLUB2 (CLUB1W in Welsh and CLUB3 in multi languages).

Jobplan

You may be referred to a Jobplan workshop if you are over 25 and have been unemployed for a year. Jobplan is a workshop lasting for four and a half days in the first week, followed by a half day session about two weeks later.

Jobplan aims to provide you with a written plan of action to help you back to work and to help you build up your confidence in one-to-one reviews with the workshop leaders. There is also an opportunity to work in small groups with others in the same position and to visit other programmes. People who have attended Jobplan have priority access to other training schemes and programmes such as Jobclub or work based training for adults.

Jobplan is a compulsory scheme (the half-day session two weeks later is not compulsory). You are not paid JSA for two weeks (four weeks in some circumstances) if you do not attend, leave early or lose your place through misconduct. See p1:377 for more about sanctions.

For further details about Jobplan ask the Employment Service for leaflet JPL1.

2. **Training**

Work based training for young people.

Work based training for young people is the umbrella term for a variety of training schemes run by Training and Enterprise Councils (TECs) including:
- Modern Apprenticeships, leading to qualifications of NVQ level 3 and above;
- National Traineeships, involving work based training of up to NVQ level 2;
- other work-based training to NVQ level 2.

If you are aged 16–18, you access work based training through the Careers Service. For most 16–18-year-olds this is the only way that you can receive any benefit (see p2:152). If you are aged 18–25 you could be referred to a National Traineeship or Modern Apprenticeship by your New Deal adviser (see p2:49).

You can receive training for work as either a non-employed status trainee receiving a training allowance or as an employee receiving a wage. As a trainee you will be eligible for a training allowance at a level set by the local TEC. It must be at least £40 a week. You may also be eligible for allowances for some expenses or a bonus for attendance or achievement. Trainees with employee status are treated exactly as other employees.

Work based training for adults

Work based training for adults replaced 'training for work' in April 1998. The scheme is delivered in England under contracts with TECs and Chambers of Commerce, Training and Enterprise (CCTEs). Within the general pattern described below, TECs/CCTE's are free to adapt the scheme to local needs, and may market and brand the scheme by a different name.

The aim is to help long-term unemployed adults aged 25–63, to find secure employment or self-employment, through an 'individually tailored' combination of guidance, structured work experience, training and approved qualifications.

You are eligible to take part if you are aged between 25 and 63 in one of the following groups:

- people with disabilities or people needing help with literacy, numeracy or basic English (eligible from day one of unemployment);
- people who have been unemployed for six months (this is not restricted to people receiving JSA);
- ex-regulars in HM Forces and ex-offenders, for whom periods in the services or in custody or on remand count towards the six month qualifying period;
- returners to the labour market, who have been out of the labour market for domestic reasons for two years or more;
- victims of specified large-scale redundancies.

Priority groups

The Employment Service gives priority to people with 'pre-vocational' educational or training needs. Where demand for places exceeds supply, priority is given in the following order:

- people referred from Employment Service advisers or employment officers (see p1:362);
- people with disabilities;
- referrals from the Employment Service Jobplan scheme (see p2:85);
- all other referrals.

The training is targeted at help with basic skills, 'work disciplines' and work experience. The programme should be tailored to meet individual need.

Occupational training and 'employed status' training are provided with the aim of matching the potential of unemployed people to 'clearly identified needs within the local labour market'. On a work based training for adults scheme you may be treated as a non-employed status trainee receiving a £10 a week training allowance on top of your benefit entitlement or as a waged employee.

Each person joining the programme has her/his training needs assessed and a training plan is agreed with her/his training provider. It covers the aims while on the programme, employment objectives, whether any qualification is being pursued and attendance requirements. Training requirements and entitlements for trainees, covering basic terms and conditions, are contained in the TEC and CCTE Planning Prospectus. Many include the terms and conditions in a Trainee's Charter.

A range of training options are available in different areas, from short courses lasting only a few weeks to courses which are job specific or customised to meet the requirements of potential employers. Training does not have to lead to an NVQ (or equivalent).

3. **Extra help for jobseekers with disabilities**

See also the New Deal for disabled people on p2:81.

Disability Employment Advisers

If you have particular problems getting a job because of your illness or disability you may be able to get extra help from a Disability Employment Adviser (DEA) to look for, and access, work.

Most job centres will have a DEA based on site. In any case, employment staff should be able to refer you to a DEA if you need to see one. The DEA will discuss the problems you face and how you might overcome them. S/he will also know of employers in the local area who might be able to offer you suitable work.

The DEA can also use special schemes, such as the two below to help you.

Work preparation (rehabilitation)

The DEA can organise for you to have a work preparation course customised to your needs. Such courses try to help you find other ways of doing tasks necessary for work that you are currently unable to do because of your disability. Courses are highly specialised and individual. On some courses expenses on top of your benefit will be covered, on others you may receive a special allowance.

Access to work

This is a fund from which the Employment Service is able to meet disability related costs which are preventing you from taking up a specific job. Typically this will cover special equipment and adaptations you would need at a place of work, or 'helpers' such as sign language interpreters, readers or support workers. However, the scheme is very flexible and many costs can be considered.

4. **Other national schemes**

Travel to interview scheme

This scheme pays the cost of travelling to a job interview which is outside your JobCentres' normal travel area. You will not be eligible unless you have been unemployed for 13 weeks or more. The job must be for at least 30 hours a week and not be seasonal, temporary or a short-term fixed contract. You must apply on form TS1 before you travel. The Employment Service confirms the interview with the prospective employer before paying. You receive either a travel warrant to exchange for train tickets or an allowance per mile by private car if that would be cheaper. Further details are given in leaflet EMPL18 (and EMPL18W – Welsh version).

Work trial

This scheme places you in a job for up to 15 working days while you remain on JSA. This gives a potential employer an opportunity to assess whether you can do the job and gives you a chance to make an informed decision about whether you want it. You will usually only be offered a work trial if you have been unemployed for six months.

You do not get paid for the work that you do but, in addition to your JSA, you receive meal expenses of up to £1.50 a day and travel expenses of up to £10 a day. You may be required to sign on while you are on work trial.

As the scheme is voluntary (unless you have been given a jobseeker's direction requiring you to attend – see p1:384), you can leave the Work trial at any time without losing your entitlement to JSA.

However, although the scheme is 'voluntary', a refusal to take part may raise a doubt as to whether you are available for work. This scheme should not be confused with employment on trial – see p1:406.

Jobfinder's grant

You may be eligible for a jobfinder's grant if you are long-term unemployed and would have difficulties taking a low paid job because of the initial costs involved. This scheme pays a one-off grant to encourage you to take jobs that you would not otherwise have considered by offsetting some of the costs of returning to work. Primarily it is aimed at jobseekers who are 25 or over but there is some discretion under the New Deal programmes. You are usually only eligible if you have been unemployed for at least two years and take a job paying under £150 a week, but some areas run slightly different schemes and your Employment Service adviser may have some discretion.

If your adviser believes that you are eligible and there are appropriate jobs available to you, they will give you Form JFL6 at a regular interview. If you get a job you simply complete the form and send it to the local payment office. The address of this office can be found on the JFL6 application form.

Jobmatch

Jobmatch is aimed at encourging people to gain work experience on a part-time job – if a full-time job cannot be found – by providing an extra weekly allowance. It is available if you are taking a subsidised job as part of the employment option on the New Deal for 18–24-year-olds, New Deal for partners of benefit claimants or the New Deal for disabled people (see pp2:45 and 2:81).

An allowance of £50 a week can be paid when you take a job of at least 16 but less than 30 hours a week. There is more flexibility if you are on a New Deal for the disabled programme and your disability means that you have placed restrictions on your hours of availability for work. In this case you may be able to get a Jobmatch allowance when you take a job of less than 16 hours a week. The allowance continues for six months as long as you remain in work.

5. **Employment Zones**

Employment Zones are 'a new approach' to helping unemployed people aged 25 and over find employment.

Pilot schemes in Employment Zones emphasise developing partnerships between a variety of organisations, such as the Employment Service, local authorities, TECs and local employers. Schemes include: 'Learning for Work' offering new approaches to training; 'Business Enterprise' which provides support if you are seeking self employment; and 'Neighbourhood Match' where a job is created to fulfil community need which is unmet from statutory sources due to lack of resources and from the private sector due to lack of profit. The participant is offered the job plus training and paid the usual rate for the job out of pooled funds. Once new powers contained in the Welfare Reform Bill are passed, schemes in Employment Zones will be able to set up Personal Job Accounts which will contain money including regeneration, training and jobsearch funds payable alongside benefit entitlement.

Prototype Employment Zones have been set up in five areas: Glasgow, Plymouth, North West Wales, Liverpool and South Tees. These pilots are due to end in April 2000, therefore it is unlikely that there will be any new placements onto existing schemes. A further 12 Employment Zones will be set up from April 2000. In Doncaster, Harringey, Newham, Nottingham, Plymouth and Southwark participation will be compulsory if you have been unemployed for 12 months or more. In Birmingham, Brent, Brighton and Hove, Liverpool and Sefton, Middlesborough and Tower Hamlets participation will be compulsory if you have been unemployed for 18 months or more. Two further Employment Zones will be located somewhere in Glasgow and Wales.

---

6. **Single work-focused gateway**

The single work-focused gateway's aim is to ensure that most benefit claimants, not just those claiming JSA, will have help and encouragement to enter work. It is also hoped that by closer involvement in claims, more people will receive their correct benefit entitlement.

The single gateway will be piloted in 12 areas in three different variants. It will apply to applications for JA, IS, widow's and bereavement benefit (except bereavement/widow's payment), IB, SDA and ICA. Claims for HB and CTB will be subject to the gateway unless the claimant is in full-time employment.

During the pilot phase, interviews with a personal adviser will only be **compulsory** for JSA claimants, who may be sanctioned under existing legislation (see p1:377).

From June 1999, the basic model will be piloted in Essex South East, Warwickshire, Clyde Coast and Renfrew, and Lea Roding (East London). When you initially contact the Benefits Agency, a 'registration and orientation' officer will take the basic details necessary for registering appropriate benefit claims.

The agencies aim to arrange an interview with your 'personal adviser' within three days of your initial contact, unless it is judged inappropriate owing to your circumstances. The interview will look at the barriers preventing you from entering work. The adviser will be able to discuss different kinds of help available to overcome these barriers and calculate in-work benefit entitlement. You will be encouraged to draw up an 'action plan' for entering work. If you enter the system through the single gateway, you will be followed up from time to time by your personal advisers and may be provided with support even after starting work.

From November 1999, variants on the basic model will be piloted. Somerset, Buckinghamshire, Calderdale and Kirklees, and Gwent Borders will test the use of call-centres as initial contact points for the benefit system.

Suffolk, North Nottinghamshire, Leeds and North Cheshire will test models involving private or voluntary organisations in managing parts of the caseload.

From April 2000 most claimants may be required to attend an interview with a personal adviser as a condition of receiving benefit.

Part 7

Claiming for others

Chapter 36

. . . .

Claiming for others: non-means-tested benefits

This chapter explains who can be included in your non-means-tested benefit claim. It covers:
1. Extra money for your adult dependant (p2:93)
2. Extra money for your children (p2:97)
3. Definition of terms (p2:99)
4. Special rules for special groups (p2:103)
5. Claims, backdating and getting paid (p2:104)
6. Tax and other benefits (p2:108)

If you are receiving a non-means-tested benefit it may be possible to claim an increase in that benefit for a dependent spouse or for an adult who looks after your child, but not for both. It may also be possible to claim increases for any dependent children you have. The rules for claiming such increases are different to those for claiming means-tested benefits for your dependants (see Chapter 37).

Increases for dependants can be included in:
* incapacity benefit (IB – see Chapter 3);
* severe disablement allowance (SDA – see Chapter 4);
* invalid care allowance (ICA – see Chapter 5);
* retirement pension (see Chapter 8);
* maternity allowance (see p1:100);
* widowed mother's allowance (see p1:114).

However, whether you can get an increase for an adult or child dependant is determined by which of these benefits you are receiving.

You can choose not to claim an increase in your non-means-tested benefit for your dependants but if you are entitled to an increase and are also receiving a means-tested benefit see p2:108.

You **cannot** get an increase in the following benefits for any of your dependants:
* statutory sick pay (SSP);
* statutory maternity pay (SMP);
* widow's pension;

- disability living allowance (DLA);
- attendance allowance (AA);
- contribution-based jobseeker's allowance (JSA);
- industrial injuries benefits (unless you are receiving disablement pension which includes unemployability supplement, a benefit which you only get if you qualified for it before 26 April 1987).

Child benefit and guardian's allowance are only paid for each eligible child see p1:240 and p1:259.

1. **Extra money for your adult dependant**

An increase for an adult dependant may be paid with:
- IB (paid at any rate);
- SDA;
- ICA;
- Category A or C retirement pensions;
- maternity allowance.

The increase can be paid for your spouse or for an adult who looks after a child for you. If you are getting Category B retirement pension (see p1:138), contribution-based JSA, SSP, SMP, DLA, AA, widow's pension or widowed mother's allowance you cannot get an increase in that benefit for an adult dependant.

Increase for your spouse

You may be entitled to an increase for your spouse if her/his earnings are not too high. An increase can be paid even if your spouse is not living with you as long as you are contributing to her/his maintenance. Your spouse is your husband or wife (see p1:121 'Who counts as a widow' for details of who can be recognised as married for these purposes, and p2:103 if your marriage is polygamous).

You cannot qualify for an increase in your benefit for your spouse if you are receiving an increase for an adult who cares for your child (see p2:95).

Who can claim
You qualify for extra money for your wife or husband if: [1]
- you make a separate claim for the increase (see p2:104);[2] *and*
- your spouse's earnings, or the payments s/he receives from an occupational or personal pension, are not too high (see p2:96 for details of this earnings rule); *and*

- you are not getting an increase for a dependent adult who is looking after your child (see p2:95); *and either*
  - you are residing with your spouse (see p2:99); *or*
  - you are 'contributing to the maintenance' of your spouse (see p2:100) at a weekly rate of at least amount of the increase (see p2:97).

Additional conditions for specific benefits

If you are getting **IB** or **SDA**, then in addition to the above conditions *either*:
- your husband or wife must be 60 or over; *or*
- if your husband or wife is under 60, you must be 'residing with' (and not merely 'contributing to the maintenance' of) your spouse and entitled to an increase of IB for a child (see p2:97).[3] If you are getting the lower rate of short term IB you cannot qualify for an increase for a child. To allow you to qualify for an increase for your spouse you are treated as entitled to an increase for a child if you would have qualified for one had you been receiving the higher rate of short-term IB or the long term rate of IB.[4] See p2:99 for the meaning of 'residing with'.

If you are getting **ICA** you must reside with (see p2:99) your spouse to get the increase. You cannot qualify just by contributing to her/his maintenance.[5]

If you are a woman and you are entitled to a **Category A retirement pension**, you can only get an increase for your husband if in addition to the general conditions of entitlement detailed above:
- immediately before you became entitled to the Category A retirement pension you were entitled to incapacity benefit including an increase for an adult dependant; *and*
- since then you have not stopped residing with (see p2:99) your husband or stopped contributing to his maintenance at the appropriate weekly rate and your husband's earnings have not been higher that the rate of the increase.[6]

This rule discriminates directly against women but the discrimination is not unlawful because it falls within an exception to the European Economic Area Equal Treatment Directive (see Chapter 43).[7]

You may not be entitled to an increase for your spouse if your husband or wife is claiming an earnings-replacement benefit (see p2:493) in her/his own right. This is a frequent source of overpayments and it is very important that when you complete the claim form you give full details of any benefits which your spouse is receiving.

See p2:97 for the amount of the increase you will receive for your spouse.

Increase for someone who cares for a child

If you are not claiming an increase in your benefit for your spouse you may get an increase for an adult dependant who is looking after a child if you are responsible for that child.

Most people who benefit under these rules are unmarried partners living together as husband and wife, with one partner looking after the child rather than working.

But other people can benefit as well. As it is not necessary for you and your dependant to be of different sexes, gay or lesbian couples may be entitled as may, for example, two people with children who live together for mutual support. You may even get an increase for someone you employ to care for your child.

Who can claim

You qualify for extra money for an adult dependant (who is not your spouse) if: [8]

- you make a separate claim for the increase (see p2:104);[9] *and*
- your dependant's earnings, or any payments s/he receives from an occupational or personal pension, are not too high (see p2:96 for details of this earnings rule); *and*
- your dependant has care of a child;
  and either
- if you are claiming an increase to **ICA**, **maternity allowance** or **retirement pension**, you are entitled to child benefit (or you are treated as entitled to child benefit) for that child (see p2:99); *or*
- if you are claiming **IB** or **SDA** you are entitled to an increase in that benefit for the child (or you are treated as entitled to such an increase) (see p2:94); *and either*
- you reside with your dependant (see p2:99); *or*
- you contribute to the maintenance (see p2:100) of your dependant at a rate equal to at least the rate of the increase; *or*
- you employ your dependant at a cost to you of at least the standard rate of the increase and the employment started before you became unemployed, incapable of work or retired, (whichever applies to you) unless the need for you to employ your dependant arose afterwards; *and*
- you do not also get an increase for your husband or wife; *and*
- your dependant is not absent from Great Britain, unless s/he is residing with you outside Great Britain and you still qualify for benefit.

If you are getting ICA you must reside with (see p2:99) your dependant to get the increase. You cannot qualify just by contributing to her/his maintenance or employing her/him.[10]

If you are a man whose wife is entitled to a **Category B or C retirement pension** on the basis of your national insurance contribution record, you are not entitled to an increase in your Category A or C retirement pension for an adult dependant who is caring for a child.[11]

As for increases for dependent wives and husbands, there is an earnings rule (see below) which means that you may not qualify for the increase if your dependant has earnings or receives payments from an occupational or personal pension. However, any money which you pay your dependant for caring for the child is ignored. Also the earnings rule does not apply if the dependant is employed by you but is not residing with you.[12]

You may not be entitled to the increase if your dependant is claiming an earnings-replacement benefit (see p2:493) in her/his own right. This is a frequent source of overpayments and it is very important that when you complete the claim form you give full details of any benefits which your dependant is receiving.

The earnings rules

You are not entitled to an increase in your benefit for a spouse or for a dependent adult who cares for your child if their earnings are too high.

If you are residing with (see p2:99) an adult dependant and are claiming an increase in **long-term incapacity benefit** (IB), **severe disablement allowance** or **Category A or C retirement pension**, your increase is not paid if, in the previous week, your dependant earned more than £51.40.[13]

This limit does not apply if you have been continuously entitled to an increase in the same benefit[14] since 14 September 1985. For further details please refer to p209 of the 17th edition of CPAG's *Rights Guide to Non-Means-Tested Benefits*.

In any other case (ie, if you are not residing with your dependant or if you are claiming an increase in any other non-means-tested benefit), your increase is not paid if your dependant's earnings in the previous week were more than the standard rate of the increase which you have claimed.[15]

Earnings include any payments received from an occupational or personal pension scheme.[16]

If you are claiming an increase for an adult dependant who is not your spouse but is looking after a child (see p2:95), your dependant's earnings do not affect your entitlement to an increase if s/he is employed by you but is not residing with you. If s/he is residing with you (see p2:99) and you are employing her/him to care for a child, then the wages that you pay to her/him for this work are ignored.

Because the earnings rule is more generous for long-term than for short-term IB, you may not be entitled to an increase during the first year of your entitlement to IB but qualify after you transfer to long-term IB. It is then necessary to make a separate claim for the increase.

For how earnings are calculated, see p2:369.

If your dependant's earnings fluctuate, you do not automatically lose your entitlement to the increase every time s/he earns too much in a particular week (although you have no right to be paid the increase during the following week if that happens).[17] This means that you do not have to make a fresh claim every time your dependant's earnings exceed the limit (although you do have to keep the Benefits Agency informed of any such changes). It also means that if you were claiming on 14 September 1985 you can continue to benefit from the more generous earnings rules which were in force before that date despite fluctuations in your dependant's earnings.

Amount of the increase for an adult dependant

Increases for spouses and adult dependants who are caring for a child are paid as follows:[18]

	£pw
Short-term incapacity benefit (claimant not over pension age)	31.15
Short-term incapacity benefit (claimant over pension age)	38.40
Long-term incapacity benefit	39.95
Severe disablement allowance	23.95
Maternity allowance	31.15
Invalid care allowance	23.90
Category A retirement pension	39.95

If you are over pension age, then for all benefits except ICA and SDA, the increase is reduced if your contribution record is incomplete (see p2:276).[19]

---

2. **Extra money for your children**

An increase for a child dependant may be paid with:
- long-term and the higher rate of short-term incapacity benefit (IB);
- severe disablement allowance;
- invalid care allowance;
- Category A, B and C retirement pensions;
- widowed mother's allowance.

An increase may also be paid with the lower rate of short-term IB but only if you are over pension age (60 for women and 65 for men). You can only qualify for an increase in widowed mother's allowance for 'qualifying children' (see p1:115).[20] If you are getting contribution-based jobseeker's allowance, maternity allowance, statutory maternity pay, statutory sick pay, disability living allowance, attendance allowance or widow's pension you cannot receive an increase in that benefit for a child.

Who can claim

You qualify for an increase for a child if:[21]
- you make a separate claim for the increase (see p2:104);[22]
and either
- you are entitled to child benefit for the child (see Chapter 12); *or*
- you are treated as entitled to child benefit for the child (see p2:99);
and either
- the child is living with you (see p2:101); *or*
- you, or you and your spouse if you reside with your spouse, contribute to the maintenance (see p2:100) of the child at a rate of at least the amount of the increase in addition to the amount of any child benefit you receive for that child; *and*
- the earnings of your spouse, or your partner if you are cohabiting (see p2:115), are not too high (see below for details of this earnings rule).

Earnings rule[23]

If you are living with your spouse or you are living with someone as husband and wife, your partner's earnings affect your entitlement to an increase for a child. You do not get an increase for your first child for any week if in the previous week your partner earned £145 or more. After that you lose entitlement for another child for each complete £19 per week s/he earns, in addition to £145. So if you have three children and your partner earns £159 a week, you get an increase for one child, not three. Earnings include any payments received by your partner from an occupational or personal pension scheme.[24]

Amount of the increase for a child dependant

The basic rate of the increase is £11.35 for each child.[25] However, if child benefit is being paid for a child at the standard rate for an eldest eligible child (ie, £14.40), any dependant's increase for that child is reduced by £1.45 to £9.90. (See p2:110 if you are getting the higher rate of child benefit for lone parents.)

The amount of the increase you receive for a child is not affected if your national insurance contribution record is incomplete.

3. **Definition of terms**

The following definitions apply for the purposes of entitlement to increases for dependent adults and children.

Who counts as a child?

The rules on who counts as a child and on when a young person stops counting as a child, are the same as for child benefit – see p1:233.

Treated as entitled to child benefit

In order to qualify for an increase for a dependent child (or for an adult who is not your spouse but is caring for a child) you must either be entitled to child benefit or be treated as entitled to child benefit for that child.

If you do not receive child benefit for a child yourself, you are still treated as doing so if:[26]

- you are residing with (see below) a parent of the child who is receiving child benefit for that child and the child is living with you; *and either*
    - you are also a parent of the child; *or*
    - you are 'wholly or mainly maintaining' the child (see p2:101); *or*
- you or your spouse, (if you are residing with your spouse – see below), would have been entitled to child benefit for that child had s/he been born at the end of the week before the week in which s/he was born.[27] (As child benefit is normally only paid from the Monday after you become entitled to it, this rule ensures that you do not have to wait a further week to qualify for an increase in a weekly non-means-tested benefit); *or*
- you are in Great Britain and would have been entitled to child benefit if you (or your spouse if you are residing with your spouse – see below) had not been receiving a family benefit from another country.[28]

This means that if a child lives with both parents and the mother receives child benefit, the father may still claim an increase for the child. But a step-father can only claim the increase if he is wholly or mainly maintaining the child (see p2:101).

If you do not benefit from these rules, you may still qualify for an increase if you arrange for child benefit to be transferred to you (see p1:238).

Residence and maintenance

'Residing with'

The term 'residing with' should be given its ordinary meaning. You and your husband, wife or other adult dependant will normally be considered to be residing with each other if you share a home. The arrangement has to have some degree of permanence – so you should not be considered to be residing with someone who has come to stay with you for a short while. This issue rarely causes difficulties in practice.

Temporary absences do not stop two people from being treated as residing with each other[29] and you are also treated as residing with your husband or wife when either or both of you are in hospital, even if the stay in hospital is likely to be permanent.[30]

'Residing with' does not mean the same as 'living with' (see p2:101) and the rules on whether a couple are residing with each other for the purposes of dependency increases are not the same as for child benefit (see p1:239).

'Contributing to the maintenance'

If you are not residing with an adult dependant you may still qualify for a dependant's increase for her/him if you are contributing to her/his maintenance at a weekly rate of at least the amount of the increase.

You only qualify for an increase for an adult dependant on this basis if:[31]

- when you were employed, or not incapable of work (see p2:15), or not a pensioner, (whichever applies to you) you were making contributions at this rate, unless the adult only became your dependant later. If you are claiming incapacity benefit (IB), and within a month of becoming entitled to the increase for an adult dependant the rate of that increase changes (because you reach pension age or start to receive long term IB) you are treated as satisfying this condition if you were contributing at least the level of the initial increase; *and*

- if the increase is payable at a reduced rate (eg, because of insufficient national insurance contributions – see p2:97), you continue to contribute at least the amount of the increase which is paid.

Similarly, if you do not live with a child you may still qualify for an increase for her/him if you (or you and your spouse, if you reside with your spouse – see p2:99), contribute to her/his maintenance at a weekly rate of at least the amount of the increase which would be paid for that child. If you (or your spouse, if you reside with your spouse), are getting child benefit for that child the amount of your contribution must be at least the amount of the increase plus the amount of child benefit payable for that child.

'Contributing to the maintenance' means that you are making payments to or on behalf of a person. A weekly payment covers you for the week after it is made, and a monthly payment for the following month etc.[32] Payments may be in kind, so money spent on clothing or an outing for a child, for example, can be counted.[33]

If you make payments for a spouse and one or more children, the total payment is allocated between those dependants in the way that is most advantageous to you (even if you pay under a court order which specifies the amounts in respect of each person).[34] However, a contribution for a spouse can only be treated as a contribution for a child and vice versa if your spouse is entitled to child benefit for that child. If the payment includes an element of arrears the amount for arrears is ignored.[35]

If you have stopped maintaining a person, you cannot later cover yourself by making a payment in arrears.[36] However, a broad view is taken of an interruption in otherwise regular payments.[37] If you are not paying enough, but think you are, a payment of arrears may be taken into account.[38]

You are treated as though you are making the required contributions if you give a written undertaking to make the contributions as soon as the increase is paid. If on receiving the increase you do not make the contributions, the decision to award the increase can be revised.[39]

Remember, the conditions of entitlement for the increases mean that it is never necessary to prove that you are contributing to the maintenance of an adult dependant if you are residing with her/him, or that you are contributing to the maintenance of a child if you live with that child (see below).

'Living with'

'Living with' has the same meaning as it does in relation to child benefit claims (see p1:237).

'Wholly or mainly maintaining'

If you are not a parent of a child and you are not getting child benefit for her/ him you are only entitled to an increase for that child if s/he is living with you and one of her/his parents and you are wholly or mainly maintaining the child.

'Wholly or mainly maintaining' means that:[40]

- while you are unemployed, incapable of work (see p2:15) or entitled to retirement pension (whichever applies to you) you are contributing to the maintenance of your dependant at a weekly rate of at least the amount of the dependant's increase; *and*
- before you became unemployed, incapable of work (see p2:15) or entitled to retirement pension you contributed more than half the actual cost of maintaining your dependant (unless s/he did not become dependent until after that time). This is determined using the 'family fund' test – see below.

If two or more people whose contributions alone are not sufficient are making contributions to a level that means that between them they are wholly or mainly maintaining the dependant they may agree by a majority that one of them gets the increase. The agreement must be in the form of a signed letter to the Secretary of State.[41]

If there is no agreement the increase is paid to the person who contributes most or, if everyone contributes equally, to the eldest.[42]

The 'family fund' test

If more than one member of a household contributes to the household income it may be difficult to assess whether you contributed more than half the cost of maintaining a dependant before you became unemployed, incapable of work or retired. In this situation, the extent to which any member of the household supports any other is calculated using the family fund test.[43]

To apply the family fund test, you first calculate the unit cost of each member of the family by dividing the net household income by the number of members of the family (treating each child of 13 or under as half an adult). If a person's contribution to the family fund is less than her/his unit cost s/he is said to have a 'deficit'. If you contribute more than your unit cost you are said to have a 'surplus' and you are treated as contributing this surplus towards the maintenance of all the other members of the household who have a deficit. The amount of your surplus which is allocated to any individual is calculated by working out the proportion of the total deficit held by each member of the family and dividing your surplus between them in the same proportions. If you are contributing more than half the unit cost of another member of the family you are considered to be wholly or mainly maintaining them.

The family fund test is applied on the basis of the family's income before you became unemployed, incapable of work, or retired.[44] Subsequent changes are ignored but you must contribute the amount of the increase to remain entitled to it.[45] If you are contributing to the family fund out of a means-tested benefit such as income support which you are claiming, you are still treated as making the contribution from your own funds.[46] Child benefit is treated as part of the general funds of the family and is used to decrease individuals' deficits.

• •

Example

Before becoming incapable of work Eva was working and had net weekly earnings of £195. She lives with her partner and his two children of 8 and 11. Her partner gets child benefit of £24 a week. She has claimed IB and, as she is not a parent of the children, she only qualifies for an increase for the children if she is wholly or mainly maintaining them. She therefore has to show that she was contributing half the cost of their maintenance before she became incapable of work. Under the family fund test the unit cost of each member of the family is:

£219 (£195 + £24) divided by 3	Eva	£73
(each child counts as half a unit)	her partner	£73
	first child	£36.50
	second child	£36.50

Eva contributed £195 into the family fund which covered her own unit cost of £73 and left a £122 surplus to be allocated between the other family members. The other members were in deficit totalling £146 (£73+£36.50+£36.50). Her partner's deficit of £73 represented 50 per cent total deficit of £146 and the deficit of each of the children was 25 per cent of the total. The child benefit is allocated between them in proportion with their share of the deficit – £12 goes to her partner (50 per cent of £24) and £6 to each of the children (25 per cent of £24). Eva's surplus is then allocated in the same way. Her partner received 50 per cent of the surplus – £61 (50 per cent of £122, the children 25 per cent – £30.50 each (25 per cent of £124). As these amount are more than half their unit cost Eva has been wholly or mainly maintaining the children and qualifies for an increase in her IB for them.

---

4. **Special rules for special groups**

There are some groups of claimants to whom special rules apply. These are covered below and in Chapters 39-41. Special rules apply to:
- people who are in hospital or whose dependants are in hospital (see p2:163);
- people who are in prison or whose dependants are in prison or detention (see pp2:183-184);
- adult dependants involved in trade disputes (see below);
- people who are abroad or whose dependants are abroad (see p2:244);
- people whose marriage is polygamous (see below).

However, it is important to note that your increase may not be affected in the same way as your basic benefit.

Trade disputes[47]

You are not entitled to an increase in benefit for an adult dependant if that dependant is involved in a stoppage of work due to a trade dispute at her/his place of work, unless you can show that s/he does not have a direct interest in the dispute. Your dependant does not have a direct interest in the dispute if s/he has nothing to gain from it either financially or in connection with her/his work conditions, for example.

Polygamous marriage

You will only qualify for an increase in your non-means-tested benefit for your spouse if you are recognised as having a valid marriage under the law of the UK (see p1:121 'Who counts as a widow' for a discussion of who can be recognised as married). You will not normally be treated as having a valid marriage unless your marriage is a monogamous one.[48] This means if your marriage is polygamous (ie, if you have more than one spouse or your husband or wife has more than one spouse) you will not generally be entitled to an increase in your benefit for your spouse.[49] However, if your marriage was formerly polygamous and is not currently (ie, if either you or your husband or wife have had other spouses in the past but all such spouses have now died or been divorced) you can qualify for an increase.

It is important to remember even if your marriage is polygamous the law may not consider it to be so (see p1:122). You should therefore seek advice about your entitlement to an increase for your spouse if you are in this situation.

Even if you do not qualify for an increase in your non-means-tested benefit for your spouse because your marriage is polygamous, you may still qualify for an increase for her/him if s/he is caring for your child – see p2:95.

5. **Claims, backdating and getting paid**

You must make a claim for an increase for a dependant[50] – a claim for basic benefit is not counted as a claim for an increase in that benefit. The rules are described in brief below. This section should be read in conjunction with Chapter 50 which explains the rules in more detail.

Making a claim

A claim for an increase should be made on the appropriate claim form, although the Secretary of State may accept a written application which is not on the appropriate form if it is sufficient in the circumstances (see p2:482).[51]

Claim forms for the relevant benefits contain claims for increases to those benefits for dependants.

Information to support your claim

If you are claiming an increase in your non-means-tested benefit for an adult dependant you will normally be asked to supply her/his national insurance number.[52] This requirement is called the national insurance number 'NINO' requirement. See p2:485 for further details of this.

You are not required to submit the national insurance number of a child for whom you are claiming an increase.

When you claim an increase in your non-means-tested benefit for a dependant you may be asked to supply 'certificates, documents, information and evidence' considered relevant to your claim.[53] This may include information about your adult dependant's earnings, for example.

If you are asked to provide evidence or documents which you do not have, ask what other evidence would be acceptable. Ask the Benefits Agency to explain what is required and why and complain if your feel any requests for information are unreasonable.

See p2:484 for further details of evidence which may be required to support your claim

Who should claim

You must normally claim benefit (including increases to that benefit for a dependant) on your own behalf. However, if your benefit is being claimed by another adult on your behalf because you are not able to act for yourself – called your appointee – the increase in that benefit should also be claimed by your appointee (see p2:480 for further details).

The date of your claim

The date of your claim (ie, the date that your claim is treated as made) is important as it determines the date from which you will be paid the increase for your dependants. Your claim for an increase in your non-means-tested benefit for a dependant is normally treated as made on the date it is received at the Benefits Agency office.[54] A claim can be counted as having been received at the Benefits Agency office even on a day when the office is closed, if that is the day it would have normally been delivered.[55] If you posted your claim it should be accepted as having been delivered unless it is proved not to have been.[56] However, in these circumstances you would have to convince the Benefits Agency that the claim was posted.

If the claim you submit is incomplete or not on the correct form you may be asked to provide further information or to complete the correct form. As long as this additional information or form is returned within a month of it being sent back to you (or longer if the Secretary of State thinks that the delay is reasonable), your claim is treated as being made on the date the initial claim was received at the Benefits Agency's office.[57]

If you reclaim severe disablement allowance (SDA) after qualifying for the higher rate of the care component of disability living allowance (DLA) in the circumstances described on p1:73, your claim for an increase in that benefit can also be treated as having been made on the date you first claimed the increase or the date from which your entitlement to DLA started, whichever is later.

Similarly, if you reclaim invalid care allowance (ICA) after a qualifying benefit was awarded to the person you care for in the circumstances described on p1:86, your claim for an increase in ICA can also be treated as having been made on the date you first claimed the increase or the date from which the qualifying benefit was awarded, if that was later.[58]

It is important to remember that you can only qualify for an increase in your benefit for a dependant if you are entitled to the benefit concerned.

It may be possible to claim in advance (see p2:106) or your date of claim may be backdated (see p2:107).

What if you claim the wrong benefit?

If you make a claim for an increase of SDA this may be treated as a claim for an increase of incapacity benefit instead, and vice versa.

If you claimed child benefit for a child, that claim may also be treated as a claim for an increase in another non-means-tested benefit for the same child.[59]

If someone has claimed benefit for her/himself (other than a claim for child benefit) and is not entitled to it but you are entitled to an increase in your non-means tested benefit for that person, her/his claim can be treated as a claim for an increase in your benefit.[60]

When someone else has claimed an increase in a benefit (other than child benefit) for an adult or child dependant but is not entitled to it, that claim may be treated as a claim for an increase in your non-means tested-benefit for the same child or adult.[61]

If you claim guardian's allowance for a child but are not entitled to it, your claim may be treated as a claim for an increase in your, or your spouse's, non-means-tested benefit for the same child.[62] See p2:486 for more details of interchanging claims in this way.

If a claim for another benefit is treated as a claim for an increase in your benefit for an adult or child dependant this may allow you to backdate your claim for the increase for more than the usual three months (see p2:107). If you satisfy the qualifying conditions for the increase and for the benefit to which the increase applies you can get the increase backdated for up to three months before the date of the claim for the other benefit.

A decision to treat a claim for one benefit (or a claim by one person) as a claim for another is made at the discretion of the Secretary of State. Although you can ask the Secretary of State to reconsider her/his decision you cannot appeal if you are unhappy with the decision (see p2:565).

Claiming in advance

You can claim an increase in your **retirement pension** up to four months before you expect to qualify for it.[63]

You can claim an increase in your **maternity allowance** for an adult dependant up to 14 weeks before your expected week of childbirth (see p1:106 for the meaning of this term) but only if you would have qualified for the increase at the time you make the claim, had maternity allowance been in payment.[64]

You can claim an increase for a dependant in any **other non-means-tested benefit** up to three months before you expect to qualify for it.[65]

It is helpful to claim in advance if you can, as it will give the Benefits Agency time to gather the information that they may need, and decide your claim in good time.

Backdating your claim

Claims for dependants' increases can be backdated for up to three months from the date you make your claim if you satisfy the conditions of entitlement to the benefit and to the dependant's increase over that period.[66] You do not have to show reasons why your claim was late to qualify for backdated benefit.

If you are claiming an increase in your **widowed mother's allowance** for a 'qualifying child' (see p1:115) that increase can be backdated for more than three months if your claim was late because you were not aware that your husband had died (see p1:128).[67]

If you might have qualified for an increase in your benefit for a dependant earlier but did not claim because you were given the wrong information by the Benefits Agency or because you were misled by them you could:
- ask for an *ex gratia* payment (see p2:663); *or*
- complain to the Ombudsman (see p2:662).

See p2:106 'What if you claim the wrong benefit' for details of whether you can be treated as having claimed an increase in your benefit for a dependant on the basis of your (or someone else's) claim for another benefit.

See p2:105 'The date of your claim' if you have previously claimed ICA or SDA but your earlier claim was refused.

See p2:487 for more details about the backdating of claims.

Note: The rules about backdating of claims for increases for dependants changed on 7 April 1997. If you made a backdated claim before that date, see the 1996/97 edition of CPAG's *Rights Guide to Non-Means-Tested Benefits*.

Getting paid

If you are claiming an increase in your non-means-tested benefit for your dependants that increase is included in payments of the benefit concerned and is paid in the same way and on the same day as that benefit. See the relevant benefit chapters for details.

Change of circumstances

It is your duty to report any changes in your circumstances which might affect your right to or the amount of your benefit, including your right to increases for your dependants.[68] So you should inform the Benefits Agency of a change in your adult dependant's earnings, for example. If you do not do this, you could be overpaid benefit (see Chapter 51). Inform the Benefits Agency of the change in your circumstances in writing and keep a copy of the letter you send in case of problems.

6. **Tax and other benefits**

Increases of retirement pensions for adult dependants are taxable.[69] Other increases (including all increases for children) are not.

Means tested benefits

If you have a low income you may also be entitled to a means-tested benefit such as income support (IS – Chapter 20), housing benefit (HB – Chapter 25), council tax benefit (CTB – Chapter 27), income-based jobseeker's allowance (JSA – Chapter 14), disability working allowance (DWA – Chapter 22), family credit (FC – Chapter 21), or earnings top up (Chapter 24).

Your entitlement to those benefits will include benefit for your partner and any dependent children who are members of your household (see Chapter 37). This is your family for the purpose of means-tested benefits. The increases you receive to your non-means-tested benefit may be for dependants who are not part of this family. If so, any increase in your non-means-tested benefit for a dependant who is not part of your family will be ignored when calculating your entitlement to means-tested benefits. Any increase in your non-means-tested benefit for a member of your family will be treated in full as income for means-tested benefits.

From October 1999 FC and DWA will be replaced by tax credits (see Chapter 23).

If you are receiving a means-tested benefit you should consider whether you will be better off claiming an increase in your non-means-tested benefit for a dependant. If the increase is for a member of your family it will affect the amount of means-tested benefit you receive and may mean that your income is too high for you to qualify for that means-tested benefit. If you lose your entitlement to IS or income-based JSA you may also lose your entitlement to free school meals for your children, community care grants or budgeting loans from the social fund, and free milk and vitamins if you are pregnant or have a child under five. In addition, your entitlement to HB and CTB may be reduced.

If you no longer qualify for IS, income-based JSA, FC, DWA, HB or CTB you also will not qualify for maternity expenses payments and funeral expenses payments from the social fund. Losing your entitlement to these benefits may make you worse off than you would have been had you not claimed an increase in your entitlement to a non-means-tested benefit for your dependant.

However, if you would be entitled to an increase in your non-means-tested benefit for a dependant but you have not claimed it, you may still be treated as receiving the increase for the purpose of calculating your entitlement to any means-tested benefit. This is because you can be treated as if you are receiving income (called notional income) which you fail to apply for if you would be entitled to it without having to satisfy further conditions (see p2:422 'Failing to apply for income').

You should only be treated as having notional income if your entitlement to an increase is straightforward. If you would have to satisfy further conditions to qualify for the increase you should not be treated as receiving it. So, for example, if your entitlement to an increase is dependant on an assessment of the earnings of your adult dependant or your partner you may be able to argue that you should not be treated as having notional income as your entitlement to the increase is not straightforward.

You should not be treated as having notional income if the increase would not be for a member of your 'family' for means-tested benefits purposes.

Non-means-tested benefits

The overlapping benefit rules apply to increases in non-means-tested benefits for dependants and mean that you may not be entitled to an increase in more than one benefit for the same child or adult and that you may not qualify for an increase if someone else is receiving an increase for your dependants.

Increases for adults and other non-means-tested benefits

You cannot receive more than one increase to a particular benefit for an adult. If you are entitled to an increase to another benefit for the same adult or for another adult, or if someone else is entitled to an increase in the same or another benefit for the same adult as you, the increase is adjusted – see p2:493 for details of the overlapping benefit rules.[70] If you are getting an increase for an adult who is employed by you to care for a child and s/he is not residing with you (see p2:99) someone else may get an increase in their benefit for the same adult.[71]

The amount of an increase for an adult dependant is reduced by any earnings-replacement benefits (see pp1:4 and 2:493) which are payable to that dependant. If the increase is less than the benefit payable to the dependant, the increase is not paid. Otherwise it is paid at a rate equal to the difference between the two rates of benefit.[72] This rule does not apply if the adult is employed by you to care for a child and s/he is not residing with you (see p2:99).

Increases for children and other non-means-tested benefits

If you are entitled to an increase in more than one benefit for a particular child or someone else is entitled to a dependant's increase for the same child the overlapping benefit rules apply (see p2:493).[73]

If you are getting an increase in widowed mother's allowance, retirement pension or invalid care allowance for a child, you cannot also get the higher rate of child benefit payable to lone parents for your eldest eligible child. Instead you receive the standard rate of child benefit (ie, £14.40).[74] If you get the higher rate of child benefit as a lone parent for your eldest eligible child, any dependant's increase to other benefits for that child are reduced by £6.75 a week.[75]

If you or someone else is receiving guardian's allowance for a child, any dependant's increase for that child is reduced by the level of guardian's allowance paid for that child.[76]

Notes

References are to statutes and regulations as amended up to 8 March 1999. All regulations are (General) Regulations unless otherwise stated. There is a full list of abbreviations in Appendix 13.

1. Extra money for your adult dependant

1 ss82-84, 86A and 90 SSCBA 1992; regs 8, 12 and Sch 2 SSB(Dep) Regs; regs 9 and 10 SS(IB-ID) Regs
2 Regs 2(3) and 19(2) and (3) SS(C&P) Regs
3 s86A SSCBA 1992; reg 9(1) SS(IB-ID) Regs
4 Reg 9(2) SS(IB-ID) Regs
5 Sch 2 para 7 SSB(Dep) Regs; s90 SSCBA 1992
6 s84 SSCBA 1992
7 Case C-420/92 *Bramhill v CAO*, ECJ 7 July 1994. The discrimination will end in April 2010 as part of the programme to equalise the rules on pensionable age and retirement pensions – Sch 4 para 2 PA 1995
8 ss82(4) and 85 SSCBA 1992; regs 10, 12 and Sch 2 SSB(Dep) Regs; regs 9 and 14 SS(IB-ID) Regs
9 Regs 2(3), 4 and 19(2) and (3) SS(C&P) Regs
10 Sch 2 para 7 SSB(Dep) Regs
11 s85(3) SSCBA 1992
12 Reg 10 and Sch 2 para 7 SSB(Dep) Regs; reg 10 SS(IB-ID) Regs
13 Regs 8(2), (3) and 12 SSB(Dep) Regs: reg 10 SS(IB-ID) Regs
14 R(P) 4/93
15 ss82 and 83(2)(b) SSCBA 1992; reg 12 and Sch 2 para 7 SSB(Dep) Regs; reg 10(1) SS(IB-ID) Regs
16 s89 SSCBA 1992; Sch 2 SSB(Dep) Regs
17 s92 and Sch 7 para 8 SSCBA 1992
18 Sch 4 SSCBA 1992
19 Reg 6(3) SS(WB&RP) Regs; reg 14 SSB(Dep) Regs; reg 13 SS(IB-ID) Regs

2. Extra money for your children

20 s80(5) SSCBA 1992
21 ss80, 81 and 90 SSCBA 1992; reg 12 and Sch 2 SSB(Dep) Regs
22 Regs 2(3), 4 and 19(2) and (3) SS(C&P) Regs
23 s80(4) SSCBA 1992; Sch 2 para 2B SSB(Dep) Regs as amended
24 s89 SSCBA 1992; Sch 2 para 9 SSB(Dep) Regs
25 Sch 4 SSCBA 1992

3. Definition of terms

26 Reg 4A SSB(Dep) Regs; reg 6 SS(IB-ID) Regs
27 Reg 4A(1)(b) SSB(Dep) Regs; reg 6(1)(b) SS(IB-ID) Regs
28 Reg 4A(4) SSB(Dep) Regs; reg 6(2) SS(IB-ID) Regs
29 Reg 2(4) SSB(PRT) Regs
30 Reg 2(2) SSB(PRT) Regs
31 Reg 11 SSB(Dep) Regs; reg 12 SS(IB-ID) Regs
32 R(S) 3/74
33 R(U) 3/66
34 Reg 3 SSB(Dep) Regs; reg 3 SS(IB-ID) Regs
35 R(U) 25/58
36 R(S) 3/74
37 R(U) 14/62
38 R(S) 1/59
39 Reg 5 SSB(Dep) Regs; reg 8 SS(IB-ID) Regs
40 Reg 2(1) SSB(Dep) Regs; reg 2(1) SS(IB-ID) Regs
41 Reg 2(2) SSB(Dep) Regs; reg 2(2) SS(IB-ID) Regs
42 Reg 2(2)(i) and (ii) SSB(Dep) Regs; reg 2(2)(i) and (ii) SS(IB-ID) Regs
43 R(I) 20/60; R(S) 12/83
44 R(S) 2/85

45 Reg 2 SSB(Dep) Regs; reg 2
SS(IB-ID)Regs
46 CS/130/1987

4. Special rules for special groups
47 s91 SSCBA 1992
48 *Hyde v Hyde* [1886]
49 Reg 2 SSFA(PM) Regs

5. Claims, backdating and getting paid
50 s1 SSAA 1992
51 Reg 4(1) SS(C&P) Regs
52 s1(1A) and (1B) SSAA 1992
53 Reg 7(1) SS(C&P) Regs
54 Reg 6(1) SS(C&P) Regs
55 R(SB) 8/89
56 CSIS/48/1992; CIS/759/1992
57 Regs 4(7) and 6(1) SS(C&P) Regs
58 Reg 6(29) SS(C&P) Regs
59 Reg 9(3) and Sch 1 Part II
SS(C&P) Regs
60 Reg 9(4) SS(C&P) Regs
61 Reg 9(5) SS(C&P) Regs
62 Reg 9(6) SS(C&P) Regs
63 Reg 15 SS(C&P) Regs
64 Reg 14 SS(C&P) Regs
65 Reg 13 SS(C&P) Regs
66 Regs 19(2) and (3) SS(C&P) Regs
67 s3 SSAA 1992; reg 19(3)(h)
SS(C&P) Regs
68 Reg 32(1) SS(C&P) Regs

6. Tax and other benefits
69 s617 ICTA 1988
70 Reg 9 SS(OB) Regs
71 Reg 9 SS(OB) Regs
72 Reg 10 SS(OB) Regs
73 Reg 7 SS(OB) Regs
74 Regs 2(4) and (5) CB&SS(FAR)
Regs
75 Reg 8(2)(b) SS(OB) Regs
76 Reg 7(4) SS(OB) Regs

Chapter 37

. . . .

Claiming for others: means-tested benefits

This chapter explains who can be included in your claim for any of the means-tested benefits (income support, income-based jobseeker's allowance, family credit, disability working allowance, earnings top-up, housing benefit and council tax benefit). The rules explained in this chapter which apply to family credit/disability working allowance will also apply to working families tax credit and disabled person's tax credit from October 1999 (see Chapter 23). It covers:
1. Who is included in your claim (below)
2. Couples (p2:114)
3. Claiming for children (p2:121).

This chapter does not deal with the non-means-tested benefits you can and cannot claim for others. The rules for non-means-tested benefits are different. Sometimes you will be able to claim both means-tested benefits and non-means-tested benefits for the same people. Sometimes you will be able to claim means-tested benefits but not non-means-tested benefits and *vice versa*. You should check Chapter 36 to see whether the rules for those benefits apply to any of the other people you may wish to claim for.

1. Who is included in your claim

You claim the following benefits for yourself and your partner (if you have one and you and your partner are considered to be a couple – see p2:114):
* income support (IS) – see Chapter 20;
* income-based jobseeker's allowance (JSA) – see Chapter 14;
* family credit (FC) – see Chapter 21;
* disability working allowance (DWA) – see Chapter 22;
* earnings top-up (ETU) – see Chapter 24;
* housing benefit (HB) – see Chapter 25;
* council tax benefit (CTB) – see Chapter 27.

You also claim IS/JSA/FC/DWA/HB/CTB for dependent children who are members of your household (you cannot apply for ETU in such circumstances – see p1:500). This is your 'family' for means-tested benefit purposes.[1] A partner can include a wife, husband or cohabitee of the opposite sex.

When your benefit is worked out, the needs of your partner (see below) and any children (see p2:121) are usually added to yours and so are your partner's income and capital. There are special rules for the treatment of the income and capital of dependent children (see pp2:382 and 2:443).

If one member of your family is claiming IS/income-based JSA/FC/DWA/ETU/HB/CTB, no other member can claim the same benefit for the same period.[2] For IS/income-based JSA/HB/CTB partners can choose which of them should be the claimant.[3] For FC, the woman must usually claim (although for WFTC couples will be able to choose which partner may apply – see p1:489).[4] For DWA (and DPTC) the disabled partner must claim, although if both of you are disabled you can choose which one of you should be the claimant.[5] For ETU, the partner in work must usually apply, although you can choose who should apply if you both work.[6] See below for who counts as your partner. For details about how to claim see p1:449 (IS), p1:281 (JSA), p1:464 (FC), p1:501 (ETU), p1:479 (DWA), p1:530 (HB) and p1:581 (CTB).

2. Couples

For means-tested benefits, you and your partner are considered to be a 'couple' if you are both 16[7] or over, *and*:[8]

- married and living in the same household (see p2:115); *or*
- not married but 'living together as husband and wife' (see p2:115) in the same household.

In these circumstances, you must claim as a couple. Your partner's income and capital are counted when assessing your entitlement to means-tested benefits. For IS, income-based JSA, HB, CTB, FC, ETU and DWA you receive the amount of benefit for couples.

If you are lesbian or gay partners, you do not count as a couple and must claim as single people.

Special rules apply if either partner is under 18 (see pp2:152 and 2:320).

Being married to someone does not necessarily mean that you cannot be treated as part of a couple with someone else instead.[9]

You count as polygamously married if you are married to more than one person and your marriages took place in a country which permits polygamy.[10] There are special rules if you are polygamously married (see p1:122).[11] Essentially, these provide that for all means-tested benefits any income and capital of a polygamous partner will be taken into account, but that for IS/JSA/HB/CTB an increased personal allowance and for FC/DWA/ETU an increased maximum award is allowed to take into account their needs.

Living in the same 'household'

The idea of sharing a household is central to whether you include a child or a partner in your claim. However, the term 'household' is not defined. Whether two people should be treated as members of the same household is very much a question of fact. A house can contain a number of separate households and if one person has exclusive occupation of separate accommodation from another they will not be considered to be living in the same household. Physical presence together is also not in itself conclusive. There must be a 'particular kind of tie' binding two people together in a domestic establishment. This could, in appropriate circumstances, include a household within, for example, a hotel or boarding house.[12] However, it must also involve two or more people living together as a unit and, as such a unit, enjoying a reasonable level of independence and self-sufficiency. It has been held that a married couple sharing a room in a residential home – because they needed someone else to help with organising their personal care and domestic activities – were not self-sufficient and therefore could not be said to live in a domestic establishment, and therefore did not share a household.[13]

There are some occasions when you and another person are regarded as members of the same household when you think you should not be. If this occurs it is important to try to show that, although you both live in the same house, you maintain separate **households**.

A separate household might exist if there are:
- independent arrangements for the storage and cooking of food;
- independent financial arrangements;
- separate eating arrangements;
- no evidence of family life;
- separate commitments for housing costs, even if the liability is to another person in the same premises.

You cannot be a member of more than one household at the same time.[14] If two people can be shown to be maintaining separate homes, they cannot be said to be sharing the same household.[15] Even if you have the right to occupy only part of a room, you may have your own household.[16]

Living together as husband and wife

If it is decided that you are 'living together as husband and wife' (cohabiting), only one of you is able to claim a means-tested benefit. The amount of benefit for a couple is usually less than that for two single people, so it is important to dispute a decision that you are cohabiting if you believe you are not. However, in some cases you may have to *prove* that you are cohabiting – eg, where you want to claim FC, and you do not work yourself, but your partner does. You should, of course, be consistent about your circumstances for each benefit. If you are awarded IS/income-based JSA, the local authority should not make a separate decision about whether you are cohabiting when considering your claim for HB/CTB.[17] However, if you have not been awarded IS/income-based JSA, the local authority has a duty to give its own consideration to whether you are cohabiting and may reach a different conclusion from that of the Benefits Agency.

The factors considered below are used as 'signposts' in determining whether or not you are cohabiting.[18] No one factor need in itself be conclusive, as it is your 'general relationship' as a whole which is of paramount importance[19] and, just as relationships between couples may often vary considerably, so each case depends on all its own particular facts and circumstances.

The Benefits Agency and local authorities often apply too narrow an interpretation of the test. There is no rule, for example, that if your partner stays with you for three nights or more a week you are *automatically* to be treated as a couple who are living together.

Cohabitation - Signposts

1. Do you live in the same household? (see below)
2. Do you have a sexual relationship? (p2:117)
3. What are your financial arrangements? (p2:117)
4. Is your relationship stable? (p2:118)
5. Do you have children? (p2:118)
6. How do you appear in public? (p2:118)

Do you live in the same household?

In all cases you must spend the major part of your time in the same household (see p2:115 for a discussion of 'household'). If one of you has a separate address where you usually live, you should not be considered to be cohabiting. You cannot be a member of more than one household at the same time so, if you are a member of one couple, you cannot also be treated as part of another.

Even if you *do* share a 'household', you may not be cohabiting. It is essential to look at *why* two people are in the same household.[20] For example, where a couple were living in the same household for reasons of 'care, companionship and mutual convenience' they were not 'living together as husband and wife'.[21]

Separated couples living under the same roof should not be treated as couples if they are maintaining separate households.[22] Where a relationship has only recently broken down, continuing financial support and shared responsibilities and liabilities may be particularly inconclusive, especially where there is evidence of active steps being taken to live apart. The way people live and their attitude of mind is more significant. Any 'mere hope' of a reconciliation is not a 'reasonable expectation' where at least one partner has accepted that the relationship is at an end.[23]

Do you have a sexual relationship?

In practice, the Benefits Agency or local authority may not ask you about the existence of a sexual relationship, in which case they will only have the information if you volunteer it. If you do not have a sexual relationship, you should tell the officer yourself – and perhaps offer to show her/him the separate sleeping arrangements.

Having a sexual relationship is not sufficient by itself to prove you are cohabiting. If you have never had a sexual relationship there is a strong (but not necessarily conclusive) presumption that you are not cohabiting.[24]

A couple who abstain from a sexual relationship before marriage on grounds of principle (eg, religious reasons) should not be counted as cohabiting until they are formally married.[25]

Even if the Benefits Agency or local authority does not go into the question of whether or not there is a sexual relationship, any tribunal or review board has a duty to ask such questions in order to determine whether or not you are cohabiting.[26]

If there is, or has been, a sexual relationship, that is evidence of the affection and trust between the parties. However, an occasional sexual relationship does not imply cohabitation if the rest of the relationship is casual and unlike a marriage.

What are your financial arrangements?

If one partner is supported by the other or household expenses are shared, this may be treated as evidence of cohabitation. However, it is important to consider how they are shared. There is a difference between, on the one hand, paying a fixed weekly contribution or rigidly sharing bills 50/50 and, on the other hand, a free common fund attributable to income and expenditure. The former does not imply cohabitation, the latter might.

The financial relationship between lodger and landlady/landlord often comes under scrutiny. The Benefits Agency or local authority sometimes claim that the payments are too high or too low and so indicate that the relationship is not purely financial. It is important to explain how payments came to be as they are. However low or high the charge may appear, it is the reasoning which led to it at the time which is important. There may be many motives for having a lodger apart from purely commercial ones or cohabitation. It may be that the relationship is entered into so that there is another adult in the house – for company or security, perhaps. Friendship between a lodger and landlady/landlord does not mean that they are cohabiting.

Is your relationship stable?

Marriage is expected to be stable and lasting. It follows that an occasional or brief association should not be regarded as cohabiting. However, the fact that a relationship is stable does not make it cohabitation – eg, you can have a stable landlord/lodger relationship but not be cohabiting.

It is important to remember that many stable relationships are not necessarily relationships where the partners are living together as husband and wife – for example, relationships between housemates or landlords and lodgers may be stable but the parties are not cohabiting. The way you spend your time together, the activities you do together and the things you do for each other are relevant, so questions such as how you spend your holidays, how you organise the shopping, the laundry and cleaning may be important.

Do you have children?

If you have had a child together, and live in the same household as the other parent, there is a strong (but not conclusive) presumption of cohabitation.

How do you appear in public?

Officers may check the electoral roll and claims for national insurance benefits to see if you present yourselves as a couple. Many couples retain their separate identity publicly as unmarried people. They should, however, be aware that they may be regarded as cohabiting.

Challenging a 'living together' decision

Sometimes benefit is stopped or adjusted because someone regularly stays overnight, even though you might have none of the long-term commitments generally associated with marriage. But couples with no sexual relationship who live together (eg, as landlord/lodger, tenant or housekeeper, or as flat-sharers) also sometimes fall foul of the rule. People who provide mutual support and share household expenses are not necessarily cohabiting – this is also the case where people of the same sex or friends of different sexes share a home.[27]

If you are at all unhappy with a decision that you are cohabiting, you should appeal (see p2:611) or apply for a review (see pp2:570 and 2:590), and carefully consider what evidence to put before the tribunal/review board in relation to each of the six questions above and any other matters that you consider relevant. Possibilities include evidence of the other person having another address[28] (eg, a rent book and other household bills), receipts for board and lodging, statements from friends and relatives or, where you have been married, evidence of a formal separation or divorce proceedings.

On an initial application for benefit it is not for you to prove that you are not cohabiting,[29] though you are required to provide the Benefits Agency or local authority with any information it reasonably requires to decide your claim.[30] Neither party has the burden of proof in this situation – a decision should simply be made on all the evidence available.[31] By contrast, if your benefit as a single person is stopped because it is alleged that you are cohabiting, the burden of proof is on the Benefits Agency or the local authority to prove that you are cohabiting.[32]

If your benefit is suspended or withdrawn because you are cohabiting, you should seek a review or reapply immediately if your circumstances change. You should also apply immediately for any other benefits for which you might qualify – eg, HB/CTB, where the local authority may reach a different decision to that of the Benefits Agency (see Chapters 25 and 27). You should apply on the basis of low income for other benefits, which you previously qualified for automatically if you were on IS or JSA – eg, health benefits (see Chapter 29).

If you are still entitled to a means-tested benefit, even though it is decided that you are cohabiting, you should be paid as a couple.

If your IS/income-based JSA stops and you have diverted a maintenance order to the Benefits Agency (see p2:291), contact the magistrates' court immediately to get payments sent direct to you. If the Child Support Agency is collecting a child maintenance assessment for you (see 2:292), ask them to start paying the money to you.

If you have no money at all, you may be able to get a social fund crisis loan (see p1:667).

Couples living apart

If you separate *permanently* you can claim as a single person immediately. However, you continue to be treated as a couple while you and your partner are *temporarily* apart.[33] Your former household need not have been in this country.[34] The following rules apply in determining whether you still count as a couple:

- **For FC, DWA or ETU.** You no longer count as a couple if you or your partner:[35]
  - are living apart and do not intend to resume living together (see p2:115); *or*
  - have been in hospital for 52 weeks or more; *or*
  - are a compulsory patient detained in hospital under the mental health provisions; *or*
  - are detained in custody serving a sentence of 52 weeks or more.

- **For CTB.** You continue to count as a couple as long as you both remain liable for the council tax at your address.[36] Note that the rules for establishing a couple's liability for council tax are not the same as the rules for establishing their entitlement to CTB (see CPAG's *Council Tax Handbook*).
- **For IS, income-based JSA and HB.** You count as a couple, even if you or your partner are temporarily living away from your family, unless you:[37]
  - have no intention of resuming living together (see p2:115); *or*
  - are likely to be separated for more than 52 weeks. However, you can still be treated as a couple if you are likely to be separated for more than 52 weeks provided it is not 'substantially' longer and there are exceptional circumstances such as a stay in hospital, or if there is no control over the length of the absence.
- **For IS and income-based JSA.** You no longer count as a couple if any of the following apply to either of you:[38]
  - you are in custody;
  - you are on temporary release from prison;
  - you are a compulsory patient detained in hospital under the mental health provisions;
  - you are staying permanently in local authority residential accommodation, or a residential care or nursing home;
  - the *claimant* is abroad and does not qualify for IS or income-based JSA. However, where your *partner* is temporarily abroad you continue to be treated as a couple, but after four weeks (eight if s/he has taken a child abroad for medical treatment) the amount of IS or income-based JSA you receive is that for a single claimant or lone parent.[39] You can get IS without signing on if you have children under 16.[40] Your partner's income and capital continue to be treated as yours for as long as the absence is held to be temporary.

If you are no longer treated as a couple for the purposes of calculating your IS or income-based JSA, you may still be liable to maintain your partner (see p2:290).

You are still treated as a couple if you are temporarily living apart and the following applies: one of you is at home or in hospital, or in local authority residential accommodation or in a residential care or nursing home, and the other is:[41]

- resident in a nursing home, but not counted as a patient; *or*
- staying in a residential care home; *or*
- in a home for the rehabilitation of alcoholics or drug addicts; *or*
- in Polish resettlement accommodation; *or*
- on a government training course and has to live away from home (see below for your right to housing costs for more than one home); *or*
- in a probation or bail hostel.

Although your income and capital are calculated in the normal way for a couple, your applicable amount is calculated as if each of you were single claimants if this comes to more than your usual couple rate. If you have children, one of you is treated as a lone parent. If you have housing costs (see Chapter 46), your applicable amount includes these as well as any costs of the temporary accommodation of the partner away from home. If you are both away from home, the costs of both sets of temporary accommodation and the family home may be met.[42] If both homes are rented see p1:518 for when HB can be paid for more than one home at a time. If you own your home and your partner is staying in rented accommodation, you may get your housing costs met by IS or income-based JSA and your partner can claim HB.

Additional points

- Where questions of 'intention' are involved (eg, in deciding whether you or your partner intend to resume living with your family), the intention must be unqualified – ie, it must not depend on some factor over which you have no control (eg, where it depends on the right of entry to the UK being granted by the Home Office[43] or on the offer of a suitable job[44]).
- See p2:344 if one of you lives away from home as a student or on a government training course and you have to pay for two homes.
- See p2:343 if your child is in hospital and you have to stay in lodgings to be nearby.
- See p2:343 if one or both of you are temporarily in local authority residential accommodation.

3. **Claiming for children**

You do not have to be a *parent* to receive benefit for a child, but you must be 'responsible' for a child who is living in your household.[45] You claim for any child under 16; or under 19 if they are still in full-time 'relevant' education[46] (see p1:329 for what this means). For earnings top-up (ETU) you must *not* be responsible for a child in your household.[47]

Where the same benefit is involved, a child can only be the responsibility of one person in any week.[48] There is no provision allowing benefit to be split between parents where a child divides her/his time equally between the homes of two parents. See p2:123 for when a child no longer counts as your dependant.

'Responsibility' for a child

You claim income support (IS), income-based jobseeker's allowance (JSA), family credit (FC), disability working allowance (DWA), housing benefit (HB) or council tax benefit (CTB) (but you cannot apply for ETU) for a child for whom you are 'responsible'. If you are in full-time work (see p2:5) and you live in an ETU pilot area (see p1:499) it is particularly important to check whether you will be treated as 'responsible' for a child before you claim. If you claim the wrong benefit you may lose money because, unlike the rules for FC/ DWA (see pp1:465 and 1:480), claims for FC/ETU are not interchangeable and you may not be able to backdate your claim for the right benefit by the time you find out that your claim for the wrong benefit has been refused. If in doubt, you should claim both FC and ETU at the same time. You are treated as 'responsible' for a child if:

- **For FC, DWA, ETU, HB and CTB** the child is 'normally living' with you.[49] This means that s/he spends more time with you than with anyone else.[50]

  Where it is unclear whose household the child lives in, or where s/he spends an equal amount of time with two parents in different homes (this may not mean literally 3½ days with each parent[51]), you are treated as having responsibility if:[52]
    - you get child benefit for the child (see Chapter 12);
    - no one gets child benefit, but you have applied for it;
    - no one has applied for child benefit, or both of you have applied, but you appear to have the most responsibility;

- **For IS and income-based JSA** you get child benefit for the child (see Chapter 12).[53]

  Where no one gets child benefit you are 'responsible' if you are the only one who has applied for it. In all other cases the person 'responsible' is the person with whom the child *usually lives*.[54]

  Where a child for whom you are 'responsible' gets child benefit for another child, you are also 'responsible' for that child.[55]

Note: For FC, ETU, DWA, HB and CTB, it is important to look at who gets child benefit only where it is unclear whose household the child *normally* lives in. For IS and income-based JSA, it is essential to look first at who gets child benefit, and only where this is not decisive is it relevant to look at where the child *usually* lives. This difference may mean that in some situations one parent may be able to claim IS or income-based JSA for a child while the other parent can claim FC, DWA, HB or CTB for the same child at the same time.

Living in the same household[56]

If you are counted as responsible for a child, then that child is usually treated as a member of your household despite any temporary absence. (For the meaning of 'household', see p2:115.) However, s/he does *not* count as a member of your household if s/he:

- **For IS, income-based JSA, FC, DWA, HB and CTB:**
  - is being fostered by you under a specific statutory provision. However, you can claim benefit for a child you are fostering privately or where social services have made a less formal arrangement for the child to live with you;
  - is living with you prior to adoption, and has been placed with you by social services or an adoption agency;
- **For IS, income-based JSA, HB and CTB:**
  - is boarded out or has been placed with someone else prior to adoption;
  - is in the care of, or being looked after by, the local authority and not living with you. You should receive IS or income-based JSA for her/him for the days when s/he comes home – eg, for the weekend or a holiday.[57] Make sure you tell the Benefits Agency in good time so they can pay you the extra money. The local authority can also increase your applicable amount to include the child for HB and CTB for all of that week whether the child returns for all or only part of it;[58]
- **For IS, income-based JSA, FC and DWA:**
  - has been in hospital or a local authority home for more than 12 weeks, and you or other members of your household have not been in regular contact with her/him. For FC/DWA this means 12 weeks prior to the claim.[59] For IS/income-based JSA, the 12 weeks run from the date s/he went into the hospital or home, or from the date you claim IS/income-based JSA, if later.[60] However, if you were getting income-based JSA immediately before your claim for IS, or if you were getting IS immediately before your claim for income-based JSA, the 12 weeks run from the date s/he went into the hospital or home;[61]
  - has been in hospital or a local authority home for 52 weeks or more because of illness or disability even if, for FC/DWA, you are still in regular contact.[62] For IS/income-based JSA, the child will still count as part of your household so long as you are still in regular contact;[63]
  - is in custody. (For FC and DWA, being in custody on remand does not count.) You should receive IS or income-based JSA for any periods your child spends at home;[64]
- **For IS and income-based JSA only:**
  - has been abroad for more than four weeks, or for more than eight weeks if the absence abroad is to get medical treatment for the child.[65] The four- or eight-week periods run from the day s/he went abroad or from the day you claim IS/income-based JSA, if later. However, if you were getting income-based JSA immediately before your claim for IS, or if you were getting IS immediately before your claim for income-based JSA, the four-

37

or eight-week periods are calculated from the day after the child went abroad;[66]

– is living with you and away from her/his parental or usual home in order to attend school. The child is not treated as a member of your family, but remains a member of her/his parent's household.[67]

When you stop claiming for a child

You stop claiming for a child for whom you are no longer responsible (see p2:122) or who is no longer a member of your household (see p2:122) or who is no longer treated as a child (see below):

- **For IS and income-based JSA.** You stop claiming for a child as soon as someone else starts receiving child benefit for her/him (see p2:122).
- **For HB and CTB.** You stop claiming as soon as the child starts normally living elsewhere (see p2:122).
- **For FC and DWA.** You are no longer entitled to make a claim for a child as soon as the child starts normally living (see p2:122) elsewhere, but see p1:468 (FC) and p1:483 (DWA) for when this may affect an award of FC/DWA which has already been made to you. For ETU, it is only when a child begins normally living elsewhere that you may make a claim.
- **For IS, income-based JSA, HB and CTB.** You claim for a child until s/he is 16, or 19 if s/he is in relevant education (see p1:329). Children count as in relevant education until the 'terminal date' (see p1:235), or until they get a full-time job if that is earlier. 'Full-time' work for dependent children means at least 24 hours a week.[68]

A 16/17-year-old who has left school or college may continue to be counted as part of your family' for a few months after the terminal date. You get benefit for them during the child benefit extension period (see p1:235 for details and dates) provided the following apply:[69]

- you were entitled to child benefit for that child immediately before the child benefit extension period started; *and*
- you have made a fresh claim for child benefit in writing for the child benefit extension period; *and*
- s/he has registered for work/work-based training for young people (formerly youth training) at the JobCentre or Careers Office; *and*
- s/he is not in full-time work (see above).

If s/he loses the job or leaves work-based training before the end of the child benefit extension period (see p1:235), s/he becomes your dependant again and you can claim for her/him as long as the above conditions are satisfied.

Some 16/17-year-olds can get IS or income-based JSA in their own right before they are 18 (see p2:152) and you cannot claim for them.[70]

- **For ETU.** Except for the rule relating to school-leavers (see p2:125), there are no express rules whereby a child for whom you would otherwise be treated as responsible (see p2:122) will nevertheless not count as a member of your household. However, as it would not appear to be consistent with the purpose of the ETU scheme for you to be denied ETU because you would be treated as responsible for a child in the very same circumstances as you may be denied FC/DWA in respect of that child, you should argue that the same rules applied to FC/DWA should apply to your claim for ETU. These circumstances would be if a child is being fostered or adopted by you (see p2:123) or has been in hospital or a local authority home for a long time or is in custody (see p2:123). You may need to seek advice (see Appendix 2) if this applies to you.

- **For FC, ETU and DWA.** A child counts as your dependant for the purposes of your FC/ETU/DWA claim where, at the date of the claim, s/he is actually undergoing full-time education. Children do not count as dependants once they have left school, even if you are still getting child benefit for them.[71] For FC (but not for DWA), your benefit will stop before the end of a 26-week award if your child leaves full-time education and you are not responsible for any other child who is still in full-time education (see p1:468). For FC/DWA, children are also not counted as dependants if they become entitled to IS or income-based JSA in their own right[72] (or would be so entitled, had a member of their family not been entitled). As soon as a child for whom you have claimed FC/DWA is awarded IS/income-based JSA, your award of FC (see p1:468) or DWA (see p1:483) will end.

Notes

References are to statutes and regulations as amended up to 8 March 1999. All regulations are (General) Regulations unless otherwise stated. There is a full list of abbreviations in Appendix 13.

1. **Who is included in your claim**

1. s137(1) SSCBA 1992; s35(1) JSA 1995; rule 3(1) ETU Scheme
2. s134(2) SSCBA 1992; s3(1)(d) JSA 1995; rule 7(4) ETU Scheme
3. **IS** Reg 4(3) SS(C&P) Regs
   JSA Reg 4(3B) SS(C&P) Regs
   HB Reg 71(1) HB Regs
   CTB Reg 61(1) CTB Regs
4. Reg 4(2) SS(C&P) Regs;
5. s129(1) SSCBA 1992; reg 4(3A) SS(C&P) Regs
6. Rule 7(2)(a) ETU Scheme and rule 5(2) ETU(A&P) Rules
7. CFC/7/1992

2. **Couples**

8. s137(1) SSCBA 1992; s35(1) JSA 1995; rule 2(1) ETU Scheme
9. R(SB) 8/85
10. **IS** Reg 2(1) IS Regs
    JSA Reg 1(3) JSA Regs
    HB Reg 2(1) HB Regs
    CTB Reg 2(1) CTB Regs
11. **IS** Regs 18 and 23 IS Regs
    JSA Regs 84 and 88(4) and (5) JSA Regs
    FC Regs 10 and 46(2) FC Regs
    DWA Regs 12 and 51(2) DWA Regs
    ETU Rules 16 and 54(5) ETU Scheme
    HB Regs 17 and 19 HB Regs
    CTB Regs 9 and 11 CTB Regs
12. *Santos v Santos* [1972] 2 All ER 246; CIS/671/1992; CIS/81/1993
13. CIS/4935/1997
14. R(SB) 8/85
15. R(SB) 4/83
16. CSB/463/1986
17. *R v HBRB of Penwith District Council ex parte Menear*, 24 HLR 120 (11 October 1991)
18. *Crake and Butterworth v SBC* [1982] 1 All ER 498
19. R(SB) 17/81; R(G) 3/71; CIS/87/1993
20. *Crake and Butterworth v SBC* quoted in R(SB) 35/85
21. R(SB) 35/85
22. para 15027 AOG
23. CIS/72/1994
24. CIS/87/1993
25. CSB/150/1985
26. CIS/87/1993
27. CSSB/145/1983
28. R(SB) 13/82
29. CIS/317/1994
30. **IS/FC/DWA** Reg 7(1) SS(C&P) Regs
    JSA Reg 24 JSA Regs
    ETU Rule 9 ETU(A&P) Rules
    HB Reg 73 HB Regs
    CTB Reg 63 CTB Regs
31. CIS/317/1994
32. R(I) 1/71
33. **IS** Reg 16(1) IS Regs
    JSA Reg 78(1) JSA Regs
    FC Reg 9 FC Regs
    DWA Reg 11 DWA Regs
    ETU Rule 15 ETU Scheme
    HB Reg 15(1) HB Regs
    CTB Reg 7(1) CTB Regs
34. CIS/508/1992
35. **FC** Reg 9 FC Regs
    DWA Reg 11 DWA Regs
    ETU Rule 15 ETU Scheme
36. Reg 7(1) CTB Regs
37. **IS** Reg 16(1) and (2) IS Regs
    JSA reg 78(2) JSA Regs
    HB Reg 15(1) and (2) HB Regs
38. **IS** Reg 16(3) IS Regs
    JSA Reg 78(3) JSA Regs
39. **IS** Sch 7 paras 11 and 11A IS Regs
    JSA Sch 5 paras 10 and 11 JSA Regs
40. Sch 1B para 23 IS Regs
41. **IS** Sch 7 para 9 IS Regs
    JSA Reg 85 and Sch 5 para 5 JSA Regs

42 **IS** Sch 7 para 9 col (2) IS Regs
JSA Reg 85 and Sch 5 para 5 col
(2) JSA Regs
43 CIS/508/1992; CIS/13805/1996
44 CIS/484/1993

3. Claiming for children

45 s137 SSCBA 1992; s35 JSA 1995;
reg 77 JSA Regs
46 **IS** Reg 14 IS Regs
JSA s35 JSA 1995; regs 1(3) and
76 JSA Regs
FC Reg 6 FC Regs
DWA Reg 8 DWA Regs
HB Reg 13 HB Regs
CTB Reg 5 CTB Regs
47 Rule 3(1) ETU Scheme
48 **IS/FC/DWA/HB/CTB** s134(2)
SSCBA 1992
IS Reg 15(4) IS Regs
JSA s3(1)(d) JSA 1995; reg 77(5)
JSA Regs
FC Reg 7(3) FC Regs
DWA Reg 9(3) DWA Regs
HB Reg 14(3) HB Regs
CTB Reg 6(3) CTB Regs
49 **FC** Reg 7(1) FC Regs
DWA Reg 9(1) DWA Regs
ETU Rule 14 ETU Scheme
HB Reg 14(1) HB Regs
CTB Reg 6(1) CTB Regs
50 CFC/1537/1995
51 CFC/1537/1995
52 **FC** Reg 7(2) FC Regs
DWA Reg 9(2) DWA Regs
ETU Rule 14(2) ETU Scheme
HB Reg 14(2) HB Regs
CTB Reg 6(2) CTB Regs
53 **IS** Reg 15(1) IS Regs
JSA Reg 77(1) JSA Regs
54 **IS** Reg 15(2) IS Regs
JSA Reg 77(3) JSA Regs
55 **IS** Reg 15(1A) IS Regs
JSA Reg 77(2) JSA Regs
56 **IS** Reg 16 IS Regs
JSA Reg 78(1) JSA Regs
FC Reg 8 FC Regs
DWA Reg 10 DWA Regs
HB Reg 15 HB Regs
CTB Reg 7 CTB Regs
57 **IS** Regs 15(3) and 16(6) IS Regs
JSA Regs 77(4) and 78(7) JSA
Regs
58 **HB** Reg 15(5) HB Regs
CTB Reg 7(4) CTB Regs

59 **FC** Reg 8(2)(a) FC Regs
DWA Reg 10(2)(a) DWA Regs
60 **IS** Reg 16(5)(b) IS Regs
JSA Reg 78(5)(c) JSA Regs
61 **IS** Reg 16(5A) IS Regs
JSA Reg 78(6) JSA Regs
62 **FC** Reg 46(6) FC Regs
DWA Reg 51(6) DWA Regs
63 **IS** Reg 16(5)(b)(ii) IS Regs
JSA Reg 78(5)(c)(ii) JSA Regs
64 **IS** Regs 15(3) and 16(6) IS Regs
JSA Regs 77(4) and 78(5)(I) and
(7) JSA Regs
65 **IS** Reg 16(5a) and (aa) IS Regs
JSA Reg 78(5)(a) and (b) JSA
Regs
66 **IS** Reg 16(5A) IS Regs
JSA Reg 78(6) JSA Regs
67 **IS** Reg 16(7) IS Regs
JSA Reg 78(8) JSA Regs
68 Regs 1(2) (definition of
'remunerative work') and 7 CB
Regs
69 **All** Reg 7D(1) CB Regs
IS Reg 15(1) IS Regs
JSA Reg 77(1) JSA Regs
HB Reg 13 HB Regs
CTB Reg 5 CTB Regs
70 s134(2) SSCBA 1992
71 **FC** Reg 6(2) FC Regs
DWA Reg 8(2) DWA Regs
ETU Rule 14(4) ETU Scheme
72 **FC** Reg 6(2) FC Regs
DWA Reg 8(2) DWA Regs

Part 8

Special rules for special groups

Chapter 38

··

Studying and claiming

This chapter contains:
1. Studying and claiming income support or jobseeker's allowance (below)
2. Studying and claiming housing benefit (p2:141)
3. Studying and claiming council tax benefit (p2:147)
4. Studying and claiming other benefits (p2:148)

Studying full or part-time can have a major impact on your entitlement to benefits if you are under pensionable age (60 for women and 65 for men). The rules about studying are different for each benefit. This means you could find you are not entitled to some benefits but other benefits are not affected by your study. If you are already claiming a benefit your entitlement may be affected if you start studying. If you are not able to claim benefit while studying someone else may be able to claim for you.

Scotland has a different education system to England and Wales. The same terms are often used within the education systems of all three countries but they can have different technical meanings, ie, 'further', 'higher' and 'advanced' education. Within benefit rules terms are used to define different levels of education, ie, 'relevant', 'non-advanced' and 'advanced', which have a technical meaning for benefit purposes. However, these are terms which are not generally used by educational institutions.

---

1. Studying and claiming income support or jobseeker's allowance

People in full-time education cannot usually qualify for income support (IS – see Chapter 20) or jobseeker's allowance (JSA – see Chapter 14), but there are some exceptions. You may be able to claim if you are studying part-time (see p2:138). The rules of entitlement depend partly on your age and partly on your course and are as follows:

- You count as in **'relevant education'** (see below) if you are under 19 and on a full-time non-advanced course. If you are in relevant education you can only claim IS in some circumstances (see below); you cannot claim JSA. If you cannot claim IS or JSA your parents (or person acting in their place) may be able to claim benefits for you (see p2:133). You should note that the term 'relevant education' does not apply for housing benefit purposes (see p2:141).

- You count as a **full-time student** (see p2:134) if:
  - you are under 19 and on a full-time advanced course;
  - you are 19 or over but under pensionable age (60 for women and 65 for men) and on a full-time advanced or non-advanced course.

To see if you are a full-time student who can claim IS or JSA see pp2:136-137.

If you are not entitled to IS or JSA but you have a partner who is not studying, s/he could be the claimant instead.

Under 19 and in relevant education

If you are under 19 and on a **full-time non-advanced course** (see p1:233) at school or college you count as being in relevant education. You usually cannot claim IS or JSA,[1] but there are exceptions (see below).

While you are in relevant education, your parents (or anyone acting as your parents) can get child benefit for you and claim additions for you if they get one of the means-tested benefits, or non-means-tested benefits (see p2:133). See below to find out if you can claim IS or JSA in your own right.

Circumstances when you qualify for IS while in relevant education

You can get IS while in relevant education (see above) if:[2]

- you are the parent of a child for whom you are treated as responsible (see p1:122);
- you are so severely disabled that you are unlikely to get a job in the next 12 months;
- you are an orphan, and have no one acting as your parent;
- you have left local authority care and of necessity you have to live away from your parents and any person acting in their place;
- you have to live away from your parents and any person acting in their place (see below), because:
  - you are estranged from them; *or*
  - you are in physical or moral danger; *or*
  - there is a serious risk to your physical or mental health.

The physical or moral danger does not have to be caused by your parents. Therefore a young person who is a refugee and cannot rejoin her/his parents can claim IS while at school.[3]

A **'person acting in place of your parents'** includes a local authority or voluntary organisation if you are being cared for by them, or foster parents – but only until you leave care.[4] It would not include a person who is your sponsor under the immigration laws.[5]

'**Estrangement**' implies emotional disharmony,[6] where you have no desire to have any prolonged contact with your parents or they feel similarly towards you. It is possible to be estranged even though your parents are providing some financial support or you still have some contact with them. If you are in care, it is also possible to be estranged from a local authority. If you are, then you could qualify for IS if you have to live away from local authority accommodation;[7]

- you live apart from your parents and any person acting in their place and they are unable to support you, *and*:
  - they are in prison; *or*
  - they are unable to come to Britain because they do not have leave to enter under UK immigration laws;[8] *or*
  - they are chronically sick or are mentally or physically disabled. This covers people who could get a disability premium or higher pensioner premium or have an armed forces grant for car costs because of disability or are substantially and permanently disabled;
- you are a refugee learning English (see p1:445).

Circumstances when you qualify for JSA while in relevant education

You cannot get JSA while in relevant education.[9] You may be able to claim IS instead if you fit into one of the groups who can claim while in relevant education (see p2:132) or your parents may be able to claim benefit for you (see below).

Circumstances in which somebody else can claim benefits for you while you are in relevant education

If you cannot claim IS or JSA because you are in relevant education somebody else may be able to claim for you as part of their own claim for benefits instead.

For means-tested benefits you can be included as part of someone else's claim if they can be treated as '**responsible**' for you (see p1:122). They cannot be treated as responsible for you if you are claiming IS in your own right.

For some non-means-tested benefits you can be included as part of someone else's claim if you are treated as their '**dependant**' (see p2:97). You cannot be treated as their 'dependant' if you are claiming IS in your own right.

In some circumstances you may count as both a person who can claim IS while you are in relevant education and as a person who can be part of someone else's claim because they can be treated as 'responsible' for you or you can be treated as their 'dependant'. You will have to decide which option is best for you.

Claiming IS or JSA when you leave relevant education

Once you have left relevant education you might be able to claim IS or JSA if you satisfy the rules for getting those benefits (see Chapters 20 and 14). However, when you have reached the official leaving date at the end of your course you continue to be treated as in relevant education during the vacation that follows. The day on which you cease to be treated as in relevant education is called the **'terminal date'** (see p1:235) but your parents continue to get benefit for you until the end of that week. While you continue to be treated as in relevant education, you are only entitled to IS in the circumstances outlined on p2:132 or from your 19th birthday if it falls after your official leaving date but before the appropriate 'terminal date'.[10] If you leave school before the legal school-leaving date, you are treated as having stayed on until that date

From the Monday following your terminal date, there are three possibilities:

- you might get IS if you fit into one of the groups of people who can claim (see Chapter 20);
- you might get JSA if you satisfy the qualifying conditions, see Chapter 14 (if you are 16 or 17 you have to satisfy special rules – see p1:328); *or*
- if you do not get IS or JSA in your own right, your parents might be able to go on claiming child benefit and some other benefits for you (see p2:133) during what is known as **the child benefit extension period** (see p1:235).

Full-time students

If you are a **full-time student** you cannot usually claim IS or JSA for the duration of your course, including vacations.[11] See pp:136 and 2:137 for exceptions to this rule. See p2:137 if you give up, change or take time out of your course and p2:138 if you are studying part-time.

You count as a **'full-time student'** if:[12]

- you are under 19 and on a **full-time course** of advanced education. 'Advanced education' means degree or postgraduate level qualifications, teaching courses, HND, diplomas of higher education, HND or HNC of the Business Technology Education Council or the Scottish Vocational Education Council and all other courses above advanced GNVQ or equivalent, OND, A-levels, highers or Scottish certificate of sixth-year studies. See below for what counts as a full-time course;
- you are 19 or over but under pensionable age (60 for women and 65 for men) and on a **full-time course** of study. If your course is full-time you are treated as a full-time student regardless of the level of the course. See below for what counts as a full-time course.

You are treated as a student until either the last day of your course or until you abandon it or are dismissed. 'Last day of the course' means the date on which the last day of the final academic year is officially scheduled to fall.[13]

Full-time courses[14]

If your course is funded by the Further Education Funding Council (FEFC) or Secretary of State for Scotland (SOSS), the main funding bodies for further education courses in England, Wales and Scotland, the definition full-time attaches to your personal pattern of attendance on the course. In England and Wales your course will be treated as full-time if:

- it is totally or partly funded by the FEFC and your personal 'learning agreement' involves more than 16 hours of **guided learning** each week.

Courses funded by the FEFC are usually academic or vocational courses leading to a recognised qualification. The FEFC also funds basic literacy and numeracy courses, English as a second language programmes, courses which prepare you to move on to qualification-bearing courses, and courses developing independent living skills for people with learning difficulties. The FEFC does not fund leisure or general interest courses.

'**Guided learning**' is not defined by the rules but the Benefits Agency says this means the hours when a member of staff is present to guide learning on a programme including lectures, tutorials and supervised study. Libraries, open learning centres and learning workshops are examples of where this may take place. Time spent by staff assessing students achievements is also included.[15] Obviously, time which you spend in meal and other breaks cannot be guided learning, nor can time spent taking examinations. The number of guided learning hours you do each week is set out in your learning agreement. This is signed by you and the college. The Benefits Agency uses this agreement to decide whether or not you are on a full-time course;

- it is not funded by the FEFC and is a **full-time course of study** (see below).

In Scotland your course counts as full-time and you will be treated as a **full-time student** if:[16]

- it is totally or partly funded by the SOSS at a college of further education, is not higher education *and* your personal learning document states that your course:
  - involves more than 16 hours a week of classroom based or work-shop based programmed learning under the guidance of a teacher; *or*
  - involves more than 21 hours study a week, 16 hours or less of which involve classroom based or workshop based programmed learning and the rest of which involve using structured learning packages with the help of a teacher.

The number of hours of 'learning' you do each week is set out in your learning document. This is signed by you and the college. The Benefits Agency uses this document to decide whether or not you are on a full-time course.

- it is not funded by the SOSS and is a full-time course of study (see below).

In England, Wales and Scotland if your course does not automatically count as full-time under the rules above, whether it counts as a **full-time course of study** depends on the college or university. Definitions are often based on local custom and practice within education authorities, or determined by the demands of course validating bodies, or by the fact that full-time courses can attract more resources. The college or university's definition is not absolutely final, but if you want to challenge it you will have to produce a good argument showing why it should not be accepted.[17] If your course is only for a few hours each week, you should argue that it is not full-time. However, a course could be full-time even though you only have to attend a few lectures a week.[18]

If you are attending a modular or similar course, whether your course is full or part-time will depend on such things as the number of modules you are taking, the number of hours you study each week and whether the course is one which you can choose to attend full or part-time.[19]

Full-time students who can claim income support

Even if you are a full-time student, you can claim IS if you are:[20]
- a lone parent, including lone foster parent, of a child under 16; *or*
- a student from abroad and entitled to an **urgent cases payment** because you are temporarily without funds (see p2:217); *or*
- a disabled student[21] and you satisfy one of the following conditions:
  - you qualify for the disability premium or severe disability premium (see pp2:325 and 2:329);
  - you have been incapable of work (see p1:39) for 28 weeks. Two or more periods when you are incapable of work are joined to form a single period if they are separated by less than eight weeks;
  - you qualify for a disabled student's allowance because you are deaf; *or*
- one of a couple who are both full-time students; *and*
  - you fit into one of the groups of people who can claim IS (see Chapter 20); *and*
  - either or both of you are responsible for a child or young person (see p1:122); *and*
  - it is the summer vacation.
  Note the different rule for HB (see p2:142); *or*
- a pensioner (aged 60 for women and 65 for men); *or*
- a refugee learning English (see p1:445); *or*
- attending a full-time course under the rules described on pp2:134-136 but were getting IS while studying part-time under the rules that applied until 7 October 1996 (see CPAG's *National Welfare Benefits Handbook*, 1996/97 edition, pp12-16 for further details). You can continue to get IS if:[22]
  - you were getting IS continuously from 31 July 1996 until 7 October 1996; *and*
  - you were not claiming JSA in the week after 7 October 1996; *and*

– you are on the same course as you were on 31 July 1996; *and*
– you satisfy the rules for entitlement to IS (see Chapter 20).
You can get IS until your course ends or you abandon it. This rule continues to apply if there is a break in your claim of 12 weeks or less.

If you are a student who cannot claim IS, check to see if you can claim JSA instead. If you have a partner who is not a full-time student, s/he might be able to claim IS or JSA for you.

Full-time students who can claim jobseeker's allowance

Even if you are a full-time student you can claim JSA if you are:

- one of a couple who are both full-time students and either or both of you is responsible for a child (see p1:122). This exception only applies during the summer vacation and if you are actually available for work;[23] *or*
- on an employment-related course of up to two weeks which has been approved in advance by your employment officer;[24] or a Venture Trust training programme of up to four weeks.[25] In either case, only one course is allowed in any 12-month period; *or*
- aged 25 or over and on an approved employment-related course including one under the New Deal (see p2:75).

If you are a student who cannot claim JSA, check to see if you can claim IS instead. If you have a partner who is not a full-time student, s/he might be able to claim IS or JSA for you.

Giving up, altering or taking time out of your course

If you abandon your course or are dismissed from it you can claim IS or JSA from that date so long as you satisfy the other rules for getting those benefits (see Chapters 20 and 14).

If you complete one course and start a different course you are not treated as a student in any period between the courses.[26]

If you are on a sandwich course, or your course includes a compulsory or optional period on placement, you count as a full-time student during the sandwich or placement period even if you have been unable to find a placement or your placement comes to an end prematurely.[27] If you are not a student who can claim IS or JSA and you have to take time off due to sickness, you might be able to claim IS once you count as a 'disabled student' (see p2:136) – eg, where you have been sick for 28 weeks.[28] If you are taking time out of your course, for any reason (including to study for and resit exams) and for however long a period, you cannot claim IS or JSA during your absence.[29]

If, due to exam failure or any other reason, you change to a different course, or your college requires you to change the level of course (eg, from 'A' level to GCSE) and this involves a change from full-time to part-time study you should argue that you are a part-time student[30] (see p2:138 - part-time students). The Government intends to amend some of these rules in the near future. If you are in any of the above circumstances you should seek specialist advice.

Housing costs - maintaining two homes

In some cases, if you qualify for IS, income-based JSA or housing benefit (HB), you may be entitled to help with the costs of more than one home if you have to live away from your normal home in order to attend a course. For further details see p1:518 and 2:344.

Calculating full-time students income and capital

The normal rules apply for assessing the income and capital of full-time students (see Chapters 48 and 49), except that there are special rules for assessing the amount of money available for grants, covenants and loans (see p409-410). These special rules do not apply if you are a part-time student or in relevant education (see p2:132). Note that the rules for HB are different (see p2:144).

Part-time students

If you are studying but are not in relevant education (see p2:132) or attending a full-time course (see p2:135) then you will be treated as a attending a part-time course.

Claiming IS while studying part-time

You can get IS while studying part-time if you are not on a full-time course, and satisfy the other rules for getting IS (see Chapter 20).

If you are attending a modular or similar course, whether your course is part-time will depend on such things as the number of modules you are taking, the number of hours you study each week and whether the course is one which you could attend part or full-time.

You may also count as studying part-time if you are currently studying part-time on a course you previously attended full-time. The Benefits Agency argue that you should still be treated as a full-time student in this situation. It may possible to challenge this interpretation[31]. You should seek specialist advice if you are in this position.

Claiming JSA while studying part-time

You count as a part-time student if your course is not full-time.[32] In effect, your course is part-time if:

- you are under 19 and spend 12 hours or less a week in non-advanced education[33] (see p1:233); *or*
- you are on a course funded by the FEFC or SOSS (see p2:135) and have a learning agreement (learning document in Scotland) from your course

stating that your course is 16 guided learning hours or less (note the slight variation in Scotland – see p2:135); *or*

- it is not a full-time course of study (see p2:136).

You can qualify for JSA while studying part-time if you meet the labour market conditions (ie, you are available for work, actively seeking work and you have a valid jobseeker's agreement – see Chapter 15). If you have agreed restrictions on the hours that you are available for work with the Employment Service there are special rules that can help you claim JSA and study part-time (see p2:140).

When you claim JSA, in addition to the JSA claim form and the 'Helping you back to work' form (see Appendix 10) you may be asked to fill in a 'student questionnaire'. Your answers are taken into account when deciding whether you are available for and actively seeking work. The Employment Service needs to be satisfied that you are genuinely available for and actively seeking work while you are studying part-time.

Availability for work and part-time study

Your availability for work should not be affected by your part-time course if your hours of study or training are at times outside your agreed pattern of availability (see p1:300) – ie, they do not clash with the times that you are willing and able to work. If the hours of your course *do* clash with the times that you say you are available for work (as set out in your jobseeker's agreement – see p1:315) you will only be accepted as available for work if either: [34]

- you are able to rearrange the hours of the course or study to fit around your job; *or*
- you are willing and able to give up the course should a job become available.

If you are under 19 and complete or leave a part-time course, you are not treated as leaving relevant education (see p1:133) and qualify for benefit straightaway as long as you satisfy the normal rules of entitlement (see p1:269).

If you are attending an employment related course as part of the New Deal you can be treated as available for and actively seeking work (see p2:75).

Factors considered when deciding whether you are available for work

The guidance for adjudication officers states that a number of factors should be considered when deciding whether you are available for work while you are studying part-time. If, for example, it appears that you are not willing or able to give up your course or that you cannot confine your study to times that would fit in with employment,[35] you will be treated as not being available for work. The factors that may be relevant include:[36]

- where you are studying or training and, if it is away from home, whether you can be contacted if a job becomes available;
- the extent of your efforts to find employment;

- how important the successful completion of the course is to your future career, including whether it will enhance your chances of finding employment;
- whether you gave up a job or training to do the course;
- the days and hours that you are required to attend the course;
- whether the times of attendance could be altered to fit in with any job you might obtain or whether successful completion of the course is possible if you miss some of the scheduled attendances;
- the duration of the study or training;
- whether a fee was paid and, if so, the amount and whether any of the fee could be refunded or transferred if you abandoned or interrupted your studies. If you have paid a fee it may be more difficult (depending on the amount) to convince the Employment Service that you are prepared to abandon the course;
- whether you received a grant and, if so, the source, the amount and whether you would have to repay any or all of it if you interrupted or abandoned the course.

The guidance for adjudication officers states that where a number of claimants are following the same course some may be able to show that they are available but others may not.[37] The Employment Service should not operate a blanket policy of treating all students on the same course as not being available (equally, you cannot assume that you will be treated as available if other people on your course are getting JSA). Each claim should be considered individually. The Employment Service assumes that you may be less willing to leave a course if you are near the end of the course or as the chance of obtaining a qualification approaches.[38]

Restricted availability for work and part-time study

There are special rules which can help you to qualify for JSA if you are a part-time student. These say that in certain circumstances the fact that you are on your course will be ignored when deciding whether you are available for work if the hours of your course fall in whole or in part within the times that you say you are available for work. (However, you still have to be available for and actively seeking work during the rest of the week when you are not on your course.)

These rules apply to you if you are a part-time student, and you are willing and able to rearrange the hours of your course to take up a job, and restrictions on your hours of availability have been agreed with the Employment Service for one of the following reasons:[39]

- your physical or mental condition (see p1:296); *or*
- your caring responsibilities (see p1:297); *or*
- you restrict your availability because you are working short-time (see p1:325); *or*

- your restrictions leave you available for work at least 40 hours a week (see p1:299).

You must also satisfy one of two conditions:
- for the three months immediately before the date you started the course you were unemployed and getting JSA, or sick and getting IS or incapacity benefit (IB – see Chapter 3), or you were on 'Work-based Training for Young People' (formerly youth training) or a 'Modern Apprenticeship'; *or*
- in the six months before you started the course, you were unemployed and getting JSA, or sick and getting IS or IB for a total of three months altogether, or on Work-based Training for Young People or a Modern Apprenticeship for a total of three months, *and*, sandwiched between these spells, you were working full-time or earning too much to qualify for benefit.

The three-month and six-month periods can only begin after you have reached your terminal date and are treated as having ceased to be in relevant education (see p1:235).

Transitional rules for part-time students

If you were unemployed, attending a course of education or training of up to 21 hours a week under the rules that applied until 7 October 1996 (see CPAG's *National Welfare Benefits Handbook*, 1996/97 edition, pp12-16 for further details) and claiming IS or unemployment benefit on 31 July 1996, and were automatically awarded JSA on 7 October 1996 without having to claim it (see CPAG's *Jobseeker's Allowance Handbook*, 1st edition, Appx 1), the old (more favourable) rules will continue to apply to you until you cease to be entitled under them.

You can continue to get JSA if:[40]
- you were getting IS on 31 July 1996; *and*
- you are on the same course as you were on 31 July 1996; *and*
- you are prepared to terminate the course at once if a suitable vacancy becomes available.

2. Studying and claiming housing benefit

If you are a **full-time student** (see below) you cannot usually qualify for housing benefit (HB – see Chapter 25) but there are some exceptions (see p2:142). You may be able to claim if you are studying part-time (see p2:138). For HB you count as a full-time student if you are in relevant education (see p2:132). This may mean that you can claim HB while in relevant education even if you cannot claim IS or JSA.

If you abandon or are dismissed from your course, or you alter or have to take time out of your course, the rules are the same as for IS and JSA (see p2:137).

Living in different accommodation during term-time

The rules about claiming HB for two homes are explained on p1:518.

If you are one of a couple and receive HB for two homes, the assessment of HB for each home is based on your joint income, your applicable amount as a couple and, in both cases, the student rent deduction (see p2:145) and corresponding income 'disregard' is applied.

Students from overseas

Most overseas students cannot claim HB because they are persons from abroad (see p2:219). Even if you are entitled, a successful claim for HB could affect your right to stay in this country and it is best to get immigration advice before making a claim.

Partners of overseas students

Where you are not eligible for HB, but there are no restrictions on your partner, either as a student or as a person from abroad, s/he may be able to claim instead.[41] However, if s/he receives HB and you are a person from abroad (see p2:219) this may affect your right to remain in the UK under the immigration rules because a claim by one partner is a claim for both (see p2:220).

Full-time students

You are a full-time student if you are on a full-time course (including a sandwich course).[42] The rules for deciding whether your course is full-time are the same as for IS and JSA (see p2:135).

You are treated as a full-time student until either the last day of your course or until you abandon or are dismissed from it. 'Last day of the course' means the date on which the last day of the final academic year is officially scheduled to fall.[43]

If you disagree with a decision made by a local authority you should seek a review (see p2:590).

Full-time students who can claim housing benefit

Full-time students are not normally entitled to HB, but there are a number of exceptions. Even if you meet one of the exceptions below there are some circumstances in which you still cannot receive HB (see p2:143). You can claim if:[44]

- you are on IS or income-based JSA;

- you are under 19 and not following a course of higher education (higher education includes degree courses, teachers' training, HND, HNC, and post-graduate courses[45]);
- you and your partner are both full-time students and either or both of you are 'responsible' for a child or young person (see p2:122). Note that, unlike IS and JSA, this provision applies throughout the year;
- you are a lone parent;
- you are a lone foster parent where the child has been formally placed with you by a local authority or voluntary agency;
- you meet the conditions for the disability premium (see p2:325), or would do if you were not disqualified from incapacity benefit (see p1:42);
- you have been incapable of work (see Chapter 3) for 28 weeks. Two or more periods when you are incapable are joined to form a single period if they are separated by less than eight weeks;
- you meet the conditions for the severe disability premium (see p2:329);
- you satisfy the conditions for a grant supplement in the form of a disabled student's allowance award because of deafness; *or*
- you are a pensioner who satisfies the conditions for one of the pensioner premiums (see p2:327).

Partners who are not themselves ineligible as students can claim HB.[46] The claim is assessed in the normal way, except that the rules about being away from term-time accommodation (see below) and the student deduction from eligible rent (see p2:145) apply to the partner's claim.[47]

Transitional protection

If you were entitled to HB on 31 July 1996 while on an FEFC-funded course, you may be able to continue to get HB even if your course would now be defined as full-time. Provided you satisfy the other conditions of entitlement, you can continue to get HB if:[48]

- you continue to attend the same course; *and*
- you have been continuously entitled to HB since 31 July 1996 (periods of up to 12 weeks during which you are not entitled after 7 October 1996 are ignored).

Note: If you are a full-time student who fits one of the exception catagories above you still cannot receive HB if either of the circumstances under the following two headings applies to you.

Being away from your term-time accommodation

If you are a full-time student who is eligible for HB (see p2:142) and your main reason for occupying your home is to enable you to attend your course, you cannot get HB on that home for any full week when you are absent from it outside your period of study (see p2:144).[49]

This rule does not apply if:

- you are away from home because you are in hospital;[50]
- the main reason for occupying your home is *not* to enable you to attend your course but for some other purpose – eg, to provide a home for your children or for yourself if you do not have a normal home elsewhere.[51] If this applies, any absences outside your period of study are dealt with under the temporary absence rules (see p1:515).

Accommodation rented from an educational establishment

If you rent your accommodation from your educational establishment you are not eligible to claim HB for it during your period of study (see below).[52]

This only applies where you pay rent to the same educational establishment as the one you attend for your studies. It does not apply where:

- your educational establishment itself rents the accommodation from a third party, unless this is on a long lease or where the third party is an education authority providing the accommodation as part of its functions;[53] *or*
- where the accommodation is owned by a separate legal body, eg, a company established under the Business Expansion Scheme to build a hall of residence.

However, the local authority can still apply this rule if it decides that your educational establishment has arranged for your accommodation to be provided by a person or body other than itself in order to take advantage of the HB scheme.[54]

If you and your partner jointly occupy accommodation rented from your educational establishment, and your partner is not a student, the restriction also applies to her/him if s/he is the claimant.[55]

Regardless of any restrictions which may apply during your period of study (see below), you can claim HB if you continue to rent your accommodation from your educational establishment outside that period.[56]

Calculating students' housing benefit

If you or your partner get IS, income based JSA or a training allowance, none of the rules below apply to you and you will be entitled to maximum HB (see Chapter 25).

If you do not get IS, JSA or a training allowance but you or your partner are eligible for HB, your entitlement is calculated in the same way as for other claimants (see p1:530), apart from the additional rules below.

The period of study

The amount of your entitlement depends on whether you are inside or outside your period of study. Your 'period of study' for HB purposes depends on the length and type of the course.[57]

- Where your course is for one year or less, the period of study is the period from the first to the last day of the course.

- Where your course is for more than one year and a grant is payable on the basis of you studying throughout the year, the period of study is the period from the first day of the course until the day before the next year of the course. In the final year the period of study ends with the last day of your final academic term. Many postgraduate courses come under this heading.
- In any other case where your course is for more than one year, the period of study is from the first day of each academic year until the day before the start of the recognised summer vacation. In the final year the period of study ends with the last day of your final academic term.

In deciding whether or not your grant has been assessed on the basis of you studying throughout the whole year (as in the second category above), the local authority should ignore supplements to your grant (eg, dependants' allowances) which are paid for the full year, regardless of the length of the course.[58]

Your period of study includes periods of practical experience outside the educational establishment for students on sandwich courses.[59]

Your HB entitlement is calculated differently during the period of study than outside it, eg, during the summer vacation. For example, the student rent deduction only applies during the period of study (see pp2:144 – and also 2:409-410 for treatment of grant and loan income). You may find, therefore, that your HB entitlement is higher – or that you are only entitled to HB – outside your period of study and that you need to make a new claim or check that your entitlement is reviewed at that time.

Assessing your rent – the student rent deduction

If you are a full-time student, your weekly eligible rent (see p1:520) is, in most cases, reduced during your period of study by (1998/99 academic year):
- £26.45 if you are attending a course in London; or
- £18.30 if you are studying elsewhere.[60]

The level of deduction depends on the area where you study rather than where you live. When it applies, it is made every week during your period of study (see p2:144), even where a grant is not paid or is paid for term-time only. It does not apply outside your period of study.

In any week in which your eligible rent is reduced, your income is also reduced by the same amount (known as an income disregard). The overall effect of this is that you get less HB.

The rent deduction applies equally where it is your partner who is a full-time student,[61] but only one rent deduction and income disregard should be made where both partners are full-time students.

When the student rent deduction does not apply

The student rent deduction is not made if:[62]

- you are on IS or income-based JSA;
- you or your partner receive a training allowance for your own maintenance or for that of your child;
- you are a student on a sandwich course during any period of work experience (industrial, professional or commercial);
- your income for HB purposes (see Chapter 48) is less than the sum of your applicable amount (see Chapter 45) and the amount of the rent deduction, and one of the following also applies:
  - you are a lone parent; *or*
  - the disability premium (see p2:325) applies (or would apply if you were not disqualified from incapacity benefit – see p1:42); *or*
  - you have been incapable of work (or treated as incapable) for a continuous 28-week period (see pChapter 3, this includes separate periods eight weeks or less apart); *or*
  - you have a partner and only one of you is a full-time student.

If none of these apply to you and the deductions result in hardship, you should ask the authority to make a discretionary addition to your HB (see p1:529). The local authority cannot increase your HB above the eligible rent figure calculated under the main rules (see p1:520) – for students this means your eligible rent before the student rent deduction has been applied.[63]

Assessing your income and capital

The normal rules apply for assessing the income and capital of students (see Chapters 47–49), except that there are special rules for assessing the amount of money available from grants, covenants and loans (see pp2:409-410). For HB, unlike IS and JSA, the special rules apply to both full and part-time students.

Payments

Students are covered by all the normal rules on the administration and payment of HB (see Chapter 25). However, there are two provisions which can apply specifically to students.

First, the local authority has the discretion to decide how long your benefit period (see p1:537) should last. For most students, there are two benefit periods a year – one during the period of study, and the other during the long summer vacation.

Secondly, the local authority may decide to pay a rent allowance once each term although students have the same right as other claimants to insist on fortnightly payments if their entitlement is more than £2 a week (see p1:540).

3. **Studying and claiming council tax benefit**

The definition of full-time student for council tax benefit purposes (CTB – see Chapter 27) is the same as for HB (see p2:142). The references given there include those for CTB.

Students who can claim council tax benefit

As with HB, most full-time students cannot get CTB, but you can claim if:[64]
- you are on income support or income-based jobseeker's allowance;
- you are a pensioner who satisfies the conditions for one of the pensioner premiums (see p2:327);
- you are a lone parent;
- you are a registered lone foster parent and a child has been placed with you by a local authority or voluntary agency;
- you and your partner are both full-time students and either or both of you are 'responsible' for a child or young person (see p1:122);
- you are under 19 and not following a course of higher education;
- you qualify for the disability premium (see p2:325) or would do if you were not disqualified from incapacity benefit (see p1:42);
- you have been incapable of work (see Chapter 3) for 28 weeks, this includes separate periods eight weeks or less apart;
- you satisfy the conditions for a grant supplement in the form of a disabled student's allowance awarded because of deafness;
- you are a work trainee on a training allowance.[65]

If you are a student who can claim, your CTB entitlement is calculated differently during the period of study (see p2:144) than outside it, eg, during the summer vacation. (For example, see p2:409-410 for treatment of grant income.) You may find, therefore, that your CTB entitlement is higher – or that you are only entitled to CTB – outside your period of study and that you need to make a new claim or check that your entitlement is reviewed at that time.

Overseas students

The rules on overseas students are the same as for HB (see p2:142). To qualify for CTB, overseas students must satisfy both the special rules that allow persons from abroad to claim (see p2:219) and the special rules for students (see above). The footnotes covering these matters include references to CTB legislation.

Students and second adult rebate

Full-time students are not precluded from getting second adult rebate and should be assessed in the normal way (see p1:579).

4. Studying and claiming other benefits

Severe disablement allowance

You cannot claim severe disablement allowance (SDA – see Chapter 4) if you are under 19 and in full-time education. Full-time means 21 hours or more a week.[66] In calculating the 21 hours, any special education or tuition designed for those with a physical or mental disability is ignored.[67] Temporary interruptions of education are disregarded. Periods of private study are also not included in the 21-hour limit. If you cannot claim SDA because you are in full-time education somebody else may be able to claim benefits for you if you are in relevant education (see p2:132).

Invalid care allowance

You cannot claim invalid care allowance (ICA – see Chapter 5) if you are in full-time education.[68] If you are attending a university , college or school for more than 21 hours a week you will be treated as being in full-time education. In calculating the 21 hours you include only hours spent in 'supervised study'. You ignore any time spent on meal breaks or unsupervised study undertaken on or off the premises of the educational establishment.[69] The ICA claim form says that supervised study includes, 'any work which the school, college or university says has to be done as part of the course. It makes no difference if you do the work at home or at school, college or university. The time spent doing it counts towards the 21-hour total.' It is difficult to see how this interpretation fits with the rules about 'unsupervised study'. If you are refused benefit for this reason you should appeal (Chapter 56) and argue that supervised means in the presence or close proximity of a teacher or tutor.[70]

The effect of this rule is that some people who might conventionally be regarded as full-time students, such as many undergraduates and postgraduates, are not disqualified from receiving the allowance. You will be treated as still being in full-time education during vacations and any temporary interruption of the course, but not if you have abandoned the course or been dismissed from it.

Child benefit

Child benefit (see Chapter 12) can be claimed for a person who is under 19 and receiving full-time non-advanced education or during the 'child benefit extension period'.

NHS benefits

You are not excluded from claiming NHS benefits (see Chapter 29) while you are studying.

Other benefits

Only those benefits covered in this chapter are potentially affected if you are studying. It is worth noting that you cannot be treated as capable of work (see Chapter 3) simply because you are studying on either a full-time or part-time course.

National insurance credits

You can receive Class 1 national insurance credits (see Chapter 42) for any week of a full-time course.

Notes

References are to statutes and regulations as amended up to 8 March 1999. All regulations are (General) Regulations unless otherwise stated. There is a full list of abbreviations in Appendix 13.

1. Studying and claiming IS/JSA

1 s124(1)(d) SSCBA 1992; s1(2)(g) JSA 1995
2 Regs 4ZA and 13(2)(a)-(e) IS Regs
3 R(IS) 9/94
4 CIS/11766/1996
5 R(IS) 9/94
6 R(SB) 2/87
7 CIS/11441/1995
8 R(IS) 9/94
9 s1(2)(g) JSA 1995; Reg 54 JSA Regs
10 **IS** Reg 12 IS Regs
 JSA Regs 54(1) and (2) and 76(1) JSA Regs
 Both s142 SSCBA 1992; reg 7 CB Regs
11 **IS** Regs 4ZA and 61 IS Regs, definition of 'student'
 JSA Regs 1(3) and 15(a) JSA Regs, definition of 'full-time student'
12 **IS** Reg 61 IS Regs, definitions of 'student' and 'course of advanced education'
 JSA Reg 1(3) JSA Regs, definitions of 'full-time student' and 'course of advanced education'
13 **IS** Reg 61 IS Regs definitions of 'student' and 'last day of the course'
 JSA Reg 15(1)(a) JSA Regs, and reg 1(3) definitions of 'full-time student', and reg 4 'period of study'
14 **IS** Reg 61 IS Regs definitions of 'full-time course of advanced education' and 'full-time course of study'
 JSA Reg 1(3) JSA Regs, definition of 'full-time student' – the definition of 'full-time course' is found within that definition
15 paras 35106 AOG
16 **IS** Reg 61 IS Regs definitions of 'full-time course of advanced education' and 'full-time course of study'
 JSA Reg 1(3) JSA Regs, definition of 'full-time student' – the definition of 'full-time course' is found within that definition
17 R(SB) 40/83; R(SB) 41/83
18 *See* note 17
19 CIS/152/1994; *CAO v Webber* (CA), *Times Law Report,* 10 July 1997
20 Regs 4ZA and 61 and Sch 1B IS Regs
21 Sch 1B paras 10, 11 and 12 IS Regs
22 Reg 8 IRBS&SF(MA) Regs; 25005 AOG
23 Reg 15(a) JSA Regs
24 Reg 14(1)(a) JSA Regs
25 Reg 14(1)(k) JSA Regs
26 R(IS) 1/96
27 CIS/368/1992; *Driver v CAO,* CA, 6 December 1996 (unreported)
28 CIS/13276/1996
29 *O'Conner v CAO,* (CA), 3 March 1999 (unreported)
30 CIS/152/1994; *CAO v Webber* (CA), *Times Law Report,* 10 July 1997
31 *CAO v Webber* (CA), *Times Law Report*, 10 July 1997; CIS/152/1994
32 Reg 1(3) JSA Regs definition of 'part-time student'
33 Reg 5(2) CB Regs
34 para 26241 AOG
35 para 26241 AOG
36 para 26242 AOG
37 para 26243 AOG
38 para 26244 AOG
39 Reg 11 JSA Regs
40 Reg 15 JSA(TP) - see *Bonner* 1998, p907 and para 42780 AOG

2. Studying and claiming HB

41 s131 SSCBA 1992; regs 6(1)(b) and 52 HB Regs
42 **HB** Reg 46 HB Regs
    CTB Reg 38 CTB Regs
43 **HB** Reg 46 HB Regs
    CTB Reg 38 CTB Regs
44 **HB** Reg 48A(2) HB Regs
    CTB Reg 40(3) CTB Regs
45 **HB** Reg 48A(3) HB Regs
    CTB Reg 40(4) CTB Regs
46 s131 SSCBA 1992; reg 6(1)(e) HB Regs
47 Reg 52 HB Regs
48 Reg 7 IRBS&SF(MA) Regs
49 Reg 48(1) HB Regs
50 Reg 48(2) HB Regs
51 para C5.26 GM
52 Reg 50(1) HB Regs
53 Reg 50(2) HB Regs
54 Reg 50(3) HB Regs
55 Reg 52 HB Regs
56 Reg 50(1) HB Regs; para C5.33 GM
57 **HB** Reg 46 HB Regs
    CTB Reg 38 CTB Regs
58 para C5.43 GM
59 **HB** Reg 46 HB Regs
    CTB Reg 38 CTB Regs
60 Reg 51(1) HB Regs
61 Reg 52 HB Regs
62 Reg 51(2) HB Regs
63 Reg 61(2) HB Regs

3. Studying and claiming CTB

64 Reg 40(3) CTB Regs
65 Reg 38 CTB Regs

4. Studying and claiming other benefits

66 Reg 8 SS(SDA) Regs; CS/20/1986
67 R(S) 2/87
68 Reg 5 SS(ICA) Regs
69 Reg 5(2) SS(ICA) Regs
70 R(F) 1/93

Chapter 39

Other special groups

This chapter covers the special rules which affect the benefit entitlement
of the following groups of claimants:

1. 16/17-year-olds (see below)
2. Hospital inpatients (see p2:154)
3. People in residential or nursing care (see p2:165)
4. Prisoners (see p2:180)
5. People without accommodation (see p2:185)
6. People involved in a trade dispute (see p2:187)

People coming from abroad or going abroad are covered in Chapters 40
and 41. People who are studying are covered in Chapter 38.

1. 16/17-year-olds

Special rules may affect your entitlement to some benefits if you are aged 16
or 17. The following checklist refers you to other parts of the *Handbook* for
further details.

Means-tested benefits

Income support

You are eligible for income support (IS) in your own right if you fall into one
of the categories of persons who can claim (see p1:441). If you are in relevant
education, you can only claim IS in specified circumstances (see p2:132).

Income-based jobseeker's allowance

You are only entitled to income-based jobseeker's allowance (JSA) in specified
circumstances (see p1:270). Otherwise, you can claim on a discretionary basis
but only if you would otherwise suffer severe hardship (see p1:425). You must
satisfy the labour market conditions and be subject to sanctions, some of
which are specific to 16/17-year-olds (see p1:335). If you are sanctioned, you
may be able to claim a hardship payment (see p2:433).

Housing benefit/council tax benefit

You can claim housing benefit (HB) if you are liable to pay rent and satisfy the other conditions of entitlement (see Chapter 25). You are not liable to pay council tax.

Family credit/disability working allowance

You can claim family credit and disability working allowance under the normal rules (see Chapters 21 and 22). **Note:** these benefits will be replaced by tax credits in October 1999 (see p1:488).

Social fund payments

You are entitled to a maternity or funeral payment if you satisfy the normal rules (see Chapter 31). If you are not receiving a qualifying benefit in your own right, a member of your family may be eligible to claim a maternity payment for you (see p1:626).

You may be eligible to claim a community care grant or budgeting loan if you are receiving IS or income-based JSA (see pp1:646 and 1:658). You can claim a crisis loan, unless you are in relevant education and not entitled to IS/income-based JSA (see p1:668).

Health benefits

You are entitled to most health benefits without charge if you are in full-time education. Otherwise you can qualify for free help if you receive a qualifying benefit or are a member of the family of someone who does, or on the grounds of low income. See Chapter 29 for full details.

Someone else claiming for you

If you are not entitled to benefit in your own right, someone else may be able to include you in their claim if:
* you live in the same household as them (see p2:122); *and*
* they are 'responsible' for you (see p2:122); *and*
* you are in, or have recently left 'relevant' education (see p2:132).

Whether or not you are included in someone else's claim, no non-dependant deductions are made from their HB/council tax benefit (CTB) or their IS/income-based JSA housing costs on account of you living with them.

Non-means-tested benefits

Disability benefits

* You are entitled to severe disablement allowance (SDA) without having to satisfy the 80 per cent disablement test (see p1:64). You are excluded from entitlement, however, if you are treated as being in full-time education (see pp2:132-134).

- You are entitled to disability living allowance, industrial injuries benefits and invalid care allowance (ICA) under the normal rules (see Chapters 10, 11 and 5). If you are a young carer, you can get advice from the National Carers' Association (tel: 0345 573369).

Other benefits

- You will rarely be able to qualify for incapacity benefit (IB) or contribution-based JSA because of the national insurance contribution conditions (see p2:255).
- You may qualify for statutory maternity pay, statutory sick pay or maternity allowance if you have been working (see Chapters 2 and 6).
- You may qualify for widows' benefits if your late husband satisfied the national insurance contributions (see p2:255).
- You are entitled to Class 3 national insurance 'starting credits' and Class 2 education and training credits in specified circumstances (see p2:269).

Someone else claiming for you

- Someone who is treated as 'responsible' for you (see p1:232) can claim child benefit for you if you are in, or have recently left, full-time non-advanced education.
- Someone may be able to claim an adult or child dependant increase for you, if they are receiving incapacity benefit, maternity allowance, SDA or ICA (see pp2:97-99).

2. **Hospital inpatients**

The amount of benefit you are entitled to may be reduced if you or your dependants are receiving free inpatient treatment in a hospital or similar institution. See p2:155 for who counts as an inpatient for benefit purposes. Not all benefits are affected and most are not reduced until someone has been an inpatient for a specified period.

It is important that you inform the relevant benefit authorities (Benefits Agency, Employment Service, local authority) about any hospital admission or discharge as soon as possible, to avoid any under- or overpayment of benefit. Depending on your circumstances, you may gain or lose entitlement to different benefits. If your income support (IS) or income-based jobseeker's allowance (JSA) stops, your housing benefit (HB)/council tax benefit (CTB) will also stop and you will need to make a new claim (see p2:479). If your benefit stops because you are an inpatient, you will normally need to make a fresh claim when you are discharged (this does not apply to attendance allowance (AA) or disability living allowance (DLA) – see p2:161). If you need to claim a benefit on the basis of incapacity, the hospital or institution you are in can normally issue medical certificates.

You can arrange for somebody else to collect your benefit while you are in hospital. If you are unable to manage your affairs, another person or the hospital can act as your appointee (see p2:493).

See Chapter 29 for details of help with fares to hospital. Help from the social fund may be available for fares to visit someone in hospital (see Chapter 30).

Who counts as an inpatient

You count as an inpatient for the purposes of benefit rules if you are being maintained free of charge while undergoing treatment as an inpatient in a hospital or similar institution under the NHS.[1] This will apply to you unless you are a fee-paying private patient in an NHS or private hospital.[2]

Hospitals include all NHS and trust hospitals, army navy and air force hospitals and special hospitals such as Broadmoor and Rampton. Prison hospital wings are not included, however.[3] You may also be treated as an inpatient if you are being treated in a nursing home, hostel or hospice under NHS contracting arrangements.[4]

Which days count

Separate stays as an inpatient which are less than 28 days apart are added together when calculating for how long you have been an inpatient.[5] For AA/DLA purposes, only days when you are entitled to benefit count.[6] This means your benefit may be reduced immediately, or sooner than normal, if you are re-admitted into hospital within 28 days of a previous stay.

Full days spent at home while receiving hospital treatment do not count as inpatient days. It is not entirely clear whether you count as an inpatient on days spent partly in hospital and partly at home, including days of admission and discharge. There have been a number of commissioners' decisions on the issue, some of which are conflicting.[7] The current legal position, which is confirmed in DSS guidance, is as follows:

- For the purposes of AA/DLA, days spent partly in hospital and partly at home count as inpatient days. This includes the day you enter and leave hospital.[8]
- For the purposes of other benefits, the circumstances which exist at the start of the day should be treated as continuing throughout the day. This means the day you enter hospital does not count as an inpatient day but the day you leave does.[9]

Note: The Government has indicated that it will be amending the regulations to bring AA/DLA into line with other benefits. See CPAG's *Welfare Rights Bulletin* for developments.

Income support

Your IS applicable amount (see p2:317) is subject to reduction after you or a member of your family (see p2:113) have been an inpatient for the periods specified below. See above for when you count as an inpatient and which days count. The 28-day linking rule means that the periods referred to below may have already partly or fully elapsed when a person is re-admitted into hospital (see p2:158). Special rules apply if you go into hospital from a residential care or nursing home (see p2:164). The date from which your IS changes is explained on p2:159. If your IS has stopped because you are an inpatient, you will need to make a fresh claim when you are discharged.

Note: IS housing costs (see p2:340) remain payable for up to 52 weeks while you are an inpatient, as long as your period of absence from home is unlikely to substantially exceed 52 weeks.[10] Housing costs may remain payable after 52 weeks if another person is treated as liable to meet them (see p2:157). No non-dependant deductions are made in respect of someone who has been an inpatient for more than six weeks.[11]

After four weeks

Your AA/DLA care component normally stops after you have been an inpatient for four weeks (see p2:162). This means your entitlement to an IS severe disability premium (see p2:329) will also cease, unless you are a member of a couple and one or both of you are in hospital, in which case you can qualify for the premium at the single person's rate.[12] Your entitlement to a disability, higher pensioner or disabled child premium is not affected by the withdrawal of AA/DLA.[13] Neither is your entitlement to a carer's premium, which can be paid for eight weeks after invalid care allowance (ICA) stops (see p2:333).[14]

After six weeks

- If you are single claimant, your IS applicable amount is reduced to £16.70 plus allowable housing costs (see note above).[15] All premiums are withdrawn. **Note:** You can be treated as a single claimant, if you are likely to be away from your family for substantially longer than 52 weeks.[16]
- If you are lone parent, your applicable amount is reduced to £16.70 plus your child(ren)'s personal allowances, the family premium, the disabled child premium (if applicable) and allowable housing costs (see note above).[17]
- If you are a member of a couple and one of you has been an inpatient for six weeks, your applicable amount is reduced by (*not to*) £13.35. If both of you have been in hospital for six weeks, your applicable amount is reduced to £33.40 plus, if applicable, personal allowances for your child(ren), the family and disabled child premiums and allowable housing costs (see note above).[18]

Note: The downrating of most non-means-tested benefits after six weeks (see p2:163) may mean that you remain, or become entitled to IS, despite the reduction in your applicable amount. If your IS stops, however, you will need to make a new claim for HB/CTB (see p1:530).

After 12 weeks

You can continue to get IS for a child or young person who has been an inpatient for 12 weeks if you remain in regular contact with them and they are unlikely to be away for substantially more than 52 weeks.[19] This should apply as long as you continue to get child benefit for them.[20] The IS personal allowance for a child or young person, however, is reduced to £13.35 after s/he has been an inpatient for 12 weeks.[21] You can still get child-related premiums including the disabled child premium, which remains payable despite the withdrawal of DLA (see p2:325) as long as the child or young person is still treated as a member of your family (see p2:122).[22]

After 52 weeks

- If you are single claimant, your applicable amount is reduced to £13.35.[23] You are not entitled to any premiums or housing costs. You can be paid less than £13.35 if:[24]
  - an appointee is acting on your behalf because you are unable to act for yourself; *and*
  - your IS is being paid to the hospital, as the appointee, or at the request of your appointee; *and*
  - the doctor treating you certifies that some or all of your IS cannot be used by you or on your behalf.

  This rule could leave you without any IS but there is a test of 'reasonableness' and the views of your relatives and hospital staff must be taken into account.

- If you are a lone parent, you are treated as a single claimant for IS purposes once your absence from your children is likely to substantially exceed 52 weeks.[25] After 52 weeks as an inpatient, your applicable amount is reduced to £13.35 or less under the rules relating to single claimants (see above) and you are not entitled to premiums or housing costs.

- If you are a member of a couple, you are treated as a single claimant for IS purposes once you are likely to be separated from your partner for substantially longer than 52 weeks.[26] After 52 weeks as an inpatient, your applicable amount is reduced to £13.35 or less under the rules relating to single claimants (see above) and you are not entitled to premiums or housing costs. If your partner is not in hospital, s/he can claim the normal rate of IS for a single claimant or lone parent, including premiums and housing costs.

- A child or young person may no longer be treated as a member of your family if s/he is likely to be away for substantially longer than 52 weeks, or you cease having regular contact.[27] You will then lose the IS personal allowance and premiums paid in respect of her/him.

Prisoners and patients detained under the Mental Health Acts

Prisoners are not normally entitled to IS while in hospital (see p2:180).[28] Single claimants detained in hospital under the Mental Health Acts after being transferred from prison, however, have an applicable amount of £13.35.[29]

Date from which benefit changes

The date from which your IS changes when you are, or cease to be, an inpatient depends on whether you are paid in arrears or in advance (see p1:454).

* If you are paid in arrears, your IS is changed from the pay day before your circumstances change or are expected to change. If your circumstances change on a pay day, your IS is changed from that day.[30] This means your IS may be reduced from up to six days before you have been an inpatient for the periods specified above. Conversely, when you leave hospital, you may be entitled to normal rate IS for up to six days before the day following your discharge.

* If you are paid in advance, your IS is changed from the pay day after your circumstances change. If your circumstances change on a pay day, your IS is changed from that day.[31] This means your IS may not be reduced for up to six days after you have been an inpatient for the periods specified above. Conversely, when you leave hospital, your IS may not be paid at the normal rate for up to six days after the day following your discharge.

* If you, or a member of your family, cease to be an inpatient for less than a week, you are entitled to normal rate IS for each complete day at home and the day of re-admission.[32]

Jobseeker's allowance

Claiming as an inpatient

You cannot generally make a claim for JSA while you are an inpatient (see p1:270) because you will not be capable of work or able to satisfy the labour market conditions (see p1:291). If you are already receiving JSA when you become an inpatient, you are treated as being capable of, available for and actively seeking work for up to two weeks. You are allowed two such periods in each year of your jobseeking period (see p1:271).[33] If you cannot satisfy the conditions for JSA, you should claim incapacity benefit or IS instead.

If your partner/dependant is an inpatient

If you are claiming income-based JSA, your personal allowance is unaffected during the first six weeks your partner is an inpatient. See p2:155 for who counts as an inpatient and which days count. You will only be entitled to the severe disability premium at the single person's rate, however, once your partner's AA/DLA care component is withdrawn (usually after four weeks – see p2:161).[34] After your partner has been an inpatient for six weeks, your applicable amount is reduced by £13.35.[35] The personal allowance for a child or young person is reduced to £13.35 after s/he has been an inpatient for 12 weeks.[36] You will not be able to claim for a member of your family once her/his absence is likely to substantially exceed 52 weeks.[37]

Date from which benefit changes

The rules governing the date from which your income-based JSA changes are the same as for IS claimants who are paid in arrears (see p1:455).[38] If you or a member of your family cease to be an inpatient for less than a week, the rules are as for IS (see p2:158).[39]

Housing benefit and council tax benefit

You remain entitled to HB and CTB for up to 52 weeks while you are an inpatient (but your entitlement may be reduced), as long as your absence from home is unlikely to substantially exceed 52 weeks.[40] You may be able to argue that you are still entitled to CTB, however, for as long as your home remains your sole or main residence (see p1:515).[41]

Entitled to income support/income-based jobseeker's allowance

Subject to the above, you are entitled to maximum HB and CTB as long as you are receiving IS or income-based JSA (see p1:518). If your IS/income-based JSA stops because of the inpatient rules (see pp2:155 and 2:158), you must make a new claim for HB/CTB.

Not entitled to income support/income-based jobseeker's allowance

If you are not getting IS or income-based JSA, your HB/CTB applicable amount (see p1:518) is affected after you or your partner (see p2:114) have been an inpatient for the following periods. See p2:155 for who counts as an inpatient and for which days count.

- After four weeks, you may lose entitlement to the severe disability premium. The rules relating to this and other premiums are the same as for IS (see p2:156).[42]

- After six weeks, your applicable amount is reduced in the same way as for IS, depending on whether you are a single claimant, lone parent, or a member of a couple (see p2:156).[43]

You can continue to claim for members of your family (see p2:113) who are inpatients as long as :
- in the case of HB, they are unlikely to be away for substantially longer than 52 weeks;[44]
- in the case of CTB, their absence remains temporary.[45]

Date from which benefit changes

Changes to your HB/CTB entitlement as a result of the above rules are not put into effect until the following Monday (see p1:537).[46] This means that when you have been an inpatient for six weeks, your benefit may not actually be reduced for up to a further seven days. Conversely, when you leave hospital, you may have to wait for up to seven days before your benefit is restored to normal.

Non-dependant deductions

No non-dependant deductions are made from your HB/CTB (see pp1:525 and 1:576) in respect of a non-dependant who has been an inpatient (see p2:155) for six weeks or more.[47]

What to do if your benefit is reduced or stopped

If your entitlement to HB or CTB is reduced because you or a member of your family is an inpatient and you are having difficulty paying your rent or council tax as a result, you can request extra benefit under the rules set out on pp1:529 and 1:597 (exceptional circumstances).

If you are no longer entitled to HB/CTB because of the inpatient rules, your partner or another person occupying your home could claim benefit as a liable person (see pp1:511 and 1:572).

If your home is no longer your sole or main residence, you are no longer a liable resident for CTB purposes. If your home is unoccupied, you can apply for it to be exempt from council tax (see CPAG's *Council Tax Handbook* for details).

Family credit and disability working allowance

An award of FC or DWA is not affected if you or a member of your family are an inpatient. If you are an inpatient when you claim or reclaim benefit, however, you may not satisfy the 16-hour working rule (see p2:5).

A child or young person who has been an inpatient for more than 12 weeks at the date of your claim continues to count as a member of your family as long as you maintain regular contact with her/him.[48] A person who has been an inpatient for 52 weeks or more no longer counts as a partner for FC/DWA purposes.[49]

Note: FC and DWA will be replaced by tax credits in October 1999 (see p1:489).

Attendance allowance and disability living allowance

If you become entitled to AA or DLA while you are an inpatient, you cannot receive any benefit until the day following your discharge.[50] If you are already entitled to AA or DLA when you become an inpatient, payment stops after you have been an inpatient for 28 days, or 84 days if you are aged under 16 (but see below for special rules relating to the mobility component).[51] The rule also applies to constant attendance allowance (see p1:217).[52] See p2:155 for who counts as an inpatient and which days count. Note that only days of *entitlement* to AA or DLA count towards the 28-day linking period and that days spent partly in hospital count as inpatient days (but see the note on p2:155 about an impending change in the rules). Special rules apply if you enter hospital from residential or nursing care (see p2:164).

It may still be worth submitting a claim while you are an inpatient so that you can start to receive benefit as soon as possible after your discharge (and for the first 28 days of any subsequent re-admission). You should not have to reclaim benefit when you are discharged if your underlying entitlement remains, but you must inform the Benefits Agency about any admission, discharge or change in your medical condition. If your condition has deteriorated, you should consider requesting a review if you may be entitled to a different or higher rate of benefit.

Disability living allowance mobility component special rules

You can continue to be paid the mobility component of DLA after 28 days as an inpatient (84 days if you are aged under 16) in the following circumstances:

• You had a Motability agreement (see p1:197) when you became an inpatient. You can continue to receive the mobility component until the agreement ends. If you renew the agreement while you are an inpatient, the mobility component stops, unless the agreement is under the Wheelchair Scheme and has been renewed the day after the previous agreement expired.[53] The mobility component will only continue to be paid at the rate payable under the agreement, so any balance being paid to you will stop after 28 (84) days.[54]

• You had been an inpatient and receiving the mobility component for a continuous period of 365 days or more on 3 to 31 July 1996. Periods of 28 days or less when you ceased to be an inpatient are ignored. You will not be covered if you were detained in hospital on 31 July 1996 under Parts II or III of the Mental Health Act 1983 or Parts V or VI of the Mental Health

(Scotland) Act 1984.[55] The mobility component can continue to be paid but only at the lower rate (see p1:181), until you cease to be an inpatient for more than 28 days, or you are committed to hospital under the Mental Health Acts, or you cease to be entitled to the mobility component.[56]

Date from which your benefit changes

Your AA/DLA will normally be stopped from the pay day following your 28th day as an inpatient (84th day if you are a child). Benefit is normally payable again from the pay day following the day you cease to be an inpatient.[57] If, however, on your day of discharge, it is expected that you will return to hospital within 28 days, you can be paid benefit from the following day at a daily rate (one-seventh of your weekly entitlement).[58]

People in hospices

If you are terminally ill (see p1:167) you can continue to receive AA or DLA while you are in a hospice.[59] A hospice is defined as a hospital or other institution whose primary function is to provide palliative care to people with a progressive disease in its final stages, other than an NHS or similar hospital, or a home owned or managed by a local authority.[60]

Invalid care allowance

You remain entitled to ICA for up to 12 weeks in any period of 26 weeks while you, or the person you are caring for, are an inpatient for a temporary period (see p1:87).[61] Dependant increases may be reduced after a dependant has been an inpatient for a specified period (see p2:100).

Your ICA stops, however, when the person you are caring for loses her/his AA or DLA care component. This will happen after s/he has been an inpatient for four weeks (12 weeks if s/he is a child), see p2:99. If s/he is discharged from hospital for part of a week and receives AA or DLA care component again, you are entitled to ICA if you satisfy the 35-hour rule (see p1:81).

If you have underlying entitlement to ICA, some of it may become payable if an overlapping benefit is reduced after six weeks because you are an inpatient (see p2:155). If you lose your ICA after 12 weeks in hospital, the person you are caring for may become entitled to the severe disability premium (see p2:329). The carer's premium (see p2:333) is normally payable for eight weeks after your ICA stops.

Other benefits

Benefits unaffected

The following benefits are unaffected while you are an inpatient (but note the conditions relating to child benefit below):

- statutory sick pay;

- statutory maternity pay;
- maternity allowance (adult dependant's increase may be reduced after the adult has been an inpatient for a specified period – see p2:100);
- industrial injuries benefits including disablement benefit, reduced earnings allowance, retirement allowance and exceptionally severe disablement allowance. (**Note:** Constant attendance allowance stops after four weeks as an inpatient, see p2:161; unemployability supplement is reduced after six and 52 weeks or eight weeks if paid with war disablement pension);
- child benefit and guardian's allowance are unaffected for the first 12 weeks the child is an inpatient and can continue after that as long as you are regularly incurring expenditure in respect of the child, or are contributing to her/his maintenance at the weekly rate of child benefit.[62] **Note:** If you are in hospital for some time, you may want to arrange for child benefit to be paid to the person looking after the child (see p1:238).

Benefits reduced

The following benefits are reduced after the periods specified below:
- retirement pension;
- widow's pension;
- widowed mother's allowance;
- incapacity benefit (IB);
- severe disablement allowance (SDA);
- unemployability supplement and industrial death benefit.

After six weeks

- After you have been an inpatient for six weeks, the weekly rate of the above benefits paid in respect of you is reduced by:
  - £26.70 if you have no dependants; *or*
  - £13.35 if you have a dependant.[63]

  Your benefit will not be reduced, however, to below £13.35. See p2:155 for when you count as an inpatient and which days count. A dependant is someone for whom you receive (or would receive but for the overlapping or earnings rules) a dependant's increase or child benefit. It also includes a spouse of any age if you are getting IB or SDA.[64]
- After your spouse has been an inpatient for six weeks, any increase of the above benefits (or ICA or maternity allowance) you are receiving for her/him is reduced by £13.35, subject to a minimum rate of £13.35 being payable.[65] An increase for a dependant other than a spouse is not affected.

After 12 weeks

After a child has been an inpatient continuously for 12 weeks, any increase of the above benefits (or ICA) you receive for her/him will only continue if you are regularly incurring expenditure for the child or making payments to her/him or to another person for her/him.[66]

After 52 weeks

- After you have been an inpatient for 52 weeks, the weekly rate of the above benefits paid for you is reduced to £13.35.[67] If you have a dependant, you should be sent a form on which you can apply for the remainder of your entitlement (including any dependant's increase) less £26.70, to be paid to your dependant.[68] The £13.35 paid to you can be reduced further if:
  - you are unable to act for yourself; *and*
  - your benefit is being paid to the hospital as your appointee or at the request of your appointee; *and*
  - the doctor treating you certifies that the benefit cannot be used for your personal comfort or enjoyment.[69]
- After your spouse has been an inpatient for 52 weeks, any increase of the above benefits (or ICA or maternity allowance) you are receiving for her/him is reduced to £13.35.[70]

Date from which your benefit changes

In the case of IB and SDA, your benefit is adjusted from the day after you, or your dependant, have been an inpatient for the specified periods or the day following your discharge.

In the case of the other benefits above, benefit is not usually adjusted until the following pay day.[71] If you are expecting to return to hospital within 28 days, however, you can be paid benefit at a daily rate (one-seventh of your weekly entitlement) from the day following your discharge.[72]

Entering hospital from residential care

If you enter hospital from residential care, special rules apply if you are receiving the following benefits when you become an inpatient.

Income support

If you enter hospital from residential or nursing care, your IS applicable amount depends on:

- whether or not you have 'preserved rights' (see p2:173);
- whether you live in a local authority home (see p2:176);
- how long you or a member of your family (see p2:113) have been an inpatient (see p2:115).

People with 'preserved rights'

- **Up to six weeks:** You remain entitled to the 'preserved rights' rate of IS (see p2:169) including the accommodation allowance (taking into account any reduction in the charge payable), while you, or a member of your family, have been an inpatient for up to six weeks.[73] If you are a single claimant and do not have to pay an accommodation charge while you are an inpatient, your applicable amount is reduced to your personal expenses and meals allowances as a home resident (see p2:170), as long as you are likely to return to the home.[74] If you are unlikely to return, your IS is calculated under the normal rules for a single claimant not in residential care.[75]

- **After six weeks:** Inpatients for more than six weeks are entitled to an IS personal allowance of £16.70. If a member of the family remains in the residential accommodation, their personal expenses and the accommodation allowance, less the inpatient's meal allowances, remain payable (taking into account any reduction in the charge). Otherwise, an amount to cover any retaining fee the inpatient is liable for, is payable.[76] A child or young person who has been an inpatient for more than 12 weeks is entitled to a personal allowance of £13.35.[77]

People without 'preserved rights'
- **Up to six weeks:** You remain entitled to your normal rate of IS, including the residential allowance (see p2:173), while you, or a member of your family, are an inpatient for up to six weeks.[78]
- **After six weeks:** Your IS is calculated under the normal rules for inpatients (see p2:156).

People in local authority homes
If you are a single claimant who is permanently resident in a home provided and managed by a local authority, your IS applicable amount is reduced to £14.75 immediately you become an inpatient.[79]

Income-based jobseeker's allowance
If you have been an inpatient for more then two weeks, you will not normally be able to satisfy the labour market conditions for JSA (see p1:291). You may be able to claim IS or IB instead. If you are receiving income-based JSA when you enter hospital from residential or nursing care, the following special rules apply.

People with 'preserved rights'
The same rules apply as for IS (see p2:164), except that:
- the 'up to six weeks rules' apply where either you have been an inpatient for up to two weeks or a member of your family has been an inpatient for up to six weeks;[80]
- the 'after six weeks rules' apply where a member of your family has been an inpatient for more than six weeks and either you are not an inpatient, or have been one for less than two weeks.[81]

People without 'preserved rights'

The rules are as for IS[82] (see p2:165) – but see above if you are an inpatient for more than two weeks.

People in local authority homes

The rules are as for IS (see p2:165).[83]

Attendance allowance/disability living allowance care component

Normally, AA/DLA care component remains payable for the first 28 days as a hospital inpatient. However, periods spent in publicly funded accommodation (including residential or nursing care) in which AA/DLA care component is not payable (see p2:177), link with periods spent as an inpatient, unless such periods are separated by more than 28 days.[84]

This means that if you enter hospital from residential or nursing care, your AA/DLA care component will not normally be reinstated for the first 28 days you are an adult inpatient.

Note, however, that:

- only periods when you have an underlying entitlement to AA/DLA care component link; *and*
- DLA mobility component remains payable for the first 28 days you are an inpatient.

Other benefits

Special rules apply if you enter hospital from residential or nursing care and are receiving any of the benefits listed on p2:163, which are normally reduced after you have been an inpatient for six and 52 weeks.

- Unless your placement is self-funded, or you are in an independent care or nursing home (see below), if you are permanently in residential or nursing care, the above benefits are reduced to £13.35 or less from the first day you become an inpatient, as if you had been an inpatient for 52 weeks (see p2:164). If you are only temporarily in a home, the period you have spent there counts towards the periods of six and 52 weeks after which your benefit is reduced.[85]
- If you are in an independent care or nursing home (see p2:174), the above rule does not take effect until you have been an inpatient for six weeks – ie, if you are a permanent resident, your benefit is reduced to £13.35 or less after six weeks in hospital.[86]

3. **People in residential or nursing care**

Special rules apply if you are in residential or nursing care and you are receiving:

- income support (IS) or income-based jobseeker's allowance (JSA) (see below);
- housing benefit (HB) and council tax benefit (CTB) (see p2:176);
- attendance allowance (AA) or disability living allowance (DLA) (care component).

Special rules do not apply to other benefits, but see p1:243 for how child benefit is affected if a child is in local authority care.

Income support/income-based jobseeker's allowance

If you are in residential or nursing care, your IS/income-based JSA applicable amount depends on whether:

- you are resident in an independent (ie, private or voluntary) residential care or nursing home; *and*
  - you have preserved rights (see p2:169); *or*
  - you do not have preserved rights (see p2:173); *or*
- you are resident in a local authority home (see p2:174).

The rules apply whether you are a permanent or temporary resident (eg, you are undergoing respite care). They do not apply, however, if you are aged under 18 and receiving residential care under the Children Act 1989. There are also more generous capital limits (£16,000 upper limit and £10,000 for tariff income) if you permanently live in residential or nursing care (see p2:442 for details).

All the following rules apply to both IS and income-based JSA. In the vast majority of cases, people in residential or nursing care will be eligible for IS rather than income-based JSA. For the sake of brevity, therefore, most of the information in this section and the related notes refer to IS only, but the rules apply equally to income-based JSA.[87]

Outline of funding arrangements

The Government's community care reforms introduced a new funding structure for residential and nursing care from 1 April 1993.[88]

Unless you have preserved rights (see p2:169), you must apply to your local authority social services or social work department for funding if you cannot afford to pay for a place in residential or nursing care. You are entitled to assistance if your capital (see p2:168) is, or falls below, £16,000,[89] and the local authority assesses that you need residential or nursing care. Local authorities have a duty to provide residential accommodation to those who need it because of age, disability or other reasons.[90] They can do this by providing a place in a local authority home, or in an independent care or nursing home, in which case they must contract to pay the full fees to the provider. The local authority is not obliged to pay more than normal for somebody with your needs, but you can choose a more expensive home if a third party can make up the shortfall.

If your placement is being provided and funded by the local authority, you will have to pay a weekly charge to the authority.[91] The charge is means-tested. The rules are laid down in national regulations.[92] Guidance on the regulations is set out in the *Charging for Residential Accommodation Guide*, issued by the Department of Health. The regulations are based on the IS Regulations but there are some significant differences. In particular, only *your* income and capital counts and not your partner's (joint savings are divided in half).

- If you have more than £16,000 capital, you must pay a charge equal to the full cost of your placement. Your capital is calculated as for IS, but:
  - property up for sale is not disregarded;
  - occupied property can be disregarded;
  - property is disregarded if you are a temporary resident for a period which does not significantly exceed 52 weeks.

  Notional capital rules are as for IS. In addition, if you give away capital in the six weeks before you were placed, the recipient can be made liable for your accommodation cost.[93] If you cannot afford to pay your charge because your capital is tied up in your property, the local authority can place a legal charge on the property and collect the debt when it is sold.[94]

- If you have less than £16,000 capital, your weekly charge is,
  - your total weekly income (including IS and any 'tariff' income but excluding most income disregarded under IS rules); *less*
  - a personal expenses allowance of at least £14.75.

  You cannot be charged more than the full cost of your home and must be left with at least £14.75 a week.

- The local authority can impose a standard reasonable charge for placements of up to eight weeks (eg, for respite care)[95] and should take into account continuing home expenses for temporary placements, of up to 52 weeks.

Prior to 1 April 1993, people in independent residential or nursing homes were entitled to special rates of IS to pay their fees. Most people who have remained in independent care since 31 March 1993 have preserved rights to these special rates of IS.

From 31 March 1993, anyone entering independent care for the first time does not have preserved rights. You can still claim IS, but only at the normal rates, plus a residential allowance of £59.40 (£66.10 in Greater London) a week. If you cannot afford to pay your home fees, you must apply to your local authority for funding (see above). In some circumstances, you may be better off not applying for funding, so that you can retain entitlement to AA/ DLA care component and the severe disability premium (see p2:180). This could apply, for example, where you will have to refund charges to the local authority when your property is sold. The issues are complex, however, and you should seek specialist advice before making a decision.

If you are in a local authority home or a local authority is funding your place in an independent home, any IS and most other benefits you are entitled to will have to be paid across to the authority to meet your weekly charge (see above).

People with preserved rights

You have preserved rights to claim special rates of IS if you were living in most types of independent residential care or nursing homes (see definition on p2:174) on 31 March 1993 *and*: [96]
- you were getting IS at the special rates; *or*
- you were not getting IS because you were able to afford to pay for the home yourself; *or*
- you were living with a partner, to whom either of the above applied; *or*
- one of the above would have applied but for the fact that you were absent from the home for:
  - up to four weeks if you were a temporary resident;
  - up to 13 weeks if you were a permanent resident;
  - up to 52 weeks if you were in hospital.

You are covered if the home you were living in was a residential care or nursing home, as defined on p2:174. Complex rules apply if you were living in a home with less than four residents or provided by a close relative or the Abbeyfield Society.[97] You should seek specialist advice if this applies to you.

You lose your preserved rights if you are absent from an independent home for:
- more than four weeks if you are a temporary resident;
- more than 13 weeks if you are a permanent resident;
- more than 52 weeks if you are in hospital. [98]

You do not lose your preserved rights if you move from one independent home to another, as long as any gap does not exceed the above periods.

You do not have preserved rights if:[99]
- your accommodation is provided in whole or part by a close relative (see p2:341) (unless via a limited company[100]) or other than on a commercial basis; *or*
- you are on holiday from your normal home for up to 13 weeks.

If you have preserved rights, your IS applicable amount consists of an amount for personal expenses plus an accommodation allowance to cover all or part of the charge made by the home. You are not entitled to any premiums. If you are a member of a couple see p2:114. AA and DLA are taken into account as income when calculating your IS/income-based JSA.[101]

Personal expenses[102]

Single claimant	£14.75
Couple	£29.50
Dependent child aged 18+	£14.75
16/17	£10.25
11/15	£ 8.85
0/10	£ 6.05

Accommodation allowance

The amount you receive covers the weekly charge for your accommodation, including meals and services where these are provided, but only up to a maximum level (see below).[103]

If you have to pay for some meals separately, your accommodation allowance includes, for each person, either an amount to cover the actual cost of the meals if they can be purchased in the home, *or*, if they cannot, the following standard amounts:[104]

- £1.10 for breakfast;
- £1.55 for lunch; *and*
- £1.55 for dinner.

The above amounts are reduced if meals are provided free or at a lower cost.

If you pay additional charges for heating, attendance needs, extra baths, laundry or a special diet you follow for medical reasons, these are included in the accommodation allowance, so long as they are provided by the home and not by an outside agency.[105]

If you receive housing benefit towards part of your accommodation charge, it is deducted from the charge and reduces your IS accordingly.[106]

Your accommodation allowance (including any charges for additional services and meals) is subject to a maximum[107] depending on the type of home you are in and the type of care you receive.[108] You may find that the amount payable does not fully cover your home fees. See p2:172 for when you can get more than the maximum and p2:172 for money from other sources.

If you are in a residential care home the maximum varies according to the type of care the home is registered to provide, or if the home is not registered, according to the type of care you receive.[109] The type of care depends on the health conditions and/or age of the residents – see the table on p2:171 for details. If more than one category could apply to you, the amount you get is decided as follows:[110]

- Where the home is registered to provide the type of care you get, you receive the amount that is allowed for that type of care.

- If the care you receive is different from the type the home is registered to provide, you receive the allowance for the lower or lowest of the categories of care which the home is registered to provide.
- In any other case you receive the amount most consistent with the care you receive.

If you are in a nursing home the maximum varies according to the type of care you actually receive. The type of care depends on your health conditions and/or age – see the table on p2:172 for details. If more than one category could apply to you, you receive the amount most consistent with the care you receive.[111] You could, for example, get the 'terminal illness' rate if that is the type and level of care you receive even though you are not, in fact, terminally ill.[112]

Some homes may be registered both as a residential care and a nursing home. In these cases your maximum accommodation allowance is decided according to whether you are receiving residential or nursing care.

The tables below list the maximum amounts payable in residential care and nursing homes. The following definitions apply to the categories of health conditions noted in the tables:

'**Mental disorder**' means 'mental illness, arrested or incomplete development of mind, psychopathic disorder, and any other disorder or disability of mind'.[113]

'**Mental handicap**' means 'a state of arrested or incomplete development of mind which includes impairment of intelligence and social functioning'.[114] 'Senility' is not mental handicap but can amount to a mental disorder.[115]

'**Disablement**' means 'blind, deaf or dumb or substantially and permanently handicapped by illness, injury or congenital deformity or any other disability prescribed by the Secretary of State'.[116]

'**Very dependent elderly**' means you are over pension age and *either*:
- registered or certified as blind; *or*
- entitled to AA or DLA care component at the highest rate (even if it is not payable because you have not met the qualifying period); *or*
- getting war or industrial injury constant attendance allowance.[117]

Residential care homes

Health condition/age	Maximum payable
Old age	£218
Past or present mental disorder but excluding mental handicap	£230
Past or present drug or alcohol dependence	£230
Mental handicap	£262
Physical disablement if under pension age, or, if over pension age, claimant had become disabled before	£298

reaching 60 (65 if a man)

Over pension age and had become physically disabled	£218
after reaching 60 (65 if a man)	
Very dependent elderly (see p2:171)	£252
Any other condition	£218

The above amounts are increased by £45 a week for homes in the Greater London area (see p2:174 for definition).

Nursing homes

Health condition/age	Maximum payable
Past or present mental disorder but excluding mental handicap	£326
Mental handicap	£262
Past or present drug or alcohol dependence	£326
Physical disablement, if under pension age, or if over pension age, claimant had become disabled before reaching 60 (65 if a man)	£367
Over pension age and had become physically disabled after reaching 60 (65 if a man)	£325
Terminal illness	£325
Any other condition (including elderly)	£325

The above amounts are increased by £50 a week for homes in the Greater London area (see p2:174 for definition).

You can get more than the maximum if one of the following applies:

- You have lived in the same accommodation for over 12 months and could afford it without IS when you moved in. You get your full accommodation charge for up to 13 weeks after you claim IS if you are trying to move but need time to find suitable alternative accommodation.[118] Income which is normally disregarded for IS may be taken into account during the 13 weeks.[119] The 13-week concession does not apply if you are being accommodated by the local authority because you are homeless or under the authority's duty to promote the welfare of children.
- You have been living in a residential care or nursing home since 28 April 1985 and your accommodation allowance under the present rules is lower than what you then received, plus £10. (For further details on this see the 22nd edition of CPAG's *National Welfare Benefits Handbook*, p78.)[120]

If your IS does not meet your accommodation fees, you will have to try to obtain the balance from other sources. Money from charities or relatives which is used to pay fees is ignored for IS/income-based JSA purposes.[121] Your local authority can only provide topping-up finance if:[122]

- you lose your preserved rights (see p2:169); *or*
- you were under pension age on 31 March 1993; *or*

- you are over pension age, have been evicted from a residential care home and need to move to another residential care home (not a nursing home), which is owned or managed by a different person.

If you have to pay a retaining fee to keep your home while you are temporarily absent from it, up to 80 per cent of your accommodation allowance is payable to cover the fee (in addition to any other IS you are entitled to) for up to four weeks, or 52 weeks if you have been in hospital for more than six weeks or you are in a local authority home.[123] In the case of income-based JSA, the retaining fee is only payable (for up to 52 weeks) if you are temporarily in a local authority home or if your partner has been in hospital for more than six weeks.[124] Commissioners disagree about your entitlement to a retaining fee if you are temporarily living in another independent residential care home.[125]

People without preserved rights in independent homes

If you do not have preserved rights (see p2:169), you are not entitled to the special rates of IS. This applies to everybody first entering an independent care or nursing home after 31 March 1993.

You are still entitled to claim IS if you satisfy the normal rules of entitlement (see Chapter 20). Your applicable amount is calculated in the normal way – ie, personal allowances plus premiums (see p2:318). You are also, in most cases, entitled to a 'residential allowance' to help pay your home fees (see below). If you are a member of a couple, see p2:119. If you go into hospital, see p2:164.

If you go into an independent home for a temporary period (either for respite care or a trial period) and you have housing costs in your own home, see p2:343. If you go into an independent home permanently, you cannot be paid housing costs on your former home or claim housing benefit to cover your residential care fees.[126]

If you cannot afford to pay your home fees, you can apply for funding from your local authority (see p2:167). If you receive local authority funding, charitable or voluntary payments used to help pay your fees are disregarded for IS/income-based JSA purposes.[127] If you are not receiving local authority funding, such payments are disregarded up to a maximum of the difference between your applicable amount (less the amounts listed as personal expenses on p2:168) and your home fees.[128]

Residential allowance[129]

You are entitled to a residential allowance if:
- you are in an independent residential care or nursing home (see p2:174 for definition); *and*

- you require and receive personal care because of old age, disablement, past or present alcohol or drugs dependence, past or present mental disorder or a terminal illness; *and*
- you are aged 16 or over and do not have preserved rights (see p2:169); *and*
- your accommodation and any meals are provided on a commercial basis and no part of your weekly charge is met by housing benefit (see chapter 25).

The residential allowance is £59.40 a week; or £66.10 a week if the home is in Greater London, which covers all the London boroughs, plus parts of Essex (Chigwell and Waltham Cross), Hertfordshire (Elstree, Ridge, Shenley, South Mimms and South Broxbourne) and Surrey (Spelthorne and part of Elmbridge).[130]

The residential allowance stops after three weeks' absence from your home, or six weeks absence if you are in hospital.[131] See p2:155 for when you count as being in hospital. Separate periods in hospital are linked if they are less than 28 days apart.

Definition of independent residential care and nursing homes

An independent residential care home is a home which is:[132]

- registered or deemed to be registered under the Registered Homes Act 1984 or the Social Work (Scotland) Act 1968 (all homes providing board and personal care are required to be registered); *or*
- run by a body established by Royal Charter or Act of Parliament (other than a local authority) and provides board and personal care; *or*
- a housing association registered with Scottish Homes which provides residential care.

An independent nursing home is a home which is:[133]

- registered as a nursing home under the Registered Homes Act 1984 or the Nursing Homes Registration (Scotland) Act 1938 or the Mental Health (Scotland) Act 1984; *or*
- run by a body established by Royal Charter or special Act of Parliament.

Note: A hospice, which has the primary function of helping those suffering from a terminal illness, does not count as a nursing home.[134] Residents are not entitled to a residential allowance and may be treated as inpatients for IS purposes (see p2:155).

In certain circumstances, you may also be classed as an inpatient if you are in a nursing home funded by the NHS (see p2:155).

People in local authority homes

If you are in a local authority home (see definition below), your IS applicable amount is worked out in a special way (see below). You do not have preserved rights (see p2:173) and you are not entitled to a residential allowance (see p2:173). You get less IS than if you were in an independent home. You also always lose your AA or DLA care component (see Chapter 10) after four weeks in a local authority home.

Definition of a local authority home

For IS purposes, you are in a local authority home if:[135]

* the home is owned or managed by a local authority; *and*
* the accommodation is provided under sections 21 and 24 of Part III of the National Assistance Act 1948 or sections 13B and 59 of the Social Work (Scotland) Act 1968 or section 7 of the Mental Health (Scotland) Act 1984; *and*
* board is provided (but if you buy and pay for food when you want – eg, in a café, or canteen on the premises, this does not count as board – this applies to many local authority hostels, the residents of which can claim ordinary rate IS and housing benefit – see chapter 25); *and*
* you are not a person who is under 18 and in the care of a local authority in Scotland.

If you were living in accommodation provided by a local authority on 31 March 1993, you may count as living in a local authority home, even if it does not fit the above definition.[136]

If you are living in a home which transferred from the local authority to the independent sector after 11 August 1991 while you were there, you are still treated as living in a local authority home for IS purposes.[137]

Income support entitlement

If you or your partner are in a local authority home, your IS applicable amount is worked out as follows:[138]

* **If you are a single person** your applicable amount (see p2:319) is a set figure of £66.75 a week (no premiums are payable). If you are only temporarily in the home, you can continue to get housing costs on your normal home (see p2:343).
* **If you are a lone parent** your applicable amount (see p2:319) is a set figure of £66.75 a week. If you are temporarily in the home, you can continue to get IS for your children (see Chapter 37), the family premium plus IS housing costs (see p2:340).
* **If you are one of a couple:**
  – If you or your partner are temporarily in the home you are still treated as a couple for IS (see p2:120). Your applicable amount (see p2:318) is £66.75 for the partner in the home plus the normal allowance (including premiums) for a single person for the other partner.
  – If you or your partner have permanently moved into a home, you are no longer treated as a couple for IS (see p2:119). The partner in the home has an applicable amount (see p2:318) of £66.75 a week. The other partner must claim IS separately as a single person or parent.

– If you are both in a home, you each have an applicable amount (see p2:318) of £66.75. If you are temporary residents, you can continue to get IS housing costs for your normal home (see p2:340).

If your child is living with you in a home you can claim the normal child allowance for her/him (see p2:322). If you go into hospital, see p2:164.

Housing benefit

People in local authority homes

You are not entitled to HB if you live in a residential home owned or managed by a local authority and you pay an inclusive charge for accommodation and meals.[139] Even if meals are not included, you are excluded from HB if you were living in such a home on 31 March 1993.[140]

People in independent homes

You are not normally entitled to HB if you live in an independent care or nursing home (see p2:174) or you are receiving a residential allowance (see p2:173).[141]

You are entitled to HB if you live in an independent care or nursing home and you fall into one of the following categories:

- You live in a home which is not required to register as a care home. This includes some small hostels and supported lodgings which do not provide board and personal care and homes set up by Royal Charter or Act of Parliament, such as Salvation Army homes.[142]
- You were entitled to HB in respect of an independent home on 29 October 1990. You remain eligible for HB in any independent home without time limit.[143]
- You were entitled to HB on 31 March 1993 and you were *either*:
  – in remunerative work; *or*
  – paying a commercial rent to a non-resident close relative (see p1:513); *or*
  – living in an unregistered home with less than four residents.
  You remain eligible for HB as long as you do not break you claim and you continue to live in the same home, disregarding temporary absences of up to 13 or 52 weeks (see p1:516).[144]

If you are entitled to HB under the above rules, the tariff income threshold is £10,000 instead of the normal £3,000 (see p2:442).

Temporary residents

You remained entitled to HB for your normal home while you are temporarily in residential or nursing care for:

- up to 13 weeks, if you are in care for a trial period; *or*

- up to 52 weeks, if you are otherwise in care and your period of absence is unlikely to substantially exceed 52 weeks.[145]

Council tax benefit

The rules are the same as for HB if you are temporarily living in residential or nursing care[146] (see above) but you may be able to argue you are entitled to CTB as long as your normal home remains your sole or main residence (see p1:572).[147] If you become a permanent resident in a care or nursing home, you will no longer be liable for council tax. If your home is unoccupied you can apply for it to be exempt from the council tax (see CPAG's *Council Tax Handbook* for details).

Attendance allowance and disability living allowance care component

Highly complex regulations restrict the payment of AA and the care component of DLA to the first 28 days spent in residential or nursing care ('special accommodation' – see below) which is, or could be, publicly funded.[148] The mobility component of DLA is not affected.

Periods spent in special accommodation which are separated by 28 days or less, link together for the purposes of calculating the 28-day limit on payability.[149] Days spent outside special accommodation, including the days you enter and leave (which do not count as days in care[150]), are normal days of entitlement, for which you can be paid one-seventh of your weekly benefit.[151]

It can be important to plan periods of respite care in the light of the linking rules. You can, for example, go into respite care every Friday and return home every Monday for 14 weekends without losing your benefit. If you then enter care on Saturday and return home on Sunday for four weeks, you will break the link and can return to your normal pattern for another 14 weeks.

If you regularly lose and regain entitlement, it is generally more convenient if you are paid by credit transfer.

You should also note that:

- periods spent as an inpatient link with periods in special accommodation, if they are separated by 28 days or less (see p2:166);
- if you become entitled to AA/DLA care in special accommodation, you cannot be paid until you leave the accommodation.[152]

When benefit is not payable

Subject to the exceptions detailed below, AA and DLA care component are not payable after 28 days in the following categories of special accommodation:[153]

- Accommodation provided under Part III of the National Assistance Act 1948, Part IV of the Social Work (Scotland) Act 1968 or section 7 of the Mental Health (Scotland) Act 1984. This will apply if:
  - you are in a local authority home (even if you are paying the full fees); *or*
  - you are in an independent home and your place was arranged, or is being funded by, a local authority (see p2:167); *or*
  - you are in respite care, funded by payments from a local authority under the Community Care (Direct Payments) Act 1996 (you cannot buy more than four weeks care in a year using such payments but the period may link with other periods in special accommodation – see p2:177).
- Accommodation, the cost of which is borne wholly or partly from public or local funds under the above enactments or under legislation relating to people with disabilities, young people or people in education or training.
- Accommodation, the cost of which *may* be borne under any of the above legislation.

Accommodation costs do not include the costs of domiciliary services to people in private dwellings or grants for improvement, furniture, equipment, motor vehicles or external recreational activities.[154]

It is not always clear whether you are in special accommodation. The Benefits Agency may send you a form asking for details from your local authority about your accommodation and the legal powers under which it is provided and funded. The view of the local authority in not always determinative, however,[155] and you should always seek specialist advice if there is a doubt about whether you are in special accommodation.

When benefit is payable

You remain entitled to AA/DLA care component after 28 days in special accommodation in any of the following circumstances:

- You are terminally ill (see p1:182) and in a hospice.
- You are not entitled to IS, income-based JSA or HB and you are meeting the whole cost of your accommodation from your own resources or with the help of another person or a charity.[156] It does not matter if a local authority is funding the home, as long as you are paying the full fees.[157] This provision, however, does not apply if you are meeting the full cost of a place in a home owned or managed by the local authority.[158]
- In the case of DLA, you are a student and the cost of your accommodation (eg, a hall of residence) is, or could be, partly or wholly met from a student grant or loan, or money from a Funding Council.[159]
- You are under 18 and receiving local authority care or services because of your age or health and you have been placed (fostered) into a private dwelling, or have been accommodated abroad by the local authority under specified legislation (eg, at the Peto Institute or Higashi School).[160]

You are not treated as being in accommodation, the cost of which *may* be borne under the legislation specified on p2:178, in any of the following circumstances:

- Your accommodation was provided under section 65 of the Housing Act 1985 or section 31 of the Housing (Scotland) Act 1987 because you were homeless.[161]
- You are living in accommodation as a privately fostered child (ie, you are under 16 and fostered with someone other than a parent, guardian or relative).[162]
- You live in a private dwelling, unless:
  - it is a residential care home (see p2:174); *or*
  - the cost of your previous accommodation was met wholly or partly out of public or local funds by a body which has placed you into a residential care home.[163]

  A private dwelling could include a house, flat, group home or supported lodgings, which is unregistered accommodation for which HB is payable. If you are receiving social services support, you may be able to argue that domiciliary services do not constitute accommodation costs (see p2:178). You may be caught by the special accommodation rules, however, if the accommodation was provided, or is funded, under the legislation specified on p2:178.
- You have preserved rights and pay and have always paid, the whole cost of your accommodation yourself (see below). You are entitled to AA/DLA care but they count as income for IS/income-based JSA purposes (see p2:406). This provision also applies if you were living in a small, unregistered home on 31 March 1993 and entitled to AA or DLA care or the special rates of IS (see p2:169).[164]

The self-funding option

If you have entered residential or nursing care since 31 March 1993 and your place is not being funded by a local authority in England and Wales (see p2:167), you should not be treated as being in accommodation, 'the cost of which may be borne' under the legislation specified on p2:178. This is because a local authority in England and Wales has no power to provide and fund accommodation which is 'otherwise available' to you.[165]

This means that if you are self-funding (with or without IS or income-based JSA), you remain entitled to AA or DLA care component, which in turn means you may also be entitled to the severe disability premium (see p2:329). Although your benefits are unlikely to be enough to meet your home fees, you may be better off meeting the shortfall from other sources, if this is possible, rather than seek local authority funding. The self-funding option is likely to be most advantageous where you have a property for sale. If you are funded by the local authority, you will lose your AA/DLA care and any severe disability premium. You will also have to refund the full cost of your accommodation to the local authority on a weekly basis, or when your property is sold. If you are self-funding you keep your AA/DLA care and none of your benefits are clawed back when your property is sold.

You can opt to be self-funding from the outset, or you can become self-funding after a period of being funded by the local authority. You should note the following points, however:

- The self-funding option is unlikely to assist you in Scotland or Northern Ireland because local authorities there have wider powers to provide and fund accommodation, so that the 'may be borne' provisions may stop you getting AA/DLA care, even if you are self-funding.[166]
- If you receive local authority funding while you are selling your property and pay your weekly accommodation charge in a lump sum when the property is sold it is unclear whether you are entitled to arrears of AA/DLA care. There have been conflicting commissioners' decisions in England and Northern Ireland on the payability of AA/DLA care in the case of 'retrospective self-funding' and some of the Northern Ireland cases have been appealed to the Court of Appeal.[167]

4. **Prisoners**

Special rules apply to most social security benefits in relation to prisoners. Most benefits are not payable while you are in prison, although in certain circumstances payment is only suspended and arrears may be payable on your release. Some benefits, however, remain payable while you are in prison, with or without restrictions. See below for details. It is important that you inform the relevant benefit authorities as soon as you, or a member of your family, enter or leave prison to avoid any under- or overpayment of benefit. Note particularly, that if your income support (IS) or income-based jobseeker's allowance (JSA) stops, you will need to make a fresh claim for housing benefit (HB). It is also important to inform the benefit authorities about your sentence, if you are being held on remand.

For details of benefits on release and help with travelling expenses, see p2:184.

Income support

You count as a prisoner for IS purposes if:[168]

- you are detained in custody (eg, prison or young offenders' institution) following a sentence of imprisonment; *or*

- you are detained in custody 'on remand' (eg, in a prison or remand centre) awaiting trial or sentence; *or*
- you are on temporary release (eg, home leave, working, attending a course).

You do not count as a prisoner if:[169]
- you are released on licence or parole; *or*
- you are in a bail or probation hostel; *or*
- you are detained in hospital (under the Mental Health Act 1983 or Scottish equivalents; *or*
- you are released under a Home Detention Curfew (electronic tagging).

If you count as a prisoner for IS purposes, you are not entitled to any IS, apart from housing costs (see p2:343), which are only payable while you are on remand, awaiting trial or sentence.[170]

A prisoner no longer counts as a member of the family for IS purposes (see p2:120).[171] If you are a prisoner, your partner can claim benefit as a single person or lone parent. If your partner or child is a prisoner, you can no longer claim IS for her/him. If you and your partner are temporarily separated because one of you is in a bail or probation hostel, you still count as a couple for IS purposes and your applicable amount is calculated at either the couple rate or double the single rate, whichever is the greater (see p2:121).[172]

Income-based jobseeker's allowance

You are not entitled to income-based JSA as you are not able to satisfy the labour market conditions while you are detained in custody or on temporary release.

A prisoner no longer counts as a member of the family for income-based JSA purposes.[173] If you are a prisoner (see p2:120), your partner can claim income-based JSA or IS as single claimant or lone parent. If your partner or child is a prisoner, you can no longer claim income-based JSA for her/him. If one of you is temporarily in a bail or probation hostel, the rules are as for IS (see above).[174]

Housing benefit

If you are remanded in custody pending trial or sentence or required to live in a bail hostel, you remain entitled to housing benefit (HB) for up to 52 weeks, as long as your absence from home is unlikely to substantially exceed 52 weeks.[175] If you are serving a custodial sentence, including where you are on temporary release, (but not when you are detained under the Mental Health Acts), you are entitled to HB for up to 13 weeks, as long as your absence from home is unlikely to exceed 13 weeks.[176] If you are serving a sentence of more than 13 weeks, you may still be entitled to HB, as prisoners serving short sentences are often released on license after serving half their sentence. The introduction of the Home Detention Curfew Scheme (tagging) means that it is possible for a prisoner serving a sentence of up to 10 months to be released within 13 weeks.

If you are no longer entitled to IS, you will need to make a new claim for HB.

If you are no longer entitled to HB, your partner or other person occupying you home may be able to claim benefit as a liable person (see p2:341). A prisoner continues to count as a member of the claimant's family as long as s/he is unlikely to be away for substantially longer than 52 weeks.[177] Non-dependant deductions are not made in respect of a non-dependant who is a prisoner.[178]

Council tax benefit

The rules are the same as for HB,[179] except that you may be able to argue that you are still entitled to council tax benefit (CTB) as long as your home remains your sole or main residence.[180] Also, a prisoner remains a member of the claimant's family, so long as s/he is only temporarily absent.[181] If your home is unoccupied while you are a prisoner, you can apply for it to be exempt from council tax, as long as you are not in prison for non-payment of a fine or the council tax. See CPAG'S *Council Tax Handbook* for details.

Family credit/disability working allowance

An award of family credit (FC) or disability working allowance (DWA) is not affected if you, or a member of your family, become a prisoner. If you are in prison when your award ends, however, you are unlikely to satisfy the 'remunerative work' rule, to reclaim (see p1:464).

A child or young person who is detained in custody under a sentence imposed by a court, does not count as a member of your family.[182] A person serving a custodial sentence of at least 52 weeks no longer counts as a partner for FC/DWA purposes.[183]

Note: FC and DWA will be replaced by tax credits in October 1999 (see p1:489).

Social fund payments

You cannot get a crisis loan while you are a prisoner (see p1:668). You are unlikely to be in receipt of a qualifying benefit to be eligible for a funeral, maternity or winter payment (see Chapter 30) or a community care grant or budgeting loan (see Chapter 31).

Non-means-tested benefits

Most non-means-tested benefits are not payable or are suspended while you are prisoner. See below for details.

You count as a prisoner for the purpose of non-means-tested benefits if you are in prison or detained in legal custody (in the UK or abroad), in connection with criminal proceedings.[184] If you are in prison for a civil offence, the following rules do not apply and you remain entitled to all benefits, provided you satisfy the normal rules of entitlement. You do not count as a prisoner if you are released on parole, license, Home Detention Curfew (tagging) or on temporary release from a young offenders institution.[185]

If you have received a sentence of imprisonment or detention and have been transferred to hospital because of a mental disorder, you are treated as prisoner until the date you were expected to be released from prison.[186] After that, you are treated as a hospital inpatient (see p2:155).

Benefits disqualified or suspended

You are disqualified from receiving the following benefits while you are a prisoner (see above), if you receive a sentence of imprisonment or detention:[187]
- incapacity benefit and severe disablement allowance;
- attendance allowance, disability living allowance and invalid care allowance (ICA);
- retirement pension and widows' benefits;
- maternity allowance;
- reduced earnings allowance and retirement allowance.

You are also disqualified from receiving an increase in the above benefits for a spouse who is a prisoner.[188]

If you are a remand prisoner awaiting trial or sentence, however, you are only disqualified from receiving the above benefits if you subsequently receive a sentence of imprisonment or detention[189] (including a suspended sentence[190]). An increase of benefit for your spouse is similarly only disqualified if s/he is sentenced to imprisonment or detention.

Payment of benefit is suspended while you are on remand. If you are not sentenced to imprisonment or detention, full arrears are payable when you are released. An increase in benefit for your spouse in suspended while s/he is on remand. Full arrears are payable if s/he is released without sentence of imprisonment or detention.[191]

Note that arrears are only payable if the normal conditions of entitlement for benefit were met while you (or your spouse) were a remand prisoner. In this context:

- you will not be able to satisfy the 'regularly and substantially caring' condition for ICA after you have been in prison for four weeks (see p1:81); *and*
- you should be treated as still 'residing with' your spouse while s/he is in prison, unless your marriage has broken down and your separation is likely to be permanent.[192]

Other benefits not payable

- You are not entitled to statutory sick pay or statutory maternity pay while you are detained in legal custody or sentenced to a term of imprisonment (except where the sentence is suspended).[193]
- You will not be able to satisfy the labour market conditions for contribution-based JSA while you are in prison.
- You are not entitled to an increase in benefit for an adult caring for a child (see p2:95) if the adult or child is a prisoner.[194]

Benefits payable

- You remain entitled to disablement benefit (but not to the increases listed on p1:217) while you are a prisoner (see p2:183) but payment is suspended until you are released and you can only be paid a maximum of 12 months arrears[195] (if you are in prison for more than a year, you should be paid for the 12-month period which gives you the most benefit[196]). In addition, you are entitled to full arrears for any period you were on remand, if you are not subsequently sentenced to imprisonment or detention.[197]
- You remain entitled to child benefit[198] and guardian's allowance[199] while you are a prisoner (see p2:183). You must continue to be responsible for the child (see p1:236). If your child is a prisoner (see p1:243), child benefit will stop after eight weeks,[200] but full arrears are payable at the end of any period of remand, if the child is not sentenced to imprisonment or detention.[201] Once child benefit stops, guardian's allowance and increases in other benefits in respect of the child will also stop.[202]

Benefits on release

- If you are on temporary release, somebody caring for you can claim a community care grant for living expenses (see p1:657). The Prison Department can also provide financial assistance while you are on temporary release.
- When you are permanently released, you should claim any benefits you are entitled to as soon as possible. Because IS and income-based JSA are generally paid in arrears, you may need to apply for a social fund crisis loan to meet your initial expenses (see p1:667). You can also apply for a community care grant if you are, or expected to be, in receipt of IS or income-based JSA (see p1:646). You may receive a discharge grant from the Prison Department,

which counts as capital for IS/income-based JSA purposes.[203] You are treated as satisfying the labour market conditions for income-based JSA for the first seven days after your release.[204]

- If you are released without being sentenced to imprisonment or detention, you should receive any arrears of non-means-tested benefits you are entitled to (see p1:4). You should also check that you have been credited with any national insurance contributions you are entitled to (see p2:266).

Help with travelling expenses

- The Prison Department can help you with travelling expenses when you are temporarily or permanently released from prison.
- The Prison Department can also help a close relative with the cost of visiting you in prison, (including, where necessary, the cost of an overnight stay), if s/he is receiving IS, income-based JSA, FC or DWA or has a low income (assessed as for health benefits – see p1:614).

5. People without accommodation

Income support and income-based jobseeker's allowance

If you are a person 'without accommodation' you are entitled to the normal income support (IS)/income-based jobseeker's allowance (JSA) personal allowances for yourself and your partner (see p2:318) but you are not entitled to any allowances for dependent children (see p2:319), nor any premiums for yourself, your partner or your children (see p2:322).[205]

The term 'accommodation' is not defined in law and should be interpreted widely and flexibly. The *Adjudication Officers' Guide* describes it as, 'An effective shelter from the elements which is capable of being heated; and in which occupants can sit, lie, cook and eat; and which is reasonably suited for continuous occupation. The site of the accommodation may alter from day to day, but it is still accommodation if the structure is habitable'.[206] This would cover tents, caravans and other substantial shelters. Cardboard boxes, bus shelters, sleeping bags[207] and cars[208] would not qualify as accommodation.

If you are temporarily absent from the accommodation you occupy as your home and are living a lifestyle as though you have no accommodation (eg, you are sleeping rough) you should be treated as having accommodation.[209]

If the Benefits Agency thinks that you have an unsettled way of life, it may refer you to a voluntary project centre. This should only be done with your consent and if a place is available. IS/income-based JSA should not be refused or delayed if you are unwilling to take the advice being offered, or are not interested in being resettled.[210]

Payment

If you are known in an area, you should receive your benefit by giro, payment card or order book in the normal way (see p1:454), but if you are 'likely to move on or mis-spend your money' you may be required to collect your benefit on a daily or part-week basis.[211]

Availability for and actively seeking work

You must be available for and actively seeking work to get JSA (see Chapter 14). You can be available for work if you do not have accommodation but it must be possible for you to be contacted at short notice if you are to satisfy the requirement that you are willing and able to take up any job immediately, or at 24 or 48 hours' notice (see p1:292). You may satisfy this requirement by daily visits to the JobCentre, or a drop-in centre or support group where a message can be left for you.

Being homeless may, of course, reduce your prospects of finding work but personal circumstances which reduce your chances of being employed should not prevent you getting JSA unless you are placing unreasonable restrictions on your availability. The fact that you are homeless should be taken into account when deciding whether you are taking reasonable steps to find work, eg, it may not be reasonable to expect you to write to employers if you have no address for them to reply to. The employment officer should also recognise that you may need time to find accommodation, and that this will leave you with less time to find work (see p1:310).

Other benefits and sources of help

Your entitlement to other benefits, including all non-means-tested benefits, is unaffected if you do not have accommodation. Note the points above about availability for and actively seeking work if you are getting contribution-based JSA.

If you become homeless and have no money, you may initially need a social fund crisis loan (see p1:672). If you set up home as part of a resettlement programme after you have been homeless, you may be entitled to a community care grant (see p1:654).

If you are homeless, the local authority may have a duty to assist you with accommodation under the Housing Acts, or, arguably under the National Assistance Act 1948, particularly if you are destitute and your health is at risk.[212] A child or young person may be entitled to help from social services under the Children Act.

6. People involved in a trade dispute

Special rules may stop or reduce the payment of some benefits if you or your partner are involved in a trade dispute. Benefits not referred to below are payable as normal during a trade dispute.

A 'trade dispute' is any dispute between employers and employees or between employees and employees about terms or conditions of employment, or the employment/non-employment of anyone.[213]

You are treated as being involved in a trade dispute if:[214]
- you are not working because of a 'stoppage of work' caused by a trade dispute at your 'place of work' (see below); *or*
- you withdraw your labour in furtherance of a trade dispute.

The 'stoppage of work' could be due to a strike, lock-out or any other stoppage caused by a trade dispute. The stoppage does not have to involve everybody,[215] or stop all work.[216] There is no 'stoppage' if normal work continues through the employment of replacement workers.[217] You are treated as involved in the trade dispute until the stoppage ends, even if you are not a party to the dispute or your contract has been terminated as part of the dispute (but see below).[218]

Your 'place of work' means the place or premises where you are employed but it does not include a separate department carrying out a separate branch of work, which is commonly undertaken as a separate business elsewhere (a colliery canteen worker, for example, laid off during a miners' strike, was not 'involved in a trade dispute at her place of work'[219]). It is often difficult, however, to establish that separate branches are commonly separate businesses and not part of integrated activities.[220]

You are treated as being involved in a trade dispute if you withdraw your labour, whether or not there is a stoppage of work at your place of work.[221]

You are not treated as being involved in a trade dispute in the following circumstances:
- You can prove you are not directly interested in the dispute,[222] ie, you will not be affected by its outcome.[223] This could apply if your terms and conditions will not be affected by the outcome of the dispute or your employment has permanently ended and you will not gain anything from the dispute.[224]
- You can prove that during a stoppage of work:[225]
  - you have been made redundant; *or*
  - you have become genuinely employed elsewhere (ie, not just to avoid the trade dispute rules[226]); *or*
  - you genuinely resume employment with your employer and then leave for a reason other than the trade dispute (note, you may be sanctioned if you voluntarily leave – see p1:395).

Whether you are involved in a trade dispute is a complex area of law. If there is any doubt, you should seek specialist advice from your trade union or from an advice or law centre. Decisions are subject to appeal.

Income support

If you or your partner are involved in a trade dispute (see above),

- you are treated as being in remunerative work and are, therefore, not entitled to income support (IS), for the first seven days either of you is so involved[227] (if the dispute causes a series of stoppages, the rule only applies for seven days from the start of the first stoppage[228]); *and*
- after that, you are not treated as being in remunerative work[229] but the amount of IS you are entitled to is reduced (sometimes to nil –see below).

You should also note the following rules:

- You can be treated as being involved in a trade dispute, pending a decision as to whether you are actually so involved. A tribunal cannot decide an appeal until a decision is made.[230]
- You do not count as involved in a trade dispute during:[231]
  - a 'period of incapacity for work' (four or more days of incapacity – see p2:22); *or*
  - a 'maternity period' (six weeks before the expected week of confinement and seven weeks after the week of confinement).
- You are no longer treated as being involved in a trade dispute from the day you return to work with the same employer (even if the dispute is continuing or you are doing a different job).[232]
- You are entitled to claim IS while you are involved in a trade dispute and for the first 15 days after you return to work (see p1:445).[233] If you are not involved in a trade dispute, but your partner is, you can only claim IS if you fall into one of the other groups of eligible claimants listed on p1:442.

Amount payable

Special rules reduce the amount of IS payable if you and/or your partner are involved in a trade dispute.

Applicable amount

Your applicable amount is calculated as follows:[234]

- If you are a single claimant, or member of a childless couple, both involved in a trade dispute, your applicable amount is nil.
- If you are a lone parent, you are only entitled to:
  - personal allowances for your children;
  - the family and disabled child premiums;
  - housing costs (see note below).

You are not entitled to a personal allowance or any premiums payable in respect of yourself. The *Adjudication Officers' Guide* suggests you are not entitled to the lone parent rate of the family premium but this is arguable.[235]

- If you are a member of a couple and one of you is involved in a trade dispute, you are eligible for:
  - half the normal personal allowance for a couple;
  - half of any premiums paid at the couple rate;
  - any premiums payable solely in respect of the person not involved in the trade dispute (eg, carer's premium, lower rate of severe disability premium);
  - personal allowances and the family and disabled child premiums for any children;
  - housing costs (see note below).

You are not entitled to any premiums payable solely for the person involved in the trade dispute (eg, carer's premium, lower rate SDP). Amounts are rounded down to the nearest lower 5 pence.

Note: Housing costs are payable unless all members of your family are involved in a trade dispute. Those members not involved are treated as responsible for the costs.[236]

Actual and 'assumed' strike pay

- Any payments you or your partner actually receive from a trade union in excess of £27.50 a week count as income. Payments of up to £27.50 are ignored. If you and your partner are both involved in a trade dispute, only £27.50 in total is ignored.[237]
- Whether or not you actually receive any payments, £27.50 is deducted from your IS as 'assumed strike pay'. If you and your partner are both involved in a trade dispute, £27.50 is still deducted.[238] This deduction may extinguish your entitlement to any IS.

Example

Cliff is on strike. He and his partner Bernice have no children. Their only income is £30 a week strike pay.

Applicable amount:	£40.30 (half normal amount)
less income:	£ 2.50 (strike pay over £27.50)
=	£37.80
less	£27.50 ('assumed strike pay')
= IS payable	£10.30

If their strike pay was £41, their income of £13.50 (strike pay over £27.50) and their 'assumed strike pay' of £27.50 would extinguish their entitlement to any IS.

Other income and capital

Other income and capital is treated as normal except that the following payments are taken into account in full as income:

- Any repayment of income tax paid or due.[239]
- Any payment received or due because the person involved in the trade dispute is not working (eg, a loan or grant from social services).[240]
- Payments made under the Children Act 1989 or Children (Scotland) Act 1995 to promote the welfare of children.[241]
- Charitable or voluntary payments (whether regular or irregular, with no £20 disregard for regular payments – see p2:413) except any payments from the Macfarlane Trusts, the Eileen Trust, the Fund or the Independent Living Funds.[242]
- Payment in kind (except payments from the above trusts or funds) paid to the person involved in the trade dispute or to a third party (unless it is used for items allowable under the notional income/capital rules – see pp2:421 and 2:461).[243]
- Holiday pay payable more than four weeks after your employment is terminated or interrupted (subject to an earnings disregard).[244]
- An advance of earnings or a loan from an employer (subject to any earnings disregard).[245]

Benefit loans on return to work

If you return to work with the same employer, whether or not the trade dispute has ended, you can receive IS for the first 15 days back at work, in the form of a loan.[246] You are not treated as being in remunerative work for this period.[247] If you are a member of a couple you are not entitled to IS if your partner is in full-time work.[248]

Your income and capital are calculated as if you were still involved in the trade dispute except that the rules about actual and assumed strike pay do not apply.[249]

Any IS that you are awarded is paid in advance.[250] You may not get IS if you are entitled to less than £5.[251]

Repayment of the loan

Any IS paid during your first 15 days back at work can be recovered by deductions from your earnings.[252] If this is not practical (eg, because you are currently unemployed) it can be recovered directly from you.[253]

The amount deducted from your earnings is worked out by comparing your protected earnings with your available earnings.

Your **'protected earnings'** are:

- your applicable amount excluding housing costs; *plus*
- £27; *less*
- child benefit paid at ordinary or lone parent rate.[254]

Your 'available earnings' are the whole of your earnings, including sick pay, after all 'lawful' deductions have been made.[255] These include tax and national insurance contributions, trade union subscriptions and any amount being deducted under a court order or, for instance, a child support deduction order. Any bonus or commission, if paid on a different day, is treated as paid on your next normal pay day.[256]

If your available earnings are less than £1 above your protected earnings, there can be no deduction. If they are £1 or more above, your employer will deduct half of the difference between your protected and available earnings. If you are paid monthly, your protected earnings are multiplied by five. If your monthly available earnings are less than £5 above this level, no deduction is made. Otherwise, half the excess is deducted. If you are paid daily, the amount of your protected earnings and the £1 figure is divided by five to determine the amount (if any) of the deduction. The calculation can be adjusted as appropriate where your wages are paid at other intervals.[257] If you are paid more than one amount of earnings on a pay day, your protected earnings and the £1 figure are multiplied to reflect this.[258]

A deduction notice is sent to your employer by the Benefits Agency setting out your protected earnings and the amount of IS to be recovered.[259] If you have not actually received IS, no deduction should be made.[260] Your employer *can* begin making the deductions from the first pay day after receiving the notice and *must* start doing so one month after getting it.[261]

A deduction notice ceases to have effect if:
- it is cancelled or replaced; *or*
- you stop working for that employer; *or*
- your IS loan has been repaid; *or*
- 26 weeks have passed since the date of the notice.[262]

If you stop work, another deduction notice can be sent if you get another job and part of your IS loan is still outstanding.[263]

You must tell the Benefits Agency within 10 days if you leave a job or start another while part of your IS loan remains unpaid.[264] If you fail to do so you can be prosecuted.[265] It is a criminal offence for your employer to fail to keep records of deductions and supply the Benefits Agency with these.[266] If your employer fails to make a deduction which should have been made from your pay, the Benefits Agency can recover the amount from your employer instead.[267]

Jobseeker's allowance

You are not entitled to contribution-based or income-based jobseeker's allowance (JSA) (including hardship payments) for the whole of any week (seven days from Sunday[268]), if you are involved in a trade dispute (see p2:187) for one or more days during that week.[269] You may, however, be entitled to IS (see p2:188). Weeks of disentitlement do not count towards your 26 weeks entitlement to contribution-based JSA.[270]

Your partner can claim income-based JSA if you are involved in a trade dispute and s/he is not,[271] but:

- you are treated as being in remunerative work precluding any entitlement to income-based JSA for the first seven days you are involved in a trade dispute unless s/he was already entitled when you became involved[272] (if the dispute causes a series of stoppages, the rule only applies for seven days from the start of the first stoppage[273]); *and*
- after that, you are not treated as being in remunerative work[274] but the amount of income-based JSA your partner is entitled to is reduced (see below).

If your partner is claiming income-based JSA, the following rules also apply, as for IS (see p2:188):

- you can be treated as involved in a trade dispute pending a decision;[275]
- you are not treated as involved in a trade dispute:
  - during a period of incapacity for work; *or*
  - during a maternity period;[276] *or*
  - after you return to work with your employer.[277]

Unlike IS, no special rules apply for the first 15 days you return to work and you are not entitled to a benefit loan of JSA during that period.

Amount payable

You are not entitled to claim JSA for any week in which you are involved in a trade dispute (see p2:187).

If your partner claims income-based JSA while you are involved in a trade dispute, as in the case of IS, the following rules reduce the amount payable.

- The applicable amount is reduced in the same way as for IS, where one member of a couple is involved in a trade dispute (see p2:188).[278]
- As with IS, the special rules relating to actual and assumed strike pay and other income and capital apply (see p2:189).[279]

Benefit is payable to your partner for part of a week if you are only involved in a trade dispute for part of a week.[280] The amount payable and the amount of assumed strike pay is worked out on a daily, pro rata basis.[281]

Back to work bonus

The following special rules apply in relation to a back to work bonus (see p1:588) if you or your partner are involved in a trade dispute (see p2:187):[282]

- Any earnings you receive while you are involved in a trade dispute are disregarded when calculating the amount of the bonus, unless you are incapable of work or in a maternity pay period (see pp2:14 and 1:106).

- The bonus is not payable when you return to work with the same employer after the trade dispute.

Housing benefit and council tax benefit

You remain entitled to HB and CTB while you or your partner are involved in a trade dispute. If your IS/income-based JSA stops because you are involved in a trade dispute, you must make a fresh claim for HB/CTB (see pp1:530 and 1:531). You may become entitled to HB/CTB as a result of a drop in income because of a trade dispute.

When assessing your earnings in connection with a claim for HB/CTB, the local authority should take into account any reduction in your income because of a trade dispute and not just consider your pre-strike earnings.[283] The local authority can average out your earnings over a different period than normal, if this results in a more accurate estimate of your earnings (see p2:392).

Family credit and disability working allowance

An existing award of family credit (FC) or disability working allowance (DWA) is not affected if you or your partner are involved in a trade dispute (see p2:187).

You will not be entitled to FC or DWA if you or your partner have not worked for at least 16 hours in the week of your claim or the two preceding weeks because of a trade dispute, unless you are expected by your employer to work at least 16 hours in the week following your claim (see p2:5).

Note: FC and DWA will be replaced by tax credits in October 1999 (see p1:488).

If your earnings are reduced because of a trade dispute when you claim FC, the assessment period for calculating your earnings (see p2:390) is shifted back, so that it contains no pay periods affected by the reduction. The length of the assessment period, however, remains unchanged.[284]

If there is a period of short-time working lasting up to 13 continuous weeks, or a trade dispute at your place of work when you claim DWA, your earnings are assessed over the five weeks (if you are paid weekly) or two months (if you are paid monthly) preceding the short-time working or trade dispute.[285]

Statutory sick pay

You are not entitled to statutory sick pay (SSP) if your period of entitlement would begin when there is a stoppage of work due to a trade dispute at your place of work, unless you can show you did not have a prior direct interest in the dispute.[286] See p2:188 for the meaning of the terms used. An overtime ban or working to grade does not count as stoppage of work.[287] You remain

39

Chapter 39: Other special groups
6. People involved in a trade dispute
. . . .

disentitled throughout your period of sickness, even if the trade dispute ends. You can, however, claim incapacity benefit and/or IS (see p1:38 and 1:441).

You remain entitled to SSP if your entitlement began before the trade dispute.

Statutory maternity pay

For the purposes of the 26-week 'continuous employment rule' (see p1:92) for statutory sick pay:[288]

- any week in which you are of working because of a stoppage of work due to a trade dispute at your place of work (see p2:187) does not break your continuity of employment; *but*
- any such week does not count towards the total of 26 weeks and if you are dismissed during the stoppage, your continuity of employment is broken, unless, in either case, you can show that you at no time had a direct interest in the trade dispute (see p2:187).

Increases for dependants

You are not entitled to an increase of incapacity benefit, severe disablement allowance, invalid care allowance, maternity allowance or retirement pension (Category A) for an adult dependant who is involved in a trade dispute (see p2:187).[289] If the adult dependant returns to work, you should reclaim the increase for her/him.

Social fund payments

Maternity expenses payment

If you or your partner are involved in trade dispute (see p2:187), you are only entitled to a maternity expenses payment (see p1:626) if:[290]

- you or your partner are receiving IS or income-based JSA and the trade dispute has been going on for at least six weeks when you claim a maternity expenses payment; *or*
- you or your partner are receiving FC or DWA, which you claimed before the trade dispute began.

Note: FC and DWA will be replaced by tax credits in October 1999 (see p1:489).

You are not treated as being involved in a trade dispute during a 'period of incapacity for work' or a 'maternity period' (see p1:106 for definitions).[291]

Note: Involvement in a trade dispute has no effect on entitlement to a funeral expenses, cold weather or winter fuel payment (see p1:626).

Community care grants

If you or your partner are involved in a trade dispute, you are not eligible for a community care grant other than for travel expenses (see p1:657) to visit somebody who is ill and then only in the following circumstances:

- You are involved in a trade dispute and are visiting:
  - your partner in hospital or a similar institution; *or*
  - a dependant in hospital or a similar institution (but only if you have no partner living with you who could get a community care grant under these provisions or if your partner is also in hospital); *or*
  - a close relative (not defined) or a member of your household who is critically ill (whether or not s/he is in hospital).
- You are not involved in a trade dispute, but your partner is, and you are visiting:
  - a close relative who is in a hospital or a similar institution or who is critically ill; *or*
  - someone else in hospital or critically ill, who was a member of your household before going into hospital or getting ill.[292]

Budgeting loans

You are not eligible for a budgeting loan if you or your partner are involved in a trade dispute (see p2:187).[293]

Crisis loans

If you or your partner are involved in a trade dispute, you are only eligible for a crisis loan for:[294]

- expenses arising from a disaster (see p1:670); *and*
- the cost of items needed for cooking (including cooking utensils) or space heating (including fireguards).

Notes

References are to statutes and regulations as amended up to 8 March 1999. All regulations are (General) Regulations unless otherwise stated. There is a full list of abbreviations in Appendix 13.

2. **Hospital inpatients**

1 Reg 2(2) SS(HIP) Regs; NHSA 1977; NHS(S)A 1978; NHSCCA 1990

2 Reg 2(2) SS(HIP) Regs; s65 NHSA 1977; s58 NHS(S)A 1978; Sch 2 para 14 NHSCCA 1990

3 paras 29335 and 67042 AOG

4 *White v CAO, The Times*, 2 August 1993; *Botchett v CAO, The Times*, 8 May 1996

5 Reg 21(2) IS Regs; reg 18(3) HB Regs; reg 10(3) CTB Regs; reg 17(4) SS(HIP) Regs; reg 8(2) SS(AA) Regs; regs 10(5)(a) and 12B(3) SS(DLA) Regs

6 Reg 8(3) SS(AA) Regs; regs 10(3) and 12B(2) SS(DLA) Regs; R(A) 4/83

7 R(S) 4/84; R(IS) 8/96; CS/249/1989; CIS/192/1991; CS/94/1992; CDLA/11099/1995

8 CDLA/11099/1995; para 77856 AOG

9 R(IS) 8/96; paras 29372-73 and 67191-92 AOG

10 Sch 3 para 3(11) and (12) IS Regs

11 Sch 3 para 18(7)(g) IS Regs

12 Sch 2 paras 13(3A) and 15(5) IS Regs

13 Sch 2 paras 12(1)(c)(ii) and 14(3) IS Regs

14 Sch 2 para 14ZA(3) IS Regs

15 Sch 7 para 1(a) IS Regs

16 Reg 16(2)(b) IS Regs

17 Sch 7 para 1(3) IS Regs

18 Sch 7 para 1(c) and Sch 2 para 12(1)(c)(ii) IS Regs

19 Reg 16(2)(b) and (5)(b) IS Regs

20 para 27070 AOG

21 Sch 7 para 3 IS Regs

22 Sch 2 para 14(b) IS Regs

23 Sch 7 para 2(b) IS Regs

24 Sch 7 para 2(a) IS Regs

25 Reg 16(2)(b) IS Regs

26 Reg 16(2)(b) IS Regs

27 Reg 16(2)(b) and (5)(b) IS Regs

28 Reg 22(3) IS Regs

29 Sch 7 para 2A IS Regs

30 Sch 7 para 7(1)(i) SS(C&P) Regs

31 Sch 7 para 7(1)(ii) SS(C&P) Regs

32 Sch 7 para 7(3)(d) and (6) SS(C&P) Regs

33 Regs 14(1)(l), 19(1)(l) and 55 JSA Regs

34 Sch 1 paras 15(5) and 20(6)(b)(i) JSA Regs

35 Sch 5 para 1 JSA Regs

36 Sch 5 para 2 JSA Regs

37 Reg 78(2)(b) JSA Regs

38 Reg 26A(4) SS(C&P) Regs

39 Reg 26A(5)(d) and (6) SS(C&P) Regs

40 Reg 5(8B)(c)(ii) and (8C) HB Regs; regs 4C(4)(c)(ii) and 5 CTB Regs

41 s131(3)(a) SSCBA 1992

42 Sch 2 paras 12(1)(a)(iii), 13(3A), 14(b), 14ZA(3) and 15(5) HB Regs; Sch 1 paras 13(1)(a)(iii), 14(3A), 15(b), 16(3) and 19(6) CTB Regs

43 Reg 18 HB Regs; reg 10 CTB Regs

44 Reg 15(2)(b) HB Regs

45 Reg 7(1) CTB Regs

46 Reg 68(1) HB Regs; reg 59(1) CTB Regs

47 Reg 63(7)(e) HB Regs; reg 52(7)(d) CTB Regs

48 Reg 8(2)(a) FC Regs; reg 10(2)(a) DWA Regs

49 Reg 9(2)(a) FC Regs; reg 11(2)(a) DWA Regs

50 Reg 8(3) SS(AA) Regs; regs 10(3) and 12B(2) SS(DLA) Regs

51 Reg 6 and 8(1) SS(AA) Regs; regs 8, 10(2), 12A and 12B(1) SS(DLA) Regs

52 Reg 21 SS(GB) Regs

53 Reg 12B(7) and (8) SS(DLA) Regs

54 Reg 12C(2) SS(DLA) Regs
55 Reg 12B(3)-(5) SS(DLA) Regs
56 Regs 12C(1) and 12B(6) SS(DLA) Regs
57 Reg 16(2) SS(C&P) Regs
58 Reg 25 SS(C&P) Regs
59 Reg 8(4) SS(AA) Regs; regs 10(6), 12B(9A) SS(DLA) Regs
60 Reg 8(5) and (7) SS(AA) Regs; regs 10(7) and (9), 12B(12) SS(DLA) Regs
61 Reg 4(2) SS(ICA) Regs
62 s143 SSCBA 1992; reg 4 CB Regs
63 Reg 5 SS(HIP) Regs
64 Reg 2(3) and Sch 1 SS(HIP) Regs
65 Regs 9 and 11(1)(a) SS(HIP) Regs
66 Reg 13 SS(HIP) Regs
67 Reg 6(2) SS(HIP) Regs
68 Regs 6(1) and (5), 10, 11(3) and 12 SS(HIP) Regs
69 Reg 16 SS(HIP) Regs
70 Reg 11(1)(b) SS(HIP) Regs
71 Reg 16 SS(HIP) Regs
72 Reg 4A SS(HIP) Regs
73 Sch 7 para 18(a)(i) and (ii) IS Regs
74 Sch 7 para 18(a)(iii) IS Regs
75 Sch 7 para 18(a)(iv) IS Regs
76 Sch 7 para 18(b) IS Regs
77 Sch 7 para 18(c) IS Regs
78 Sch 7 para 2A(4A) IS Regs
79 Sch 7 para 13(2) IS Regs
80 Sch 5 para 17(a) JSA Regs
81 Sch 5 para 17(b) JSA Regs
82 Sch 1 para 3(5)(a) JSA Regs
83 Sch 5 para 15(2) JSA Regs
84 Reg 8(2) SS(AA) Regs; reg 10(5) SS(DLA) Regs
85 Reg 17(2) SS(HIP) Regs
86 Reg 17(3) SS(HIP) Regs

3. People in residential or nursing care

87 Regs 85 and 86, Schs 1, 3, and 4 and Sch 5 paras 7-9 and 15 JSA Regs
88 NHSCCA 1990
89 s21 NAA 1948, as amended by the Community Care (Residential Accommodation) Act 1998
90 s21 NAA 1948; Social Work (Scotland) Act 1968
91 s22(1) NAA 1948
92 NA(AR) Regs
93 s21 HSS&SSA Act 1983

94 s22 HSS&SSA Act 1983
95 s22(5A) NAA 1948
96 Reg 19(1ZB)-(1ZR) IS Regs
97 Reg 19 IS Regs
98 Reg 19(1ZF) IS Regs
99 Sch 4 paras 14 and 15 IS Regs
100 R(SB) 9/89; para 29047 AOG
101 Sch 9 para 9 IS Regs; Sch 7 para 10 JSA Regs
102 Sch 4 para 13 IS Regs
103 Sch 4 para 1(1)(a) IS Regs
104 Sch 4 para 2(2) IS Regs
105 Sch 4 para 2(1) IS Regs
106 Sch 4 para 3 IS Regs
107 Sch 4 para 5 IS Regs
108 Sch 4 paras 6 and 7 IS Regs
109 Sch 4 para 9 IS Regs
110 Sch 4 para 10 IS Regs
111 Sch 4 paras 9(b) and 10(4) IS Regs
112 CIS/263/1991
113 s55 RHA 1984
114 Reg 1(2) RCH Regs
115 CSB/1171/1986
116 s20(1) RHA 1984
117 Sch 4 para 6(2) IS Regs
118 Sch 4 para 12(1) and (2) IS Regs
119 Sch 4 para 12(1) and (2) IS Regs
120 Sch 4 para 12(3) and (4) IS Regs
121 Sch 9 para 30(1)(e) IS Regs; Sch 7 para 31(1)(e) JSA Regs
122 s26A NAA 1948; RA(RPORE) Regs
123 Sch 7 para 16 IS Regs
124 Sch 5 para 16 JSA Regs
125 CIS/5415/1995; CSIS/833/1995
126 Sch 3 para 4(1)(b) IS Regs; Sch 2 para 4(1)(b) JSA Regs; reg 7(1)(e) HB Regs
127 Sch 9 para 15A IS Regs; Sch 7 para 16 JSA Regs
128 Sch 9 para 30A IS Regs; Sch 7 para 32 JSA Regs
129 Sch 2 para 2A IS Regs
130 Sch 3C IS Regs
131 Sch 2 para 2A(4A) IS Regs
132 Reg 17(1)(bb) and Sch 2 para 2A(3) IS Regs
133 Reg 19(3) and Sch 2 para 2A(3) IS Regs
134 Sch 2 para 2A(4) IS Regs
135 Reg 21(3)-(4) IS Regs
136 Reg 21(3B)-(3E) IS Regs
137 Reg 21(3A) IS Regs
138 Sch 7 paras 10A-10C and 13 IS Regs

139 Reg 8(2)(b) HB Regs
140 Reg 8(2ZA) and (2ZB) HB Regs
141 Regs 7(1)(k), (2) and (3) and 8(2)(a) HB Regs
142 Regs 7(1)(e) and (3) HB Regs
143 Reg 7(2)(c) and (d) HB Regs
144 Reg 7(4)-(12) HB Regs
145 Reg 5(7B), (7C), (8B) and (8C) HB Regs
146 Reg 4C(1), (2), (4) and (5) CTB Regs
147 s131(3) SSCBA 1992
148 Regs 7, 7A and 8 SS(AA) Regs; regs 9, 9A and 10 SS(DLA) Regs
149 Reg 8(2) SS(AA) Regs; reg 10(5) SS(DLA) Regs
150 para 77854 AOG
151 Reg 25 SS(C&P) Regs
152 Reg 8(3) SS(AA) Regs; reg 10(3) SS(DLA) Regs
153 Reg 7(1) SS(AA) Regs; reg 9(1) SS(DLA) Regs
154 Reg 7(5) SS(AA) Regs; reg 9(6) SS(DLA) Regs
155 CA/2985/1997
156 Reg 8(6) SS(AA) Regs; reg 10(8) SS(DLA) Regs
157 *Steane v CAO and Another* (HL), 24 July 1996
158 Reg 8(7) SS(AA) Regs; reg 10(9) SS(DLA) Regs
159 Reg 9(1A) SS(DLA) Regs
160 Reg 9(2) and (2A) SS(DLA) Regs; para 77736 AOG
161 Reg 7(3)(a) SS(AA) Regs; reg 9(4)(b) SS(DLA) Regs
162 Reg 9(4)(a) SS(DLA) Regs; para 77771 AOG
163 Reg 7(3)(c), (4) and (4A) SS(AA) Regs; reg 9(4)(d), (5) and (5A) SS(DLA) Regs
164 Regs 7(3)(b) and 7A and Sch 1 SS(AA) Regs; regs 9(4)(c) and 9A and Sch 3 SS(DLA) Regs
165 s21(1)(a) NAA 1948; CA/2985/1997; *Steane v CAO*; paras 77721-24 AOG
166 paras 77925-26 AOG; para 77721 Northern Ireland AOG
167 CA/7126/1995, CA/11185/1995 and CA/84/1996 reject payability; CA/4723/1995, C3/95(AA), C4/95(AA), C2/96(AA), C3/96(AA) and C15/96(AA) accept payability.

4. Prisoners

168 Reg 21(3) IS Regs
169 Reg 21(3) IS Regs; para 29526 AOG
170 Sch 7 para 8 IS Regs
171 Reg 16(3)(b) and (5)(f) IS Regs
172 Sch 7 para 9 IS Regs
173 Reg 78(3)(b) and (5)(i) JSA Regs
174 Sch 5 para 5 JSA Regs
175 Reg 5(8B)(c)(i) HB Regs
176 Reg 5(8) and (8A) HB Regs
177 Reg 15(2) HB Regs
178 Reg 63(7)(e) HB Regs
179 Regs 4C(3), (4) and (5) and 52(8)(b) CTB Regs
180 s131(3)(a) SSCBA 1992
181 Reg 7(1) CTB Regs
182 Reg 8(2)(e) FC Regs; reg 10(2)(e) DWA Regs
183 Reg 9(2)(c) FC Regs; reg 11(2)(c) DWA Regs
184 s113(1)(b) SSCBA 1992; reg 2(9) and (10) SS(GB) Regs; R(S) 8/79
185 paras 17018-19 AOG
186 Reg 2(3) and (4) SS(GB) Regs
187 s113(1)(b) SSCBA 1992; reg 2 SS(GB) Regs
188 s113(1)(b) SSCBA 1992
189 Reg 2(2) and (8)(c) SS(GB) Regs
190 R(S) 1/71
191 Reg 3 SS(GB) Regs
192 CS/541/1950
193 Reg 3(1) SSP Regs; reg 9 SMP Regs
194 Reg 10(2)(d) and Sch 2 para 7(b)(ii) SSB(Dep) Regs
195 Reg 2(6) and (7) SS(GB) Regs
196 Reg 2(7) SS(GB) Regs; para 17048 AOG
197 Reg 2(2) and (7) SS(GB) Regs
198 s113(1)(b) SSCBA 1992
199 Reg 2(5) SS(GB) Regs
200 Sch 9 para 1(a) SSCBA 1992; reg 16(6) SS(GB) Regs
201 Reg 16(2) CB Regs; reg 3(1)(b) SS(GB) Regs
202 s80 SSCBA 1992
203 Reg 48(7) IS Regs; reg 110(7) JSA Regs
204 Regs 14(1)(h) and 19(1)(h) JSA Regs

5. People without accommodation

205 Sch 7 para 6 IS Regs; Sch 5 para 3 JSA Regs

206 paras 29503-504 AOG
207 para 29504 AOG
208 CIS/16772/1996
209 para 29506 AOG
210 para 15 HC Handbook
211 para 42 HC Handbook
212 s12 NAA 1948; *R v Hammersmith and Fulham LBC and others*, CA, *The Times*, 19 February 1997

6. People involved in a trade dispute

213 s35(1) JSA 1995
214 s14(1) and (2) JSA 1995
215 R(U) 7/58
216 R(U) 1/87
217 para 37107 AOG
218 R(U) 1/65; paras 37121-25 and 37160-61 AOG
219 CU/66/1986(T)
220 R(U) 4/62; R(U) 1/70
221 s14(2) JSA 1995
222 s14(1) JSA 1995
223 *Presho v Insurance Officer* [1984] (HL) (*see* R(U) 1/84); *Cartlidge v CAO* [1986] (CA) 2 All ER 1
224 See note 223; R(U) 1/87; paras 37210 and 37245-49 AOG
225 s14(3) JSA 1995
226 R(U) 6/74
227 Reg 5(4) IS Regs
228 paras 37677-78 AOG
229 Reg 6(e) IS Regs
230 Reg 56(1)(b), (2) and (3)(a) SS(Adj) Regs
231 s126(1) and (2) SSCBA 1992
232 s127(a) SSCBA 1992
233 Sch 1B para 20 IS Regs
234 s126(3) and (4) SSCBA 1992
235 s126(3)(b) SSCBA 1992; para 37639 AOG
236 Sch 3 para 2(2) IS Regs
237 Sch 9 para 34 IS Regs
238 s126(5)(b) and (7) SSCBA 1992
239 s126(5)(a)(ii) SSCBA 1992; reg 48(2) IS Regs
240 s126(5)(a)(i) SSCBA 1992
241 Reg 41(3), Sch 9 para 48 and Sch 10 para 17 IS Regs
242 Reg 48(9), (10)(a) and (c), Sch 9 paras 15 and 39 and Sch 10 para 22 IS Regs
243 Reg 42(4) and Sch 9 para 21 IS Regs
244 Reg 35(1)(d) IS Regs
245 Reg 48(5) and (6) IS Regs

246 s127 SSCBA 1992; Sch 1B para 20 IS Regs
247 Reg 6(e) IS Regs
248 s127(b) SSCBA 1992
249 s127(a) SSCBA 1992; regs 35(1)(d), 41(3) and (4), 42(4), 48(6), 48(10) and Sch 9 paras 15, 21, 28 and 39 IS Regs
250 para 37790 AOG
251 Reg 26(4) SS(C&P) Regs
252 s127(c) SSCBA 1992; reg 18 SS(PAOR) Regs
253 Reg 26 SS(PAOR) Regs
254 Reg 19(3), (4) and (5) SS(PAOR) Regs
255 Reg 18(2) SS(PAOR) Regs
256 Reg 22(2) SS(PAOR) Regs
257 Reg 22(3) SS(PAOR) Regs
258 Reg 22(4) SS(PAOR) Regs
259 Reg 20(1) and (2) SS(PAOR) Regs
260 Reg 22(5)(a) SS(PAOR) Regs
261 Reg 22(6) SS(PAOR) Regs
262 Reg 21(1) SS(PAOR) Regs
263 Reg 25 SS(PAOR) Regs
264 Reg 28 SS(PAOR) Regs
265 Reg 29 SS(PAOR) Regs
266 Regs 27 and 29 SS(PAOR) Regs
267 Reg 27(5) SS(PAOR) Regs
268 s35(1) JSA 1995
269 s14 JSA 1995
270 s5 JSA 1995
271 s15 JSA 1995
272 Reg 52(2) JSA Regs
273 paras 37677-78 AOG
274 Reg 53(g) JSA Regs
275 Reg 56A(1) and (2) SS(Adj) Regs
276 s15 JSA 1995
277 s15 JSA 1995
278 s15(2)(a) and (b) JSA 1995; Sch 2 para 2(2) JSA Regs
279 s15(2)(c) and (d) JSA 1995; regs 98(1)(c), 104(3), 105(10), 110(5), (6), (9), (10)(a) and (c), Sch 7 paras 15, 22, 29, 36 and 41 and Sch 8 paras 22 and 27 JSA Regs
280 s15(5) JSA 1995
281 Reg 155 JSA Regs
282 Reg 19 SS(BTWB) Regs
283 *R v HBRB London Borough of Ealing ex parte Saville* [1986] HLR 349
284 Reg 14(3) FC Regs
285 Reg 16(3), (4) and (9) DWA Regs

286 Sch 11 paras 2(g) and 7 SSCBA
1992
287 R(SSP) 1/86
288 Reg 13 SMP Regs
289 s91 SSCBA 1992
290 Reg 6 SFM&FE Regs
291 Reg 3(1) SFM&FE Regs; s126(1)
and (2) SSCBA 1992
292 SF Dir 26
293 SF Dir 8(1)(b)
294 SF Dir 17(a) and (f)

Chapter 40

Coming from abroad

This chapter covers:
1. Immigration status (below)
2. Non-means-tested benefits (p2:205)
3. Means-tested benefits (p2:206)
4. The rights of European Economic Area nationals (p2:223)
5. Reciprocal agreements (p2:228)
6. Residence conditions (p2:229)
7. The habitual residence test (p2:234)

This chapter covers some complicated rules. It is beyond the scope of this book to cover the issues in detail. The following sections contain general principles only. For detailed advice, particularly if you are advising persons from abroad, you should consult CPAG's *Migration & Social Security Handbook* (2nd Edition).

If you have come from abroad there are a number of factors to take into account:
- Your immigration status. In recent years there has been as alignment of social security and immigration policy. As a result most benefits now contain rules relating to immigration status. The rules differ according to the particular benefit that you are claiming.
- European Community (EC) law and reciprocal agreements provide additional rights to benefit for certain groups.
- There are special rules for people from Northern Ireland, the Isle of Man and the Channel Islands.
- Even if your immigration status is not restricted you may not qualify for benefit because you do not satisfy the residence conditions for the benefit in question. The type of residence test varies according to the benefit claimed.

1. **Immigration status**

Introduction

It is important, before making a claim for benefit, to know what your immigration status is. This is not only because your immigration status can determine your right to social security benefits but also because a claim for benefit can affect your right to remain in the UK. If you are unsure as to your immigration status you should seek specialist advice.

Most people, apart from British Citizens, are subject to immigration control. This means that you cannot freely enter the UK, but will be subject to scrutiny by the immigration authority. The degree of control varies according to your nationality, for example European Economic Area (EEA) nationals enjoy much greater freedom to enter by virtue of EC law. They do not need leave to enter or remain. (See CPAG's *Migration & Social Security Handbook* for further details.)

If you are subject to immigration control you will require leave, or permission, to enter or remain. Such leave can be:
- limited leave to enter or remain;
- indefinite leave to enter or remain;
- exceptional leave to enter or remain.

If you have limited leave you are only permitted to remain in the UK for a limited period of time. Certain conditions are frequently attached to a grant of limited leave. For example, a restriction may be made on you working or claiming benefits. If you breach these conditions you may put your right to remain in the UK at risk.

The interrelationship between immigration and social security law is extremely complex. For more information, you should consult CPAG's *Migration & Social Security Handbook* and JCWI's *Immigration, Nationality and Refugee Law Handbook* (listed in Appendix 3).

Your immigration status may not always be clear. There are close links between the Benefits Agency and the Home Office. Making a claim for benefit could alert the immigration authorities to the fact that you are here unlawfully, or that you have broken your conditions of entry by claiming 'public funds'. It is vitally important, therefore, to get specialist advice before claiming if you are unsure about your position. You can get advice from your local law centre, citizens advice bureau or other advice agency which deals with immigration problems. You can also get specialist advice from the Joint Council for the Welfare of Immigrants (JCWI), 115 Old Street, London EC1V 9RT (tel: 0171 251 8706) or the Immigration Advisory Service (various offices – tel: 0171 357 6917). If you are a refugee or asylum-seeker, you can contact the Refugee Council, 3 Bondway, London SW8 1SJ (tel: 0171 582 6922/1162).

Immigration conditions

Many social security benefits now have immigration conditions attached to them which render a person ineligible for benefit purely because of their immigration status. The condition varies according to the benefit involved, however, you may be ineligible for some benefits because:

- you have a limit or condition on your stay given within the immigration rules; *or*
- you are defined as a 'person from abroad' in social security law because of your immigration status; *or*
- you have been granted temporary admission.

Benefits affected by immigration status

Attendance allowance (AA)	Housing benefit (HB)
Child benefit	Income-based Jobseeker's allowance
Council tax benefit (CTB)	(JSA)
Disability living allowance (DLA)	Income support (IS)
Disability working allowance (DWA)	Invalid care allowance (ICA)
Family credit (FC)	Severe disablement allowance (SDA)

If you have indefinite leave to enter or remain, you can claim all benefits. However, if you are here permanently and another person has signed an undertaking to maintain and accommodate you, special rules apply which affect your right to get certain means-tested benefits for the first five years of your stay (see p2:209).

'Public Funds'

Most people admitted to the UK as:

- visitors;
- students;
- business and self-employed people;
- people with a work permit;
- artists;
- writers;
- au pairs;
- fiance(e)s

are given limited leave to stay here on condition that they do not have recourse to public funds. If you have recourse to 'public funds' in breach of your permission to stay (your 'leave conditions') you could be liable to deportation, refusal of further leave and prosecution. Spouses or dependent relatives may have limited or unlimited leave. People of independent means are initially given limited leave. Where leave is limited it is subject to the public funds condition. Limited leave given outside the terms of the Immigration Act 1971 and the immigration rules means the person is not subject to the public funds test.

'Public funds' is defined in the immigration rules as AA, child benefit, CTB, DLA, DWA, FC, HB, IS, income-based JSA, ICA, SDA, and housing provided by local authorities.[1]

If you are eligible for urgent cases payments of IS or JSA, you can claim without jeopardising your immigration status (see p2:217).

Home Office policy that a person should not have recourse to public funds has so far meant not having recourse to *additional* public funds. If you are in the UK and should not have recourse to public funds but your partner is claiming a benefit which counts as public funds (see above) you should seek advice. You could be treated as having recourse to public funds if your partner claims benefit for you and is treated as maintaining you. This could result in you being refused leave to remain in the UK or even being deported. However, no additional payment of benefit is paid because of the presence of a partner who is a person from abroad if the claim by the settled, or British, partner is for any one of the following benefits:

- AA;
- DLA;
- DWA,
- FC;
- IS; *or*
- income-based JSA.

For HB and CTB, no additional benefit is payable if the claimant also receives IS or income-based JSA.

The question of additional recourse to public funds mights arise where:

- a couple including a person from abroad claim HB/CTB and are not receiving either IS or income-based JSA. Benefit in this case would then be paid at a higher rate than would have been paid for the single partner before the claim was made;
- a family including a child who is a person from abroad, where the settled, or British, adult claims HB, CTB, SDA, ICA, child benefit, FC or DWA. Benefit may be increased to take account of the person from abroad child. See p2:215 for more details about claiming IS or income-based JSA where one child and/ or adult is a person from abroad;
- the person changes the benefit they claim. A move from IS to FC could result in a higher level of benefit being paid.

To check whether Home Office policy on public funds has changed, you should get in touch with a lawyer experienced in immigration matters or contact JCWI (see p2:202).

You should also always seek advice before claiming a 'public funds' benefit (see above) if your fiance(e) or spouse is applying for entry clearance to join you in the UK, or for indefinite leave to remain in the UK after being here with limited leave. This is because leave to enter or remain may be refused if you are unable to maintain yourselves without recourse to 'public funds' (see CPAG's *Migration & Social Security Handbook* for more details).

Note: once your spouse is here and has been given limited leave (for the trial 12-month period), s/he will receive a letter from the Home Office telling her/him that her/his British, or settled, spouse can claim any benefit to which s/he is entitled in her/his own right.

2. **Non-means-tested benefits**

Contributory benefits

Your immigration status does not, by itself, prevent you from getting contributory benefits, but in practice you may have paid insufficient contributions (see pp2:272-276) to be entitled. Moreoever, to qualify for benefits depending on Class 1 contributions (see p2:261), you will normally have had to work in the UK (see CPAG's *Migration & Social Security Handbook* for further details).

Non-contributory benefits

You should be aware of your immigration status before claiming non-contributory benefits (see p1:4) – ie, AA, child benefit, DLA, ICA and SDA. These are 'public funds', (see p2:203). A claim could have serious consequences for your immigration status.

Attendance allowance, disability living allowance, invalid care allowance and severe disablement allowance

If your immigration status is 'subject to any limitation or condition' then the basic rule is that you cannot get AA, DLA, ICA or SDA. If you have indefinite leave to remain and/or 'settled status' you are treated as having no conditions or limitations on your stay. You are also not considered subject to a condition or limitation if:[2]

- you have refugee status;
- you have exceptional leave to remain or enter;
- you are an EEA national or family member of an EEA national (see p2:223);
- you, or if you are living with them, a member of your family are lawfully working in GB and are a citizen of a state with which the EC has an agreement concerning equal treatment in social security. This applies to citizens of Algeria, Morocco, Slovenia or Tunisia (and possibly Turkey);
- you are a person who was receiving benefit before 5 February 1996 (see p2:206).

Child benefit[3]

If you are a person who is 'subject to immigration control' (ie, you need leave to enter or remain) you cannot get child benefit. However, regulations exempt you from this if:

- you have indefinite leave to remain;
- you have refugee status;
- you have exceptional leave to enter or remain;
- you are an EEA national, or family member of an EEA national;
- you, or if you are living with them, a member of your family are lawfully working in GB and are a citizen of a state with which the EC has an agreement concerning equal treatment in social security. This applies to citizens of Algeria, Morocco, Slovenia or Tunisia (possibly Turkey);
- you are a citizen of a country with which the UK has a reciprocal agreement;
- you were paid child benefit immediately before 7 October 1996.[4]

Transitional protection

If you were entitled to AA, DLA, DWA, FC, ICA or SDA before the introduction of the immigration conditions on 5 February 1996 or for child benefit if you received benefit before 7 October 1996, you can continue to receive the benefit until such time as it is reviewed (see p2:570). This is what is known as transitional protection. For your award of benefit to be reviewed there must be grounds for review (see p2:572).

If you have transitional protection **do not ask for a review** without advice, eg, simply requesting a higher component of DLA may give rise to a review, and result in the termination of your current entitlement. The change in law by itself is not a relevant change of circumstance and therefore is not grounds for a review.[5] The birth of a further child does not give rise to a review of your existing child benefit entitlement.[6] You continue to get child benefit for your existing child and child benefit for the new child. A social security commissioner has, however, now held[7] that when you make a renewal claim for FC (a means-tested benefit, to which the same immigration status test applies – see below), ie, after the award which was current on 5 February 1996 expired, **you lose your transitional protection**. Although only concerned with FC, the principle would also apply to DWA. A similar approach has been taken by the court of appeal in a case involving DLA.[8]

3. **Means-tested benefits**

You should be aware of your immigration status before claiming means-tested benefits. These are 'public funds' (see p2:203). Claiming additional public funds could affect your right to stay or chance of getting indefinite leave to stay.

Family credit and disability working allowance

You are not entitled to family credit (FC) or disability working allowance (DWA) if your right to be in Great Britain (GB) is subject to any limitation or condition (see p2:202).[9] This rule does not apply to you if:[10]

* you are a refugee;
* you are a person who has been granted exceptional leave to enter or remain in the UK;
* you, or a member of your family, are an EEA national (see p2:223);
* you are lawfully working in GB and you, or a member of your family, is a national of a state which the EC has an agreement with concerning equal treatment of workers in social security. This applies to citizens of Algeria, Morocco, Slovenia and possibly Turkey.
* you were receiving benefit before 5 February 1996 (see p2:206).

The transitional protection rules for FC and DWA are the same as that for attendance allowance (AA), disability living allowance (DLA), iinvalid care allowance (ICA) and severe disablement allowance (SDA) (see p2:206).

In addition to satisfying the immigration conditions, you must also satisfy residence rules (see p2:233). For more details, see CPAG's *Migration & Social Security Handbook*.

Income support and income-based jobseeker's allowance

The income support (IS) and income-based jobseeker's allowance (JSA) regulations both contain a definition of a 'person from abroad'. The definition is a legal term rather than a literal description of the claimant. Certain categories of claimants are classed as 'persons from abroad' under the regulations because of their immigration status (see p2:202). *All* claimants, including British citizens and EEA nationals, who fail to satisfy or gain exemption from the 'habitual residence' test (see p2:234) are also classed as 'persons from abroad'. If you are a 'person from abroad' you are not entitled to IS or income-based JSA unless you are entitled to urgent cases payments of IS or JSA which are paid at a reduced rate (see p2:217).

If your partner is not a 'person from abroad', s/he can claim IS or JSA but cannot receive any benefit for you (see p2:215).

This section gives a brief outline of the rights of claimants who are classed as 'persons from abroad' for IS and JSA purposes.

Who counts as a 'person from abroad' for income support and jobseeker's allowance

If you are classed as a 'person from abroad' under the IS or JSA regulations, you are not entitled to normal rate benefit. Your applicable amount is nil, unless you are entitled to urgent cases payments (see p2:217).[11]

The claim forms ask whether you, or anyone you are claiming for, have come to live in the UK in the last five years. If the answer is 'yes', you are likely to be interviewed to determine whether any one of you is a 'person from abroad'. The forms also ask whether you have come to the UK under a sponsorship undertaking (see p2:209).

You are classed as a 'person from abroad' under the regulations if you fall into any of the following categories.[12] The first category can apply to *any* person including a British citizen. The remaining categories apply to people who are subject to immigration control and refer to various types of immigration status.

- You are not 'habitually resident' or treated as 'habitually resident' in the UK, Republic of Ireland, Channel Islands or the Isle of Man. The 'habitual residence' test is discussed on pp2:234-238.
- You have 'limited leave' to enter or remain in the UK subject to the condition or requirement that you do not have recourse to 'public funds' (see below).
- You have been allowed temporary admission to the UK (this applies to people about whom a decision to give or refuse leave to enter has not yet been made).
- You have been in the UK for less than five years, subject to a *sponsorship undertaking* (see p2:209). You are entitled to normal rate of benefit after five years' residence, and to urgent cases payments if, before five years' residence, your sponsor dies (see p2:217).
- Your immigration status has not been determined by the Secretary of State.
- You are an asylum-seeker (but see p2:210). Some asylum-seekers are entitled to urgent cases payments (see p2:217).
- You are a European Union national (see p2:224), 'required to leave the UK' by the Secretary of State – ie, you are subject to a deportation or removal order – see p2:214.
- The immigration authorities have decided that you are an illegal entrant with no permission to stay.
- You are an 'overstayer' – ie, your limited leave has expired and you have not applied for permission to stay prior to that expiry.
- You are subject to a deportation order.

If you come within the last three categories you should always seek independent advice before approaching the Benefits Agency.

Limited leave and public funds

- 'Limited leave' means that you only have permission to enter, or remain in, the UK for a specified period of time, but see p2:216 if you have been given exceptional leave to enter or remain for a specific period.
- Having recourse to 'public funds' in breach of your leave conditions could render you liable to deportation, refusal of further leave and prosecution. See

p2:203 for further information. Claiming IS or JSA urgent cases payments, however, is usually safe.

- Nationals of the European Economic Area (EEA) States (see p2:224) do not require leave to enter or remain in the UK, and are specifically excluded from the limited leave category of 'persons from abroad'.[13] However, EEA nationals can be classed as persons from abroad if they fail the habitual residence test (see p2:234). See p2:214 for information about EU nationals and 'requirement to leave'.
- Cypriot nationals with limited leave are not classed as persons from abroad. Nor are Maltese or Turkish nationals, unless they have applied for a variation of their conditions of leave.[14]

Sponsorship and undertakings

Most people subject to immigration control are admitted to the UK on the condition that they can maintain and accommodate themselves. A relative or friend in the UK can act as a sponsor to help satisfy this condition.

In some cases, sponsors are required to give a written undertaking under the terms of the Immigration Act 1971 (on a special form – RON 112 or SET (F)), that they will provide maintenance and accommodation. Such undertakings are only usually required for dependent elderly relatives and *not* for spouses. They may be required for children over 16. Other sorts of voluntary or informal sponsorship which are commonly used to support applications to enter the UK are *not* undertakings (this distinction is often misunderstood by the Benefits Agency).

If you have been resident in the UK subject to a mandatory sponsorship undertaking for less than five years, you are not entitled to normal rate IS or JSA. After five years, you are entitled to IS under the normal rules (see Chapter 20). The five years runs either from your date of entry into the UK, or the date the undertaking was given, whichever was later.[15] You are entitled to urgent cases payments of IS (see p2:217) during the five-year period if your sponsor dies.[16]

If you were entitled to IS before 5 February 1996 as a person subject to a mandatory sponsorship undertaking, the above rules do not apply to you and you remain entitled to IS.[17] Caselaw has now determined that you must have been entitled to IS on 4 February 1996 (see p2:212 – Asylum seekers entitled to IS before 5 February 1996). Virtually the same transition rules apply, but the position for broken claims is unclear for sponsored immigrants. If you are in this position you should seek specialist advice.

If you have 'worker' status under EC law (see p2:226), you should not be denied IS or JSA because of a sponsorship undertaking.

If you are paid benefit as a sponsored immigrant and your sponsor signed an undertaking, the Benefits Agency can recover the amount of benefit paid to you from your sponsor.[18] It has been government policy not to enforce this power if your sponsor cannot afford to pay. If the undertaking was given before 23 May 1980, the Benefits Agency does *not* have the power to recover any money from the sponsor.[19]

Asylum-seekers

You are treated as an 'asylum-seeker' while you are waiting for a Home Office decision on an application for refugee status (see p2:215). If you applied for asylum when you arrived in the UK, you will normally have been given 'temporary admission' while your case is considered (although you can be detained or removed in certain circumstances). You may also have applied for asylum while you were in the UK with limited leave or as an illegal entrant or overstayer. If your application for asylum is refused, you have the right of appeal. It can take a long time before your application is finally decided, although the Government has now introduced quicker procedures and curtailed appeal rights for many asylum-seekers.

You can apply to the Home Office for permission to work after six months as an asylum-seeker (including while you are appealing). Claiming IS, JSA or other 'public funds' benefits (see p2:204) should not affect your application for asylum, but in most cases, you are excluded from entitlement by the benefit rules (see below). See p2:216 if you have been recognised as a refugee.

Entitlement to income support and jobseeker's allowance

Only certain asylum-seekers are now eligible for IS or JSA and if you are eligible you are not entitled to normal rate of benefit because you are classed as a 'person from abroad' (see p2:207).[20] You are entitled to urgent cases payments (see p2:217) if you fall into one of the following categories:
- you applied for asylum 'on arrival' (see below);
- you applied for asylum following an 'upheaval' declaration by the Secretary of State (see p2:211);
- you were entitled to IS as an asylum-seeker before 5 February 1996 and have not had a negative determination of your asylum claim since then;
- for JSA you must also have a work permit or written permission from the Secretary of State.

Applying for asylum 'on arrival' in the UK[21]

The term 'on arrival' is not defined in the regulations. A social security commissioner has decided that it means 'while clearing immigration control at the port of entry'. He does recognise, however, that there may be cases when a person cannot clear immigration control immediately while at the port of entry – eg, because there is no interpreter available.[22] Other cases might include where you are too ill to make an application immediately or you arrive secretly at an entry point with no immigration officer. In such cases, your application should be treated as made on arrival if you make it as soon as is practicable after arrival.[23] Another commissioner however has decided that your application for asylum, or at least an indication of your intention to claim asylum, does not necessarily have to be made before leaving immigration control, simply before you leave the port of arrival.

- Your application for asylum does not have to be made in any particular form. It could be verbal or written, in any language, and doesn't necessarily have to include the words 'asylum' or 'refugee'. The application must be made to the 'Secretary of State'. In practice, this should mean any immigration officer. The claim must be recorded as having been made (again not in any particular form).
- You must have arrived in the UK from a country outside the 'Common Travel Area' of Northern Ireland, the Republic of Ireland, the Channel Islands or the Isle of Man (see p2:234).
- You must not be re-entering the UK on your arrival. It is not entirely clear what 're-entry' means. Presumably, the rule is designed to prevent people going abroad for a short period, in order to apply for asylum on re-entry. Arguably, however, it should only apply to re-entry during the period covered by your previous grant of leave to enter the UK.
- Decisions about whether you applied for asylum on arrival in accordance with the above rules are made by adjudication officers (see p2:561) and not the Home Office. You have the right to appeal any question to a social security appeal tribunal (see p2:630).
- If you claimed asylum on arrival in the UK, you can claim urgent cases payments of IS until your entitlement ends in accordance with the rules on p2:212.[24]

Applying for asylum following an 'upheaval declaration'[25]
- The declaration is a written announcement from the Home Office that because a country is subject to such a fundamental change of circumstances, a person would not be ordered to return there by the Secretary of State.
- You must be a national of the country concerned. Stateless people are not covered.
- You must submit your application for asylum within three months of the date of the declaration and your application must be recorded by the Secretary of State. If you have an asylum application or appeal awaiting determination when the declaration is made, you are only covered if you make a fresh application for asylum within the three-month time limit. You should always seek advice before you do this, however, because a fresh application could prejudice your case for asylum. You do not have to make your claim for IS within the three-month time limit for asylum applications, referred to above.
- At the time of writing, only two countries have been subject to declarations – Zaire (May 1997) and Sierra Leone (July 1997).

40

Chapter 40: Coming from abroad
3. Means-tested benefits
· ·

- You can claim urgent cases payments until your entitlement ends in accordance with the rules below.[26]

Asylum-seekers entitled to income support before 5 February 1996[27]

- All asylum-seekers were eligible for urgent cases payments of IS (see p2:217) before 5 February 1996. If you were entitled to IS as an asylum-seeker before that date, you can continue to claim it until your entitlement ends in accordance with the rules below.[28]
- Although the regulations do not state that you must have been entitled to IS 'immediately before' 5 February 1996, the Court of Appeal and a social security commissioner have ruled that you must have been entitled to IS on 4 February 1996.[29] There may be further challenges on the scope of transitional protection, however. See CPAG's *Welfare Rights Bulletin* for developments.
- Although the rules imposing restrictions on an asylum-seeker's rights to claim benefit were only validly in force from 24 July 1996 (see the 1998 edition of CPAG's *National Welfare Benefits Handbook*), transitional protection was only given to asylum-seekers entitled to IS before 5 February 1996. The Court of Appeal rejected a challenge that the relevant date for transitional protection should have been 24 July 1996.[30] Asylum-seekers first claiming IS between 5 February and 24 July 1996 were therefore entitled to benefit under the old rules but lost their entitlement from 24 July unless they satisfied the new rules.
- Transitional protection is also extended to anyone who was a member of your family (see p2:113) on 5 February 1996, allowing them to claim IS urgent cases payments (see p2:217) if, for example, they leave your household, leave education or you 'swap' claimants (see p1:451).[31] They can claim until their entitlement ends in accordance with the rules below.

Notes:

- If you have worked in the EEA (see p2:224), you may be able to argue that you are a refugee entitled to normal rate IS/JSA under EC law (see p2:224). The argument is complex so seek specialist advice if this applies to you.[32]
- You are only excluded from normal rate IS if you apply for asylum when you are already classed as a 'person from abroad' because you fall into one of the categories listed on p2:208. Get advice if you think you may not fall into any of those categories.
- It is normally better to claim IS, rather than income-based JSA, to avoid having to satisfy the labour market conditions (see Chapter 15) and sanctions (see p1:377). If you are entitled to contribution-based JSA, you cannot claim IS (although your partner may be able to).[33]

When your entitlement ends

- You are only normally entitled to urgent cases payments as an asylum-seeker until the Home Office makes and records an initial decision on your asylum application.[34] There is no requirement that you must be notified of the asylum decision before your IS can be stopped, although according to Home Office policy, you should be notified at the same time as the Benefits Agency.[35] The asylum decision, however, must be clearly recorded and dated to be valid.[36]

- You are not entitled to IS while you are appealing against an asylum decision, unless that decision was made before 5 February 1996 and an appeal was pending on that date or was submitted within the time limits laid down in the immigration rules.[37] The appeal could be to an adjudicator, immigration appeal tribunal or court. In these circumstances, you are entitled to IS until the appeal is determined. It is unclear whether you remain entitled while you appeal against an appeal decision. Seek advice in this situation (see Appendix 2).

Documentation

There are often problems in providing acceptable evidence of identification and status when you claim IS/JSA as an asylum-seeker if you have come to the UK without the usual travel and identity documents, or with false documentation.

If you apply for asylum 'on arrival in the UK' (see p2:210), you should be issued with a 'standard acknowledgement letter' (SAL1). You may also be given a form IS96 confirming that you have been granted 'temporary admission' to the UK. These documents should be accepted by the Benefits Agency as proof of your identity (see p2:484) and a SAL is proof of status.

Other sources of help

If you are not entitled to benefit, you could try to access the following alternative sources of help:

- If you have children, you should approach your local authority social services department for help under the Children Act 1989. The local authority has a duty under the Act to safeguard the welfare of children and can provide services such as accommodation, food, heat and emergency cash payments.[38]
- The Court of Appeal has ruled that destitute asylum-seekers are entitled to assistance from local authorities under s21 of the National Assistance Act 1948, which covers accommodation, board and other services.[39] Local authorities cannot make cash payments, but you do not have to be homeless to qualify for help.[40] You should contact the social services department or your local authority for help.
- You are entitled to apply for a crisis loan from the social fund to alleviate the consequences of a disaster (see p1:670). The *Social Fund Guide* advises social fund officers to give particular attention to the clothing needs of asylum-seekers.[41] The problem is that you must be able to show that you are likely to be able to repay the loan (see p1:667).

• You can qualify for health service benefits on the grounds of low income (see p1:614).
• You could ask your MP to request an extra-statutory payment (a discretionary payment) from the Secretary of State for Social Security. The more MPs are aware of the hardship caused by the rules, the more likely it is that the law will be changed.
• For advice on charitable sources of help, contact the Refugee Council (see Appendix 1). A network of emergency provision has been established to alleviate the effects of the rules.

Right to reside and requirement to leave

Under EC law, EC nationals (see p2:224) generally have more rights than other foreign nationals. However, until recently, an EEA national who was not exercising treaty rights (as a worker, work-seeker or being self-sufficent) and who claimed IS or income-based JSA for more than six months, could be sent a letter by the Home Office requesting that s/he makes arrangements to leave the UK. Simultaneously benefit was withdrawn, as the issue of the so-called 'requirement to leave' letter meant the person was treated as a person from abroad for purposes of IS, income–based JSA, HB and CTB (see p2:220). A House of Lords ruling has said that such letters do *not* amount to 'requirement to leave' and benefit cannot be stopped on the basis of their issue.[42] The House of Lords ruled that requirement to leave existed only where a final decision to remove or deport had been taken after full rights of appeal had been exhausted.

In practice, regardless of status, you are only likely to be deported on grounds of public policy, security or health – eg, you have committed a serious offence.[43]

Provided you satisfy the particular conditions for the means-tested benefit that you are claiming, your status as worker/work-seeker/person not financially independent and not available to work, appears now to be irrelevant. It may, however, affect the application of the habitual residence test (see p2:237).

People entitled to normal rate income support and jobseeker's allowance

If you are not a 'person from abroad' (see p2:207) you are entitled to benefit at the normal rate.[44] In practical terms, this means you are entitled to normal rate IS/JSA if you satisfy (or are exempt from) the 'habitual residence' test (see p2:234) and you fall into any of the following categories:
• You are a British citizen.
• You have the right of abode in the UK or a certificate of patriality.

- You have 'indefinite leave' to enter, or remain in, the UK (ie, 'settled' status), unless you have been in the UK for less than five years, subject to a sponsorship undertaking (see p2:209).
- You have been granted refugee status (see p2:216).
- You have been given exceptional leave to enter or remain in the UK (see p2:216).
- You are a national of Northern Ireland, the Channel Islands, or the Isle of Man (see p2:208).
- You are a national of Cyprus, Malta or Turkey (unless in the case of Malta or Turkey, you have applied for your leave conditions to be varied).
- You are an EEA national – see p2:223 – (but see p2:214).
- You are in GB and you left Montserrat after 1 November 1995 because of a volcanic eruption there.

Couples and families

The following rules apply where one or more members of your family (see Chapter 37 for who counts as your family) are 'persons from abroad' (see p2:208):

- If you claim IS/JSA as a 'person from abroad', you are not entitled to any benefit for yourself or for any members of your family, unless you qualify for an urgent cases payment (see p2:217).[45]
- If your partner is not a 'person from abroad' but you are, s/he can claim IS/JSA under the normal rules but does not receive any benefit for you or any other family member who is a 'person from abroad'.[46] Full housing costs (see Chapter 46) are payable.[47] You are still treated as a couple for IS purposes (see p2:114), so your joint resources are taken into account.
- Couples where both partners are not 'persons from abroad' and lone parents who are not 'persons from abroad', can claim IS for children who are.[48] But claimants who are 'persons from abroad' cannot claim benefit for children even if the children are *not* 'persons from abroad'.[49]
- Foreign fiancé(e)s and spouses who are admitted for settlement on the condition that they can maintain and accommodate themselves, count as 'persons from abroad' and are not entitled to IS/JSA until they are granted indefinite leave to remain in the UK.[50]

Refugees

The UK is a signatory to the 1951 United Nations Convention on the Status of Refugees which gives refugees certain rights in a foreign country, including the right to public relief and assistance. A refugee is defined under the Convention as someone who is unable or unwilling to return to his own country because of a '... well founded fear of persecution for reasons of race, religion, nationality, membership of a particular social group or political opinion ...'

If the Home Office accepts that you are a refugee, you and your family are entitled to remain in the UK and claim IS or income-based JSA under the normal rules (see Chapters 20 and 14) from the date you are recorded as a refugee by the Secretary of State.[51] You do not have to satisfy the 'habitual residence' test (see p2:234).[52]

You, or your partner, can also claim backdated urgent cases payments of IS (see p2:217) for any period following the first refusal of your asylum claim (if you claimed asylum 'on arrival in the UK' – see p2:210), or the date of your asylum claim (if you claimed asylum other than 'on arrival in the UK'). You cannot, however, get IS for any period prior to 5 February 1996 and you must submit your claim for IS within 28 days of being notified that you have been accepted as a refugee. The normal restrictions on backdating IS do not apply.[53] Any IS already paid to you or your partner for the backdated period is offset against the amount you get. You cannot get backdated payments for any week in which you were receiving contribution-based JSA.[54] If your partner has been recognised as a refugee and was not getting contribution-based JSA, s/he could claim instead. Only IS, and not income-based JSA, can be backdated when you are granted refugee status. If you are only entitled to income-based JSA on becoming a refugee, you must submit a separate claim for backdated IS within the 28-day time limit to receive your arrears of urgent cases payments. The arrears are disregarded as capital for 52 weeks from the date of receipt.[55]

You may be able to get backdated IS at the normal rate (rather than the 90 per cent urgent cases rate – see p2:217) if you have worked in the UK (see p2:224) by arguing that you are entitled to equal treatment with British citizens under EC law.[56] So far the courts have been largely unsympathetic to the argument, but a case is currently being pursued to the House of Lords. Seek advice if this applies to you (see Appendix 2).

See p2:210 if you are an asylum-seeker.

People with 'exceptional leave'

In some circumstances, the Home Office will not accept that you are a refugee but will grant you 'exceptional leave' to enter or remain in the UK on humanitarian grounds or because of the political situation in your country (your family is not normally allowed to join you until you have been in the UK for four years). Some people are also granted exceptional leave for other reasons. Exceptional leave may initially be given for a year but this does not count as 'limited leave' (see p2:202). A person applying for an extension of their exceptional leave, continues to be treated as a person with exceptional leave, provided their application was made before their original leave had expired.

If you are granted exceptional leave to enter or remain in the UK, you are entitled to claim IS or income-based JSA under the normal rules (see Chapters

20 and 14). You do not have to satisfy the 'habitual residence' test (see p2:234).[57] There is normally no prohibition on claiming 'public funds' (see p2:203) if you are granted exceptional leave to remain, but if you have any doubts about this, you should get advice (see Appendix 2). The Benefits Agency sometimes wrongly refuses benefit to people with exceptional leave because it mistakenly thinks they have limited leave (see p2:202).

Urgent cases payments of income support and jobseeker's allowance

Urgent cases payments are payments of IS/JSA payable at a reduced rate. The two categories of claimant eligible are:
* certain persons from abroad; *and*
* claimants who are treated as possessing income which is due but has not been paid (see p2:422).

If you are not entitled to normal rate IS because you are classed as a 'person from abroad' (see p2:208), you are entitled to urgent cases payments if any of the following circumstances apply to you:
* You have 'limited leave' to remain in the UK on the condition that you do not have recourse to public funds (see p2:203), but you are temporarily without money. You are entitled to urgent cases payments of IS/JSA for a maximum of 42 days if:
  – you have supported yourself without recourse to public funds during your limited leave; *and*
  – you are temporarily without funds because remittances from abroad have been disrupted; *and*
  – there is a reasonable expectation that your supply of funds will be resumed.[58]
* You are an asylum-seeker and you satisfy the rules set out on pp2:210-2:212.[59]
* You have been in the UK subject to a sponsorship undertaking for less than five years and your sponsor has died (see p2:209).[60]

How you claim

There is no special procedure for claiming urgent cases payments. You claim IS or income-based JSA in the normal way (see pp1:499 and 1:353). You do not have to make a separate claim for an urgent cases payment. A claim for income-based JSA is treated as a claim for any entitlement you may have under the rules for urgent cases payments.[61] In practice, you may need to request the urgent cases payment and should not rely on the Benefits Agency to automatically decide whether you are entitled.

How much you can get

Urgent cases payments of IS and income-based JSA are paid at a reduced rate. Your applicable amount (see p2:317) is:

- a personal allowance for you (and your partner) – see p2:114. It is paid at 90 per cent of the personal allowance that would have been paid had you qualified for benefit in the normal way; *plus*
- full personal allowances for your children (see p2:320); *plus*
- premiums (see p2:322) and housing costs (see Chapter 46) or residential allowance (see p2:173), if any, and any 'protected sum' paid because you were a boarder prior to 10 April 1989.[62]

If you are living in a residential or nursing home and have 'preserved rights' (see p2:169), you receive 90 per cent of the personal allowance for you (and your partner) plus full personal allowances for any children plus the amount normally allowed for your accommodation. You get 98 per cent of the amount paid if you are in a local authority home.[63]

Income

All of your income counts, but the following is ignored:[64]

- any tariff income from capital between £3,000 and £8,000 (£10,000 and £16,000 if you live in a residential or nursing home – see p2:442);
- backdated payments of IS made to you once the Home Office accepts you are a refugee (see p2:216);
- concessionary urgent cases payments of IS or income-based JSA;
- any HB and/or CTB;
- any payment made to compensate you for the loss of entitlement to HB;
- social fund payments;
- any payment from any of the Macfarlane Trusts, the Eileen Trust, the Fund, or the Independent Living Funds;
- payments made by people with haemophilia to their partner or children, out of money originally provided by one of the Macfarlane Trusts. If the person with haemophilia has no partner or children, payments made to a parent, step-parent or guardian are also disregarded, but only for two years. These payments are also disregarded if the person with haemophilia dies and the money is paid out of the estate;
- payments arising from the Macfarlane Trusts which are paid by a person to a partner who has haemophilia, or to their child(ren).

Certain income is treated as capital if you get IS under the normal rules (see p2:447). However, if you apply for an urgent cases payment the following capital is treated as income:[65]

- any lump sum paid to you not more than once a year for your work as a part-time firefighter, part-time member of a lifeboat crew, auxiliary coastguard or member of the Territorial Army;

- any refund of income tax;
- holiday pay which is not payable until more than four weeks after your job ended;
- any irregular charitable or voluntary payment.

Capital

Your capital is calculated in the usual way (see Chapter 49) but the usual disregards do not apply to urgent cases payments. Any capital taken into account affects your urgent cases payment, not just that over the capital limit (see p2:448). The following cannot be disregarded:
- money from the sale of your home which you intend to use to buy another;
- the liquid assets of a business (eg, cash in hand);
- arrears of the following: mobility supplement, DLA or DWA, AA, earnings top-up, FC or any concessionary payments made to compensate for non-payment of any of these benefits;
- arrears of IS or income-based JSA **but not:**
  - arrears of urgent cases payments;
  - concessionary urgent cases payments;
- backdated payments of IS, HB or CTB made to you once the Home Office accepts you are a refugee (see p2:216);
- money which had been deposited with a housing association and which is now to be used to buy a home;
- up to £200 of a training bonus received after being on Training for Work;
- a refund of tax on a mortgage or loan taken out to buy, or to do repairs and/ or improvements to your home.

Housing benefit and council tax benefit for 'persons from abroad'

As with IS and income-based JSA, HB regulations contain a definition of a 'person from abroad'. The definition is a legal term rather than a literal description of the claimant. If you are classed as a person from abroad, you are not entitled to HB/CTB. The term applies to some foreign nationals but also to British nationals who fail the habitual residence test (see p2:234 for an explanation).

Local authorities have been advised to add questions to their claim forms asking about your nationality and whether you have come to this country in the last five years. Some local authorities substitute two years for five years. Detailed guidance has been issued to them to decide if you are a 'person from abroad', but there is sometimes liaison between them and the Immigration and Nationality Directorate of the Home Office to check your immigration status. You should be advised if they are intending to contact the Home Office. There is also liaison between the local authority and the Benefits

Agency if you are claiming IS as well, and information which you give to one department could be passed to the other.[66]

You may be interviewed to check out whether you are entitled to claim and you will certainly be asked to produce proof of your identity and immigration status. You do not have to produce your passport, but you need some other way of verifying your status. If you do not have this, the local authority should interview you and make a decision on the balance of probabilities.

If you are a couple and your partner is not classed as a 'person from abroad', s/he can claim for you both and you are paid the full amount for a couple. However, in some cases your immigration status could be jeopardised by your partner's claim for HB, as it counts as 'public funds' under the immigration rules (see p2:203). If you are here subject to the condition that you should not have recourse to public funds, it may not be wise for your partner to claim. You should seek independent immigration advice before your partner claims HB, see p2:202.

If you are a married or unmarried couple and both of you are 'persons from abroad', you are not entitled to HB.

If you are unsure about how a claim for HB might affect your right to remain in the UK, you should get independent advice about this before making a claim. If you subsequently discover that you can claim with no problems, you should ask for your benefit to be backdated on the grounds that you have 'good cause for a late claim' (see p1:534).

Who counts as a 'person from abroad'

You are classed as a person from abroad under the HB and CTB regulations if you fall into one of the following groups:
- you have limited leave to enter or remain in the UK subject to the requirement that you have no recourse to public funds[67] but this does not apply if *either*:[68]
  - either you are a national of the EEA (see p2:224 for a list of countries), Malta, Turkey or Cyprus; *or*
  - your funds from abroad have been temporarily disrupted and there is a reasonable expectation that they will resume (provided you have not been without funds for more than 42 days in one period of limited leave);
- you were given limited leave to enter or remain in the UK and have overstayed the period of your leave;[69]
- you are subject to a deportation order unless your removal has been deferred in writing by the Secretary of State;[70]
- you are an illegal entrant unless you have the Secretary of State's written consent to stay;[71]
- you are an EEA national who has been required to leave by the Secretary of State (but as for IS see p2:214);[72]
- you are an asylum-seeker (see p2:221);

- you are a sponsored immigrant in certain circumstances (see below);
- you are not habitually resident (see p2:234).

The rules on persons from abroad for HB/CTB are slightly different to that of IS/JSA and there is no equivalent urgent cases provisions, but certain groups are exempt from the person from abroad definitions. You are **not classed as a person from abroad** under the immigration status test if:

- you are an **asylum-seeker** and satisfy certain conditions (see below); *or*
- you are a **sponsored immigrant** and satisfy certain conditions; *or*
- you are in receipt of **IS/income-based JSA**; *or*
- you are in GB and left **Montserrat** after 1 November 1995 because of the effects of a volcanic eruption;[73] *or*
- you are a 'worker' under EC law; *or*
- you are a refugee; *or*
- you have exceptional leave to remain; *or*
- you have temporary admission.

Asylum-seekers

If you are an asylum-seeker, you are entitled to HB/CTB if either:

- you applied for asylum on arrival in the UK (for the meaning of this see pp2:210-211); *or*
- you applied for asylum within the three months following a declaration by the Secretary of State that your country is subject to such a fundamental change of circumstances that you would not normally be ordered to return there (see p2:211);[74] *or*
- you were entitled to HB as an asylum-seeker immediately before 5 February 1996.[75] This means that you must have been in receipt of HB on 4 February – a period of entitlement prior to that is insufficient.[76] If you were receiving HB on 4 February, the fact that you have subsequently made a renewal claim ought not to prevent you getting HB.[77] However the position remains unclear if you break your claim. If you were getting HB on 4 February 1996, you remain entitled until you receive a decision on your application. You are not entitled pending an appeal unless the decision was made before 5 February 1996;[78]
- you have temporary admission. This applies even where you have been refused asylum.[79] You are likely to have temporary admission if you applied for asylum at the port of entry.

For more about asylum-seekers, see p2:210.

People with sponsorship undertakings

If you were given leave to enter the UK subject to a sponsorship undertaking, you are entitled to HB if:[80] *either*

- you have been resident in the UK for at least five years; *or*

- the person who gave the undertaking has died; *or*
- you were entitled to or were receiving HB/CTB before 5 February 1996.[81]

For more about sponsorship undertakings and benefit, see p2:209.

Backdating housing benefit and council tax benefit when you get refugee status

If you are notified that you have been granted refugee status, you no longer count as a 'person from abroad' (see p2:219) and can therefore claim HB/CTB from that date. If, while you were seeking asylum, you were not entitled to HB/CTB because you were classed as a person from abroad, you may be entitled to a retrospective award of HB/CTB for that past period.

Claims

You must make a claim for retrospective HB/CTB within 28 days of the date you are notified by the Secretary of State that you have been recorded as a refugee.[82] You must claim within the time limit as a late claim cannot be backdated.[83] If you have lived in more than one local authority area, you should make your claim to the local authority in whose area you last lived before being granted refugee status.[84]

The date from which a backdated payment is made

Your HB/CTB claim is treated as made on:[85]
- *if you applied for asylum on arrival* in the UK, the date your application for asylum was first refused or 5 February 1996, whichever is later; *or*
- *if you applied for asylum other than on arrival* in the UK (see p2:210), the date of your asylum application or 5 February 1996, whichever is later.

HB/CTB can be paid for the whole or part of the period from the date the claim is treated as made until the date you were notified of your refugee status. Any HB/CTB which has already been paid to you or any partner of yours over this period is deducted from your award.[86]

- -

Example

Meral applied for asylum on arrival in the UK in December 1995. She was paid HB until March 1996, when her asylum application was refused. In October 1996, she started living as a couple with Barry who has since been claiming HB for both of them. In April 1997, she is granted refugee status. She claims HB immediately. Meral is entitled to retrospective HB from March 1996 (when her asylum application was refused) until April 1997 when she was granted refugee status. However, the award is reduced by the amount of HB paid to her partner for both of them from October 1996 onwards.

- -

How your claim is assessed

You must provide any evidence and information you have or could reasonably get which the local authority may reasonably require to determine your entitlement.[87] The authority can ask for information from your landlord, from the person you paid rent to, from any person who paid the rent on your behalf or from another local authority.[88]

You must notify the local authority of any changes of circumstances which might be relevant to your HB/CTB entitlement over the period for which you are claiming (see p1:537).[89] Where you are unable to provide the necessary evidence, the local authority must determine your claim on the basis of the information you have been able to provide.[90]

Your HB claim is assessed using the rules for rent and rent restrictions as they stood on 1 January 1996.[91] In particular, this means that the rent officer's assessment of the appropriate rent for your home is not conclusive (see p1:554).

Payment of benefit

Once the local authority decides you are entitled to retrospective HB/CTB it must make payment within 14 days.[92] CTB is paid into your council tax account if there is any outstanding council tax liability for the period covered by the award. Any remaining CTB is paid to you. If your rent has not been paid, part or all of your HB award can be paid direct to the landlord. If your landlord was a local authority, any eligible rent owing to them is deducted from your award and only the balance paid to you.[93] Otherwise, HB can be paid to your landlord where the local authority considers it reasonable to do so.[94] The landlord must show that you have not paid your rent for part or all of the period of your award and the local authority must give you an opportunity to give reasons why payment should not be made to the landlord.

Residence rules and means-tested benefits

In addition to satisfying the immigration conditions, you must also satisfy residence rules – these are different for different means-tested benefits (see p2:229). For more details, see CPAG's *Migration & Social Security Handbook*.

4. **The rights of European Economic Area nationals**

Social security benefits are not governed by British law alone. There are also laws made by the European Community (EC) which apply directly in the UK and throughout the European Economic Area (EEA).

The EEA consists of the 15 member states of the European Union (EU): Austria, Belgium, Denmark, Finland, France, Germany, Greece, the Irish Republic, Italy, Luxembourg, the Netherlands, Portugal Spain, Sweden and the UK, which have joined together with three other countries from the European Free Trade Area (EFTA): Iceland, Liechtenstein and Norway.

If you are a national of any of the EEA states, you and your dependants, even if they are non-EEA nationals have rights under EC law. These rights stem from the Treaty of Rome and have been added to and expanded upon over the years by a variety of Regulations, Directives and caselaw.

If there is a conflict between rights given in EC law and the UK social security system, the EC law overrides the British rules.

Although primarily concerned with 'freedom of movement' there are two main areas of EC law which can assist you, in respect of benefits, if you go to another EEA country.

European Community Regulation 1408/71

The first area of law is that based on EC Regulation 1408/71, a detailed Regulation that is intended to co-ordinate the various social security systems of the EEA. It does this by:

* prohibiting discrimination in matters of social security on grounds of nationality;
* allowing you to rely on periods of employment, residence and contributions paid in one EEA country towards entitlement to benefit in others (this is called the principle of aggregation);
* allowing you to take with you certain benefits abroad to another EEA country with you (this is called the principle of exportation);
* generally allowing you to claim benefit only from the state in which you last worked (this is called the single state principle).

Who is covered by the Regulation?

In order to rely on the Regulation you must have been an employed or self-employed person. This is not the same as the term worker for other areas of EC law. You will be treated as an employed or self-employed person if you are insured under a national social security scheme. In the UK this means that you pay, have in the past paid, or ought to pay national insurance contributions.

The Regulation does not apply only to EEA nationals – stateless persons and refugees are also covered.

Benefits covered

The Regulation applies to state benefits which are designed to protect against certain risks and relevant UK benefit:

Risk	UK Benefit
Sickness and maternity	Incapacity benefit, maternity benefit, statutory sick pay, statutory maternity pay
Invalidity	Incapacity benefit, severe disablement allowance
Old age	Retirement pension, graduated retirement pension, Christmas bonus
Survivors, benefits and death grants	Widows' benefits, widowed mother's allowance
Accidents at work and occupational diseases	Industrial disablement benefit, reduced earnings allowance
Family benefits	Child benefit, guardian's allowance, child dependency increases
Unemployment	Jobseeker's allowance

In addition, since 1992 the Regulation has been extended to include 'special non-contributory benefits'.

The UK Government states that the following are 'special non-contributory' benefits:

* attendance allowance;
* disability living allowance;
* family credit;
* income support (IS);
* incapacity benefit (IB);
* income-based jobseeker's allowance (JSA);
* disability working allowance;
* invalid care allowance.

Special non-contributory benefits cannot be exported but they do appear to attract all the other rights contained in the Regulation such as non-discrimination and the right to rely on periods of residence in other member states.

Exporting benefits

If a benefit can be exported, you can continue to receive the benefit at the full rate for as long as you continue to satisfy the conditions for that benefit. However, only certain benefits can be exported to another member state. These are for 'invalidity, old age or survivors, pensions for accidents at work or occupational diseases and death benefits'.

Unemployment benefits can be exported but only for a maximum period of three months. You must register as unemployed for at least four weeks before you leave the state in which you are living and must register in the second EEA country within seven days. At present the UK Government will only allow contribution-based JSA to be exported as it considers income-based JSA to be a special non-contributory benefit and therefore non-exportable. This point has yet to be challenged.

Family benefits cannot be exported, however, they can be paid for family members living in another member state.

The rights of 'workers'

The second area of EC law that may affect your entitlement to benefit is that based on the rights given by EC law to workers.

This area of EC law is primarily concerned with allowing freedom of movement to enter and take up employment, be self-employed, or provide or receive a service in any member state. However, if you are economically active in one of the above ways you are entitled to the same tax, housing and social advantages as offered to nationals of the member state. The courts have ruled that this term applies to social security benefits, including means-tested benefits such as IS. Therefore, if you are a 'worker' you cannot be denied a benefit such as income-based JSA on the basis of your nationality. In order to rely on the social advantage route you must have worked in the member state in which you seek to claim benefit, but this can be for a short period and includes part-time work. (See below and pp2:227-8 for more detail on workers).

'Workers'

The term 'worker' is not defined in EC legislation. Its meaning and scope remain somewhat unclear and have been the subject of complex and sometimes contradictory caselaw. What is clear, however, is that many people who are not actually working are still classed as 'workers'.[95]

Workers under Regulation 1612/68

Regulation 1612/68 covers freedom of movement and equality of treatment for 'workers'. You should be treated as a worker for the purposes of the Regulation if you fall into any of the following categories:

- You are working in the UK, whether full- or part-time. Any 'genuine' and 'effective work' should count, so long as it is not so irregular and limited that it is a purely marginal and ancillary activity.[96]
- You have worked in the UK (at any time and even for a short period) but have become involuntarily unemployed or temporarily incapable of work.[97]
- You have worked in the UK, have become involuntarily unemployed and must take on occupational retraining to compete in the job market.[98]

- You have voluntarily given up work in the UK to take up vocational training linked to your previous job.[99] If you have voluntarily given up work for other reasons, your position is not entirely clear. Benefits Agency guidance suggests you are not a worker[100] but you may be able to argue otherwise if you remain in the labour market and are trying to find alternative work, or are seeking reinstatement.[101]
- You have been temporarily laid off and are seeking to return to work with the same employer in the UK.[102]

Note: Work-seekers – if you are looking for work, but have not worked in the UK before, you have some EC rights but you do not have the right to the same 'social advantages'.[103]

Workers under Regulation 1251/70
Regulation 1251/70 allows certain incapacitated or retired workers to remain in the State where they have worked.

You are a worker for the purposes of the Regulation if you fall into one of the following categories:
- You have given up work in the UK because of permanent incapacity *and either*:
  - you had resided continuously in the UK for at least two years when you gave up work; *or*
  - your incapacity resulted from an industrial injury or disease (see p1:204) which entitles you to a disability benefit or IB (see Chapters 10 and 3); *or*
  - your spouse is (or was before marrying you) British.[104]
- You retired on or after pensionable age *and either*:
  - you had resided continuously in the UK for at least three years and were employed in the UK for at least 12 months immediately before retiring; *or*
  - your spouse is (or was before marrying you) British.[105]

Notes:[106]
- Absences from the UK of up to three months a year (or longer for military service) are ignored when calculating your period of residence.
- Periods of unemployment recorded by the JobCentre and absences from work because of illness or accident are ignored when calculating your period of employment.
- Periods of employment as a 'frontier worker' in another EEA State can count if you returned to your home in the UK at least once a week.

Right to reside in the UK
EC Directives 68/360 and 73/148 deal with residence rights and the issuing of residence permits.

You have the right to reside in the UK under the Directives if you fall into one of the following categories:

- You are a 'worker' for the purposes of EC Regulation 1612/68 (see p2:226).[107] Caselaw has so far held that if you are a work-seeker, who has not worked in the UK, your right of residence does not derive from Directive 68/360, which means you cannot secure exemption from the habitual residence test on that basis.[108]
- You are self-employed or provide a service on a commercial basis in the UK.[109]
- You are receiving commercial services in the UK.[110] These could include tourism, private education or health care and business or professional services.[111]
- You are a member of the family of any of the above. This covers spouses, children under 21, and other dependent relatives.[112]

Your right to reside in the UK is confirmed by the issue of a residence permit but the lack of a permit does not negate that right.[113] Permits are normally issued for five years on confirmation of employment.

---

5. **Reciprocal agreements**

There are several countries with which Great Britain (GB) has reciprocal agreements. These mean that you receive some British benefits while in the other country and *vice versa*.

Each reciprocal agreement is different from the others. The arrangements for particular countries are described in detail in CPAG's *Migration & Social Security Handbook*.

Special rules for people from Northern Ireland, the Isle Of Man and the Channel Islands

Technically, the rules described in this *Handbook* apply only to GB. GB consists of England, Wales and Scotland. It does not include Northern Ireland, the Isle of Man or the Channel Islands which have their own social security legislation. GB is not the same as the UK, which does include Northern Ireland.

However, because of the close links between GB, Northern Ireland and the Isle of Man, you do not lose any non-means-tested benefit by moving between them[114] and national insurance contributions (see p2:255) paid in one of those jurisdictions count as though they were paid in each of the others. For most practical purposes the systems in GB, Northern Ireland and the Isle of Man may be treated as identical.

The Channel Islands, Jersey and Guernsey (including Alderney, Herm and Jethou), have their own social security systems but there is a reciprocal agreement (see p2:228) under which you can receive some British benefits (see DSS leaflet SA4, from the Overseas Branch, see above).[115] You also remain entitled to benefits (other than jobseeker's allowance under British legislation while in any part of the Channel Islands.[116]

6. Residence conditions

The following benefits have residence requirements:
- Attendance allowance (AA – see p2:231);
- Child benefit (see p2:231);
- Disability living allowance (DLA – see p2:231);
- Disability working allowance (DWA – see p2:233);
- Family credit (FC – see p2:233);
- Guardian's allowance (see p2:231);
- Invalid care allowance (ICA – see p2:231);
- Category D retirement pension (see p2:234);
- Severe disablement allowance (SDA – see p2:233).
- Income support (IS), income-based jobseeker's allowance (JSA), housing benefit (HB), council tax benefit (CTB) (see p2:234).

Present, resident and ordinarily resident

In addition to any immigration conditions, entitlement to many benefits depends on whether you satisfy the particular residence conditions for that benefit. The type of residence conditions varies according to the type of benefit claimed, but you may be required to be:
- present;
- resident;
- ordinarily resident; *or*
- habitually resident.

Present

To be '**present**', you must prove that you were present throughout any day in question – ie, from midnight to midnight.[117] 'Absent' is the opposite of present. If the adjudication officer seeks to disqualify you because you are absent from Great Britain (GB), the burden is upon her/him to prove that you were absent throughout any day in question.[118]

For the purpose of satisfying the presence conditions for AA, DLA, ICA and SDA you still count as being in GB if you are:[119]
- a member of the armed forces serving abroad;
- a spouse, son, daughter, parent or parent-in-law of a member of the armed forces serving abroad and living with her/him;
- a master, member of crew or other person employed on board a ship under a contract entered into in the UK;
- a pilot or member of crew or other person employed on board an aircraft under a contract entered into in the UK;
- a person employed on an oil or gas rig on the continental shelf.

A worker on an oil or gas rig on the continental shelf is not disqualified from benefit if s/he is in the area of an oil or gas field or is travelling to it from another such area or from a European Economic Area (EEA) state (see p2:224).[120]

Presence in an EEA state (see p2:224) may count as presence in GB (see p2:225).

Resident and ordinarily resident

You are usually '**resident**' in the country where you have your home for the time being.[121] It is possible to be resident in more than one place at a time but it is unusual.[122] You can remain resident in a place during a temporary absence but this depends on the circumstances.[123] So if you go abroad to work on one particular project of limited duration, intending to return on its completion, you remain resident in GB. But if you go abroad for a considerable period, you may not remain resident in GB even if you do expect to return eventually. Important factors in deciding the issue are where the rest of your family live, the sort of accommodation you have – a hotel does not suggest residence – and where your furniture and other personal effects are kept. If you move intending to settle at your new address, you are regarded as resident there from the very first day.

You are '**ordinarily resident**' if there is a degree of continuity about your residence so that it can be described as settled.[124] So if you live mostly in GB but also live elsewhere from time to time, you remain ordinarily resident in GB throughout the shorter periods of residence elsewhere.

The burden of proof lies on you to show that you are or were resident in GB at the relevant time if you are claiming benefit.[125]

Residence in another EEA country (see p2:225) may count as residence in GB (see below). Some reciprocal agreements with other countries (see p2:228) contain similar rules.

Residence tests and benefits

Attendance allowance, disability living allowance and invalid care allowance

To qualify for AA, DLA and ICA, you must:[126]
- be ordinarily resident in GB (see p2:230); *and*
- be present in GB (see p2:229); *and*
- have been present in GB for a total of 26 weeks, in the last 12 months.

People claiming DLA or AA on the basis that they are terminally ill (see p1:182), are exempted from the rule that they have to have been present in GB for the last 26 weeks.[127] There are exemptions from the presence tests for, among others, serving members of the armed services and their families, mariners, and off-shore workers.[128] If claims are made for DLA for babies who are less than six months old they only have to have been present for 13 of the last 26 weeks.[129]

For DLA and AA, you are treated as being present during any temporary absence of less than 26 weeks, and during any further absence for the purpose of treatment if you obtain a certificate from the Secretary of State to the effect that the further absence is reasonable.[130]

For ICA you are treated as being present during any temporary absence of up to four weeks. You are also treated as present during any temporary absence for the purpose of caring for your patient, provided of course, that your patient's DLA care component, AA or constant attendance allowance is still payable.[131]

Child benefit and guardian's allowance

The residence conditions for child benefit are complicated. There are separate conditions for the child, the claimant and, if different, the child's parents.

Generally speaking:
- the child must be in GB;[132]
- the claimant must be in GB, and have been in GB for more than 182 days (six months) in the last year; [133]
- the claimant and either the child or one of the parents must have been in GB for more than 182 days in the last year.[134]

There are exceptions to each of these rules.

Exceptions to the rule that the child must be present in Great Britain

Child benefit can be paid while the child is abroad if:[135]
- someone was entitled to receive child benefit immediately before the child went abroad; *and*

- the child's absence abroad was intended to be temporary when it began and continues to be temporary; *and either*
- the child has not been abroad for more than eight weeks; *or*
- the child has not been abroad for more than 156 weeks receiving full-time education at a recognised education establishment; *or*
- the child is abroad during a period agreed by the Secretary of State which is for the specific purpose of medical treatment for a condition which existed before s/he left.

There are special rules if a child was born abroad during a temporary absence of the mother (see below).[136]

Exception to the rule that the claimant must be in Great Britain

If you are already receiving child benefit you may continue to do so for up to eight weeks while abroad on an absence which was intended when it began, and continues, to be temporary[137] or you leave GB in the week you give birth or you give birth while absent and are in the first eight weeks of a temporary absence and would otherwise qualify for child benefit.[138]

Exceptions to the 182-day rule

Normally, a person coming into GB from abroad for the first time cannot get child benefit until s/he and the child have been in the country for at least six months (182 days) (see p2:231).

There are a number of exceptions:[139]

- if the child is actually in GB and guardian's allowance would be payable for her/him (but for the disqualification from child benefit) then it is not necessary for either the child or one of her/his parents to satisfy the 182-day rule as long as the claimant does;
- you, as the claimant, are exempt from the 182-day rule, where you are treated as having been in GB for six months because:
  - you are in GB; *and*
  - you are likely to remain here for a period of at least 183 consecutive days including the time already here (but excluding up to 28 days' temporary absence); *and*
  - one of the following applies:
    - you are employed or self employed during this time;[140] *or*
    - you have been entitled to child benefit for any child during the last three years;[141] *or*
    - you have a spouse who was entitled to child benefit for any child in the last three years and who was either living with you at that time or is living with you now.[142]

Guardian's allowance

Entitlement to guardian's allowance depends upon entitlement to child benefit, so the above conditions must be satisfied. However, if the only bar to your entitlement to child benefit and, therefore to guardian's allowance, is that neither the child nor either of her/his parents had been in GB for 182 days during the last year, that condition is waived.[143]

A further condition of entitlement to guardian's allowance is that at least one of the child's parents was born in the UK or had, at some time after reaching the age of 16, spent a total of 52 weeks in any two-year period in the UK.[144]

Family credit and disability working allowance

To be entitled to FC or DWA as well as satisfying the immigration test (see p2:205) you must be in GB.[145] You can be treated as being in GB if:[146]
- you are present (see p2:229) and ordinarily resident (see below) in GB; *and*
- your partner (if any) is ordinarily resident in the UK (but see below); *and*
- at least part of your earnings (or your partner's earnings) are derived from full-time work in the UK; *and*
- your earnings (or those of your partner) do not come wholly from paid work done outside the UK.

You are 'ordinarily resident' here if you normally live in GB (or, if relevant, the UK.[147] This means that the residence here has been adopted voluntarily and for settled purposes, although not necessarily with the intention of remaining indefinitely, or for more than a limited period.[148] If you and your partner used to live together abroad but you now live in this country and s/he lives abroad, s/he is counted as your 'partner' for social security purposes if you intend to resume living together (see p2:119).[149] The fact that s/he is not ordinarily resident in the UK would therefore disentitle you. The position is the same if your partner was living with you in this country but is now living abroad – if you intend to resume living together s/he is still regarded as your 'partner' (see p2:114). Again, the fact that s/he is not ordinarily resident in the UK would therefore disentitle you.[150]

You cannot be treated as being in GB during any period you or your partner are entitled to FC or DWA in Northern Ireland.[151]

There is no requirement that a child for whom you are responsible and who is a member of your household (see p2:115) should be present in GB.[152]

Severe disablement allowance

For SDA you must, at the start of your claim:[153]
- be 'ordinarily resident' in Great Britain (see p2:230); *and*

- be present in GB (see p2:229); *and*
- have been present for at least 26 weeks in the past year.

If the first day of your claim is during a period in which you receive income that is exempt from UK income tax under certain international treaties, you must also have spent at least 156 weeks (ie, three years) out of the last four years in GB.[154]

As can be seen above, the rule imposes a residence condition and two presence conditions. This may be unlawful.[155] People who are ordinarily resident in GB, but have not been present here for 26 weeks in the past year – or *vice versa* – should seek advice.

Category D pension

You are only entitled to the Category D pension if you are over 80 and are not entitled to any other pension in excess of the present rate of this pension.[156] The residence conditions are:[157]

- you must have been 'resident' (see p2:230) in GB for at least 10 in any continuous period of 20 years ending on or after your 80th birthday; *and*
- you were 'ordinarily resident' (see p2:230) in GB either on the day you reached the age of 80, or on the date of the claim.

Income support, income-based jobseeker's allowance, housing benefit and council tax benefit

For all of these benefits you must be habitually resident in the 'common' travel area (see below).

7. **The habitual residence test**

The benefits affected by the habitual residence test are :
- income support (IS);
- income-based jobseeker's allowance (JSA);
- housing benefit (HB);
- council tax benefit (CTB).

You are not entitled to IS, income-based JSA, HB or CTB unless you are habitually resident, or are treated as habitually resident, in the '**common travel area**' which is comprised of the Republic of Ireland, the Channel Islands, the Isle of Man and the UK. If you do not satisfy the habitual residence test, you are classed as a 'person from abroad' (see pp2:207 and 2:219 for how this affects your entitlement to benefit).[158]

The habitual residence test is applied to all claimants of these benefits (but not partners or dependants), including British citizens. The following people, however, are automatically treated as habitually resident in the UK and are therefore exempt from the test: [159]

For income support and income-based jobseeker's allowance

- European Economic Area (EEA) nationals who are classed as 'workers', in European Community (EC) law, and their dependants. See p2:226 for details.
- Refugees or people who have been granted 'exceptional leave to enter or remain' in the UK (see pp2:215 and 2:216).
- People in Great Britain (GB) who left Montserrat after 1 November 1995 because of a volcanic eruption there.

For housing benefit and council tax benefit

- Asylum-seekers who satisfy certain conditions (see p2:221).
- Sponsored immigrants whose sponsor has died.
- People in receipt of IS or income-based JSA.
- People in GB who left Montserrat after 1 November 1995 because of a volcanic eruption there.
- EEA workers and their dependants.
- Refugees.
- People with exceptional leave to enter or remain (see pp2:221 and 2:216).
- People whose funds from abroad have been temporarily disrupted and there is a reasonable expectation that they will resume (provided you have not been without funds for more than 42 days in one period of limited leave).
- People subject to a deportation order but whose deportation has been deferred in writing by the Secretary of State.
- Illegal entrants who have the Secretary of State's written consent to stay.

If you are entitled to IS or income-based JSA urgent cases payments as a 'person from abroad' (see p2:217), you do not have to satisfy the habitual residence test.

If you get IS or income-based JSA, the local authority has to treat you as habitually resident. The local authority may not proceed to carry out the test itself.

The meaning of 'habitually resident'

The term 'habitually resident' is not defined in the benefit regulations. Although there is a certain amount of caselaw, 'habitual residence' remains a problematic and imprecise concept. The 'habitual residence test' is therefore open to highly subjective, restrictive and inconsistent decision-making by adjudication officers (AOs), local authorities and social security appeal tribunals (SSATs). Particular groups tend to be targeted, including nationals and people (especially from ethnic minority communities) who spend lengthy periods overseas.

The concept of habitual residence occurs in law relating to migrant workers[160] but the Benefits Agency appears to have accepted that this interpretation is not applicable to means-tested benefits.[161]

Two social security commissioner decisions which considered the meaning of 'habitual residence' in the context of IS (and are now the basis for Benefits Agency guidance), have established the following principles:[162]

- The term 'habitual residence' must be given its ordinary and natural meaning. There is no definitive definition or list of factors which determines a person's habitual residence. Each case must be considered on its merits, taking into account all the relevant circumstances and facts.

- To be habitually resident in a country, you must have a 'settled intention' to reside there – ie, to make your home there for a temporary or permanent period. Events subsequent to your arrival can help confirm that your intentions were settled from the outset.

- You must be actually resident for an 'appreciable period of time' before you become 'habitually resident'. What counts as an appreciable period of time depends on the facts of each case. There is no minimum period but habitual residence cannot be acquired immediately. One of the commissioner's decisions suggested, by way of example, that a UK citizen could establish habitual residence after three to six months.[163] The other commissioner's decision, however, said such examples should not be relied upon as normal or minimum 'appreciable periods'.[164] In spite of this, AOs and SSATs often treat three months as an unofficial minimum period. There is no legal basis for this. Family caselaw has found an 'appreciable period' to be as little as a month[165] and each case must be decided on its own circumstances. Previous visits to the UK to prepare for settled status can form part of the 'appreciable period' (see above).

- If you go abroad for a temporary period, you may retain your habitual residence in the UK, so that you will be habitually resident from the first day of your return. You can also be habitually resident in more than one country at the same time.

- The appreciable period should be for a period that is viable. This relates to the practicality of your arrangements for residence. However, the viability of your residence is only one relevant factor to be taken into account. In one case a commissioner held that living arrangements dependent on public funds, including IS, were not viable,[166] another firmly stated that there was no condition that only residence without recourse to public funds counted towards the required 'appreciable period'.[167]

Note: One of the commissioners' decisions referred to above was appealed to the Court of Appeal on the issue of whether you need to be resident for an 'appreciable period' of time to be considered habitually resident. The Court decided by a majority that it was necessary for residence to be for an appreciable period of time before residence could become habitual.[168] This decision is being appealed to the House of Lords. See *Welfare Rights Bulletin* for further developments.

European Economic Area nationals

Certain EEA nationals (see p2:224) are automatically treated as satisfying the 'habitual residence' test. You are automatically treated as habitually resident in the UK and therefore exempt from the test if you are:[169]

- a 'worker' for the purposes of EEC Regulations 1612/68 or 1251/70 (see below); *or*
- a person with the right to reside in the UK under EC Directives 68/360 or 73/148 (see p2:227).

If you are a British citizen, you can only be a 'worker' or person with the right to reside in the UK under the above provisions, if you are returning after working or exercising an EC right in another EEA country and you have also worked in the UK.[170]

Following a recent test case, if you are a British citizen who has worked in another EEA country and moved back to GB as a work-seeker the appreciable period of the residence test cannot be applied to you.[171] This may effectively undermine this element of the test for all EEA work-seekers. See CPAG's *Welfare Rights Bulletin* for further developments.

Tactics

- Only the claimant is subject to the habitual residence test. If you cannot satisfy the test, your partner could be the claimant if s/he would satisfy the test (eg, s/he has been in the UK longer than you) or would be exempt (eg, as an EEA worker – see p2:224).
- Since the habitual residence test operates as an exclusion from IS and income-based JSA, HB and CTB the onus of proof lies with the Benefits Agency or local authority to establish that you are *not* habitually resident.[172] It is vital, nevertheless, that you produce as much evidence as possible to show that you *are* habitually resident, taking into account the above points on the meaning of the term. You should prepare your case thoroughly before attending a Benefits Agency or local authority interview or a tribunal or housing benefit review board.
- If you fail the test, you may be able to satisfy it at a later date, particularly if there is a change in your circumstances, or simply through the passage of time. Repeated claims for benefit can highlight your determination to remain in the UK, as well as the unfairness of the test. Some local offices are refusing to accept repeat claims if there is an appeal pending. This is wrong – the local

office should accept the claim and make a decision. It is also now essential to make repeat claims because tribunals cannot take into account circumstances between the date of the SSAT's hearing and the date of the original decision (see p2:624).

- If you are refused benefit because of the habitual residence test, you can request a review, or (for IS/JSA) appeal to a tribunal (see Chapters 54 and 56). You can ask for an expedited hearing of your appeal if you are suffering hardship. Always ask for an oral hearing, so that you can explain your circumstances in person.

- If you have no money to live on because you have failed the habitual residence test, you could:
  - apply to the Benefits Agency for an 'extra-statutory payment' (see p2:662);
  - apply to your local social services department for financial assistance if you have children. (If you do not have children then you can ask your local authority to pay you under the National Assistance Act if you face destitution – see asylum-seekers, p2:213);
  - apply for a social fund crisis loan (see p1:667). Although you have to be able to repay a loan, if you are likely to be counted as habitually resident in the near future you will then qualify for benefit and will be in a position to repay the loan.

- If you qualify for IS or income-based JSA by virtue of EC Regulation 1408/71 (see p2:224), you cannot be denied benefit under the habitual residence test.[173]

- The future of the habitual residence test may now be in doubt as a result of the *Swaddling* case (see p2:237). See future editions of CPAG's *Welfare Rights Bulletin* for latest developments.

Notes

· ·

References are to statutes and regulations as amended up to 8 March 1999. All regulations are (General) Regulations unless otherwise stated. There is a full list of abbreviations in Appendix 13.

1. **Immigration status**
   1 para 6 HC 395 as amended by para 1 HC 324

2. **Non-means-tested benefits**
   2 Reg 2(1A) SS(AA) Regs; reg 2(1A) SS(DLA) Regs; reg 9(IA) SS(ICA) Regs; reg (IB) 3 SS(SDA) Regs
   3 s146A SSCBA 1992
   4 Reg 14B CB Regs
   5 Reg 3 CB(Amdt) Regs 1996; SS(PFA) MA Regs 1996; AM(AOG) 42 11 August 1997; AM(AOG) 41 11 August 1997;
   6 CF/1015/1995; AM(AOG) 41 11 August 1997
   7 CIS/16992/1996; CIS/2809/ 1997; CFC/1580/1997
   8 *R v CAO ex parte 'B'*

3. **Means-tested benefits**
   9 Reg 3(1)(aa) FC Regs; reg 5(1)(aa) DWA Regs
   10 Reg 3(1A) FC Regs; reg 12 SS(PFA)MA Regs; reg 5(1A) DWA Regs
   11 Regs 70 and 71 and Sch 7 para 17 IS Regs; regs 147, 148 and Sch 5 para 15 JSA Regs
   12 Reg 21(3) IS Regs
   13 s7(1) Immigration Act 1988; reg 23(3)(a) IS Regs
   14 Reg 21(3)(a) IS Regs
   15 Reg 21(3)(i) IS Regs
   16 Reg 70(3)(c) IS Regs
   17 Reg 12(2) SS(PFA)MA Regs
   18 ss105 and 106 SSAA 1992
   19 ss78(6)(c), 105 and 106 SSAA 1992
   20 Regs 21(3)(j) and 70(3)(b) IS Regs
   21 Reg 70(3)(b) and (3A)(a) IS Regs
   22 CIS/143/1997
   23 para 36144 AOG
   24 Reg 70(3A)(b)(i) IS Regs
   25 Reg 70(3A)(aa) IS Regs
   26 Reg 70(3A)(b)(i) IS Regs
   27 Reg 12(1) SS(PFA)MA Regs; Sch 1 para 6(2)(a) AIA 1996
   28 Reg 70(3A)(b)(ii) IS Regs
   29 *R v Secretary of State for Social Security ex parte Okito, Zaheer, Vijeikis* (10 July 1997); CIS/ 16992/1996
   30 *R v Secretary of State for Social Security ex parte 'T'* (18 March 1997)
   31 Sch 1 *para 5* AIA 1996
   32 *Krasniqi v Secretary of State for Social Security*
   33 s124(1)(f) SSCBA 1992
   34 Reg 70(3A)(b)(i) IS Regs
   35 *R v Secretary of State ex parte Karaoui and Abbad* (HC, 11 March 1997)
   36 See note 35
   37 Reg 70(3A)(b)(ii) IS Regs
   38 s17(6) CA 1989
   39 *R v Hammersmith and Fulham London Borough and others*, CA, *The Times*, 19 February 1997
   40 *R v Newham ex parte Gorenkin*, HC, 14 May 1997
   41 para 5205 SFG
   42 *Wolke and Remilien v Secretary of State for Social Security and CAO*, (27 November 1997)
   43 Art 15 1(EEA)O 1994
   44 s124 SSCBA 1992; reg 21(3) IS Regs
   45 Reg 21(3) and Sch 7 para 17 IS Regs
   46 Sch 7 para 17(c)(i) IS Regs
   47 Sch 7 para 17(c)(i) IS Regs
   48 Sch 7 para 17 IS Regs; para 28831 AOG
   49 Sch 7 para 17(b) and (c)(ii) and (iii) IS Regs
   50 Reg 21(3)(a) IS Regs
   51 Reg 21ZA(1) IS Regs; reg 85(4) JSA Regs

52 Reg 21(3) IS Regs; reg 85(4) JSA Regs
53 Reg 21ZA(2) and (4) IS Regs; reg 4(3C) and 19(1A) SS(C&P) Regs
54 s124(1)(f) SSCBA 1992
55 Sch 10 para 49 IS Regs; Sch 8 para 12(b) JSA Regs
56 Arts 2 and 3 EEC Reg 1408/71; CIS/564/1994
57 Reg 21(3) IS Regs; reg 85(4) JSA Regs
58 Reg 70(3)(a) IS Regs; reg 85(3)(a) JSA Regs
59 Reg 70(3)(b) IS Regs; reg 85(3)(b) JSA Regs
60 Reg 70(3)(c) IS Regs; reg 85(3)(c) JSA Regs
61 para 36133 AOG
62 Reg 71(1)(a) IS Regs; reg 148(1)(a) JSA Regs
63 Reg 71(1)(b) and (c) IS Regs; regs 148(1)(b) and (c) JSA Regs
64 Reg 72(1) IS Regs; reg 149(1) JSA Regs
65 Reg 72(1)(c) IS Regs; regs 149(1)(c) and 110(1)-(3) and (9) JSA Regs
66 Circular HB/CTB A7/94
67 Reg 7A(2) HB Regs
68 Reg 7A(3) HB Regs
69 Reg 7A(4)(a) HB Regs
70 Reg 7A(4)(b) HB Regs
71 Reg 7A(4)(c) HB Regs
72 Reg 7A(4)(d) HB Regs
73 Reg 7A(5) HB Regs
74 Reg 7A(5) HB Regs
75 Reg 12(1) SS(PFA)MA Regs
76 *R v Secretary of State for Social Security ex parte Vijeikis*, 10 July 1997, QBD; CIS/16992/1996
77 CIS/16992/1996
78 Reg 7A(5A) HB Regs
79 HB/CTB Circular A5/98
80 Reg 7A(4)(f) and (5) HB Regs
81 Reg 12(2) SS(PFA)MA Regs
82 Sch A1 para 2(4) HB Regs; Sch A1 para 2(4) CTB Regs
83 Sch A1 para 2(5) HB Regs; Sch A1 para 2(5) CTB Regs
84 Sch A1 para 2(1) HB Regs; Sch A1 para 2(1) CTB Regs
85 Sch A1 para 1(2) HB Regs; Sch A1 para 1(2) CTB Regs
86 Sch A1 para 9 HB Regs; Sch A1 para 8 CTB Regs

87 Sch A1 para 5(1) HB Regs; Sch A1 para 4(1) CTB Regs
88 Sch A1 paras 4 and 5(2) HB Regs; Sch A1 para 4(2) and (4) CTB Regs
89 Sch A1 para 6 HB Regs; Sch A1 para 5 CTB Regs
90 Sch A1 para 5(3) HB Regs; Sch A1 para 4(3) CTB Regs
91 Reg 7B(1)(b) HB Regs; reg 10(5A) HB(Amdt) Regs as amended
92 Sch A1 para 8(1) HB Regs; Sch A1 para 7(1) CTB Regs
93 Sch A1 para 8(5) HB Regs
94 Sch A1 para 8(4) HB Regs

4. **The rights of EEA nationals**
95 *Levin* Case 53/81 [1982] ECR 1035; EEC Reg 1251/70
96 *Levin; Kempf* Case 139/85 [1986] ECR 1741; *Raulin* Case 357/89 [1992] ECR 1027
97 *Scrivner* Case 122/84 [1985] ECR 1027; Art 7 I(EEA)O; CIS/12909/1996
98 *Lair* Case 39/86 [1988] ECR 3161; *Raulin*; Art 7(2) EEC Reg 1612/68
99 *Raulin*; Art 7(2) EEC Reg 1612/68
100 para 22680 AOG
101 CIS/4521/1995, para 13; Art 7(1) EEC Reg 1612/68
102 *Lair*; Art 7(1) EEC Reg 1612/68
103 *Lebon* Case 316/85 [1989] ECR 2811
104 Art 2(b) EEC Reg 1251/70
105 Art 2(a) EEC Reg 1251/70
106 Arts 2(c) and 4 EEC Reg 1251/70
107 Arts 1 and 4 EEC Dir 68/360
108 *Antonissen*, Case 292/88 [1991] ECR 1745; CIS/4521/1995
109 Arts 1 and 4 EC Dir 73/148
110 Art 1(b) EC Dir 73/148
111 *Cowan* Case 186/87 [1989] ECR 195; *Humbel* Case 263/86 [1988] ECR 5365; *Luisi* Case 286/82 [1988] ECR 5365
112 Art 1 EC Dir 68/360; Art 10 EEC Reg 1612/68; Art 1 EC Dir 73/148
113 *Royer* [1976] ECR 497; *Echternach* [1989] ECR 723; *Raulin*

5. Reciprocal agreements

114 Reg 2 and Sch 1 SS(NIRA) Regs;
Art 2 and Sch 1 SS(IoM)O
115 Sch 1 SS(J&G)O
116 Reg 12(1) SSB(PA) Regs

6. Residence conditions

117 R(S) 1/66
118 R(S) 1/66
119 Reg 2(2) SS(AA) Regs; reg 2(2)
SS(DLA) Regs; reg 6(2) SS(GA)
Regs; reg 9(3) SS(ICA) Regs; reg
3(2) SS(SDA) Regs
120 Reg 11 SSB(PA) Regs as amended
121 R(P) 1/78
122 R(G) 2/51
123 CG/204/1949
124 R(P) 1/78
125 R(G) 2/51
126 Reg 2(1) SS(AA) Regs; reg 2(1)
SS(DLA) Regs; reg 9(1) SS(ICA)
Regs
127 Reg 2(4) SS(DLA) Regs
128 Reg 2(2) SS(AA) Regs; reg 2(2)
SS(DLA) Regs
129 Reg 2(5) SS(DLA) Regs
130 Reg 2(2)(d) and (e) SS(AA) Regs;
reg 2(2)(d) and (e) SS(DLA) Regs
131 Reg 9(2) SS(ICA) Regs
132 s146(2)(a) SSCBA 1992
133 s146(3)(a) SSCBA 1992
134 s146(2)(b) and (3)(b) SSCBA
1992
135 Reg 2(2) CB(RPA) Regs
136 Reg 2(3) CB(RPA) Regs
137 Reg 4 CB(RPA) Regs as amended
138 Reg 4(3) CB(RPA) Regs
139 Regs 3 and 5 CB(RPA) Regs
140 Reg 5(2)(b) CB(RPA) Regs
141 Reg 5(2)(d)(i) CB(RPA) Regs
142 Reg 5(2)(d)(ii) CB(RPA) Regs
143 Reg 3(2)(b) CB(RPA) Regs
144 Reg 6(1) SS(GA) Regs as
amended
145 s128(1) SSCBA 1992
146 Reg 3(1) FC Regs
147 R(P) 1/78; R(M) 1/85
148 *Shah v Barnet LBC* [1983] All ER
226
149 Reg 9(1) FC Regs; CIS/508/1992
150 R(FC) 2/93
151 Reg 3(2) FC Regs
152 para 50100 AOG
153 Regs 3(1)(a) and (3) SS(SDA)
Regs

154 Reg 3(1)(b) SS(SDA) Regs
155 There are three conflicting
commissioners' decisions on this
point. CS/118/1989 holds that
the Secretary of State can impose
residence conditions, or presence
conditions, but not both. CS/46/
1988 and CS/137/1993 reject
this view.
156 s78(3) SSCBA 1992
157 Reg 10 SS(WB&RP) Regs

7. The habitual residence test

158 Reg 21(3) IS Regs; reg 85 JSA
Regs; reg 7A(4)(e) HB Regs; reg
7A(4)(e) CTB Regs
159 Reg 21(3) and (3F) IS Regs; reg
85(4) and (4A) JSA Regs; reg
7A(4)(e) and (5) HB Regs
160 EEC Reg 1408/71; *Di Paolo v
Office National de l'Emploi*, Case
76/76 [1977] ECR 315; R(U) 8/
88
161 CIS/2326/1995; paras 20747-48
AOG
162 CIS/1067/1995; CIS/2326/1995;
paras 20747-48 AOG
163 CIS/1067/1995, para 28
164 CIS/2326/1995, para 24
165 *Re F (child abduction)* [1992] 1
FLR 548
166 CIS/1067/1995, para 29
167 CIS/2326/1995, para 28
168 CIS/2326/1995; *Nessa v CAO*
169 Reg 21(3) IS Regs
170 *R v Immigration Appeal Tribunal
and Surinder Singh ex parte
Secretary of State for the Home
Department* (ECJ) Case 370/90
[1992] 3 All ER 798
171 *Swaddling v AO* (Case C-90/97)
ECJ, 25 February 1999
172 CIS/1067/1995, para 15
173 CIS/7201/1995; *Swaddling v AO*
(Case C-90/97) ECJ, 25 February
1999

CHAPTER 41

· ·

Going abroad

This chapter covers all the rules about claiming benefits when you go abroad. It contains:
1. Benefits when you go abroad (below)
2. Benefits when you move within the European Economic Area (p2:248)
3. Reciprocal agreements (p2:250)

If you go abroad your benefit may be affected. This is because in order to receive most benefits, generally you must be living in Great Britain (GB). However there are exceptions which allow certain benefits to continue to be paid. In addition these rules are enhanced by European Community (EC) law (see p2:223) and by reciprocal agreements.

1. Benefits when you go abroad

Some benefits can be paid abroad once you qualify for them. The rules are complicated – for further details see CPAG's *Migration & Social Security Handbook*. Some benefits have no residence and presence conditions, and may always be payable abroad eg, some retirement pensions. Despite being subject to residence and presence conditions, it may be possible to receive some benefits during temporary absences. Other benefits can be paid once you return from a temporary absence abroad.

Whether an absence is temporary is a question which depends on the circumstances of each individual case. An absence does not cease to be temporary because no date is fixed for your return: but the absence must be for a limited period only.[1] If you spend longer abroad than the permitted periods you may no longer satisfy the residence condition for your benefit.

Unless a reciprocal agreement (see p2:228) applies, the time you spend working abroad does not usually count towards the residence conditions if you claim severe disablement allowance (SDA – see Chapter 4), invalid care allowance (ICA – see Chapter 5), disability living allowance (DLA) or attendance allowance (AA) (see Chapter 10), or child benefit (see Chapter 12) on your return to GB. The residence conditions for each of these benefits are described on pp2:231-2:234. For the meaning of presence, residence, and ordinarily resident see p2:229.

For details of the rules which allow you to be paid certain benefits if you go abroad but not to work (eg, for medical treatment, because you want to retire there or take a holiday) see CPAG's *Migration & Social Security Handbook*.

Payment of benefit while you are abroad

If you are not working, you may want your British benefits to be paid to you while you are abroad. Unfortunately, unless you can benefit from a reciprocal agreement (see p2:228), this is only possible in the circumstances listed below.

Widows' benefits, retirement pensions, and guardian's allowance

These are payable while you are abroad, but your benefit is not normally uprated each year once you have ceased to be ordinarily resident (see p2:230) in GB.[2] You cannot de-retire (see p1:142) while abroad.[3]

In the case of widow's payment (see p1:113), there are two further conditions:[4]
* you or your husband must have been in GB when he died; *or*
* the contribution conditions for widowed mother's allowance or widow's pension are satisfied (see p2:274).

Attendance allowance, disability living allowance, and invalid care allowance

As long as you remain 'resident' (see p2:230) in Great Britain, a temporary absence does not affect your entitlement to DLA, ICA and AA and you can continue to receive benefit for up to 26 weeks. However, on your return you may experience difficulties in requalifying for benefit if your absence has been for more than 26 weeks. This is because you must have been present in GB for 26 out of the last 52 weeks in order to satisfy the residence conditions (see p2:231).

Disablement benefit, reduced earnings allowance and retirement allowance

Disablement benefit (except constant attendance allowance and exceptionally severe disablement allowance) and retirement allowance are unaffected while you are abroad.[5]

Constant attendance allowance and exceptionally severe disablement allowance are payable during a temporary absence for up to six months or such longer period as the Secretary of State may allow.[6]

Reduced earnings allowance is payable during a temporary absence if:[7]
* you have been away for less than three months, or such further period as the Secretary of State shall allow; *and*

- your absence is not for work purposes; *and*
- you claim before you go; *and*
- you are entitled before you go.

Increases for dependants

You may be eligible for an increase for dependants for:
- incapacity benefit (IB);
- ICA;
- maternity allowance;
- category A retirement pension;
- SDA;
- widowed mother's allowance.

If your spouse is abroad, you remain entitled to an increase (see p2:93) during any period your spouse is counted as 'residing with you' (see p2:99).[8] No increase is paid while another adult dependant is abroad.

If your child dependant (see p2:97) is abroad, you remain entitled to an increase while you are entitled to child benefit (see Chapter 12). If the only reason you are not entitled to child benefit is that you are abroad, you are still entitled to the increase if there is no one else who is entitled to child benefit in respect of that child.[9]

Incapacity benefit and severe disablement benefit

IB (see Chapter 3) and SDA (see Chapter 4) are payable during the first 26 weeks of any temporary absence if the Secretary of State has certified that payment would be 'consistent with the proper administration of the Act' and:[10]
- your absence from GB is for the specific purpose of being treated for an illness or industrial injury (see p1:204) which began before you left this country; *or*
- when you left this country you had been continuously incapable of work (see p2:15) for six months and you have been continuously incapable since your departure.

Maternity allowance

Maternity allowance (see p1:100) can be paid to you abroad. You should tell your benefit office before you go.

The rules for remaining entitled to maternity allowance while abroad are identical to those for IB (see above) except that maternity allowance is only payable for a period of 18 weeks.

Statutory sick pay and statutory maternity pay

There are no longer any requirements of presence or residence for statutory sick pay (see Chapter 2) or statutory maternity pay (see p1:91). You remain entitled if you are abroad for as long as you meet the normal entitlement rules.[11]

Child benefit

If you are claiming child benefit (see Chapter 12), your benefit could be affected if you or the child spend more than eight weeks abroad (see p2:231).

Income support

Once you have established your right to income support (IS) in GB, it is possible to claim during temporary absences abroad. GB means England, Scotland and Wales only, therefore a trip to Northern Ireland counts as going abroad. If you are going to Northern Ireland for more than four weeks you should claim under the Northern Ireland social security system. Benefit can continue to be paid for up to either four or eight weeks. To qualify for IS while abroad you must:[12]

* have been entitled to IS before you left the country;
* not expect to be away for more than a year; *and*
* continue to satisfy the other rules for getting IS described in Chapter 20 while you are away.

You can get IS for up to **four weeks** if you fall within one of the following groups:[13]

* you are going to Northern Ireland;
* you and your partner are both abroad and your partner qualifies for a pensioner, enhanced pensioner, higher pensioner, disability or severe disability premium (see pp2:325-329);
* you are incapable of work (see p2:14) *and*:
  – you have been continuously incapable for the previous 28 weeks and you are terminally ill or receiving the highest rate of disability living allowance care component; *or*
  – you have been continuously incapable for 364 days.
  Two or more periods when you are incapable of work are joined together to form a single period if they are separated by less than eight weeks;
* you are incapable of work (see p2:14) and are going abroad specifically for treatment of the incapacity from an appropriately qualified person. Before you go you should check that the Benefits Agency accepts that this rule applies to you;
* you fit into one of the groups of people who can claim IS (see p1:442). However, you must *not* be:
  – in 'relevant education' (see p2:132);
  – involved in a trade dispute, or in the first 15 days after you have returned to work following the dispute (see p2:187);
  – receiving an urgent cases payment of IS as a 'person from abroad' (see p2:217);
  – incapable of work for less than 28 weeks or appealing a decision of the Benefits Agency not to treat you as incapable of work (see p2:37).

You can get IS for up to **eight weeks** if you are taking a child abroad specifically for medical, physiotherapy or similar treatment from an appropriately qualified person. The child must count as part of your family (see p2:123).

If your partner is abroad temporarily you may still be treated as a couple for IS purposes (see p2:120), which means your partner's income and capital are taken into account and if s/he is in full-time work, you are not entitled to benefit.[14] This can apply even if you have not lived together in the UK, because the rules relate to absence from each other, not absence from home. You will not be treated as a couple if:

- you do not intend to resume living together; or
- your absence from one another is likely to be for 52 weeks or more.

If your partner is waiting for entry clearance to come to the UK, you can argue that because this is a lengthy process and refusal rates are high, your separation is likely to exceed 52 weeks substantially, so you should not be treated as a couple (see p2:120). [15] Alternatively, you can argue that you should not be treated as a couple because your intention to live together depends on entry clearance being granted.[16]

If you qualify for IS under the four- or eight-week rule, your benefit is normally paid to you on your return, but if you are a member of a couple you can ask for it to be paid to your partner during your absence instead. If you are not entitled to IS while abroad or you have already used up your four- or eight-week entitlement, your partner has to make a claim in her/his own right (see p1:449).

If it is your partner who goes abroad, your benefit is reduced after four weeks (eight weeks if your partner is taking a child abroad for medical treatment). You are then paid as if you were a single claimant or lone parent, but your joint income and capital counts.[17]

Housing benefit and council tax benefit

While you are temporarily out of the country, you may be entitled to housing benefit (HB) to cover your rent, and council tax benefit (CTB) towards your council tax (see pp1:516 and 1:572). If your IS stops, you must make a fresh claim for these benefits to qualify:

- your absence must be temporary and unlikely to exceed 13 weeks; or
- your absence is temporary and for a period of up to 52 weeks and:
  - you are providing or receiving medically approved care abroad; or
  - you are undertaking a training course approved or provided by Government.

If your partner goes abroad temporarily you will continue to be treated as a couple unless:
- you do not intend to resume living together; *or*
- your absence form one another is likely to exceed 52 weeks.

Jobseeker's allowance

You cannot normally get JSA if you are not in GB. However, JSA can be paid when you are absent from GB:
- for up to four weeks if you satisfy the conditions for being treated as available for work (see p1:291) and your partner satisfies the conditions for one of the pensioner premiums, a disability premium or a severe disability premium (see p2:322);
- for up to eight weeks if you are taking a child or young person abroad for treatment if that child or young person is a member of your family (see p2:113);
- for up to seven days if you are attending a job interview;
- for up to three months if you are unemployed and looking for work in another European Economic Area (EEA) country (see below).

National insurance contributions

If you go to work in a country which is not a member of the EEA (see p2:224), then your benefit and liability to pay national insurance contributions may be affected.
- If you are 'ordinarily resident' (see p2:230) in GB; *and*
- If you were 'resident' (see p2:230) in GB before you went abroad to work; *and*
- your employer has a place of business in GB

you must pay Class 1 national insurance contributions for the first year of your absence.[18] In all other cases, you may pay Class 3 contributions (see p2:259). This is probably something which you should do because it is unlikely that time spent working abroad in a non-EEA country will count towards your retirement pension in GB. There may be reciprocal agreements with some countries which are an exception to this. You should check with the Overseas Branch. For more on how an inadequate contribution record can affect your pension, see p2:276.

Other points to note

On your return to GB, you will probably have to show that you are still 'habitually resident' here if you want to claim means-tested benefits (see p2:234).

2. **Benefits when you move within the European Economic Area**

Social security benefits are not governed by British law alone. There are also laws made by the EC which apply directly in the UK and throughout the EEA.

The EEA consists of the 15 member states of the European Union, ie, Austria, Belgium, Denmark, Finland, France, Germany, Greece, the Irish Republic, Italy, Luxembourg, the Netherlands, Portugal, Spain, Sweden and the UK, which have joined together with three other countries from the European Free Trade Area (EFTA) – Iceland, Liechtenstein and Norway.

If you are a national of any of the EEA states, you and your dependants, even if they are non-EEA nationals, have rights under EC law. These rights stem from the Treaty of Rome and have been added to and expanded upon over the years by a variety of Regulations, Directives and caselaw.

If there is a conflict between rights given in EC law and the UK social security system, the EC law overrides the British rules.

Although primarily concerned with 'freedom of movement' there are two main areas of EC law which can assist you, in respect of benefits, if you go to another EEA country.

EC Regulation 1408/71

The first area of law is that based on EC Regulation 1408/71, a detailed Regulation that is intended to co-ordinate the various social security systems of the EEA. It does this by:
- prohibiting discrimination in matters of social security on grounds of nationality;
- allowing you to rely on periods of employment, residence and contributions paid in one EEA country towards entitlement to benefit in others (this is called the principle of aggregation);
- allowing you to take certain benefits abroad with you to another EEA country (this is called the principle of exportation);
- generally, allowing you to claim benefit only from the state in which you last worked (this is the single state principle).

Who is covered by the Regulation

In order to rely on the Regulation you must have been an employed or self-employed person. This is not the same as the term worker for other areas of EC law. You will be treated as an employed or self-employed person if you are insured under a national social security scheme. In the UK this means that you pay, have in the past paid, or ought to pay national insurance contributions.

The Regulation does not only apply to EEA nationals. Stateless persons and refugees are also covered.

Benefits covered

The Regulation applies to state benefits which are designed to protect against certain risks. The risks are laid down in EC law and each EEA country has to state which of its benefits fall under each of the headings. All benefits specified are covered but the fact that a benefit is not specified does not necessarily mean it is excluded.

The following table gives the risks and relevant UK benefit:

Risk	UK benefit
Sickness and maternity	IB, maternity benefit, SSP, SMP
Invalidity	IB, SDA
Old age	RP, graduated retirement pension, Christmas bonus
Survivors, benefits and death grants	Widows' benefits, widowed mother's allowance
Accidents at work and occupational diseases	Industrial disablement benefit, reduced earnings allowance
Family benefits	Child benefit, guardian's allowance, Child dependency increases
Unemployment	JSA

In addition, since 1992 the Regulation has been extended to include 'special non-contributory benefits'. The UK Government states that the following are 'special non-contributory' benefits:

- AA;
- DLA;
- FC;
- IS;
- income-based JSA;
- DWA; *and*
- ICA.

Special non-contributory benefits cannot be exported but they do appear to attract all the other rights contained in the Regulation such as non-discrimination and the right to rely on periods of residence in other member states.

Exporting benefits

If a benefit can be exported, you can continue to receive the benefit at the full rate for as long as you continue to satisfy the conditions for that benefit. However, only certain benefits can be exported to another member state.

These are for 'invalidity, old age or survivors, pensions for accidents at work or occupational diseases and death benefits'.

Unemployment benefits can be exported, but only for a maximum period of three months. You must register as unemployed for at least four weeks before you leave the UK and must register in the second EEA country within seven days. At present the UK Government will only allow contribution-based JSA to be exported as it considers income-based JSA to be a special non-contributory benefit and therefore non-exportable. This point has yet to be challenged.

Family benefits cannot be exported, however, they can be paid for family members living in another member state.

The rights of workers

The second area of EC law that may benefit you if you go abroad is that based on the rights given by EC Regulation 1612/68 to workers.

This Regulation and other related areas of law are concerned mainly with your rights to enter and take up employment, be self-employed, and provide or receive a service in any member state. However, if you are economically active in one of the above ways you are entitled to the same tax, housing and social advantages as offered to nationals of the member state. The courts have ruled that this term applies to social security benefits, including means-tested benefit, such as IS. In order to rely on the social advantage route you must have worked in the member state in which you seek to claim benefit, but this can be for a short period and includes part-time work (see p2:226 for more details and for a more detailed explanation of 'worker').

3. **Reciprocal agreements**

The UK has reciprocal agreements covering social security with both EEA and non-EEA states. You may claim benefit either in the UK or in the country with which the UK has a reciprocal agreement.

If the EEA rules do not apply to you, you may benefit from a reciprocal agreement (see p2:228) with the EEA country in which you have been living. But if EEA law does apply to you, you cannot rely on a reciprocal agreement even if that would be more favourable to you.[19] If you are not covered by either the EEA rules or a reciprocal agreement, then your position is the same as if you were working in a non-EEA country – see p2:242.

For the detailed rules on reciprocal agreements see CPAG's *Migration & Social Security Handbook*.

Notes

References are to statutes and regulations as amended up to 8 March 1999. All regulations are (General) Regulations unless otherwise stated. There is a full list of abbreviations in Appendix 13.

1. **Benefits when you go abroad**
   1 Akbar, *The Times*, 6 November 1992
   2 Reg 4 SSB(PA) Regs
   3 Reg 6 SSB(PA) Regs
   4 Reg 4(2)(a) SSB(PA) Regs
   5 Reg 9(3) SSB(PA) Regs
   6 Reg 9(4) SSB(PA) Regs
   7 Reg 9(5) SSB(PA) Regs
   8 Reg 13 SSB(PA) Regs
   9 Reg 13A SSB(PA) Regs
   10 Reg 2 SSB(PA) Regs
   11 Reg 10 SSP(MAPA) Regs and Reg 3(4) SS; reg 2A SMP(PAM) Regs
   12 Reg 4(1) and (2)(a) and (b) IS Regs
   13 Reg 4(2)(c) IS Regs
   14 Reg 16 IS Regs
   15 CIS/13805/1996
   16 CIS/508/1992; CIS/13805/1996
   17 Sch 7 paras 11 and 11A IS Regs
   18 Reg 120 SS(Con) Regs

3. **Reciprocal agreements**
   19 Art 6 Reg 1408/71/EEC; R(U) 4/84

Part 9

General rules

Chapter 42

. . . .

National insurance contributions

This chapter covers:
1. Introduction (below)
2. Payment of contributions (p2:258)
3. Credits and home responsibilities protection (p2:226)
4. Contribution conditions for benefits (p2:272)

1. Introduction

As was mentioned in Chapter 1, many of the benefits described in this *Handbook* are financed from the national insurance fund which is made up of payments from the Treasury and the social security contributions made by employees, their employers, the self-employed and other people who choose to pay them.

In turn, entitlement to those benefits – and, in some cases the amount paid – depends upon the contribution record of the claimant or, in the case of widows' benefits and Category B retirement pensions, of the claimant's spouse. For the contribution conditions for benefits, see p2:272.

A percentage of social security contributions goes to the National Health Service. The rest is paid into the national insurance fund.[1]

Contributions are collected for the DSS by the Inland Revenue. From April 1999 the Inland Revenue National Insurance Contributions Office (NICO) keeps the records of your contributions throughout your working life.

Classes of contribution

There are five different classes of contribution.[2] The class you pay depends upon whether you are an employee, self-employed or a voluntary contributor. Not all classes of contributions count for all benefits.[3]

Class of contribution	Payable by	Giving entitlement to
Class 1	employed earners and their employers	all benefits with contribution conditions
Class 1A	employers of employed earners	no benefits
Class 2	self-employed earners	all benefits with contribution conditions except contribution-based JSA (p1:272)
Class 3	voluntary contributors	widows' benefits and retirement pensions
Class 4	self-employed earners	no benefits

The amount of Class 1 or Class 4 contributions you pay depends upon your earnings. However, you do not necessarily gain more benefit by paying higher contributions.

Employed earners and self-employed earners

The distinction between being employed and self-employed is usually clear but there are sometimes grey areas.

An employed earner is defined as 'a person who is gainfully employed in Great Britain either under a contract of service, or in an office (including elective office) with emoluments chargeable to income tax under Schedule E'[4]: in other words if income tax is – or should be – deducted from your earnings before you receive them under the Pay As You Earn Scheme (PAYE) then you are an 'employed earner'.

A self-employed earner is anyone 'gainfully employed in Great Britain otherwise than in employed earner's employment'.[5] If you have two jobs it is possible to be both employed and self-employed.

There is not usually much dispute over whether you hold an office or not. Office-holders are such people as judges, company directors, registrars of births, deaths and marriages.

The usual area of dispute is whether you are employed under a *contract of service* (in which case you are an employee) or a *contract for services* (in which case you are self-employed). This can be a complicated question and the Secretary of State must take into account a number of factors such as how closely your work is supervised, whether you can employ a substitute to do your job for you, the method of payment, whether the contract is for a fixed period, whether you have to provide your own equipment, where you work and the amount of freedom you have to decide when you work and how much work you must do. No one criterion is conclusive and different aspects may have different weight attached to them in different cases.[6]

Certain people are deemed to be employed earners.[7] These are office cleaners, many agency workers, people employed by their spouses for the purposes of their spouses' employment, lecturers, teachers and instructors (but not if the instruction is for no more than three days in any three months or is given as public lectures) and most ministers of religion. Conversely examiners, moderators and invigilators are deemed to be self-employed.[8]

You do not have to pay contributions if your job is:[9]

- employment in your home by a close relative if you both live in the home and the employment is not for the purposes of any trade or business carried on there. Close relatives are parent, grandparent, step-parent, son, daughter, step-son, step-daughter, brother, sister, half-brother or half-sister;
- employment by your spouse if it is not for the purposes of your spouse's employment;
- employment as a self-employed earner if you are not ordinarily self-employed;
- employment as a returning officer at an election;
- employment by certain international organisations or foreign armed forces (but only in certain circumstances).

Upper and lower earnings limits

Contributions are now paid by reference to the tax year (ie, 6 April to 5 April).[10] For each tax year there is an upper earnings limit and a lower earnings limit.[11] Employees are liable to pay Class 1 contributions on weekly earnings between those limits. The earnings limits for the years from 1997/98 to 1999/00 are as follows:

Year	Lower earnings limit	Upper earnings limit
1997/98	£62	£465
1998/99	£64	£485
1999/00	£66	£500

A list of the earnings limits for each year since the present system was adopted in 1975/76 can be found in Appendix 9.

Earnings factors

Payment of Class 1, 2 and 3 contributions gives rise to an 'earnings factor' which is used to calculate your entitlement to contributory benefits (including the additional pension payable under the State Earnings-Related Pension Scheme – see Chapter 9). For Class 1 contributions, the earnings factor is the amount of earnings upon which those contributions have been paid. Each Class 2 and Class 3 contribution gives rise to an earnings factor equal to that year's lower earnings limit.[12]

Decisions relating to contributions

These are made by the Secretary of State[13] and not by an adjudication officer, which means that you cannot appeal to a tribunal if there is a dispute, although there are other ways of contesting a decision (see p2:565). One issue the Secretary of State must decide is whether you are employed or self-employed. Disputes can also arise over a person's contribution record. The Secretary of State relies heavily on the Inland Revenue's records but will often accept that the computer record is not perfect if you can explain why you think the computer record is wrong.

2. **Payment of contributions**

Age limits

Contributions are intended to be paid during a normal working life. They are not, therefore, payable by those under the minimum school-leaving age of 16,[14] nor by those over pensionable age (65 for men, 60 for women).[15] The DSS should send you a certificate of age exemption when you reach pensionable age. Ask at your local Benefits Agency office if it does not. Employers of employees over pensionable age still have to pay their contributions at the full (contracted-in) rate.

These rules discriminate against men (and in some circumstances also against women) on the grounds of gender but the European Court has held that they are not contrary to EC law (see p2:283).[16]

Residence and presence in Great Britain

Class 1 contributions must usually be paid by employees who are employed in Great Britain[17] and who are resident, present (except for temporary absence) or ordinarily resident in Great Britain at the time.[18]

However, if you are employed by an overseas employer and are not ordinarily resident or employed in the UK, you are not liable for Class 1 contributions until you have been resident in Great Britain for a year.[19] This also applies to certain foreign students and apprentices.[20]

If you are working abroad, you must still pay Class 1 contributions for the first year if your employers have a place of business in Great Britain, you were resident in Great Britain before your employment started and you are still ordinarily resident in Great Britain.[21] After that year you are entitled, but not obliged, to pay Class 3 contributions.[22]

Class 2 contributions are compulsory if you are self-employed in Great Britain and are either ordinarily resident in Great Britain, or have been resident here for at least 26 weeks during the last year.[23] If you are present in

Great Britain, they may be paid voluntarily if you are not required to pay them.[24] If you are self-employed outside Great Britain, you may pay Class 2 contributions if you wish, provided you were employed or self-employed immediately before you left Great Britain and, *either*:

- you have been resident in Great Britain for a continuous period of at least three years at some time in the past; *or*
- you have paid contributions producing an earnings factor of at least 52 times the lower earnings limit in each of three years in the past. Each set of 52 flat-rate contributions paid before April 1975 counts as satisfying that condition in respect of one year.[25]

You may also pay Class 2 contributions if you are a **volunteer development worker** resident in Great Britain but employed outside Great Britain and not liable to pay Class 1 contributions. These are paid at a special rate and give entitlement to contribution-based jobseeker's allowance (JSA), but are payable only if the Secretary of State certifies that it would be consistent with the proper administration of the legislation to allow you to do so.[26]

Class 3 contributions are always voluntary. They may be paid if you are resident in Great Britain during the course of the year in respect of which you wish to pay the contributions. They are payable while you are abroad if you satisfy either of the conditions which would allow you to pay Class 2 contributions but it is not necessary for you to have been employed or self-employed before you left Great Britain. You may also pay them if you have been paying Class 1 contributions while abroad.[27]

Class 4 contributions are payable only if you are resident in the UK for income tax purposes.[28]

If you pay Class 2 or 3 contributions, the National Insurance Contribution Office (NICO) sends a bill each quarter or you may pay by direct debit. For more details, see DSS leaflet CA05 – Self-Employed and Voluntary Contributors – 'Payment by Quarterly Bill'.

If you wish to pay contributions while abroad, obtain DSS leaflet NI38 which contains an application form.

When you return to Great Britain, it is a good idea to notify the Inland Revenue so that you can be told of any deficiency in your contribution record that you might remedy, and so that your future contribution record is accurately tied in with your past record.

The meaning of the terms 'resident' and 'present' are explained on p2:229. Members of the armed forces are deemed always to be present in Great Britain and there are special rules for aircrew, mariners, share fishermen and offshore workers on the continental shelf.

For the factors which are taken into account in deciding where you are ordinarily resident see p2:230.

It should also be noted that Northern Ireland and Isle of Man contributions count towards British benefits and so can contributions paid in other countries in some circumstances. Also you may be entitled to benefits from other countries while you are in this country (see Chapter 32).

Reduced liability for married women and widows

Newly married or widowed women now pay the same level of contributions as anyone else. Until 5 April 1977 they could choose to pay a reduced Class 1, or no Class 2, contribution.[29] Women who had done so were able to choose to continue payment at this reduced level of contribution. The disadvantage is that there is no later entitlement to any benefit (except for industrial injury) and no right (except for widows) to receive credits when these would otherwise be made, eg, during sickness or unemployment.[30]

A married woman whose husband dies while she is taking advantage of this provision loses her right to continue to do so unless she is receiving a widow's benefit. The right is lost at the end of the tax year in which her husband dies or the end of the next year if he dies after 30 September.[31]

The right to opt for reduced liability is also automatically lost:[32]

- on divorce or annulment of marriage;
- at the end of the tax year in which she stops receiving a widow's benefit;
- after two tax years with no earnings;
- at the end of a tax year in which a Class 1 contracted-out contribution (see p2:261) is paid by mistake but the woman wishes to pay such contributions;
- when a Class 1 contracted-in contribution (see below) is paid by mistake but the woman wishes to continue paying it, has asked for no refund, has not since paid any reduced or contracted-out rate contributions and confirms to the Secretary of State that she wishes to pay the full rate before the end of the calendar year after the tax year in which she starts to pay the full contributions, eg, 31 December 2001 for the tax year 1999/00.

It is worth thinking carefully about your position if you are currently taking advantage of the reduced liability. Once lost, the right cannot be reclaimed.

On the one hand, if you continue with the reduced liability, you are not accumulating entitlement to contributory benefits. On the other hand, you can still receive widows' benefits and Category B retirement pension on your husband's record, non-contributory benefits (such as attendance allowance or disability living allowance), and means-tested benefits (such as income support). The following considerations are relevant:

- the extent to which your pension entitlement would be improved by paying contributions now (see p2:274); *and*
- although you could gain an additional pension under the State Earnings-Related Pension Scheme (SERPS) if you start paying full Class 1 contributions, it might be better to continue to pay reduced contributions and put the money into a private scheme instead. This is a point on which you will probably need advice from a financial adviser, but remember that many

financial advisers will only give advice on certain products and may have a vested interest in telling you to start a private pension because of the commission that they will receive. It is always a good idea to ask how much commission your adviser will get if you follow her/his advice and s/he is obliged to disclose this information if you ask for it;

- (if you are looking after an invalid or child(ren) for whom you receive child benefit) home responsibilities protection (see p2:271) is only available if the election to pay the reduced amount is revoked; *and*
- if you are unemployed or too ill to work or if you work but have low earnings and receive family credit or disability working allowance, you may be entitled to credits (see pp2:267 and 2:270) if you revoke the election.

It is very difficult to give general advice. Quite a lot depends on individual circumstances, such as the amount you earn, the security of your employment, your state of health, your age and whether you are sufficiently well off not to be entitled to means-tested benefits. Ask your union or local citizens advice bureau for advice.

To revoke your election, fill in the form in DSS leaflet CA13 for married women or CA09 for widows.

Class 1 contributions

Class 1 contributions are paid both by employed earners (see p2:256 – known as primary contributors) and their employers (secondary contributors).[33] Both your liability and your employers' liability depend upon the amount of your earnings in relation to the lower and upper earnings limits (see p2:257). These earnings limits are currently £66 and £500 a week. If your earnings are monthly, the earnings limits are multiplied by 41/3 to give monthly equivalents.[34]

If you are not contracted-out of SERPS (see p1:154), the rate of your contribution is 10 per cent of your earnings between the lower and upper earnings limits.[35] The old rule which also required employees to pay 2 per cent of their earnings up to the lower earnings limit has been abolished with effect from 6 April 1999.

Example
If your weekly earnings are £164 your Class 1 contribution is:
$10\% \times (£164 - £66) = 10\% \times £98 = £9.80$

The most an employee has to pay is £43.40 a week (ie, 10 per cent of £434).

If you are **contracted out of SERPS** (see Chapter 9), the rate of your contribution is 8.4 per cent of your earnings between the lower and upper earnings limits.[36] So, the most you can have to pay is £36.46 a week.

Although your contributions to the national insurance fund are lower if you are contracted-out, you probably pay more than 2 per cent of your earnings into your occupational pension scheme instead.

If you are a member of an appropriate personal pension scheme (see p1:154), you pay Class 1 contributions at the contracted-in rate but the Secretary of State then pays to the scheme a sum equal to the difference between the contracted-in and contracted-out rates.[37]

If you are a **married woman or widow with reduced liability** for contributions (see p2:260), you pay 3.85 per cent of your earnings up to the upper earnings limit but your employers pay at the usual rate.[38]

There are also **special rates** for members of the armed forces and the employers of certain mariners employed on foreign-going ships.[39]

If you have **more than one job**, the basic rule is that your liability to pay Class 1 contributions is calculated for each job as if the others did not exist.[40]

- -

Example

Mary earns £50 a week working part time serving dinners at a school and £60 a week working behind the bar of a pub in the evenings. Although her total earnings are £110 a week neither she nor her employers pay any Class 1 contributions because her earnings in each job are below the lower earnings limit. As a result, Mary is not earning any entitlement to contribution-based JSA, incapacity benefit (IB) or a Category A retirement pension.

- -

This rule is subject to two exceptions. The first is that if you have more than one job, you can claim a refund if, during a contribution year, you pay more than 53 times the maximum weekly amount that anyone can pay in Class 1 contributions (ie, £2,300.20 in 1999/00 – 53 x £43.40 – see above).[41]

The second exception is that if you have two different jobs for the same employer or employers who carry on business in association with each other, then your earnings from those jobs are added together and you have to pay national insurance contributions based on your total earnings.[42] This is to stop employers avoiding the liability to pay contributions.[43]

Your employers' liability is calculated differently from yours. There is no liability in respect of that part of your earnings which are below the 'earnings threshold' (which is set at the rate of the basic single person's personal allowance for income tax – currently £83 a week). but, unless you are contracted out of SERPS, your employer pays a contribution calculated as 12.2 per cent of your earnings above that level including any earnings above the upper earnings limit.[44]

If you are contracted out of SERPS, then:[45]

- if your pension is a salary-related scheme your employers pay 3 per cent less on that part of your earnings between the earnings threshold and the upper earnings limit;

- if your pension is a money-purchase scheme your employers pay 0.6 per cent less on that part of your earnings between the earnings threshold and the upper earnings limit.

Your employers should deduct your Class 1 contributions from your earnings and pay them with their own contributions to the Inland Revenue.[46] See p2:265 for what happens if they do not.

Class 1A contributions[47]

Class 1A contributions are paid by employers. They are only payable if an employee has the use of a company car and are charged at 10 per cent of the 'cash equivalent' of the benefit to the employee of the car and any fuel. This is calculated in the same way as for income tax.

Class 2 contributions

Class 2 contributions must be paid by self-employed earners (see p2:396) unless you have a certificate of exemption on the grounds that your income is below a certain level (£3,770 in 1999/00, £3,590 in 1998/99, £3,480 in 1997/98 and £3,430 in 1996/97).[48]

You must apply for a certificate as soon as possible because it can only be backdated for up to 13 weeks before the date of application,[49] although repayment of contributions is now possible – see below. The application form is included in DSS leaflet CA03. It is sometimes possible to have the calculation of your earnings deferred until the end of the year and so wait to see if you do or do not have sufficiently low earnings. Usually your earnings are estimated; your earnings will be estimated as below the minimum level if they were below that level in the previous year and there has been 'no material change of circumstances'. Expenses are deducted when calculating earnings.[50]

You must pay contributions unless you have a certificate; you may pay them even if you do have a certificate.[51] Married women and widows with reduced liability for contributions (see p2:260) are not liable for Class 2 contributions.

Class 2 contributions are payable at a flat rate.[52] The current and recent rates are:

1997/98	£6.15 a week
1998/99	£6.35 a week
1999/00	£6.55 a week

Volunteer development workers overseas (see p2:259) and share fishermen pay contributions at special rates (£6.45 and £7.20 a week respectively) which count towards contribution-based JSA, unlike other Class 2 contributions.[53]

The methods of payment are set out in DSS leaflet CA03. If you are self-employed part of the time and also have a job as an employed earner you pay both Class 1 and Class 2 contributions, subject to a maximum.[54]

If you have paid Class 2 contributions, you can apply to have them repaid to you if your earnings in that year were in fact low enough to entitle you to exception. The application must be made in writing after the end of the relevant contribution year (5 April) and no later than 31 December of the same calendar year.[55]

Class 3 contributions

Class 3 contributions are purely voluntary.[56] They give entitlement only to widows' benefits and retirement pensions and are not payable if your earnings factor is otherwise sufficient in that tax year to meet the second contribution condition for those benefits (see p2:275).[57] Any accidental overpayment of contributions should be refunded if you make a written application.[58]

Class 3 contributions are paid at a flat rate. The current and recent rates are:[59]

1997/98	£6.05 a week
1998/99	£6.25 a week
1999/00	£6.45 a week

The introduction of home responsibilities protection (see p2:271) has lessened the need for payment of Class 3 contributions. However, if your contribution record for long-term benefits would otherwise be imperfect (eg, because you have been abroad or in prison) you may still consider it a good idea to pay them. Ask at your local Benefits Agency office if you are in doubt.

Class 4 contributions

Class 4 contributions are paid by self-employed earners (see p2:256). They are levied as a percentage of profits or gains between certain sums.[60] The current and recent rates are:

Year	Payable on earnings between	Percentage
1996/97	£6,860 and £23,660	6.0
1997/98	£7,010 and £24,180	6.0
1998/99	£7,310 and £25,220	6.0
1999/00	£7,530 and £26,000	6.0

The profits and gains are those chargeable to income tax under Schedule D, and Class 4 contributions are usually collected with your income tax by the Inland Revenue. You may apply for permission to defer payment for a specified period if the amount to be paid has not yet been established.[61]

If you are liable to pay both Class 1 and Class 4 contributions, the total is limited to the maximum which could be paid under one class only.[62]

Pre-1975 contributions

The present contribution system was introduced on 6 April 1975. Between 5 July 1948 and 5 April 1975 there were no Class 4 contributions, and Class 1 contributions were paid by way of a 'flat-rate stamp' in the same way as Class 2 and Class 3 contributions. Graduated contributions giving entitlement to graduated retirement benefit (see p1:140) were introduced in 1961 but were collected separately.

Before 6 April 1975, contribution years were not the same as tax years – as they are now. Instead, each person was allocated a contribution year which might have begun in December, March, June or September depending on the last letter of your national insurance number. There were complicated transitional arrangements in both 1948 and 1975 so that you may well have had a contribution year which was not 12 months long. That may explain what would otherwise be anomalies in your contribution record.

Before 5 July 1948, there was a contributory scheme under the Widows', Orphans' and Old Age Contributory Pension Acts 1936/41, which may still give entitlement to an enhanced rate of pension.

Non-payment or late payment of contributions

It is an offence not to pay contributions on time (unless, of course, they are voluntary).[63] As far as Class 1 contributions are concerned, it is your employers' responsibility to make sure that contributions are deducted from your earnings and then paid to the Inland Revenue. But if you connive with your employers in order to avoid paying contributions, you too could be prosecuted. In practice, the Inland Revenue is usually more interested in collecting the appropriate contributions than in prosecuting people.

All employees have the right to receive an itemised pay statement from their employer every time that they are paid.[64] The statement must show all the deductions which have been made, including income tax and national insurance contributions. If you are not given a pay-slip which complies with these rules, you can take your employer to an industrial tribunal which can award you compensation if money has been deducted without your being told.[65]

If your employers have deducted Class 1 contributions from your earnings but have failed to pay them to the Inland Revenue, you are treated as though they had been paid unless you have been negligent, or consented to or connived in that arrangement.[66]

Class 2 contributions should technically be paid in the week in respect of which they are due.[67] In practice, payment is by quarterly bill or direct debit.

(See Contributions Agency leaflet CA04) At the end of the tax year you will know whether or not it is necessary to pay Class 3 contributions if you want to fill any gap in your record.

In any event, contributions may still count for benefit purposes if paid late provided that they are paid within two years (Class 1) or six years (Class 2 or Class 3) after the end of the tax year in which they were due.[68] Students, apprentices and prisoners may pay Class 3 contributions to cover their period of education, apprenticeship or imprisonment at any time before the end of the sixth complete tax year after that period finished.[69] However, contributions give no entitlement to benefits, until they have actually been paid (and, in the case of contribution-based JSA or IB, until six weeks after they have been paid).[70]

Voluntary contributions may be paid on behalf of a contributor after her/his death provided they are paid no later than s/he would have been allowed to pay them.[71] This may be useful to gain entitlement to – or increase the rate of – widow's pension or widowed mother's allowance (see pp1:118 and 1:114).

3. **Credits and home responsibilities protection**

If you do not pay social security contributions, there will be gaps in your contribution record. However, in a large number of circumstances you will be 'credited' with a contribution. A credited contribution is usually known simply as a 'credit'.

Credits help you satisfy the second contribution condition for benefits with two contribution conditions (ie, contribution-based jobseeker's allowance (JSA), incapacity benefit (IB), Category A and B retirement pensions, widowed mother's allowance and widow's pension). It is important to note that credits cannot help you to satisfy the first contribution condition for such benefits or to qualify for maternity allowance or widow's payment (both of which have a single contribution condition).

In practice, this means that if you are claiming a retirement pension, widowed mother's allowance or widow's pension, you (or your late spouse) must actually have paid a full year's contributions[72] at some point during your working life in order to benefit from the rules on credits.[73] If you are claiming contribution-based JSA or IB you must actually have paid contributions with an earnings factor of at least 25 times the lower earnings limit for the year in question and, in the case of contribution-based JSA these must have been paid in one of the last two years before the 'relevant year' (see p2:273).

You are credited with an amount of earnings equal to the lower earnings limit (except starting credits, which give you a Class 3 credit).

You receive only sufficient credits in any tax year to meet the minimum contribution condition.[74] For example, if you earn £4,000 as an employee between April and October 1999 you receive no credits during the rest of 1998/99 because you have already paid contributions with an earnings factor of more than £3,432 (the minimum required to count for long-term benefits; 52 times the lower earnings limit of £66).

Married women currently opting for reduced liability for contributions (see p2:260) are not entitled to credits other than starting credits (see p2:269).[75]

Home responsibilities protection (see p2:271) helps you satisfy the second contribution condition for long-term benefits by reducing the years for which you would otherwise have to satisfy the contribution condition.

Credits for weeks of unemployment or incapacity for work

You can get a credit for a week in which you are signing on as unemployed or covered by a medical certificate. More precisely, you get one Class 1 credit[76] for *either*:

- each complete week (ie, the seven days from Monday to Sunday) for which you receive JSA; *or*
- each complete week for which you have (either from the first day you claim or else within any reasonable period of time) made a written claim for credits and provided the DSS with evidence that you satisfy (or satisfied) the conditions of entitlement to JSA (see Chapter 14) except those requiring you to:
  - meet the contribution conditions (or the means test for the purposes of income-based JSA); *and*
  - have a jobseeker's agreement; *and*
  - be in Great Britain.

  You will also get credits under this rule if the only reason a week would not otherwise qualify is that you were incapable of work (see Chapter 3) for part of it;
- each complete week during which you were incapable of work (or would have been if you had claimed short-term IB or maternity allowance in time) or during which you were entitled to statutory sick pay (SSP).

In any of these cases, you must claim your credits by writing to the DSS no later than the end of the benefit year (see p2:273) following the one in which you were ill (although the time may be extended if it is reasonable to do so.[77]

So, for example, if you are incapable of work at any time between Sunday 3 January 1999 and Saturday 1 January 2000, the DSS must (in practical terms[78]) receive your claim by Friday 30 December 2000. For the 2000 benefit year (ie, Sunday 2 January 2000 to Saturday 6 January 2001) the closing date for claiming credits is (again in practical terms) Friday 4 January 2002. These are the maximum times allowed: it is much better to claim your credits as soon as you are well enough to do so.

Entitlement to credits is one reason why you might continue to sign on at the JobCentre, even though you are getting no immediate benefit from doing so. Therefore, if you do not have a good enough contribution record to claim contribution-based JSA or your entitlement to contribution-based JSA has run out and you are unable to claim income-based JSA or income support (IS) in your own right, you should consider whether it is still worth signing on to protect your right to benefits.

However, you will still not get credits for any period of unemployment during which:[79]

- you are involved in a trade dispute; *or*
- you are not getting JSA (or your income-based JSA is paid at the reduced 'hardship' rate) because you have been 'sanctioned' (eg, because you left or failed to take a job without good reason – see p1:395); *or*
- you receive IS or income-based JSA solely because you are a 16/17-year-old in 'severe hardship' (see p1:328).

These credits will only help you towards qualification for short-term IB if, during the relevant contribution year, *either*:[80]

- you have actually paid contributions giving an earnings factor of at least 25 times the lower earnings limit in one of the two years before the beginning of the relevant benefit year (see p2:273); *or*
- you received long-term (or the higher rate of short-term) IB or invalid care allowance (ICA) or would have done if you had not been receiving another earnings replacement benefit instead (see p2:493); *or*
- you made an earlier claim for short-term IB, disability working allowance (DWA), JSA or maternity allowance and you satisfied the contribution conditions for short-term IB at the time of the earlier claim; *or*
- you were credited with a contribution for approved training (see below); *or*
- you received SSP but would have been entitled to short-term IB if you had claimed it.

Credits for caring for an invalid

You receive a Class 1 credit for each week you receive ICA (see Chapter 5).[81] You also receive credits if the only reason that you do not receive ICA is that you are receiving a widow's benefit instead.

If you are looking after an invalid but are not entitled to credits under these provisions, you may receive home responsibilities protection instead (see p2:271).

Starting credits

You receive Class 3 credits for the contribution year in which you were 16 and for the next two years if you would otherwise have an insufficient contribution record for long-term benefits.[82]

This is intended to help those who have stayed on at school after the minimum school-leaving age. No credits are made under this provision in respect of years before 6 April 1977.

Education and training credits

You receive Class 1 credits for the purposes only of contribution-based JSA and IB for any week of a course of full-time education or full-time (or, for a person who is registered as disabled, part-time – at least 15 hours a week) training to acquire occupational or vocational skills or apprenticeship provided that:

- in one of the two contribution years in which you must satisfy the second contribution condition for the benefit (see p2:273), you have an earnings factor of 50 times the lower earnings limit without recourse to this provision; *and*
- you are 18 or will become 18 during the current tax year; *and*
- you were under 21 when the course started.[83]

You also receive Class 1 credits for the purposes of **all benefits** for each week you are undertaking an approved training course[84] provided that:

- the training is full-time unless either you are disabled or it is an introductory course; *and*
- the training is not part of your job; *and*
- the training is intended to run for less than one year (except in certain circumstances if it is a course for disabled people); *and*
- you were 18 or over at the beginning of the contribution year in which the credit is claimed.

All courses run by the Training Enterprise and Education Directorate count. Other courses are considered on their merits. You should apply through your local DSS office on form CF55C.

Credits for maternity pay period

You are entitled to a Class 1 credit for each week of the maternity pay period (see p1:93) for which you receive statutory maternity pay.[85] This will be important only if you are receiving maternity pay at a rate less than the lower earnings limit (currently £66 a week). You must claim these credits in writing before the end of the 'benefit year' (see p2:273) following the tax year in which the week falls, (see p2:273) but the time may be extended if it is reasonable to do so.

Credits for jury service

You are entitled to a Class 1 credit for each week after 6 April 1988 when you spend part of the week on jury service.[86] Again, you must claim these credits in writing before the end of the benefit year following the tax year in which the week falls (or such further period as is reasonable).

Credits for widows

If you are a widow, you may receive credits to enable you to satisfy the second contribution condition for contribution-based JSA or IB. This is, of course, important only if you are not receiving widowed mother's allowance or widow's pension at the full rate.

You receive Class 1 credits for each year in which widow's allowance (a benefit abolished in April 1988) or widowed mother's allowance was paid, if payments have ceased for a reason other than remarriage or cohabitation.[87] Since a widow in this position is deemed to satisfy the first contribution condition for contribution-based JSA or IB,[88] the effect of this provision is effectively to waive the contribution conditions for widows altogether.

Credits for men aged 60 or over

Women are not entitled or required to pay contributions once they are 60 or over. Men aged over 60 must continue to pay contributions if they are liable even if their contribution records are already sufficient to qualify them for a full Category A retirement pension. This rule discriminates against men (and also in some limited circumstances against women) on grounds of their sex but is not contrary to European Economic Area law (see p2:283) because it is a consequence of having a different pensionable age for men and women.[89]

Men receive Class 1 credits for the contribution year in which they become 60 and for the next four years if credits are needed to allow the year to count for the purposes of the second contribution condition for any benefit.[90] This means that if you take early retirement at 60 you will still have the last five years of your 'working life' counted in full towards satisfaction of the second contribution condition for your retirement pension when you reach 65. These are sometimes known as 'autocredits'.

Credits for family credit and disability working allowance claimants

Family credit (FC) is a means-tested benefit for people who work 16 hours a week or more and have low earnings and dependent children. DWA is a means-tested benefit paid to people who work 16 hours a week or more but who have a disability which puts them at a disadvantage in the labour market. For more details see Chapter 22.

You are entitled to a Class 1 credit if you are getting FC or DWA during any week and *either*:[91]

- you are employed and earn less than the lower earnings limit (currently £66); *or*
- you are self-employed but have been granted exemption from paying Class 2 contributions because your earnings are below the small earnings limit (see p2:263).

If you are receiving FC, these rules apply from 6 April 1996 but only if you will reach pensionable age after 5 April 1999.[92] If you are receiving FC as a member of a married or cohabiting couple and both partners have earnings, then the credit is given to the partner with the higher earnings or, if the earnings of both partners are the same, to the one to whom the FC is actually paid.[93] The rules do not apply to married women or widows who have elected to pay reduced contributions (see p2:260).[94]

This provision will be carried over into working families tax credit and disabled person's tax credit, which will replace FC and DWA from 5 October 1999 (see Chapter 23).

Home responsibilities protection

A year of home responsibilities protection is one:[95]
- throughout which you receive child benefit for a child aged under 16; *or*
- throughout which you are allowed to receive IS on the basis that you are looking after an invalid; *or*
- in 48 weeks of which you spend 35 hours looking after someone receiving either the higher or middle rates of disability living allowance care component (see p1:169), attendance allowance (see p1:180) or constant attendance allowance (under the industrial injuries scheme or war pensions scheme).

A year should be automatically recorded as a year of home responsibilities protection if you qualify because you receive child benefit or you receive IS while caring for an invalid. If you qualify only on the third of the above grounds, or you qualify for part of the year on one ground and the rest on another, you should apply at your local DSS office. This should be done at the end of any contribution year when your earnings do not exceed 50 times that year's lower earnings limit. Ask your local office for form CF411.

Note that for the first of the above grounds, you have to be entitled to child benefit. If you are a man *and*:
- you are looking after children and *either*:
  - you do not work; *or*
  - you do not earn sufficient to pay national insurance contributions; *and*
- their mother lives with you *and*:
  - is in work; *and*

– earns enough to pay national insurance contributions; *and*
– is receiving child benefit

you should ask her to stop claiming the child benefit so that you can claim it instead. When you claim the child benefit, you should include a letter from her saying that she no longer wishes to claim. It is not enough for you to say that your name is or should be on the child benefit order book together with hers.

A year in which a woman has elected reduced liability for contributions cannot be a year of home responsibilities protection.[96] It may be worth revoking such an election (see p2:260).

No year before 6 April 1978 can be a year of home responsibilities protection.

Home responsibilities protection helps towards satisfaction of the second contribution condition for the long-term benefits (see p2:275). Years of home responsibilities protection in which you do not satisfy the contribution conditions are deducted from the number of years for which you would otherwise have to satisfy the contribution conditions.[97]

Example

Florence left school at age 16 in 1976. Because she was born after 6 April 1955, she will reach pensionable age at 65 (see p1:142), ie, in 2025. Her working life for retirement pension purposes will be 49 years and the number of years in which she would normally have to satisfy the contribution conditions is 44 (see below). The effect of home responsibilities protection for 10 complete years of looking after children, and three of looking after a disabled relative receiving attendance allowance (or a similar benefit – see Chapter 5), is to reduce the requisite number of years in which she must satisfy the contribution conditions for a retirement pension on the basis of her own contributions to 31 (ie, 44 – 13).

Home responsibilities protection can reduce the requisite number of years to 20 or half what it would otherwise be, whichever is lower.

4. Contribution conditions for benefit

Contributory benefits have two contribution conditions except maternity allowance and widow's payment. To help you satisfy the second condition, you may be credited with contributions to fill gaps in your record (see p2:266). However, the first contribution condition must always be satisfied by contributions which have actually been paid.

Contribution-based jobseeker's allowance and incapacity benefit

The first condition

You must have actually paid, in one contribution year, the appropriate class of contributions producing an earnings factor (see p2:257) at least 25 times that year's lower earnings limit (eg, £1,550 in 1997/98, 25 times £62),[98] or 25 flat-rate contributions paid before 6 April 1975.[99] For incapacity benefit (IB), they may have been paid in any tax year; but for contribution-based jobseeker's allowance (JSA) they must have been paid in one of the last two complete tax years before the 'relevant benefit year' (see below).

The contributions may be either Class 1 or 2 for IB; they must be Class 1 for contribution-based JSA (except for share fishermen and volunteer development workers, see p2:263).[100] They must be paid before a claim for contribution-based JSA or IB is made.

Benefit years are almost the same as calendar years and run from the first Sunday in January.[101] The 'relevant benefit year' for contribution-based JSA is the benefit year in which the jobseeking period (see p1:274) begins. For IB it is the year in which the period of incapacity for work (see p1:40) begins.[102]

A widow who loses her entitlement to widowed mother's allowance for some reason other than remarriage or cohabitation (ie, because her children grow up) will be deemed to have satisfied this contribution condition (and may well be credited with contributions to satisfy the second condition – see p2:270).[103]

The second condition

You must have either paid or been credited with contributions producing an earnings factor (see p2:257) equal to 50 times the lower earnings limit in each of the last two complete contribution years ending before the relevant benefit year (see above).[104]

Credited contributions will not always help you fulfil the second contribution condition (see p2:266).

In rare cases, the rules about when contributions must have been paid in order to satisfy the second contribution condition may mean that you should delay a claim for contribution-based JSA so that you can draw on a different year's contribution record. This is because the relevant contribution year for contribution-based JSA depends on the benefit year in which the first day of your jobseeking period (see p1:274) falls. Thus, if you claim on or after Monday 4 January 1999, the relevant contribution years for contribution-based JSA purposes will be 1996/97 and 1997/8, whereas if you claim on or after Monday 3 January 2000 they would be 1997/98 and 1998/99.

Any day for which you do not claim does not count as part of your jobseeking period (see p1:274),[105] so it is easy to postpone when that period begins. However, if you claim and are refused benefit because the contribution conditions are not satisfied, your period of interruption of employment will have started.[106] You would then have to stop claiming for more than eight weeks and make a fresh claim after that period. The eight-week gap would break the period of interruption of employment.

Example

During 1996/97, Doug spent time at home looking after his children and has only done paid work and made contributions since April 1997. In 1999, he is made redundant and (after payments in lieu of notice were taken into account), his period of interruption of employment is due to start on 13 December 1999. His wife is in full-time employment so he is not entitled to income support or income-based JSA. It is plainly in his interest to wait until Monday 3 January 2000 before he claims contribution-based JSA.

Maternity allowance

The only contribution condition for maternity allowance is that you must actually have paid Class 1 or Class 2 contributions for at least 26 weeks in the 52 weeks ending at the end of the 15th week before the expected week of confinement (see p1:100). The earnings factor is immaterial, but contributions paid by a married woman or widow at the reduced rate do not count.[107]

Widow's payment

The only contribution condition for widow's payment is that your husband must actually have paid, in any one tax year before his death, contributions of Classes 1, 2 or 3 producing an earnings factor (see p2:257) of at least 25 times the lower earnings limit (eg, £1,600 in 1998/99, 25 times £64).[108]

Any paid contributions may be counted if he became liable to pay contributions only in the tax year in which he died or the previous tax year, or if he had ever successfully claimed contribution-based JSA or IB.[109] The payment of 25 flat-rate contributions in a contribution year prior to 6 April 1975 satisfies this condition.[110]

Widowed mother's allowance, widow's pension and Category A and B retirement pensions

The first condition

The contributor (ie, you for Category A retirement pensions, your late husband for widow's pension and either you, your husband or your late spouse for Category B retirement pensions) must actually have paid in any one tax year before death or pensionable age, contributions with an earnings factor of 52 times that year's lower earnings limit (eg, £3,328 in 1998/99, 52 times £64).[111]

This condition is deemed to be satisfied if the contributor was receiving long-term IB in the year of death or of reaching pensionable age, or in the preceding year.[112] Fifty flat-rate payments in a contribution year before 6 April 1975 also satisfy this condition.[113]

The second condition

The contributor must have paid or been credited with contributions with an earnings factor of at least 52 times that year's lower earnings limit for each of the requisite number of years.[114]

The number of years you need to satisfy this condition depends on the length of your 'working life'. This is the period inclusive of the tax year in which you reach the age of 16 up to but exclusive of the year in which you reach pensionable age or in which you die.[115]

If you were over 16 on 5 July 1948, your working life is taken as having started either on 6 April 1948 or on 6 April of the year between 1936 and 1948 that you first started paying contributions, if you paid contributions before 5 July 1948.[116]

A year of home responsibilities looking after a child or invalid does not count as a year of your working life unless your earnings factor in that year was at least 52 times the lower earnings limit (see p2:257 for exactly how this works).

The requisite number of years is then calculated as follows:[117]

Length of 'working life'	Requisite number of years
1-10 years	Length of working life minus 1
11-20 years	Length of working life minus 2
21-30 years	Length of working life minus 3
31-40 years	Length of working life minus 4
41-50 years	Length of working life minus 5

Since contributions paid before 6 April 1975 do not produce an earnings factor (see p2:257), the number of years before that date in which the contribution condition is satisfied is calculated by adding together all the contributions paid or credited before 6 April 1975, and dividing the answer by 50. If that does not produce a whole number the result is rounded up, as long as that would not produce a number greater than the number of years of the working life before 6 April 1975. A credit is given for each of the 13 weeks between 6 April and 4 July 1948 if those form part of your working life but you did not contribute then.[118]

Example

Gerald reached pensionable age in July 1999. He reached 16 in the year 1950/51 and therefore did not contribute to any pre-1948 scheme. He paid or had credited 1,250 contributions between 1950 and 1975. For every year from 6 April 1975 to 5 April 1999 he paid contributions with earnings factors above the minimum level of 52 times the lower earnings limit. His working life began on 6 April 1950 and ended on 5 April 1999 – a total of 49 years. The requisite number of years is therefore 44. He has satisfied 23 years since 1975. Between 1950 and 1975 he paid or had credited 1,300 contributions, which equals 25 years (1,250 divided by 50). He therefore satisfies the condition for 48 years, four more than the number that he needs.

Widows, widowers and divorcees may be able to combine their own contribution records with those of their late or former spouses in order to claim a Category A retirement pension (see p1:138).

Insufficient contributions

Benefits are paid at a reduced rate if the second contribution condition is not satisfied for the requisite number of years, provided it is satisfied in at least 25 per cent of the requisite number. The benefit is paid at a percentage of the amount which would otherwise be paid; the percentage is calculated by expressing the number of years in which the condition is satisfied as a percentage of the requisite number of years and rounding it up to the nearest whole number.[119] Thus, if you are a widow and your husband's working life was 12 years, so that the requisite number of years is 10, and if he only satisfied the condition in eight years, you receive 80 per cent of the standard rate of widowed mother's allowance.

Increases for adult dependants are reduced in the same proportion, but increases for children are always paid in full.[120]

It may be possible for you to pay voluntary contributions (see p2:264) to bring the number of years in which the second contribution condition is satisfied up to the 25 per cent figure needed for a minimum pension or to enhance the rate at which the pension will be paid. This can be very worthwhile. For example, if you are only one year short of the minimum number of years, payment of £332.80 (52 Class 3 contributions at £6.45 each) may secure you a pension of £16.68 a week (66.75 x 25 per cent) uprated annually for the rest of your life. You will get your money back in a little over 20 weeks.

Notes

. . . .

References are to statutes and regulations as amended up to 8 March 1999. All regulations are (General) Regulations unless otherwise stated. There is a full list of abbreviations in Appendix 13.

1. Introduction

1 s1(1) SSCBA 1992; s162 SSAA 1992
2 s1(2) SSCBA 1992
3 s21(1) and (2) SSCBA 1992
4 s2(1)(a) SSCBA 1992
5 s2(1)(b) SSCBA 1992
6 *Ready Mixed Concrete South East Ltd v Ministry of Pensions and National Insurance* [1968] 2 QB 497 (QBD); *Global Plant v Secretary of State for Health and Social Security* [1971] 3 All ER 385 (QBD)
7 Sch 1 paras 1-5 SS(CatE) Regs
8 Sch 1 para 6 SS(CatE) Regs
9 Sch 1 paras 7-12 SS(CatE) Regs
10 s21(5)(d) SSCBA 1992
11 s5(1) SSCBA 1992
12 Sch 1 SS(EF) Regs as amended
13 s17(1)(b) SSAA 1992; and see generally *Secretary of State v Scully, Independent,* 22 June 1992 and *Welfare Rights Bulletin 109* (August 1992), p10

2. Payment of contributions

14 ss6(1)(a) and 13(1) SSCBA 1992; reg 60 SS(Con) Regs
15 s6(2) SSCBA 1992; reg 58 SS(Con) Regs but see discussion on 'autocredits' in section 3 below
16 *Equal Opportunities Commission v Secretary of State for Social Security,* ECJ Case C-9/91, reported at [1992] 3 CMLR 233
17 s2(1)(a) SSCBA 1992
18 Reg 119(1)(a) SS(Con) Regs
19 Reg 119(2) SS(Con) Regs
20 Reg 119(3) SS(Con) Regs
21 Reg 120 SS(Con) Regs
22 Reg 120(2)(b) SS(Con) Regs
23 s2(1)(b) SSCBA 1992; reg 119(1)(d) SS(Con) Regs
24 Reg 119(1)(c) SS(Con) Regs

25 Regs 121 and 122 SS(Con) Regs
26 Reg 123A SS(Con) Regs
27 Regs 119(1)(e), 120(2)(b), 121 and 122 SS(Con) Regs
28 Reg 58(b) SS(Con) Regs
29 Reg 100 SS(Con) Regs
30 s22(4) SSCBA 1992; regs 5(2), 7(3), 7A(2)(b), 8(2)(b), 8A(5)(e) and 9(6) SS(Cr) Regs as amended
31 Reg 103 SS(Con) Regs
32 Reg 101(1) SS(Con) Regs as amended
33 ss6 and 7 SSCBA 1992
34 Regs 8(2) and 8A(2) SS(Con) Regs
35 s8(1) and (2) SSCBA 1992
36 s27 SSPA 1975 as amended (not consolidated); para 2(a) SS(CICCP)O
37 s3 SSA 1986 (not consolidated)
38 s3 SSPA 1975 as amended (not consolidated); reg 104 SS(Con) Regs
39 Regs 89 and 115 SS(Con) Regs as amended
40 Regs 10, 11, 12, 12A and 17 SS(Con) Regs as amended
41 Reg 17 SS(Con) Regs
42 Regs 10, 11, 12 and 12A SS(Con) Regs as amended. There are also special rules which affect some people who work for agencies and for barristers' clerks and some ministers of religion.
43 If the rule did not exist, employers could (for example) set up five different companies and have Company A employ you on Monday, Company B on Tuesday and so on. In many cases, this would mean that there would be no liability to pay contributions (and no entitlement to contributory benefits) because your earnings

with each individual company would be below the lower earnings limit.

44 s9(2), (3) and (4) SSCBA 1992

45 s27(2) SSPA 1975 (not consolidated); para 2(b) SS(CICCP)O

46 Sch 1 para 3 SSCBA 1992

47 s1(2) SSCBA 1992

48 s11 SSCBA 1992

49 s11(5) SSCBA 1992

50 Reg 25 SS(Con) Regs

51 Reg 26 SS(Con) Regs

52 s11(1) SSCBA 1992 as amended

53 Regs 98 and 123A-F SS(Con) Regs; reg 2 SS(Con) Amdt 4 Regs; reg 13B SSB(PA) Regs as amended

54 Reg 17 SS(Con) Regs as amended

55 Reg 26A SS(Con) Regs as amended

56 s13 SSCBA 1992

57 s14 SSCBA 1992

58 Reg 34 SS(Con) Regs

59 s13(1) SSCBA 1992 as amended

60 s15(1) and (3) SSCBA 1992

61 Regs 62-66 SS(Con) Regs as amended

62 Reg 67 SS(Con) Regs as amended

63 s114 SSAA 1992

64 s8 ERA 1996

65 s13 ERA 1996. However, as with all disputes with your employer, you should remember that not all employees have a right not to be unfairly dismissed and that, even if you have that right, compensation for unfair dismissal may be a poor second to keeping your job.

66 Reg 39 SS(Con) Regs

67 Reg 39 SS(Con) Regs

68 Reg 38 SS(Con) Regs

69 Reg 27(3)(b) SS(Con) Regs as amended

70 Reg 38(5) and (6) SS(Con) Regs as amended

71 Reg 43 SS(Con) Regs

3. **Credits and home responsibilities protection**

72 More accurately, contributions with an earnings factor of at least 52 times the lower earnings limit for the year in question (or 50 flat-rate pre-1975 contributions).

73 This does not apply if the contributor was receiving long-term IB in the year s/he reached pensionable age (or died) or the preceding year. See Sch 3 para 5(6) SSCBA 1992.

74 Reg 3 SS(Cr) Regs as amended

75 Regs 5(2), 7(3), 7A(2)(b), 8(2)(b), 9B(3) and 9C(3) SS(Cr) Regs as amended

76 Regs 8A and 8B SS(Cr) Regs as amended

77 Reg 8B(4)(b) SS(Cr) Regs as amended

78 Technically, the claim could be received up to the Saturday but DSS offices do not open on Saturdays. On the principle of R(SB) 8/89, it is arguable that the claim would be in time if received by the following Monday.

79 Reg 8A(5) SS(Cr) Regs as amended

80 Reg 9 SS(Cr) Regs as amended

81 Reg 7A SS(Cr) Regs as amended

82 Reg 4 SS(Cr) Regs

83 Reg 8 SS(Cr) Regs

84 Reg 7 SS(Cr) Regs

85 Reg 9C SS(Cr) Regs as amended

86 Reg 9B SS(Cr) Regs as amended

87 Reg 3(1)(b) SSB(MW&WSP) Regs

88 Reg 3(1)(a) SSB(MW&WSP) Regs

89 *Equal Opportunities Commission v Secretary of State for Social Security*, ECJ, Case C-9/91, reported at [1992] 3 CMLR 233

90 Reg 9A SS(Cr) Regs as amended

91 Regs 7B and 7C SS(Cr) Regs

92 Reg 7C(5) SS(Cr) Regs

93 Reg 7C(3) SS(Cr) Regs

94 Reg 7C(4)(b) SS(Cr) Regs

95 Reg 2(2) and (3) SSP(HR) Regs

96 Sch 3 para 5(7) SSCBA 1992

97 Sch 3 para 5(7)(a) SSCBA 1992

4. Contribution conditions for benefit

98 s21 and Sch 3 paras 1 and 2 SSCBA 1992
99 Reg 15 SS(STB)(T) Regs
100 s21(1) and (2) SSCBA 1992
101 s21(6) SSCBA 1992
102 Sch 3 paras 1(6) and 2(6) SSCBA 1992
103 Reg 3(1) SSB(MW&WSP) Regs as amended
104 s21 and Sch 3 paras 1 and 2 SSCBA 1992
105 Reg 47(3)(a) JSA Regs
106 CS/174/1949; R(U) 13/80
107 Sch 3 para 3 SSCBA 1992
108 Sch 3 para 4 SSCBA 1992
109 Sch 3 para 7 SSCBA 1992
110 Reg 13(1) SS(STB)(T) Regs
111 Sch 3 para 5 SSCBA 1992
112 Sch 3 para 5(6) SSCBA 1992
113 Reg 6 SS(WBRP&OB)(T) Regs
114 Sch 3 para 5 SSCBA 1992
115 Sch 3 para 5(8) SSCBA 1992
116 Reg 7(7) SS(WBRP&OB)(T) Regs; s20 Sch 3 para 5(5) SSCBA 1992
117 Sch 3 para 5(5) SSCBA 1992
118 Reg 7(7) SS(WBRP&OB)(T) Regs
119 Reg 6 SS(WB&RP) Regs
120 s60(4)-(6) SSCBA 1992; regs 13 and 14 SSB(Dep) Regs as amended; reg 6(2) SS(WB&RP) Regs

Chapter 43

. . . .

Equal treatment

This chapter covers:
1. The principle of equal treatment (p2:281)
2. The material scope of the Directive (p2:282)
3. The personal scope of the Directive (p2:282)
4. Exceptions to the principle of equal treatment (p2:283)
5. The effect of the principle of equal treatment on British social security benefits (p2:285)

Social security benefits are not governed by British law alone. There are also Regulations and Directives made by the European Community which apply directly in the UK and throughout the European Economic Area (EEA) (see p2:223).

In particular, there are a number of Directives which are designed to ensure that (subject to limited exceptions which are kept under review) social security benefits, occupational pensions, pay and other benefits from employment are received on an equal basis by both men and women.

British courts (including adjudication officers, tribunals and social security commissioners) are obliged to apply EC law as well as domestic British law and although British law has been amended to take these Directives into account, the EC rules override the British rules where the two still conflict.[1] Cases which involve new points of EC law may be referred to the European Court of Justice (ECJ) in Luxembourg, for a ruling.

There has been a vast amount of caselaw in the ECJ and national courts on these anti-discrimination provisions and a book the length of this *Handbook* could not begin to cover the subject comprehensively.[2] What follows is an outline of the general principles and a discussion of what these mean in practical terms for people claiming non-means-tested benefits. If you think there is a chance that you may benefit from the principle of equal treatment, there is no substitute for getting proper advice on the particular circumstances of your claim. See Appendix 2 for the names and addresses of organisations which may be able to help you with this.

For non-means-tested benefits the most important Directive is the Council Directive of 19 December 1978 on the progressive implementation of the principle of equal treatment for men and women in matters of social security.[3] This Directive, which became binding on all Member States on 22

December 1984, has direct effect. This means that individual citizens of the EEA countries can rely on it to claim benefits from their governments on a non-discriminatory basis even if those governments have not introduced national legislation putting the Directive into operation or if they have implemented it only in part.

1. **The principle of equal treatment**

The 'Principle of Equal Treatment' established by the Directive is that:

> There shall be no discrimination whatsoever on ground of sex either directly, or indirectly by reference in particular to marital or family status ...[4]

Discrimination simply means treating one person less favourably than another. Indirect discrimination occurs when a rule appears to be neutral but in practice can be complied with by fewer members of one sex than the other and that rule cannot be justified for reasons other than discrimination based on sex.

For example, a rule which said that applicants for a job had to be at least 6'3" tall would be indirectly discriminatory even though it applied equally to women and men. This is because, in practice, fewer women than men would qualify. Such a rule would be unlawful unless the employer could show a good, non-discriminatory, reason for employing only tall people.

It is often necessary to rely on statistical evidence to prove indirect discrimination. Governments may not rely upon purely financial reasons to justify a discriminatory practice.[5]

The principle of equal treatment only prohibits discrimination 'on ground of sex'. It does not prevent a government from discriminating on the ground of marital or family status unless that amounts to a form of indirect discrimination on the ground of sex. So a rule is not necessarily contrary to the Directive just because it differentiates between married (or cohabiting) people and single people.[6] On the other hand, a rule which differentiates between married men and married women or single men and single women is directly discriminatory on grounds of sex.

If the principle of equal treatment applies to you, then your claim for benefit should be decided using the rules which would have applied had you been a member of the opposite sex where those rules would be more favourable.[7]

However, this broad general principle is subject to a number of limitations and to exceptions (known as 'derogations'). In practice this means that you have to ask three questions before you can know whether the principle of equal treatment applies in your case:

- Is the benefit you are claiming (or your liability to pay contributions) covered by the Directive? Only schemes for benefits which cover certain risks (see below) are subject to the principle of equal treatment. This is sometimes referred to as the material scope (or *scope rationae materiae*) of the Directive.
- Does the Directive apply to you? You are only entitled to benefit from the principle of equal treatment if you are a member of the working population (see p2:283). This is sometimes referred to as the personal scope (or *scope rationae personae*) of the Directive.
- Does the Directive include a derogation which applies in your case? If so, the government is allowed to discriminate against you even if you are within both the personal and material scope of the Directive.

2. **The material scope of the Directive**

The Directive applies to schemes for state benefits which are designed to protect against the following risks:[8]

- sickness;
- invalidity;
- old age;
- accidents at work and occupational diseases;
- unemployment.

This means that all the benefits discussed in Chapters 2-19 (except for maternity benefits and widows' benefits[9]) are covered by the Directive.

The Directive also applies to means-tested benefits (referred to as social assistance) to the extent that they are intended to supplement or replace the schemes referred to above.[10] For example, income-based jobseeker's allowance should be covered as an unemployment type benefit.[11]

The fact that the Directive applies only to state schemes means that other schemes (such as occupational pensions schemes) are beyond its scope. These are, however, covered by a later Directive[12] which is in similar terms.

3. **The personal scope of the Directive**

The Directive applies to you if you are a member of the working population. If you are not a member of the working population then you cannot use the Directive to stop the government discriminating against you even if the benefit which you are claiming is within the material scope of the Directive.

The working population is defined as being:[13]
- workers (ie, people in employment);
- the self-employed;
- people seeking employment;
- workers and self-employed people whose jobs have been interrupted by illness, accident or involuntary unemployment;
- workers and self-employed people who have retired or become unable to work because of invalidity.

This means that to be covered by the Directive you must have been either working or actively looking for work when you became affected by one of the risks set out on p2:282.[14] So, for example, the Directive does not apply to you if:
- you have been so ill or disabled since before you reached the age of 16 that you have never been able to contemplate working or looking for work; *or*
- you stopped working for a reason which is not included in the list of risks on p2:282 (eg, because you were pregnant) and before you began to look for work again you became too ill to work.

It is not, however, necessary for the risks to be suffered by you personally. In one case, a woman who gave up work to look after her severely disabled mother was held to be a member of the working population because her work had been interrupted by invalidity, even though it was the invalidity of her mother and not her own personal invalidity.[15]

4. **Exceptions to the principle of equal treatment**

The Directive permits Member States to adopt or continue discriminatory rules on certain aspects of entitlement to benefits even if they are within its material scope.

The types of discriminatory rule which may be lawful are:[16]
- rules which set a different age for men and women to become entitled to retirement pensions. This derogation also covers rules which deal with the possible consequences for other benefits of having a differential pensionable age;
- rules which allow people who have looked after children to claim retirement pensions and other benefits on advantageous terms. In Britain, this derogation would seem to permit the rules about home responsibilities protection (see p2:271) which discriminate indirectly against men;
- rules which allow wives to derive entitlement to old age pensions and incapacity benefits on the basis of their husbands' contributions or periods of

insurance. This permits the British rules on Category B and C retirement pensions which discriminate directly against men;

- rules which cover increases for a dependent wife of incapacity benefits, retirement pensions and industrial injuries benefits. This allows the discrimination in the different rules for dependency increases in Category A retirement pensions (see p1:138);
- rules which allow special treatment for people who before 22 December 1984 have opted 'not to acquire rights or incur obligations under a statutory scheme'. This is intended to cover the British rules on the married woman's reduced national insurance contribution (see p2:260).

The derogations should not be regarded as a carte blanche to discriminate. As part of the progressive implementation of the principle of equal treatment, European Economic Area States are supposed to keep these discriminatory rules under review to ensure that they are still justified in the light of social developments[17] and to notify the European Commission of the measures that they have taken so to do.[18]

Perhaps more importantly, the European Court of Justice has repeatedly held that the elimination of discrimination based on sex is a fundamental right which it has a duty to protect. In the past it has therefore scrutinised the validity of rules which rely on the derogations very carefully to ensure that the principle of proportionality is observed.[19]

This meant that it did not follow that a discriminatory rule was lawful just because it had one of the effects allowed by the derogations. In each case it was for the government of the Member State which made the rule to establish that the discriminatory means which it adopted were an appropriate way of achieving the ends permitted by the derogation.

One case suggests that the principle of proportionality will not be applied in the future and that where the discrimination is within the wording of the derogation, the principle of proportionality has no application to it.[20] This is contrary to the earlier caselaw and may have been prompted by the particular facts of that case (which the Court saw as threatening the implementation of the principle of equal treatment by making it impossible for states to abolish discrimination in the areas covered by the derogations a little at a time[21]). It therefore remains to be seen what attitude the Court will take on this point in other cases.

5. The effect of the principle of equal treatment on British social security benefits

The principle of equal treatment has had a significant impact on claimants' entitlement to non-means-tested benefits. Even before the Directive came into force, many discriminatory rules about entitlement to benefit were abolished in order to comply with Britain's community obligations. Since December 1984, the Directive has been used by the European Court of Justice (ECJ) to extend entitlement for many women by overruling many discriminatory laws which still remained.

For British social security law, the most important issue has been the scope of the derogation for 'the possible consequences' for other benefits of different retirement ages,[22] ie, whether it is lawful to withdraw or reduce earnings replacement benefits (eg, contribution-based jobseeker's allowance (JSA), incapacity benefit (IB), severe disablement allowance (SDA), invalid carer's allowance (ICA) and reduced earning allowance (REA)) when a claimant reaches pensionable age with the effect – in most cases – that women are denied benefits which would be paid to a man of the same age.

It is clear that not just any connection between a benefit and pensionable age is sufficient for the derogation to apply. To take a far-fetched example, a country could not (say) pay contribution-based JSA to women aged over 20 while making men wait until they were 25 and then justify the discrimination against men by claiming that the qualifying age was pensionable age less 40 years. The question is how close the link must be before it is covered by the derogation.

This question has been the subject of three decisions of the ECJ in the *Thomas* and *Equal Opportunities Commission (EOC)* cases[23] and, most recently, in the *Graham*[24] case. In the *Thomas* case the Court ruled that different pensionable ages for men and women in non-contributory benefits such as ICA and SDA was contrary to EC Directive 79/7 and therefore unlawful. As a result, British law was amended to bring the rules on non-contributory benefits into line with the law as declared by the ECJ.

In the *EOC* case, the Court held that inequality with respect to the number of contributions required to be paid in order to gain entitlement to a full retirement pension was justified. Men could be required to pay contributions for 44 years but women only 39 years for the same amount of benefit.

The decision in the *Graham* case was that the DSS could lawfully:
* reduce invalidity benefit (now abolished) to pension rate at 60 for women and 65 for men;
* take invalidity benefit away altogether from women at 60 and men at 65; *and*

43

Chapter 43: Equal treatment
5. The effect of the principle of equal treatment on British social security benefits

- pay extra benefit to men who became incapable of work between the ages of 55 and 60 and not to women in the same position.

Although the Court's reasoning is wholly unconvincing,[25] there is no appeal against a decision of the ECJ so there can be no doubt that the *Graham* decision is an effective statement of the law. There is also no realistic doubt that the reasoning in *Graham* also applies to IB (which replaced invalidity benefit) and contribution-based JSA.

The combined effect of the *Thomas, EOC* and *Graham* cases is that, in order to be covered by the derogation for 'the possible consequences for other benefits' of setting different pensionable ages for men and women, the discriminatory rule must be necessary *either*:
- to avoid disturbing the financial equilibrium of the social security system; *or*
- to ensure coherence between the retirement pension scheme and other benefit schemes.

Applying these tests, the Court has held (in general terms) that for contributory benefits (*Graham*) or the liability to pay national insurance contributions (*EOC*), a discriminatory link to pensionable age is lawful but for non-contributory benefits (*Thomas*) such discrimination is unlawful. For a list of which benefits are contributory and which non-contributory see p1:4.

In the light of this, the status of the discriminatory rules on REA (see p1:217) is unclear. REA is not strictly contributory although the requirement that the claimant must have been an 'employed earner' at the time of the industrial accident or the onset of the prescribed disease means that in practice many REA claimants would actually have been paying, or liable to pay, Class 1 contributions.[26] A reference to the ECJ has been made in five test cases seeking a preliminary ruling on whether the different cut off ages for male and female REA claimants infringe the Equal Treatment Directive and if so what the consequences are.[27]

Those affected are women aged between 60 and 65 whose REA is stopped because they are regarded as having 'given up regular employment'.
- Men, who, if they were women, would be entitled to frozen REA for life and who are therefore now worse off since the definition of 'regular employment' was changed on 24 March 1996.
- Women who are on a life award of frozen REA and who are therefore better off than the men above but are nevertheless worse off than they were before they reached 60.

You should appeal on the grounds that this is contrary to the Directive. You need to argue that REA should be treated as a non-contributory benefit because it has no contribution conditions and that, as with ICA or SDA, it is not 'necessary to ensure coherence' between the contributory pension scheme and the industrial injuries scheme, for REA to be withdrawn from women at 60 rather than at 65. You should also seek advice (see Appendix 2).

Notes

. . . .

References are to statutes and regulations as amended up to 8 March 1999. All regulations are (General) Regulations unless otherwise stated. There is a full list of abbreviations in Appendix 13.

1 s2 ECA 1972
2 For a detailed account see *Equal Treatment Between Women and Men in Social Security*, McCrudden, ed Butterworths (1994)
3 Directive 79/7/EEC (*Official Journal of the European Communities* (OJ) No. L6, 10 January 1979, p24)

1. The principle of equal treatment
4 Art 4(1) Directive 79/7/EEC
5 C-343/92, *M. A. De Weerd (núe Roks) & Others v Bestuur van de Bedrijfsvereniging voor de Gezondhid, Geestelijke en Maatschappenlijke Belangen & Others*
6 eg, *Blaik v Department of Health & Social Security*, (CA) 19 July 1990
7 eg, C-286/85, *Cotter and McDermott v Minister for Social Welfare and Another*

2. The material scope of the Directive
8 Art 3(1)(a) Directive 79/7/EEC
9 Art 3(2) Directive 79/7/EEC
10 Art 3(1)(b) Directive 79/7/EEC
11 The UK Government dispute that income-based JSA falls within the scope of the Directive and the point has yet to be challenged.
12 Directive 86/378/EEC (OJ No. L225, 12 August 1986, p40)

3. The personal scope of the Directive
13 Art 2 Directive 79/7/EEC
14 C-48/88, C-106-107/88, *Achterberg-te Riele & others v Social Verzekeingsbank*
15 *Drake v Chief Adjudication Officer* ECJ Case No.150/85

4. Exceptions to the principle of equal treatment
16 Art 7(1) Directive 79/7/EEC
17 Art 7(2) Directive 79/7/EEC
18 Art 8(2) Directive 79/7/EEC
19 *Johnston v Chief Constable of the Royal Ulster Constabulary* (ECJ) [1986] ECR 723
20 C-420/92, *Bramhill v Chief Adjudication Officer*, para 23 of Judgment dated 7 July 1994
21 *See note 21,* para 21

5. The effect of the principle of equal treatment on British social security benefits
22 Art 7(1)(a) Directive 79/7/EEC
23 *R v Secretary of State for Social Security ex parte Equal Opportunities Commission*, ECJ Case C-9/91
24 *Secretary of State for Social Security and Chief Adjudication Officer v Rose Graham*, ECJ Case C-92/94 (11 August 1995)
25 It is interesting to compare the Court's decision with the opinion of the Advocate-General in the same case.
26 It is possible to be an employed earner but not liable to pay national insurance contributions if you are in part-time or low-paid work and earn less than the lower earnings limit – see Chapter 12.
27 C-196/98, *Hepple and Others v CAO*

Chapter 44

Maintenance

This chapter is about maintenance and how this affects your entitlement to benefit. It covers:
1. Getting maintenance (below)
2. Child support maintenance (p2:292)
3. How maintenance affects your income support and income-based jobseeker's allowance (p2:303)
4. How maintenance affects your family credit, disability working allowance, housing benefit and council tax benefit (p2:311)
5. Benefits if you are contributing to someone's maintenance (p2:313)

This chapter tells you how to go about getting maintenance for you and your child(ren) and the effect any maintenance payments have on your means-tested benefits. For:
- income support (IS) see p2:303;
- jobseeker's allowance (JSA) see p2:303;
- family credit (FC) see p2:311;
- disability working allowance (DWA) see p2:311;
- housing benefit (HB) see p2:313; *and*
- council tax benefit (CTB) see p2:313.

Some of the provisions affect sponsors who have signed undertakings to maintain people from abroad; the implications for them are dealt with on p2:290.

This chapter also covers the benefits you might get if you are contributing to the maintenance of a child or a person caring for a child (see p2:313).

1. Getting maintenance

If you have separated from your partner or from the other parent of your child(ren) you might be able to get maintenance. You are entitled to maintenance payments for your child(ren) whether or not you were married and possibly for yourself if you were married. You are required to apply for child support maintenance if you claim IS, income-based JSA, FC or DWA, unless you are exempt (see p2:293). The maintenance you get affects your means-tested benefits (see pp2:303, 2:311 and 2:313).

For information about the rules about maintenance for children under the Child Support Act 1991 see p2:292. These are covered where they affect your right to benefit or the amount to which you are entitled. For further information about the child support scheme, see CPAG's *Child Support Handbook*.

Payments of maintenance for yourself could be on a voluntary basis or under a court order. Detailed advice about maintenance orders is beyond the scope of this *Handbook*. You should see a solicitor for advice about these. If you are on a low income you can apply for legal aid for court proceedings. In addition, you can get free advice from a solicitor under what is known as the Green Form scheme.

While you are on IS or income-based JSA, certain people are 'liable to maintain' you or your children. For further information, see p2:290. In some cases, the Benefits Agency can take action to obtain maintenance from them on your behalf (see p2:291).

If you are on IS, income-based JSA, FC, DWA, HB or CTB, voluntary payments from your former partner or the parent of your child(ren) are dealt with under the maintenance rules in this chapter and *not* under the normal rules on charitable and voluntary payments (see p2:412).[1]

Note: If you have been getting child maintenance (see p1:598) and you or your partner start working full time (see p2:5) or increase your earnings and stop getting IS or income-based JSA, you might be able to get a child maintenance bonus (see p1:598).

Amount of maintenance

The Child Support Agency (CSA) have a rigid formula for calculating **child support maintenance.** However, departures from the formula are allowed in certain circumstances, for example, where you or a non-resident parent have a disabled child or where a non-resident parent's travel costs to see your child(ren) are expensive or if a parent's life style is more extravagant than her/his declared income allows. See the *Child Support Handbook* for an explanation of the formula and details of the departure rules.

There is more flexibility about how much **maintenance your spouse is required to pay for you.** S/he can negotiate with the Benefits Agency to pay an amount s/he can afford given her/his outgoings. As a starting point for negotiations, the Benefits Agency compares your spouse's net income with the total of:[2]

- the IS personal allowances and premiums s/he would qualify for if entitled to IS (see Chapter 45);
- household expenses including rent, mortgage and council tax (excluding arrears);

- 15 per cent of her/his net wage (to cover expenses for work); *and*
- the balance of any other expenses exceeding the 15 per cent margin that are considered essential.

If your spouse has a new partner, two calculations are performed – one as if s/he was single and the other using joint incomes. The lower figure is used as the basis for negotiation.

If the Benefits Agency feels that your spouse is not paying enough it has the right to take her/him to court (see p2:291).

Who is 'liable to maintain' you while you are on income support or income-based jobseeker's allowance?

If someone is 'liable to maintain' you or your child(ren), s/he must pay maintenance. The Secretary of State can take proceedings against anyone who has a liability to maintain you or your child(ren) while you are on IS or income-based JSA. If that person fails to maintain you or your children, s/he can be prosecuted (see p2:291).

While you are on IS or income-based JSA:
- **You** must be maintained by your spouse, if you are married or separated.[3] If you have to live apart from your spouse because you need care or treatment (eg, in hospital, or in a residential or nursing home) you may be assessed and paid as separate individuals for benefit purposes (see p2:119). However, your spouse is still 'liable to maintain' you and may be asked to make a financial contribution towards your care.

While you are on IS:
- **Your child(ren)** must be maintained by both their parents.[4] A parent is not 'liable to maintain' children over 16 who are independent or any children over the age of 19.
- If you are a '**person from abroad**', you must be maintained by a sponsor who has given an undertaking to support you (see p2:209). This includes your ex-spouse after you are divorced.

Your right to claim benefit is not affected by the fact that the Benefits Agency can get money back from someone who is liable to maintain you. You should therefore not be refused IS or income-based JSA while maintenance is being pursued. However, maintenance that is recovered might affect your benefit (see p2:203).

Note: A parent who does not live with the person who is looking after her/his child(ren) is expected to pay child support maintenance on a regular basis to that person.[5] If you are the parent looking after the child(ren) and claiming IS, income-based JSA, FC or DWA you are required to apply for this maintenance unless you are exempt (see p2:294). However, you can opt not to apply for maintenance and have your benefit paid at a reduced rate (but see p2:298 before you decide to do this).

Prosecution

A person who is 'liable to maintain' you or your child(ren) (see above) can be prosecuted if IS or income-based JSA is paid as a result of her/his persistently refusing or neglecting to pay maintenance. You can even be prosecuted for failing to maintain yourself (this is uncommon). Although the power remains in respect of children, it is very unlikely to be used given that child maintenance is now being dealt with by the CSA (see p2:292). In either case, the maximum penalty is three months' imprisonment or a fine of £2,500 or both.[6] If you are charged with such an offence, see a solicitor. Legal aid may be available to help meet the cost.

Maintenance orders

While you are on IS or income-based JSA, the Secretary of State can take proceedings against anyone who is 'liable to maintain' you or your child(ren) (see p2:290) if s/he fails to do so. This enables the Benefits Agency to pursue maintenance on your behalf while you are on IS or income-based JSA. However, the Benefits Agency says it does not intend to use these rules to seek maintenance for your children. Instead, you can apply for child support maintenance (see p2:292).

The magistrates' court can make an order telling the person who is liable what s/he has to pay.[7] The fact that there was an agreement that you would not ask for maintenance is not a bar to an order being made,[8] although all the circumstances must be taken into account.[9] The court is entitled to refuse to make an order for maintenance if you have been guilty of adultery, cruelty or desertion.[10]

Since 5 April 1993, the courts have not had the power to make new orders for maintenance for children, other than consent orders.[11] Instead, you can apply for child support maintenance (see p2:292).

Collection of maintenance by the Benefits Agency

While you are on IS or income-based JSA, if maintenance is payable through a magistrates' court (including orders made in the county court or High Court but registered in the magistrates' court) it can be paid direct to the Benefits Agency.[12] In return, the Benefits Agency pays you the amount of IS or income-based JSA you would receive if no maintenance was being paid. The Benefits Agency does not usually accept this sort of arrangement unless payments have actually been missed, but may if you have a good reason for wanting it done and you explain why.

Collection of child support maintenance by the Child Support Agency

Child support maintenance (see below) can be paid to the CSA rather than direct to you as the person looking after the child(ren), if the Secretary of State agrees.[13] If you want this to happen, ask the CSA. You can request this on the maintenance application form or at a later date. This is useful where maintenance payments are likely to be irregular or unreliable, or where you do not want to be located by the other party. If the CSA is collecting the payments for you, enforcement action should begin automatically when a payment is missed. Where payment should be made direct to you, it is up to you to contact the CSA and the Benefits Agency when a maintenance payment does not arrive.

If you are on IS or income-based JSA and your child(ren)'s other parent is making payments to the CSA, your child support maintenance is paid in the same order book/girocheque as your IS or income-based JSA. The CSA retains the payments made by the non-resident parent. If the Agency does not receive your child support maintenance payment, you can still cash the full amount of IS or income-based JSA.

2. **Child support maintenance**

You should look at this section if you do not live with your child(ren)'s other parent and are claiming (or thinking about claiming):
- income support (IS);
- income-based jobseeker's allowance (JSA);
- family credit (FC); *or*
- disability working allowance (DWA).

Maintenance for children is dealt with by the Child Support Agency (CSA) and is called child support maintenance. If you are getting maintenance for a child under a voluntary agreement or court order, this can continue until the CSA takes on your case. If you want to apply for child support maintenance and have not been approached by the CSA, you can request a maintenance application form.

If you are a lone parent or are looking after children on your own, and claim or are paid IS, income-based JSA, FC or DWA, you must apply to the Child Support Agency (CSA) for a maintenance assessment unless you are exempt (see p2:293). Maintenance you receive counts as income when calculating your benefit. However, if you are claiming FC, DWA, housing benefit (HB) or council tax benefit (CTB), £15 is disregarded (see p2:311). Your benefit claim should not be held up by the CSA, but failure to apply for child support maintenance could affect the amount of benefit you receive (see p2:294). The CSA may collect other types of maintenance at the same time as child support maintenance.[14]

A child must be maintained by both parents (see p2:290). If you are a child's non-resident parent (sometimes called an absent parent – see p2:301) and are on IS or JSA, a deduction is made from your benefit as a contribution towards your child's maintenance (see pp2:301-303).

The CSA assessment overrides any previous maintenance agreement you have for your child(ren), including a court order.

Note: Working families tax credit and disabled person's tax credit are due to replace family credit and disability working allowance in October 1999 (see pp1:489 and 1:490). The Government says that people getting these tax credits will not have to apply to the CSA for a maintenance assessment.

Pursuing maintenance

On your claim form, you are asked if any child for whom you are claiming has another parent who does not normally live with you. If so, you are asked whether you are willing, if required, to authorise the CSA to pursue child support maintenance on your behalf (the 'requirement to co-operate' – see below). If you think you or your child(ren) would be at risk of harm or undue distress were you required to co-operate (see p2:295), there is a space on the form for you to say so. You are given time (currently 14 days) to decide what you want to do.

If you are making a new claim for **IS or income-based JSA** and are not getting child support maintenance currently – unless you have indicated there is a risk of harm or undue distress (see p2:295) – you are visited by an officer of the Benefits Agency. If you said on your form that you are willing to authorise the CSA to pursue maintenance, s/he helps you complete a maintenance application form. Otherwise, s/he explains your obligations and how to claim exemption (see p2:294). You are given more time to decide what you want to do if you need this. After 14 days, an officer of the Benefits Agency visits you again. If you think there is a risk of harm or undue distress, a Benefits Agency officer interviews you.

If you are making a new claim for **FC or DWA** and are not currently getting child support maintenance, the Benefits Agency notifies the CSA, who send you a form to complete. If you are willing to authorise the CSA to pursue maintenance, you are sent an application form to complete. However, if you indicate there is a risk of harm or undue distress (see p2:295) you are interviewed either by telephone or in person. If you prefer to be interviewed in person you can request this.

It is a child support officer who decides if you are required to co-operate. See CPAG's *Child Support Handbook* for full details of the child support scheme.

The requirement to co-operate

If you are claiming IS, income-based JSA, FC or DWA the Secretary of State may require you to apply for child support maintenance from your child(ren)'s other parent (the absent parent) where you are living apart and you have care of your child(ren) for at least part of the week[15] (see the *Child Support Handbook* for details of shared care situations). This is what is known as the 'requirement to co-operate' with the CSA. You are required to:
- authorise the CSA to pursue child support maintenance for your child(ren) (see below); *and*
- provide information and evidence to the CSA (see p2:295).

You are generally required to apply for child support maintenance. However:
- the Secretary of State has the discretion not to require you to co-operate and must consider the welfare of any children involved;[16]
- you can be exempt from the requirement to co-operate where you or your child(ren) would be put at risk of suffering '**harm or undue distress**' if you gave your authorisation for child support maintenance to be pursued (see p2:295).

The requirement to co-operate applies not only to lone parents, but also to couples where any of the children in the family has a parent who is living elsewhere. It even applies if you are not receiving any benefit for the child (see p2:321).[17] The requirement does not apply where a child lives with neither parent. In this case, an application for child support maintenance from the person looking after the child is voluntary.

Refusal to co-operate with the Child Support Agency

If you refuse to authorise the CSA to seek maintenance for your child(ren) or to provide information to help them do so (see p2:295), your benefit (IS, income-based JSA, FC or DWA) may be paid at a reduced rate (see p2:297).[18] However, your benefit claim must still be processed by the Benefits Agency. You do not need to withdraw your benefit claim to avoid child support maintenance being pursued. If you do not want to apply for child support maintenance, do not sign the maintenance application form.

If you or your child(ren) would be at risk of 'harm of undue distress', you should be notified in writing if you are required to co-operate. In this case, your benefit should not be paid at a reduced rate.

Providing authorisation

Unless you have given the CSA details of a risk of 'harm or undue distress' (see below), if you claim IS, income-based JSA, FC or DWA you are asked to complete a child support maintenance application form. If you sign the form, you are giving your authorisation to the CSA to pursue child support maintenance. Without your signature, the CSA cannot take any action to pursue maintenance. **Do not sign the maintenance application form unless you are sure that you want to apply for child support maintenance.** You can opt not to authorise the CSA to pursue maintenance but your benefit may be paid at a reduced rate (see p2:298).

If you are looking after children who have different parents, see the *Child Support Handbook.*

Withdrawing authorisation

If you sign the maintenance application form and later find that you or your children are at risk of 'harm or undue distress' (see below) as a result of the maintenance assessment, you can ask the CSA to stop pursuing maintenance.[19]

The CSA goes through the same procedure as if you had refused to co-operate at the beginning. If the child support officer decides you are no longer required to co-operate (see p2:294), the CSA must stop pursuing the maintenance. Otherwise, the CSA continues to act on the original authorisation and pursues the maintenance. You do not have the option of having your benefit paid at a reduced rate (see p2:298) at this stage. You may want to contact your MP for support.

Providing information

Unless you or your child(ren) would be at risk of harm or undue distress (see below), as well as providing authorisation (see above) you must provide information and evidence to enable the CSA to trace your child(ren)'s absent parent and to assess and collect child support maintenance.[20] See the *Child Support Handbook* for details of the information the CSA can expect you to provide.

Harm or undue distress

You do not have to provide authorisation or information (see above) if the CSA argues that doing so would put you or your child(ren) at risk of 'harm or undue distress'.

When you claim benefit you are asked if you or your child(ren) would be put at risk of suffering harm or undue distress if you were required to pursue maintenance. If you think this applies to you, you should say so and give details of your situation. This is then followed up by the CSA. See the *Child Support Handbook* for further details.

There is no legal definition of **'harm or undue distress'**. It certainly covers situations where there is a possibility of violence or where there has been rape, sexual abuse, threats or other harassment.[21] There does not need to have been a history of actual violence – fear of violence is enough. A child support officer decides if a fear of violence is reasonably held.

There are many other situations in which you might find it distressing to pursue maintenance. Examples are where:

- you have not had any contact with the other parent for many years;
- you had a clean-break divorce;
- the other parent is threatening to contest who the child lives with;
- you chose to have the child against the father's wishes;
- you believe that seeking child support maintenance would threaten the arrangement between the child(ren) and their other parent.

You have to persuade the CSA that you or your child(ren) would suffer harm or undue distress. Each case is decided on its merits. Your word should be accepted without any supporting evidence unless you contradict yourself or the child support officer thinks the information is improbable.[22]

It can take the CSA time to decide whether you have to provide authorisation or information (see p2:294). It is important not to sign a maintenance application form in the meantime. See below for the procedure the CSA must follow if you refuse to co-operate.

The procedure

If you are required to provide authorisation and information (see p2:294), you are warned in writing that your benefit could be paid at a reduced rate (see p2:297) unless you do so.[23] You must respond within two weeks, giving your reasons why you think you or your child(ren) would suffer 'harm or undue distress' (see p2:295) if you were required to co-operate. You can submit supporting letters – eg, from friends and relatives, your doctor, child's school, or other helpful organisations – if you wish. It is important to do this to avoid having your benefit paid at a reduced rate (see p2:297).

If you do submit further information, the Secretary of State should let you know if it is accepted that there would be a risk of 'harm or undue distress' (see p2:295) if you were required to co-operate. If it is not accepted, your case is referred to the area manager of the CSA. S/he writes to you asking you either to provide the authorisation or information requested, or to explain why you have not done this. You are given 14 days in which to respond.[24] Even at this stage, you should not sign the maintenance application form if you believe you should not be required to co-operate (see p2:294). You do not have a right of appeal until the end of the procedure. See the *Child Support Handbook* for more details about the procedure.

To ensure that your benefit is not paid at a reduced rate (see below) it is important that you explain the 'harm or undue distress' (see p2:295) which could arise if you authorise the CSA to pursue child support maintenance. Make it clear that this is why you do not wish to co-operate. You do not have to reply in writing – a telephone call is acceptable.[25] Nor do you have to provide evidence to prove that you would be under threat. Your word should be accepted,[26] though it is always useful to point to specific examples of problems which have occurred in the past or reasons why you believe they might occur in the future, to help illustrate what effect your co-operation might have. If there are reasonable grounds for believing that you or your child(ren) would suffer 'harm or undue distress' were authorisation to be given, no further action is taken and you are advised of this.[27]

Payment of benefit at a reduced rate

Your IS, income-based JSA, FC and DWA can be paid at a reduced rate if:
- you refuse to provide authorisation or information to enable the CSA to pursue child support maintenance for your child(ren) (see pp2:295); *and*
- the child support officer does not accept that there is any risk of harm or undue distress to you or your child(ren) (see p2:295).

If this is the case, the child support officer makes what is known as a **'reduced benefit direction'**.[28] When deciding whether to issue a 'reduced benefit direction', the child support officer must consider whether the welfare of any child involved would be adversely affected, for example, because of her/his age or state of health or that of her/his parents.[29] See p2:298 for more information about the amount by which your benefit can be reduced.

A 'reduced benefit direction' cannot be issued if:[30]
- IS or income-based JSA is paid to you or your partner which includes a disabled child premium, a disability premium or a higher pensioner premium – see pp2:325 and 2:327 – (this applies even if it is your partner who has the disability);
- FC or DWA is paid to you and the disabled child premium or the disability premium – see pp2:325 – is included in your exempt income for child support maintenance purposes (see the *Child Support Handbook* for details). (A 'reduced benefit direction' can be issued if it is your partner who has the disability, not you or your child.)

You have a right of appeal to a child support appeal tribunal against a 'reduced benefit direction' (see p2:301).

Note: Working families tax credit and disabled person's tax credit are due to replace family credit and disability working allowance in October 1999 (see pp1:489 and 1:490). The Government says that people getting these tax credits will not have to apply to the CSA for a maintenance assessment. This could mean that you will no longer be affected by these rules.

The reduced rate of benefit

The adjudication officer (AO) at the Benefits Agency must follow a 'reduced benefit direction' (see p:2:297) issued by a child support officer. Your benefit should be paid in full until a direction is issued but it is then adjusted. A current award of FC or DWA can be changed immediately if a 'reduced benefit direction' is issued, cancelled or suspended (see p1:468) and not at the end of your current award as is usually the case.

Benefit can be paid at a reduced rate even if it does not include an amount for the child(ren) for whom maintenance is being claimed.[31] However, no reduction is made if you are getting IS or income-based JSA while in hospital, a residential care or nursing home, or a local authority residential home.[32]

If your FC or DWA is being paid at a reduced rate and you then go on to IS or income-based JSA, this is paid at a reduced rate.[33]

Only one 'reduced benefit direction' (see p2:297) can be in operation at a time even if you refuse to co-operate in seeking maintenance for children from different relationships.[34] However, if another child is born or joins your household you can be asked to give authorisation and information (see pp2:293) in relation to that additional child. A second 'reduced benefit direction' could be issued if you again fail to co-operate. The second direction replaces the original one which ceases even if it would otherwise have run for several more months.[35]

The amount by which benefit is reduced and how long this lasts

If a 'reduced benefit direction' is issued (see p2:297), unless it ends early (see p2:299), your benefit is reduced by £20.56 a week for three years.[36] If the reduction would take your IS or income-based JSA to below 10 pence or your FC or DWA to below 50 pence, a lower reduction is made so that you are left with this minimum amount of benefit.[37] When benefit rates are increased in April the amount of the reduction also increases. For IS and income-based JSA, this happens straightaway but with FC or DWA it is adjusted when your claim is next renewed.[38]

If you are claiming housing benefit (HB) or council tax benefit (CTB) – see Chapters 25 and 27 – as well as FC or DWA, you should seek a review of your HB or CTB when a 'reduced benefit direction' is issued. Ask the local authority to take the reduction in your FC or DWA into account.

The three-year period begins on the first day of the second benefit week after the AO has reviewed and revised your claim.[39] At the end of the three-year period, if you still refuse to co-operate, another 'reduced benefit direction' can be issued (see p2:299).

The rules about the amount of the reduction and how long it lasts changed on 7 October 1996. If your 'reduced benefit direction' began before that date, the old rules still apply.[40] You cannot get more than one 'reduced benefit direction' for the same child(ren). See the *Child Support Handbook* 1996/97 edn, pp112-14.

Second 'reduced benefit directions'

If a second 'reduced benefit direction' (see p2:297) is made against you because you refuse to co-operate in relation to an additional child (see above), the original direction lapses and the reduction under the new direction lasts for a fresh three years.[41]

Example

Paula has been paid benefit at a reduced rate for seven months because she refused to sign a maintenance application form for her first child. She has now refused to authorise the CSA to pursue maintenance for her new baby. The first 'reduced benefit direction' ends early. However, she is penalised for a further three years under a new 'reduced benefit direction'.

If the second 'reduced benefit direction' terminates because it is reviewed (see p2:301) or because you decide to provide the required authorisation or information (see p2:293), the original direction can be brought back into operation for the balance of the three-year period. This can only be done if you are still refusing to co-operate in relation to the original child support maintenance application.[42]

Example

After a second 'reduced benefit direction' (RBD) has been in operation for one year, Paula has decided to co-operate with the CSA in seeking child support maintenance for her baby. However, she still does not want to seek maintenance for her first child. The original RBD had been in place for seven months. It is reinstated for one year and five months.

3 years – 1 year (second RBD) – 7 months (original RBD)
= 1 year and 5 months.

The rules about what happens when a second 'reduced benefit direction' ends early changed on 7 October 1996. If your earlier 'reduced benefit direction' was made before 7 October 1996, the old rules still apply, even if the second direction was made after that date.[43] See the *Child Support Handbook* 1996/97 edn, p114.

When a 'reduced benefit direction' ends early

A 'reduced benefit direction' (see p2:297) can end early:

- It is **cancelled** if it was made in error, or not ended earlier due to an error (in this case the money is repaid).[44] This can include situations where the child support officer did not at first accept your explanation why you or your children were at risk of 'harm or undue distress' (see p2:295) but now does;
- It **terminates** if you decide to provide the authorisation (see p2:293) or information (see p2:295) requested by the CSA.[45] It can also be terminated on review (see p2:301);
- It is **suspended or withdrawn** where:
  - you stop getting IS, income-based JSA, FC and DWA.[46] However, if you claim one of these benefits again within 52 weeks, the 'reduced benefit direction' is reinstated for the remainder of the three-year period. You must be given 14 days notice of this. If you make your new claim more than 52 weeks after you last received IS, income-based JSA, FC or DWA the direction is no longer valid. However, the requirement to co-operate (see p2:294) still applies and you will be asked to complete a maintenance application form. A new direction could be made, though it should only run for the balance of the three years which was not used up on the previous claim;
  - your child(ren) cease(s) to be eligible for maintenance because they are over 16 and have left non-advanced education (see p2:132), or are 19 or over. If they become eligible again (eg, because they return to full-time education) the reduced benefit direction can be reinstated;[47]
  - you stop living with and caring for the child(ren). The reduced benefit direction can be reinstated if you resume your role as carer;[48]
  - you are paid IS or income-based JSA at a special rate because you are in hospital, a residential care or nursing home or a local authority residential home (see Chapter 39). Initially the reduced benefit direction is suspended, but if you stay there for more than 52 weeks it ceases completely;[49]
  - your child(ren) (if in Scotland) or their absent parent successfully apply to the CSA for a maintenance assessment.[50]

Both you and the Benefits Agency AO should be notified if a 'reduced benefit direction' ceases, and given an explanation.[51]

The rules about what happens when a 'reduced benefit direction' ends early changed on 7 October 1996. If your earlier 'reduced benefit direction' was made before 7 October 1996, the old rules still apply, even if the second direction was made after that date.[52] See the *Child Support Handbook* 1996/97 edn, p114.

Reviewing a 'reduced benefit direction'

A 'reduced benefit direction' (see p2:297) must be **reviewed** if you, or someone on your behalf, provides additional reasons explaining why:[53]
- you failed to co-operate with the CSA (see p2:295);
- you are no longer obliged to co-operate (see p2:295).

It should also be reviewed if the child(ren)'s welfare is likely to be put in jeopardy by the continuing existence of a direction.

The review is done by a child support officer (but not the one who issued the direction). S/he may decide to terminate the direction from the date that the reasons were supplied. You should be given a full written decision and informed of your right of appeal if the direction is not terminated.

Right of appeal

If you disagree with a 'reduced benefit direction, you have a right of appeal. Your appeal must be made to an independent child support appeal tribunal against the 'reduced benefit direction',[54] (not to a social security appeal tribunal against the reduction in your benefit). You must appeal within 28 days of the decision being sent to you, although a late appeal can be accepted if you have special reasons.[55] The special reasons do not have to relate to your own personal circumstances or actions. They could include things like the amount of money involved or how strong your case is. The reduced benefit direction is imposed in the meantime, unless you decide to co-operate by providing the authorisation or information (see p2:297) after it is issued.

Note: The time limit and procedures for appealing are due to change when the Social Security Act 1998 comes into effect. See p2:648 for further information.

Child support maintenance paid by non-resident parents on income support or jobseeker's allowance

If you are a non-resident parent (known as an absent parent) you are liable to maintain your children (see p2:290). Deductions for child support maintenance can be made from your weekly IS or income-based JSA. Deductions for arrears of child support maintenance can be made from contribution-based JSA (see p2:203).

Income support and income-based jobseeker's allowance

If you are on IS or income-based JSA, deductions of £5.20 a week can be made from your benefit as a contribution towards the maintenance of your child(ren).[56] This does not apply if you:[57]
- are aged under 18;

- qualify for a family premium or have day-to-day care of any child (see the *Child Support Handbook* for details of 'day-to-day care');
- receive incapacity benefit, maternity allowance, statutory sick pay or maternity pay, severe disablement allowance, attendance allowance, disability living or working allowances, invalid care allowance, industrial injuries disablement benefit, a war pension or a payment from either of the Independent Living Funds. If this benefit is not paid solely because of overlapping benefit rules, or an inadequate contribution record, you are still exempt from deductions.

If you are a non-resident parent on IS or income-based JSA and have children from two or more different relationships, only one deduction can be made and the £5.20 is apportioned between the people who care for the children.[58] If deductions for other debts of a higher priority are being made from your benefits (see p2:500), half of the deduction is made, ie; £2.60.

Challenging a decision to make deductions

If you think that a decision to make deductions from your IS or income-based JSA is wrong, you should apply in writing to the CSA (not the Benefits Agency) for a review. You should try to show that the decision was:

- given in ignorance of relevant facts; *or*
- based on a mistake about the facts; *or*
- wrong in law.

A different child support officer reviews the decision. If you still do not agree with the decision you can appeal to a child support appeal tribunal but must do this within 28 days.[59] If your circumstances change you can also apply for a review.

Note: The time limits and procedures for seeking reviews and appealing are due to change when the Social Security Act 1998 comes into effect. See p2:581 for further information.

Procedure for making deductions

If you are not exempt from the deductions, the CSA sends a notification to the Benefits Agency. This request for deductions to be made is binding on the adjudication officer of the Benefits Agency, unless other deductions are being made from your IS or income-based JSA which are of a higher priority (see p2:500). Deductions for child support maintenance cannot be made from any benefit other than IS or JSA, unless incapacity benefit, severe disablement allowance or retirement pension are paid in the same girocheque or order book. If you are a non-resident parent who is not exempt from the deductions but disagree that the Benefits Agency can make them because other higher priority deductions are being made from your benefit, you have a right of appeal to a social security appeal tribunal (see Chapter 56).

Contribution-based jobseeker's allowance

Deductions for arrears of child support maintenance can be made from your *contribution-based* JSA.[60] You must have been served with a notice that you are in arrears of maintenance before a deduction can be made. The Secretary of State generally only applies for a deduction to be made from your benefit if the payment of child support maintenance cannot be obtained by other means. Your consent is not needed.

The amount that can be deducted depends on your age as follows:

- if you are aged 16 or 17, £10.31;
- if you are aged 18 to 24, £13.56;
- if you are aged 25 or over, £17.13.

No deduction can be made if deductions are already being made for community charge arrears, a fine or council tax arrears (see p2:500).[61]

If you disagree that the Benefits Agency can make deductions, you have a right of appeal to a social security appeal tribunal (see Chapter 56).

---

3. **How maintenance affects your income support and income-based jobseeker's allowance**

The following are taken into account in working out the amount of income support (IS) or income-based JSA to which you are entitled:

- child support maintenance (see below);
- other maintenance payments made by 'liable relatives' (see p2:304).

If someone is paying your child(ren)'s school fees, see p2:383.

Different rules apply if you are claiming family credit, disability working allowance, housing benefit or council tax benefit. For these rules, see p2:310.

Note: Maintenance is not taken into account in working out the amount of *contribution-based* JSA to which you are entitled.

Child support maintenance

All payments of child support maintenance are treated as income and are taken into account in full on a weekly basis.[62] Where payments are made monthly, multiply by 12 and divide by 52 to obtain a weekly amount. Where regular payments are made at intervals other than each week or month, the payments are spread over the period, including any part week. It is the actual payments made, and not the amount due under the Child Support Agency (CSA) assessment, which are taken into account in this way.[63]

The Benefits Agency should not calculate IS or income-based JSA on the assumption that child support maintenance payments are being made where this has not been happening. So a parent who would lose entitlement to IS or income-based JSA if payments were made can continue to receive it if the child support maintenance is not received. If there is a delay in obtaining increased or reinstated IS or income-based JSA you should seek advice.

Child support maintenance can be paid direct to the CSA rather than to you. See p2:292 for further details.

Arrears at the beginning of the child support assessment

Arrears of child support maintenance have usually accrued by the time an assessment is made. Usually these arrears are paid to, and retained by, the CSA if you are on IS or income-based JSA. However, if the payment is made to you, the IS or income-based JSA which has been overpaid to you can be recovered by the Benefits Agency.[64]

Arrears due during a claim

The CSA is responsible for collecting arrears of child support maintenance if you are on IS or income-based JSA. The CSA retains an amount equal to the IS or income-based JSA you were paid because the maintenance was not paid when it was due.[65]

Arrears paid for a period before the claim

Only child support maintenance both due for and received in the weeks of the claim can be taken into account by the Benefits Agency. A payment of child support maintenance due before but paid after you claim IS or income-based JSA is treated as paid in the week in which it was due.[66]

Other maintenance payments made by 'liable relatives'

If someone who is a 'liable relative' (see p2:304) makes maintenance payments to you which are not child support maintenance (see p2:292) these are dealt with in a special way.[67] (To find out how child support maintenance affects your IS or income-based JSA, see p2:302.)

How such a payment affects your benefit depends on whether it:
- counts as a 'liable relative payment', and is *either:*
  - a regular payment – known as a 'periodical payment' (see p2:305); *or*
  - a lump sum (in one go or by instalments) treated as income or capital (see p2:307); *or*
- does not count as a 'liable relative payment' (see p2:309).

You and your solicitor should look at these rules carefully *before* negotiating payments from your former partner.

Most payments by 'liable relatives' (see below) count as 'liable relative payments'. These are usually treated as income and are taken into account fully to reduce your IS or income-based JSA (see below). If you are receiving IS or income-based JSA, it is usually not a good idea to have a lump sum instead of 'periodical payments' (see below). This is because a lump sum is usually treated as income (see p2:307) at a sufficiently high level to disqualify you from benefit altogether even if the amount is well below the usual capital limit (see p2:442).

For information about lump sums which can be treated as capital, see p2:447. For information about payments which do not count as 'liable relative payments', see p2:307. Some of these do not affect your benefit (see p2:308).

'Liable relatives payments'

Unless it is a payment that does not count (see p2:307) payments from the following people (known as **'liable relatives'**) count as 'liable relative payments':[68]

- a husband or wife. This includes one from whom you are separated or divorced;
- a parent of a child or young person under 19 for whom you are claiming (this could include a step-parent);
- a parent of a young person under 19 who is claiming IS or JSA in her/his own right (this could include a step-parent);
- a person who has been living with and maintaining a child or young person under 19 or maintaining a young person under 19 who is claiming IS or JSA in her/his own right and can therefore reasonably be treated as her/his parent;
- if you are a 'person from abroad', a sponsor who has given an undertaking to support you financially (see p2:209).

There are special rules about how payments to you or to someone else on your behalf by one of the people above are taken into account (see below and p2:307). However, it is important to note that not all of them are legally 'liable to maintain' you (see p2:290). The Secretary of State can only pursue those who are 'liable to maintain' you (see p2:291).

Periodical payments

Periodical payments are any of the following payments made by 'liable relatives' (see above):[69]

- any payment made, or due to be made, regularly, whether voluntarily or under a court order or other formal agreement;
- any other small payment no higher than your weekly IS or income-based JSA;
- any payment made instead of one or more regular payments due under an agreement (whether formal or voluntary), either as payment in advance or

arrears. This does not include any arrears due before the beginning of your entitlement to IS or income-based JSA (see p2:307).

Periodical payments which are received on time are each spread over a period equal to the interval between them – eg, monthly payments are spread over a month. Payments are converted to a weekly amount – eg, monthly payments are multiplied by 12 and divided by 52 to produce a weekly income figure.[70]

Arrears of periodical payments due during your claim

When a payment arrives during a claim and it includes a lump sum for arrears (or in advance), the payment is spread over a period calculated by dividing it by the weekly amount of maintenance you should have received.[71]

Example

Tia should receive maintenance of £80 a month. It is not paid for three months and she then receives £200.

£80 a month is treated as producing a weekly income of:

$$\frac{£80 \times 12}{52} = £18.46$$

The £200 is taken into account for:

$$\frac{£200}{18.46} = 10.83 \text{ weeks}$$

Tia is assumed to have an income of £18.46 for the next 10 weeks and six days. The maintenance payments due are still two weeks and one day in arrears (£40).

If a payment is specifically identified as being arrears of maintenance for a particular period, the Benefits Agency can:
- take it into account for a forward period from the week you report you have received it; *or*
- attribute it to the past period which it was intended to cover, unless it is 'more practicable' to choose a later week.[72] In this case the Secretary of State can recover the full amount of extra benefit paid to you while maintenance was not being received.[73] (This can still be done when you receive a payment after your claim ends which is for arrears of maintenance that should have been paid while you were still claiming.)

It is important to work out how you would be better-off financially. You should then argue for the payment to be spread over whichever period is more advantageous to you. This depends on the amount of IS or income-based JSA you would otherwise receive, the amount of the payment and whether any other periodical payments (see p2:305) are being made. You should appeal if your argument is not accepted.

Example 1

Connie should have been receiving maintenance at the rate of £25 a week. Her husband misses eight weeks and she has to claim IS at the rate of £15 a week to top up her part-time earnings. When she reduces her hours her entitlement to IS increases to £30 a week. Then her husband pays her eight weeks' arrears of maintenance (£200).

The Benefits Agency might try to take the maintenance into account for eight weeks at the rate of £25 a week from the date it is paid to Connie. If it does this, she loses £200 (£25 × 8 weeks).

Connie argues that the maintenance should be attributed to the eight-week period it was intended to cover. The Benefits Agency can then recover the IS she was paid for that period. She says that she will pay the Benefits Agency what she owes out of the arrears of maintenance. This is a very good case for arguing that it is not 'more practicable' to spread the payment forwards rather than over the past period. She loses £120 (£15 × 8 weeks).

Example 2

Gwen is in exactly the same position as Connie. However, when her husband paid her arrears of maintenance of £200, he also started making regular maintenance payments. She is better off having the payment of arrears spread forwards from the date of payment. The new maintenance payments of £25 a week reduce her IS to £5 a week (£30 − £25). If the Benefits Agency takes the arrears into account for eight weeks from the date it is paid to Gwen, she only loses £40 (£5 × 8 weeks).

Arrears of periodical payments due before your claim

If arrears of maintenance are paid for a period before the date of your claim they do not count as periodical payments (see p2:305).[74] The Benefits Agency deals with such payments as lump sums treated as income (see p2:308). This means that they spread them over a future period (see p2:308). You should try to argue that this is wrong and that such payments should be treated as capital. The benefit rules do not exclude arrears from the definition of periodical payments just to have them brought back into the calculation in this way. Any other interpretation is unfair and gives the Secretary of State an unwarranted windfall at your expense.[75] It is also contrary to the rule for arrears of child support maintenance (see p2:304).

Lump sum payments treated as capital

If a 'liable relative' (see p2:305) is already paying you 'periodical payments' (see p2:305) equal to:

- your IS or income-based JSA if the payments include payments for you; *or*

- your child's applicable amount and any family premium (see pp2:321 and 2:323) if the payments are only for a child, *then*

a lump sum payment from her/him counts as capital.[76]

If you stop getting 'periodical payments' (see p2:305) or get less than the amounts shown above, any of the lump sum you still have is taken into account as income (see below).[77] Lump sum payments that count as capital do not affect your IS or income-based JSA unless they take your capital over £3,000 (£10,000 if you live in a residential care or nursing home). See Chapter 49 for more information about the capital rules.

Lump sum payments treated as income

Unless they do not count as 'liable relative payments' (see p2:309) or are lump sums treated as capital (see above), lump sums are treated as income.[78] They are spread over a period so as to disqualify you from IS or income-based JSA for as long as possible.

If you are **not receiving 'periodical payments'** (see p2:305), the lump sum is treated as producing a weekly income equal to:[79]

- if the lump sum is for you or for you and any children, your weekly IS or income-based JSA plus £2;
- if the lump sum is just for a child or children, the personal allowance for you and each child for whom you get maintenance, any disabled child premium or family premium, and any carer's premium (see pp2:325, 2:323 and 2:333) if it is paid because you are caring for a disabled child for whom you receive maintenance. However, if your weekly IS or income-based JSA entitlement plus £2 would be less than this amount (eg, because you had other income), the lower amount is used. This means that the lump sum disqualifies you from IS or income-based JSA for a longer period.

If you are **also receiving 'periodical payments'** (see p2:305), the lump sum is treated as producing a weekly income equal to the difference between the 'periodical payment' and:[80]

- the weekly amount of IS or income-based JSA plus £2 which would be paid if you did not get the 'periodical payment' when it is paid for you alone or for you and your children;
- the child's personal allowance plus family premium (see pp2:321 and 2:323) if the 'periodical payment' is just for a child.

If the 'periodical payments' are varied or stop, the calculation is done again taking the balance of the lump sum into account.[81]

You are then disqualified from getting IS or income-based JSA for a period beginning on the first day of the benefit week in which the payment is received and lasting for a number of weeks calculated by dividing the amount of the payment by the weekly income. The period can start in a later week if that is more practical.[82]

Example

Fiona receives a lump sum of £2,000 from her husband. Her IS is £48. Under the rules, the lump sum is treated as producing a weekly income of £50. She does not receive IS for 40 weeks (£2,000 divided by £50 = 40 weeks).

If you receive a lump sum which is treated as income, and are disqualified from receiving IS or income-based JSA under the rules described above, you should ask the Benefits Agency to recalculate the period of your disqualification whenever:

* your circumstances change so that your entitlement to IS or income-based JSA would be higher; *or*
* benefit rates increase (April of every year).

Arrears of 'periodical payments' due before your claim are often treated as described above so as to disqualify you from benefit. However, you should try to argue that that is wrong (see p2:307).

Payments that do not count as 'liable relative payments'

Certain types of payment from 'liable relatives' (see p2:305) do not count as 'liable relative payments'.[83] They are therefore dealt with under the normal income and capital rules (see Chapters 48 and 49) and you are usually better off. You should ensure that your solicitor takes account of this in negotiating payments with your former partner. For example:

* some payments can be disregarded as income or capital (see pp2:381 and 2:448 for more information about disregarded income and capital);
* some payments made to someone else for the benefit of you or a member of your family, or paid to you or a member of the family to pay to someone else (see p2:310), do not count as your income or capital (see pp2:381 and 2:448 for more information about notional income and notional capital which does not affect your IS or income-based JSA).

If you receive a payment which does not count as a 'liable relative payment' (see below), it is usually better if it can be treated as capital. If it is treated as capital it does not affect your benefit if it does not take your capital over £3,000 (£10,000 if you live in a residential care or nursing home). If the payment is more than the capital limit (see p2:442), you will not receive any means-tested benefit whether it is capital or a lump sum treated as income (see p2:455), but you might be able to reclaim sooner if it is capital.

The following types of payment from 'liable relatives' (see p2:305) do not count as liable relative payments:[84]

* any payment arising from a 'disposition of property' (see p2:310) in consequence of your separation, divorce or the nullity of your marriage;
* any gifts not exceeding £250 in any period of 52 weeks (and not so regular as to amount to periodical payments – see p2:305);

- payments made after the 'liable relative' has died;
- any payment in kind;
- any payment made to someone else for the benefit of you or a member of your family (such as mortgage capital payments), or paid to you or a member of your family to pay to someone else, which it is unreasonable to take into account – you can appeal to a tribunal which may take a different view from the adjudication officer about what is reasonable;
- any boarding school fees (but see p2:383);
- any payment to, or for, a child or young person who does not count as a member of your household;
- money from a liable relative which has already been taken into account under a previous claim, or which has already been recovered out of overpaid IS or income-based JSA;
- any payment which you have used before the adjudication officer makes her/ his decision provided that you did not use it for the purpose of gaining entitlement to IS or income-based JSA. It should not be taken into account if you have used it to clear debts such as your solicitor's bill.

'Disposition of property'

Any payment arising from a 'disposition of property' does not count as a liable relative payment (see p2:309). It is therefore vital to distinguish between payments arising from a disposition of property and those that are not. 'Property' is not confined to houses and land, but includes any asset such as the contents of your former home or a building society account. There is a 'disposition' when those contents are divided up or your former partner buys out your interest.[85] Therefore, any lump sum which is paid in settlement of a claim to a share in any property does not count as a 'liable relative payment'. It is only those lump sums which are paid instead of income which are liable to be treated as income.[86] It is important to take this into account in any negotiations with your former partner. You should make sure your solicitor knows about this rule.

It is best that court orders are drawn up to make it clear that any lump sum is in settlement of a claim to an interest in property. However, this is not essential and the Benefits Agency should accept a letter from your solicitor explaining why a lump sum was asked for and agreed.

Note that the proceeds of sale of your former home may be disregarded altogether for a period of time (see p2:448). Other capital, such as the home itself and its contents, may also be disregarded (see p2:448). There is therefore an advantage, while you are on benefit, to ask for a greater share of the home and accept less in the way of income or capital which would be taken into account to reduce your benefit.

4. How maintenance affects your family credit, disability working allowance, housing benefit and council tax benefit

The following are taken into account in working out the amount of family credit (FC), disability working allowance (DWA), housing benefit (HB) or council tax benefit (CTB) to which you are entitled:
- child support maintenance;
- other maintenance paid for a member of your family (see p2:113 for who counts as your 'family').

How payments are taken into account depends on whether they are treated as income or capital (see below and p2:312). It is important to remember that some payments made to someone else for the benefit of you or a member of your family, or paid to you or a member of the family to pay to someone else, do not always count as your income or your capital (see pp2:421 and 2:455 for more information about notional income and capital which does not affect your FC, DWA, HB or CTB).

If someone is paying your child(ren)'s school fees, see p2:383.

The rules which say who is 'liable to maintain' you or your child(ren) and about 'liable relatives payments' if you are claiming income support (IS) and income-based jobseeker's allowance (JSA) (see p2:290) do not apply to FC, DWA, HB and CTB.

Different rules apply if you are claiming IS or income-based JSA. For these rules, see p2:303.

Disregarded maintenance

If you are a lone parent, or a couple with a child, for FC, DWA, HB and CTB, £15 of any maintenance payment made by your former partner, or your partner's former partner, or the parent of any child in your family is disregarded in working out the amount of your benefit. If you receive maintenance from more than one person, only £15 of the total is disregarded.[87] See Chapter 48 for further information about the income rules.

Family credit and disability working allowance

If you claim FC or DWA and regular amounts of maintenance payments, or child support maintenance payments, are being (or are due to be) made, these are taken into account as income. Any other payments are taken into account as capital (see p2:312).

Maintenance payments to or for a child in your family (see p2:121) are treated as yours but only if the payments are actually made.

Some payments made to someone else for the benefit of you or a member of your family, or paid to you or a member of the family to pay to someone else (see p2:423), do not count as your income (see p2:381). If they *do* count as your income, you should ensure the Benefits Agency disregards £15 (see pp2:311 and 2:400).

Regular child support maintenance and other maintenance payments are taken into account as income as follows:

- If regular amounts of child support maintenance or other maintenance are being paid at regular intervals (eg, weekly or monthly) before you claim, the normal weekly amount counts as income.[88] If any child support maintenance payments made are more than the amount due under a maintenance assessment (see p2:292), only the amount due under the assessment is taken into account.

- If regular child support maintenance payments are due to be paid but are not being paid regularly, the average of the payments made over the last 13 weeks, or, if the maintenance assessed was notified to you within the last 13 weeks, over the period since the notification, counts as income. However, if that average is more than the maintenance assessment (see p2:292), only the amount due under the assessment is taken into account.[89]

- If other maintenance payments are due to be paid regularly but are not being so, the average of the payments made in the 13 weeks up to the week of your claim counts as income.[90]

Payments are taken into account from the date they are received by you, not the date they are received into court or by the Benefits Agency (if appropriate).[91]

FC and DWA are awarded for a period of 26 weeks. If your circumstances change during that period, this does not usually affect the amount you are paid (see p1:468). A change in the amount of your maintenance is not a change of circumstances that affects your FC or DWA. For this reason, it is important to think about when to claim. See p1:466 for further information.

Maintenance treated as capital

Any payments of maintenance which are not paid (or due to be paid) regularly count as capital.[92] The normal capital rules apply (see Chapter 49). However, any payments made by the Secretary of State as compensation for a reduction in child support maintenance assessment are disregarded as income and (for 52 weeks) as capital.[93]

You are usually better off if maintenance can be treated as capital. If it is treated as capital it does not affect your benefit if it does not take your capital over £3,000 (£10,000 if you live in a residential care or nursing home). If the payment is more than the capital limit (see p2:442), you will not receive any means-tested benefit whether it is capital or income, but you might be able to reclaim sooner if it is capital. You should ensure that your solicitor takes account of this in negotiating payments with your former partner. For example:

- some payments can be disregarded as capital (see p2:448 for more information about disregarded capital);
- some payments made to someone else for the benefit of you or a member of your family, or paid to you or a member of the family to pay to someone else (see p2:461), do not count as your capital (see p2:455 for more information about notional capital which does not affect your FC or DWA).

Housing benefit and council tax benefit

If you are claiming HB or CTB, there are no special rules for how child support maintenance or other maintenance are taken into account. If you are receiving payments regularly, they are taken into account as income. If you are paid irregularly or in lump sums, they are taken into account as capital. See Chapters 48 and 49 for information about the income and capital rules. See pp2:421 and 2:455 for information about notional income and capital which does not affect your HB or CTB.

Maintenance paid to or for your dependent child counts as yours.[94]

If are also claiming FC or DWA and have been given a 'reduced benefit direction' (see p2:297), you should seek a review of your HB and CTB. Ask the local authority to take the reduction in your income into account.

5. **Benefits if you are contributing to someone's maintenance**

If you are 'contributing to the maintenance' of someone you might qualify for an increase of a non-means-tested benefit even if you are not living with her/him. See Chapter 36 for details of the rules. You might also qualify for child benefit (see Chapter 12) or guardian's allowance (see Chapter 13).

You might qualify for an increase for a child dependant (see p2:97) to be paid with your:

- long-term or higher rate of short-term incapacity benefit;
- severe disablement allowance;
- invalid care allowance;
- category A, B or C retirement pension;
- widowed mother's allowance.

You might qualify for an increase for your spouse or someone who cares for a child (see pp2:93 and 2:95) with your:
- incapacity benefit (any rate);
- severe disablement allowance;
- invalid care allowance;
- category A or C retirement pension;
- maternity allowance.

'Contributing to the maintenance' of someone on income support or income-based jobseeker's allowance

There are special rules that allow the Benefits Agency to recover money from you if you are meant to be 'contributing to the maintenance' of someone who is claiming income support (IS) or income-based jobseeker's allowance (JSA) but fail to do so. If you do not pay what you are meant to pay, that person's IS or income-based JSA might be increased to make up the difference. The IS or income-based JSA that would not have been paid to her/him had you paid the maintenance can be recovered from your child benefit, guardians' allowance or the increases in benefit listed above.[95]

Notes

References are to statutes and regulations as amended up to 8 March 1999. All regulations are (General) Regulations unless otherwise stated. There is a full list of abbreviations in Appendix 13.

1. **Getting maintenance**
   1 **IS** Sch 9 para 15(3) IS Regs;
     JSA Sch 7 para 15(3) JSA Regs
     FC Sch 2 para 13(3) FC Regs
     DWA Sch 3 para 12(3) DWA Regs
     HB Sch 4 para 13(3) HB Regs
     CTB Sch 4 para 13(3) CTB Regs
   2 *Residual Liable Relative and Proceedings Guide,* paras 1630-42
   3 ss78(6)-(9) and 105(3) & (4) SSAA 1992
   4 ss78(6)-(9) and 105 SSAA 1992
   5 s1 CSA 1991
   6 s105(1) SSAA 1992
   7 **IS** s106 SSAA 1992
     JSA s23 JSA 1995
   8 *NAB v Parkes* [1955] 2 QBD 506; *Hulley v Thompson* [1981] 1 WLR 159
   9 **IS** s106(2) SSAA 1992
     JSA s23 JSA 1995, reg 169 JSA Regs
   10 *NAB v Parkes* [1955] 2 QBD 506
   11 ss8(3) and 9 CSA 1991
   12 **IS** s106(4)(a) SSAA 1992
     JSA s23 JSA 1995, reg 169 JSA Regs
   13 s29(3) CSA 1991; reg 2 CS(C&E) Regs

2. **Child support maintenance**
   14 s30(1) CSA 1991; CS(CEOFM) Regs
   15 s6(1) CSA 1991; reg 34 CS(MAP) Regs
   16 s2 CSA 1991
   17 s6(8) CSA 1991
   18 s46(5) CSA 1991
   19 s6(1) and (11) CSA 1991
   20 s6(9) CSA 1991; regs 2 and 3 CS(IED) Regs
   21 App 1 CSRCG
   22 para 2553 CSAG
   23 Reg 35 (1) and (2) CS(MAP) Regs

   24 Reg 35(3) CS(MAP) Regs
   25 s46(10) CSA 1991
   26 R(SB) 33/85
   27 s46(3) and (4) CSA 1991
   28 s46(5) CSA 1991
   29 s2 CSA 1991; para 2556 CSAG; CCS/1037/1995
   30 Reg 35A CS(MAP) Regs
   31 s6(8) CSA 1991
   32 Regs 40 and 40ZA CS(MAP) Regs
   33 Reg 39 CS(MAP) Regs
   34 Reg 36(8) CS(MAP) Regs
   35 Reg 47(1) CS(MAP) Regs
   36 Reg 36(2) CS(MAP) Regs
   37 Reg 37 CS(MAP) Regs
   38 Reg 36(7) CS(MAP) Regs
   39 Reg 36(4) CS(MAP) Regs
   40 Reg 25(3) and (4) CS(MA) Regs
   41 Reg 47(2) CS(MAP) Regs
   42 Reg 47(4) and (5) CS(MAP) Regs
   43 Reg 25(4) CS(MA) Regs
   44 Reg 46 CS(MAP) Regs
   45 Reg 41 CS(MAP) Regs
   46 Reg 38 CS(MAP) Regs
   47 Reg 48 CS(MAP) Regs
   48 Reg 48 CS(MAP) Regs
   49 Regs 40 and 40ZA CS(MAP) Regs
   50 Regs 43 and 44 CS(MAP) Regs
   51 Reg 49 CS(MAP) Regs
   52 Reg 25(4) CS(MA) Regs
   53 Reg 42 CS(MAP) Regs
   54 s46(7) CSA 1991
   55 Reg 3 CSAT(P) Regs
   56 s43 CSA 1991; regs 13 and 28 CS(MASC) Regs
   57 Reg 28(1) and Sch 4 CS(MASC) Regs
   58 s43 and Sch 1 para 5(4) CSA 1991; reg 28(3) CS(MASC) Regs; Sch 9 para 7A SS(C&P) Regs
   59 Reg 28(5) and Sch 5 CS(MASC) Regs
   60 Sch 9 para 7B SS(C&P) Regs
   61 Sch 9 para 7B(4) (C&P) Regs

3. **How maintenance affects your IS
and income-based JSA**

62 **IS** Reg 60B IS Regs
JSA Reg 126 JSA Regs
63 **IS** Reg 60C IS Regs
JSA Reg 128 JSA Regs
64 s74(1) SSAA 1992; reg 7
SS(PAOR) Regs
65 s41(2) CSA 1991; reg 8
CS(AIAMA) Regs
66 **IS** Reg 60D(1)(aa) IS Regs
JSA Reg 129(1)(aa) JSA Regs
67 **IS** Regs 54-60 IS Regs
JSA Regs 117-124 JSA Regs
68 **IS** Reg 54 IS Regs
JSA Reg 117 JSA Regs
69 **IS** Reg 54 IS Regs, definition of
'periodical payment';
JSA Reg 117 JSA Regs, definition
of 'periodical payment'
Both *Bolstridge v CAO*
70 **IS** Reg 58 IS Regs
JSA Reg 122 JSA Regs
71 **IS** Reg 58(4) IS Regs
JSA Reg 122(4) JSA Regs
72 **IS** Reg 59(1) IS Regs
JSA Reg 123(1) JSA Regs
73 s74(1) SSAA 1992; reg 7(1)
SS(PAOR) Regs
74 **IS** Reg 54 IS Regs, definition of
'periodical payment'
JSA Reg 117 JSA Regs, definition
of 'periodical payment'
75 *Regina v West London SBAT ex
parte Taylor* [1975] 1 WLR 1048
(DC); *McCorquodale v CAO* (CA)
reported as an appendix to R(SB)
1/88
76 **IS** Reg 60 IS Regs
JSA Reg 124 JSA Regs
77 **IS** Reg 60(2) IS Regs
JSA Reg 124(2) JSA Regs
78 **IS** Reg 54 IS Regs, definition of
'payment' and reg 55 IS Regs
JSA Reg 117 JSA Regs, definition
of 'payment' and reg 118 JSA
Regs
79 **IS** Reg 57(1) IS Regs
JSA Reg 121(1) JSA Regs
80 **IS** Reg 57(2) IS Regs;
JSA Reg 121(2) JSA Regs
81 **IS** Reg 57(3) IS Regs
JSA Reg 121 (3) JSA Regs

82 **IS** Regs 57(4) and 59(2) IS Regs
JSA Regs 121 (4) and 123(2) JSA
Regs
83 **IS** Reg 54 IS Regs, definition of
'payment';
JSA Reg 117 JSA Regs, definition
of 'payment'
84 **IS** Regs 54, definition of
'payment', 55 and 60(1) IS Regs;
JSA Reg s117 JSA Regs,
definition of 'payment',118 and
124(1) JSA Regs
85 CSB/1160/1986; R(SB) 1/89
86 R(SB) 1/89

4. **How maintenance affects your
FC, DWA, HB and CTB**

87 **FC** Sch 2 paras 13(3) and 47 FC
Regs
DWA Sch 3 paras 12(3) and 13
DWA Regs
HB Sch 4 paras 13(3) and 47 HB
Regs
CTB Sch 4 paras 13(3) and 46
CTB Regs
88 **FC** Reg 16(2)(a) and (2A)(a) FC
Regs
DWA Reg 18(2)(a) and (2A)(a)
DWA Regs
89 **FC** Reg 16 (2A)(b) FC Regs
DWA Reg 18 (2A)(b) DWA Regs
90 **FC** Reg 16(2)(b) FC Regs
DWA Reg 18(2)(b) DWA Regs
91 CFC/ 48/ 1993
92 **FC** Reg 31(6) FC Regs
DWA Reg 34(6) DWA Regs
93 **FC** Sch 2 para 55 and Sch 3 para
48 FC Regs
DWA Sch 3 para 53 and Sch 4
para 47 DWA Regs

5. **Benefits if you are contributing
to someone's maintenance**

94 s136(1) SSCBA 1992
95 s74(3) SSAA 1992; reg 9
SS(PAOR) Regs

Chapter 45

- -

Applicable amounts

This chapter explains the different amounts allowed for meeting your needs for the purposes of calculating your entitlement to income support, income-based jobseeker's allowance, housing benefit and council tax benefit. It covers:

1. Personal allowances (p2:319)
2. Premiums (p2:322)
3. Backdating of premiums (p2:334)

Income support, income-based jobseeker's allowance, housing benefit and council tax benefit

For income support (IS), income-based jobseeker's allowance (JSA), housing benefit (HB) and council tax benefit (CTB) the 'applicable amount' is a figure representing your weekly needs for the purpose of calculating your benefit. For IS/income-based JSA, your applicable amount is the amount you are expected to live on each week. For HB/CTB, it is the amount used to see how much help you need with your rent or council tax. This chapter explains how you work out your applicable amount for those benefits. For the way benefit payable is calculated, see p1:446 for IS, p1:280 for income-based JSA, p1:518 for HB and p1:573 for CTB.

Family credit, disability working allowance and earnings top-up

This chapter does not deal with the applicable amounts for family credit (FC), disability working allowance (DWA) or earnings top-up (ETU).

The applicable amount for FC is always £80.65. For DWA it is £60.50 for single people (other than lone parents) and £80.65 for couples/lone parents. For the way FC and DWA are calculated, see pp1:462 and 1:477 respectively. For ETU, your applicable amount depends on the area in which you live and may vary according to your age and whether you are single or have a partner. For the different applicable amounts and the way ETU is calculated, see p4:4.

For the applicable amounts for working families tax credit and disabled person's tax credit, which replace FC/DWA from October 1999, see Chapter 23.

What is included in your applicable amount

For IS, income-based JSA, HB and CTB, your applicable amount is made up of:
- personal allowances: this is the amount the law says you need for living expenses (see p1:319);
- premiums: this is the amount given for certain extra needs you or your family may have (see p1:322);
- for IS and income-based JSA only, housing costs: (see Chapter 46).

For IS and income-based JSA, your applicable amount is different if you live in a residential care home, nursing home or local authority residential accommodation (see p2:167). Your applicable amount is reduced if, for IS/income-based JSA/HB/CTB, you are:
- receiving an urgent cases payment (see p2:217);
- in hospital (see p2:154);
- a 16/17-year-old, in certain circumstances (see p2:152);
- trade disputes (see p2:187);
- a couple, one of whom is a person from abroad (see p2:215);
- without accommodation (see p2:185);
- a prisoner (see p2:180);
- for IS only, appealing against a decision that you are not incapable of work under the 'all-work' test[1] (see p2:41 for entitlement to IS in this situation and p2:22 for more information on the all-work test);
- for income-based JSA only, you are getting JSA on hardship grounds (see p1:425).

When your benefit might be paid at a lower rate

There are a number of other reasons why your benefit might be reduced, such as:
- for IS/income-based JSA, you are subject to a benefit penalty for refusing to co-operate with the Child Support Agency (see p2:297);
- you are repaying an overpayment of benefit (see p2:525);
- for IS/income-based JSA, you are repaying a social fund loan (see p1:662);
- for IS/income-based JSA, the Benefits Agency is making direct payments on your behalf in respect of housing costs, water charges, fuel debts, council tax and community charge arrears, fines or child support maintenance (see p2:500).

Some IS, income-based JSA and HB claimants get an amount of transitional protection on top of their ordinary IS or HB (see pp1:448 and 1:529).

1. Personal allowances

The amount of your personal allowance for income support (IS), income-based jobseeker's allowance (JSA), housing benefit (HB) and council tax benefit (CTB) depends on your age and whether you are claiming as a single person or a couple. You also get an allowance for each dependent child (but see pp2:382 and 2:443 for the rules on income and capital belonging to children).

If you are polygamously married (see p2:114) you usually receive an extra amount for each additional partner in your household.[2] This amount is equivalent to the difference between the rates for a couple over the age of 18 and a single person over the age of 25. For IS and income-based JSA, where any additional partner is under the age of 18, you only receive an extra amount if s/he is responsible for a child (see p2:122) or would otherwise meet the special conditions for qualifying for JSA as a 16/17-year-old[3] (see p2:152). For the treatment of additional partners in polygamous marriages for family credit (FC), disability working allowance (DWA) and earnings top-up (ETU), see pp2:462, 2:477 and 2:500.

Rates of personal allowances (ages 18 and over)[4]

The rates of personal allowances for people aged 18 or over are the same for IS, income-based JSA and HB/CTB. If you and/or your partner (if any) are aged 16 or 17, the rates for IS/income-based JSA may be different to the rates for HB/CTB (see p2:321).

Single claimant:	
Aged 18/24	£40.70
Aged 25 or over	£51.40
Lone parent:	
Aged 18 or over	£51.40
Couple:	
Both aged 18 or over	£80.65
One aged under 18 (some IS/JSA cases – see p2:321 – and all HB and CTB cases)	£80.65
One aged under 18 (other IS/JSA cases only – see p2:321)	
either	£51.40
or	£40.70
Polygamous marriages: Each additional qualifying partner living in the same household[5]	£29.25

Rates of personal allowances (16/17-year-olds)

Special rates of IS and income-based JSA personal allowances are paid if you are aged 16 or 17. These depend partly on your age and that of your partner, if you have one. For HB, if you or your partner or both of you are under 18, your personal allowance is the same as the rate for 18/24-year-olds (see above). CTB is not payable for single people under 18, or for couples if both of you are under 18 because you cannot be liable to pay council tax at that age (see p2:572). If one of you is 18 or over you will get the same personal allowance as for all couples aged 18/24 (see 2:319).

Single people and lone parents (income support and income-based jobseeker's allowance)

There are two levels of payment.[6]

Lower rate	£30.95
Higher rate	£40.70

You are paid at the higher rate if:[7]
- you qualify for the disability premium (see p2:325); *or*
- you are an orphan with no one acting as your parent (which includes foster parents, a local authority or a voluntary organisation if you are in care or are being looked after by them, or any other person with parental responsibility for you); *or*
- you are living away from parents and any person acting as your parent, and immediately before you were 16 you were in custody, or being looked after by a local authority who placed you with someone other than a close relative (see p2:332); *or*
- you are living away from parents and any person acting as your parent, and instead are living elsewhere:
  - as part of a programme of resettlement or rehabilitation under the supervision of the probation service or a local authority; *or*
  - to avoid physical or sexual abuse; *or*
  - because you need special accommodation due to mental or physical illness or handicap; *or*
- you are living away from your parents and any person acting as your parent, they are unable to support you financially and they are:
  - in custody; *or*
  - unable to enter Great Britain (eg, because of the immigration laws); *or*
  - 'chronically sick or mentally or physically disabled'; *or*
- you have to live away from parents and any person acting as your parent, because:
  - you are estranged from them (see p1:331); *or*

- you are in physical or moral danger; *or*
- there is a serious risk to your physical or mental health;
- for income-based JSA only, you qualify for JSA either because you are claiming during or after the child benefit extension period or because you are entitled to a special hardship payment (see p1:338).

Couples[8] (income support and income-based jobseeker's allowance)

The amount paid to couples depends on your ages and whether one or both of you are or would be eligible for IS or income-based JSA (including JSA discretionary severe hardship payments – see p1:338) if you were a single person. For some couples the amount may be no more than that for a single person.

One partner aged 18 or over and the other under 18 *and* entitled to IS or income-based/discretionary JSA (or would be if not a member of a couple)	£80.65
Both under 18 *and both* entitled to IS or income-based/ discretionary JSA (or would be if not a member of a couple)	£61.35
Both under 18 and one is responsible for a child	£61.35
For IS, the claimant, or for JSA, either partner is aged 25 or over and the other under 18 *and* not entitled to IS or income-based/discretionary JSA (even if s/he were not a member of a couple)	£51.40
For IS, the claimant, or for JSA, either partner is 18/24 and the other under 18 *and* not entitled to IS or income-based/ discretionary JSA (even if s/he was not a member of a couple)	£40.70
Both under 18 and one is entitled to IS or income-based/ discretionary JSA at the higher rate for single under-18s	£40.70
Both under 18 and one is entitled to IS or income-based/ discretionary JSA at the lower rate for single under-18s	£30.95

Note: If you are a couple claiming IS, any of the above references to a person being entitled or not entitled to IS means any of the 'people who can claim IS' listed on p1:441 and not those who could claim IS as a 16/17-year-old single person or lone parent listed on p1:448. If you are a couple claiming JSA, any such reference means either those listed on p1:441 or those listed on p1:448.

Children

The rates for your dependent children are the same for IS, income-based JSA, HB and CTB and are not affected by your (or your partner's) own age.

Children:

Under 11	£20.20 (From October 1999 £24.90)
11/15	£25.90
16/18	£30.95

For the purpose of calculating the personal allowances above, a child is not treated as being aged 11 or 16 until the first Monday in September following her/his 11th or 16th birthday.[9]

2. **Premiums**

Premiums are added to your basic personal allowances and are intended to help with extra expenses caused by age, disability or the cost of children. They are:

- family premium (see p2:323);
- disabled child premium (see p2:325);
- disability premium (see p2:325);
- pensioner premium (see p2:327);
- higher pensioner premium (see p2:327);
- severe disability premium (see p2:329); *and*
- carer's premium (see p2:333).

See p2:334 for information about backdating of premiums. See the box below for the premium rates.

Except for the lone parent increase of the family premium (which is higher for housing benefit (HB) and council tax benefit (CTB) than for income support (IS) and income-based jobseeker's allowance (JSA), the rates of premiums are the same for all claimants (even if you are under 18 or under 25) of all benefits.

Premium rates

The following premiums can be paid on top of any other premiums:

Family premium (ordinary rate)	£13.90
Disabled child premium (for each qualifying child)	£21.90
Severe disability premium	
Single (or one partner qualifying)	£39.75
Couple (both partners qualifying)	£79.50
Carer's premium	
Single (or one partner qualifying)	£13.95
Couple (both partners qualifying)	£27.90

Only one of the following premiums can be paid; if you qualify for more than one you get whichever is the highest:[10]

Family premium (lone parent increase)

IS/JSA	£ 1.85
HB/CTB	£ 8.15

Disability premium

Single	£21.90
Couple	£31.25

Pensioner premium

(i) if aged 60/74

Single	£23.60
Couple	£35.95

(ii) if aged 75/79

Single	£25.90
Couple	£39.20

Higher pensioner premium

Single	£30.85
Couple	£44.65

Entitlement to some premiums depends on receipt of other benefits. Once you have qualified for a premium, if you or your partner cease to receive a qualifying benefit because of the overlapping benefit rules (ie, because you are receiving another benefit at the same or a higher rate – see p2:493), or because you or your partner are on an employment training course or getting a training allowance, you continue to receive the relevant premium.[11] In addition, you or your partner (if any) must be getting the benefit for yourself (or for your partner), and not on behalf of someone else – eg, as an appointee (see p2:480).[12]

Sometimes, you may be able to get payment of a premium backdated (see p2:334).

Family premium[13]

You are entitled to this if your family includes a child (see p2:121). It is paid even if you are not the parent of the child and even if you do not receive a personal allowance for any child because they have capital over £3,000.

Only one family premium is payable regardless of the number of children you have. Where a child who is in the care of or being looked after by a local authority or who is in custody, comes home for part of a week, your IS or income-based JSA includes a proportion of the premium, according to the number of days the child is with you.[14] For HB and CTB you may be paid the full premium if your child who is in care or being looked after by a local authority is part of the household for any part of the week – how often and for how long the child visits are taken into account.[15]

Lone parents[16]

Prior to 6 April 1998, a higher rate of the family premium was payable to lone parents than to couples (unless they were also entitled to the disability premium – see p2:325 – or one of the pensioner premiums – see p2:327 – which would be payable instead). The lone parent rate of the family premium is now only payable if:

For IS and income-based JSA:
- you were both a lone parent and entitled to IS or income-based JSA on 5 April 1998, *or*, if you were not, you were on any day within 12 weeks before or after that date and you have not ceased to be, both a lone parent and entitled to IS or income-based JSA for more than 12 weeks in this time; *and*
- you do not subsequently cease to be both a lone parent and entitled to IS or income-based JSA, although any periods of less than 12 weeks during which you may cease to be either a lone parent or entitled to IS or income-based JSA, or both, are ignored.

For HB and CTB:
- you were entitled or treated as entitled to HB/CTB and the lone parent increase on 5 April 1998; *and*
- you do not cease to be a lone parent; *and*
- you do not cease to be entitled or treated as entitled to HB/CTB; *and*
- you do not become or cease to be entitled to IS or income-based JSA; *and*
- the disability (see p2:325) or one of the pensioner premiums (see p2:327) does not become payable instead.

You are treated as entitled to HB and CTB on 5 April 1998 if you were entitled to the other benefit (ie, CTB or HB) as a lone parent from 5 April 1998 to the day before you eventually claim it. You are also treated as entitled to HB during any rent-free weeks.

Note: Unlike IS and income-based JSA, there are no linking periods for HB and CTB, so if you lose the increase even for a short period you will not be able to claim it back (although a change of address does not break your entitlement).[17]

If you have been getting the lone parent rate of the family premium with IS/income-based JSA continuously since 5 July 1998 (or if you have been getting a pensioner or disability premium as a lone parent since 5 April 1998), and you do not already get the lone parent rate of child benefit (see Chapter 12), you will still be able to claim that benefit so long as you claim within one month of your entitlement to IS/income-based JSA ending (see p2:241).

If you lose your entitlement to the lone parent increase for IS, income-based JSA, HB or CTB, you may still be entitled to the ordinary rate of the family premium instead.

Disabled child premium[18]

You are entitled to a disabled child premium for each of the children in your family who gets disability living allowance (DLA – see p1:160) or who is blind.

A child is treated as blind if s/he is registered as blind and for the first 28 weeks after s/he has been taken off the register on regaining her/his sight.[19] If DLA stops because the child has gone into hospital, see p2:156. Where your child is in local authority care or in custody for part of the week, this premium is affected in the same way as the family premium (see above). For how to qualify for DLA, see Chapter 10.

If the child has over £3,000 capital, you do not get this premium.[20]

Disability premium[21]

The way in which you can get a disability premium differs depending on whether you have a partner or not (see p2:114). In either case, the person who satisfies the qualifying conditions set out below has to be aged under 60. If you or your partner (if any) are aged 60 or over you may instead get the higher pensioner premium (see p2:327). You qualify for a disability premium if:

- you or your partner (if any) are getting a qualifying benefit. These are:
  - DLA (see Chapter 10);
  - attendance allowance (AA – see Chapter 10) – but note that this can only be claimed if you are aged 65 or over and will therefore be a qualifying benefit not for the disability premium but for the higher pensioner premium (see p2:327) instead – or an equivalent benefit paid to meet attendance needs because of an injury at work (see Chapter 11) or a war injury;[22]
  - war pensioner's mobility supplement;
  - disability working allowance (DWA – see Chapter 22);
  - severe disablement allowance (SDA – see Chapter 4); *or*
  - incapacity benefit (IB) paid at the long-term rate (see Chapter 3); *or*
  - special short-term rate of IB because you are terminally ill (see p2:45).[23]

Extra-statutory payments to compensate you or your partner (if any) for not getting these benefits also count.[24]

You must be getting the benefit in question for yourself, not on behalf of someone else – eg, as an appointee (see p2:480). The same applies if it is your partner who gets the benefit.[25]

Once you qualify for the premium, you, or your partner (if any), are treated as still getting a qualifying benefit you no longer in fact get, if you would have got it but for the overlapping benefit rules (see p2:493) – eg, your SDA stops because you start to get a widow's pension;[26]

- you, or your partner (if any), are registered as blind with a local authority. If you, or your partner, regain your sight you still qualify for 28 weeks after being taken off the register;[27]
- you, or your partner (if any), have an NHS invalid trike or private car allowance because of disability;[28]
- you, or your partner (if any), were getting IB paid at the long-term rate (or at the short-term rate because of terminal illness) which stopped when retirement pension became payable, since when you have been continuously entitled to IS/income-based JSA/HB/CTB.[29] If it is your partner who began receiving a retirement pension, s/he must still be alive (IS/income-based JSA),[30] or still be a member of your family (HB/CTB).[31] In the case of IS or income-based JSA only, you or your partner (if any), must have previously qualified for a disability premium;[32]
- you, or your partner, were getting AA or DLA but payment of that benefit was suspended when one of you became a hospital inpatient.[33] In the case of IS and income-based JSA only, you or your partner must have previously qualified for a disability premium.
- for IS/HB/CTB but not for income-based JSA, the Benefits Agency has decided that you are 'incapable of work' or you are treated as incapable and you have been so entitled, incapable of work or treated as incapable of work for a continuous period of:[34]
  - 196 days if you have been certified as 'terminally ill' – ie, it can reasonably be expected that you will die within six months in consequence of a progressive disease;[35]
  - 364 days in all other cases;

  provided you have claimed IB (whether you are entitled to it or not) or (for IS only) you are entitled to statutory sick pay (SSP).

  Breaks in entitlement/incapacity of up to 56 days (or 52 weeks if you are a 'welfare to work beneficiary'[36] – see Chapter 34) are included in these periods. See pp1:15 and 2:14 for more details about SSP and 'incapacity for work'.

  If you consider you have been incapable of work for 364/196 days or more, but you have not previously been certified or assessed as incapable of work, you should claim IB (see Chapter 3). You do not have to be awarded IB, you only have to show that you have been incapable of work. A medical note is not necessary for any period after 13 April 1995, although one is still helpful as you have to persuade an adjudication officer that you have been incapable of work throughout. Even if you have not yet been incapable of work for 364/196 days, it is advisable to claim IB as soon as possible so that the disability premium can be awarded to you as soon as you reach the qualifying period.

Note: Although the rules for the disability premium include reference to receipt of AA and retirement pension (see above), if you or your partner receive either of these benefits you are certain to be entitled to one of the pensioner premiums (see below) instead of the disability premium.

If you are a couple, you get the disability premium at the couple rate (£31.25) provided that one of you meets one of the above qualifying conditions, except in the case of the condition concerning SSP and incapacity for work. In that case, you do not get the premium at all unless the person who qualifies is the claimant of the IS/HB/CTB paid to you as a couple.[37] You may, therefore, need to swap who is the claimant of your IS/HB/CTB (see pp2:114 and 2:480). This does not apply to income-based JSA because you cannot claim JSA while you are incapable of work. If your partner is incapable of work s/he should claim IS instead of your claim for JSA so that you may benefit from the disability premium.

If you go on a Training for Work or Work-based Training for Young People (formerly Youth Training), or for any period you receive a training allowance, you keep the disability premium even though you may cease to receive one of the qualifying benefits, or cease to be entitled to SSP or be incapable of work during the course, as long as you continue to be entitled to IS, income-based JSA, HB or CTB. After the course, the premium continues (except for income-based JSA) if you remain entitled to SSP (for IS only), are still incapable of work, or getting a qualifying benefit.[38]

Pensioner premium[39]

The pensioner premium is paid at two rates according to age:
- the lower rate if you or your partner are aged 60/74 inclusive;
- the enhanced rate if you or your partner are aged 75/79 inclusive (sometimes known as the 'enhanced pensioner premium').

The couple rate for either is paid even if only one partner fulfils the condition. You are paid the highest rate which may apply to you. If you or your partner are sick or disabled check to see if you could get the higher pensioner premium instead (see below).

Higher pensioner premium

You qualify for higher pensioner premium if one of the following applies:[40]
- you or your partner are 80 or over;
- you were getting a disability premium as part of your IS, income-based JSA, HB or CTB before you were 60 and you have continued to claim that benefit since reaching that age. You must have been getting a disability premium at some time during the eight weeks (or 52 weeks if you are a 'welfare to work beneficiary' – see Chapter 34)[41] before you were 60, and have received that

benefit continuously since you reached 60.[42] But you can have a period off that benefit of up to eight (or 52) weeks and still qualify.

For HB and CTB, if you were entitled to a higher pensioner premium for one benefit in the previous eight (or 52) weeks you will get a higher pensioner premium with the other if you then qualify or requalify for that benefit.[43] Previous entitlement to a premium while on HB or CTB does not help you qualify for the higher pensioner premium when you claim IS or income-based JSA, and *vice versa*, but whereas previous entitlement while on IS helps you qualify when you claim income-based JSA,[44] the reverse does not apply.

In the case of couples, the person who was the claimant for that benefit before s/he was 60 must continue to claim after that, but it is not necessary for the claimant to have been the person who qualified for the disability premium;[45]

- you or your partner are aged 60/79 *and* either of you receive a qualifying benefit (as for the disability premium – see p2:325), are registered blind, or have an NHS trike or a private car allowance.

  - If your AA or DLA stops because you go into hospital – see p2:156 (IS and income-based JSA), p2:159 (HB and CTB).

  - If you (for IS/HB/CTB), or your partner (for IS/income-based JSA/HB/CTB), stop getting IB (or if in the past you stopped getting invalidity benefit) because you get retirement pension instead, you still get a higher pensioner premium with your IS, income-based JSA, HB or CTB, if you remain continuously entitled (apart from breaks of eight weeks – or 52 weeks if you are a 'welfare to work beneficiary' – or less) to the same benefit.[46] In the case of HB and CTB, if you were entitled to a higher pensioner premium for one of these benefits in the previous eight or 52 weeks, you get a higher pensioner premium with the other if you then qualify or requalify for that benefit.[47] Previous entitlement within this period to the higher pensioner premium with IS will also count when you claim income-based JSA, but the reverse will not apply.[48] If it is your partner who had changed to a retirement pension, s/he must still be alive (IS/income-based JSA), or still be a member of your family (HB and CTB).[49] In the case of IS and income-based JSA, the higher pensioner premium or a disability premium must also have been applicable to you or your partner.[50] So, if, up to the time your IB (or invalidity benefit) ceased, your applicable amount was calculated by a method that did not include premiums (eg, because you were in a hostel prior to 9 October 1989, or you lived in a residential care or nursing home before 31 March 1993), you are not able to qualify in this way.[51]

  - If you are getting SDA by the time you reach 65, you will be awarded it for life even if you no longer satisfy the incapacity or disability conditions. You will therefore continue to qualify for the higher pensioner premium.[52] This also applies even if it ceases to be paid because you get retirement pension at a higher rate.[53]

Severe disability premium[54]

You qualify for a severe disability premium if all of the following apply to you:

- you **receive a qualifying benefit.** For the severe disability premium this is either AA (or the equivalent war pension or industrial injury benefit,[55] or the middle or higher rate care component of DLA (or extra-statutory payments to compensate you for not receiving any of these[56]). If you are a couple (or polygamously married), whichever one of you is claiming IS, income-based JSA, HB or CTB must be getting a qualifying benefit and your partner(s) must also either be getting a qualifying benefit or else s/he must be registered blind (or treated as blind).[57] However, in either case you are treated as getting the qualifying benefit while still in hospital (see p2:154). The qualifying benefit must be paid in respect of yourself/selves, as receipt of benefit for someone else (eg, a child) does not count;[58]

- **no non-dependant** aged 18 or over is **'normally residing with you'** (see p2:330) – eg, a grown-up son or daughter, or your parents. It does not matter whose house it is, yours or the non-dependant's.[59] For IS, income-based JSA and HB, someone is only counted as living with you if you share accommodation apart from a bathroom, lavatory or a communal area such as a hall, passageway or a room in common use in sheltered accommodation. If s/he is separately liable to make payments for the accommodation to the landlord, s/he does not count as living with you.[60] This is not explicitly stated in the rules for CTB, although the same test may in practice be applied for consistency;

- **no one gets invalid care allowance (ICA) for looking after you**, or, if you are a couple (or polygamously married), no one gets ICA for both (or all) of you (but see below for an exception when you and/or your partner(s) go into hospital). Only payments of ICA count,[61] so no account is taken of any underlying entitlement to ICA where it is awarded but not paid because of the overlapping benefit rules, or of any extra-statutory payments to compensate for it not being paid. Similarly, no account is taken of any backdated payments or arrears ICA[62] (see 'Carers and the severe disability premium', p2:333).

Couples and the severe disability premium

Couples get the couple rate if both (or, in a polygamous marriage, all) of you are getting a qualifying benefit and no one gets ICA for either one (or any) of you. However, if your partner does not get a qualifying benefit but is registered blind (or treated as blind), or if ICA is paid for one of you, you still get the single rate. (In polygamous marriages the single rate is awarded in respect of each partner who gets a qualifying benefit while ICA is not paid.)

Note that for couples (and polygamous marriages) only, you and/or your partner(s) are treated as getting AA (or the higher or middle rate care component of DLA), even though it has stopped because you/your partner(s) have been in hospital for more than four weeks. Similarly, for couples (and polygamous marriages) only, a person is treated as receiving ICA even if the qualifying benefit of the person for whom s/he is caring has stopped because that person has been in hospital for more than four weeks.[63]

Non-dependants[64]

The following people who live with you do *not* count as non-dependants:

For IS, income-based JSA, HB and CTB:

- anyone aged under 18;
- any member of your family (see p2:113 for who counts as part of your family). This may include any child up to the age of 19 (see p2:121) as well as your partner, although your partner must be getting a qualifying benefit (or would be but for being in hospital, see above) or be registered or treated as blind (see p1:443) if you are to be paid the severe disability premium (see p2:329);
- anyone else who receives a qualifying benefit;[65]
- anyone who is registered blind (or treated as blind);[66]
- anyone staying in your home who normally lives elsewhere. In deciding whether someone normally lives with you or elsewhere it may be relevant to consider: why the residence started; the relationship and its history, if any, between those concerned; the motivations involved; the purpose for which residence has been taken up; its duration; and whether there is any other home in which residence is or could be taken up;[67]
- any person (and, for IS and income-based JSA only, her/his partner) employed by a charitable or voluntary body as a resident carer for you or your partner if you pay a charge for that service (even if the charge is only nominal).[68]

For IS and income-based JSA only:

- any person (or her/his partner) who jointly occupies (see p2:232) your home and is either the co-owner with you or your partner, or jointly liable with you or your partner to make payments to a landlord in respect of occupying it. If this person is a close relative (see p2:232), however, s/he *will* count as a non-dependant *unless* the co-ownership or joint liability to make payments to a landlord existed either before 11 April 1988 or by the time you or your partner first moved in (but, for IS only, see transitional provisions below);
- any person (or any member of their household) who is liable to pay you or your partner on a commercial basis (see p2:232) in respect of occupying the

dwelling (eg, tenants or licensees), unless s/he is a close relative of you or your partner (but, for IS only, see transitional provisions below);

- any person (or any member of her/his household) to whom you or your partner are liable to make such payments on a commercial basis, unless s/he is a close relative (see p2:232) of you or your partner (but, for IS only, see transitional provisions below);
- if someone (other than those listed above) comes to live with you in order to look after you, or your partner, your severe disability premium remains in payment for the first 12 weeks.[69] After that, you lose the premium (or get a lower rate premium). The carer should then consider claiming ICA (see Chapter 5).

In the first three situations above, the presence of close relatives (see p2:232) does *not* prevent you from continuing to get the severe disability premium if you fall within the scope of the *transitional provisions* which applied to IS claimants entitled to this premium before 21 October 1991. These were set out in the 22nd edition of the *National Welfare Benefits Handbook* (1992/93).

For HB only:[70]

- any person who jointly occupies your home and is either the co-owner with you or your partner, or liable with you or your partner to make payments in respect of occupying it. A joint occupier who was a non-dependant at any time within the previous eight weeks counts as a non-dependant if the local authority thinks that the change of arrangements was created to take advantage of the HB scheme;
- any person who is liable to pay you or your partner on a commercial basis in respect of occupying the dwelling unless s/he is a close relative (see p2:232) of you or your partner, or if the local authority thinks that the rent or other agreement has been created to take advantage of the HB scheme (but this cannot apply if the person was otherwise liable to pay rent for the accommodation at any time during the eight weeks before the agreement was made);
- any person, or any member of her/his household, to whom you or your partner are liable to make payments in respect of your accommodation on a commercial basis unless s/he is a close relative of you or your partner.

For CTB only:[71]

- any person who is jointly and severally liable (see p2:232) with you to pay council tax. If s/he was a non-dependant at any time within the eight weeks before s/he became liable for council tax, s/he counts as a non-dependant if the local authority thinks that the change of arrangements was created to take advantage of the CTB scheme;
- any person who is liable to pay you or your partner on a commercial basis in respect of occupying the dwelling unless s/he is a close relative (see below) of you or your partner, or if the local authority thinks that the liability to make

payments in respect of the dwelling has been created to take advantage of the CTB scheme (but this cannot apply if the person was otherwise liable to pay rent for the accommodation at any time during the eight weeks before that liability arose).

Definitions

'**Close relative**' means parent, parent-in-law, son, son-in-law, daughter, daughter-in-law, step-parent, step-son, step-daughter, brother, sister, or partners of any of these.[72]

'**Jointly occupies**' has a technical meaning. It is a legal relationship involving occupation by two or more persons (whether as owner-occupiers or as tenants or licensees), with one and the same legal right.[73] It does not exist if people merely have equal access to different parts of the premises (as had previously been decided by a commissioner[74]).

'**Commercial basis**' has no technical meaning, and there is no requirement that there need be any intention to make a profit.[75] It may be sufficient if a 'reasonable' charge is made, even if this does not fully cover the cost of the accommodation and meals being provided.[76] The reasonableness of the charge made should be judged solely against the cost of occupying the dwelling, disregarding the additional costs of providing food, clothing and care for the claimant.[77] A useful, but not conclusive, test to apply is to consider whether the same arrangement *might* have been entered into with a lodger rather than with the claimant.[78] It is not relevant to the question of whether the arrangement is on a commercial basis to consider either whether the non-dependant depends financially on the charge being paid or if s/he would take action against the claimant if s/he did not pay.[79] However, these last two matters are relevant to whether there is a *liability* (see below).

'**Liability**' means a legal or contractual liability (as distinct from a moral or ethical obligation), although this can always be inferred from the circumstances, there being no requirement that any arrangements need be evidenced in writing.[80] It has been held, however, that even though a landlord may have expected relatives of a liable person to share their home in order to provide care, it cannot be inferred that they are also liable. Nor can it be assumed that someone is owed a liability in recompense merely for allowing another person to occupy their home, particularly if the gains (eg, when someone depends on another person for their care) exceed any possible loss.[81] Any liability must arise from the costs of occupying the home. People with no contractual capacity (eg, people with very severe learning disabilities) cannot establish liability under English law. However, there is always a presumption that capacity exists and the test of capacity may not be very stringent. In any case, a commissioner has urged a consistency of approach for England and Scotland where the law is different in that a liability can exist even where contractual capacity is not established.[82]

Carer's premium[83]

You qualify for this if you or your partner are getting, or are treated as getting, ICA.

- For how to qualify for ICA, see Chapter 5. Note that if you are entitled to invalid care allowance by the time you reach the age of 65, you continue to be entitled to it for life even if you stop providing care to a severely disabled person or if you start full-time work (see p2:5).[84]
- You are treated as getting ICA even if you do not receive it but:
  - you would get it but for the overlapping benefit rules – see p2:493 – (eg, you get long-term IB instead), provided you claimed (or reclaimed) it on, or after, 1 October 1990, and the person you are claiming for continues to get AA (see Chapter 10) or the care component (middle or higher rate) of DLA (see Chapter 10).[85] The Benefits Agency may argue that you can only benefit from this if you originally claimed ICA on or after 1 October 1990, but you should argue that that was not the intention of the rule and that the claim you made before that date should be treated as if it had continued to be made on and after that date. Alternatively, you could simply make a new claim for ICA even though it has already been awarded to you;
  - you are awarded an extra-statutory payment to compensate you for non-payment of ICA.[86]
- If you stop getting, or being treated as getting, ICA, your entitlement to a carer's premium continues for a further eight weeks, even if you first claim IS, income-based JSA, HB or CTB in this time.
- A double premium is awarded where both you and your partner satisfy the conditions for it.

Carers and the severe disability premium

Before claiming ICA, you should consider how your claim may affect the entitlement to the severe disability premium (see p2:329), of the disabled person you are caring for, particularly where the only financial advantage to you as the carer is the amount of the carer's premium which may be worth considerably less than the severe disability premium (but see p2:329 for the rules on notional income).

Any backdated award of ICA does not affect a disabled person's entitlement to the severe disability premium.[87] There may therefore be scope for careful planning to take advantage of this rule so that carers can be paid ICA or the carer's premium for the same period that the disabled person has already received the severe disability premium.

45

3. **Backdating of premiums**

To qualify for the disability premium (p2:325), higher pensioner premium (p2:327), severe disability premium (p2:329), disabled child premium (p2:325) and/or carer's premium (p2:333), you and/or a member of your family usually have to have been awarded the qualifying benefit which applies to each premium. The date you may begin to get your premium may therefore depend on the date from which your qualifying benefit is awarded. However, because of the time it may take to deal with your claim for the qualifying benefit, or because your claim is backdated, or because it is initially refused but awarded some time later after a review or appeal, you may not get your premium straightaway and you may have to apply for it to be backdated.

- If you are already getting income support (IS), income-based jobseeker's allowance (JSA), housing benefit (HB) or council tax benefit (CTB), you should ask for your award of this benefit to be reviewed and for your premium to be backdated either to the same date that your qualifying benefit is awarded from, or to when you first got (or claimed) IS, income-based JSA, HB or CTB if that is later. In such circumstances there is no limit to the period for which IS or income-based JSA arrears can be paid to you, but any new or increased entitlement to HB or CTB is limited to 12 months.[88]

- If you have previously claimed IS/income-based JSA/HB/CTB, but your claim was refused solely because you did not at that time get the qualifying benefit for your premium, the DSS has argued that for IS/income-based JSA, even though the rules were not intended to operate in this way, it is not possible to review your claim in these circumstances. However, you should seek advice if this applies to you as the DSS may be wrong (see Appendix 2). In the meantime, you may have to make a fresh claim for IS/income-based JSA in order to get your premium, even though this may only be backdated for a maximum period of three months if you have a specified reason for a late claim (see p2:490).

    For HB/CTB, it may also be argued that your earlier disallowed claim cannot be reviewed in these circumstances. You should also seek advice if this applies to you. In the meantime, you may also have to make a fresh claim for HB/CTB and in these circumstances it should be accepted that you clearly have 'good cause' for your late claim so that it should be backdated, although it cannot be backdated for more than 12 months (see pp1:534 and 1:582).

- If as a result of getting a qualifying benefit backdated you now qualify for but have not previously claimed IS, income-based JSA, HB or CTB, you should make a new claim and ask for it to be backdated for up to three months (for IS/income-based JSA) or 12 months (for HB and CTB). However, for IS/income-based JSA, backdating of up to three months is only possible if you have a specified reason for making a late claim (see p2:487). For HB/CTB, backdating is possible if you have 'good cause' for not claiming earlier (see pp1:534 and 1:582).

If your premium has been missed out on an earlier refused claim or on your current claim, because your entitlement to the premium has been overlooked or because of some other error in assessing your entitlement, you can also apply for your claim to be reviewed in order to get your claim backdated. In such circumstances there is no limit to the period for which IS/income-based JSA arrears can be paid to you, and although the rules may limit any arrears of any new or increased entitlement to HB or CTB to 12 months,[89] you may be able to get compensation for any longer period (see p2:663).

Additional points to note

- Although a later award of invalid care allowance may entitle you to have your carer's premium backdated, this will not affect the severe disability premium of the person you are looking after (see p2:329).
- For HB and CTB, if you are one of a couple and the person who is incapable of work is not the claimant, you can swap the claimant role and s/he can apply to backdate a new claim if s/he has 'good cause' (see pp1:534 and 1:582). In this way you can get the disability premium backdated for up to 12 months.[90] For IS/income-based JSA, it will not be possible to backdate your claim unless one of the specified reasons for making a late claim apply (see p2:490).

Notes

· ·

References are to statutes and regulations as amended up to 8 March 1999. All regulations are (General) Regulations unless otherwise stated. There is a full list of abbreviations in Appendix 13.

1 Reg 22A IS Regs
2 **IS** Reg 18 IS Regs
 JSA Reg 84 JSA Regs
 HB Reg 17 HB Regs
 CTB Reg 9 CTB Regs

1. Personal allowances

3 **IS** Reg 18(2) IS Regs
 JSA Reg 84(2) JSA Regs
4 **IS** Sch 2 Part I IS Regs
 JSA Sch 1 paras 1 and 2 JSA Regs
 HB Sch 2 Part I HB Regs
 CTB Sch 1 Part I CTB Regs
5 **IS** Reg 18(1)(b) IS Regs
 JSA Reg 84(1)(b) JSA Regs
 HB Reg 17(b) HB Regs
 CTB Reg 9(b) CTB Regs
 HB/CTB paras C4.05-06 GM
6 **IS** Sch 2 para 1(1)(a), (b) and (c) and (2)(a), (b) and (c) IS Regs
 JSA Sch 1 para 1(1)(a)-(c) and (2)(a)-(c) JSA Regs
7 **IS** Sch 2 paras 1(1)(b) and (c), (2)(b) and (c) and 1A IS Regs
 JSA Sch 1 para 1(1)(b)-(c) and (2)(b)-(c) JSA Regs
8 **IS** Sch 2 para 1(3) IS Regs
 JSA Sch 1 para 1(3) JSA Regs
9 **IS** Sch 2 para 2 IS Regs
 JSA Sch1 para 2 JSA Regs
 HB Sch 2 para 2 HB Regs
 CTB Sch 1 para 2 CTB Regs

2. Premiums

10 **IS** Sch 2 para 5 IS Regs
 JSA Sch 1 para 6 JSA Regs
 HB Sch 2 para 5 IS Regs
 CTB Sch 1 para 5 HB Regs
11 **IS** Sch 2 para 7 IS Regs
 JSA Sch 1 para 8 JSA Regs
 HB Sch 2 para 7 HB Regs
 CTB Sch 1 para 7 CTB Regs

12 **IS** Sch 2 para 14B IS Regs
 JSA Sch 1 para 19 JSA Regs
 HB Sch 2 para 14B HB Regs
 CTB Sch 1 para 18 CTB Regs
 See also R(IS) 10/94
13 **IS** Sch 2 para 3 IS Regs
 JSA Sch 1 para 4 JSA Regs
 HB Sch 2 para 3 HB Regs
 CTB Sch 1 para 3 CTB Regs
14 **IS** Regs 15(3) and 16(6) IS Regs
 JSA Regs 74(4) and 78(7) JSA Regs
15 **HB** Reg 15(4)-(5) HB Regs
 CTB Reg 7(3)-(4) CTB Regs
16 **IS** Sch 2 para 3 IS Regs
 JSA Sch 1 para 4 JSA Regs
 HB Sch 2 para 3 HB Regs
 CTB Sch 1 para 3 CTB Regs
17 **HB/CTB** A45/97 and A10/98
18 **IS** Sch 2 paras 14 and 15(6) IS Regs
 JSA Sch 1 para 16 JSA Regs
 HB Sch 2 paras 14 and 15(6) HB Regs
 CTB Sch 1 paras 15 and 19(7) CTB Regs
19 **IS** Sch 2 paras 12(1)(a)(iii) and (2) and 14(c) IS Regs
 JSA Sch 1 paras 14(1)(h) and (2) JSA Regs
 HB Sch 2 paras 12(1)(a)(v) and (2) and 14(c) HB Regs
 CTB Sch 1 paras 13(1)(a)(v) and (2) and 15(c) CTB Regs
20 **IS** Sch 2 para 14(a) IS Regs
 JSA Sch 1 para 16(a) JSA Regs
 HB Sch 2 para 14(a) HB Regs
 CTB Sch 1 para 15(a) CTB Regs
21 **IS** Sch 2 para 11 IS Regs
 JSA Sch 1 paras 13 and 14 JSA Regs
 HB Sch 2 para 11 HB Regs
 CTB Sch 1 para 12 CTB Regs
22 **IS** Reg 2(1) IS Regs
 JSA Reg 1(3) JSA Regs
 HB Reg 2(1) HB Regs

CTB Reg 2(1) CTB Regs
All Definition of 'attendance allowance'

23 **IS** Sch 2 para 12(6) IS Regs
JSA Sch 1 para 14(1)(d) JSA Regs
HB Sch 2 para 12(7) HB Regs
CTB Sch 1 para 13(6A) CTB Regs

24 **IS** Sch 2 para 14A IS Regs
JSA Sch 1 para 18 JSA Regs
HB Sch 2 para 14A HB Regs
CTB Sch 1 para 17 CTB Regs

25 **IS** Sch 2 para 14B IS Regs
JSA Sch 1 para 19 JSA Regs
HB Sch 2 para 14B HB Regs
CTB Sch 1 para 18 CTB Regs
See also R(IS) 10/94

26 **IS** Sch 2 para 7(1)(a) IS Regs
JSA Sch 1 para 8(1)(a) JSA Regs
HB Sch 2 para 7(1)(a) HB Regs
CTB Sch 1 para 7(1)(a) CTB Regs

27 **IS** Sch 2 para 12(1)(a)(iii) and (2) IS Regs
JSA Sch 1 para 14(1)(h) and (2) JSA Regs
HB Sch 2 para 12(1)(a)(v) and (2) HB Regs
CTB Sch 1 para 13(1)(a)(v) and (2) CTB Regs

28 **IS** Sch 2 para 12(1)(a)(ii) IS Regs
JSA Sch 1 paras 14(1)(e) and (f) JSA Regs
HB Sch 2 para 12(1)(a)(iv) HB Regs
CTB Sch 1 para 13(1)(a)(iv) CTB Regs

29 **IS** Sch 2 para 12(1)(c)(i) IS Regs
JSA Sch 1 para 14(1)(g)(i) JSA Regs
HB Sch 2 para 12(1)(a)(ii) HB Regs
CTB Sch 1 para 13(1)(a)(ii) CTB Regs

30 **IS** Sch 2 para 12(1)(c)(i) IS Regs
JSA Sch 1 para 14(1)(g)(i) JSA Regs

31 **HB** Sch 2 para 12(1)(a)(ii) HB Regs
CTB Sch 1 para 13(1)(a)(ii) CTB Regs

32 **IS** Sch 2 para 12(1)(c) IS Regs
JSA Sch 1 para 14(1)(g) JSA Regs

33 **IS** Sch 2 para 12(1)(c)(ii) IS Regs
JSA Sch 1 para 14(1)(g)(ii) JSA Regs
HB Sch 2 para 12(1)(a)(iii) HB Regs
CTB Sch 1 para 13(1)(a)(iii) CTB Regs

34 **IS** Sch 2 para 12(1)(b) IS Regs
HB Sch 2 para 12(1)(b) HB Regs
CTB Sch 1 para 13(1)(b) CTB Regs

35 s30B(4) SSCBA 1992

36 **IS** Sch 2 para 12(1A) IS Regs
JSA Sch 1 para 12(3) JSA Regs
HB Sch 2 para 12(8) HB Regs
CTB Sch 1 para 13(8) CTB Regs

37 **IS** Sch 2 paras 11(b) and 12 IS Regs
HB Sch 2 paras 11(b) and 12 HB Regs
CTB Sch 1 paras 12(b) and 13 CTB Regs

38 **IS** Sch 2 paras 7(1)(b) and 12(5) IS Regs
JSA Sch 1 para 8(1)(b) JSA Regs
HB Sch 2 paras 7(1)(b) and 12(5) HB Regs
CTB Sch 1 paras 7(1)(b) and 13(5) CTB Regs

39 **IS** Sch 2 paras 9 and 9A IS Regs
JSA Sch 1 paras 10 and 11 JSA Regs
HB Sch 2 paras 9 and 9A HB Regs
CTB Sch 1 paras 9 and 10 CTB Regs

40 **IS** Sch 2 para 10 IS Regs
JSA Sch 1 para 12 JSA Regs
HB Sch 2 para 10 HB Regs
CTB Sch 1 para 11 CTB Regs

41 **IS** Sch 2 para 10(4) IS Regs
JSA Sch 1 para 12(3) JSA Regs
HB Sch 2 para 10(4) HB Regs
CTB Sch 1 para 11(4) CTB Regs

42 **IS** Sch 2 para 10(1)(b)(ii) and (3) IS Regs
JSA Sch 1 para 12(2) JSA Regs
HB Sch 2 para 10(1)(b)(ii) and (3) HB Regs
CTB Sch 1 para 11(1)(b)(ii) and (3) CTB Regs

43 **HB** Sch 2 para 10(3)(c) HB Regs
CTB Sch 1 para 11(3)(c) CTB Regs

44 Sch 1 para 12(1)(a)(ii) JSA Regs

45 **IS** Sch 2 para 10(2)(b)(ii) IS Regs
JSA Sch 1 para 12(1)(c) JSA Regs
HB Sch 2 para 10(2)(b)(ii) HB Regs
CTB Sch 1 para 11(2)(b)(ii) CTB Regs

46 **IS** Sch 2 para 12(1)(c)(i) and (1A) IS Regs
JSA Sch 1 paras 14(1)(g)(i) and 12(3) JSA Regs
HB Sch 2 para 12(1)(a)(ii) and (8) HB Regs
CTB Sch 1 para 13(1)(a)(ii) and (8) CTB Regs

47 **HB** Sch 2 para 10(3)(c) HB Regs
CTB Sch 1 para 11(3)(c) CTB Regs

48 Sch 1 para 12(2) JSA Regs

49 **IS** Sch 2 para 12(1)(c)(i) IS Regs
JSA Sch 1 para 14(1)(g)(i) JSA Regs
HB Sch 2 para 12(1)(a)(ii) HB Regs
CTB Sch 1 para 13(1)(a)(ii) CTB Regs

50 **IS** Sch 2 para 12(1)(c) IS Regs
JSA Sch 1 para 14(1)(g) JSA Regs

51 CIS/458/1992

52 CIS/458/1992

53 **IS** Sch 2 para 7(1)(a) IS Regs
JSA Sch 1 para 8(1)(a) JSA Regs
HB Sch 2 para 7(1)(a) HB Regs
CTB Sch 1 para 7(1)(a) CTB Regs

54 **IS** Sch 2 para 13 IS Regs
JSA Sch 1 para 15 JSA Regs
HB Sch 2 para 13 HB Regs
CTB Sch 1 para 14 CTB Regs

55 **IS** Reg 2(1) IS Regs
HB Reg 2(1) HB Regs
CTB Reg 2(1) CTB Regs

56 **IS** Sch 2 para 14A IS Regs
JSA Sch 1 para 18 JSA Regs
HB Sch 2 para 14A HB Regs
CTB Sch 1 para 17 CTB Regs

57 **IS** Sch 2 para 13(2A) IS Regs
JSA Sch 1 para 15(3) JSA Regs
HB Sch 2 para 13(2A) HB Regs
CTB Sch 1 para 14(2A) CTB Regs

58 **IS** Sch 2 para 14B IS Regs
JSA Sch 1 para 19 JSA Regs
HB Sch 2 para 14B HB Regs
CTB Sch 1 para 18 CTB Regs

See also R(IS) 10/94, upheld in *Rider v CAO* (CA), *The Times*, 30 January 1996

59 *Bate v CAO* [1996] 2 All ER 790 (HL)

60 **IS** Reg 3(4) and (5) IS Regs
JSA Reg 2(6) and (7) JSA Regs
HB Reg 3(4) HB Regs

61 **IS** Sch 2 para 13(2)(a)(iii) and (b) IS Regs
JSA Sch 1 para 15(1)(c) and (2)(d) JSA Regs
HB Sch 2 para 13(2)(a)(iii) and (b) HB Regs
CTB Sch 1 para 14(2)(a)(iii) and (b) CTB Regs

62 **IS** Sch 2 para 13(3ZA) IS Regs
JSA Sch 1 para 15(7) JSA Regs
HB Sch 2 para 13(4) HB Regs
CTB Sch 1 para 14(4) CTB Regs

63 **IS** Sch 2 para 13(3A) IS Regs
JSA Sch 1 para 15(5) JSA Regs
HB Sch 2 para 13(3A) HB Regs
CTB Sch 1 para 14(3A) CTB Regs

64 **IS** Reg 3 and Sch 2 para 13 IS Regs
JSA Reg 2 and Sch 1 para 15 JSA Regs
HB Reg 3 and Sch 2 para 13 HB Regs
CTB Reg 3 and Sch 1 para 14 CTB Regs

65 **IS** Sch 2 para 13(3)(a) IS Regs
JSA Sch 1 para 15(4)(a) JSA Regs
HB Sch 2 para 13(3)(a) HB Regs
CTB Sch 1 para 14(3)(a) CTB Regs

66 **IS** Sch 2 para 13(3)(d) IS Regs
JSA Sch 1 para 14(1)(h) and (2) JSA Regs
HB Sch 2 para 13(3)(c) HB Regs
CTB Sch 1 para 14(3)(c) CTB Regs

67 CIS/14850/1996 para 10

68 **IS** Reg 3(2)(c) and (d) IS Regs
JSA Reg 2(2)(c) and (d) JSA Regs
HB Reg 3(2)(f) HB Regs
CTB Reg 3(2)(f) CTB Regs

69 **IS** Sch 2 para 13(3)(c) and (4) IS Regs
JSA Sch 1 para 15(4)(b) and (5) JSA Regs

70 Regs 3 and 7(1) HB Regs

71 Reg 3 CTB Regs

72 **IS** Reg 2(1) IS Regs
    JSA Reg 1(3) JSA Regs
    HB Reg 2(1) HB Regs
    CTB Reg 2(1) CTB Regs
    All Definition of 'close relative'
73 *Bate v CAO* [1996] 2 All ER 790
    (HL)
74 CIS/180/1989
75 CIS/529/1994 (Tribunal of
    Commissioners)
76 CSIS/43/1989
77 CIS/754/1991 and CIS/529/1994
    para 12
78 CIS/529/1994 para 8
79 CIS/529/1994 paras 10 and 11
80 CIS/754/1991
81 CSIS/641/1995
82 CIS/754/1991 referring to CSIS/
    28/1992 and CSIS/40/1992
83 **IS** Sch 2 para 14ZA IS Regs
    JSA Sch 1 para 17 JSA Regs
    HB Sch 2 para 14ZA HB Regs
    CTB Sch 1 para 16 CTB Regs
84 s70(6) SSCBA 1992; reg 11
    SS(ICA) Regs
85 **IS** Sch 2 paras 7 and 14ZA(2) IS
    Regs
    JSA Sch 1 para 17(2) JSA Regs
    HB Sch 2 paras 7 and 14ZA(2)
    HB Regs
    CTB Sch 1 paras 7 and 16(2)
    CTB Regs
86 **IS** Sch 2 para 14A IS Regs
    JSA Sch 1 para 18 JSA Regs
    HB Sch 2 para 14A HB Regs
    CTB Sch 1 para 17 CTB Regs
87 **IS** Sch 2 para 13(3ZA) IS Regs
    JSA Sch 1 para 15(7) JSA Regs
    HB Sch 2 para 13(4) HB Regs
    CTB Sch 1 para 14(4) CTB Regs

3. Backdating of premiums

88 **IS** Reg 63(1A) SS(Adj) Regs
    JSA Reg 63A(1A) SS(Adj) Regs
    HB Reg 79 HB Regs
    CTB Reg 69 CTB Regs
89 **IS** Reg 63(1A) SS(Adj) Regs
    JSA Reg 63A(1A) SS(Adj) Regs
    HB Reg 79 HB Regs
    CTB Reg 69 CTB Regs
90 CSIS/66/1992; CIS/706/1992

46

Chapter 46

· ·

Housing costs

This chapter covers the rules for getting income support or income-based jobseeker's allowance to cover your housing costs. It contains:
1. When you can get help with your housing costs (below)
2. Mortgages and loans (p2:345)
3. Loans for repairs and improvements (p2:350)
4. Help with 'other housing costs' (p2:352)
5. The amount of housing costs you get (p2:353)

If you own or are buying your home, income support (IS) or *income-based* jobseeker's allowance (JSA) can include a variety of payments for your housing costs. Housing costs are not included as part of *contribution-based* JSA. However, if you satisfy the means test (see p1:280) you can claim income-based JSA to top this up.

If you are a tenant you can get IS or income-based JSA for some types of housing costs, but not for your rent. This is covered by housing benefit (HB) instead (see Chapter 25). If you live in a residential care or nursing home your fees are treated differently (see p2:167) and you do not get housing costs for these.[1]

If you are paying a mortgage, it is worth checking to see if you can qualify for IS or income-based JSA, even if you think your income might be too high.

You cannot get extra help with your housing costs if you are claiming family credit (FC), disability working allowance (DWA) or earnings top-up (ETU) – see Chapters 21, 22 and 24. However, you can get HB to help you with your rent (see Chapter 25).

1. When you can get help with your housing costs

You can get help with your housing costs if:[2]
- the type of housing costs can be met by IS or income-based JSA (see p2:341);
- you, or someone in your family, are liable to pay the housing costs (see p2:341);
- the housing costs are for the home in which you normally live (see p2:342).

There are some situations in which you might not get help with housing costs. These are:
- for the first few weeks after you claim. You are expected to rely on mortgage protection payments or other income or savings initially (see p2:358);
- where you take out a loan while you are on IS or income-based JSA or during a period of 26 weeks between two claims (see p2:346).

There are restrictions on the amount you can be paid if:
- your housing costs are too high (see p2:353);
- you increase a loan while on IS or income-based JSA (see p2:346).

Which housing costs can be met[3]

Your IS or income-based JSA can include the following housing costs:
- interest:
  - on mortgages and other house purchase loans;
  - under a hire purchase agreement taken out to buy your home.
  See p2:345 for further information;
- interest on loans used to pay for repairs and improvements or to meet a service charge for repairs and improvements (see p2:350);
- 'other housing costs' (see p2:352):
  - rent or ground rent (feu duty in Scotland) if you have a lease of more than 21 years;
  - service charges (though some are excluded – see p2:352);
  - rentcharge payments;
  - payments under a co-ownership scheme;
  - rent if you are a Crown tenant (minus any water charges);
  - payments for a tent and its pitch if that is your home.

Are you liable to pay housing costs?[4]

You count as liable to pay housing costs (see above for the types that can be met) if:
- you, or your partner, are liable to pay them. You do not have to be legally liable.[5] However, you do not count as liable to pay housing costs if you pay these to someone who is a member of your household (see p2:115 for the meaning of household);
- you are treated as liable to pay them. You are treated as liable if:
  - you share the costs with other members of your household (see p2:115 for the meaning of household); *and*
  - at least one of those with whom you share is liable.
  In this case, you can be paid for your share,[6] as long as those you share with are not 'close relatives' of yourself or your partner and it is reasonable to treat you as sharing. ('Close relative' means a parent, parent-in-law, son, son-in-law, daughter, daughter-in-law, step-parent, stepson, stepdaughter,

brother, sister or the partner of any of these. Sister or brother includes a half-sister or half-brother. An adopted child ceases to be related to her/his natural family on adoption and becomes the relative of her/his adoptive family[7]);

- someone else is liable to pay them but is not paying so you have to meet the cost yourself in order to continue to live in your home. You must show that it is reasonable for you to pay instead of her/him – eg, where you have given up your home to live with and care for someone and s/he has now gone into a nursing home, or where you have separated from your partner.

If you are not required to pay any housing costs currently, for example, if under the terms of your mortgage do not have to pay interest, you cannot receive IS or income-based JSA for housing costs. This applies to special mortgage schemes for pensioners where the mortgage is repaid from your estate when you die rather than by regular monthly payments.[8]

If you are on strike your partner is treated as liable for housing costs to enable her/him to make a claim.[9]

Are the housing costs for the home in which you normally live?

Housing costs are paid for the home in which you or a member of your family normally live (see Chapters 36 and 37 for who counts as your family). You cannot usually be paid for any other home,[10] but if you have to make payments on two properties, see p2:344 for exceptions to this rule. If you are liable to pay the mortgage on a property but have no immediate intention of living there you cannot get help with the cost.[11]

Your home is defined as the building, or part of the building, in which you live. This includes any garage, garden, outbuildings and other premises and land which it is not reasonable or practicable to sell separately.[12]

There are special rules if:

- you have just moved into your home (see below);
- you are temporarily away from home (see p2:343);
- you are liable to pay housing costs on more than one home (see p3:344).

Moving house[13]

If you have just moved into your home but were liable to pay housing costs before moving in, your IS or income-based JSA can include these costs for a period of up to four weeks before your move if your delay in moving was reasonable, you claimed IS or JSA before moving in, *and*:

- you were waiting for adaptations to be finished that meet needs you or a member of your family have because of a disability (see p2:113 for who counts as your family); *or*

- you became responsible for the housing costs while you were in hospital or residential care; *or*
- you were waiting for a social fund payment to help you set up home – eg, for help with removal costs or furniture and bedding. This only applies if you have a child of five or under, or you qualify for a pensioner, enhanced pensioner, higher pensioner, disability, severe disability or disabled child premium.

The amount for housing costs is not actually paid until you move in. If the earlier IS or JSA claim you made before you moved was turned down you must claim again within four weeks of moving in to qualify.

Temporary absence from home

If you are temporarily away from home but are still entitled to IS or income-based JSA, have not rented out your home and intend to return, your housing costs continue to be paid for a period.

You can get housing costs for **13 weeks** if you are unlikely to be away for longer than this.[14] However, you can get housing costs for **52 weeks** if you are unlikely to be away for longer than this (or in exceptional circumstances, unlikely to be away for substantially longer than this) and you are:[15]

- in hospital. If you are claiming JSA, you must be treated as capable of work (ie, during a short spell of sickness – see p1:271);
- receiving care (approved by a doctor) in the UK or abroad, as long as this is not in a residential care or nursing home;
- receiving medical treatment or convalescing in the UK or abroad (approved by a doctor) or your partner or a dependent child is, as long as this is not in a residential care or nursing home;
- attending a training course away from home in the UK or abroad. Your training course counts if it is provided by or on behalf of or by arrangement with or approved by a government department, the Secretary of State, Scottish Enterprise or Highlands and Islands Enterprise;
- in a bail hostel;
- for IS only, in prison on remand. If you were claiming JSA before going into prison you must claim IS instead to cover your housing costs;
- in a residential care or nursing home for short-term or respite care. However, if you are in the home for a trial period to see if you wish to move there permanently, you can only get your housing costs met for 13 weeks.[16] You must intend to return home if the accommodation is not suitable. If the home does not suit your needs you can have further trial periods in other homes, so long as you are not away from home for more than 52 weeks in total;
- providing care for someone living in the UK or abroad (approved by a doctor);

- caring for a child whose parent or guardian is receiving medical treatment or care (approved by a doctor) away from home;
- away from home through fear of violence (see below if you need to claim for two homes and for what counts as violence); *or*
- a full-time student (see p2:134) who is neither able to get housing costs for two homes nor who is a single claimant or a lone parent who is liable to pay housing costs on one but not both of a term time and a home address (see p2:344).

There is no linking rule with these provisions, which means that a new period can start if you return home even for a short stay – eg, a day or a weekend.[17]

If you have to live in temporary accommodation while essential repairs are done to your normal home and you only have to pay for housing costs for one of the homes, your IS or income-based JSA covers those costs.[18] This is not subject to the normal limits on temporary absence from home (see p2:343).[19] If you have to pay housing costs for both homes, you may be able to claim IS or income-based JSA for both for up to four weeks (see below). After that you are only paid for one home. This could be your normal home if you are unlikely to be away for more than 13 or 52 weeks (see p2:343) or your temporary home if you will be away for longer.

Housing costs for more than one home

In most cases you can only be paid housing costs for one home. However, if you have to pay housing costs for two homes you can get IS or income-based JSA for both:[20]

- for up to four weeks if you have moved into a new home and cannot avoid having to pay for the other one as well;
- indefinitely if you left your home because of either domestic violence or fear of other violence in that home. Remember that your garden and garage, for example, count as your home (see p2:342). So long as you left home because of the violence and are still away from home because of it, it does not matter if you were away from home for some other reason during this period – for example, because you were in prison.[21]
  'Violence' means violence against you and not caused by you[22] and includes violence in your old home or from a former member of your family. Fear of a racial attack should be covered provided the attack would take place *in* the old home (see p2:342 for what counts as your home). You have to show that it is reasonable for you to get payment for two homes. Thus, if you do not intend to return home or someone else is paying the mortgage, you might not get IS or income-based JSA for both homes;
- indefinitely if you are one of a couple and you or your partner are a student (see p2:136) or on a training course (see p2:343) and living away from your home (see p2:345).

If you have to live in temporary accommodation while essential repairs are done to your normal home see p2:342.

If you have to live away from your normal home because you are a student (see p2:136) **or on a training course** (see p2:343) IS or income-based JSA can cover the housing costs as follows:

- if you are one of a couple and have to live apart, you can get IS or income-based JSA for both of your homes if it is reasonable for you to get help with both;[23]
- if you are a single person or lone parent and are having to pay housing costs for *either* your normal home or your term-time accommodation but not both, you can get IS or income-based JSA for the home for which you pay.[24]

If neither of the above apply you may only get help with your normal home for up to 52 weeks (see p2:343).[25]

If you are getting IS or income-based JSA for your term-time accommodation and you stop living there during a vacation, you cannot get housing costs unless you are away because you are in hospital.[26]

2. **Mortgages and loans**

An amount for mortgage payments is included in your IS or income-based JSA applicable amount (see pp1:280 and 1:446) under the rules described below. The term 'mortgage' refers to mortgages, hire purchase agreements or loans.

It is important to remember that:

- not all loans qualify for help;
- restrictions might be made – eg, if your total housing costs are thought to be too high (see p2:353) or if you took out or increased your loan while on IS or income-based JSA (see p2:347). For circumstances in which you are allowed to take out or increase your loan, see p2:346;
- your IS or income-based JSA for housing costs only covers interest on your loan(s) and the amount you are paid is calculated in a special way (see p2:350);
- you might not get your full housing costs met during the first weeks of your claim (see p2:358);
- deductions can be made if other people live in your home (see p2:356);
- payment is usually made direct to the lender (see p2:492).

Loans that qualify

You are only paid where your loan qualifies. If your loan was taken out to pay for repairs or improvements, see p2:350. If you have other housing costs, see p2:352.

Your loan qualifies if it was:[27]

- **taken out to buy the home in which you live.** Loans taken out to buy an existing property as well as those to pay for materials and labour to build your own home are covered.[28] If all or part of your loan was taken out to pay for something other than your home (eg, to buy a car or set up a business) you cannot get help with the cost even if the loan is secured on your home (but see p2:361);
- **taken out to buy an additional interest in the home in which you live** for example:
  - by buying out your ex-partner's share in your home after you separated. However, where your ex-partner has registered a right to occupy your home (what is known as a 'Class F land charge') you cannot get help with a loan to pay her/him to remove it;[29]
  - by purchasing the freehold on a leasehold property;[30]
  - by buying your partner's share back from a trustee in bankruptcy if s/he is bankrupt;[31]
  - by buying out sitting tenants;[32]
- **taken out to repay a loan which itself would have qualified** (see above). However, if the second loan is also for things that do not qualify for help (eg, to pay debts or to pay for a holiday) you only get help with the amount of the original loan.

Example

Mr Clay took out a new mortgage of £60,000. £45,000 was to pay off the mortgage he took out to buy his home and £15,000 was to pay off business debts. He will get help with the loan for £45,000.

Loans taken out for any costs necessary to help you buy the home or the additional interest are covered.[33] These could include things like search or valuation fees, legal fees and stamp duty.

Remember that even if all of your loan qualifies, you might not get help if you took it out or increased it while on IS or income-based JSA (see below). Where your home is used for both business and domestic purposes and neither part can be sold off separately, you can only get help with the interest payable on the loan for the part where you live.[34]

Taking out or increasing loans while on income support or income-based jobseeker's allowance[35]

Even if your loan qualifies (see p2:345) you cannot get IS or income-based JSA to help you pay the cost if you took it out or increased it:[36]

- when you were on IS or income-based JSA; *or*

- when you were living as a member of the family with someone who was on IS or income-based JSA (see Chapters 36 and 37 for who counts as your family); *or*
- during a period of 26 weeks between two IS or income-based JSA claims as described above.

For these purposes, you and your partner are treated as being on IS or income-based JSA when you are on a New Deal programme or scheme (see Chapter 34), but only if as a result you:
- count as in full-time work (see p2:5); *or*
- have too much income (see p1:446).[37]

You can get IS for your housing costs even if you took out your loan during one of the periods listed above if:[38]
- your loan was taken out before 2 May 1994;
- your loan was taken out between 2 May 1994 and 2 October 1995 and you got IS for it under the rules that applied between those dates;
- your loan was taken out after 2 May 1994 but you have since stopped getting IS and income-based JSA for more than 26 weeks;
- you have taken out, or increased, your loan to buy a home which is better suited than your former home to the needs of a disabled person.[39] The person has to qualify as disabled at the time the loan is taken out.[40] S/he does not have to be a member of your family nor to have previously lived with you. A 'disabled person' is anybody for whom you or someone living with you is getting a disabled child, disability, enhanced pensioner or higher pensioner premium (see pp2:325 and 2:327) as well as other people living in your home who would get one of these premiums if they were on IS. It also includes a person who is sick, but, under the incapacity rules, is either disqualified from receiving benefit or is treated as capable of work (see pp1:442 and 2:16);
- you have a boy and a girl aged 10 or over and you increased your loan to move to a home where they could have separate bedrooms.[41] You can argue that this should apply if one of the children is 10 or over and the other will be 10 in the reasonably near future.[42]

You can get IS for your housing costs even if you took out your loan during one of the periods listed above (although the amount you get might be restricted) if:
- you re-mortgaged your home to pay off your original house purchase loan,[43] *or* you sold your previous home, paid off a loan which you took out to buy a home or pay for repairs or improvements, and have now taken out a new loan for a new property, even if this is some time later.[44]
The original loan must have qualified (see above) and be one for which you can get IS or income-based JSA even if it was taken out during any of the periods described above. Unless the loan was to buy a home for a

disabled person (see p2:347) or to provide separate bedrooms for a boy and girl aged 10 or over (see p2:347) you cannot get help with any increase in your housing costs. Thus, if your original mortgage was £30,000 and you took out a new loan for £35,000 to buy a new home, you can only get housing costs on £30,000 of the second loan.

It seems that the rule *is* intended to apply if, following divorce or separation, you buy out your former partner's share of your home – you will not get the mortgage interest paid in relation to that share. Similarly, if you take out a loan or increase an existing loan to buy a home after separation, the rule will in principle apply. However, where couples on IS or income-based JSA separate, it can be argued that each should be entitled to housing costs up to the amount of the loan they were liable to pay when they were together.[45] So, for example, if you were liable to pay a mortgage of £50,000 when you were together, you can argue that you should each be entitled to housing costs on a mortgage of up to £50,000 when you separate;

- you buy your home and immediately beforehand you were in rented accommodation and getting housing benefit (HB – see Chapter 25). Your housing costs are restricted to the amount of HB you previously received plus any 'other housing costs' (see p2:352) you were already getting.[46] You get any subsequent increases in the standard rate of interest (see below) or the 'other housing costs' and do not lose these if the interest rate or costs go down again;[47]

- you were only getting 'other housing costs' (see p2:352) paid with your IS or income-based JSA (eg, as a Crown tenant) and you then buy a home.[48] To begin with you only get the amount you had been getting for those other costs. You get any subsequent increases in the standard rate of interest or the 'other housing costs' and do not lose these if the interest rate or costs go down again.

How your mortgage payments are calculated

Your IS or income-based JSA does not cover the whole of your mortgage payments. You can get help with interest on the loan(s) but not with capital repayments or the cost of associated insurance premiums.[49] Thus claimants with an endowment mortgage do not get the insurance element paid.

There is therefore a short-fall between the IS or income-based JSA you get for your housing costs and what you have to pay your lender. Your lender may be prepared to accept interest-only payments for a while and it is important to discuss this with them so that you do not fall into arrears and risk losing your home. If you have to make capital repayments you may be able to increase your income by taking in lodgers (see p2:414 for how this affects your IS or income-based JSA). Payments made direct to the lender by relatives, friends or a charity towards the capital repayments can also be ignored in calculating your entitlement to IS or income-based JSA (see p2:423).

The weekly housing costs that you get are worked out using a special formula.[50] The amount of your loan which qualifies (see p2:345) is taken into account less any restrictions that have been made (see pp2:347 and 2:353). Housing costs are worked out net of tax relief (known as MIRAS) provided this is deducted at source by your lender.

Unless your rate of interest is less than 5 per cent (see below), a **standard rate of interest** is used, not what you actually have to pay.[51] The standard rate of interest is set by the DSS. At the time this *Handbook* was written it was 7.75 per cent. If your repayments are higher because your lender charges a higher rate of interest you have to meet the shortfall yourself.

If you are paying less than 5 per cent interest (eg, under a special low-start mortgage scheme) your housing costs are calculated using the interest rate you pay. If the interest rate on your mortgage goes above 5 per cent, the standard rate will be used.

Your housing costs for repairs and improvements (see p2:350) are calculated in the same way as for mortgages.

Example

Mr and Mrs Khan have a repayment mortgage. The outstanding loan of £30,000 qualifies (see p2:345). Tax relief is deducted at source. They pay interest at the rate of 9%.

£30,000 × 90% (loan net of tax relief at 10%) × 7.75% (standard interest rate) = £2,092.50

Their weekly IS housing costs are £2,092.50 ÷ 52 = £40.24.

When are housing costs re-calculated?

Interest is met on the amount of your loan which is outstanding when your housing costs are first included in your IS or income-based JSA. If you were previously getting one of these with housing costs and are now getting the other, the same calculation is automatically used if:[52]

- you or your partner were getting (or were treated as entitled to) IS or income-based JSA in the 12 weeks before one of you became entitled to the other. This period is extended to 26 weeks if:
  - you or your partner were unable to get IS or income-based JSA because you were receiving child support maintenance which has now reduced as a result of child support rule changes in April 1995 or because an interim maintenance assessment has been replaced or terminated (see CPAG's *Child Support Handbook,* 1999/2000 edition, for details);
  - you were unable to get IS or income-based JSA because your housing costs were met by an insurance policy covering loss of employment which has since run out; *and*

- you or your partner were getting an amount for housing costs (either for a mortgage or a loan for repairs and improvements); *and*
- there has been no change of circumstances affecting your housing costs since they were last calculated.

If there has been a change of circumstances since you started getting IS or income-based JSA, your housing costs are re-calculated afresh, unless the change of circumstances is a reduction in the amount of your outstanding loan.[53] If there has been a reduction, your housing costs can only be reviewed on the anniversary of when they were first met with IS or income-based JSA, if you have been continuously entitled, or treated as entitled, to one of these benefits.[54] In all other cases, your benefit is reviewed annually on the anniversary of the date you first became entitled to IS or income-based JSA for housing costs. Interest is met on the amount of the loan outstanding at the date of review.[55]

Note: The rules for calculating your weekly housing costs changed on 2 October 1995. If you have been claiming IS or income-based JSA since before that date, see p2:361 to see if you are entitled to transitional protection.

Limits on the amount that can be paid

There can be a limit on how much interest is paid. If your loan is for more than £100,000 you might only be paid interest on this figure (see p2:353). If your housing costs are lower than this but still thought to be too high they might be restricted (see p3:354).

3. **Loans for repairs and improvements**

IS and income-based JSA do not meet the cost of repairs and improvements to the home or the cost of service charges for these (but see p2:352). However, if you take out a loan to pay for the repairs and improvements or the service charge (or to pay off an earlier loan taken out for this purpose) you might get help with the interest.[56] See below for what repairs or improvements qualify. You must use the loan for the repairs and improvements or service charge within six months (longer if this is reasonable). A bank overdraft which you arrange to pay for the repairs or improvements counts as a loan.[57]

It is important to remember that:
- not all loans for repairs and improvements qualify for help;
- you might not get your full costs met initially (see p2:358);
- the amount you are paid might be restricted if your total housing costs are thought to be too high (see p2:353);
- deductions can be made if other people live in your home (see p2:356);

- your IS or income-based JSA only covers interest on your loan(s) and there is a special way the amount you can be paid is calculated (see p2:348);
- payment is usually made direct to the lender (see p2:492).

Repairs and improvements that qualify

You can only get help with loans for repairs or improvements to maintain your current home,[58] or any part of the building in which it is contained, in a habitable condition. Loans towards the cost of necessary survey work should also be included.[59] You can get interest on a loan for any of the following:

- provision of a bath, shower, toilet, wash basin and the necessary plumbing and hot water;
- repairs to your heating system;
- damp-proof measures;
- provision of ventilation and natural lighting;
- provision of drainage facilities;
- facilities for preparing and cooking food (but not for storing it[60]);
- home insulation;
- provision of electric lighting and sockets;
- storage facilities for fuel or refuse;
- repairs of unsafe structural defects;
- adaptations for a disabled person (see p2:347 for who counts);
- providing separate bedrooms for children of different sexes aged 10 or over who are part of your family (see p2:114 for who counts as your family). You can argue that this should apply if one of the children is 10 or over and the other will be 10 in the reasonably near future.[61]

If your loan is also for other repairs and improvements, you are only paid housing costs for the proportion which relates to any of the items listed above. If your loan is for the right sort of repairs or improvements, the amount payable is calculated as for mortgages – you do not get your interest charges paid in full when you first claim (see p2:358) and the standard interest rate is used (see p2:348). The restriction on taking out loans while on IS or income-based JSA does not apply to those taken out for repairs and improvements.

Note: The rules for help with loans for repairs and improvements changed on 2 October 1995. If you took out your loan before that date, you might be able to get help under the old, more favourable rules (see p2:361).

4. **Help with 'other housing costs'**

You are paid the normal weekly charge for all other housing costs covered by IS or income-based JSA.[62] These are:

- service charges (though some are excluded – see p2:352);
- rent or ground rent (feu duty in Scotland) if you have a lease of more (than 21 years;
- rentcharge payments;
- payments under a co-ownership scheme;
- rent if you are a Crown tenant (minus any water charges);
- payments for a tent and its pitch if that is your home.

Where you pay your 'other housing costs' annually or irregularly, the weekly amount is worked out by dividing what is payable for the year by 52.

It is important to remember that:

- you might not get your full costs met initially (see p2:358);
- the amount you are paid might be restricted if your total housing costs are thought to be too high (see p2:353).

If your other housing costs have been waived because you have paid for repairs or redecoration which are not your responsibility, you can still get IS or income-based JSA for them for up to eight weeks.[63]

Service charges

A 'service' is something which is agreed and arranged on your behalf and for which you are required to pay. So, for example, if you own a flat and the lessor arranges the exterior painting of the building for which you have to pay a share of the cost, your IS or income-based JSA includes this as a service charge. Some service charges are specifically excluded (see the list of ineligible service charges listed on p1:523). Some service charges only count if they relate to the provision of 'adequate accommodation' (see p1:523).[64] See below for charges which cannot be met.

House insurance paid under the terms of your lease can be a service charge, but insurance required by a building society as a condition of your mortgage is not.[65] Service charges to cover minor repairs and maintenance are covered but service charges for repairs and improvements listed on p2:350 are not – you must take out a loan to pay for these, and the interest on the loan can be covered by IS or income-based JSA (see p2:350).

Services provided by an outside authority which you arrange yourself are not covered. Thus charges for water and sewerage paid to a water board are not met.[66]

If you normally pay service charges annually you have to ask if you can make weekly payments.

Charges for the items that follow cannot be met[67]
- Fuel but only where this is included in your housing costs. If there is no specific charge for fuel, set deductions are made as follows:

heating	£9.25	lighting	£0.80
hot water	£1.15	cooking	£1.15

- Repairs and improvements listed on p2:350. You are expected to take out a loan to pay for these and can claim help with the interest (see p2:350).
- Ineligible services listed on p1:523. See above for further information about service charges.

5. **The amount of housing costs you get**

Once you have worked out which housing costs can be met by IS or income-based JSA you need to:
- calculate the weekly amount of:
  - mortgage interest (see p2:345);
  - interest on loans for repairs and improvements (see p2:350);
  - other housing costs (see p2:352);
- add these amounts together;
- deduct any restrictions being made because your housing costs are too high (see below);
- deduct any amounts for other people living in your home (known as non-dependants – see p2:356).

Remember that a reduced amount might be paid for the early weeks of your claim (see p2:358).

Restrictions if your housing costs are too high

Your housing costs can be restricted if:
- your loans exceed an upper limit (see p2:354); *or*
- your total housing costs are thought to be excessive (see p2:354).

If you are left with insufficient money to pay your housing costs you may be in danger of losing your home, particularly if you are on IS or JSA for a long time. You should inform your lender and discuss with them how to resolve the situation. You should also seek independent debt advice.

Ultimately, you may have to sell your home and buy somewhere cheaper but you could try and make up any shortfall by taking in a lodger (see p2:414) or finding a part-time job and benefiting from an earnings disregard (see p2:399). Another way around the problem is to move out and put your house up for sale. The capital value of your house can be disregarded for a period while you take reasonable steps to sell it (see p2:448).[68] If you also rent it out while trying to sell, the income from any tenants can be disregarded up to the value of any mortgage outgoings which you have on the property.[69]

The upper limit

If your loans amount to more than £100,000 in total, your housing costs might not be met in full.[70] This includes all mortgages taken out to buy your home and also any loans for repairs and improvements. The restriction is applied proportionately to each loan. If a loan was taken out to adapt your home for a disabled person (see p2:347 for who counts), it is ignored when working out if your loans exceed the upper limit. If you are getting housing costs on more than one home (see p2:344) you can be paid up to the limit for each.[71]

Upper limits for loans have only existed since 2 August 1993 and have changed twice since that date. The limit has been £100,000 since 10 April 1995. However:

- your limit is £125,000 if you have been entitled to IS or income-based JSA since 11 April 1994;
- your limit is £150,000 if you have been entitled to IS or income-based JSA since 2 August 1993;
- there is no limit if you have been entitled to IS or income-based JSA from before 2 August 1993.

If you are uncertain about which limit applies to you, you should seek advice. If you are considering increasing your mortgage or loan, see p2:346.

Excessive housing costs

Whether your loan is higher or lower than the upper limit (see above), your housing costs can be restricted if:[72]

- your home (excluding any part which you let) is too big for you and your family. When deciding if your home is too big, a comparison is made with other accommodation which would be suitable given the size of your household. Any non-dependants (see p2:356) or foster children in your home count as part of your family for this purpose. The needs of everyone in your family must be considered. For example, if a member of your family needs extra space because of a disability, or you have a child or elderly relative in care who regularly comes to stay with you, your need for a large home may be justified;
- the area in which you live is more expensive than other areas where there is accommodation suitable for your needs. An area is 'something more confined, restricted and compact than a locality or district ... It might

consist of ... a number of roads, refer to a neighbourhood and even to a large block of flats'.[73] The area should not be chosen on too wide a basis – ie, you should not be expected to move to a completely different part of the country;
- the outgoings on your home which are met by IS or income-based JSA housing costs (see pp2:345, 2:350 and 2:352) are higher than on other properties in the area which are suitable for your needs.

The capital value of your home cannot be taken into account.[74]

When no restriction should be made

No restriction should be made even if suitable accommodation is available if it is not reasonable for you to look for cheaper accommodation. Account should be taken of:[75]
- the general level of housing costs in the area and whether a suitable alternative is available. This means that property must be generally available, not necessarily available to you personally;[76]
- your family circumstances – eg, your employment prospects, the age and state of health of your family members and whether the move would have a detrimental effect on a child's education if s/he would have to change schools.

These are not the only situations which count.[77] A move may not be reasonable where:
- the size of your family would make it difficult to find accommodation;
- you need to be near relatives or friends to provide (or receive) care or support;
- you have moved a number of times recently;
- it would be difficult to sell your property[78] or you have negative equity or selling would cause you financial hardship;[79]
- you have lived in your home for many years and it is now too large because you are separated or divorced, or your children have left home, or your partner has died;
- prior to your claim you were advised by the Benefits Agency that full mortgage interest would be paid;[80]
- you could not get another mortgage on a property.[81]

Even if it is reasonable for you to move, your housing costs should not be restricted for 26 weeks if you, or a member of your family, were able to meet these costs when they were first taken on. Your housing costs are not restricted for a further 26 weeks if you are trying to find cheaper accommodation. If full payment is made initially but later, following a review, your housing costs are restricted, the 26-week periods begin from the date of the review.[82] Periods of 12 weeks or less when you were not getting IS or income-based JSA are included when calculating these periods. If you have only recently become one of a couple or separated from your partner and you make a new claim within 12 weeks, periods when your partner was in receipt of IS or income-based JSA count towards the 26-week period. You should be notified of any intention to restrict your benefit.[83]

If it is appropriate to restrict your housing costs, the amount paid is limited to what you would have to pay for a suitable alternative property. This is a subjective test – if the equity in your property was sufficient to buy a new home outright your IS or income-based JSA housing costs could be nil.[84]

Deductions for other people living in your home[85]

If other people normally live with you in your home who are not part of your family for benefit purposes (see p2:114) – they are called **'non-dependants'** – a set deduction is usually made from your housing costs. Thus, if an adult son or daughter, or an elderly relative shares your home, you may need to ask her/him for a contribution towards your outgoings.

A person can only be treated as living with you if s/he shares rooms with you. This includes the kitchen (unless it is only used by someone else to prepare food for her/him[86]), but not a bathroom, toilet or common access areas.[87] A person who is separately liable to pay rent to a landlord is not counted as living with you.

When no deduction is made

No deduction is made from your housing costs if **the person living with you is not treated as a 'non-dependant'** (though any rent or lodging charges they pay to you affects the amount of your IS or income-based JSA, see p2:414). A person does not count as a non-dependant if s/he:[88]

- is liable to pay you, or your partner, in order to live in your home – eg, a sub-tenant, licensee or boarder. This also applies to other members of her/his household. The payment must be on a commercial basis. A low charge does not necessarily mean that the arrangement is not commercial, nor do you have to make a profit. An arrangement between friends can be commercial.[89] Close relatives (see p2:341) count as non-dependants even if they pay for their accommodation;

- is someone other than a close relative (see p2:341) to whom you, or your partner, are liable to make payments on a commercial basis (ie, as a sub-tenant, licensee or boarder) in order to live in her/his property. Other members of her/his household do not count as non-dependants either;

- jointly occupies your home and is a co-owner or joint tenant with you or your partner. Your joint occupier's partner is not a non-dependant. Close relatives (see p2:341) who jointly occupy your home are treated as non-dependants unless they had joint liability prior to 11 April 1988 or joint liability existed on or before the date you first lived in the property (or your partner did if s/he is the joint owner/tenant). However, no non-dependant deduction is made for them even though they are non-dependants;

- is employed by a charitable or voluntary organisation as a resident carer for you, or your partner, and you pay for that service (even if the charge is nominal). If the carer's partner also lives in your home s/he does not count as a non-dependant.

Even **if you do have a non-dependant** in your home no deduction is made if:[90]
- a deduction is already being made from your HB (see p1:525);
- you, or your partner, are blind or treated as blind (see p1:443);
- you, or your partner, get attendance allowance (or equivalent benefits paid because of injury at work or a war injury) or the care component of disability living allowance.

In addition no deduction is made for a non-dependant who is:
- staying with you but who normally lives elsewhere;
- 16 or 17 years old, or getting a work-based training for young people (formerly youth training) allowance;
- a full-time student (see p2:314). This also applies during the summer vacation as long as s/he is not working full time (see p2:5 for the meaning of full-time work);
- 18–24 years old and getting IS or income-based JSA;
- not living with you at present because s/he has been in hospital for more than six weeks, or is in prison;
- a co-owner or joint tenant with you, or your partner, even if s/he is a close relative (see p2:341).

The amount of deductions

If you have a non-dependant living with you who is 18 or over, a fixed amount is usually deducted from your housing costs, whatever s/he pays you. If your non-dependant is working full-time (see p2:5), the amount depends on her/his weekly gross income as follows:

Gross weekly income	Non-dependant deduction
£255 or more	£46.35
£204–254.99	£42.25
£155–203.99	£37.10
£118–154.99	£22.65
£80–117.99	£16.50
Less than £80	£ 7.20

In all other cases, a £7.20 deduction is made, but see p2:356 for situations when no deduction is made.

Gross income includes wages before tax and national insurance are deducted plus any other income the non-dependant has (but not attendance allowance, disability living allowance or payments from the Macfarlane

Trusts, the Eileen Trust, the Fund or the Independent Living Funds – see p2:412).[91]

A deduction is made for each non-dependant in your home, but if there is more than one and they include a couple only one deduction is made for the couple. In this case their joint income counts and the highest possible deduction is made.

If you are a joint owner with someone other than your partner, any deductions are shared proportionally between you and the other owner(s).

Reduced payment during the first weeks of your claim

Even if you are entitled to IS or income-based JSA to cover your housing costs, the amount for your housing costs is not usually paid until you have been claiming for a number of weeks – what is known as a 'waiting period'.[92] This applies to mortgages and loans (see p2:345), loans for repairs and improvements (see p2:350) and 'other housing costs' (see p2:352). To help you get help with your housing costs sooner, you are treated as being on IS or income-based JSA for certain weeks prior to your claim even though you were not actually receiving it (see p2:359).

You can be paid straight away if:[93]

- you have already been entitled to IS or income-based JSA for the relevant number of weeks when you take out your loan or agreement to pay 'other housing costs' (but see p2:356 for the rules restricting housing costs if you take out or increase a loan while on IS or income-based JSA);
- you or your partner are 60 or over;
- you are claiming for payments as a Crown tenant, under a co-ownership scheme or for a tent.

All other claimants get a reduced amount of help initially. How long your waiting period is depends on when you took out your mortgage or loan or agreed to pay 'other housing costs' (see p2:352) and how long you have been on (or treated as on) IS or income-based JSA (see below). You are expected to use mortgage protection policy payments, savings or disregarded income to meet any shortfall. If you do not have enough to pay the shortfall you should approach your lender to discuss how you can protect your home.

'Existing housing costs'

If you took your loan out or agreed to pay 'other housing costs' (see p2:352) before 2 October 1995 (the Benefits Agency calls these 'existing housing costs') you get:[94]

- nothing for the first eight weeks of your claim;
- 50 per cent of your housing costs for the next 18 weeks;
- full housing costs after 26 weeks on IS or income-based JSA.

This 26-week waiting period can also apply if you take out a loan after 2 October 1995, provided it replaces a loan taken out before that date and is with the same lender, for the same property and for the same amount (or lower) as the earlier loan.

'New housing costs'

If you took your loan out or agreed to pay 'other housing costs' (see p2:352) after 1 October 1995 (the Benefits Agency calls these 'new housing costs') you get:[95]

- nothing for the first 39 weeks of your claim;
- full housing costs after 39 weeks on IS or income-based JSA.

However, if the loan replaces another loan taken out before 2 October 1995, see above.

Certain claimants are exempt from this 39-week waiting period. Instead the 26-week waiting period described above applies. This is the case if you:[96]

- are a lone parent and have claimed IS or income-based JSA because your partner has abandoned you[97] or died, unless you become one of a couple again;
- are claiming IS or JSA *and:*
  - you are a carer getting invalid care allowance; *or*
  - you are caring for someone getting attendance allowance (AA – see Chapter 10) or disability living allowance (DLA) higher or middle rate care component; *or*
  - you are caring for someone who has claimed AA or DLA and the claim has not yet been decided, for a maximum of 26 weeks from the date of claim;
  - for IS only, it is more than eight weeks since you have ceased to meet those conditions or have stopped being a carer;
- are claiming IS and are in prison awaiting trial or sentence; *or*
- have been refused payments under a mortgage protection policy due to a pre-existing medical condition or because you are HIV positive.

If you have two loans or agreements to pay 'other housing costs' and one was taken out before and one after 1 October 1995, the relevant waiting periods apply to each.[98]

Getting full housing costs earlier

To help you get full housing costs earlier, you are treated as being on IS or income-based JSA for certain weeks prior to your claim even though you were not actually receiving it. You are treated as in receipt of IS or income-based JSA:[99]

- for any period when you were getting or were treated as entitled to the other benefit;[100]

- during a period of 12 weeks or less between two periods when:
  - you were getting IS or income-based JSA; *or*
  - you were treated as entitled to IS or income-based JSA.

  This period is extended to 26 weeks if you were getting full housing costs but stopped getting IS or income-based JSA because you received child support maintenance, and this has now reduced as a result of child support rule changes in April 1995 or because an interim maintenance assessment has been replaced or terminated (see the *Child Support Handbook*, 1998/99 edition for details);
- during any period for which you are awarded IS or income-based JSA after a review or an appeal (see pp2:570 and 2:611);
- during any period when you were getting contribution-based JSA immediately before starting on a New Deal programme or scheme (see Chapter 34);
- during the time when your partner was claiming IS or income-based JSA on her/his own, provided you make a claim for IS or income–based JSA within 12 weeks of becoming a couple;
- during the time when your ex-partner was claiming IS or income-based JSA for you both, provided you claim IS or income-based JSA within 12 weeks of separating;
- during the time when your partner was claiming IS or income-based JSA for you both, if you take over the claiming role;
- during the time when you or your partner were on a New Deal programme or scheme (see Chapter 34) so long as your partner was claiming IS or income-based JSA for you immediately before this and you claim IS or income-based JSA immediately after;
- during the time when someone who was not your partner was claiming IS or income-based JSA for you and another dependent child or young person. You must claim within 12 weeks of this and you must be a member of another family (see p2:114 for who counts as your family) and be claiming for that other child;
- during periods when you stop getting IS or income-based JSA because you or your partner are:
  - doing an employment training rehabilitation course;
  - on a New Deal programme or scheme (see Chapter 34) and as a result count as in full-time work (see p2:5) or have too much income (see p2:446);
- for up to 39 weeks where you were not entitled to IS or income-based JSA because your income or capital was too high (including where your contribution-based JSA was the same as or higher than your income-based JSA 'applicable amount' – see p1:280) *and*:[101]
  - you have been getting contribution-based JSA, statutory sick pay or incapacity benefit (or credits for unemployment or incapacity); *or*
  - you are a lone parent or for IS, a carer (see p1:443) or for JSA, a carer who is allowed to restrict the hours you are available for work (see p1:297) and

you or someone claiming on your behalf has previously been refused IS or JSA. This does not apply if you or your partner count as in full-time paid work (see p2:5), or you are a full-time student who cannot claim IS or JSA (see p2:134) or are temporarily absent from Great Britain and not entitled to IS or JSA (see pp2:245-7);

- for any period where you were not entitled to IS or income-based JSA because your income was too high and you were getting payments under a mortgage protection policy. You are treated as entitled to IS or income-based JSA for any period for which the payments were made. This could be longer than 39 weeks.[102]

If you reclaim IS or income-based JSA within 26 weeks of a previous claim during which you were getting housing costs and you have been receiving payments under an employment insurance policy which has since run out, periods when you were getting those payments are ignored in calculating the 26/39-week waiting periods (see pp2:358 and 2:359). This means that you can requalify for housing costs sooner.

Transitional protection if you have been claiming since before 2 October 1995

The rules on payment of housing costs changed on 2 October 1995. Some people qualify for a lower amount of housing costs than they did before that date. However, there are two types of transitional protection which ensure that you should be no worse off than you were under the old rules.

- You can continue to get certain types of housing costs which could be paid with IS before 2 October 1995, but which can no longer be paid by IS or income-based JSA. These are:[103]
  - accumulated arrears of interest;
  - interest on a secured loan which was not for house purchase, taken out when you were one of a couple, where your partner had left and could not or would not pay the cost or had died;
  - interest on a loan for repairs and improvements under the pre-2 October 1995 rules.

  You can continue to get these if they were included in your housing costs before 2 October 1995, if you fulfil the qualifying conditions *and* you remain on (or are treated as being on – see p2:359) IS or income-based JSA. See the *National Welfare Benefits Handbook*, 1995/96 edition, pp30-32 for more details on how these costs were assessed.
- If you were on IS both on and after 1 October 1995 and the amount of IS or income-based JSA housing costs to which you are now entitled is less because of the new rules, you can get an extra payment to make up the loss.[104]

  This payment is called an 'add-back' and is equal to the difference between your IS housing costs in the week including 1 October 1995 and your entitlement in the next week. Where you have more than one loan, the 'add-back' for each is calculated separately.

You continue to be paid the 'add-back' so long as you remain on IS or income-based JSA. However, you lose the 'add-back' if you stop getting (or being treated as getting – see p2:359) IS or income-based JSA for more than 12 weeks or if you cease to qualify for housing costs. If you lose the 'add-back' but your partner makes a claim for you within 12 weeks, s/he can continue to get the 'add-back' to which you were entitled.

The 'add-back' reduces if your new entitlement to housing costs increases. You lose the 'add-back' when your new entitlement equals what you used to get under the old rules.

If you are on a fixed-rate mortgage, where your interest rate stays the same throughout, the way the 'add-back' rule is applied means you lose out if the standard rate of interest used to calculate your housing costs goes down. However, although the rule is unfair, it is lawful.[105]

Notes

References are to statutes and regulations as amended up to 8 March 1999. All regulations are (General) Regulations unless otherwise stated. There is a full list of abbreviations in Appendix 13.

1 **IS** Sch 3 para 4(1) IS Regs
JSA Sch 2 para 4(1) JSA Regs

1. When you can get help with your housing costs

2 **IS** Sch 3 para 1 IS Regs;
JSA Sch 2 para 1 JSA Regs
3 **IS** Sch 3 paras 15-17 IS Regs
JSA Sch 2 paras 14-16 JSA Regs
4 **IS** Sch 3 para 2 IS Regs
JSA Sch 2 para 2 JSA Regs
5 CSB/213/1987
6 **IS** Sch 3 para 5(5) IS Regs
JSA Sch 2 para 5(5) JSA Regs
Both CIS/743/1993
7 **IS** Reg 2(1) IS Regs
JSA Reg 1(3) JSA Regs
HB Reg 2(1) HB Regs
All R(SB) 22/87
8 CIS/636/1992 (confirmed by the Court of Appeal in *Brain v CAO*, 2 December 1993)
9 **IS** Sch 3 para 2(2) IS Regs
JSA Sch 2 para 2(2) JSA Regs
10 **IS** Sch 3 para 3(1) IS Regs
JSA Sch 2 para 3(1) JSA Regs
11 CIS/297/1994
12 s137(1) SSCBA 1992, definition of 'dwelling'; reg 2(1) IS Regs and reg 1(3) JSA Regs, definition of 'dwelling occupied as the home'
13 **IS** Sch 3 para 3(7) IS Regs
JSA Sch 2 para 3(7) JSA Regs
14 **IS** Sch 3 para 3(10) IS Regs
JSA Sch 2 para 3(10) JSA Regs
15 **IS** Sch 3 para 3(11) IS Regs
JSA Sch 2 para 3(11) JSA Regs
16 **IS** Sch 3 para 3(8) and (9) IS Regs
JSA Sch 2 para 3(8) and (9) JSA Regs
17 *R v Penwith District Council ex parte Burt*
18 **IS** Sch 3 para 3(5) IS Regs;
JSA Sch 2 para 3(5) JSA Regs

19 CIS/719/1994
20 **IS** Sch 3 para 3(6) IS Regs
JSA Sch 2 para 3(6) JSA Regs
21 CIS/543/1993
22 CIS/339/1993
23 **IS** Sch 3 para 3(6)(b) IS Regs
JSA Sch 2 para 3(6)(b) JSA Regs
24 **IS** Sch 3 para 3(3) IS Regs
JSA Sch 2 para 3(3) JSA Regs
25 **IS** Sch 3 para 3(11)(c)(viii) IS Regs;
JSA Sch 2 para 3(11)(c)(viii) JSA Regs
26 **IS** Sch 3 para 3(4) IS Regs
JSA Sch 2 para 3(4) JSA Regs

2. Mortgages and loans

27 **IS** Sch 3 para 15 IS Regs
JSA Sch 2 para 14 JSA Regs
28 R(IS) 11/94
29 R(IS) 4/95
30 R(IS) 7/93
31 R(IS) 6/94
32 CIS/465/1994
33 R(IS) 11/94
34 **IS** Sch 3 para 5 IS Regs
JSA Sch 2 para 5 JSA Regs
35 **IS** Sch 3 para 4 IS Regs
JSA Sch 2 para 4 JSA Regs
36 **IS** Sch 3 para 4(4) IS Regs
JSA Sch 2 para 4(4) JSA Regs
37 **IS** Sch 3 para 4(4A) IS Regs
JSA Sch 2 para 4(4A) JSA Regs
38 **IS** Sch 3 para 4(2) and (4) IS Regs
JSA Sch 2 para 4(2) and (4) JSA Regs
Both paras 28481 and 28486-87 AOG, definition of 'relevant period'
39 **IS** Sch 3 paras 1(3) and (4) and 4(9) IS Regs
JSA Sch 2 paras 1(3) and (4) and 4(9) JSA Regs
40 CIS/7273/1995

41 **IS** Sch 3 para 4(10) IS Regs
JSA Sch 2 para 4(10) JSA Regs
42 CIS/14657/1996
43 **IS** Sch 3 para 4(6)(a) IS Regs
JSA Sch 2 para 4(6)(a) JSA Regs
44 **IS** Sch 3 para 4(6)(b) IS Regs
JSA Sch 2 para 4(6)(b) JSA Regs
Both CIS/7273/1995
45 CIS/11293/1995
46 **IS** Sch 3 para 4(8) IS Regs
JSA Sch 2 para 4(8) JSA Regs
47 R(IS) 8/94
48 **IS** Sch 3 para 4(11) IS Regs
JSA Sch 2 para 4(11) JSA Regs
49 **IS** Sch 3 para 10 IS Regs
JSA Sch 2 para 9 JSA Regs
Both R(SB) 46/83
50 **IS** Sch 3 para 10 IS Regs
JSA Sch 2 para 9 JSA Regs
51 **IS** Sch 3 para 12 IS Regs
JSA Sch 2 para 11 JSA Regs
52 **IS** Sch 3 para 1A(1) IS Regs
JSA Sch 2 para 1A(1) JSA Regs
53 **IS** Sch 3 para 1A(2) IS Regs
JSA Sch 2 para 1A(2) JSA Regs
54 **IS** Sch 3 paras 6(1B) and 8(1B)
IS Regs
JSA Sch 2 paras 6(3) and 7(2A)
JSA Regs
Both Regs 63(7), 63A(9) and
63B SS(Adj) Regs
55 **IS** Sch 3 paras 6(1A) and 8(1A)
IS Regs
JSA Sch 2 paras 6(2) and 7(2)
JSA Regs

3. Loans for repairs and improvments

56 **IS** Sch 3 para 16 IS Regs
JSA Sch 2 para 15 JSA Regs
57 CIS/6010/1995
58 R(IS) 5/96
59 CIS/14657/1996
60 CIS/14468/1996
61 CIS/14657/1996

4. Help with 'other housing costs'

62 **IS** Sch 3 para 17 IS Regs
JSA Sch 2 para 16 JSA Regs
63 **IS** Sch 3 para 17(4) IS Regs
JSA Sch 2 para 16(4) JSA Regs
64 R(IS) 3/91; R(IS) 4/91; CIS/1460/
1995
65 R(IS) 4/92; R(IS) 19/93
66 CIS/4/1988

67 **IS** Sch 3 para 17(2) IS Regs
JSA Sch 2 para 16(2) JSA Regs

5. The amount of housing costs you get

68 **IS** Sch 10 para 26 IS Regs
JSA Sch 8 para 6 JSA Regs
69 **IS** Sch 9 para 22 IS Regs
JSA Sch 7 para 23 JSA Regs
70 **IS** Sch 3 para 11(4) and (5) IS
Regs
JSA Sch 2 para 10(3) and (4) JSA
Regs
71 **IS** Sch 3 para 11(6) IS Regs
JSA Sch 2 para 10(5) JSA Regs
72 **IS** Sch 3 para 13 IS Regs
JSA Sch 2 para 12 JSA Regs
73 R(IS) 12/91
74 **IS** Sch 3 para 13(2) IS Regs
JSA Sch 2 para 12(2) JSA Regs
75 **IS** Sch 3 para 13(4) and (5) IS
Regs
JSA Sch 2 para 12(4) and (5) JSA
Regs
76 R(SB) 7/89
77 R(SB) 6/89; R(SB) 7/89
78 R(IS) 10/93
79 CIS/347/1992
80 CSB/617/1988. This case has
been reported as R(SB) 4/89, but
the reported version omits the
relevant paragraphs.
81 R(SB) 7/89
82 **IS** Sch 3 para 13(6) and (7) IS
Regs
JSA Sch 2 para 12(6) and (7) JSA
Regs
Both *Secretary of State for Social
Security v Julien*, reported as
appendix to R(IS) 13/92
83 R(SB) 7/89
84 R(IS) 9/91
85 **IS** Sch 3 para 18 IS Regs
JSA Sch 2 para 17 JSA Regs
86 CSIS/185/1995
87 **IS** Reg 3(4) and (5) IS Regs
JSA Reg 2(6) and (7) JSA Regs
88 **IS** Reg 3 IS Regs
JSA Reg 2 JSA Regs
89 CSB/1163/1988
90 **IS** Sch 3 para 18(6) and (7) IS
Regs
JSA Sch 2 para 17(6) and (7) JSA
Regs

91 **IS** Sch 3 para 18(8) IS Regs
   JSA Sch 2 para 17(8) JSA Regs
92 **IS** Sch 3 paras 6 and 8 IS Regs
   JSA Sch 2 paras 6 and 7 JSA
   Regs
93 **IS** Sch 3 para 9 IS Regs
   JSA Sch 2 para 8 JSA Regs
94 **IS** Sch 3 paras 1(2) - definition of
   'existing housing costs' - and 6
   IS Regs;
   JSA Sch 2 paras 1(2) - definition
   of 'existing housing costs' - and
   6 JSA Regs
95 **IS** Sch 3 paras 1(2) - definition of
   'new housing costs' and 8 IS
   Regs
   JSA Sch 2 paras 1(2) - definition
   of 'new housing costs' - and 7
   JSA Regs
96 **IS** Sch 3 para 8(2) and (3) IS
   Regs;
   JSA Sch 2 para 7(3)-(6) JSA Regs
97 CIS/5177/1997
98 **IS** Sch 3 para 11(2) IS Regs
   JSA Sch 2 para 10(1) JSA Regs
99 **IS** Sch 3 para 14 IS Regs
   JSA Sch 2 para 13 JSA Regs
100 Reg 32 IS(JSACA) Regs
101 **IS** Sch 3 paras 14(4), (5), (5A)
   and (5B) IS Regs
   JSA Sch 2 paras 13(5), (6), (7)
   and (8) JSA Regs
102 **IS** Sch 3 para 14(6) IS Regs
   JSA Sch 2 para 13(9) JSA Regs
103 Reg 3 IS(AT) Regs
104 Sch 3 para 7 IS Regs and Sch 2
   para 18 JSA Regs
105 s16 IA 1978; CIS/1939/1997

Chapter 47

Income – non-means-tested benefits

This chapter explains the income rules for non-means-tested benefits. It covers:

1. Earnings-related income for non-means-tested benefits (except for contribution-based jobseeker's allowance) (p2:367)
2. Earnings-related income for contribution-based jobseeker's allowance (p2:376)

Earnings-related income includes earnings from employment and self-employment, as well as payments from occupational and personal pension schemes.

If you are claiming invalid care allowance, incapacity benefit or severe disablement allowance, only your earnings can affect your entitlement to benefit, but the earnings-related income of an adult dependant may affect any increase you can claim with these and certain other non-means-tested benefits for any adult or child dependant (see Chapter 37). If you are claiming contribution-based jobseeker's allowance (JSA), both your earnings and pension payments could affect your entitlement (no increases for dependants are payable with JSA).

This chapter explains which benefits are affected, what counts as earnings and pension payments, how they are calculated, and how they affect your entitlement.

No other forms of income you or any member of your family or anyone else receives affects your entitlement to any non-means-tested benefit you may be able to claim for yourself or anyone else.

For the treatment of earnings-related and other income on claims for means-tested benefits, see Chapter 48.

1. Earnings-related income for non-means-tested benefits

Most non-means-tested benefits are not affected by income. However, some non-means-tested benefits are intended as earnings-replacement benefits and they may be affected by earnings-related income.

You will not be entitled to any benefit if you earn more than a certain amount (but any pension payments you receive will not be counted) if you are claiming:

- invalid care allowance (ICA) (see Chapter 5); *or*
- incapacity benefit (IB) (see Chapter 3); *or*
- severe disablement allowance (SDA) (see Chapter 4)

For ICA, the earnings limit is £50 a week. For IB and SDA (which you can claim if the work you do is 'therapeutic work' – see p2:16), the therapeutic earnings limit is £58 a week. IB and SDA will also be paid at a reduced rate if you are a local councillor and your net allowances exceed £49.50 a week (see p2:389).

The earnings-related income of an adult dependant (see p2:93) may affect your entitlement to any increase of benefit you may be able to claim for her/him (for the earnings limits for each benefit see p2:96), if you are claiming:

- ICA; *or*
- IB; *or*
- SDA; *or*
- retirement pension (see Chapter 8); *or*
- maternity allowance (see Chapter 6).

The earnings-related income of an adult dependant may affect your entitlement to an increase of benefit you may be able to claim for a child dependant (see p2:97 for who counts as a child dependant and for the earnings limits) if you are claiming:

- ICA; *or*
- IB; *or*
- SDA; *or*
- retirement pension; *or*
- widowed mother's allowance (see Chapter 7)

If you are claiming contribution-based jobseeker's allowance (JSA), see p2:376 for the rules on how your own earnings-related income may affect your own entitlement to benefit for yourself.

Note: The rules for calculating earnings changed on 25 November 1996. Some appeals may still involve calculating earnings for periods prior to that date. If so, the old rules still apply and are probably more favourable to you.[1]

You should consult of CPAG's *Rights Guide to Non-Means-Tested Benefits,* 19th edition, p265.

Earnings

It is important to distinguish between 'earnings' and other types of income because only earnings and certain pension payments (see p2:375) can affect your entitlement to non-means-tested benefits – but see p2:377 for the rules for contribution-based JSA.

Earnings are what you get in return for working as opposed to, for example, interest on your savings or social security benefits. What counts as earnings depends on whether you are an employee (see below) or self-employed (see p2:370).

Employees

If you are employed by someone else (including employment by a limited company in which you have shares) earnings means 'any remuneration or profit derived from ... employment'. The main type of income which counts as earnings is therefore your wages. But the following are also included:[2]

- any bonus or commission (including tips);
- holiday pay (but not if it is payable more than four weeks after your job ends or is interrupted);
- any payment in lieu of notice;
- compensation for unfair dismissal and certain other types of compensation under the Employment Rights Act;[3]
- any payments made by your employer for expenses not 'wholly, exclusively and necessarily' incurred in carrying out your job, including any travel expenses to and from work, and any payments made to you for looking after members of your family;
- a retainer fee (eg, you may be paid during the school holidays if you work for the school meals service) or a guarantee payment;[4]
- maternity pay and sick pay.[5]

The following **do not** count as earnings:
- periodic payments made as part of a redundancy scheme;[6]
- payments towards expenses that are 'wholly, exclusively and necessarily' incurred in the performance of your employment, such as travelling expenses during the course of your work.[7] In appropriate circumstances these could, for example, include:
  - tools or work equipment;
  - special clothing or uniform;[8]
  - telephone costs (including rental);[9]
  - postage;
  - fuel costs (including standing charges);

- secretarial expenses;[10] *and*
- the costs of running a car (including petrol, tax, insurance, repairs and maintenance and rental on a leased car).[11]

Where any expenditure serves a dual purpose for both business and private use it should be apportioned as appropriate to the circumstances (and any determination by the inland revenue – which commonly allows for 85 per cent business usage – should normally be followed).[12]

If you are a local councillor, travelling expenses and subsistence payments are (and basic allowances may be[13]) ignored as expenses 'wholly, exclusively and necessarily' incurred in your work. However, allowances for attending meetings etc, are counted as earnings.[14]

Calculating net earnings from employment

For the earnings rules for the non-means-tested benefits in this *Handbook* (other than contribution-based JSA – see p2:376), your 'earnings' are your net earnings. 'Net' earnings are your 'gross' earnings (calculated as set out above) less any deductions made for income tax, Class 1 national insurance contributions (but not Class 3 voluntary contributions[15]) and half of any contribution you make towards a personal or occupational pension scheme.[16]

The date from which earnings from employment are counted

You are usually treated as having received earnings on the first day of the benefit week in which they are due to be paid.[17] The benefit week is the seven days corresponding to the week for which the particular benefit you are claiming is paid (see the relevant chapter for the benefit you are claiming).[18]

The exception to this is if you are claiming:

- an increase in maternity allowance or ICA for an adult dependant (see p2:93); *or*
- an increase in your Category A retirement pension for an adult dependant who does not live with you (see p2:93),

in which case earnings are treated as having been paid on the first day of the benefit week after the week in which they are due to be paid.[19]

The date that a payment is due may well be different from the date of actual payment. Earnings are due on the employee's normal pay day. If your contract of employment does not reveal the date of due payment and there is no evidence to suggest differently, the date the payment was received should be taken as the date it was due.[20] If your contract of employment is terminated without proper notice, outstanding wages, wages in hand, holiday pay and any pay in lieu of notice are due on the last day of employment and are treated as paid on that day, even if this does not happen.[21] If you receive compensation for, say, being dismissed in circumstances constituting sex discrimination, the relevant date is the date when the earnings in question were due to be paid, not when the compensation was awarded.[22]

The period covered by earnings from employment

Once it has been calculated, your earnings count for a future period. The length of that period is worked out as follows:

- Where a payment of income is made in respect of an identifiable period, it is taken into account for a period of equal length.[23] For example, a week's part-time earnings are taken into account for a week.
- If the payment does not relate to a particular period, the amount of the payment is divided by the amount of the weekly earnings limit (see p2:367) plus one penny and then rounded down to the nearest whole number. If part of the payment should be disregarded (see p2:371), the weekly earnings limit is increased (for the purpose of this calculation only) by the amount of the appropriate disregard (see p2:371). The result of this calculation is the number of weeks for which you will not get benefit.[24]

Example

Bob receives a Category A retirement pension with an increase for his wife who lives with him. She receives £700 net earnings for work which cannot be attributed to any specific period of time. The £700 figure includes a tax refund of £150 paid through the PAYE system.

The earnings limit for the dependant's increase is £51.40.

The £150 tax refund is disregarded.

The period over which the income is taken into account is

£700 ÷ (£51.40 + £0.01 + £150) =

£700 ÷ 201.41 = 3.475 weeks

This means that Bob is not entitled to his dependency increase for three weeks.

Self-employed people

If you are self-employed, your weekly earnings – see below – (including any allowance from an Employment Service Scheme to assist you with your business[25]) are averaged over a period of a year unless:

- you have recently become self-employed; *or*
- there has been a change which is likely to affect the normal pattern of your business,

in which case, your earnings are averaged over whatever other period the adjudication officer (AO) considers will give the most accurate figure.[26] This means that when you first claim, the AO will need you to provide an up-to-date set of accounts. If you receive royalties from copyrights, the period for which these payments will count is calculated in a similar way to payments made for unspecified periods to employees (see above).[27]

The figure used for your earnings is your 'net profit' from self-employment or, if you are a member of a partnership or a share fisherman, your share of the net profit. Unless you are a childminder (in which case see below) your net profit is calculated taking your earnings over the period and deducting:[28]

- expenses incurred during the period wholly and exclusively for the purposes of the business. Where a car or telephone, for example, is used partly for business and partly for private purposes, the costs of it can be apportioned and the amount attributable to business use can be deducted;[29]
- income tax and national insurance contributions;[30] *and*
- half of any contributions you have made during the period towards a private pension.

Childminders are always treated as self-employed. If you are a childminder, your net profit is deemed to be one-third of your earnings less income tax, your national insurance contributions and half of certain pension contributions[31] (see p2:369). The rest of your earnings are completely ignored.

Disregarded earnings

Some of your income which might otherwise be classed as earnings is specifically disregarded and does not affect your benefit. Some care and childcare costs can also be disregarded (see pp2:373 and 2:372). The same earnings disregards apply whether you are an employee or self-employed (and, if you are a childminder, they apply in addition to the other disregards explained above).

Earnings which can be disregarded are:[32]

- any payment made to you by someone who normally lives with you on an informal or non-contractual basis as part of their contribution towards shared living expenses;
- the first £4 of any income you receive each week for renting out room(s) in your home. This disregard is increased to £13.25 a week if your tenant(s) pay for their heating as part of the rent rather than, for example, through a separate electricity meter;
- the first £20 of any income you receive each week for providing board and lodging in your home. If you receive more than £20 a week, then 50 per cent of the excess is also disregarded. This disregard applies to each person who lodges with you so, for example, if you are providing bed & breakfast accommodation and in one week five different people each stay for one night and pay £20, then the full £100 is disregarded;
- earnings payable abroad which cannot be brought into Britain (eg, because of exchange control regulations);
- if your earnings are paid in another currency, any bank charges for converting them into sterling are deducted before taking them into account;
- payments from a local authority or voluntary organisation for fostering or accommodating a child under formal arrangements, or payments from a

health authority or local authority or voluntary organisation for providing temporary respite care;
- refunds of Schedule D or Schedule E income tax;
- if you are an employee, any loan or advance of earnings from your employer;
- certain bounty payments made to part-time firefighters, auxiliary coast-guards, members of the territorial or reserve armed forces and part-time lifeboat crews.

Childcare costs[33]

In addition to the earnings disregards set out above, certain childcare costs may also be deducted from earnings. The following rules apply to claims for those benefits and dependency increases listed on p2:367, except that different rules (see below) apply to the treatment of childcare costs if you are claiming ICA (although the following rules do apply to ICA dependency increases).

An allowance of up to a maximum of £60 a week may be deducted from your earnings if:
- you are a single parent; *or*
- you are a member of a couple (see p2:93) and both you and your partner are working (full- or part-time); *or*
- you are a member of a couple and your partner is incapacitated (see below).

This will only apply if you have any child(ren) in your family under the age of 11 for whom you are paying charges for childcare (not counting charges paid to or by your partner, or charges in respect of compulsory education) which is provided:
- by a registered childminder or other registered childcare provider (such as a nursing or after-school club for the under-8's); *or*
- by (for children between the ages of 8 and 11) a school on school premises or by a local authority (eg, an out-of-hours or holiday play scheme); *or*
- by a childcare scheme operating on Crown property; *or*
- in schools or establishments exempt from registration.[34]

Your partner counts as 'incapacitated' if:[35]
- s/he is getting long-term IB, SDA, attendance allowance, disability living allowance (see pp1:45, 1:62 and 1:160) (or an equivalent award under the war pensions or industrial injuries schemes), or would have been if s/he were not a hospital inpatient (see p2:154); *or*
- s/he is provided with an invalid carriage or other vehicle by the NHS; *or*
- you or your partner are getting housing benefit or council tax benefit (see Chapters 25 and 27) and either childcare costs have been allowed for under the rules applying to claims for those benefits (see p2:401) or else a disability premium or higher pensioner premium in respect of your partner has been awarded (see pp2:325 and 2:327).

Because childcare costs are likely to vary considerably between term time and holiday periods, a formula is used to assess the costs that will be taken into account.

Where charges are paid monthly, the amount will be:
- if the charge is for a fixed amount, that amount multiplied by 12 and divided by 52; *or*
- if the charge is variable, 1/52 of the aggregate of charges over the previous 12 months.

Where charges are paid other than monthly, the amount will be either:
- 1/52 of the aggregate of:
  - the average weekly charge in the four most recent complete weeks falling in term time, multiplied by 39; *and*
  - the average weekly charge in the two most recent complete weeks falling out of term time, multiplied by 13: *or*
- if your child does not yet attend school, the average weekly charge in the four most recent complete weeks.

However, if there is no, or insufficient, information available to calculate your childcare costs in these ways (eg, you have just started to use a childminder), an estimate will be made based on the information provided by the childcare provider or, if that is not available, by whoever is paying the charges. [36]

Care costs and invalid care allowance[37]

If you are getting invalid care allowance (ICA – see Chapter 5) and because of your work you have to pay for someone (other than a 'close relative' – see below) to look after the severely disabled person you care for or to look after a child under 16 for whom you or your partner are getting child benefit (see Chapter 12) then (in addition to any disregarded earnings – see p2:371), those care costs can be deducted when your earnings are calculated. The maximum deduction is 50 per cent of the figure which would otherwise be your net earnings. Any disregarded income is deducted from your net earnings before calculating the 50 per cent figure. 'Close relative' means a parent, son, daughter, brother, sister or partner of you or the severely disabled person you care for. There is therefore no restriction on charges paid to someone who is only a close relative of the child being looked after (eg, the parent of the child if s/he is not also your partner).

Notes on childcare costs
- Childcare allowances apply separately to each individual in respect of whom benefit is claimed. The same childcare costs may therefore sometimes be allowed in respect of more than one claim. For example, the childcare costs you and your partner pay may be deducted from your earnings on a claim for IB for yourself, as well as from your partner's earnings on a claim for IB for

her/himself, or on your claims for child and adult dependency increases of IB in respect of your partner's earnings.

- Similarly, the same childcare costs may apply to a claim for ICA for yourself, as well as on a claim for an ICA dependency increase. Because different rules apply on the treatment of childcare costs, however, the same childcare costs may be allowed on one claim but not on the other (eg, if your child is over 11, your costs may be deducted from your earnings on a claim for yourself, but will not be deducted from your partner's earnings on a claim for a dependency increase).

- Whether or not childcare costs are taken into account on a claim for a non-means-tested benefit, different rules apply on claims for any means-tested benefit (see p2:401) or tax credit (see p1:492).

Notional earnings[38]

In some circumstances you will be treated as having some earnings even if you have none, or as having more earnings than you actually receive. This is called 'notional earnings' which applies to work from employment or self-employment.

You will be deemed to have notional earnings if:

- it is not possible to work out your earnings when your claim is decided. This may apply if, eg, you have just started employment and your pay will depend on your performance, or you have just started a business and there is no way of calculating what profits you will make. If so, you will be treated as earning such amount as is considered reasonable taking into account the number of hours you work and the earnings paid for comparable work in the area;

- you provide a service for someone else, but either you are not paid for it, or you are paid less than for comparable work in the area. If so, you will be treated as earning whatever is considered reasonable for that work unless *either*:
  - you can show that whoever you are working for cannot afford to pay you, or pay you more; *or*
  - you work for a charitable or voluntary organisation or as a volunteer and it is accepted that it is reasonable for you to give your services free of charge.

(For more details on how these rules may apply, see p2:424 when similar considerations apply to 'cheap or unpaid labour' while claiming means-tested benefits.)

Estimates of the appropriate deductions for income tax and national insurance contributions, and half of any occupational or personal pension contributions, are deducted from your notional earnings, as are any earnings disregards or allowances for childcare or care costs (see above).

Pension payments

For all claims for dependency increases (see p2:367), certain pension payments are now also counted as earnings[39] (unless the 'transitional protection' rules below apply).

All the following periodical payments of an occupational or personal pension count as earnings[40] which are made in connection with the ending of a person's employment, and are paid:
- out of money provided wholly or partly by or under arrangements made by an employer; *or*
- under an approved personal pension, contract of trust scheme; *or*
- under a statutory scheme.

This covers most pension payments, including early retirement schemes for those who retire early on health grounds or for other reasons[41], or, in some cases, those who volunteer for redundancy.[42]

However, it does not include lump sum or redundancy payments which are not related to a specific period, even if you have chosen to receive a lump sum instead of a periodical payment (although if you choose to receive payments in instalments, even if you do not have to, they will count).[43]

Only pension payments made in respect of the person for whom benefit is being claimed count. Payments made because of the ending of someone else's employment (eg, the pension received by a widow on account of her late husband's employment) do not count.[44]

Calculation of weekly pension payments

The amount of the pension to be taken into account is the *gross* amount paid before any deductions for income tax,[45] although deductions will be made from any payments in respect of any compulsory reductions made by the pension scheme if the rules of the scheme require this for the purpose of acquiring additional pension rights.[46]

All pension payments are converted into equivalent weekly amounts[47] and any pension payment is counted from the first day of the benefit week in which it is actually made. If you therefore postpone receipt of a pension payment it will not be taken into account immediately, but when it is paid later any award of benefit paid in the meantime may be reviewed (although no payment will count if it is foregone completely).[48]

Transitional rules for pension payments

For dependency increases of all benefits except ICA, *occupational pension* payments will not be counted if benefit was in payment in the week before these rules were introduced on 26 November 1984 and benefit would have remained continuously in payment since then if the pension payments did

47

Chapter 47: Income – non-means-tested benefits
2. Earnings-related income for contribution-based jobseeker's allowance

not count.[49] For ICA, the same protection will apply to benefit in payment in the week before 6 April 1987.[50]

For all dependency increases, *personal pensions* will not be counted if benefit was in payment in the week before the rules were introduced on 9 October 1989 and benefit would have remained continuously in payment since then if the pension payments were not counted.[51]

2. Earnings-related income for contribution-based jobseeker's allowance

Any earnings and pension payments you receive can also affect your entitlement to contribution-based JSA. Any other income you receive will not affect your contribution-based JSA. Similarly, any savings you have, and any income (including earnings and pension payments) or savings of any member of your family will not affect your entitlement to contribution-based JSA. For the rules on the treatment of any income or savings of you, or any member of your family, on a claim for income-based JSA, see Chapters 48 and 49.

Earnings

The rules on the treatment of earnings for contribution-based JSA are different from the rules which apply to non-means-tested benefits explained on p2:367). However, although all other rules on the treatment of income are otherwise different, most of the earnings rules for income-based JSA apply in the same way to contribution-based JSA. For an explanation of how each of the following applies to contribution-based JSA, you should therefore read the relevant section of Chapter 48 as it applies to income-based JSA:
- what counts as earnings (p2:388);
- how earnings are assessed (p2:390);
- calculating net earnings from employment (p2:390);
- calculating net earnings from self-employment (p2:396);
- working out average earnings from self-employment (p2:397);
- childminders (p2:399);
- payments at the end of a job (p2:392);
- converting income into a weekly amount (p2:384);
- the period covered by income (p2:385);
- the date from which a payment is counted (p2:386).

Chapter 47: Income – non-means-tested benefits
2. Earnings-related income for contribution-based jobseeker's allowance

47

Although these rules are the same, different rules apply to disregarded earnings and how earnings affect your contribution-based JSA. These are explained below.

Disregarded earnings

For contribution-based JSA, £5 a week of your earnings are disregarded. £15 a week is disregarded if you are a share fisherman, an auxiliary coastguard, a part-time member of a fire brigade, a part-time member of a lifeboat crew or a member of the territorial or reserve forces.[52] Your benefit is reduced pound for pound by the amount of any earnings you receive over the disregarded amount.

How earnings affect your contribution-based jobseeker's allowance

You are *not entitled* to contribution-based JSA for any week in which your earnings exceed a prescribed amount (see below). The days in any week when your earnings exceed the prescribed amount do not count towards your maximum 182 days of contribution-based JSA (see p1:272).[53] The prescribed amount is not the same for everyone. It is calculated by adding the amount of relevant earnings disregard to the rate of contribution-based JSA paid to someone your age, and then deducting one penny (see below).

Calculating the 'prescribed amount'

The prescribed amount is calculated by using a formula: $(A + D) - £0.01$ where A = the age-related amount of contribution-based JSA for your age (see p1:276) and D = the amount to be disregarded when calculating the amount of your earnings (see above). An example is given below.

> *Example*
> Maggie, aged 35, is entitled to contribution-based JSA of £51.40 a week. She works part-time. Her earnings disregard is £5 a week. Applying the formula: (£51.40 + £5) – £0.01 = £56.39, if Maggie earns more than £56.39 a week she is not entitled to contribution-based JSA – the week will not be counted towards her maximum 182 days entitlement to contribution-based JSA.

Pension payments

Certain pension payments you receive may also affect your contribution-based JSA.[54] Your contribution-based JSA is reduced by the amount of weekly pension *above* £50 a week, regardless of your age. A pension of less than £50 a week is ignored for contribution-based JSA.[55] In this context, 'pension payments' means[56] periodical payments paid under:

47

Chapter 47: Income – non-means-tested benefits
2. Earnings-related income for contribution-based jobseeker's allowance

- a personal pension scheme; *or*
- a pension connected with the ending of your employment as an earner, such as an occupational pension scheme or a public service pension scheme.

Although the meaning of pension payments is slightly different than that applying to other non-means-tested benefits, it should still cover most periodical pension payments as explained on p2:375, and the same exclusions (eg, lump sum payments) will also apply, as will identical rules on the calculation of weekly pension payments.[57]

The amount of your pension payments may mean that you are not paid any JSA. However, unless your earnings also exceed the prescribed amount (see p2:377) you remain *entitled* to contribution-based JSA even though it is not paid because your pension payments are too high (so long as you also satisfy the other conditions for getting JSA – see p1:269). Any day on which you are entitled to JSA even if it is not paid counts towards your 182 days' entitlement to contribution-based JSA (see p1:272). A combination of earnings and pension payments may also mean that you are not paid any JSA, even though you may remain entitled to it.

As for non-means-tested benefits dependency increases, any payments you receive under a personal pension scheme because of the death of the person who was a member of the pension scheme are ignored when calculating your contribution-based JSA.[58] For example, if your late partner was a member of a scheme, any payment made to you following her/his death does not affect your contribution-based JSA.

As for non-means-tested benefits dependency increases, any pension payment you receive is counted from the first day of the benefit week (see p2:375) in which the payment is actually made to you.[59]

Example

Brian claims JSA and is entitled to contribution-based JSA from Wednesday, 4 November 1998. His benefit week begins on a Friday (his signing-on day is Thursday). He starts receiving a personal pension of £68 a week from Monday 9 November 1998. £18 a week is deducted from his contribution-based JSA (£68 – £50) from the benefit week starting Friday, 6 November 1998.

If your pension is increased when you are on contribution-based JSA, the change should be taken into account from the first day of the benefit week in which the increase is paid.[60]

Notes

• •

References are to statutes and regulations as amended up to 8 March 1999. All regulations are (General) Regulations unless otherwise stated. There is a full list of abbreviations in Appendix 13.

1. Earnings-related income for non-means-tested benefits

1 Reg 18(2) SS(CE) Regs
2 Reg 9 SS(CE) Regs
3 Regs 9(1)(b), (g)-(i) and (4) SS(CE) Regs; s112(3) SSCBA 1992
4 CIS/743/1992
5 Reg 9(1)(j) SS(CE) Regs
6 Reg 9(1)(b) SS(CE) Regs
7 Reg 9(3) SS(CE) Regs; *Parsons v Hogg* [1985] 2 All ER 897, CA (also reported as an appendix to R(FIS) 4/85)
8 R(FC) 1/90
9 CFC/26/1989
10 R(FIS) 4/85
11 R(IS) 13/91; R(IS) 16/93; CFC/26/1989
12 R(U) 2/72; R(FIS) 4/85; R(FC) 1/91; R(IS) 13/91
13 CIS/77/1993; CIS/89/1989
14 R(IS) 6/92
15 CIS/521/1990
16 Reg 10(4) SS(CE) Regs
17 Reg 7(b) SS(CE) Regs
18 Reg 2(1) SS(CE) Regs
19 Reg 7(a) SS(CE) Regs
20 R(SB) 33/83
21 R(SB) 22/84; R(SB) 11/85
22 CIS/590/1993
23 Reg 6(2)(a) SS(CE) Regs
24 Reg 6(2)(b) SS(CE) Regs
25 Reg 12(1) SS(CE) Regs
26 Reg 11(1) SS(CE) Regs
27 Reg 11(2) SS(CE) Regs
28 Reg 13(1)(a) and (b), (4) and (5) SS(CE) Regs
29 R(IS) 13/91; R(FC) 1/91; CFC/26/1989
30 See also reg 14 SS(CE) Regs
31 Reg 13(10) SS(CE) Regs
32 Sch 1 SS(CE) Regs
33 Regs 10(2), 13(2) and Sch 2 SS(CE) Regs
34 Sch 2 para 2 SS(CE) Regs
35 Sch 2 para 8 SS(CE) Regs
36 Sch 2 para 4 SS(CE) Regs
37 Regs 10(3), 13(3) and Sch 3 SS(CE) Regs
38 Reg 4 SS(CE) Regs
39 s89 SSCBA 1992; Sch 2 para 9 SSB(Dep) Regs
40 s122(1) SSCBA 1992
41 CP/7/1987
42 CU/66/1993
43 R(U) 5/85
44 para 61264 AOG
45 R(U) 8/83
46 R(U) 4/83; para 61267 AOG
47 Reg 9A SSB(Dep) Regs; paras 61272-73 AOG
48 para 61266 AOG
49 para 61276 AOG
50 Sch 2 para 9(2) SSB(Dep) Regs
51 para 61286 AOG

2. Earnings-related income for contribution-based JSA

52 Reg 99(3) and Sch 6 JSA Regs
53 s2(1)(c) JSA 1995; reg 56(1) and (2) JSA Regs
54 s4(1) JSA 1995
55 Reg 81(1) JSA Regs
56 s35(1) JSA 1995
57 Reg 81 JSA Regs; para 28923 AOG
58 Reg 81(2)(c) JSA Regs
59 Reg 81(1A) JSA Regs
60 Reg 81(1B) JSA Regs

Chapter 48

Income – means-tested benefits

This chapter explains the rules for working out your weekly income for income support, income-based jobseeker's allowance, family credit, disability working allowance, earnings top-up, housing benefit and council tax benefit. It contains:

1. Some general rules about income (p2:381)
2. Earnings of employed earners (p2:387)
3. Earnings from self-employment (p2:396)
4. Disregarded earnings (p2:399)
5. Other income (p2:404)
6. Notional income (p2:421)

Note

The same rules which apply to the treatment of income when claiming family credit (FC)/disability working allowance (DWA), and the treatment of FC/DWA as income when claiming other benefits, will also apply to the new tax credits which will replace FC and DWA from October 1999 (see Chapter 23), except that different rules will apply to the treatment of childcare expenses (for FC/DWA, see pp1:463 and 1:477; for tax credits, see p1:492) and maintenance payments (for FC/DWA, see p2:401; for tax credits, see pp1:489 and 1:491).

Your entitlement to income support (IS – Chapter 2), income-based jobseeker's allowance (JSA – Chapter 14), family credit (FC – Chapter 21), disability working allowance (DWA – Chapter 22), earnings top-up (ETU – Chapter 24), housing benefit (HB – Chapter 25) and council tax benefit (CTB – Chapter 27) and the amount you receive depends on how much income you have. Note that if you get IS or income-based JSA you do not need to work out your income again for HB or CTB purposes (see pp1:519 and 1:574).[1]

The rules for working out your income are very similar for each of the means-tested benefits. Where there are differences these are indicated. Some of your income may be completely ignored, *or* partially ignored, *or* counted in full. Some income may be treated as capital (see p2:455), and some capital may be treated as income (see p2:416). There are some important differences in the rules on income for urgent cases payments under the IS and income-based JSA schemes. These are set out at p2:210.

The rules in this chapter about *earnings* (as opposed to other forms of income) are also relevant when applying the earnings rules for contribution-based JSA. However, for contribution-based JSA, only the claimant's earnings are relevant, not the earnings of other members of her/his family.[2] For further information about the earnings rules for contribution-based JSA, see p2:376.

For information about the earnings rules for certain other non-means-tested benefits, see Chapter 47.

Note that, except when special rules apply on the treatment of income from certain pension schemes (see Chapter 47), no other forms of income other than earnings count for any other non-means-tested benefit. However, although you may be able to claim certain non-means-tested benefits in spite of any income or earnings you may have, these benefits themselves may be taken into account (see p2:405) when calculating your entitlement to any means-tested benefit.

For the treatment of earnings and other income on claims for certain health benefits, see p2:623.

---

1. **Some general rules about income**

This section explains the rules about whose income counts when working out your entitlement to means-tested benefits, how the income of your partner or a dependent child is treated, how any income is converted into weekly amounts so as to calculate your entitlement to these weekly benefits, and the special rules on the periods covered by income in claims for income support (IS) and income-based jobseeker's allowance (JSA).

Whose income counts

Income of a partner

If you are a member of a couple (see p2:93), your partner's income is added to yours.[3]

If, for IS/income-based JSA, you receive the reduced rate of the normal personal allowance for a couple because your partner is under 18 and not eligible for IS or income-based JSA (see p2:370), an amount of her/his income equivalent to the reduction is ignored.[4]

Example

Kalid is 19. His partner, Kate, is 17 and is not able to claim IS or income-based JSA.
Kalid's personal allowance is £40.70 (the rate for a single person aged 18/24). If Kate
was eligible for IS or income-based JSA, their personal allowance would be £80.65.
Up to £39.95 (£80.65 – £40.70) of any income that Kate has is ignored.

Similar rules apply to additional partners in polygamous marriages for whom, for IS/income-based JSA, you do not receive an increase in your personal allowance because the additional partner is under 18 (see p2:320), so that any income equivalent to the increase you would receive is ignored.[5]

Income of a dependent child

If your child has over £3,000 capital, you do not get benefit for her/him[6] (although for IS, income-based JSA, HB and CTB, the ordinary or lone parent rate of the family premium may still be payable – see p2:323) and her/his income is not counted as yours. However, maintenance paid to, or for, a child does count as yours (see p2:303).[7]

If your child has capital of £3,000 or less, any of her/his income (subject to disregards) is usually treated as yours.[8]

With IS, income-based JSA, HB and CTB, if that income comes to more than your child's personal allowance (plus any disabled child premium payable for her/him), the extra is ignored and not counted as yours.[9] In the case of FC and DWA, if your child's income (ignoring any maintenance payments) comes to more than the child credit – see pp1:463 and 1:478 – (plus, for DWA, any disabled child allowance payable for your child) the whole of your child's income is ignored, but you do not get any child credit, or disabled child allowance for her/him.[10] However, in all cases, any maintenance that is not disregarded and which is paid to, or for, your child counts in full as your income.[11]

As you cannot apply for earnings top-up while a child for whom you are responsible lives in your household (see Chapter 24), there are no rules on the treatment of a child's income (above) or earnings (below) in the earnings top-up scheme.

Child's earnings

Your child's earnings (as opposed to other forms of income) while s/he is *at school* do not normally count,[12] but if you are on IS, income-based JSA, HB and CTB (not FC or DWA), and your child gets a *full-time* job *after leaving school* but while you are still claiming for her/him (eg, during the summer holiday), her/his earnings over £5 count as your income.[13] If the child qualifies for the disabled child premium (see p2:325) – or would, but for her/his being in a residential care or nursing home – and her/his earning capacity is not, as a result of the disability, less than 75 per cent of what it otherwise would be, £15 is ignored.[14] In either case, any income that exceeds her/his personal allowance and any disabled child premium is also ignored.[15] However, earnings from part-time work (up to 24 hours a week) are still completely ignored.

School fees

School fees paid by someone other than you or your partner are dealt with differently for each benefit.

Your entitlement to IS or income-based JSA is not affected if someone is paying school fees directly to the school,[16] except that any payments for the child's living expenses at a boarding school count as the child's income (up to the amount of the child's personal allowance and, if applicable, the disabled child premium) for the period that the child is there.[17] If your child comes home for part of the week, you receive full benefit for the child for the days s/he is at home and any payments towards the child's living expenses are averaged over the period the child is at school.[18] If your child spends a night with you s/he does not count as at the boarding school on that day.[19]

If your child goes away to school and this is paid for by the local education authority, the child is treated as having income equal to the amount of her/his IS or income-based JSA child's personal allowance (and disabled child premium, if applicable) for the days s/he is at school.[20] You are entitled to full benefit for the child for the days s/he spends at home.

There are no special rules about school fees for FC or DWA. However, for both benefits all fees paid to a school by someone else or by a local education authority should be ignored even during periods when your child stays overnight at a boarding school.[21]

For HB/CTB, the local authority is advised that boarding school fees met by, for example, a child's grandparents should be ignored unless they are already broken down into separate amounts for education and maintenance. In that case, the education element is disregarded and the living expenses part, if it is taken into account as the child's income under the rules for payments made to someone else on your behalf (see p2:423), is treated as a charitable or voluntary payment and qualifies for the £20 disregard (see p2:412).[22] (See p2:382 for how a child's income is counted.) The education element of school fees paid by a former partner is also ignored, but the living expenses part, if taken into account as income under the rules for payments made to someone else on your behalf (see p2:423), counts as maintenance (see p2:288) and qualifies for the £15 disregard (see p2:400).[23]

Converting income into a weekly amount

IS, income-based JSA, FC, DWA, ETU, HB and CTB are all calculated on a weekly basis so your earnings and other income have to be converted into a weekly amount if necessary.

The following rules apply to income from employment.[24]

For income from self-employment, see p2:396.

For other income, see p2:404.

For income from employment:

- if the payment is for less than a week it is treated as the weekly amount;
- if the payment is for a month, multiply by 12 and divide by 52;
- for IS, income-based JSA, FC, DWA and ETU, multiply a payment for three months by 4 and divide by 52;
- for IS, income-based JSA, FC, DWA and ETU, divide a payment for a year by 52;
- for all benefits, multiply payments for any other periods by 7 and divide by the number of days in the period.

If you work on certain days but are paid monthly, it is necessary to decide whether the payment is for the days worked or for the whole month. This, generally, depends on the terms of your contract of employment,[25] but may depend on how your employer has arranged to make payments to you.[26]

For IS and income-based JSA, where your income fluctuates or your earnings vary because you do not work every week, your weekly income may be averaged over the cycle, if there is an identifiable one; or, if there is not, over five weeks, or over another period if this would be more accurate.[27] If the cycle involves periods when you do no work, those periods are included in the cycle, but not other absences – eg, holidays, sickness.

Example

Ahmed works a cycle of two weeks on and one week off. He works 20 hours a week in the weeks he works for which he is paid £60. In the third week he is paid a retainer of £30. He claims income-based JSA in the third week. His average weekly earnings are £50 a week (£60 + £60 + £30 = £150 ÷ 3 = £50) which will be taken into account in calculating his income-based JSA entitlement.

For IS and income-based JSA, there are a number of rules about the calculation of income for part-weeks. They are:

- Where income covering a period up to a week is paid before your first benefit week, and part of it is counted for that week; or, if, in any case, you are paid for a period of a week or more, and only part of it is counted in a particular benefit week – multiply the whole payment by the number of days it covers in the benefit week, then divide the result by the total number of days covered by the payment.[28]

- Where any payment of maternity allowance, incapacity benefit, or severe disablement allowance falls partly into the benefit week, only the amount paid for those days is taken into account. For any payment of IS or JSA, that amount is the weekly amount multiplied by the number of days in the part-week and divided by 7.[29]

For IS or income-based JSA, where you have regularly received a certain kind of payment of income from one source, and in a particular benefit week you receive that payment and another of the same kind from the same source (eg, where your employer first pays you sick pay in arrears and this then overlaps with a payment in advance), the maximum amount to be taken into account is the one paid first.[30]

This does not apply if the second payment was due to be taken into account in another week, but the overlapping week is the first in which it could practically be counted (see p2:386).

See p1:454 for definition of IS benefit week and p1:274 for the definition of a JSA benefit week.

The period covered by income for income support and income-based jobseeker's allowance

For FC/DWA/ETU/HB/CTB a past period is normally looked at to assess what your current normal weekly income is. If you are claiming IS or income-based JSA, however, there are special rules for deciding the length of the period for which and the date from which payments of earnings and other income count. These rules are designed to give a clearer indication of how you are expected to make use of any earnings or other income you receive for each week of your claim for IS/income-based JSA. These rules do not, however, apply to self-employed earnings (see p2:396).

- Where a payment of income is made in respect of an identifiable period, it is taken into account for a period of equal length.[31] For example, a week's part-time earnings is taken into account for a week.
- If the payment does not relate to a particular period, the amount of the payment is divided by the amount of the weekly IS or income-based JSA to which you would otherwise be entitled. If part of the payment should be disregarded, the amount of IS or income-based JSA is increased by the appropriate disregard. The result of this calculation is the number of weeks that you are not entitled to IS or income-based JSA.[32]

Example

Conor receives £700 net earnings for work which cannot be attributed to any specific period of time. He and his partner are both aged 28. They have one child aged 8. Their rent and council tax are met by HB or CTB. Conor's income-based JSA is £100.35 (applicable amount of £114.75 less child benefit of £14.40). As a couple they are entitled to a £10 earnings disregard.

$$£700 \div (£100.35 + £10 = £110.35) = 6 \text{ with } £37.90 \text{ left over}$$

This means that Conor is not entitled to income-based JSA for six weeks and the remaining £37.90 (less a £10 earnings disregard, leaving £27.90) is taken into account in calculating his benefit for the following week.

- Payments made on leaving a job are taken into account for a forward period (see p2:392).

The date from which a payment is counted

The date from which a payment of earnings and/or other income counts depends on when it was due to be paid. If it was due to be paid before you claimed IS or income-based JSA, it counts from the date on which it was due to be paid.[33] Otherwise it is treated as paid on the first day of the benefit week in which it is due, or on the first day of the first benefit week after that in which it is practical to take it into account.[34] Payments of IS, JSA, maternity allowance, incapacity benefit or severe disablement allowance are treated as paid on the day they are officially due.[35]

The benefit week for IS or JSA is the seven days running from the day of the week on which benefit is paid. It often overlaps two calendar weeks.[36]

The date that a payment is due may well be different from the date of actual payment. Earnings are due on the employee's normal pay day. If the contract of employment does not reveal the date of due payment, and there is no evidence pointing in another direction, the date the payment was received should be taken as the date it was due.[37] If your contract of employment is terminated without proper notice, outstanding wages, wages in hand, holiday pay and any pay in lieu of notice are due on the last day of employment and are treated as paid on that day, even if this does not happen.[38] If income due to you has not been paid you may be entitled to an urgent cases payment (see p2:217) or a crisis loan from the social fund (see p1:667). For the treatment of payments at the end of a job, see p2:392. If you receive compensation for, say, being dismissed in circumstances constituting sex discrimination, the relevant date is the date when the earnings in question were due to be paid, not when the compensation was awarded.[39]

2. **Earnings of employed earners**

This section explains how any earnings of you or anyone you are claiming for (see p2:113) are treated for the purposes of any claim for any means-tested benefits. The same rules apply to your (but not your partner's or child's) earnings if you are claiming contribution-based JSA (for further information, see p2:376). For the rules on earnings for non-means-tested benefits, see Chapter 47; for health benefits, see p1:614.

Calculating net earnings from employment

Both your 'gross' earnings and 'net' earnings need to be calculated so that a proper assessment can be made of your income from employment.

'Gross' earnings means the amount of earnings received from your employer less deductions for any expenses wholly, necessarily and exclusively incurred by you in order to carry out the duties of your employment.[40] In appropriate circumstances deductions could, for example, be made for expenditure on tools or work equipment, special clothing or uniform,[41] telephone costs (including rental),[42] postage, fuel costs (including standing charges) and even secretarial expenses,[43] and the costs of running a car (including petrol, tax, insurance, repairs and maintenance and rental on a leased car).[44] It has also been held that an armed forces local overseas allowance (representing the additional cost of essential living expenses incurred from working overseas) should also be deducted,[45] although lodgings allowances to those stationed in the UK cannot be deducted,[46] and rent allowances for police officers probably cannot be deducted.[47] Where any expenditure serves a dual purpose for both business and private use it should be apportioned as appropriate to the circumstances (and any determination by the Inland Revenue – which commonly allows for 85 per cent business usage – should normally be followed).[48]

'Net' earnings means your 'gross' earnings less any deductions made for income tax, Class 1 national insurance contributions (but not Class 3 voluntary contributions[49]) and half of any contribution you make towards a personal or occupational pension scheme.[50] For FC, DWA, HB and CTB, a deduction is also made in certain cases for some childcare costs (see p2:401).

If your earnings are estimated the authorities estimate the amount of tax and national insurance you would expect to pay on those earnings, and deduct this plus half of any pension contribution you are paying.[51]

For HB and CTB, the local authority has the discretion to ignore changes in tax or national insurance contributions for up to 30 benefit weeks. This can be used, for example, where Budget changes are not reflected in your actual income until several months later. When the changes are eventually taken into account and your benefit entitlement is either increased or reduced accordingly, you are not treated as having been underpaid or overpaid benefit during the period of the delay.[52]

What counts as earnings

Earnings means 'any remuneration or profit derived from ... employment'. As well as your wages, this includes:[53]

- any bonus or commission (including tips);
- holiday pay, except if it is not payable until more than four weeks after your job ends or is interrupted, in which case it is treated as capital.[54]
  Note: For IS and income-based JSA, this rule does not apply if you are involved in, or, for IS only, returning to work after a trade dispute[55] (see p2:188). For more detail on payments at the end of a job, see p2:392;
- for FC/DWA/ETU/HB/CTB, any sick pay.[56] For IS and income-based JSA all sick pay is treated as other income (see p2:404 – and therefore does not attract an earnings disregard – see p2:399) and counted in full less any tax, Class 1 national insurance contributions and half of any pension contributions;[57]
- for HB and CTB, any maternity pay.[58] For FC, DWA and ETU, any statutory maternity pay and maternity allowance (see Chapter 6) is ignored altogether,[59] although any additional non-statutory contributions that may be made by an employer should be treated as earnings. For IS and income-based JSA all maternity pay is treated as other income (see p2:404 – and therefore does not attract an earnings disregard – see p2:399) and counted in full less any tax, Class 1 national insurance contributions and half of any pension contributions;[60]
- any payments made by your employer for expenses not 'wholly, exclusively and necessarily' incurred in carrying out your job, including any travel expenses to and from work, and any payments made to you for looking after members of your family;
- a retainer fee (eg, you may be paid during the school holidays if you work for the school meals service[61]) or a guarantee payment;[62]
- for DWA, any payment made by your employer towards your council tax;[63]
- certain compensation payments in respect of your employment.

For all benefits, these include any awards payable by an industrial tribunal as compensation for loss of earnings due to unfair dismissal[64] or sex or race discrimination[65] or for loss of maternity pay if an employer becomes insolvent, or for arrears of pay in respect of a reinstatement order or because of a 'protective' award when an employer fails to comply with redundancy procedures.[66]

For IS/income-based JSA/HB/CTB these also include any payment in lieu of wages (eg, on the termination of a fixed-term contract) – except for periodic payments following a redundancy (which count instead as other income).[67] For IS/income-based JSA/HB/CTB, pay in lieu of notice also counts as earnings.[68] For HB/CTB, however, pay in lieu of notice only counts in so far as it represents loss of income (and not, therefore, any *ex gratia* award). Note that for IS/income-based JSA any payment in lieu of wages or notice will count for the period for which the payment relates so that you will be treated as if you are still in work in that period and may not be entitled to benefit (see p2:392).

For income-based JSA, industrial tribunal awards in respect of guaranteed payments, pay while suspended from work on medical or maternity grounds, or compensatory awards in respect of trade union activity, and certain other awards[69] are also expressly treated as earnings.

For IS/JSA, compensatory refunds of contributions to an occupational scheme[70] and any lump sum payments made under the Iron and Steel Re-adaptation Benefits Scheme,[71] are not treated as earnings.

The following are examples of payments not counted as earnings:
- payments in kind (eg, petrol)[72] are ignored[73] unless you are on IS or income-based JSA and involved in a trade dispute (see p2:187), but the notional income rules may be applied instead (see p2:421).[74]

  The value of any accommodation provided as part of your job is ignored for IS and income-based JSA.[75] For FC/DWA/ETU, if it is free, the Benefits Agency takes account of its value by adding £12 to the calculation of your weekly earnings. If your employer charges you less than £12 rent, the difference between that amount and £12 is added instead. If the accommodation is worth less to you – eg, it is provided but you never use it,[76] no amount is added. For CTB, and for HB where job-related accommodation is in addition to the normal home, argue that this is payment in kind[77] and should be disregarded;
- an advance of earnings or a loan from your employer. This is treated as capital[78] (although it is still treated as earnings for IS or income-based JSA if you or your partner are involved in a trade dispute, or have been back at work after a dispute for no longer than 15 days[79]);
- payments towards expenses that are 'wholly, exclusively and necessarily' incurred, such as travelling expenses during the course of your work.[80] Such disregards from payments by your employer may be in addition to the allowances to be taken into account for expenses incurred by you in the assessment of your 'gross' earnings (see p2:387);
- if you are a local councillor, travelling expenses and subsistence payments are (and basic allowances may be[81]) ignored as expenses 'wholly, exclusively and necessarily' incurred in your work. However, allowances for attending meetings etc are counted as earnings;[82]
- earnings payable abroad which cannot be brought into Britain – eg, because of exchange control regulations.[83] If your earnings are paid in another

currency, any bank charges for converting them into sterling are deducted before taking them into account;[84]

- any occupational pension.[85] This counts as other income and the net amount is taken into account in full.[86] See p2:377 for the occupational pension rules for contribution-based JSA;
- certain payments made by the Employment Service for taking part in one of the options of the New Deal programme are treated as other income and may be disregarded (see p2:420).

How earnings are assessed

For IS and income-based JSA, it is necessary to work out the period which payments cover (see p2:385). However, for FC, DWA, ETU, HB and CTB a past period is usually used to assess your 'normal weekly earnings'.

For family credit and earnings top-up

Unless you are employed as a director (see p2:391), the normal rule is to average your weekly earnings over an 'assessment period' of:

- six consecutive weeks immediately preceding the week you claim (or the week before that if this information is not available) if you are paid weekly; *or*
- three consecutive fortnights immediately preceding the week you claim (or, if this information is not available, the three consecutive fortnights leading up to the week before you claim) if you are paid fortnightly; *or*
- three months or three four-week periods if you are paid monthly or four-weekly; *or*
- six consecutive pay periods if you are paid at another interval that is less than a month (eg, daily); *or*
- one year if your pay period is longer than a month.

In the last three cases, the periods in question must immediately precede the week of your claim.[87]

In all cases, it is the earnings which you *received* during the assessment period which count, even though some of these earnings may be for a period falling outside the assessment period – eg, an early payment of holiday pay.[88]

Any weeks or months in the assessment period are ignored and replaced by the next earliest 'normal' pay period if your earnings are reduced because you have been involved in a trade dispute[89] or if you have deliberately chosen to reduce the number of hours you work with the intention of becoming entitled to, or increasing your entitlement to, FC or ETU.[90]

Any pay period in which your earnings are 20 per cent or more above or below your average earnings are left out. If this applies to all the weeks or months in your assessment period, only those in which you received no pay or received pay for a longer period than usual (eg, two weeks' holiday pay in one week) are left out. If this still results in all the weeks or months in your assessment period being left out, your employer is required to provide an estimate of your likely earnings for the period for which you are normally paid.[91]

Where your earnings vary widely you may find that the figure arrived at can be based on just one wage slip which could be up to 20 per cent above or below your real average earnings. Therefore it may sometimes be sensible to delay your claim in order to allow for the lowest possible rate of pay to be taken into account and thus maximise the amount of FC/ETU you will receive for the next 26 weeks.

Earnings of directors

If you are employed as a director of a company, different rules apply.[92] Your normal weekly earnings are worked out by looking at how much you received in the year immediately before the week of your claim. If you have been employed for less than a year, an estimate is made of what you are likely to earn in the first year, taking into account what you have already received. Any week when you do no work and do not get paid is ignored in calculating your weekly earnings.[93]

For disability working allowance

The normal rule is to calculate your weekly earnings over an 'assessment period' of:

- five consecutive weeks in the last six weeks if you are paid weekly; *or*
- two months if you are paid monthly;

immediately before the week of your claim.[94]

As with FC/ETU, it is the earnings which are *received* during the assessment period which count, whether or not they were actually earned in respect of that period.[95]

However, any time in the assessment period during which your earnings were irregular or unusual does not count[96] – eg, any week in which you received, for instance, a one-off bonus included in your weekly wage (eg, a special Christmas bonus) or holiday pay, or in which large deductions were made from your wages.

If your earnings fluctuate, or in the five-week or two-month period before your claim do not represent your normal earnings (eg, because you are on unpaid maternity leave[97]), a different period before the week of your claim can be used if this gives a more accurate picture of your normal weekly earnings.[98]

If there is a period of short-time working of not more than 13 weeks or a trade dispute at your place of work, your normal weekly earnings are taken as those prior to the period of short-time working or dispute. Trade dispute includes a work-to-rule or overtime ban as well as a strike.[99]

For family allowance, disability working allowance and earnings top-up

A bonus or commission paid separately, or for a longer period than other earnings, and which is paid in the year prior to your claim, counts as earnings.[100] The net amount is divided by 52 before it is taken into account.[101]

If you have just started a job or returned to work after a break of more than, for FC/ETU four weeks, or, for DWA 13 weeks, or your hours have just changed, and the period since the start or resumption of your employment or the change in hours is less than your assessment period, your employer will be required (for FC/DWA), or requested (for ETU), to provide an estimate of your likely earnings for the period for which you are normally paid.[102] If your actual earnings turn out to be lower than the estimate, this does not result in your FC, DWA or ETU being reviewed and increased, so it is important that your employer does not overestimate your earnings.

For housing benefit and council tax benefit

Earnings as an employee are usually averaged out over:
- the previous five weeks if you are paid weekly; *or*
- two months if you are paid monthly.[103]

Where your earnings vary, or if there is likely to be or has recently been a change (eg, you usually do overtime but have not done so recently, or you are about to get a pay rise), the local authority may average them over a different period where this is likely to give a more accurate picture of what you are going to earn during the benefit period.[104]

If you are on strike, the local authority should not take into account your pre-strike earnings and average them out over the strike period.[105]

If you have only just started work and your earnings cannot be averaged over the normal period (ie, five weeks or two months), an estimate is made based on any earnings you have been paid so far if these are likely to reflect your future average wage. Where you have not yet been paid or your initial earnings do not represent what you will normally earn over the benefit period, your employer must provide an estimate of your average weekly earnings.[106] Where your earnings change during your benefit period, your new weekly average figure is estimated on the basis of what you are likely to earn over the remainder of the benefit period.[107]

Payments at the end of a job

Redundancy payments are normally treated as capital for all benefits (see Chapter 49). However, for IS/JSA, if an employer makes a redundancy payment in excess of the statutory amount, the excess will be treated as earnings for the period it covers[108] (see p2:394).

Some redundancy schemes make periodic payments after leaving work; for all benefits, these are treated as other income (see p2:417).[109]

Other payments can cause problems, and are dealt with separately for each benefit.

For income support and income-based jobseeker's allowance

In most cases, when you finish a job you need to claim income-based JSA (see Chapter 14) rather than IS (see Chapter 20). However, if you do not need to register for work, you may need to claim IS instead.

If you retire from a full-time job (16 hours or more a week) and you are aged at least 60 (women) or 65 (men), any payments counted as earnings (eg, final wages, holiday pay, etc) that you receive are disregarded in full.[110] You are not treated as in full-time work for any period covered by those earnings after the end of your job.

Leaving a full-time job

In all other cases, only the following final payments that you receive when you leave a *full-time* job affect your right to IS or income-based JSA (because you will still be treated as if you are still in that job for the period for which these payments are made):[111]

* holiday pay which counts as earnings (see p2:388);
* pay in lieu of notice;
* pay in lieu of wages;
* for IS, any other compensation payments in respect of that job, but only if you have not had any or all of the pay in lieu of notice due to you, and not counting any compensation payments that are counted as if they are or are not earnings (see p2:388). In practice, this will mean any *ex gratia* payments or payments in settlement of a claim to an industrial tribunal. Any payment is divided by the maximum payable under the statutory redundancy scheme (usually uprated yearly). The result is the number of weeks the payment will cover up to a maximum of your notice period, whether statutory, contractual or customary.[112] If the amount is less than the statutory maximum for one week or if the calculation creates a fraction, these are treated as capital.[113] If the *ex gratia* payment is not compensation but a gift (eg, a 'golden handshake') you should argue that it should be treated as capital, not income;
* for income-based JSA, any other compensation payments in respect of that job, except for any awards payable by an industrial tribunal which are treated as earnings (see p2:388), refunds of pension contributions or any payments in respect of wages earned before you lost your job.

Period payment taken into account

You are treated as in full-time work (and therefore ineligible for IS/JSA) for the number of weeks covered by these payments after your employment ended.[114] These payments are taken into account consecutively and in the following order:

- any pay in lieu of wages or in lieu of notice; *then*
- payments of compensation for loss of employment; *then*
- holiday pay.[115]

The period for which you are treated as in full-time work starts on the earliest date that any of these payments are due to be paid.[116]

Example

Mary leaves her full-time job with a final week's wages, a week in hand and one week's holiday pay. All three amounts are due to be paid on 30 May. Only the holiday pay will be taken into account, starting from 30 May. Mary will not be entitled to IS/income-based JSA for one week.

If you receive an award of compensation for unfair dismissal or certain other awards of pay from an industrial tribunal, these are taken into account as earnings in calculating the amount of your IS or income-based JSA from when the award is made (see p2:388).

If your employment is interrupted (eg, you are laid off), any holiday pay which is treated as your earnings affects your right to IS/income-based JSA; all other payments are disregarded except that any retainer you are paid is taken into account as earnings in calculating the amount of your IS/income-based JSA.[117] If you have been suspended, any payment you receive is taken into account and affects your right to IS/income-based JSA.

Leaving a part-time job

If you were working part time (less than 16 hours a week) before you claimed IS or income-based JSA, any payments you receive when the job ends or is interrupted (unless you have been suspended), are ignored and do not affect your IS or income-based JSA except, (for IS/income-based JSA), any retainer or, (for income-based JSA), any compensation payments, holiday pay or awards payable by an industrial tribunal which are treated as earnings (see p2:388).[118] If, however, you were claiming IS or income-based JSA while you were in part-time work, any payments made to you when that job ends are taken into account as earnings in the normal way except that, for IS only, this is taken into account for a period of one week only.[119] Your wages, including any final wages, are counted first (for both IS and income-based JSA), then (for IS only) any pay in lieu of wages or notice, then (for IS/income-based JSA) any compensation paid by your employer for loss of employment, and then any holiday pay.[120]

Once the period covered by payments at the end of a full- or part-time job has ended, any money remaining is treated as capital.[121]

Because sick pay does not count as earnings for IS/income-based JSA, any arrears of sick pay you receive when a job ends will be treated as income from when it is paid for the same length of time for which the arrears cover.[122]

For family credit, disability working allowance and earnings top-up

There are no special rules for payments received at the end of a job for FC, DWA or ETU. However, if, for example, your partner has just lost her/his job and you apply for FC/DWA/ETU because you are working full time, you should argue that any payments that s/he received at the end of the employment (and indeed the amount of previous wages) should not be included as part of your 'normal' weekly income,[123] unless there is evidence that the job will resume while you are getting your current FC/DWA/ETU award.

For housing benefit and council tax benefit

If you retire from a full-time job (16 hours or more) and have reached the age of 65 (men) or 60 (women), any payments counted as earnings (see p2:388) that you receive are disregarded from the day after your job ends.[124]

If you leave a full-time job for any reason other than retirement any payments you receive should be disregarded except:[125]
- holiday pay which counts as earnings (see p2:388);
- pay in lieu of wages (except for periodical redundancy payments);
- pay in lieu of notice or other compensation for loss of employment, but only in so far as it represents loss of income;
- an award of compensation for unfair dismissal, or certain other awards of pay from an industrial tribunal (see p2:388);
- any sick pay or maternity pay;
- any retainer fee.

However, this only applies if you leave your job before you claim HB/CTB. If you are already getting HB/CTB when you leave your job, all payments in respect of that job count as earnings.

If your work is interrupted, your earnings are disregarded except for holiday pay which counts as earnings (see p2:388), sick pay, maternity pay and any retainer paid to you.[126]

Where you were in part-time work (ie, less than 16 hours a week) before claiming HB or CTB, any earnings paid when your job ended or was interrupted are disregarded, *except* where that payment is a retainer or sick pay or maternity pay.[127] This disregard does not apply to earnings paid when your job ends if you are already getting HB/CTB.

Disregarded earnings

Some earnings can be disregarded (see p2:399). There is also a childcare costs allowance (see p2:401) which can be deducted from your earnings if you are claiming FC, DWA, HB or CTB (but not if you are claiming IS, income-based JSA or ETU).

---

3. **Earnings from self-employment**

Even if you are an employee, any other earnings from work you do as a self-employed person is assessed under the following rules.

Calculating net earnings

Your 'net profit' over the period before your claim must be worked out. This consists of your self-employed earnings, including any allowance from an Employment Service scheme to assist you with your business (unless paid during a period of test trading to those undertaking the self-employment option of the New Deal – see p2:61),[128] minus:[129]

- reasonable expenses (see below); *and*
- income tax and national insurance contributions; *and*
- half of any premium paid in respect of a personal pension scheme or a retirement annuity contract which is eligible for tax relief.[130] For IS and income-based JSA, if you and your partner (if any) are aged under 60, you must supply certain information about the scheme or annuity contract to the relevant authority if requested.[131]

For FC, DWA and ETU, the Business Start-Up Allowance does not count if it ended before you claimed – so it may be worthwhile delaying your claim.[132] In calculating your earnings any capital grant to set up a business, or a loan of working capital, or the sale of capital assets is excluded,[133] and any capital (eg, a legacy) not generated by the business cannot be treated as earnings.[134]

For IS, income-based JSA, HB and CTB, if you receive payments for fostering from a local authority or voluntary organisation, and for IS, income-based JSA, FC, DWA, ETU, HB and CTB if you receive payments for providing temporary respite care under community care arrangements from a health authority, local authority, voluntary organisation or from the person being looked after, these do not count as earnings[135] but are ignored[136] (although in either case the person you are being paid to look after may not count as a member of your family – see p1:121). For IS, income-based JSA, HB and CTB, if you receive payments for board and lodging charges these do not count as earnings[137] but as other income (less any disregards, see p2:399). For FC, DWA and ETU, these are treated as earnings if, after discounting all the disregards on pp2:399-421 (other than the boarder's allowance on p2:414), they form a *major part* of your total income.[138] Otherwise they are treated as other income, as for IS and income-based JSA.

For the treatment of payments made by the Employment Service for taking part in the self-employment option of the New Deal programme, see p36A:74a.

Reasonable expenses

Expenses must be reasonable and 'wholly and exclusively' incurred for the purposes of your business.[139] This involves similar considerations to those that apply in the allowances permitted in the assessment of 'gross' earnings of employed earners (see p2:387). Where a car or telephone, for example, is used partly for business and partly for private purposes, the costs of it can be apportioned and the amount attributable to business use can be deducted.[140]

Reasonable expenses include:[141]
- repayments of capital on loans for replacing equipment and machinery;
- repayment of capital on loans for, and income spent on, the repair of a business asset except where this is covered by insurance;
- interest on a loan taken out for the purposes of the business;
- excess of VAT paid over VAT received.

Reasonable expenses do not include:[142]
- any capital expenditure;
- depreciation. However, the normal accountancy practice in valuing stock should be applied so that the 'cost of sales' (the cost of any opening stock plus purchases less any closing stock) should be set against actual sales;[143]
- money for setting up or expanding the business – eg, the cost of adapting the business premises;
- any loss incurred before the beginning of the current assessment period. If the business makes a loss, the net profit is nil. The losses of one business cannot be offset against the profit of any other business in which you are engaged, or against your earnings as an employee,[144] (although where two businesses or employments share expenses these may be apportioned and offset);[145]
- capital repayments on loans taken out for business purposes;
- business entertainment expenses;
- for HB and CTB only, debts (other than proven bad debts), but the expenses of recovering a debt can be deducted.

Working out your average earnings from self-employment

There are different rules for each benefit.

For income support and income-based jobseeker's allowance

The weekly amount is the average of earnings:[146]

- over a period of any one year (normally the last year for which accounts are available);
- over a more appropriate period where you have recently taken up self-employment or there has been a change which will affect your business or for any other reason if a different period may enable any part or all of your income and expenditure to be calculated more accurately.[147]

If your earnings are royalties or copyright payments, the amount of earnings is divided by the weekly amount of IS or income-based JSA which would be payable if you had not received this income plus the amount which would be disregarded from those earnings.[148] You are not entitled to IS/income-based JSA for the resulting number of weeks.

For family credit, disability working allowance and earnings top-up

Your normal weekly earnings are worked out by looking at:[149]

- your profit and loss account (and your trading account and/or balance sheet if appropriate), if this covers a period of at least six but not more than 15 months, which ends within 12 months before the date of your claim; *or*
- if you do not provide such a profit and loss account, but do provide a statement of your earnings and expenses, for FC/DWA, for the six calendar months or, for ETU, the 52 weeks, up to and including the month (for FC/DWA) or week (for ETU) before your claim, your earnings over that period; *or*
- if you do not provide a profit and loss account or statement of earnings and expenses, the six calendar months (for FC/DWA) or 52 weeks (for ETU) up to and including the month (for FC/DWA) or week (for ETU) preceding your claim; *or*
- a different past period, if this represents your normal weekly earnings more accurately.

Your weekly earnings are worked out by averaging the earnings you have received or can expect to receive over the assessment period or, where you have provided a profit and loss account, by averaging the earnings relevant to the period covered by that account.[150]

For FC/DWA only, complete week(s) in the assessment period when you are not actually working (eg, because you are sick or on holiday) are ignored.[151]

If you have just started being self-employed (ie, for less than seven calendar months), for FC your normal weekly earnings are worked out over six calendar months, beginning with the month after the one in which you started the business. If you provided a statement of earnings and expenses for those months, up to and including the last month before the month in which you claim, the earnings of those months are taken; if you do not provide such a statement, the earnings up to and including the month before the one preceding your claim are taken. In either case, the amount you can expect to earn for the remainder of the six-month period is added. Any week where you do not work for the business is ignored.[152]

For DWA and ETU, if you have been self-employed for less than 26 weeks (for DWA) or 52 weeks (for ETU), an estimate is made of your likely weekly earnings over the next 26 weeks from the date of your claim.[153]

If your actual earnings turn out to be lower than the estimate this will not result in your FC, DWA or ETU being reviewed and increased.[154]

Note that for ETU, if your self-employed earnings amount to no more than £20 on four separate assessments for which you have been paid ETU, you cannot be paid another award of ETU as a self-employed earner.[155]

For housing benefit and council tax benefit

The amount of your weekly earnings is averaged out over an 'appropriate' period (usually based on your last year's trading accounts) which must not be longer than a year.[156]

Childminders

Childminders, in practice, are always treated as self-employed. Your net profit is deemed to be one-third of your earnings less income tax, your national insurance contributions and half of certain pension contributions (see p2:396).[157] The rest of your earnings are completely ignored.

Disregarded earnings[158]

Some earnings can be disregarded (see below). There is also a childcare costs allowance (see p2:401) which can be deducted from your earnings if you are claiming FC, DWA, HB or CTB (but not if you are claiming IS, income-based JSA or ETU). Different rules on the treatment of childcare costs will apply to tax credits from October 1999 (see p1:492) than those which apply to FC/DWA.

4. Disregarded earnings

For FC, DWA and ETU, your earnings, worked out in the way described above, are taken into account in full (but see p2:401 for the provisions on deductions for certain childcare costs for FC and DWA and p1:492 for tax credits).

For IS, income-based JSA, HB and CTB, some of your earnings from employment or self-employment are disregarded and do not affect your benefit. The amount of the 'disregard' depends on your circumstances. There are three levels. For the amount of disregarded earnings for contributions-based JSA, see p2:376.

£25 disregard

Lone parents on HB or CTB have £25 of their earnings ignored.[159] This does not apply to anyone claiming IS or income-based JSA (see below).

£15 disregard

£15 of your earnings (including those of your partner, if any) is disregarded if:
- for IS or income-based JSA, you are a lone parent;[160]
- you or your partner (if any) qualifies for a disability premium (see p2:325).[161] For IS and income-based JSA, you are treated as qualifying for the premium if you would do so but for being in hospital, or a local authority home or because you are a person in a residential care or nursing home with preserved rights (see p2:169);
- you or your partner (if any) qualifies for the higher pensioner premium (see p2:327, and you or your partner are over 60 and, immediately before reaching that age, you or your partner were in employment (part time for IS and income-based JSA) and you were entitled to a £15 disregard because of qualifying for a disability premium. For HB and CTB this includes where, in the case of a couple, you would have qualified for a disability premium but for the fact that a higher pensioner premium was payable. Since reaching 60, you or your partner must have continued in employment (part time for IS and income-based JSA), although breaks of up to eight* weeks when you were not getting IS or income-based JSA (or HB/CTB where you claim either of these benefits) are ignored. For IS and income-based JSA you are treated as qualifying for the higher pensioner premium even if you are in hospital etc (as for the disability premium, see p2:325);[162]
- you are a member of a couple, your benefit would include a disability premium but for the fact that one of you qualifies for the higher pensioner premium or the enhanced rate of pensioner premium (see p2:327), one of you is under 60 and either of you are in employment. For IS and income-based JSA, you are treated as qualifying for the higher or enhanced pensioner premium if you would do so, but for being in hospital, etc (see above);[163]
- you are a member of a couple, one of you is aged 75-79 and the other over 60, and immediately before that person reached 60 either of you were in part-time employment and you were entitled to a £15 disregard because of qualifying, or being treated as qualifying, for an enhanced pensioner premium (see above). Since then either of you must have continued in part-time employment, although breaks of up to eight* weeks when you were not getting IS or income-based JSA (or HB or CTB where you claim either of these benefits), are ignored;[164]

- you or your partner (if any) qualifies for a carer's premium (see p2:333). The disregard applies to the carer's earnings. For a couple, if both partners get the carer's premium, £15 is disregarded from their combined earnings. If the carer is the claimant and her/his earnings are less than £15, the remainder of the disregard can be used up on her/his partner's earnings as an auxiliary coastguard, etc (see below), or up to £5 (for HB and CTB up to £10) of it can be used up on her/his partner's earnings from another job but the total disregard cannot be more than £15;[165]

- you or your partner (if any) are an auxiliary coastguard, part-time firefighter or a part-time member of a lifeboat crew, or a member of the Territorial Army.[166] If you earn less than £15 for doing any of these services you can use up to £5 (for HB and CTB up to £10 if you have a partner) of the disregard on another job[167] or a partner's earnings from another job.[168]

* **Note:** for IS and income-based JSA, this is increased to 12 weeks if you stopped getting IS/income-based JSA because you or your partner started full-time work (see p2:5 for the detailed rules on this). Any period when you were not entitled to IS/income-based JSA because you or your partner went on a government training scheme is ignored. But it counts as a period that you were in receipt of IS/income-based JSA if you qualify for the £15 disregard as a long-term claimant (see above).[169]

If you qualify under more than one category you still have a maximum of only £15 of your earnings disregarded.

Basic £10 or £5 disregard

If you do not qualify for a £25 or £15 disregard, £5 of your earnings is disregarded if you are single. If you claim as a member of a couple, £10 of your total earnings is disregarded – whether or not you are both working.[170]

Childcare costs [171]

For FC/DWA/HB/CTB (but not IS/income-based JSA/ETU), an allowance may be deducted from your (or your partner's) earnings for certain childcare costs (see below). Different rules on the treatment of childcare costs will apply to tax credits (see p1:492) when they replace FC/DWA in October 1999. Allowances for childcare costs may also be made when calculating earnings for claims for certain non-means-tested benefits. The rules for those benefits are similar but not the same and the effect may be quite different so you will need to check Chapter 47 if you or your partner may be entitled to one of those benefits instead, or as well. Note that the same childcare costs may be allowed once for means-tested benefits and once for non-means-tested benefits, so they may help you to become entitled to or gain an increased award of both types of benefit (but see p2:405 for how any amount of a non-means-tested benefit is treated as income when claiming a means-tested benefit).

For FC/DWA/HB/CTB an allowance – of up to £60 a week for one child or up to £100 a week for two or more children – may be deducted from your (or your partner's) earnings (from employment or self-employment) in respect of childcare costs if you are:
- a lone parent working 16 hours a week or more; *or*
- a couple and both of you work 16 hours a week or more, or else one of you works 16 hours a week or more and the other is 'incapacitated' (see below).

This only applies if you have any child(ren) in your family under the age of 12 for whom you are paying charges for childcare (not counting charges in respect of compulsory education or charges paid by you to your partner for a child in your family) which is provided:
- by a registered childminder or other registered childcare provider (such as a nursery or after-school club catering for the under-8s); *or*
- by (for children between the ages of 8 and 12) a school on school premises or a local authority – eg, an out-of-hours or holiday play scheme. For FC and DWA it is the age of the child at the start of the claim which counts; *or*
- by a childcare scheme operating on Crown property; *or*
- in schools or establishments exempt from registration.

Note: A child is not treated as having reached the age of 12 until the day before the first Tuesday (for FC and DWA) or first Monday (for HB and CTB) in September *following* her/his 12th birthday.[172]

You (or your partner) are treated as 'incapacitated' if:
- you get short-term (higher rate) or long-term incapacity benefit (see Chapter 3); *or*
- you get severe disablement allowance (see Chapter 4); *or*
- you get attendance allowance, disability living allowance (see Chapter 10) or constant attendance allowance (or an equivalent award under the war pensions or industrial injuries schemes), or else you would receive one of these benefits but for the fact that you (or your partner) are in hospital; *or*
- you have an invalid carriage or similar vehicle; *or*
- HB and CTB is payable and includes (or would include, but for a disqualification of up to six weeks for misconduct) a disability or higher pensioner premium (see Chapter 45) in respect of the incapacity; *or*
- for HB and CTB, you (but not your partner) have been treated as incapable of work for a continuous period of 196 days or more (disregarding any break of up to 56 days or 52 weeks if you are a 'welfare to work beneficiary' – see Chapter 34); *or*
- for FC and DWA, you have already been awarded an allowance for childcare costs in HB or CTB.

Calculating childcare costs
For family credit and disability working allowance[173]

Because childcare costs are likely to vary considerably between term time and holiday periods, a formula is used to assess the costs that are taken into account. Where charges are paid other than monthly, the amount is *either*:
- 1/52 of the aggregate of:
  - the average weekly charge in the four most recent complete weeks falling in term time, multiplied by 39; *and*
  - the average weekly charge in the two most recent weeks falling out of term time, multiplied by 13; *or*
- where your child does not yet attend school, the average weekly charge in the four most recent complete weeks.

Where charges are paid monthly:
- if the charge is for a fixed amount, that amount multiplied by 12 and divided by 52; *or*
- if the charge is variable, 1/52 of the aggregate of charges over the previous 12 months.

However, where there is no, or insufficient, information available in order to assess the childcare costs in any of these ways, an estimate will be made based on information provided by the care provider or, if that is not available, by you.

For housing benefit and council tax benefit[174]

The costs to be taken into account are estimated over whatever period, not exceeding a year, that will give the best estimate of the average weekly charge over the 'benefit period' (see pp1:533 and 1:583), based on information to be provided by the childminder or care provider.

Additional points to note
- These rules do *not* apply to IS, JSA or ETU.
- There are separate childcare costs rules for non-means-tested benefits (see p2:372).
- £60 is the maximum amount that can be deducted for one child even if the actual cost of your childcare is more. £100 is the maximum even if you have to pay for childcare for more than two children and even if the actual cost is more.
- If you are claiming FC or DWA only, the net gain to you of the £60/£100 allowance is a maximum of £42/£70 (because of the 70 per cent taper used in the calculation of FC and DWA – see pp1:463 and 1:478) but you do not get an allowance for your childcare costs if your income is less than the appropriate 'applicable amount' (£80.65 for FC – see p1:463; £60.50 or £80.65 for DWA – see p1:478), because you are getting the maximum award

of FC or DWA anyway. Similar considerations also apply if you are claiming HB and/or CTB only (see pp1:519 and 1:574 for the taper rules).

- The childcare costs calculation applies both on your claim for FC or DWA and your claims for HB and CTB. If you are claiming more than one of these benefits the effect of their combined tapers is that the maximum gain to you of the allowance may be more than the £42/£70 (70 per cent) if you were claiming FC or DWA only.

- Local authorities may not charge you for nursery services provided under the Children Act if you are on FC or DWA.[175] If your income, but for the childcare allowance, would be too high to qualify for FC or DWA, any charges a local authority makes could be used to enable you to qualify. You should then be able to keep your FC or DWA throughout the 26-week period of the award even though, as soon as you are awarded it, the local authority has to stop charging you. When your award expires, the local authority can charge you again, and you can then claim again. If, however, you are also claiming HB or CTB, your HB or CTB award may be revised and reduced as soon as you no longer have to pay any childcare charges.

- The costs of any childcare provided by a relative or friend (other than your partner – but a former partner, who may even be the child's parent, is not excluded) may be allowed so long as s/he is a registered childminder.

- It is not necessary for the childcare to be provided only while you are at work, nor for it to be in any way work-related, and there is no requirement for the charges to be reasonable (so the £60/£100 charge could be incurred for only one hour of childcare). Note that while the notional income rules (see p2:421) could apply if you intentionally reduced your income, they would not appear to apply just because you increased your expenditure.

5. **Other income**

As well as income from earnings, most other forms of income are taken into account for each of the means-tested benefits (income support (IS)/income-based jobseeker's allowance (JSA)/family credit (FC)/disability working allowance (DWA)/earnings top-up (ETU)/housing benefit (HB)/council tax benefit (CTB), although there are different rules as to how they are treated for each benefit.

By contrast, any income other than earnings does not affect your, or your partner's, entitlement to any non-means-tested benefit (except that some income from certain pension schemes may sometimes also count as earnings) – see Chapter 47. If, however, you are entitled to a non-means-tested benefit, this may affect your entitlement to a means-tested benefit (see p2:405).

For each of the means-tested benefits, most other types of income are taken into account less any tax due on them.[176] For HB and CTB, changes in tax and national insurance rates may be ignored for up to 30 weeks,[177] as for earnings (see p2:392).

There are special rules for the treatment of payments from Work-based Training for Young People and Work-based Training for Adults (formerly Training for Work) schemes (see p2:419) and for those participating in any of the New Deal programmes (see p2:420).

All income is converted into a weekly amount (see p2:384). For IS and income-based JSA, this amount is attributed to a forward period (see p2:385) and affects the benefit payable for that period.

For FC, DWA, ETU, HB and CTB, a past period is used where possible to assess normal weekly income, and this figure is used to calculate benefit.

For HB and CTB, an estimate of income is made by looking at an appropriate period (not exceeding one year). The period chosen must give an accurate assessment of your income.[178]

For FC, DWA and ETU, your income during the 26 weeks immediately before the week of your claim is used, unless a different period immediately before your claim would produce a more accurate assessment.[179]

Benefits

Benefits that count in full:
- contribution-based JSA (see Chapter 14);
- incapacity benefit (IB – see Chapter 3) and severe disablement allowance (SDA – see Chapter 4);
- except for FC, DWA and ETU (when it is completely ignored – see p2:407), maternity allowance (see Chapter 6);
- invalid care allowance (ICA – see Chapter 5);
- widows' benefits (see Chapter 7) (including industrial death benefit – see Chapter 11). Note that the widow's payment is treated as capital (see p2:443);
- retirement pensions (see Chapter 8);
- industrial injuries benefits (except constant attendance allowance and exceptionally severe disablement allowance which are disregarded) – see Chapter 11;
- except for FC, DWA and ETU (when it is completely ignored – see p2:407), child benefit (see Chapter 12);
- for IS and income-based JSA only, guardian's allowance (see Chapter 13);
- child's special allowance and war orphan's pension;
- for IS and income-based JSA only, FC, DWA or ETU. For HB and CTB, any additional FC, DWA or ETU paid because you, or your partner, are working 30 hours or more a week is ignored (see pp2:462, 2:477 and 2:500). Otherwise, FC, DWA and ETU are taken into account;[180]
- for IS and income-based JSA only,[181] statutory sick pay (SSP – see Chapter 2) and statutory maternity pay (SMP – see Chapter 6) – less any Class 1 national insurance contributions and half of any pension contributions and any tax.

For HB and CTB, SSP and SMP are treated as earnings (see p2:388) and you may, therefore, benefit from an earnings disregard (see p2:388).
- For FC, DWA and ETU, SSP is counted as earnings but SMP is ignored (see p2:388).

Problems can arise where, for example, the Benefits Agency or local authority try to take into account a benefit you are not receiving, such as child benefit that has been delayed. In such a case, the benefit should not be treated as income possessed by you. For IS and income-based JSA, you should get your full benefit and leave the Benefits Agency to deduct the difference from arrears of the delayed benefit when it is eventually awarded.[182]

For IS, income-based JSA, FC, DWA, ETU, HB and CTB, arrears of all means-tested and those disability benefits which are disregarded as income (see below) should be treated as capital and ignored for 52 weeks (see p2:452).[183] This rule only applies to arrears of benefit which you actually receive. Therefore, for IS and income-based JSA, it only applies to arrears of benefit which are paid to you *after* the Benefits Agency has made any deductions because the award of the benefit was delayed.

Benefits that are ignored completely:
- attendance allowance (AA) (or constant attendance allowance, exceptionally severe disablement allowance or severe disablement occupational allowance paid because of an injury at work or a war injury) or any care component of disability living allowance (DLA – see Chapter 10). For IS and income-based JSA only, it is taken into account in full up to the amount of the highest rate of attendance allowance (£59.95 a week) if you went to live in a residential care or nursing home before 31 March 1993 and you are a person with preserved rights (see p2:169), or you are accommodated under The Polish Resettlement Act;[184]
- pensioner's Christmas bonus (see Chapter 8);[185]
- either of the mobility components of DLA;[186]
- mobility supplement under the War Pensions Scheme;[187]
- any extra-statutory payment made to you to compensate for non-payment of IS, income-based JSA, mobility allowance, mobility supplement, AA or DLA;[188]
- for FC, DWA[189] (or any extra-statutory compensation for non-payment of it[190]) and ETU[191];
- for DWA, FC[192] and ETU[193];
- for ETU, DWA and FC (or any extra-statutory compensation for non-payment of either);[194]
- social fund payments.[195] For FC, DWA and ETU, they are not specifically disregarded, but they should not count as part of your 'normal weekly' income.[196] For IS, income-based JSA, FC, ETU, HB and CTB, social fund payments are disregarded as capital indefinitely;[197]

- except for DWA, resettlement benefit paid to certain patients who are discharged from hospital and who had been in hospital for more than a year before 11 April 1988;[198]
- except for income-based JSA and ETU, any transitional payment made to compensate you for loss of benefit due to the changes in benefit rules in April 1988;[199]
- any payment made to the Secretary of State to compensate for the loss of housing benefit (whether due to the 1988 changes in benefit rules or not);[200]
- HB, CTB or, formerly (except for ETU), community charge benefit;[201]
- except for ETU, any payment in consequence of a reduction in liability for council tax (or, formerly, community charge);[202]
- IS and income-based JSA are ignored for FC, DWA, ETU, HB and CTB.[203] There are special HB and CTB rules for IS and income-based JSA claimants (see pp1:519 and 1:574);
- certain special war widows' payments,[204] including any special or supplementary payments (currently £56.45) to pre-1973 war widows;[205]
- for FC, DWA, ETU, HB and CTB, guardian's allowance (see Chapter 13);[206]
- for FC, DWA and ETU, child benefit (see Chapter 12);[207]
- for FC and DWA, maternity allowance and SMP (see Chapter 6);[208]
- for HB and CTB, any additional payment of FC, DWA or ETU made because you or your partner (if any) are working for 30 hours or more a week;[209]
- any increase for adult or child dependants who are not members of your family (see p2:113), where you are getting IB, maternity allowance, widowed mother's allowance, retirement pension, industrial injuries benefits (including unemployability supplement), ICA or a service pension.[210]

For the treatment of payments of arrears of benefits, see p2:406. For the treatment of payments of child maintenance bonuses, see p1:603, and back to work bonuses, p1:597.

Benefits that have £10 ignored:
- war disablement pension (including any tax-free service invaliding pension or 'service attributable pension'[211]);
- war widow's pension;
- widow's pension payable to widows of members of the Royal Navy, Army or Royal Air Force who were disabled or died in consequence of service in the armed forces;
- an extra-statutory payment made instead of the above pensions;
- similar payments made by another country;
- a pension from Germany or Austria paid to the victims of Nazi persecution.[212]

Only £10 in all can be ignored, even if you have more than one payment which attracts a £10 disregard.[213] However, the £10 disregard allowed on these war pensions is additional to the total disregard of any mobility supplement or attendance allowance (ie, constant attendance allowance, exceptionally severe disablement allowance and severe disablement occupational allowance) paid as part of a war disablement pension. The £10 disregard may, however, overlap with other disregards on student loans (see p2:410) and charitable or voluntary payments (see p2:412) when a combined maximum of £20 is allowed.

Local authorities are given a limited discretion to increase the £10 disregard on war disablement, war widows' pensions and the pension payable to widows of members of the Royal Navy, Army or Royal Air Force, when assessing income for HB and CTB.[214] Some local authorities disregard the full amount of these pensions, and some do not increase the disregard at all, so you should check your own local authority's policy on this issue.

Maintenance payments

For IS/income-based JSA/FC/DWA/HB/CTB (but not ETU) there are special rules for the treatment of any payments of maintenance or child support maintenance which you and/or your partner receive for yourself/selves and/or any child(ren) in your family. These are explained in Chapter 44.

Most (see Chapter 44 for exceptions) maintenance counts in full while you are claiming IS or income-based JSA, but you should check to see if you are accruing an entitlement to a child maintenance bonus (see p2:598). (Note, however, that the Government intends to introduce a £10 a week disregard on certain child support maintenance payments for IS/income-based JSA claimants from the year 2001.)

For FC/DWA/HB/CTB, £15 of any maintenance payments made by your or your partner's former partner or the parent of any child in your family is disregarded, but only if you are a lone parent or a couple with a child. If you receive maintenance from more than one person only £15 of the total is disregarded.[215]

For ETU, there is no disregard of any payment of maintenance if it forms part of your normal weekly income, even if it is paid on a voluntary basis.[216]

From October 1999, FC and DWA will be replaced by tax credits (see Chapter 23). All payments of maintenance will be completely disregarded as income when assessing entitlement to tax credits.

If you *pay* maintenance to a former partner or a child not living with you, your payments are not disregarded for the purpose of calculating your income for IS, income-based JSA, FC, DWA, ETU, HB, CTB.[217] Even if you are on IS or income-based JSA you may still have to pay child support maintenance (see p2:598).

Grants to students

The term grant includes bursaries (including those paid to Project 2000 nurses[218]), scholarships and exhibitions as well as grants or awards from education authorities.[219] An educational award which is paid by way of a loan does not count as a grant for IS or income-based JSA,[220] but is nevertheless taken into account as 'other income' (see p2:404). You are treated as having the parental or partner's contribution to your grant whether or not it has been paid to you. However, if you are (for IS) a lone parent, a single foster parent or (for IS/income-based JSA) a disabled student, only the amount of any contribution that you actually receive counts for IS or income-based JSA.[221]

Grant income is taken into account for the academic year, excluding the summer vacation, unless the grant expressly covers a different period. In each case, it is divided equally over the weeks in the period.[222] In the case of a sandwich course, grant income is averaged out over the period of study excluding the periods of experience – ie, in industry or commerce.[223] Any grant income paid under the Education (Mandatory Awards) Regulations that is intended for the maintenance of a student's dependants or which is an allowance for mature students or lone parents[224] is spread over 52 or 53 weeks.[225] (Benefit weeks and academic years sometimes run to 53 weeks, including part-weeks.) However, for other grants the normal rule (period of study or period for which grant payable) applies. So where a student on a sandwich course received a grant from the Department of Health, the element for his dependants was spread over the period of study only.[226]

The following grant income is ignored:[227]

- a fixed amount of £295 or whatever you get in your grant towards the cost of books and equipment (so that, eg, an additional initial expenses allowance of £55 paid to Project 2000 nurses is also ignored[228]);
- a fixed amount for travelling expenses. Where you are in receipt of a mandatory grant, and living away from your parents' home, this is usually £166. If you are living at your parents' home it is usually £256. There is no additional disregard even if your actual travelling expenses are higher;[229]
- any allowance for tuition and examination fees;
- any allowance to meet extra expenses because you are a disabled student;
- any allowance to meet the cost of attending a residential course away from your normal student accommodation during term time;
- any allowance for the costs of your normal home (away from college) but, for IS and income-based JSA, only if your rent is not met by HB;
- any amount for a partner or children abroad is ignored for IS, income-based JSA, HB and CTB, but not FC, DWA and ETU.

These disregards apply only to the maintenance grant you receive during the academic year, and not to any element for dependants you may receive during the summer vacation.[230]

General points about grant income

- If you receive any payments over and above your grant or top-up loan, to help you with certain expenses (see p2:138), and these payments are greater than the amounts for those expenses disregarded from your grant income, the excess amount is ignored.[231]
- If you have been required by your education authority to make a contribution to your own grant (eg, because you have other income such as maintenance or part-time earnings), an amount equivalent to that contribution is disregarded as income for IS, income-based JSA, FC, DWA, ETU, HB and CTB.[232] In the case of a couple, the amount of any contribution that one member has been assessed to pay to her/his partner who is a student does not count as the non-student's income.[233]
- For HB only, if your eligible rent is subject to a flat-rate deduction (see p2:145), the same amount is disregarded from your income. If your income does not cover the deduction, the balance is ignored from your partner's income.[234]
- For IS and income-based JSA only, if you either give up or are dismissed from your course before it finishes, any grant you have received is taken account of as if you were still a student[235] until you either repay the grant or the academic term or vacation in which you ceased to be a student ends, or until the end of the period covered by the last instalment of your grant, whichever is the earlier.[236]

Student loans[237] under the statutory scheme are treated as income. Weekly income is calculated by dividing the loan over the 52 (or 53) weeks of the academic year. In the final year of the course, or for a one-year course, the loan is divided by the number of weeks from the start of the academic year to the end of the course – ie, the last day of the last term.[238]

There is a £10 disregard on loan income, but it may overlap with other disregards on income from certain war pensions (see p2:407) and charitable or voluntary payments (see p2:412). With charitable or voluntary payments, a combined maximum of £20 is allowed.[239]

If you give up your course before it finishes, your loan continues to be counted in the same way, but without any disregard, for each remaining benefit week covered by the loan period following the date you gave it up.[240]

If you fail to take reasonable steps to get a loan to which you are entitled, the maximum amount payable to you is counted as weekly income, calculated as if you actually received it.[241] This does not apply if you have given up your course early (see above), since you are no longer a student.

Career development loans paid under section 2 of the Employment and Training Act 1973 are taken account of as income.[242] For IS and income-based JSA, the weekly income is calculated by dividing the loan by the number of weeks of education and training which the loan was paid for.[243] However, for all means-tested benefits, this income is ignored – except where it was paid for and is used to meet the cost of food, clothing and footwear, household fuel, rent, mortgage interest charges, certain other accommodation charges, council tax and water charges.[244]

For IS and income-based JSA only, any grant income, student loan or career development loan which you have left over at the end of your course is ignored.[245]

Access Fund payments[246] made to students by educational establishments to prevent hardship are treated as voluntary or charitable payments (see below).

Loans to students from overseas are neither grants nor awards, but should be taken into account as income.[247]

Adoption, fostering and residence order (in Scotland custody) payments

An **adoption allowance** paid in respect of any child who is a member of your family (see p2:121) counts in full for IS, income-based JSA, FC, DWA, HB and CTB up to the amount of the adopted child's personal allowance or credit and disabled child premium or allowance, if any. Above that level it is ignored completely.[248] No such rules apply to ETU because you cannot apply for ETU if you have a child (see Chapter 24).

If the child has capital over £3,000, you are not entitled to any benefit for the child (see p2:443) and the entire adoption allowance is ignored.[249]

For all means-tested benefits, the way that a **fostering allowance** is treated depends on whether the arrangement is an official or a private one. If a child is placed or boarded out with you by the local authority or a voluntary organisation under specific legal provisions, the child is not counted as a member of your family (see p2:121) so you are not entitled to any benefit for her/him, but any fostering allowances you receive are ignored altogether.[250]

If the fostering arrangement is a private one, any money you receive from the child's parent(s) is counted as maintenance (see p2:290). If the money you receive is not from the child's parent(s), you should probably be treated as a childminder (see p2:399).

If you are paid a **residence order allowance** (in Scotland, custody allowance) by the local authority, this is treated in the same way as an adoption allowance (see above).[251] Arrears of residence order (in Scotland, custody) allowances are treated as capital for IS and income-based JSA.[252] Any payments made by the biological parents count as maintenance (see p2:290).

If the local authority makes a lump sum payment to enable you to make adaptations to your home for a disabled child, this is treated as capital and ignored.[253]

Charitable and voluntary payments

Payments from the Macfarlane and similar trusts

For all means-tested benefits, any payments, including payments in kind, from the Macfarlane Trust, the Macfarlane (Special Payments) Trust, the Macfarlane (Special Payments) (No. 2) Trust, the Fund, the Eileen Trust or either of the Independent Living Funds are disregarded in full.[254]

The Macfarlane Trusts make payments to haemophiliacs. The Fund was set up on 24 April 1992 for people who are not haemophiliacs who have contracted HIV through blood or tissue transfusions.

If you are, or were, a haemophiliac, or have received a payment from the Fund or the Eileen Trust, the following payments from money that originally came from any of the three Macfarlane Trusts, the Fund or the Eileen Trust are also disregarded in full:[255]

- any payment made by you, or on your behalf, to, or for the benefit of:
  - your partner, or former partner from whom you are not estranged or divorced;
  - (except for ETU) any child who is a member of your family (see p1:121), or who was but is now a member of another family; or
- if you have no partner or former partner (other than one from whom you are estranged or divorced), or children, any payment made by you (or from your estate in the event of your death) to:
  - your parent or step-parent; or
  - your guardian if you have no parent or step-parent and were a child (see p1:233) or student at the date of the payment (or at the date of your death).

In the case of a payment to a parent, step-parent or guardian, this is only disregarded until two years after your death;

- any payment made by your partner, or former partner from whom you are not estranged or divorced, or on her/his behalf, to, or for the benefit of:
  - you;
  - any child who is a member of your family, or who was and is now a member of another family.

Any income or capital that derives from any such payment is also disregarded.

Other payments

Most other charitable or voluntary payments that are made irregularly and are intended to be made irregularly are treated as capital and are unlikely to affect your claim unless they take your capital above the limit.[256] However, if you are on IS or income-based JSA it counts as income:

- if you are involved in a trade dispute and for IS only, for the first 15 days following your return to work after a dispute (see p2:187);[257] *or*
- where payments made to a child's boarding school are treated as the child's notional income (see p2:382).[258]

Charitable or voluntary payments made, or due to be made regularly, are completely ignored if:[259]

- for IS, income-based JSA, HB and CTB, they are intended, and used, for anything *except* food, ordinary clothing or footwear, household fuel, council tax, water rates and rent (less any non-dependant deductions) for which HB is payable; and, for IS and income-based JSA only, housing costs met by IS or income-based JSA and residential care or nursing home accommodation charges for people with preserved rights (see p2:169) met by IS or income-based JSA or by a local authority. Where you do not have a preserved right (see p2:169) and the local authority has placed you in a residential care or nursing home that is more expensive than normal for a person of your needs because you preferred that home, a charitable or voluntary payment towards the *extra* cost is ignored for IS and income-based JSA;[260]
- for FC, DWA and ETU, they are intended, and used, for anything *except* food, ordinary clothing or footwear, household fuel, council tax and any housing costs.

School uniform and sportswear are examples of clothing and footwear that is not ordinary.

If not ignored altogether, charitable or voluntary payments have a £20 disregard, although this disregard may overlap with other disregards for certain war pensions (see p2:407) or student loans (see p2:410) when a combined maximum of £20 is allowed.[261] Note that this is a weekly disregard so payments spread over different or successive benefit weeks attract a £20 disregard for each.

For HB and CTB, discretionary grants to Canadian war veterans or their widows settled in the UK should also be treated as voluntary payments and attract a £20 disregard.[262] It is arguable that this disregard should also apply to IS, income-based JSA, FC, DWA and ETU and to any other discretionary grants paid to any other overseas war veterans (or their widows) who are settled in the UK.

For IS and income-based JSA, these rules do not apply where you are involved in a trade dispute and, for IS only, for the first 15 days following your return to work after a trade dispute. For IS, income-based JSA, FC, DWA, ETU, HB and CTB, payments from a former partner, or the parent of your child, are dealt with as maintenance (see p2:305).

See also, payments made to someone else on your behalf, p2:423, and payments disregarded under miscellaneous income, p2:417.

Concessionary coal or cash in lieu

Coal that is provided free by British Coal to a former employee or widow is ignored as income in kind for all benefits (for IS and income-based JSA, if you or your partner are involved in a trade dispute, see p2:187).[263] Cash in lieu of coal is not a voluntary payment[264] but counts in full as income, or as earnings if paid to a current employee.[265]

Income from tenants and lodgers

Lettings without board

For all means-tested benefits, if you let out room(s) in your home to tenants, sub-tenants, licensees under a formal contractual arrangement, £4 of your weekly charge for each tenant, sub-tenant, licensee (and her/his family) is ignored, and an extra £9.25 if the charge covers heating costs.[266] The balance counts as income.

If someone shares your home under an informal arrangement, any payment made by them to you for their living and accommodation costs is ignored,[267] but a non-dependant deduction may be made from any HB/CTB or housing costs paid with IS/income-based JSA (see pp1:526, 1:577 and 2:357).

Boarders

If you have a boarder(s) on a commercial basis in your own home, and the boarder or any member of her/his family is not a close relative of yours, the first £20 of the weekly charge is ignored and half of any balance remaining is then taken into account as your income.[268] (With HB and CTB, there is no specific reference to non-commercial arrangements or close relatives, but the rules on contrived tenancies could possibly apply – see p1:514.) This applies for each boarder you have. The charge must normally include at least some meals.[269]

Note: Whether you let part of your home to a tenant, sub-tenant, licensee or to a boarder, any income left after applying the above disregards may be considered to be intended to be used to meet any housing costs of your own which are not met by IS, income-based JSA or HB, and may also therefore be offset accordingly.[270]

Tenants in other properties

If you have a freehold interest in a property other than your home and you let it out, the rent is treated as capital.[271] This rule also applies if you have a leasehold interest in another property which you are sub-letting. There is disagreement between commissioners as to whether it is the gross rent which should be taken into account, or only the sum left after deducting expenses.[272]

Income from capital

In general, actual income generated from capital (eg, interest on savings) is ignored as income[273] but counts as *capital*[274] from the date you are due to receive it. However, income derived from the following categories of disregarded capital (see p2:448) is treated as income:[275]

- your home;
- your former home if you are estranged or divorced;
- property which you have acquired for occupation as your home but which you have not yet been able to move into;
- property which you intend to occupy as your home but which needs essential repairs or alterations;
- property occupied wholly or partly by a partner or relative of any member of your family who is 60 or over or incapacitated;
- property occupied by your former partner, but not if you are estranged or divorced (unless – for HB and CTB only – s/he is a lone parent);
- property up for sale;
- property which you are taking legal steps to obtain to occupy as your home;
- your business assets;
- a trust of personal injury compensation.

Income from any of the above categories (other than your current home, business assets or a personal injuries trust) is ignored up to the amount of the total mortgage repayments (ie, capital and interest, and any payments that are a condition of the mortgage such as insurance or an endowment policy),[276] council tax and water rates paid in respect of the property for the same period over which the income is received.[277]

Tariff income from capital over £3,000[278]

If your capital is over £3,000, you are treated as having an assumed income from it, called your tariff income. You are assumed to have an income of £1 for every £250, or part of £250, by which your capital exceeds £3,000 but does not exceed £8,000 (IS, income-based JSA, FC and ETU) or £16,000 (DWA, HB and CTB). Note that for IS, income-based JSA and HB, if you are in residential care or similar accommodation (see p2:167), tariff income applies between £10,000 and £16,000.

If you are underpaid because of a reduction in your capital affecting your tariff income, you should ask for a review (see p1:456 for IS, p1:287 for JSA, p2:590 for HB and CTB). You should report any increase in your capital to the Benefits Agency for IS and income-based JSA,[279] and to the local authority for

HB/CTB, except where the increase does not stop you getting some IS/ income-based JSA.[280] If there is a change in your capital which increases the amount of your tariff income and as a result of which you are overpaid, see p2:525 for IS and income-based JSA, p2:531 for HB CTB on recovery of overpayments. For FC, DWA and ETU, any increase or reduction in the amount of your capital during the period of your award does not affect your entitlement (see pp2:468 and 2:483) and you do not need to notify the Benefits Agency unless or until you renew your claim.

Capital which counts as income

The following count as income:
- Instalments of capital outstanding when you claim benefit if they would bring you over whichever capital limit is applicable. For IS and income-based JSA, the instalments to be counted are any outstanding either when your benefit claim is decided, or when you are first due to be paid benefit, whichever is earlier, or at the date of any subsequent review.[281] For FC, DWA and ETU it is any instalments outstanding at the date of your claim.[282] For HB and CTB it is any instalments outstanding when your claim is made or treated as made, or when your benefit is reviewed.[283] Any balance over the capital limit counts as income, by spreading it over the number of weeks between each instalment.[284] Note that for IS and income-based JSA, there are two capital limits of £8,000 and £16,000 (see p2:442).

  If instalments are outstanding in this way on your child's capital, a similar rule applies (except for ETU which is not payable to those with children). If the total of these instalments and your child's existing savings come to more than £3,000, the outstanding instalments should count as your child's income,[285] and be spread over the period between each instalment.[286]
- Any payment from an annuity[287] (see p2:451 for when this is disregarded).
- Any career development loan paid under section 2 of the Employment and Training Act 1973[288] (see p2:411 for how such loans are treated).
- For IS and income-based JSA only, any educational maintenance grant paid to you as a student if you leave the course before the end of the period for which the grant has been paid (see p2:409).
- For IS only, a tax refund if you or your partner have returned to work after a trade dispute (see p2:187).[289]
- For IS and income-based JSA, a payment from a social services department under sections 17 and 24 of the Children Act 1989 or, in Scotland, a payment from a social work department under sections 12, 24 and 26 of the Social Work (Scotland) Act 1968 – ie, payments from social services to assist children in need or young people who have previously been in care or been looked after by them, if you or your partner are involved in or, for IS only, have returned to work after a trade dispute (see p2:187).[290]

- For HB and CTB, a local authority sometimes treats withdrawals from a capital sum as income.[291] This is most likely where a sum was intended to help cover living expenses over a particular period – eg, a bank loan taken out by a mature student. If this is not the intended use of any capital sum, you should dispute the decision. Even where the sum is intended for living expenses, you should argue that unless it is actually paid in instalments it should be treated as capital.[292]

  Any payments of capital, or any irregular withdrawals from a capital sum, which are clearly for one-off items of expenditure and not regular living expenses, should be treated as capital. Further, whatever the intention behind the sum, if no withdrawals are in fact made, it should be treated as capital.[293]
- Some lump sums from liable relatives (see p2:303).

For all means-tested benefits, capital which is counted as income cannot also be treated as producing a tariff income (see p2:442).[294]

Income tax refunds

PAYE income tax refunds are not payable to unemployed people receiving IS or income-based JSA until the end of the tax year, or until they obtain a job, whichever comes first. Strikers can only get a tax refund on return to work. Other people who are not entitled to IS or JSA can still get tax refunds when they fall due.
- PAYE refunds (employed earners) and tax refunds under Schedule D (self-employed) are treated as capital.[295]
- For IS only, if you or your partner have returned to work after a trade dispute (see p2:187), tax refunds are treated as income and are taken into account in full.[296]

For treatment of income tax refunds on mortgage interest or loans for repairs and improvements, see below.

Miscellaneous income

The following are counted in full:
- An occupational pension, income from a personal pension or retirement annuity contract (except any discretionary payment from a hardship fund and, for IS and income-based JSA, half of a pension or retirement annuity contract in some residential care situations where at least half of it is for your spouse).[297]
- Payments from an annuity. *Except* that in the case of 'home income plans', income from the annuity equal to the interest payable on the loan with which the annuity was bought is ignored if the following conditions are met:

- you used at least 90 per cent of the loan made to you to buy the annuity; *and*
- the annuity will end when you and your partner die; *and*
- you or your partner are responsible for paying the interest on the loan; *and*
- you, or both your partner and yourself, were at least 65 at the time the loan was made; *and*
- the loan is secured on a property which you or your partner owns or has an interest in, and the property on which the loan is secured is your home, or that of your partner.

If the interest on the loan is payable after income tax has been deducted, it is an amount equal to the net interest payment that is disregarded, otherwise it is the gross amount of the interest payment.[298]

The following are ignored:
- For IS and income-based JSA only, payments you receive under a mortgage protection policy which you took out, and which you use, to pay the housing costs which are not being met by the Benefits Agency in your IS or income-based JSA[299] (for restrictions on housing costs see p2:353). However, if the amount you receive exceeds the total of:
  - the interest you pay on a qualifying loan which is not met by the Benefits Agency;
  - capital repayments on a qualifying loan; *and*
  - any premiums you pay on the policy in question and any building insurance policy;
  then the excess is counted as your income.
- For IS and income-based JSA only, and as long as you have not already used insurance payments for the same purpose, *any* money *you* receive which is given, and which *you* use to make:[300]
  - payments under a secured loan which do not qualify under the housing costs rules (see Chapter 46);
  - interest payments which are not met under the housing costs rules, even though some interest payments under the loan in question are met;
  - capital repayments on a qualifying loan;
  - payments of premiums on an insurance policy which you took out to insure against the risk of not being able to make the payments in the above three categories, and premiums on a building insurance policy;
  - any rent that is not covered by HB (see Chapter 25);
  - the part of your accommodation charge that is above the maximum payable by IS if you live in a nursing home or residential care home and you are a person with preserved rights (see p2:169) or above that payable by a local authority.
- For HB, CTB, FC, DWA and ETU only (see above for IS/income-based JSA), payments you receive under an insurance policy you took out to insure

against the risk of being unable to maintain payments on a loan secured on your home. However, anything you get above the total of the following counts as your income:
- the amount you use to maintain your payments; *and*
- any premium you pay for the policy; *and*
- any premium for an insurance policy which you had to take out to insure against loss or damage to your home.[301]
- For all benefits, payments you receive under an insurance policy you took out to insure against the risk of being unable to maintain hire purchase or similar payments or other loan payments, for example for credit card debts. However, anything you get above the amount you use to make your payments and the premium for the policy counts as your income.[302]
- For FC and DWA, compensation for a reduced child support maintenance assessment.[303]
- Except for ETU, educational maintenance allowances paid by local authorities or (in Scotland) the Board of Management of Colleges.[304] These allowances are payable for the prevention or relief of hardship of a child or young person staying on at school beyond school-leaving age. The rules suggest that the disregard may only apply if the allowance is paid in respect of a child in your family, but it is arguable that they also apply even if the allowance is paid to you and you are able to claim benefit for yourself while studying (see Chapter 38). You may need to seek advice if this applies to you.
- Any payment to cover expenses if you are working as a volunteer.[305]
- Payments in kind (unless, for IS or income-based JSA, you or your partner are involved in a trade dispute, see p2:187).[306] These may include food, fuel, cigarettes,[307] clothing, holidays, gifts, accommodation, transport,[308] or nursery education vouchers[309] (but see p2:421 for the rules on notional income).
- For FC, DWA and ETU, a Jobmatch allowance paid under the Employment and Training Act 1973 if the payments are before your award begins.[310]
- A payment (other than a training allowance) to a disabled person under the Employment and Training Act 1973 or the Disabled Persons (Employment) Act 1944 to assist them to obtain or retain employment.[311]
- If you are participating in arrangements for training under section 2 of the Employment and Training Act 1973 or, in Scotland, section 2 of the Enterprise and New Towns (Scotland) Act 1990 (or an employment rehabilitation course under the 1973 Act), certain travel expenses, living away from home expenses and training premiums[312] (for the treatment of payments for taking part in a New Deal programme – see Chapter 34).
- Any payments, other than for loss of earnings or of a benefit, made to jurors or witnesses for attending at court.[313]
- A payment from a social services department under sections 17 or 24 of the Children Act 1989, or, in Scotland, a payment from a social work department

under sections 12, 24 or 26 of the Social Work (Scotland) Act 1968 – ie, payments from social services to assist children in need or young people who have been in care or been looked after by them.[314] For IS and income-based JSA, such payments are not ignored if you or your partner are involved in or, for IS only, have returned to work after a trade dispute (see p2:187).

- Any payments made under the Community Care (Direct Payments) Act 1996 or under section 12B of the Social Work (Scotland) Act 1968.[315]
- Any payment you receive for looking after a person temporarily in your care if it is paid under community care arrangements by a health authority, local authority, voluntary organisation or by the person being looked after.[316]
- Victoria Cross or George Cross payments or similar awards.[317]
- Income paid outside the UK which cannot be transferred here.[318]
- If income is paid in another currency, any bank charges for converting the payment into sterling.[319]
- Fares to hospital.[320]
- Payments instead of milk tokens and vitamins.[321]
- Payments to assist prison visits.[322]
- For HB and CTB, if you make a parental contribution to a student's grant, an equal amount of any 'unearned' income you have for the period the grant is paid, is ignored.[323] If your 'unearned' income does not cover the contribution the balance can be disregarded from your earnings.[324] If you are a parent of a student under 25 who does not get a grant (or who only gets a smaller discretionary award) and you contribute to her/his living expenses, the amount of your 'unearned' income that is ignored is the amount equal to your contribution up to a maximum of £40.70 (less the weekly amount of any discretionary award the student has).[325] This is only ignored during the student's term. Again, any balance can be disregarded from your earnings.[326]

Income from New Deal programmes

There are special rules for the treatment of payments you may receive from the Employment Service for taking part in one of the options of the New Deal programme (see Chapter 34).

For all means-tested benefits, the following payments made for taking part in a New Deal programme will be disregarded:[327]
- any travel expenses;
- any living away from home allowance (in respect of housing costs not met by HB);
- any training premium; *and*
- (except for ETU) any childcare expenses.

In addition, any mandatory top-up payment to participants in the Voluntary Sector Option, the Environment Task Force Option, or the Self-Employment Option, and any discretionary payments for special needs made to participants in the Full-Time Education and Training Options will also be disregarded.[328]

Similarly (except for ETU) any childcare expenses or mandatory top-up payments or (until 29 November 1999) payments under a written agreement between the Secretary of State and the person who has arranged for your participation, for taking part in the intensive activity period of the New Deal pilot for those aged 25 or over will also be disregarded.[329]

For those taking part in the Self-Employment Option, or (except for ETU) in the intensive activity period of the New Deal pilot for those aged 25 or over, any payments to meet expenses 'wholly and necessarily' incurred while trading, and any payments used for the repayments of a loan necessary for the business are also disregarded[330] (provided these payments are from a special account set up for the purposes of this programme). Once you have completed your (up to) 26-week period of 'test-trading', any income you have received from trading and which has accrued in your special account is released to you. For HB/CTB/FC/DWA/ETU, these are treated as capital.[331] For IS/income-based JSA, these are treated as income and spread over the same number of weeks in the future (usually 26) for which you have been receiving assistance, less any income tax due on the profits and an earnings disregard appropriate to your circumstances (see p2:396).[332]

6. **Notional income**

For all means-tested benefits you may, in certain circumstances, be treated as having income although you do not possess it, or have used it up.

Deprivation of income in order to claim or increase benefit

If you deliberately get rid of income in order to claim or increase your benefit, you are treated as though you are still in receipt of the income.[333] The basic issues involved are the same as those for the deprivation of capital (see p2:456). Note that the rule can only apply if the purpose of the deprivation is to gain benefit for *yourself* (or your family). It should not apply if, for example, you stop claiming invalid care allowance solely so that another person (who is not a member of your family) can become entitled to the severe disability premium (see p2:329).[334] However, if you do not claim a benefit which would clearly be paid if you did, it may be argued that you have failed to apply for income (see below).

A deliberate decision to 'de-retire' and give up your retirement pension (in the expectation of achieving an overall increase in benefit in the future) can come within this deprivation rule.[335] For an explanation of de-retirement, see p1:142.

Failing to apply for income[336]

If you fail to apply for income to which you are entitled without having to fulfil further conditions, you are deemed to have received it from the date you could have obtained it.

This does not include income from:
- a discretionary trust; *or*
- a trust set up from money paid as a result of a personal injury; *or*
- funds administered by a court as a result of a personal injury or the death of a parent of someone under 18; *or*
- an Employment Service Rehabilitation Allowance; *or*
- where you are under 60, a personal pension scheme or retirement annuity. However, if you are 60 or over, you are treated as receiving income in certain circumstances if you fail to purchase an annuity.[337]

For income support (IS) and income-based jobseeker's allowance (JSA) only, the lone parent element of child benefit, JSA, family credit (FC), disability working allowance (DWA) and earnings top-up (ETU) are also exempted.

For other income or benefits it must still be certain that it would be paid upon application. It may therefore be difficult to establish that there is 'no doubt' that invalid care allowance, for example, would be paid to a carer who does not wish to claim it because of the effect on another person's severe disability premium (see p2:329).[338]

Previously, DSS guidance for housing benefit (HB) and council tax benefit (CTB) said that FC (and presumably other benefits as well) should not count as notional income if you might be entitled but had not applied for it, although local authorities should notify the Family Credit Unit where it appeared to them a successful claim could be made. It also said that if you applied for FC or DWA but had not yet been paid, it did not count as income or notional income and should be ignored until you actually received it. Current guidance does not deal with these points, but you should argue that the same still applies.

Any such income must also be available to *you* (or your family) *for your own benefit*. For example, income could not be attributed to the leaseholder of a shop he was forced to sublet to tenants in order to meet his liabilities to the landlord. Although their rents were technically available to him, they were immediately passed on to the landlord so no profit was ever available.[339]

Income due to you that has not been paid

This applies to IS and income-based JSA only.[340] You are treated as possessing any income owing to you. Examples could be wages legally due but not paid, or an occupational pension payment that is due but has not been received. However, this does not apply where an occupational pension has not been paid, or fully paid, because the pension scheme has insufficient funds.[341] The rule also does not apply if any social security benefit has been delayed, or you are waiting for a late payment of a pension under the Job Release Scheme, a government training allowance or a benefit from a European Economic Area country. Nor does it apply in the case of money due to you from a discretionary trust, or a trust set up from money paid as a result of a personal injury.

As above, the income must be due to *you* (or your family) and *for your own benefit*.[342]

If this rule is applied, an urgent cases payment should be considered (see p2:217).[343]

Unpaid wages

This applies to IS and income-based JSA only. If you have wages due to you, but you do not yet know the exact amount or you have no proof of what they will be, you are treated as having a wage similar to that normally paid for that type of work in that area.[344] If your wages cannot be estimated you might qualify for an interim payment (see p2:499).[345]

Income payments made to someone else on your behalf[346]

For all means-tested benefits, if money is paid to someone on your behalf (eg, the landlord for your rent) this can count as notional income. This has been held to apply in the case of a claimant whose husband, from whom she had separated, continued to pay the mortgage on the home the claimant lived in. Because both spouses had a 'joint and several' liability to pay the mortgage, half of the payments were treated as the notional income of the claimant, and the other half was disregarded (because it was paid not on behalf of the claimant, but in respect of the husband's own share of the liability).[347] In this case, because the payments were made by way of maintenance, the maintenance disregard (see p2:408) applied to the notional income in assessing the claimant's entitlement to FC. The proportions of the payment to be taken into account as notional income or disregarded related to the share of the liability, so that if the claimant owned two-thirds of the property, two-thirds of the payment would count as notional income.[348]

These rules are the same as for notional capital (see p2:455).

For IS and income-based JSA, payments of income in kind are ignored, unless you or your partner are involved in a trade dispute, but even then they are ignored if they are from the Macfarlane Trusts, the Fund, the Eileen Trust or either of the Independent Living Funds (see p2:412) or in the form of concessionary coal under the Coal Industry Act 1994 or if they are paid in respect of participation in a Government training scheme or a New Deal programme (see Chapter 34).[349]

For the treatment of school fees paid for your child(ren) by someone else, see p2:383.

Income payments paid to you for someone else[350]

If you or a member of your family get a payment for somebody not in the 'family' (see p2:113) (eg, a relative living with you) it counts as your income if you keep any of it yourself or spend it on your family. This does not apply if the payment is from the Macfarlane Trusts, the Fund, the Eileen Trust or either of the Independent Living Funds or in the form of concessionary coal under the Coal Industry Act 1994, or if the payment is a mandatory or discretionary grant for participating in a government training scheme or in a New Deal programme (see Chapter 34). Note that the same exception for payments in kind applies for IS and income-based JSA as for income payments made to someone else on your behalf.

Cheap or unpaid labour

If you are helping another person or an organisation by doing work of a kind which would normally command a wage, or a higher wage, you are deemed to receive a wage similar to that normally paid for that kind of job in that area.[351] The burden of proving that the kind of work you do is something for which an employer would pay, and what the comparable wages are, lies with the adjudicating authority.[352]

The rule does not apply if *either*:

- you can show that the person ('person' in this context includes a limited company[353]) cannot, in fact, afford to pay, or pay more; *or*
- you work for a charitable or voluntary organisation or as a volunteer, and it is accepted that it is reasonable for you to give your services free of charge, or where your services are provided because you are participating in a government training scheme or in a New Deal programme (see Chapter 34) for which you are not being paid an allowance (this may apply where you are, eg, sampling a New Deal 'taster' before committing yourself to it).[354] A 'volunteer' in this context is someone who, without any legal obligation, performs a service for another person without expecting payment.[355]

Even if you are caring for a sick or disabled relative or another person, it may be considered reasonable for her/him to pay you from her/his benefits, unless you can bring yourself within these exceptions.[356] It may, for example, be more reasonable for a close relative to provide services free of charge out of a sense of family duty,[357] particularly if a charge would otherwise break up a relationship.[358] Whether it is reasonable to provide care free of charge depends on the basis on which the arrangement is made, the expectations of the family members concerned, the housing arrangements and the reasons (if appropriate) why a carer gave up any paid work. The risk of a carer losing entitlement to invalid care allowance if a charge were made should also be considered[359] as should the likelihood that a relative being looked after would no longer be able to contribute to the household expenses.[360] If there is no realistic alternative to the carer providing services free to a relative who simply will not pay, this may also make it reasonable not to charge.[361] It may also be worth arguing that carers should not charge because they will otherwise lose their statutory right to an assessment of their needs by social services.[362]

Sometimes it may also be reasonable to do a job for free out of a sense of community duty, particularly if the job would otherwise have remained undone, and there would be no financial profit to an employer.[363]

Reducing the number of hours you work

For FC and ETU only, if you deliberately choose to reduce the number of hours you work in order to be able to claim or increase your entitlement to FC or ETU, any period of reduced hours is ignored when assessing your normal weekly earnings.[364]

Notes

References are to statutes and regulations as amended up to 8 March 1999. All regulations are (General) Regulations unless otherwise stated. There is a full list of abbreviations in Appendix 13.

1 **HB** Sch 3 para 10 and Sch 4 para 4 HB Regs
CTB Sch 3 para 10 and Sch 4 para 4 CTB Regs
2 Reg 80(2) JSA Regs

1. Some general rules about income
3 **IS/FC/DWA/HB/CTB** s136(1) SSCBA 1992
JSA s13(2) JSA 1995
ETU Rule 16 ETU Scheme
4 **IS** Reg 23(4) IS Regs
JSA Reg 88(3) JSA Regs
5 **IS** Reg 23(5) IS Regs
JSA Reg 88(4) and (5) JSA Regs
6 **IS** Reg 17(b) IS Regs
JSA Reg 83(b) JSA Regs
FC Reg 46(4) FC Regs
DWA Reg 51(4) DWA Regs
HB Reg 16(b) HB Regs
CTB Reg 8(b) CTB Regs
7 **IS** Regs 25 and 44(5) IS Regs
JSA Reg 89 JSA Regs
FC Reg 27(3) FC Regs
DWA Reg 30(3) DWA Regs
HB Reg 36(2) HB Regs
CTB Reg 27(2) CTB Regs
8 **IS/FC/DWA/HB/CTB** s136(1) SSCBA 1992
JSA s13(2) JSA 1995
9 **IS** Reg 44(4) IS Regs
JSA Reg 106(4) JSA Regs
HB Reg 36(1) HB Regs
CTB Reg 27(1) CTB Regs
10 **FC** Regs 27(2) and 46(5) FC Regs
DWA Regs 30(2) and 51(5) DWA Regs
11 **IS** Reg 25 IS Regs
JSA Reg 89 JSA Regs
FC Reg 27(2) FC Regs
DWA Reg 30(2) DWA Regs
HB Reg 36(1) HB Regs
CTB Reg 27(1) CTB Regs

12 **IS** Sch 8 para 14 IS Regs
JSA Sch 6 para 17 JSA Regs
FC Sch 1 para 2 FC Regs
DWA Sch 2 para 2 DWA Regs
HB Sch 3 para 13 HB Regs
CTB Sch 3 para 13 CTB Regs
13 **IS** Sch 8 para 15(b) IS Regs
JSA Sch 6 para 18(b) JSA Regs
HB Sch 3 para 14(b) HB Regs
CTB Sch 2 para 14(b) CTB Regs
14 **IS** Sch 8 para 15(a) IS Regs
JSA Sch 6 para 18(a) JSA Regs
HB Sch 3 para 14(a) HB Regs
CTB Sch 3 para 14(a) CTB Regs
15 **IS** Reg 44(4) IS Regs
JSA Reg 106(4) JSA Regs
HB Reg 36(1) HB Regs
CTB Reg 27(1) CTB Regs
16 **IS** Reg 42(4)(a)(ii) IS Regs
JSA Reg 105(10) JSA Regs
17 **IS** Reg 44(2)(a) and (4) IS Regs
JSA Reg 106(2)(a) JSA Regs
18 **IS** Reg 44(2)(b) IS Regs
JSA Reg 106(2)(b) JSA Regs
19 **IS** Reg 44(9) IS Regs
JSA Reg 106(9) JSA Regs
20 **IS** Reg 44(3) IS Regs; CIS/164/1994
JSA Reg 106(3) JSA Regs
21 **FC** Reg 26(3)(a) FC Regs
DWA Reg 29(3)(a) DWA Regs
22 **HB** Reg 35(3)(a) and Sch 4 para 13(1), (2) and (5) HB Regs
CTB Reg 26(3)(a) and Sch 4 para 13(1), (2) and (5) CTB Regs
Both paras C3.107 and C3.112 GM
23 **HB** Reg 35(3)(a) and Sch 4 paras 13(3) and 47 HB Regs
CTB Reg 26(3)(a) and Sch 4 paras 13(3) and 46 CTB Regs
Both paras C3.89, C3.110 and C3.112 GM
24 **IS** Reg 32(1) IS Regs
JSA Reg 97 JSA Regs
FC Reg 18(1) FC Regs

DWA Reg 20(1) DWA Regs
ETU Rule 25(1) ETU Scheme
HB Reg 25 HB Regs
CTB Reg 17 CTB Regs
25 R(IS) 3/93
26 CIS/242/1989 (apparently to be
reported as R(IS) 10/95)
27 **IS** Reg 32(6) IS Regs
JSA Reg 97(6) JSA Regs
28 **IS** Reg 32(2) and (3) IS Regs
JSA Reg 97(2) and (3) JSA Regs
29 **IS** Reg 32(4) IS Regs
JSA Reg 97(4) JSA Regs
30 **IS** Reg 32(5) and Sch 8 para 10
IS Regs
JSA Reg 97(5) and Sch 6 para
13 JSA Regs
31 **IS** Reg 29(2)(a) IS Regs
JSA Reg 94(2)(a) JSA Regs
32 **IS** Reg 29(2)(b) IS Regs
JSA Reg 94(2)(b) JSA Regs
33 **IS** Reg 31(1)(a) IS Regs
JSA Reg 96(1)(a) JSA Regs
34 **IS** Reg 31(1)(b) IS Regs
JSA Reg 96(1)(b) JSA Regs
35 **IS** Reg 31(2) IS Regs
JSA Reg 96(2) JSA Regs
36 **IS** Reg 2(1) IS Regs
JSA Reg 1(3) JSA Regs
37 R(SB) 33/83
38 R(SB) 22/84; R(SB) 11/85
39 CIS/590/1993

2. **Earnings of employed earners**
40 *Parsons v Hogg* [1985] 2 All ER
897, CA, appendix to R(FIS) 4/85
41 R(FC) 1/90
42 CFC/26/1989
43 R(FIS) 4/85
44 R(IS) 13/91; R(IS) 16/93; CFC/
26/1989
45 CCS/318/1995 (applying the
identical provisions in child
support law)
46 CCS/5352/1995
47 CCS/2320/1997, following CCS/
10/1994 and CCS/12598/1996,
but rejecting CCS/12769/1996
which had held that police rent
allowances were deductible.
48 R(U) 2/72; R(FIS) 4/85; R(FC) 1/
91; R(IS) 13/91
49 CIS/521/1990

50 **IS** Reg 36(3) IS Regs
JSA Reg 99(1) and (4) JSA Regs
FC Reg 20(3) FC Regs
DWA Reg 22(3) DWA Regs
ETU Rule 27(3) ETU Scheme
HB Reg 29(3) HB Regs
CTB Reg 20(3) CTB Regs
51 **FC** Regs 14(2) and 20(4) FC
Regs
DWA Regs 16(7) and 22(4)
DWA Regs
ETU Rules 20(2) and 27(4) ETU
Scheme
HB Regs 22(2) and 29(4) HB
Regs
CTB Regs 14(2) and 20(4) CTB
Regs
HB/CTB para C3.22 GM
52 **HB** Reg 26 HB Regs
CTB Reg 18 CTB Regs
HB/CTB paras C3.03-04 GM
53 R(SB) 21/86
IS Reg 35(1) IS Regs
JSA Reg 98(1) JSA Regs
FC Reg 19(1) FC Regs
DWA Reg 21(1) DWA Regs
ETU Rule 26(1) ETU Scheme
HB Reg 28(1) HB Regs
CTB Reg 19(1) CTB Regs
54 **IS** Reg 48(3) IS Regs
JSA Reg 110(3) JSA Regs
FC Reg 31(2) FC Regs
DWA Reg 34(2) DWA Regs
ETU Rule 37(2) ETU Scheme
HB Reg 40(3) HB Regs
CTB Reg 31(3) CTB Regs
55 **IS** Regs 35(1)(d) and 48(3) and
(10)(a) IS Regs
JSA Regs 98(1)(c) and 110(3)
and (10)(a) JSA Regs
56 **FC** Reg 19(1)(g)-(h) FC Regs
DWA Reg 21(1)(g)-(h) DWA
Regs
ETU Rule 26(1)(g) ETU Scheme
HB Reg 28(1)(i)-(j) HB Regs
CTB Reg 19(1)(i)-(j) CTB Regs
57 **IS** Regs 35(2)(b) and 40(4) and
Sch 9 paras 1, 4 and 4A IS Regs
JSA Regs 98(2)(c) and 103(6)
and Sch 7 paras 1, 4 and 5 JSA
Regs
58 **HB** Reg 28(1)(i)-(j) HB Regs
CTB Reg 19(1)(i)-(j) CTB Regs

59 **FC** Sch 2 paras 27 and 31 FC
Regs
DWA Sch 3 paras 27 and 31
DWA Regs
ETU Sch 4 paras 24 and 25 ETU
Scheme

60 **IS** Regs 35(2)(b) and 40(4) and
Sch 9 paras 1, 4 and 4A IS Regs
JSA Regs 98(2)(c) and 103(6)
and Sch 7 paras 1, 4 and 5 JSA
Regs

61 **IS** Reg 35(1)(e) IS Regs
JSA Reg 98(1)(d) JSA Regs
FC Reg 19(1)(c) FC Regs
DWA Reg 21(1)(c) DWA Regs
ETU Rule 26(1)(c) ETU Scheme
HB Reg 28(1)(e) HB Regs
CTB Reg 19(1)(e) CTB Regs

62 R(IS) 9/95

63 Reg 21(1)(i) DWA Regs

64 **IS** Reg 35(1)(g) IS Regs
JSA Reg 98(1)(f) JSA Regs
FC Reg 19(1)(e) FC Regs
DWA Reg 19(1)(e) DWA Regs
ETU Rule 26(1)(e) ETU Scheme
HB Reg 28(1)(g) HB Regs
CTB Reg 19(1)(g) CTB Regs

65 CIS/590/1993

66 **IS** Reg 35(1)(h) IS Regs
JSA Reg 98(1)(b) JSA Regs
FC Reg 19(1)(f) FC Regs
DWA Reg 21(1)(f) DWA Regs
ETU Rule 26(1)(f) ETU Scheme
HB Reg 28(1)(h) HB Regs
CTB Reg 19(1)(h) CTB Regs

67 **IS** Reg 35(1)(b) IS Regs
JSA Reg 98(1)(b) and (2)(b) JSA
Regs
HB Reg 28(1)(b) HB Regs
CTB Reg 19(1)(b) CTB Regs

68 **IS** Reg 35(1)(c) IS Regs
JSA Reg 98(1)(b) JSA Regs
HB Reg 28(1)(c) HB Regs
CTB Reg 19(1)(c) CTB Regs

69 **JSA** Reg 98(1)(f), (ff) and (g) JSA
Regs

70 **IS** Reg 35(3)(iv)
JSA Reg 98(3)(d)

71 **IS** Reg 35(2)(e) IS Regs
JSA Reg 98(2)(g) JSA Regs

72 **IS** Reg 35(2)(a) IS Regs
JSA Reg 98(2)(a) JSA Regs
FC Reg 19(2)(a) FC Regs
DWA Reg 21(2)(a) DWA Regs

ETU Rule 26(2)(a) ETU Scheme
HB Reg 28(2)(a) HB Regs
CTB Reg 19(2)(a) CTB Regs

73 **IS** Sch 9 para 21 IS Regs
JSA Sch 7 para 22 JSA Regs
FC Sch 2 para 20 FC Regs
DWA Sch 3 para 20 DWA Regs
ETU Sch 4 para 18 ETU Scheme
HB Sch 4 para 21 HB Regs
CTB Sch 4 para 22 CTB Regs

74 CIS/11482/1995

75 **IS** Reg 35(2)(a) IS Regs
JSA Reg 98(2)(a) JSA Regs
Both para 29126 AOG

76 **FC** Reg 19(3) FC Regs
DWA Reg 21(3) DWA Regs
ETU Rule 26(3) ETU Scheme

77 **HB** Reg 28(2)(a) HB Regs
CTB Reg 19(2)(a) CTB Regs

78 **IS** Reg 48(5) IS Regs
JSA Reg 110(5) JSA Regs
FC Reg 31(5) FC Regs
DWA Reg 34(5) DWA Regs
ETU Rule 37(5) ETU Scheme
HB Reg 40(5) HB Regs
CTB Reg 31(5) CTB Regs

79 **IS** Reg 48(6) IS Regs
JSA Reg 110(6) JSA Regs

80 **IS** Reg 35(2)(c) IS Regs
JSA Reg 98(2)(d) JSA Regs
FC Reg 19(2)(b) FC Regs
DWA Reg 21(2)(b) DWA Regs
ETU Rule 26(2)(b) ETU Scheme
HB Reg 28(2)(b) HB Regs
CTB Reg 19(2)(b) CTB Regs

81 CIS/77/1993; CIS/89/1989

82 R(IS) 6/92
IS/JSA paras 29155-166 AOG
HB/CTB para C3.10 GM

83 **IS** Sch 8 para 11 IS Regs
JSA Sch 6 para 14 JSA Regs
FC Sch 1 para 1 FC Regs
DWA Sch 2 para 1 DWA Regs
ETU Sch 3 para 1 ETU Scheme
HB Sch 3 para 11 HB Regs
CTB Sch 3 para 11 CTB Regs

84 **IS** Sch 8 para 12 IS Regs
JSA Sch 6 para 15 JSA Regs
FC Sch 1 para 3 FC Regs
DWA Sch 2 para 3 DWA Regs
ETU Sch 3 para 2 ETU Scheme
HB Sch 3 para 12 HB Regs
CTB Sch 3 para 12 CTB Regs

85 **IS** Reg 35(2)(d) IS Regs
JSA Reg 98(2)(e) JSA Regs
FC Reg 19(2)(c) FC Regs
DWA Reg 21(2)(c) DWA Regs
ETU Rule 26(2)(c) ETU Scheme
HB Reg 28(2)(c) HB Regs
CTB Reg 19(2)(c) CTB Regs

86 **IS** Reg 40(4) and Sch 9 para 1 IS Regs
JSA Reg 103(6) and Sch 7 para 1 JSA Regs
FC Reg 24(5) and Sch 2 para 1 FC Regs
DWA Reg 27(4) and Sch 3 para 1 DWA Regs
ETU Rule 33(5) and Sch 4 para 1 ETU Scheme
HB Reg 33(4) and Sch 4 para 1 HB Regs
CTB Reg 24(5) and Sch 4 para 1 CTB Regs

87 **FC** Reg 14(1) and (2) FC Regs
ETU Rule 20(1) and (2) ETU Scheme

88 **FC** Reg 14(1) FC Regs
ETU Rule 20(1) ETU Scheme

89 **FC** Reg 14(3) FC Regs
ETU Rule 20(4) ETU Scheme

90 **FC** Reg 14(2A) FC Regs
ETU Rule 14(3) ETU Scheme

91 **FC** Reg 20(5) FC Regs
ETU Rule 27(5) ETU Scheme

92 **FC** Reg 14A FC Regs
ETU Rule 21 ETU Scheme

93 **FC** Regs 14(1), 14A, 17(b) and 18(3) FC Regs
ETU Rules 20(1), 21, 22 and 25(3) ETU Scheme

94 Reg 16(2)-(4) DWA Regs

95 Reg 16(1) DWA Regs

96 Reg 19(a) DWA Regs

97 R(FIS) 1/87; R(FIS) 2/87

98 Reg 16(5) DWA Regs

99 s27(3)(b) SSCBA 1992; reg 16(3), (4)(b) and (9)(b) DWA Regs; R(U) 5/87

100 **FC** Regs 14(4) and 20A FC Regs
DWA Regs 16(6) and 23 DWA Regs
ETU Rules 20(5) and 29 ETU Scheme

101 **FC** Reg 20A FC Regs
DWA Reg 23 DWA Regs
ETU Rule 29 ETU Scheme

102 **FC** Reg 14(5) and (6) FC Regs
DWA Reg 16(7) and (8) DWA Regs
ETU Rule 20(6) and (7) ETU Scheme

103 **HB** Reg 22(1)(a) HB Regs
CTB Reg 14(1)(a) CTB Regs
HB/CTB para C3.16 GM

104 **HB** Reg 22(1)(b) HB Regs
CTB Reg 14(1)(b) CTB Regs
HB/CTB para C3.17 GM

105 *R v HBRB of the London Borough of Ealing ex parte Saville* [1986] 18 HLR 349

106 **HB** Reg 22(2)(a)-(b) HB Regs
CTB Reg 14(2)(a)-(b) CTB Regs
HB/CTB para C3.19 GM

107 **HB** Reg 22(3) HB Regs
CTB Reg 14(3) CTB Regs

108 **IS** Regs 35(1)(i) and (3) and 5(5) IS Regs
JSA Regs 98(1)(b) and 52(3) JSA Regs

109 **IS** Regs 35(1)(b) and 40(1) IS Regs
JSA Regs 98(2)(b) and 103(1) JSA Regs
FC Regs 19 and 24 FC Regs
DWA Regs 21 and 27 DWA Regs
ETU Rule 26 and 33 ETU Scheme
HB Regs 28(1)(b) and 33(1) HB Regs
CTB Regs 19(1)(b) and 24(1) CTB Regs

110 **IS** Sch 8 para 1(a)(i) IS Regs
JSA Sch 6 para 1(a)(i) JSA Regs

111 **IS** Sch 8 para 1(a)(ii) and reg 35(1)(b)-(e) and (g)-(i) IS Regs
JSA Sch 6 para 1(a)(ii) and regs 98(1)(b), (c), (f) and (g) JSA Regs

112 Reg 29(4B) and (4D)(b) IS Regs

113 Reg 48(11) IS Regs

114 **IS** Regs 5(5) and 29(3)(a) IS Regs
JSA Regs 52(3) and 94(3)(a) JSA Regs

115 **IS** Reg 29(4) IS Regs
JSA Reg 94(4) JSA Regs

116 **IS** Reg 29(3)(b) IS Regs
JSA Reg 94(3)(b) JSA Regs

117 **IS** Reg 5(5) and Sch 8 para 1(b) IS Regs
JSA Reg 52(3) and Sch 6 para 1(b) JSA Regs

118 **IS** Sch 8 para 2 IS Regs
JSA Sch 6 para 2 JSA Regs

119 Regs 29(4C) and 32(7) IS Regs
120 **IS** Reg 29(4) and (4C) IS Regs
  JSA Reg 94(4) JSA Regs
121 R(IS) 3/93; CIS/104/1989
122 CIS/4312/1997
123 **FC** Reg 16(1) FC Regs
  DWA Reg 18(1) DWA Regs
  ETU Rule 24(1) ETU Scheme
124 **HB** Sch 3 para 1(a) HB Regs
  CTB Sch 3 para 1(a) CTB Regs
125 **HB** Sch 3 para 1(aa) HB Regs
  CTB Sch 3 para 1(aa) CTB Regs
126 **HB** Sch 3 para 1(b) HB Regs
  CTB Sch 3 para 1(b) CTB Regs
127 **HB** Sch 3 para 2 HB Regs
  CTB Sch 3 para 2 CTB Regs

3. **Earnings from self-employment**
128 **IS** Reg 37(1) IS Regs
  JSA Reg 100(1) JSA Regs
  FC Reg 21(1) FC Regs
  DWA Reg 24(1) DWA Regs
  ETU Rule 30(1) ETU Scheme
  HB Reg 30 HB Regs
  CTB Reg 21 CTB Regs
129 **IS** Reg 38(3) IS Regs
  JSA Reg 101(4) JSA Regs
  FC Reg 22(3) FC Regs
  DWA Reg 25(3) DWA Regs
  ETU Rule 31(3) ETU Scheme
  HB Reg 31(3) HB Regs
  CTB Reg 22(3) CTB Regs
130 **IS** Reg 2(1) IS Regs
  JSA s35(1) JSA 1995
  FC Regs 2(1) and 22(12)-(13) FC
  Regs
  DWA Regs 2(1) and 25(14)-(15)
  DWA Regs
  ETU Rules 2(7) and 31(14)-(15)
  ETU Scheme
  HB Regs 2(1) and 31(11)-(12)
  HB Regs
  CTB Regs 2(1) and 22(11)-(12)
  CTB Regs
131 Reg 32(3) SS(C&P) Regs
132 **FC** Reg 21(1) FC Regs
  DWA Reg 24(1) DWA Regs
  ETU Rule 30(1) ETU Scheme
133 CFC/24/1989; CFC/3/1992
134 CFC/4/1991 (*Kostanczwk v CAO*);
  CFC/23/1991
135 **IS** Reg 37(2) IS Regs
  JSA Reg 100(2)(b) JSA Regs
  FC Reg 21(3) FC Regs
  DWA Reg 24(3) DWA Regs

ETU Rule 30(3) ETU Scheme
  HB Reg 30(2) HB Regs
  CTB Reg 21(2) CTB Regs
136 **IS** Sch 9 paras 26-27 IS Regs
  JSA Sch 7 paras 27 and 28 JSA
  Regs
  FC Sch 2 para 24 FC Regs
  DWA Sch 3 para 24 DWA Regs
  ETU Sch 4 para 21 ETU Scheme
  HB Sch 4 paras 24-25 HB Regs
  CTB Sch 4 paras 25-26 CTB Regs
137 **IS** Reg 37(2)(a) IS Regs
  JSA Reg 100(2)(9) JSA Regs
  HB Sch 4 para 42 HB Regs
  CTB Sch 4 para 21 CTB Regs
138 **FC** Reg 21(2) FC Regs
  DWA Reg 24(2) DWA Regs
  ETU Rule 30(2) ETU Scheme
139 **IS** Reg 38(3)(a), (4), (7) and
  (8)(a) IS Regs
  JSA Reg 101(4) and (8) JSA Regs
  FC Reg 22(3)(a), (4), (7) and
  (8)(a) FC Regs
  DWA Reg 25(3)(a), (4)(a), (5),
  (6), (9) and (10)(a) DWA Regs
  ETU Rule 31(3)(a), (5), (9) and
  (10)(a) ETU Scheme
  HB Reg 31(3)(a), (4), (7) and
  (8)(a) HB Regs
  CTB Reg 22(3)(a), (4), (7) and
  (8)(a) CTB Regs
140 R(IS) 13/91; R(FC) 1/91; CFC/26/
  1989
141 **IS** Reg 38(6) and (8)(b) IS Regs
  JSA Reg 101(7) and (9) JSA Regs
  FC Reg 22(6) and (8)(b) FC Regs
  DWA Reg 25(8) and (10)(b)
  DWA Regs
  ETU Rule 31(8) and (10)(b) ETU
  Scheme
  HB Reg 31(6) and (8)(b) HB
  Regs
  CTB Reg 22(6) and (8)(b) CTB
  Regs
142 **IS** Reg 38(5) IS Regs
  JSA Reg 101(6) and (8) JSA Regs
  FC Reg 22(5) FC Regs
  DWA Reg 25(7) DWA Regs
  ETU Rule 31(7) ETU Scheme
  HB Reg 31(5) HB Regs
  CTB Reg 22(5) CTB Regs

143 R(FC) 1/96 (formerly CFC/41/
   1993), following CFC/19/1993
   and disagreeing with CFC/22/
   1989, CFC/19/1992 and CFC/
   10/1993
144 **IS** Reg 38(11) IS Regs
   JSA Reg 101(12) JSA Regs
   FC Reg 22(11) FC Regs
   DWA Reg 25(13) DWA Regs
   ETU Rule 31(13) ETU Scheme
   HB Reg 31(10) HB Regs
   CTB Reg 22(10) CTB Regs
   See also R(FC) 1/93
145 CFC/836/1995
146 **IS** Reg 30 IS Regs
   JSA Reg 95 JSA Regs
147 **IS** Regs 30(1)(b) and 38(10) IS
   Regs; CIS/166/1994; CIS/14409/
   1996
   JSA Regs 95(1)(b) and 101(11)
   JSA Regs
148 **IS** Reg 30(2) IS Regs
   JSA Reg 95(2) JSA Regs
149 **FC** Reg 15 FC Regs
   DWA Reg 17 DWA Regs
   ETU Rule 23 ETU Scheme
150 **FC** Reg 18(2) FC Regs
   DWA Reg 20(2) DWA Regs
   ETU Rule 25(2) ETU Scheme
151 **FC** Reg 17 FC Regs
   DWA Reg 19(b) DWA Regs
152 Regs 15(2) and (4) and 17(a) FC
   Regs
153 **DWA** Reg 17(3) DWA Regs
   ETU Rule 23(3) ETU Scheme
154 **FC** s128(3) SSCBA 1992
   DWA s129(6) SSCBA 1992
   ETU Rule 10(1) ETU Scheme
155 Rule 7(5) ETU Scheme
156 **HB** Regs 23(1) and 25(2) HB
   Regs
   CTB Regs 15(1) and 17(2) CTB
   Regs
157 **IS** Reg 38(9) IS Regs
   JSA Reg 101(10) JSA Regs
   FC Reg 22(9) FC Regs
   DWA Reg 25(11) DWA Regs
   ETU Rule 31(11) ETU Scheme
   HB Reg 31(9) HB Regs
   CTB Reg 22(9) CTB Regs
158 **IS** Reg 38(2) IS Regs
   JSA Reg 101(2) and (3) and Sch
   6 paras 1-16 JSA Regs
   FC Reg 22(2) FC Regs

DWA Reg 25(2) DWA Regs
HB Reg 31(2) HB Regs
CTB Reg 22(2) CTB Regs

4. **Disregarded earnings**
159 **HB** Sch 3 para 4 HB Regs
   CTB Sch 3 para 4 CTB Regs
160 **IS** Sch 8 para 5 IS Regs
   JSA Sch 6 para 6 JSA Regs
161 **IS** Sch 8 para 4(2) IS Regs
   JSA Sch 6 para 5(1) and (2) JSA
   Regs
   HB Sch 3 para 3(2) HB Regs
   CTB Sch 3 para 3(2) CTB Regs
162 **IS** Sch 8 para 4(4) IS Regs
   JSA Sch 6 para 5(4) JSA Regs
   HB Sch 3 para 3(4) HB Regs
   CTB Sch 3 para 3(4) CTB Regs
163 **IS** Sch 8 para 4(3) and (5) IS
   Regs
   JSA Sch 6 para 5(5) and (3) JSA
   Regs
   HB Sch 3 para 3(3) and (5) HB
   Regs
   CTB Sch 3 para 3(3) and (5) CTB
   Regs
164 **IS** Sch 8 para 4(6) IS Regs
   JSA Sch 6 para 5(6) JSA Regs
   HB Sch 3 para 3(6) HB Regs
   CTB Sch 3 para 3(6) CTB Regs
165 **IS** Sch 8 paras 6A and 6B IS Regs
   JSA Sch 6 paras 7 and 8 JSA Regs
   HB Sch 3 paras 4A and 4B HB
   Regs
   CTB Sch 3 paras 4A and 4B CTB
   Regs
166 **IS** Sch 8 para 7(1) IS Regs
   JSA Sch 6 para 9(1) JSA Regs
   HB Sch 3 para 6(1) HB Regs
   CTB Sch 3 para 6(1) CTB Regs
167 **IS** Sch 8 para 8 IS Regs
   JSA Sch 6 para 10 JSA Regs
   HB Sch 3 para 7 HB Regs
   CTB Sch 3 para 7 CTB Regs
168 **IS** Sch 8 para 7(2) IS Regs
   JSA Sch 6 paras 9 and 10 JSA
   Regs
   HB Sch 3 para 6(2)(b) HB Regs
   CTB Sch 3 para 6(2)(b) CTB
   Regs
169 **IS** Reg 3A and Sch 8 para 4(7) IS
   Regs
   JSA Sch 6 paras 5(7) and 21 and
   reg 87(7) JSA Regs

170 **IS** Sch 8 paras 6 and 9 IS Regs
JSA Sch 6 paras 11 and 12 JSA Regs
HB Sch 3 paras 5 and 8 HB Regs
CTB Sch 4 paras 5 and 8 CTB Regs

171 **FC** Regs 13(1)(c) and 13A FC Regs
DWA Regs 15(1)(c) and 15A DWA Regs
HB Regs 21(1)(c) and 21A HB Regs
CTB Regs 13(1)(c) and 13A CTB Regs

172 **FC** Reg 13A(2) FC Regs
DWA Reg 15A(2) DWA Regs
HB Reg 21A(2) HB Regs
CTB Reg 13A(2) CTB Regs

173 **FC** Reg 13A FC Regs
DWA Reg 15A DWA Regs

174 **HB** Reg 21A HB Regs
CTB Reg 13A CTB Regs

175 s29 CA 1989

5. Other income

176 **IS** Reg 40 and Sch 9 para 1 IS Regs
JSA Reg 103(1) and (2) and Sch 7 para 1 JSA Regs
FC Reg 24 and Sch 2 para 1 FC Regs
DWA Reg 27 and Sch 3 para 1 DWA Regs
ETU Rule 33 and Sch 4 para 1 ETU Scheme
HB Reg 33 and Sch 4 para 1 HB Regs
CTB Reg 24 and Sch 4 para 1 CTB Regs

177 **HB** Reg 26 HB Regs
CTB Reg 18 CTB Regs

178 **HB** Reg 24 HB Regs
CTB Reg 16 CTB Regs

179 **FC** Reg 16(1) FC Regs
DWA Reg 18(1) DWA Regs
ETU Rule 24(1) ETU Scheme

180 **HB** Sch 4 paras 57, 58 and 60 HB Regs
CTB Sch 4 paras 56, 57 and 59 CTB Regs

181 **IS** Reg 35(2) and Sch 9 para 4 IS Regs
JSA Sch 7 para 5 JSA Regs

182 s74(2) SSAA 1992

183 **IS** Sch 10 para 7 IS Regs
JSA Sch 8 para 12(b) JSA Regs
FC Sch 3 para 8 FC Regs
DWA Sch 4 para 8 DWA Regs
ETU Sch 5 para 8 ETU Scheme
HB Sch 5 para 8 HB Regs
CTB Sch 5 para 8 CTB Regs

184 **IS** Sch 9 para 9 IS Regs
JSA Sch 7 para 10 JSA Regs
FC Sch 2 paras 4 and 7 FC Regs
DWA Sch 3 paras 4 and 7 DWA Regs
ETU Sch 4 para 4 ETU Scheme
HB Sch 4 paras 5 and 8 HB Regs
CTB Sch 4 paras 5 and 8 CTB Regs

185 **IS** Sch 9 para 33 IS Regs
JSA Sch 7 para 35 JSA Regs
FC Sch 2 para 28 FC Regs
DWA Sch 3 para 28 DWA Regs
ETU Sch 4 para 26 ETU Scheme
HB Sch 4 para 31 HB Regs
CTB Sch 4 para 32 CTB Regs

186 **IS** Sch 9 para 6 IS Regs
JSA Sch 7 para 7 JSA Regs
FC Sch 2 para 4 FC Regs
DWA Sch 3 para 4 DWA Regs
ETU Sch 4 para 4 ETU Scheme
HB Sch 4 para 5 HB Regs
CTB Sch 4 para 5 CTB Regs

187 **IS** Sch 9 para 8 IS Regs
JSA Sch 7 para 9 JSA Regs
FC Sch 2 para 6 FC Regs
DWA Sch 3 para 6 DWA Regs
ETU Sch 4 para 6 ETU Scheme
HB Sch 4 para 7 HB Regs
CTB Sch 4 para 7 CTB Regs

188 **IS** Sch 9 paras 7 and 8 IS Regs
JSA Sch 7 paras 8 and 9 JSA Regs
FC Sch 2 paras 5 and 6 FC Regs
DWA Sch 3 paras 5 and 6 DWA Regs
HB Sch 4 paras 6 and 7 HB Regs
CTB Sch 4 paras 6 and 7 CTB Regs

189 Sch 2 para 4 FC Regs
190 Sch 2 paras 5(a) and 4 FC Regs
191 Sch 2 para 56 FC Regs
192 Sch 3 para 46 DWA Regs
193 Sch 3 para 54 DWA Regs
194 Sch 4 paras 4 and 5 ETU Scheme

195 **IS** Sch 9 para 31 IS Regs
JSA Sch 7 para 33 and Sch 8 para 23 JSA Regs
HB Sch 4 para 30 HB Regs
CTB Sch 4 para 31 CTB Regs

196 **FC** Reg 16(1) FC Regs
DWA Reg 16(1) DWA Regs
ETU Rule 24(1) ETU Scheme

197 **IS** Sch 10 para 18 IS Regs
JSA Sch 8 para 23 JSA Regs
FC Sch 3 para 19 FC Regs
DWA Sch 4 para 19 DWA Regs
ETU Sch 5 para 19 ETU Scheme
HB Sch 5 para 19 HB Regs
CTB Sch 5 para 19 CTB Regs

198 **IS** Sch 9 para 38 IS Regs
JSA Sch 7 para 40 JSA Regs
FC Sch 2 para 33 FC Regs
ETU Sch 4 para 30 ETU Scheme
HB Sch 4 para 37 HB Regs
CTB Sch 4 para 39 CTB Regs

199 **IS** Sch 9 paras 40-42 IS Regs
FC Sch 2 paras 35-37 FC Regs
DWA Sch 2 paras 34-36 DWA Regs
HB Sch 4 paras 35, 36 and 48 HB Regs
CTB Sch 4 paras 37, 38 and 47 CTB Regs

200 **IS** Sch 9 para 40 IS Regs
JSA Sch 7 para 42 JSA Regs
FC Sch 2 para 35 FC Regs
DWA Sch 4 para 34 DWA Regs
ETU Sch 4 para 32 ETU Scheme
HB Sch 4 para 35 HB Regs
CTB Sch 4 para 37 CTB Regs

201 **IS** Sch 9 paras 5, 45 and 52 IS Regs
JSA Sch 7 paras 6, 44 and 51 JSA Regs
FC Sch 2 paras 3, 41 and 49 FC Regs
DWA Sch 3 paras 3, 39 and 47 DWA Regs
ETU Sch 4 paras 3 and 40 ETU Scheme
HB Sch 4 paras 40 and 51 HB Regs
CTB Sch 4 paras 36 and 50 CTB Regs

202 **IS** Sch 9 para 46 IS Regs
JSA Sch 7 para 45 JSA Regs
FC Sch 2 para 42 FC Regs
DWA Sch 3 para 40 DWA Regs
HB Sch 4 para 41 HB Regs
CTB Sch 4 para 41 CTB Regs

203 **FC** Sch 2 para 3 FC Regs
DWA Sch 3 para 3 DWA Regs
ETU Sch 4 para 3 ETU Scheme
HB Sch 4 para 4 HB Regs
CTB Sch 4 para 4 CTB Regs

204 **IS** Sch 9 para 47 IS Regs
JSA Sch 7 para 46 JSA Regs
FC Sch 2 para 43 FC Regs
DWA Sch 3 para 41 DWA Regs
ETU Sch 4 para 35 ETU Scheme
HB Sch 4 para 43 HB Regs
CTB Sch 4 para 42 CTB Regs

205 **IS** Sch 9 paras 54-56 IS Regs
JSA Sch 7 paras 53-55 JSA Regs
FC Sch 2 paras 52-54 FC Regs
DWA Sch 3 paras 50-52 DWA Regs
ETU Sch 4 paras 42-44 ETU Scheme
HB Sch 4 paras 53-55 HB Regs
CTB Sch 4 paras 52-54 CTB Regs

206 **FC** Sch 2 para 50 FC Regs
DWA Sch 3 para 48 DWA Regs
ETU Sch 4 para 46 ETU Scheme
HB Sch 4 para 50 HB Regs
CTB Sch 4 para 49 CTB Regs

207 **FC** Sch 2 para 15 FC Regs
DWA Sch 3 para 15 DWA Regs
ETU Sch 4 para 45 ETU Scheme

208 **FC** Sch 2 paras 27 and 31 FC Regs
DWA Sch 3 paras 27 and 31 DWA Regs

209 **HB** Sch 4 paras 57, 58 and 60 HB Regs
CTB Sch 4 paras 56, 57 and 59 CTB Regs

210 **IS** Sch 9 para 53 IS Regs
JSA Sch 7 para 52 JSA Regs
FC Sch 2 para 51 FC Regs
DWA Sch 3 para 49 DWA Regs
ETU Sch 4 para 41 ETU Scheme
HB Sch 4 para 52 HB Regs
CTB Sch 4 para 51 CTB Regs

211 CIS/276/1998

212 **IS** Sch 9 para 16 IS Regs
JSA Sch 7 para 17 JSA Regs
FC Sch 2 para 14 FC Regs
DWA Sch 3 para 14 DWA Regs
ETU Sch 4 para 13 ETU Scheme
HB Sch 4 para 14 HB Regs
CTB Sch 4 para 14 CTB Regs

213 **IS** Sch 9 para 36 IS Regs
JSA Sch 7 para 38 JSA Regs
FC Sch 2 para 29 FC Regs
DWA Sch 3 para 29 DWA Regs
ETU Sch 4 para 27 ETU Scheme
HB Sch 4 para 33 HB Regs
CTB Sch 4 para 34 CTB Regs
214 ss134(8) and 139(6) SSAA 1992;
regs 7 and 8 IRBS(Amdt 2) Regs
215 **FC** Sch 2 paras 13(3) and 47 FC
Regs
DWA Sch 3 paras 12(3) and 13
DWA Regs
HB Sch 4 paras 13(3) and 47 HB
Regs
CTB Sch 4 paras 13(3) and 46
CTB Regs
216 Rule 24(1) and Sch 4 para 12(3)
ETU Scheme
217 CIS/683/1993
218 CIS/450/1997
219 **IS** Reg 61 IS Regs
JSA Reg 130 JSA Regs
FC Reg 37 FC Regs
DWA Reg 41 DWA Regs
ETU Rule 44 ETU Scheme
HB Reg 46 HB Regs
CTB Reg 38 CTB Regs
All Definition of 'grant'
220 R(IS) 16/95
221 **IS** Reg 61 IS Regs
JSA Reg 130 JSA Regs
FC Reg 37 FC Regs
DWA Reg 41 DWA Regs
ETU Rule 44 ETU Scheme
HB Reg 46 HB Regs
CTB Reg 38 CTB Regs
All Definition of 'grant income'
222 **IS** Reg 62(3) IS Regs
JSA Reg 131(4) JSA Regs
FC Reg 38(3) FC Regs
DWA Reg 42(3) DWA Regs
ETU Rule 45(4) ETU Scheme
HB Reg 53(3) HB Regs
CTB Reg 42(4) CTB Regs
223 **IS** Reg 62(4) IS Regs
JSA Reg 131(6) JSA Regs
FC Reg 38(4) FC Regs
DWA Reg 42(5) DWA Regs
ETU Rule 45(6) ETU Scheme
HB Reg 53(4) HB Regs
CTB Reg 42(5) CTB Regs
224 R(IS) 15/95

225 **IS** Reg 62(3A) IS Regs
JSA Reg 131(5) JSA Regs
FC Reg 38(3A) FC Regs
DWA Reg 42(4) DWA Regs
ETU Rule 45(5) ETU Scheme
HB Reg 53(3)(b) HB Regs
CTB Reg 42(4)(b) CTB Regs
HB/CTB para C5.47 and Annex
A GM
226 CIS/109/1991
227 **IS** Reg 62(2) IS Regs
JSA Reg 131(2) JSA Regs
FC Reg 38(2) FC Regs
DWA Reg 42(2) DWA Regs
ETU Rule 45(2) ETU Scheme
HB Reg 53(2) HB Regs
CTB Reg 42(2) CTB Regs
228 **HB/CTB** A29/98 page 10
229 R(IS) 7/95
230 CIS/91/1994
231 **IS** Reg 66(1) IS Regs
JSA Reg 135 JSA Regs
FC Reg 42 FC Regs
DWA Reg 46 DWA Regs
ETU Rule 50 ETU Scheme
HB Reg 57 HB Regs
CTB Reg 46 CTB Regs
232 **IS** Reg 67A IS Regs
JSA Reg 137A JSA Regs
FC Reg 43A FC Regs
DWA Reg 48A DWA Regs
ETU Rule 51A ETU Scheme
HB Reg 58A HB Regs
CTB Reg 48A CTB Regs
233 **IS** Reg 67 IS Regs
JSA Reg 137 JSA Regs
FC Reg 43 FC Regs
DWA Reg 48 DWA Regs
ETU Rule 51 ETU Scheme
HB Reg 58(1) HB Regs
CTB Reg 48 CTB Regs
234 Reg 58(2) HB Regs
235 **IS** Reg 32(6A) IS Regs
JSA Reg 97(7) JSA Regs
236 **IS** Reg 29(2B) IS Regs
JSA Reg 94(2B) JSA Regs
237 **IS** Reg 66A IS Regs
JSA Reg 136 JSA Regs
FC Reg 42A FC Regs
DWA Reg 47 DWA Regs
ETU Rule 50 ETU Scheme
HB Reg 57A HB Regs
CTB Reg 47 CTB Regs

238 **IS** Reg 61 IS Regs
JSA Reg 136(2)(b) JSA Regs
FC Reg 37 FC Regs
DWA Reg 41 DWA Regs
ETU Rule 44 ETU Scheme
HB Reg 46 HB Regs
CTB Reg 38 CTB Regs
All Definition of 'last day of the course'

239 **IS** Sch 9 para 36 IS Regs
JSA Sch 7 para 38 JSA Regs
FC Sch 2 para 29 FC Regs
DWA Sch 3 para 29 DWA Regs
ETU Sch 4 para 27 ETU Scheme
HB Sch 4 para 33 HB Regs
CTB Sch 4 para 34 CTB Regs

240 **IS** Reg 40(3A) IS Regs
JSA Reg 103(5) JSA Regs
FC Reg 24(4A) FC Regs
DWA Reg 27(5) DWA Regs
ETU Rule 33(4) ETU Scheme
HB Reg 33(3A) HB Regs
CTB Reg 24(4) CTB Regs

241 **IS** Reg 66A(3) IS Regs
JSA Reg 136(3) JSA Regs
FC Reg 42A(3) FC Regs
DWA Reg 47(3) DWA Regs
ETU Rule 50(3) ETU Scheme
HB Reg 57A(3) HB Regs
CTB Reg 47(3) CTB Regs

242 **IS** Reg 41(6) IS Regs
JSA Reg 104(5) JSA Regs
FC Reg 25(3) FC Regs
DWA Reg 28(3) DWA Regs
ETU Rule 34(3) ETU Scheme
HB Reg 34(4) HB Regs
CTB Reg 25(4) CTB Regs

243 **IS** Reg 29(2A) IS Regs
JSA Reg 94(2A) JSA Regs

244 **IS** Sch 9 para 59 IS Regs
JSA Sch 7 para 57 JSA Regs
FC Sch 2 para 58 FC Regs
DWA Sch 3 para 56 DWA Regs
ETU Sch 4 para 48 ETU Scheme
HB Sch 4 para 63 HB Regs
CTB Sch 4 para 63 CTB Regs

245 **IS** Sch 9 paras 60 and 61 IS Regs
JSA Reg Sch 7 paras 58 and 59 JSA Regs

246 Excluded from definition of 'grant' in:
IS Reg 61 IS Regs
JSA Reg 130 JSA Regs
FC Reg 37 FC Regs
DWA Reg 41 DWA Regs

ETU Rule 44 ETU Scheme
HB Reg 46 HB Regs
CTB Reg 38 CTB Regs

247 R(IS) 16/95

248 **IS** Sch 9 para 25(1)(a) and (2)(b) IS Regs
JSA Sch 7 para 26 JSA Regs
FC Sch 2 para 22(1)(a) and (2)(b) FC Regs
DWA Sch 3 para 22(1)(a) and (2)(b) DWA Regs
HB Sch 4 para 23(1)(a) and (2)(b) HB Regs
CTB Sch 4 para 24(1)(a) and (2)(b) CTB Regs

249 **IS** Sch 9 para 25(2)(a) IS Regs
JSA Sch 7 para 26(2)(a) JSA Regs
FC Sch 2 para 22(2)(a) FC Regs
DWA Sch 3 para 22(2)(a) DWA Regs
HB Sch 4 para 23(2)(a) HB Regs
CTB Sch 4 para 24(2)(a) CTB Regs

250 **IS** Sch 9 para 26 IS Regs
JSA Sch 7 para 27 JSA Regs
FC Sch 2 para 23 FC Regs
DWA Sch 3 para 23 DWA Regs
ETU Sch 4 para 20 ETU Scheme
HB Sch 4 para 24 HB Regs
CTB Sch 4 para 25 CTB Regs

251 **IS** Sch 9 para 25(1)(b) and (2) IS Regs
JSA Sch 7 para 26(1) JSA Regs
FC Sch 2 para 22(1)(b) and (2) FC Regs
DWA Sch 3 para 22(1)(b) and (2) DWA Regs
HB Sch 4 para 23(1)(b) and (2) HB Regs
CTB Sch 4 para 24(1)(b) and (2) CTB Regs

252 **IS** Reg 48(8) IS Regs
JSA Reg 110(8) JSA Regs

253 **IS** Sch 10 para 8(b) IS Regs
JSA Sch 8 para 13(b) JSA Regs
FC Sch 3 para 9(b) FC Regs
DWA Sch 4 para 9(b) DWA Regs
HB Sch 5 para 9(b) HB Regs
CTB Sch 5 para 9(b) CTB Regs

254 **IS** Reg 48(10)(c) and Sch 10 para 22 IS Regs
JSA Sch 7 para 41(1) JSA Regs
FC Sch 2 para 34 FC Regs
DWA Sch 3 para 33 DWA Regs

ETU Sch 4 para 31 ETU Scheme
HB Sch 4 para 34 HB Regs
CTB Sch 4 para 35 CTB Regs
255 IS Sch 9 para 39 IS Regs
JSA Sch 7 para 41(2) JSA Regs
FC Sch 2 para 34 FC Regs
DWA Sch 3 para 33 DWA Regs
ETU Sch 4 para 31 ETU Scheme
HB Sch 4 para 34 HB Regs
CTB Sch 4 para 35 CTB Regs
256 IS Reg 48(9) IS Regs
JSA Reg 110(9) JSA Regs
FC Reg 31(3) FC Regs
DWA Reg 34(3) DWA Regs
ETU Rule 37(3) ETU Scheme
HB/CTB There are no specific
provisions for HB/CTB but such
payments are obviously capital
257 IS Reg 48(10)(a) IS Regs
JSA Reg 110(10) JSA Regs
258 IS Reg 48(10)(b) IS Regs
JSA Reg 110(10)(b) JSA Regs
259 IS Sch 9 para 15 IS Regs
JSA Sch 7 para 15 JSA Regs
FC Sch 2 para 13 FC Regs
DWA Sch 3 para 12 DWA Regs
ETU Sch 4 para 12 ETU Scheme
HB Sch 4 para 13 HB Regs
CTB Sch 4 para 13 CTB Regs
260 IS Sch 9 para 15A IS Regs
JSA Sch 7 para 16 JSA Regs
261 IS Sch 9 paras 15(4) and 36 IS
Regs
JSA Sch 7 paras 15(4) and 38
JSA Regs
FC Sch 2 paras 13(4) and 29 FC
Regs
DWA Sch 3 paras 12(4) and 29
DWA Regs
ETU Sch 4 paras 12(4) and 27
ETU Scheme
HB Sch 4 paras 13(4) and 33 HB
Regs
CTB Sch 4 paras 13(4) and 34
CTB Regs
262 HB/CTB Circular A17/97
263 IS Sch 9 para 21 IS Regs
JSA Sch 7 para 15 JSA Regs
FC Sch 2 para 20 FC Regs
DWA Sch 3 para 20 DWA Regs
ETU Sch 4 para 18 ETU Scheme
HB Sch 4 para 21 HB Regs
CTB Sch 4 para 22 CTB Regs

264 *R v Doncaster MBC ex parte
Boulton* [1992] 25 HLR 195; R(IS)
4/94
265 IS para 31047 AOG
JSA para 33496 AOG
FC/DWA para 51166 AOG
HB/CTB para C3.90 GM
266 IS Sch 9 para 19 IS Regs
JSA Sch 7 para 20 JSA Regs
FC Sch 2 para 19 FC Regs
DWA Sch 3 para 19 DWA Regs
ETU Sch 4 para 17 ETU Scheme
HB Sch 4 para 20 HB Regs
CTB Sch 4 para 20 CTB Regs
267 IS Sch 9 para 18 IS Regs
JSA Sch 7 para 19 JSA Regs
FC Sch 2 para 18 FC Regs
DWA Sch 3 para 18 DWA Regs
ETU Sch 4 para 16 ETU Scheme
HB Sch 4 para 19 HB Regs
CTB Sch 4 para 19 CTB Regs
268 IS Sch 9 para 20 IS Regs
JSA Sch 7 para 21 JSA Regs
FC Sch 2 para 40 FC Regs
DWA Sch 3 para 38 DWA Regs
ETU Sch 4 para 34 ETU Scheme
HB Sch 4 para 42 HB Regs
CTB Sch 4 para 21 CTB Regs
269 All Definition of 'board and
lodging accommodation'
IS Reg 2(1) IS Regs
JSA Reg 1(3) JSA Regs
HB Sch 4 para 42(2) HB Regs
CTB Sch 4 para 21(2) CTB Regs
270 CIS/13059/1996
271 All *CAO v Palfrey and Others, The
Times,* 17 February 1995
IS Reg 48(4) IS Regs
JSA Reg 110(4) JSA Regs
FC Reg 31(4) FC Regs
DWA Reg 34(4) DWA Regs
ETU Rule 37(4) ETU Scheme
HB Reg 40(4) HB Regs
CTB Reg 31(4) CTB Regs
272 *See* CIS/25/1989; CIS/563/1991;
CIS/85/1992 (*Palfrey*)
273 IS Sch 9 para 22(1) IS Regs
JSA Sch 7 para 23 JSA Regs
FC Sch 2 para 16(1) FC Regs
DWA Sch 3 para 16(1) DWA
Regs
ETU Sch 4 para 14(1) ETU
Scheme
HB Sch 4 para 15(1) HB Regs
CTB Sch 4 para 15(1) CTB Regs

274 **IS** Reg 48(4) IS Regs
JSA Reg 110(4) JSA Regs
FC Reg 31(4) FC Regs
DWA Reg 34(4) DWA Regs
ETU Rule 37(4) ETU Scheme
HB Reg 40(4) HB Regs
CTB Reg 31(4) CTB Regs

275 **IS** Sch 9 para 22(1) IS Regs
JSA Sch 7 para 23(2) JSA Regs
FC Sch 2 para 16(1) FC Regs
DWA Sch 3 para 16(1) DWA Regs
ETU Sch 4 para 14(1) ETU Scheme
HB Sch 4 para 15(1) HB Regs
CTB Sch 4 para 15(1) CTB Regs

276 CFC/13/1993

277 **IS** Sch 9 para 22(2) IS Regs
JSA Sch 7 para 23(2) and (3) JSA Regs
FC Sch 2 para 16(2) FC Regs
DWA Sch 3 para 16(2) DWA Regs
ETU Sch 4 para 14(2) ETU Scheme
HB Sch 4 para 15(2) HB Regs
CTB Sch 4 para 15(2) CTB Regs

278 **IS** Reg 53 IS Regs
JSA Reg 116 JSA Regs
FC Reg 36 FC Regs
DWA Reg 40 DWA Regs
ETU Rule 43 ETU Scheme
HB Reg 45 HB Regs
CTB Reg 37 CTB Regs

279 **IS** Reg 32(1) SS(C&P) Regs
JSA Reg 24(7) JSA Regs

280 **HB** Reg 75 HB Regs
CTB Reg 65 CTB Regs

281 **IS** Reg 41(1) IS Regs
JSA Reg 104(1) JSA Regs

282 **FC** Reg 25(1) FC Regs
DWA Reg 28(1) DWA Regs
ETU Rule 34(1) ETU Scheme

283 **HB** Reg 34(1) HB Regs
CTB Reg 25(1) CTB Regs

284 **IS** Reg 29(2)(a) IS Regs
JSA Reg 94(2)(a) JSA Regs
FC Reg 18 FC Regs
DWA Reg 20 DWA Regs
ETU Rule 25 ETU Scheme
HB Reg 25 HB Regs
CTB Reg 17 CTB Regs

285 **IS** Reg 44(1) and (5) IS Regs
JSA Reg 106(1) and (5) JSA Regs
FC Reg 27(1) and (3) FC Regs

DWA Reg 30(1) and (3) DWA Regs
HB Reg 36(2) and (5) HB Regs
CTB Reg 27(2) and (5) CTB Regs

286 **IS** Reg 32(1) IS Regs
JSA Reg 97(1) JSA Regs
FC Reg 18(1) FC Regs
DWA Reg 20(1) DWA Regs
HB Reg 25(1) HB Regs
CTB Reg 17(1) CTB Regs

287 **IS** Reg 41(2) IS Regs
JSA Reg 104(2) JSA Regs
FC Reg 25(2) FC Regs
DWA Reg 28(2) DWA Regs
ETU Rule 34(2) ETU Scheme
HB Reg 34(2) HB Regs
CTB Reg 25(2) CTB Regs

288 **IS** Reg 41(6) IS Regs
JSA Reg 104(5) JSA Regs
FC Reg 25(3) FC Regs
DWA Reg 28(3) DWA Regs
ETU Rule 34(3) ETU Scheme
HB Reg 34(4) HB Regs
CTB Reg 25(4) CTB Regs

289 Regs 41(4) and 48(2) IS Regs

290 **IS** Reg 41(3) IS Regs
JSA Reg 104(3) JSA Regs

291 *R v SBC ex parte Singer* [1973] 1 All ER 931; *R v Oxford County Council ex parte Jack* [1984] 17 HLR 419; *R v West Dorset DC ex parte Poupard* [1988] 20 HLR 295; para C3.118 GM

292 paras C2.09(xix) and 3.118 GM

293 *R v West Dorset DC ex parte Poupard* [1988] 20 HLR 295

294 **IS** Sch 10 para 20 IS Regs
JSA Sch 8 para 25 JSA Regs
FC Sch 3 para 21 FC Regs
DWA Sch 4 para 21 DWA Regs
ETU Sch 5 para 21 ETU Scheme
HB Sch 5 para 21 HB Regs
CTB Sch 5 para 21 CTB Regs

295 **IS** Reg 48(2) IS Regs
JSA Reg 110(2) JSA Regs
FC Reg 31(1) FC Regs
DWA Reg 34(1) DWA Regs
ETU Rule 37(1) ETU Scheme
HB Reg 40(2) HB Regs
CTB Reg 31(2) CTB Regs

296 Regs 41(4) and 48(2) IS Regs

297 **IS** Reg 40(4) and Sch 9 para 15B IS Regs
JSA Regs 103(6) and 98(2)(e) JSA Regs

FC Reg 24(5) FC Regs
DWA Reg 27(4) DWA Regs
ETU Rule 33(5) ETU Scheme
HB Reg 33(4) HB Regs
CTB Reg 24(5) CTB Regs
All Definition of 'occupational pension' in reg 2(1) of each of those regs

298 **IS** Reg 41(2) and Sch 9 para 17 IS Regs
JSA Reg 104(2) and Sch 7 para 18 JSA Regs
FC Reg 25(2) and Sch 2 para 17 FC Regs
DWA Reg 28(2) and Sch 3 para 17 DWA Regs
ETU Rule 34(2) and Sch 4 para 15 ETU Scheme
HB Reg 34(2) and Sch 4 para 16 HB Regs
CTB Reg 25(2) and Sch 4 para 16 CTB Regs

299 **IS** Sch 9 para 29 IS Regs; para 33240 AOG
JSA Sch 7 para 30 JSA Regs

300 **IS** Sch 9 para 30(a)-(d) IS Regs
JSA Sch 7 para 31 JSA Regs

301 **FC** Sch 2 para 25A FC Regs
DWA Sch 3 para 25A DWA Regs
ETU Sch 4 para 22A ETU Scheme
HB Sch 4 para 28 HB Regs
CTB Sch 4 para 29 CTB Regs

302 **IS** Sch 9 para 30ZA IS Regs
JSA Sch 7 para 31A JSA Regs
FC Sch 2 para 25A FC Regs
DWA Sch 3 para 25A DWA Regs
ETU Sch 4 para 22A ETU Scheme
HB Sch 4 para 28 HB Regs
CTB Sch 4 para 29 CTB Regs

303 **FC** Sch 2 para 55 FC Regs
DWA Sch 3 para 53 DWA Regs

304 **IS** Sch 9 para 11 IS Regs
JSA Sch 7 para 12 JSA Regs
FC Sch 2 para 9 FC Regs
DWA Sch 3 para 9 DWA Regs
HB Sch 4 para 10 HB Regs
CTB Sch 4 para 10 CTB Regs

305 **IS** Sch 9 para 2 IS Regs
JSA Sch 7 para 2 JSA Regs
FC Sch 2 para 2 FC Regs
DWA Sch 3 para 2 DWA Regs
ETU Sch 4 para 2 ETU Scheme
HB Sch 4 para 2 HB Regs
CTB Sch 4 para 2 CTB Regs

306 **IS** Sch 9 para 21 IS Regs
JSA Sch 7 para 22 JSA Regs
FC Sch 2 para 20 FC Regs
DWA Sch 3 para 20 DWA Regs
ETU Sch 4 para 18 ETU Scheme
HB Sch 4 para 21 HB Regs
CTB Sch 4 para 22 CTB Regs

307 para C3.73(xiii) GM

308 *See* para 63596 AOG on related provisions for child benefits

309 **HB/CTB** Circular A17/97

310 **FC** Sch 2 para 12 FC Regs
DWA Sch 3 para 11A DWA Regs
ETU Sch 4 para 11 ETU Scheme

311 **IS** Sch 9 para 51 IS Regs
JSA Sch 7 para 50 JSA Regs
FC Sch 2 para 48 FC Regs
DWA Sch 3 para 45 DWA Regs
ETU Sch 4 para 39 ETU Scheme
HB Sch 4 para 49 HB Regs
CTB Sch 4 para 48 CTB Regs

312 **IS** Sch 9 para 13 IS Regs
JSA Sch 7 para 14 JSA Regs
FC Sch 2 para 11 FC Regs
DWA Sch 3 para 11 DWA Regs
ETU Sch 4 para 10 ETU Scheme
HB Sch 4 para 11 HB Regs
CTB Sch 4 para 11 CTB Regs

313 **IS** Sch 9 para 43 IS Regs
JSA Sch 7 para 43 JSA Regs
FC Sch 2 para 38 FC Regs
DWA Sch 3 para 37 DWA Regs
ETU Sch 4 para 33 ETU Scheme
HB Sch 4 para 38 HB Regs
CTB Sch 4 para 40 CTB Regs

314 **IS** Sch 9 para 28 IS Regs
JSA Sch 7 para 29 JSA Regs
FC Sch 2 para 25 FC Regs
DWA Sch 3 para 25 DWA Regs
ETU Sch 4 para 22 ETU Scheme
HB Sch 4 para 26 HB Regs
CTB Sch 4 para 27 CTB Regs

315 **IS** Sch 9 para 58 IS Regs
JSA Sch 7 para 56 JSA Regs
FC Sch 2 para 57 FC Regs
DWA Sch 3 para 55 DWA Regs
ETU Sch 4 para 47 ETU Scheme
HB Sch 4 para 67 HB Regs
CTB Sch 4 para 62 CTB Regs

316 **IS** Sch 9 para 27 IS Regs
JSA Sch 7 para 28 JSA Regs
FC Sch 2 para 24 FC Regs
DWA Sch 3 para 24 DWA Regs

ETU Sch 4 para 21 ETU Scheme
HB Sch 4 para 25 HB Regs
CTB Sch 4 para 26 CTB Regs
317 **IS** Sch 9 para 10 IS Regs
JSA Sch 7 para 11 JSA Regs
FC Sch 2 para 8 FC Regs
DWA Sch 3 para 8 DWA Regs
ETU Sch 4 para 8 ETU Scheme
HB Sch 4 para 9 HB Regs
CTB Sch 4 para 9 CTB Regs
318 **IS** Sch 9 para 23 IS Regs
JSA Sch 7 para 24 JSA Regs
FC Sch 2 para 21 FC Regs
DWA Sch 3 para 21 DWA Regs
ETU Sch 4 para 19 ETU Scheme
HB Sch 4 para 22 HB Regs
CTB Sch 4 para 23 CTB Regs
319 **IS** Sch 9 para 24 IS Regs
JSA Sch 7 para 25 JSA Regs
FC Sch 2 para 30 FC Regs
DWA Sch 3 para 30 DWA Regs
ETU Sch 4 para 28 ETU Scheme
HB Sch 4 para 32 HB Regs
CTB Sch 4 para 33 CTB Regs
320 **IS** Sch 9 para 48 IS Regs
JSA Sch 7 para 47 JSA Regs
FC Sch 2 para 44 FC Regs
DWA Sch 3 para 42 DWA Regs
ETU Sch 4 para 36 ETU Scheme
HB Sch 4 para 44 HB Regs
CTB Sch 4 para 43 CTB Regs
321 **IS** Sch 9 para 49 IS Regs
JSA Sch 7 para 48 JSA Regs
FC Sch 2 para 45 FC Regs
DWA Sch 3 para 43 DWA Regs
ETU Sch 4 para 37 ETU Scheme
HB Sch 4 para 45 HB Regs
CTB Sch 4 para 44 CTB Regs
322 **IS** Sch 9 para 50 IS Regs
JSA Sch 7 para 49 JSA Regs
FC Sch 2 para 46 FC Regs
DWA Sch 3 para 44 DWA Regs
ETU Sch 4 para 38 ETU Scheme
HB Sch 4 para 46 HB Regs
CTB Sch 4 para 45 CTB Regs
323 **HB** Sch 4 para 17 HB Regs
CTB Sch 4 para 17 CTB Regs
324 **HB** Sch 3 para 9 HB Regs
CTB Sch 3 para 9 CTB Regs
325 **HB** Sch 4 para 18 HB Regs
CTB Sch 4 para 18 CTB Regs
326 **HB** Sch 3 para 9 HB Regs
CTB Sch 3 para 9 CTB Regs

327 **IS** Sch 9 para 13 IS Regs
JSA Sch 7 para 14 JSA Regs
FC Sch 2 para 11 FC Regs
DWA Sch 3 para 11 DWA Regs
ETU Sch 4 para 10 ETU Scheme
HB Sch 4 para 11 HB Regs
CTB Sch 4 para 11 CTB Regs
328 **IS** Sch 9 paras 62, 63 and 65 IS Regs
JSA Sch 7 paras 60, 61 and 63 JSA Regs
FC Sch 2 paras 59, 60 and 62 FC Regs
DWA Sch 3 paras 57, 58 and 60 DWA Regs
ETU Sch 4 paras 49, 50 and 52 ETU Scheme
HB Sch 4 paras 64, 65 and 68 HB Regs
CTB Sch 4 paras 64, 65 and 68 CTB Regs
329 **IS** Sch 9 paras 67 and 68 IS Regs
JSA Sch 7 paras 65 and 66 JSA Regs
FC Sch 2 paras 63 and 64 FC Regs
DWA Sch 3 paras 61 and 62 DWA Regs
HB Sch 4 paras 69 and 70 HB Regs
CTB Sch 4 paras 68 and 69 CTB Regs
330 **IS** Sch 9 paras 62 and 64 IS Regs
JSA Sch 7 paras 60 and 62 JSA Regs
FC Sch 2 paras 59 and 61 FC Regs
DWA Sch 3 paras 57 and 59 DWA Regs
ETU Sch 4 paras 49 and 51 ETU Scheme
HB Sch 4 paras 64 and 66 HB Regs
CTB Sch 4 paras 64 and 66 CTB Regs
331 **FC** Reg 31(7) FC Regs
DWA Reg 34(7) DWA Regs
ETU Rule 37(6) ETU Scheme
HB Reg 40(7) HB Regs
CTB Reg 31(7) CTB Regs
332 **IS** Regs 39C and 39D IS Regs
JSA Regs 102C and 102D JSA Regs

6. **Notional income**
    333 **IS** Reg 42(1) IS Regs
        JSA Reg 105(1) JSA Regs
        FC Reg 26(1) FC Regs
        DWA Reg 29(1) DWA Regs
        ETU Rule 35(1) ETU Scheme
        HB Reg 35(1) HB Regs
        CTB Reg 26(1) CTB Regs
    334 paras 33608-16 AOG; *see also*
        CIS/15052/1996
    335 CSIS/57/1992
    336 **IS** Reg 42(2) IS Regs
        JSA Reg 105(2) JSA Regs
        FC Reg 26(2) FC Regs
        DWA Reg 29(2) DWA Regs
        ETU Rule 35(2) ETU Scheme
        HB Reg 35(2) HB Regs
        CTB Reg 26(2) CTB Regs
    337 **IS** Reg 42(2A) IS Regs
        JSA Reg 105(3) JSA Regs
        FC Reg 26(2A) FC Regs
        DWA Reg 29(2A) DWA Regs
        ETU Rule 35(2) ETU Scheme
        HB Reg 35(2A) HB Regs
        CTB Reg 26(2A) CTB Regs
    338 paras 33608-16 AOG
    339 CIS/15052/1996, para 11
    340 **IS** Reg 42(3) IS Regs
        JSA Reg 105(6) JSA Regs
    341 **IS** Reg 42(3A) and (3B) IS Regs
        JSA Reg 105(7)(a), (8) and (9)
        JSA Regs
    342 CIS/15052/1996, para 10
    343 **IS** Reg 70(2)(b) IS Regs
        JSA Regs 147-149 JSA Regs
    344 **IS** Reg 42(5) IS Regs
        JSA Reg 105(12) JSA Regs
    345 Reg 2 SS(PAOR) Regs
    346 **IS** Reg 42(4)(a)(ii), (4A) and (9)
        IS Regs
        JSA Reg 105(10)(a)(ii) JSA Regs
        FC Reg 26(3)(a) FC Regs
        DWA Reg 29(3)(a) DWA Regs
        ETU Rule 35(6)(a) ETU Scheme
        HB Reg 35(3)(a) and (8) HB Regs
        CTB Reg 26(3)(a) and (8) CTB
        Regs
    347 CFC/13585/1996
    348 AM(AOG)77, 29 April 1998
    349 **IS** Reg 42(4) and (4ZA) IS Regs
        JSA Reg 105(10) and (10A) JSA
        Regs
    350 **IS** Reg 42(4)(b) IS Regs
        JSA Reg 105(10)(b) JSA Regs
        FC Reg 26(3)(b) FC Regs

    DWA Reg 29(3)(b) DWA Regs
    ETU Rule 35(6)(b) ETU Scheme
    HB Reg 35(3)(b) HB Regs
    CTB Reg 26(3)(b) CTB Regs
    351 **IS** Reg 42(6) IS Regs; CIS/191/
        1991
        JSA Reg 105(13) JSA Regs
        FC Reg 26(4) FC Regs
        DWA Reg 29(4) DWA Regs
        ETU Rule 35(7) ETU Scheme
        HB Reg 35(5) HB Regs
        CTB Reg 26(5) CTB Regs
    352 R(SB) 13/86
    353 R(SB) 13/86
    354 **IS** Reg 42(6) IS Regs
        JSA Reg 105(13) JSA Regs
        FC Reg 26(4) FC Regs
        DWA Reg 29(4) DWA Regs
        ETU Rule 35(7) ETU Scheme
        HB Reg 35(5) HB Regs
        CTB Reg 26(5) CTB Regs
    355 R(IS) 12/92
    356 *Sharrock v CAO*, (CA) 26 March
        1991; CIS/93/1991
    357 CIS/93/1991
    358 CIS/422/1992
    359 CIS/701/1994
    360 CIS/422/1992
    361 CIS/701/1994
    362 s1(3)(a) Carers (Recognition and
        Services) Act 1995 excludes
        those who care 'by virtue of a
        contract of employment or other
        contract' which according to
        policy guidance issued by the
        Department of Health means,
        'anyone who is providing
        personal assistance for payment
        either in cash or in kind'.
    363 CIS/147/1993
    364 **FC** Reg 14(2A) FC Regs
        ETU Rule 20(3) ETU Scheme

Chapter 49

· ·

Capital

This chapter explains how capital affects your entitlement to any means-tested benefit. It covers:
1. The capital limit (p2:442)
2. Whose capital counts (p2:443)
3. What counts as capital (p2:443)
4. Disregarded capital (p2:448)
5. Notional capital (p2:455)
6. How capital is valued (p2:463)

How much capital you have may affect your entitlement to the following means-tested benefits:
- income support (IS);
- income-based jobseeker's allowance (JSA);
- family credit (FC);
- disability working allowance (DWA);
- earnings top-up (ETU);
- housing benefit (HB); *and*
- council tax benefit (CTB).

The same rules which apply to the treatment of capital when claiming FC/DWA, and the treatment of FC/DWA as capital when claiming other benefits, will also apply to the new tax credits which will replace FC/DWA from October 1999 (see Chapter 23).

Similar rules on the treatment of capital, and different capital limits apply to social fund payments (see Chapter 30), grants and loans (see Chapter 31) and certain health benefits (see Chapter 29). The different rules are explained in those chapters.

If you get IS or income-based JSA, you do not need to work out your capital again for HB and CTB purposes because you receive your maximum HB (see p1:519) or CTB (see p1:574),[1] less any deductions for non-dependants (see pp1:525 and 1:576). There are no capital rules for any of the non-means-tested benefits. Your entitlement to any non-means-tested benefit is therefore not affected by any capital you may have.

1. **The capital limit**

If you have over £8,000 (IS, income-based JSA, FC and ETU)[2] or £16,000 (DWA, HB and CTB)[3] you are not entitled to benefit (but for CTB, see p1:571 for second adult rebate).

Different capital limits apply if you live in a residential or nursing care home (see below).

If you have up to £3,000, it is ignored and does not affect your weekly benefit at all. If you have between £3,000.01 and £8,000 (IS, income-based JSA, FC and ETU)/£16,000 (DWA, HB and CTB), you may be entitled to benefit but some income from your capital is assumed.[4] This is known as tariff income (see p2:415).

Some capital is disregarded (see p2:448), but you may also be treated as having some capital which you do not actually possess (see p2:455).

There are some important differences in the rules on capital for urgent cases payments under the IS and income-based JSA schemes (see p2:219).

Residential care

There are higher capital limits if you live permanently in residential or similar accommodation (see below). For IS, income-based JSA and HB (but not for FC/DWA and ETU), tariff income starts at £10,000 (instead of £3,000) and the upper limit is £16,000 (for HB and DWA that is the limit even if you are not in residential care). You cannot claim CTB if you are permanently in residential or nursing care because you will not then be liable for council tax.

For IS and income-based JSA[5] the higher limits apply if you live permanently in:
- residential care or a nursing home and in either case you are given board and personal care because of:
  - old age;
  - disablement;
  - past or present dependence on alcohol or drugs; *or*
  - past or present mental disorder;
- residential accommodation. For what is meant by residential accommodation see p2:167, but note that for the higher capital rules the exceptions for people under 18 or for people not receiving board do not apply;
- Abbeyfield Society homes; *or*
- a home provided under the Polish Resettlement Act in which you are receiving personal care because of:
  - old age;
  - disablement;

- past or present dependence on alcohol or drugs;
- past or present mental disorder; *or*
- a terminal illness.

Note that you are treated as living permanently in one of these homes for periods of absence of up to 13 weeks. However, if you are over pensionable age or (in some cases) were getting supplementary benefit as a residential care home boarder before 27 July 1987, it can be up to 52 weeks.

For HB[6] the higher limits apply, broadly speaking, if you live permanently in one of the limited categories of accommodation referred to on p2:176. Some temporary absences (see p2:515) are again ignored.

2. **Whose capital counts**

Your partner's capital is added to yours.[7] Your child's capital does not count as belonging to you,[8] but if it is over £3,000 you will not get benefit for that child[9] (although, for IS, income-based JSA, HB and CTB, the ordinary or lone parent rate of the family premium is still payable – see p2:323), in which case any income of the child will not be counted as yours either.[10] However, maintenance paid to, or for, a child does count as yours.[11] The rules used to work out your capital also apply to your child's capital.[12] There are no rules on the treatment of a child's capital for ETU purposes, because families with children cannot apply for ETU (see Chapter 24).

3. **What counts as capital**

The term 'capital' is not defined. In general, it means lump sum or one-off payments rather than a series of payments.[13] It includes, for example, savings, property and redundancy payments. It also includes any payments of child maintenance bonus[14] (see p2:598) or back to work bonus[15] (see p2:588).

Capital payments can normally be distinguished from income because they are not payable in respect of any specified period or periods, and they do not form nor are intended to form part of a regular series of payments[16] (although capital can be paid by instalments).

However, some capital is treated as income (see p2:416), and some income is treated as capital (see p2:447).

Savings

Your savings generally count as capital – eg, cash you have at home, premium bonds, stocks and shares, unit trusts, and money in a bank account or building society.

Your savings from past earnings can only be treated as capital when all relevant debts, including tax liabilities, have been deducted.[17] Savings from other past income (including social security benefits) will be treated as capital (see p2:452). There is no provision for disregarding money put aside to pay bills.[18] If you have savings just below the capital limit, it may be best to pay bills for gas, electricity, telephone etc by monthly standing order, or by use of a budget account, to prevent your capital going above the limit.

Fixed-term investments

Capital held in fixed-term investments counts. However, if in reality it is presently unobtainable, it may have little or no value (but see p2:464 for jointly held capital). If you can convert the investment into a realisable form, sell your interest, or raise a loan through a reputable bank using the asset as security, its value counts. If it takes time to produce evidence about the nature and value of the investment, you may be able to get an interim payment for IS, income-based JSA, FC or DWA (see p2:499) or HB[19] (see p1:543) or a crisis loan from the social fund (see p1:667).

Property and land

Any property or land which you own counts as capital. Many types of property are disregarded (see p2:448). See also proprietary estoppel – p2:445.

Loans

A loan usually counts as money you possess. However, a loan granted on condition that you only use the interest but do not touch the capital should not be counted as part of your capital because the capital element has never been at your disposal.[20] Where you have been paid money to be used for a particular purpose on condition that the money must be returned if not used in that way, it should not be treated as part of your capital.[21] Where you have bought a property on behalf of someone else who is paying the mortgage,[22] or where you are holding money in your bank account on behalf of another person which is to be returned to them at a future date,[23] the capital should not count as yours.

For HB and CTB, some loans might be treated as income even though paid as a lump sum (see p2:417).

Trusts

A trust is a way of owning an asset. In theory, the asset is split into two notional parts: the legal title owned by the trustee, and the beneficial interest owned by the beneficiary. A trustee can never have use of the asset, only the responsibility of looking after it. An adult beneficiary, on the other hand, can ask for the asset at any time. Anything can be held on trust – eg, money, houses, shares etc.

If you are the adult beneficiary of:
- a non-discretionary trust, you can obtain the asset from the trustee at any time. You effectively own the asset, and so its market value counts as your capital;
- a discretionary trust, you cannot insist on receiving payments from the trust. Payments are at the discretion of the trustee within the terms of the trust. Any payments made are treated in full as income or capital depending on the nature of the payment. The trust asset itself would not normally count as your capital because you cannot demand payment (of either income or capital);
- a trust which gives you the right to receive payments in the future (eg, on reaching 25). This is a right that has a present capital value, unless disregarded (see p2:452).

If you have a life interest (or, in Scotland, a life rent) only in an asset (ie, if you have the right to enjoy an asset in your life time, but the asset will pass on to someone else when you die), the value of your right to receive income is disregarded[24] (see p2:452), but not the income itself if you get any.

If the beneficiary is under 18, even with a non-discretionary trust, s/he has no right to payment until s/he is 18 (or later if that is what the trust stipulates). Her/his interest may nevertheless have a present value.[25]

If you hold an asset as a trustee, it is not part of your capital. You are only a trustee either if someone gives you an asset on the express condition that you hold it for someone else (or use it for their benefit), or if you have expressed the clearest intention that your own asset is for someone else's benefit, and renounced its use for yourself[26] (assets other than money may need to be transferred in a particular way to the trust).

It is not enough to only *intend* to give someone an asset. However, in the case of property and land, proprietary estoppel may apply. This means that if you lead someone to believe that you are transferring your interest in some property to them, but fail to do so (eg, it is never properly conveyed), and they act on the belief that they have ownership (eg, they improve or repair it, or take on a mortgage), it would then be unfair on them were they to lose out if you insisted that you were still the owner.[27] In this case, you can argue the capital asset has been transferred to them, and you are like a trustee. Thus you can insist that it is not your capital asset, but theirs, when claiming benefit.

If money (or another asset) is given to you to be used for a special purpose, it may be possible to argue that it should not count as your capital. This is called a purpose trust.[28]

Trust funds from personal injury compensation

Where a trust fund has been set up out of money paid because of a personal injury, the value of the trust fund is ignored.[29] Although the regulations refer to 'personal injury to the claimant' only, the capital value of the trust fund is ignored regardless of whether the money was paid in respect of you, your partner (if any), or your children.[30]

It is not necessary for the trust to be set up by a formal deed. For these purposes, personal injuries compensation held by the Court of Protection (because the injured person is incapable of managing her/his own affairs) and administered by that Court and/or the Public Trustee is treated in the same way as a trust.[31] The important point is that the person who is awarded the compensation should not be able to have any direct access to it.

In this context, 'personal injury' includes not only accidental and criminal injuries, but also any disease and injury suffered as a result of a disease. Thus, a trust fund for a child who had both legs amputated following meningitis and septicaemia could be disregarded for the purposes of the parent's claim.[32]

Any payments actually made to you from these trusts may count in full as income or capital depending on the nature of the payment.[33] However, trustees may have a discretion to use such funds to purchase items that would normally be disregarded as capital such as personal possessions (see p2:450) – eg, a wheelchair, car, new furniture – or to arrange payments that would normally be disregarded as income – eg, for IS, income-based JSA, HB and CTB, ineligible housing costs. Similarly, they may have discretion to clear debts or pay for a holiday, leisure items or educational or medical needs. See p2:412 for the treatment of voluntary payments and pp2:412 and 2:423 for the treatment of payments made to third parties. Note that the notional income and capital rules (see pp2:421 and 2:455) cannot apply to trusts or funds administered by the court which, in either case, have been set up as a result of a personal injury.

If there is no trust, or until one can be set up, the whole of the compensation payment counts as capital, even if the money is held by your solicitor.[34]

Infant funds in court[35]

Where damages are awarded to minors (ie, under the age of 18) in respect of personal injury or compensation for the death of one or both parents, the money may be paid into a special fund to be administered by, and at the discretion of, the court. The same rules on capital disregards, notional income, and treatment of payments apply to these funds as to other funds from personal injuries administered by the court (see p2:466).

Income treated as capital

Certain payments which appear to be income are nevertheless treated as capital. These are:[36]
- an advance of earnings or loan from your employer;*
- holiday pay which is not payable until more than four weeks after your employment ends or is interrupted;*
- income tax refunds;*
- income from capital (eg, interest on a building society account) and income from rents on properties let to tenants (see p2:414). However, income from disregarded property listed on p2:448 (eg, a home you are trying to move into or sell, or which is occupied by elderly relatives) and income from business assets or personal injury trusts counts as income not capital;
- for IS, income-based JSA, HB and CTB, a lump sum or 'bounty' paid to you not more than once a year as a part-time firefighter or part-time member of a lifeboat crew, or as an auxiliary coastguard or member of the Territorial Army – for FC, DWA and ETU this will normally count as earnings;[37]
- irregular (one-off) charitable payments;*
- for IS only, the part, or the whole, of a compensation payment for loss of employment that is treated as capital under the IS rules (see p2:393);[38]
- for IS and income-based JSA only, a discharge grant paid on release from prison;
- for IS and income-based JSA only, arrears of residence order (in Scotland, custody) payments from a local authority (see p2:411);
- for FC and DWA only, irregular maintenance payments (see p2:312).[39]

* Except:
- for IS, in the case of people involved in, or returning to work after, a trade dispute; *or*
- for income-based JSA, when it is paid to someone involved in a trade dispute or, if paid in consequence of the dispute, to a member of her/his family (see p2:187).

Any income treated as capital is disregarded as income.[40]

4. **Disregarded capital**

Your home

If you own the home you normally live in, its value is ignored.[41] Your home includes any garage, garden, outbuildings and land, together with any premises that you do not occupy as your home but which it is impractical or unreasonable to sell separately – eg, croft land.[42] If you own more than one property, only the value of the one normally occupied is disregarded under this rule.[43]

The value of property can be disregarded even if you do not live in it, in the following circumstances.

- **If you have left your former home following a marriage or relationship breakdown**, the value of the property is ignored for six months from the date you left. It may also be disregarded for longer if any of the steps below are taken. For HB and CTB, if it is occupied by your former partner who is a lone parent its value is ignored as long as s/he lives there.[44]

- **If you have sought legal advice or have started legal proceedings in order to occupy property** as your home, its value is ignored for six months from the date you first took either of these steps.[45] The six months can be extended, if it is reasonable to do so, where you need longer to move into the property.

- **If you are taking reasonable steps to dispose of any property**, its value is ignored for six months from the date you *first* took such steps.[46] This may include a period before you claimed benefit.[47] The definition of 'property' here includes land on its own, even if there are no buildings on it.[48] Putting the property in the hands of an estate agent or getting in touch with a prospective purchaser should constitute 'reasonable steps'.[49] The test for what constitutes 'reasonable steps' is an objective one. Any period when the house is advertised at an unrealistic sale price would not count.[50] But if you need longer to dispose of the property, the disregard can continue for years if it is reasonable – eg, where a husband or wife attempts to realise their share in a former matrimonial home but the court orders that it should not be sold until the youngest child reaches a certain age.

- **If you are carrying out essential repairs or alterations** which are needed so that you can occupy a property as your home, the value of the property is ignored for six months from the date you first began to carry them out.[51] If you cannot move into the property within that period because the work is not finished, its value can be disregarded for as long as is reasonable.

- **If you sell your home** and intend to use the money from the sale to buy another home, the capital is ignored for six months from the date of the sale.[52] This also applies even if you do not actually own the home but, for a price, you surrender your tenancy rights to a landlord.[53] If you need longer to complete a purchase, the authorities can continue to ignore the capital if it is reasonable to do so. You do not have to have decided within the six months to buy a *particular* property. It is sufficient if you intend to use the proceeds to buy *some* other home although your 'intention' must involve more than a mere 'hope' or 'aspiration'.[54] There must be an element of 'certainty' which may be shown by evidence of a practical commitment to another purchase, although this need not involve any binding obligation.[55] If you intend to use only part of the proceeds of sale to buy another home, only that part is disregarded even if, for example, you have put the rest of the money aside to renovate your new home.[56]

- **If you have acquired a house or flat for occupation** as your home but have not yet moved in, its value is ignored if you intend to live there within six months.[57] If you cannot move in by then the value of the property can be ignored for as long as seems reasonable.
- **If your home is damaged or you lose it altogether**, any payment, including compensation, which you intend to use for its repair, or for acquiring another home, is ignored for a period of six months, or longer if it is reasonable to do so.[58]
- **If you have taken out a loan or been given money for the express purpose of essential repairs and improvements** to your home, it is ignored for six months, or longer if it is reasonable to do so.[59] If it is a condition of the loan that the loan must be returned if the improvements are not carried out, you should argue that it should be ignored altogether.[60]
- **If you have deposited money with a housing association as a condition of occupying your home**, this is ignored indefinitely.[61] If money which was deposited for this purpose is now to be used to buy another home, this is ignored for six months, or longer if reasonable, in order to allow you to complete the purchase.[62]
- **Grants made to local authority tenants to buy a home or do repairs/ alterations** to it can be ignored for up to 26 weeks, or longer if reasonable, to allow completion of the purchase or the repairs/alterations.[63]
- **For ETU only, if you have moved into a pilot scheme area** (see p1:499), the value of the home you lived in outside the area will be ignored for six months from the date of your application for ETU[64] (but its value may not be ignored for more than six months under this particular rule). If you also own the home you have moved into, its value should also be disregarded.

When considering whether to increase the period of any disregard, all the circumstances should be considered – particularly your and your family's personal circumstances, any efforts made by you to use or dispose of the home[65] (if relevant) and the general state of the market (if relevant). In practice, periods of around 18 months are not considered unusual.

It is possible for property to be ignored under more than one of the above paragraphs in succession.[66]

Some income generated from property which is disregarded is ignored (see p2:414).

The home of a partner or relative

The value of a house is also ignored if it is occupied wholly or partly as their home by:[67]

- *either* your partner[68] – ie, your husband/wife, provided you are both still treated as living in the same household (see p2:114) or your cohabitee, provided you are still treated as living together as husband and wife (see p2:115);

  or a relative of yours, or any member of your family;

  who in either case, is aged 60 or over or is incapacitated (see below);
- your former partner from whom you are not estranged or divorced. This means your husband/wife where you are not still treated as living in the same household or your former cohabitee where you are not still treated as living together as husband and wife;
- for HB and CTB only, your former partner from whom you are estranged or divorced if s/he is a lone parent.[69]

'Incapacitated' is not defined, but guidance suggests it refers to someone who is getting an incapacity or disability benefit, or who is sufficiently incapacitated to qualify for one of those benefits.[70] However, you should argue for a broader interpretation, if necessary. For FC, DWA and ETU, the relative must have been incapacitated throughout the 13 weeks before you claim.[71]

'Relative' includes: a parent, son, daughter, step-parent/son/daughter, or parent/son/daughter-in-law; brother or sister; or a partner of any of these people; or a grandparent or grandchild, uncle, aunt, nephew or niece.[72] It also includes half-brothers and sisters and adopted children.[73]

Personal possessions

All personal possessions, including items such as jewellery, furniture or a car, are ignored unless you have bought them in order to be able to claim or get more benefit[74] (in which case the sale value, rather than the purchase price, is counted as actual capital, and the difference is treated as notional capital[75] – see p2:455).

Compensation for damage to, or the loss of, any personal possessions, which is to be used for their repair or replacement is ignored for six months, or longer if reasonable.[76]

Business assets

If you are self-employed, your business assets are ignored for as long as you continue to work in that business. Guidance for IS, income-based JSA, FC, DWA and ETU suggests that, as little as half an hour's work a week may be sufficient.[77] If you cannot work because of physical or mental illness, but intend to work in the business when you are able, the disregard operates for 26 weeks, or for longer if reasonable in the circumstances.[78] If you stop working in the business, you are allowed a reasonable time to sell these assets without their value affecting your benefit. For FC, DWA and ETU, if you have sold a business asset but intend to reinvest the proceeds in that business within 13 weeks (or longer if reasonable) the money is ignored.[79] It is sometimes difficult to distinguish between personal and business assets. The test is whether the assets are 'part of the fund employed and risked in the business'.[80] Note that letting out a single house does not constitute a business.[81] For the treatment of business assets if you are taking part in the self-employment route under the Employment Option of the New Deal, see p2:454.

Tax rebates

Tax rebates for the tax relief on interest on a mortgage or loan obtained for buying your home or carrying out repairs or improvements are ignored.[82]

Personal pension schemes and retirement annuity contracts

The value of a fund held under a personal pension scheme or retirement annuity is ignored.[83]

Insurance policy and annuity surrender values

The surrender value of any life assurance or endowment policy is ignored. Note that the life assurance aspect need not be the sole or even the main aspect of the policy (although the other features of any policy may still be considered under the actual or notional income and capital rules – see pp2:443 and 2:455).[84] The surrender value of any annuity is also ignored.[85] Any payment under the annuity counts as income[86] (but see p2:417 for when this is ignored).

Personal injuries trust funds

The value of a trust fund or fund administered by the court and set up out of money paid because of personal injury is ignored (see p2:451).

Future interests in property

A future interest in most kinds of property is ignored.[87] A future interest is one which will only revert to you, or become yours for the first time, when some future event occurs.

However, this does not include a freehold or leasehold interest in property which has been let *by you* to tenants. If you did not let the property to the tenant (eg, because the tenancy was entered into before you bought the property), then your interest in the property should be ignored as a future interest in the normal way. In addition, a commissioner has suggested that if you grant someone an '*irrevocable* licence' to occupy property, your interest in that property is a future one and should be ignored.[88]

An example of a future interest is where someone else has a life interest (see p2:455) in a fund and you are only entitled after that person has died.

The right to receive a payment in the future

If you know you will receive a payment in the future, you could sell your right to that payment at any time so it has a market value and therefore constitutes an actual capital resource. The value of this is ignored where it is a right to receive:

- income under a life interest or, in Scotland, a life rent.[89] When the income is actually paid, it counts in full (see p2:415);
- any earnings or income which are ignored because they are frozen abroad (see pp2:389 and 2:420);[90]
- any outstanding instalments where capital is being paid by instalments (see p2:416);[91]
- an occupational or a personal pension;[92]
- any rent if you are not the freeholder or leaseholder;[93]
- any payment under an annuity (see p2:417);[94]
- any payment under a trust fund that is disregarded (see p2:445).[95]

Benefits and other payments

Arrears of certain benefits are ignored for 52 weeks after they are paid.[96] These are attendance allowance (or, for FC, DWA and ETU only, an equivalent benefit paid because of a war or work injury), mobility supplement, disability living allowance (DLA), income-based JSA, IS, FC, DWA, ETU, HB and CTB (as well as, formerly, supplementary benefit, family income supplement and mobility allowance which have now been replaced by IS, FC and DLA), or concessionary payments made instead of any of these, certain war widows' payments,[97] and refunds on council tax or, formerly (except for ETU), community charge liability.[98]

For IS, any backdated payments of IS, HB and CTB made once the Home Office has accepted you are a refugee (see p2:222) are ignored for 52 weeks from the date of receipt.[99] The same rule also applies in relation to backdated payments of IS and HB (for HB)[100] and IS and CTB (for CTB).[101] For special capital rules and urgent cases, see p2:217.

For FC, DWA, ETU, HB and CTB only, any child maintenance bonus (see p2:598) or back to work bonus (see p2:588) is ignored for 52 weeks from the date you receive it.[102]

The following payments are ignored for 52 weeks from receipt:
- fares to hospital;[103]
- payments in place of milk tokens or vitamins;[104]
- payments to assist prison visits;[105]
- for FC and DWA only, payments made by the Secretary of State as compensation for a reduction in your child support maintenance assessment;[106]

For the treatment of payments for taking part in a New Deal programme, see p2:454.

Social fund payments are ignored indefinitely.[107]

A payment to a disabled person under the Disabled Persons (Employment) Act 1944 or the Employment and Training Act 1973 (other than a training allowance or training bonus) to assist with employment, or a local authority payment to assist blind homeworkers is ignored.[108]

Any payments made to holders of the Victoria or George Cross are ignored.[109]

Compensatory payments made by the Secretary of State for the loss of entitlement to HB are ignored indefinitely for all benefits, as are, for IS/FC/DWA/HB/CTB only, compensatory payments for the loss of entitlement to supplementary benefit or housing benefit supplement as a consequence of the 1988 changes to the means-tested benefits scheme.[110]

Payments by social services

A payment under section 17 of the Children Act 1989 from a social services department or, in Scotland, a payment from a social work department under section 12 of the Social Work (Scotland) Act 1968 (see Appendix 1), is ignored. 'Section 24' (or, in Scotland, 'section 24 or 26') payments made by local authorities to young people who have previously been in care or been looked after by social services are also ignored. But if you or your partner are involved in a trade dispute or, for IS, it is paid during the first 15 days following your return to work after the dispute, it counts as income for IS and income-based JSA.[111]

Charitable payments

Any payment in kind by a charity is ignored.[112] All payments from the Macfarlane Trusts, the Fund, the Eileen Trust and either of the Independent Living Funds (see p1:679) are ignored.[113] Payments from the Macfarlane Trusts, the Fund or the Eileen Trust do not have to be declared for HB and CTB at all, or to the Benefits Agency, if they are kept separately from the claimant's other capital and income.[114] Certain payments from money that originally came from any of the three Macfarlane Trusts, the Fund or the Eileen Trust are also ignored – the rules are the same as for income (see p2:412).

Payments to jurors and witnesses

Any payments made to jurors or witnesses for attending at court are ignored, except for payments for loss of earnings or of benefit.[115]

Training bonus

A training bonus of up to £200 is ignored,[116] but only for a year for HB, CTB, FC, DWA and ETU.

New Deal payments

There are special rules for the treatment of payments you may receive from the Employment Service for taking part in one of the options of the New Deal programme (see Chapter 34 for more details about the New Deal).

For all means-tested benefits the following payments are ignored for 52 weeks:
- mandatory top-up payments for taking part in:
  - the Voluntary Sector Option;
  - the Environment Task Force Option;
  - the self-employment route of the Employment Option.

and (for all means-tested payments except ETU);
- payments for taking part in the intensive activity period of the pilot programme for those aged 25 or over, including:
  - any top-up payments; *or*
  - payments under a written agreement between the Secretary of State and the person who has arranged for your participation.[117]

Similarly, any discretionary payments for special needs for taking part in the full-time Education and Training option or (except for ETU) in a qualifying course, and (except for ETU) any payments of childcare expenses for taking part in the intensive activity period of the pilot programme for those aged 25 or over, are also ignored for 52 weeks.[118]

Any sum of capital acquired for the purposes of participating in the self-employment option will also be ignored for 52 weeks,[119] and any capital assets acquired for such purposes will be ignored for as long as you are receiving assistance for taking part in the programme and, after you have ceased trading, for as long as reasonable in order to dispose of the assets.[120]

For the treatment of payments under the New Deal as income, notional income and notional capital, see pp2:420, 2:421and 2:455.

Payments in other currencies

Any payment in a currency other than sterling is taken into account after disregarding banking charges or commission payable on conversion to sterling.[121]

Capital treated as income

Some payments which appear to be capital are treated as income. See p2:416 for the detailed rules.

Any capital treated as income is ignored as capital.[122]

5. **Notional capital**

In certain circumstances, you are treated as having capital which you do not, in fact, possess. This is called 'notional capital'.[123] There is a similar rule for notional income (see p2:421). Notional capital counts in the same way as capital you actually do possess except that a 'diminishing notional capital rule' (see p2:458) may be applied so that the value of the notional capital you are treated as having will be considered to reduce over time.

There are five circumstances in which you will be treated as having notional capital:

- where you deliberately deprive yourself of capital in order to claim or increase benefit (see p2:456);
- where you fail to apply for capital which is available to you (see p2:461);
- where someone else makes a payment of capital to a third party on your behalf (see p2:461);
- where you (or a member of your family) receive a payment of capital on behalf of a third party and, instead of handing it on, you (or the member of your family) use or keep the capital (see p2:462); *and*
- where you are a sole trader or a partner in a business which is a limited company (see p2:462).

Note: The 'diminishing notional capital rule' (see p2:458) can only apply where you are treated as having notional capital under the first circumstance.

Deprivation of capital in order to claim or increase benefit

If you deliberately get rid of capital in order to claim or increase your benefit, you are treated as still possessing it.[124] You are likely to be affected by this rule if, at the time of using up your money, you know that you may qualify for benefit (or more benefit) as a result, or qualify more quickly. It should not be used if you know nothing about the effect of using up your capital (eg, you do not know about the capital limit for claiming benefit),[125] or if you have been using up your capital at a rate which is reasonable in the circumstances. Knowledge of capital limits can be inferred from a reasonable familiarity with the benefit system as a claimant,[126] but if you fail to make enquiries about the capital limit, this does not constitute an intention to secure benefit. This is because you cannot form the required intention if you do not know about the capital rules.[127]

Even if you do know about the capital limits, it still has to be shown that you intended to obtain, retain or increase your benefit.[128] For example, where a claimant, facing repossession of his home, transferred ownership to his daughter (who, he feared, would otherwise be made homeless), in spite of having been warned by Benefits Agency staff that he would be disqualified from benefit if he did so, it was held that, under the circumstances, he could not be said to have disposed of the property with the intention of gaining benefit.[129] The longer the period that has elapsed since the disposal of the capital, the less likely it is that it was for the purpose of obtaining benefit.[130] However, no matter how long it has been since you may have disposed of an asset, there is no set 'safe' period after which it may be said that benefit can be claimed without the need for further enquiry.[131]

A person who uses up her/his resources may have more than one motive for doing so. Even where qualifying for benefit as a result is only a subsidiary motive for your actions, and the predominant motive is something quite different (eg, ensuring your home is in good condition by spending capital to do necessary repairs and improvements) you may still be counted as having deprived yourself of a resource in order to gain benefit.[132] Local authorities tend to apply this test less stringently in the case of HB and CTB. Examples of the kinds of expenditure that could be caught by the rule are an expensive holiday and putting money in trust.[133] (For IS, income-based JSA, FC, DWA and ETU, putting money in trust for yourself does not constitute deprivation if the capital being put in trust came from compensation paid for any personal injury.[134]) But the essential test is not the kind of item that the money has been spent on but the *intention* behind the expenditure.

If you pay off a debt which you are required by law to repay immediately, you will not be counted as having deprived yourself of money in order to gain benefit.[135] However, even if you pay off a debt which you are not required by law to repay immediately, it is still for the Benefits Agency (for IS, income-based JSA, FC, DWA and ETU) or the local authority (for HB and CTB) to prove that you did so in order to get benefit.[136]

In practice, arguing successfully that you have not deprived yourself of capital to get or increase benefit may boil down to whether you can show that you would have spent the money in the way you did (eg, to pay off debts or reduce your mortgage), regardless of the effect on your benefit entitlement. Where this is unclear, the burden of proving that you did it in order to get benefit lies with the Benefits Agency (IS, income-based JSA, FC, DWA and ETU) or local authority (HB and CTB). In one case a man lost over £60,000 speculating on the stock market. Due to his wife's serious illness which affected his own health and judgement, he did not act to avoid losses when the stock market crashed. It was held that the adjudication officer had not discharged the burden of proving that this had been done for the purpose of obtaining IS.[137]

For IS, income-based JSA, FC, DWA and ETU, you can only be treated as having notional capital under this rule if the capital of which you have deprived yourself is *actual* capital.[138] So if you are counted as owning half a joint bank account under the rule about jointly held capital (see p2:464), but your real share is only a quarter, you should not be caught by the deprivation rule in relation to the other quarter. It is also arguable that the deprivation rule should not apply even to the quarter you actually hold.[139] There is no express rule spelt out in HB and CTB law that for the notional capital rule to apply you must have deprived yourself of actual capital, but you should argue that the same principle applies.

Note that where a disposal of capital is not effective (eg, where there is a disposal between the serving of a bankruptcy notice and the appointment of a trustee in bankruptcy) the notional capital rules will not apply (but the actual capital rules will apply if you still own the asset in question).[140] If, on the other hand, a person acting on your behalf as your attorney has misspent your money for her/his own benefit, the amount spent cannot be notional capital (because the disposal was unlawful) or actual capital (because you no longer have it), but your right to recover the money may still have an actual capital value.[141]

If you are treated as possessing notional capital, it is calculated in the same way as if it were actual capital[142] and the same disregards usually apply. The only possible exception is that you may not be able to rely on the disregard for the 26 weeks (or longer) you would otherwise be allowed to take steps to dispose of a property, even if the new owner is trying to sell it. However, there is conflicting caselaw on this.[143]

Other points on deprivation of capital

Any deprivation must be found to have been for the purposes of claiming or increasing your entitlement to that benefit.[144]

Deprivation for the purposes of obtaining supplementary benefit cannot be said to have been deprivation for the purposes of obtaining IS,[145] because IS did not exist at that time. It should also, therefore, be argued that there could have been no deprivation for the purposes of obtaining FC prior to April 1988, DWA prior to April 1992, CTB prior to April 1993 or ETU prior to April 1996, as those benefits did not come into existence until those dates. The only exception is that a deprivation for the purposes of gaining IS may be treated as a deprivation for the purposes of gaining income-based JSA (but not *vice versa*).

Where an intentional deprivation has been found for the purposes of obtaining IS, for example, it does not necessarily follow that there has also been any intention to gain HB and CTB. Where your circumstances change (eg, you start work and claim FC) any finding of intentional deprivation for IS will not necessarily be relevant to your claim for FC.

Each adjudicating authority must reach its own decision on each benefit. Even decisions on deprivation for HB must be made independently of decisions for CTB.[146] This may result in different conclusions being drawn on any disposal for each benefit. And even where intent is found in two different benefits, there may be different views about the amount of capital that has been intentionally disposed of.[147]

However, where you are held to have deprived yourself of capital for the purposes of claiming HB and CTB, and you then submit a successful claim for IS, the notional capital rules for HB and CTB should be put in abeyance for as long as IS remains in payment.[148]

The diminishing notional capital rule

This rule provides a calculation for working out how your notional capital may be treated as *spent*.[149] It only applies if you have deliberately deprived yourself of capital.[150] Prior to 1 October 1990 there was a different rule (see p2:460). The rule starts to operate from the first week (or, for IS, income-based JSA and CTB only, part-week) after the week in which it is first decided that the notional capital is to be taken into account. The rule provides that:

- **where your benefit has been refused altogether** because of your notional capital, the amount of your notional capital is reduced by the weekly total of any of the following benefits (or the additional amounts of the benefits, unless it is IS or income-based JSA) that you would have been entitled to but for the notional capital rule:

for IS	–	IS, HB and CTB (or, formerly community charge benefit (CCB))
for income-based JSA	–	income-based JSA, HB and CTB
for FC	–	FC, HB and CTB (or CCB)
for DWA	–	DWA, HB and CTB (or CCB)
for ETU	–	ETU, HB and CTB
for HB	–	IS, income-based JSA, FC, DWA, HB and CTB (or CCB)
for CTB	–	IS, income-based JSA, FC, DWA, HB and CTB

In order to ensure that account is taken of as many other benefits as possible, it is important (where you are not already doing so) to make a claim for any of the other benefits (where appropriate) as soon as the notional capital rule has been applied. Any notice you are then given of any amounts of benefits you have 'lost' can then be supplied as evidence of the total weekly aggregate that should be taken into account;

- **where your IS, income-based JSA, FC, DWA, ETU, HB and CTB is reduced because of tariff income (see p2:442) from your notional capital**, that capital is diminished by the amount of that reduction each week (or part-week). For example, if your notional capital is £3,750, giving a tariff income of £3 a week, the reduction is £3 a week until it reaches £3,500, when it will be £2 and so on. Except for ETU, account should be taken of any anticipated reduction in your tariff income band during any assessment period.[151]

For FC, DWA, ETU, HB and CTB, the amount of your notional capital is also reduced by the weekly aggregate of the following benefits (or any additional amounts of these benefits, unless it is IS or income-based JSA) which you would have been entitled to but for the notional capital rule:

for FC	–	HB and CTB (or CCB)
for DWA	–	HB and CTB (or CCB)
for ETU	–	HB and CTB
for HB	–	IS, income-based JSA, FC, DWA and CTB (or CCB)
for CTB	–	IS, income-based JSA, FC, DWA and HB

- **the reduction in your notional capital is calculated on a weekly basis**. However, where your benefit has been stopped altogether because of the notional capital rule, the amount is fixed for a period of 26 weeks. Even if the amount you would have been entitled to increases during this period, there will be no change in the amount by which the capital is reduced (except for HB and CTB where guidance[152] states that in circumstances not related to capital – eg, you have married or a baby has been born – a new assessment can be made). The aggregate of your benefit entitlement can, however, be recalculated from the end of this 26-week period when you reclaim benefit, and is increased if it is more than it was before, but it stays the same as in the earlier assessment if it is unchanged or less. You do not have to reclaim at the end of every 26-week period but there can be no recalculation unless and until you do. However, you cannot renew a claim until at least 26 weeks (IS, income-based JSA, HB and CTB), 22 weeks (FC and ETU) or 20 weeks (DWA) have passed since the last assessment. Once the amount of reduction has been recalculated in this way, it is again fixed for the same period.

For IS or income-based JSA, you should ask the Benefits Agency for a forecast of when your notional capital will reduce to a point where a further claim might succeed, but the onus will be on you to reclaim when it is to your advantage to do so[153] – ie, when you may qualify for an increased assessment, or because you have requalified for benefit. Timing will be important. If you delay you may lose out as new assessments cannot take effect before you reclaim. However, if you reclaim too soon you have to wait until the fixed periods have lapsed before you can apply for a fresh determination;

- **where you have both actual and notional capital**, you may have to draw on your actual capital to meet your living expenses, which may include (and will probably exceed) amounts equivalent to benefits you have 'lost'. There is no reason why this should affect the amount by which your notional capital is diminished, even if this effectively results in double-counting. Any reduction in your actual capital should be taken into account in calculating any tariff income arising from your combined actual and notional capital, unless, of course, you have spent it at such a rate and in such a way that it raises questions of intent, when you may find that the notional capital rules are applied all over again.

Note: It has been decided that these rules on how your capital was *spent* only apply from 1 October 1990. Prior to that date, any reasonable living and other expenditure was counted, which was far more generous.[154] Any notional capital you have been held to possess until 30 September 1990 is reduced under the earlier rules, and any notional capital carried forward to 1 October 1990 and onwards is reduced under the current rules.[155] Note that the current rules apply to deprivation of capital only; the earlier rules still apply to other forms of notional capital (see below).

For IS or FC, where the current more restrictive rules have been applied to you for any period before 1 October 1990, you should consider submitting a late appeal (see p2:645) to take advantage of the more generous treatment. For HB, the position on how the rules should have applied in earlier periods is less clear, although you should argue that as the law was essentially the same, the more generous rules should apply.

Failing to apply for capital[156]

Under this rule you are treated as having capital you could get if you applied for it. Examples of failure to apply could be where money is held in court which would be released on application, or even an unclaimed premium bond win! For IS, income-based JSA, HB and CTB, you are only treated as having such capital from the date you could obtain it. Although the FC, DWA and ETU rules do not make the same point, you should argue that the same applies.

This rule does not apply if you fail to apply for:
- capital from a discretionary trust; *or*
- capital from a trust (or fund administered by the court[157]) set up from money paid as a result of a personal injury; *or*
- capital from a personal pension scheme or retirement annuity contract; *or*
- a loan which you could only get if you gave your home or other disregarded capital (see p2:448) as security.

Capital payments made to a 'third party' on your behalf

If someone else pays an amount to a 'third party' (eg, the electricity board or a building society) for you or a member of your family (if any), this may count as your capital.[158] It counts if the payment is to cover certain of your or your family's normal living expenses – ie, food, household fuel, council tax or ordinary clothing or footwear. (School uniforms and sportswear are not ordinary clothing;[159] nor are, for example, special shoes because of a disability.[160])

It also counts if it is to cover:
- **for IS, income-based JSA, HB and CTB**, rent for which HB is payable (less any non-dependant deductions) or water charges;
- **for IS and income-based JSA only**, housing costs met by IS or income-based JSA or a residential care or nursing home accommodation charge for a person with preserved rights (see p2:173) met by IS or income-based JSA;
- **for FC and DWA**, any housing costs (or any outstanding community charge, but not any standard community charge);
- **for ETU**, any housing costs.

If the payment is for other kinds of expenses – eg, children's school fees (see p2:383), a TV licence, accommodation charges above the IS/income-based JSA limit, or (except for FC, DWA and ETU) mortgage capital repayments – it does not count. Payments from the Macfarlane Trusts, the Fund, the Eileen Trust or either of the Independent Living Funds do not count, whatever their purpose.

Payments for participating in any of the employment, education or training options of the New Deal (see Chapter 34) also do not count, whatever they are for, except for payments from the intensive activity period of the New Deal pilot programme for those aged 25 or over which (except for ETU) will only be ignored if they are not used for any of the normal living expenses listed on p2:454.[161]

Payments made for the food etc, of any member of the family, count as the capital of the member of the family in respect of whom they are paid. Since a child's capital is not counted as belonging to the claimant, a payment to, for example, a clothes shop for your child, should count as the child's notional capital and not yours.

For IS and income-based JSA only, payments *derived* from certain social security benefits (including war disablement pensions and war widows' pensions) and paid to a third party count:

- as yours, if you are entitled to the benefit; *and*
- as a member of your family's, if it is the family member who is entitled to the benefit.[162]

For IS and income-based JSA, there are different rules if you could be liable to pay maintenance as a liable relative (see p2:290).

Capital payments paid to you for a 'third party'[163]

If you or a member of your family get a payment for someone not in your family (eg, a relative who does not have a bank account) it only counts as yours if it is kept or used by you. Payments from the Macfarlane Trusts, the Fund, the Eileen Trust or either of the Independent Living Funds, or any of the payments made for participating in the New Deal (see Chapter 34), do not count at all.

Companies run by sole traders or a few partners

You will also be treated as possessing notional capital if, as a sole trader or a small partnership, you have registered your business as a limited company. For IS, income-based JSA, FC, DWA and ETU the value of your shareholding is ignored but you are treated as possessing a proportionate share of the capital of the company.[164] This does not apply while you are working for the company.[165] Even if you work for the company for, say, only half an hour a week, this will suffice.[166] DSS guidance for FC and DWA indicates that it is not necessary for the work to be paid.[167] It has, however, been held that a 'sleeping partner' in a business managed and worked exclusively by others may not benefit from this disregard. As well as having a financial commitment to the business you must also be involved or engaged in it in some practical sense as an earner.[168]

For HB and CTB, the local authority has a discretion whether to apply the same rules as for IS, income-based JSA, FC, DWA and ETU, but if it decides to, it must apply them all.[169]

6. **How capital is valued**

Market value

Apart from national savings certificates (see below), your capital is valued at its current market or surrender value.[170] This means the amount of money you could raise by selling it or raising a loan against it, etc. The test is the price that would be paid by a willing buyer to a willing seller on a particular date.[171] So if an asset is difficult, or impossible, to realise, its market value should be very heavily discounted or even nil.[172]

In the case of a house, an estate agent's figure for a quick sale is a more appropriate valuation than the District Valuer's figure for a sale within three months.[173]

It is not uncommon for an unrealistic assessment to be made of the value of your capital. You should consider challenging any decision you disagree with.

Expenses of sale

If there would be expenses involved in selling your capital, 10 per cent is deducted from its value for the cost of sale.[174]

Debts

Deductions are made from the 'gross' value of your capital for any debt or mortgage secured on it.[175] If a creditor (eg, a bank), holds the land certificate to your property as security for a loan and has registered notice of deposit of the land certificate at the Land Registry, this counts as a debt secured on your property.[176] Where a single mortgage is secured on a house and land and the value of the house is disregarded for benefit purposes, the whole of the mortgage can be deducted when calculating the value of the land.[177]

If you have debts which are not secured against your capital (eg, tax liabilities), these cannot be offset against the value of your capital.[178] However, once you have paid off your debts, your capital may well be reduced. You can be penalised if you deliberately get rid of capital in order to get benefit (see p2:456).

National savings

For IS and income-based JSA, a certificate bought from an issue which ceased before the 1 July before your claim is decided, or your benefit is first payable (whichever is earlier), or the date of any subsequent review, has the value it would have had on that 1 July if purchased on the last day of the issue. For FC, DWA and ETU, it is the 1 July before the date of your claim; for HB and

CTB, it is the 1 July before your claim is made or treated as made or when your benefit is reviewed. In any other case, the value is the purchase price.[179] DSS guidance contains a convenient valuation table for each issue.[180]

Capital that is jointly owned with someone else

If you jointly own any capital asset (except as a partner in a company when the rules explained on p2:462 will apply instead) you are treated as owning an equal share of the asset with all other owners. This applies regardless of the actual proportion of your real share in the asset.[181] For example, if you actually own 30 per cent of an asset and your brother owns the other 70 per cent, each of you are treated as owning a 50 per cent share. Similarly, if you actually own 90 per cent of an asset and one other person owns the other 10 per cent, you are treated as owning only 50 per cent and the value of the extra 40 per cent you actually own does not count as your capital.

The value of any deemed share should be calculated in the same way as your actual capital (see p2:463). However, it is only the value of your deemed share looked at in isolation which counts, and this will usually be worth rather less than the same proportion of the value of the whole asset. If the asset is, eg, a house, the value of any deemed share, even if it is larger than your actual share, may be very small or even worthless, particularly if the house is occupied and the other owner(s) are unwilling to buy your share or sell their share(s) and there is a possibility that the sale of the property cannot be forced. This is because even a willing buyer could not be expected to pay much for an asset s/he would have difficulty making use of or selling on to someone else.[182]

The rules do not apply to assets which are not really jointly owned. In the case of savings held in a joint bank account, for example, with a separated spouse, there is a presumption that both parties have joint beneficial ownership of the whole account. But if there is clear evidence that part of the sum belongs to one party alone, and the joint account has merely been used for convenience, that part will count as if it is in her/his sole ownership.[183]

If, because you jointly own an asset, you are treated as owning an asset of greater value than it is actually worth to you, you should consider selling your share if possible because as soon as it is sold only the actual proceeds of your actual share should be treated as your capital. Unless you sell it for less than it is actually worth, the notional capital rules (see p2:455) should not apply. Even if you (or any other co-owner(s)) sell only part of your (or their) share(s), the deemed value of your asset will reduce as the number of co-owners increases. In the meantime, you may be able to apply for a crisis loan from the social fund (see p1:667).

The current rules on the treatment of jointly owned capital were introduced on 12 October 1998[184] following a commissioner's decision on 21 May 1998[185] which held that earlier rules, which usually applied even more harshly in over-valuing shares in joint assets, were unlawful. If you have lost benefit because of the way the rules were previously applied you should seek advice from one of the agencies in Appendix 2.

Treatment of assets following the breakdown of a relationship

When partners separate, assets such as their former home or a building society account may be in joint or sole names. For example, if a building society account is in joint names, under the rule about jointly owned capital, you and your former partner are treated as having a 50 per cent share each (see above). But if your former partner is claiming sole ownership of the account, DSS guidance for FC and DWA says that your interest in the account should count as having a nil value until the question of ownership is settled.[186] Arguably, the same should apply to IS, income-based JSA, ETU, HB and CTB. The guidance deals only with a marriage breakdown, but there is no reason why the same should not apply if you were not married. If your former partner puts a stop on the account, in effect freezing it, the account should be disregarded until its ownership is resolved.

On the other hand, a former partner may have a right to some or all of an asset that is in your sole name – eg, s/he may have deposited most of the money in a building society account in your name. If this is established, then the partner in whose name the account is held may well, depending on the circumstances, be treated as not entitled to the whole of the account but as holding part of it as trustee for her/his former partner.[187] In that event, the rule about jointly owned capital may have the effect of treating you as owning half of the amount in the account. However, the point made in the DSS guidance referred to above should logically apply equally here, so you should not be treated as owning half the capital (or indeed any of it) unless or until it is established that you do own at least some share of it, and the value of your interest can be assessed.

Shares

Shares are valued at their current market value less 10 per cent for the cost of sale[188] and after deducting any lien held by brokers for sums owed for the cost of acquisition and commission. Market value should be calculated in accordance with Inland Revenue guidance which is based on the bid price plus a quarter of the difference between this and the offer price (rather than *Financial Times* figures which rely on the mean between the bid and offer prices).[189] Fluctuations in price between routine reviews of your case are normally ignored. Where a claimant has a minority holding of shares in a company, the value of the shares should be based on what the claimant could realise on them, and not by valuing the entire share capital of the company and attributing to the claimant an amount calculated according to the proportion of shares held.[190] Although there may be some practical difficulties in selling shares held by children, there are no obstacles to sale that cannot be overcome by courts, if necessary. They would, therefore, still have a value, even though allowance would have to be made for some inducement to overcome the reluctance of stockbrokers, registrars and potential purchasers in contracting with minors for an immediate sale.[191]

Unit trusts

These are valued on the basis of the 'bid' price quoted in newspapers. No deduction is allowed for the cost of sale because this is already included in the 'bid' price.[192]

The right to receive a payment in the future

The value of any such right that is not ignored (see p2:452) is its market value – what a willing buyer will pay to a willing seller.[193] For something which is not yet realisable this may be very small.

Overseas assets

If you have assets abroad, and there are no exchange controls or other prohibitions that would prevent you transferring your capital to this country, your assets are valued at their current market or surrender value in that country.[194] If there are problems getting benefit because it is difficult to get the assets valued, you may be able to get an interim payment of IS, income-based JSA, FC or DWA (see p2:499), or a 'payment on account' of HB (see p1:543).

If you are not allowed to transfer the full value of your capital to this country, you are treated as having capital equal to the amount that a willing buyer in this country would give for those assets.[195] It seems likely that the price such a person (if there is one) would be willing to pay may bear little relation to the actual value of the assets.

The same deductions of 10 per cent if there are expenses of sale, and for any debts or mortgage secured on the assets abroad, are made. If the capital is realised in a currency other than sterling, charges payable for converting the payment into sterling are also deducted.[196]

Notes

References are to statutes and regulations as amended up to 8 March 1999. All regulations are (General) Regulations unless otherwise stated. There is a full list of abbreviations in Appendix 13.

1 **HB** Sch 5 para 5 HB Regs
CTB Sch 5 para 5 CTB Regs

1. The capital limit

2 **IS** Reg 45 IS Regs
JSA s13(1) JSA 1995; reg 107(a) JSA Regs
FC Reg 28 FC Regs
ETU Rule 7(2)(d) ETU Scheme

3 **DWA** Reg 31 DWA Regs
HB Reg 37 HB Regs
CTB Reg 28 CTB Regs

4 **IS** Reg 53 IS Regs
JSA Reg 116(1) JSA Regs
FC Reg 36 FC Regs
DWA Reg 40 DWA Regs
ETU Rule 43 ETU Scheme
HB Reg 45 HB Regs
CTB Reg 37 CTB Regs

5 **IS** Regs 45 and 53(1A), (1B), (1C) and (4) IS Regs
JSA Regs 107(b) and 116(1A) JSA Regs

6 Regs 7(9) and 45(1A), (1B), (1C), (4) and (5) HB Regs

2. Whose capital counts

7 **IS/FC/DWA/HB/CTB** s136(1) SSCBA 1992
JSA s13(2) JSA 1995
ETU Rule 7(2)(d) ETU Scheme

8 **IS** Reg 47 IS Regs
JSA Reg 109 JSA Regs
FC Reg 30 FC Regs
DWA Reg 33 DWA Regs
HB Reg 39 HB Regs
CTB Reg 30 CTB Regs

9 **IS** Reg 17(1)(b) IS Regs
JSA Reg 83(b) JSA Regs
FC Reg 46(4) FC Regs
DWA Reg 51(4) DWA Regs
HB Reg 16(b) HB Regs
CTB Reg 8(b) CTB Regs

10 **IS** Reg 44(5) IS Regs
JSA Reg 106(5) JSA Regs
FC Reg 27(3) FC Regs

DWA Reg 30(3) DWA Regs
HB Reg 36(2) HB Regs
CTB Reg 27(2) CTB Regs

11 **IS** Regs 25 and 44(5) IS Regs
JSA Regs 89 and 106(5) JSA Regs
FC Reg 27(3) FC Regs
DWA Reg 30(3) DWA Regs
HB Reg 36(2) HB Regs
CTB Reg 27(2) CTB Regs

12 **IS** Reg 17(1)(b) IS Regs
JSA Reg 83(b) JSA Regs
FC Reg 46(4) FC Regs
DWA Reg 51(4) DWA Regs
HB Reg 16(b) HB Regs
CTB Reg 8(b) CTB Regs

3. What counts as capital

13 para C2.09 GM; para 34020 AOG

14 Reg 14 SS(CMB) Regs

15 Reg 22 SS(BTWB) Regs

16 *R v SBC ex parte Singer* [1973] 1 WLR 713

17 R(SB) 35/83

18 CIS/654/1991

19 **IS/JSA/FC/DWA** Reg 2 SS(PAOR) Regs
HB Reg 91(1) HB Regs

20 R(SB) 12/86

21 R(SB) 53/83; R(SB) 1/85

22 R(SB) 49/83

23 R(SB) 23/85

24 **IS** Sch 10 para 13 IS Regs
JSA Sch 8 para 18 JSA Regs
FC Sch 3 para 14 FC Regs
DWA Sch 4 para 14 DWA Regs
ETU Sch 5 para 14 ETU Scheme
HB Sch 5 para 14 HB Regs
CTB Sch 5 para 14 CTB Regs

25 *Peters v CAO* reported as an appendix to R(SB) 3/89

26 R(IS) 1/90

27 R(SB) 23/85

28 *Barclays Bank v Quistclose Investments Ltd* [1970] AC 567; R(SB) 49/83; CFC/21/1989

29 **IS** Sch 10 para 12 IS Regs
JSA Sch 8 para 18 JSA Regs
FC Sch 3 para 13 FC Regs
DWA Sch 4 para 13 DWA Regs
ETU Sch 5 para 13 ETU Scheme
HB Sch 5 para 13 HB Regs
CTB Sch 5 para 13 CTB Regs

30 **IS** Reg 23(1) IS Regs
JSA Reg 88(1) JSA Regs
FC Reg 10(1) FC Regs
DWA Reg 12(1) DWA Regs
ETU Rule 16(1) ETU Scheme
HB Reg 19(1) HB Regs
CTB Reg 11(1) CTB Regs

31 **IS** Sch 10 paras 44 and 45 IS Regs
JSA Sch 8 paras 42 and 43 JSA Regs
FC Sch 3 paras 46 and 47 FC Regs
DWA Sch 4 paras 45 and 46 DWA Regs
ETU Sch 5 paras 44 and 45 ETU Scheme
HB Sch 5 paras 46 and 47 HB Regs
CTB Sch 5 paras 46 and 47 CTB Regs
All CIS/368/1994

32 R(SB) 2/89

33 **IS** Regs 40 and 46 IS Regs
JSA Regs 103 and 108 JSA Regs
FC Regs 24 and 29 FC Regs
DWA Regs 27 and 32 DWA Regs
ETU Rules 33 and 36 ETU Scheme
HB Regs 33 and 38 HB Regs
CTB Regs 24 and 29 CTB Regs
All CIS/559/1991

34 *Thomas v CAO* (appendix to R(SB) 17/87)

35 **IS** Sch 10 paras 44 and 45 IS Regs
JSA Sch 8 paras 42 and 43 JSA Regs
FC Sch 3 paras 46 and 47 FC Regs
DWA Sch 4 paras 45 and 46 DWA Regs
ETU Sch 5 paras 44 and 45 ETU Scheme
HB Sch 5 paras 46 and 47 HB Regs
CTB Sch 5 paras 46 and 47 CTB Regs

36 **IS** Reg 48 IS Regs
JSA Reg 110 JSA Regs
FC Reg 31 FC Regs
DWA Reg 34 DWA Regs
ETU Rule 37 ETU Scheme
HB Reg 40 HB Regs
CTB Reg 31 CTB Regs

37 paras 51162 and 51172 AOG

38 Reg 48(11) IS Regs

39 **FC** Reg 31(6) FC Regs
DWA Reg 34(6) DWA Regs

40 **IS** Sch 9 para 32 IS Regs
JSA Sch 7 para 34 JSA Regs
FC Sch 2 para 26 FC Regs
DWA Sch 3 para 26 DWA Regs
ETU Sch 5 para 23 ETU Scheme
HB Sch 4 para 29 HB Regs
CTB Sch 4 para 30 CTB Regs

4. Disregarded capital

41 **IS** Sch 10 para 1 IS Regs
JSA Sch 8 para 1 JSA Regs
FC Sch 3 para 1 FC Regs
DWA Sch 4 para 1 DWA Regs
ETU Sch 5 para 1 ETU Scheme
HB Sch 5 para 1 HB Regs
CTB Sch 5 para 1 CTB Regs

42 **IS** Reg 2(1) IS Regs meaning of 'dwelling occupied as the home'; R(SB) 3/84; CIS/427/1991
JSA Reg 1(3) JSA Regs meaning of 'dwelling occupied as the home'
FC Sch 3 para 1 FC Regs
DWA Sch 4 para 1 DWA Regs
ETU Sch 5 para 1 ETU Scheme
HB Sch 5 para 1 HB Regs
CTB Sch 5 para 1 CTB Regs

43 **IS** Sch 10 para 1 IS Regs
JSA Sch 8 para 1 JSA Regs
FC Sch 3 para 1 FC Regs
DWA Sch 4 para 1 DWA Regs
ETU Sch 5 para 1 ETU Scheme
HB Sch 5 para 1 HB Regs
CTB Sch 5 para 1 CTB Regs

44 **IS** Sch 10 para 25 IS Regs
JSA Sch 8 para 5 JSA Regs
FC Sch 3 para 26 FC Regs
DWA Sch 4 para 26 DWA Regs
ETU Sch 5 para 27 ETU Scheme
HB Sch 5 para 24 HB Regs
CTB Sch 5 para 24 CTB Regs

45 **IS** Sch 10 para 27 IS Regs
JSA Sch 8 para 7 JSA Regs
FC Sch 3 para 28 FC Regs

DWA Sch 4 para 28 DWA Regs
ETU Sch 5 para 29 ETU Scheme
HB Sch 5 para 26 HB Regs
CTB Sch 5 para 26 CTB Regs
46 IS Sch 10 para 26 IS Regs
JSA Sch 8 para 6 JSA Regs
FC Sch 3 para 27 FC Regs
DWA Sch 4 para 27 DWA Regs
ETU Sch 5 para 28 ETU Scheme
HB Sch 5 para 25 HB Regs
CTB Sch 5 para 25 CTB Regs
All CIS/6908/1995; CIS/7319/1995
47 CIS/562/1992
48 CIS/7319/1995
49 R(SB) 32/83
50 CIS/7319/1995, para 22
51 IS Sch 10 para 28 IS Regs
JSA Sch 8 para 8 JSA Regs
FC Sch 3 para 29 FC Regs
DWA Sch 4 para 29 DWA Regs
ETU Sch 5 para 30 ETU Scheme
HB Sch 5 para 27 HB Regs
CTB Sch 5 para 27 CTB Regs
52 IS Sch 10 para 3 IS Regs
JSA Sch 8 para 3 JSA Regs
FC Sch 3 para 3 FC Regs
DWA Sch 4 para 3 DWA Regs
ETU Sch 5 para 3 ETU Scheme
HB Sch 5 para 3 HB Regs
CTB Sch 5 para 3 CTB Regs
53 R(IS) 6/95
54 CIS/685/1992
55 CIS/8475/1995; CIS/15984/1996
56 R(SB) 14/85
57 IS Sch 10 para 2 IS Regs
JSA Sch 8 para 2 JSA Regs
FC Sch 3 para 2 FC Regs
DWA Sch 4 para 2 DWA Regs
ETU Sch 5 para 2 ETU Scheme
HB Sch 5 para 2 HB Regs
CTB Sch 5 para 2 CTB Regs
58 IS Sch 10 para 8(a) IS Regs
JSA Sch 8 para 13(a) JSA Regs
FC Sch 3 para 9(a) FC Regs
DWA Sch 4 para 9(a) DWA Regs
ETU Sch 5 para 9(a) ETU Scheme
HB Sch 5 para 9(a) HB Regs
CTB Sch 5 para 9(a) CTB Regs
59 IS Sch 10 para 8(b) IS Regs
JSA Sch 8 para 13(b) JSA Regs
FC Sch 3 para 9(b) FC Regs
DWA Sch 4 para 9(b) DWA Regs

ETU Sch 5 para 9(b) ETU Scheme
HB Sch 5 para 9(b) HB Regs
CTB Sch 5 para 9(b) CTB Regs
60 Barclays Bank v Quistclose Investments Ltd [1970] AC 567; CSB/975/1985
61 IS Sch 10 para 9(a) IS Regs
JSA Sch 8 para 14(a) JSA Regs
FC Sch 3 para 10(a) FC Regs
DWA Sch 4 para 10(a) DWA Regs
ETU Sch 5 para 10(a) ETU Scheme
HB Sch 5 para 10(a) HB Regs
CTB Sch 5 para 10(a) CTB Regs
62 IS Sch 10 para 9(b) IS Regs
JSA Sch 8 para 14(b) JSA Regs
FC Sch 3 para 10(b) FC Regs
DWA Sch 4 para 10(b) DWA Regs
ETU Sch 5 para 10(b) ETU Scheme
HB Sch 5 para 10(b) HB Regs
CTB Sch 5 para 10(b) CTB Regs
63 IS Sch 10 para 37 IS Regs
JSA Sch 8 para 9 JSA Regs
FC Sch 3 para 39 FC Regs
DWA Sch 4 para 38 DWA Regs
ETU Sch 5 para 37 ETU Scheme
HB Sch 5 para 37 HB Regs
CTB Sch 5 para 36 CTB Regs
64 Rule 36(3) ETU Scheme
65 para 34578 AOG
66 CIS/6908/1995
67 IS Sch 10 para 4 IS Regs
JSA Sch 8 para 4 JSA Regs
FC Sch 3 paras 4 and 30 FC Regs
DWA Sch 4 paras 4 and 30 DWA Regs
ETU Sch 5 paras 4 and 31 ETU Scheme
HB Sch 5 para 4 HB Regs
CTB Sch 5 para 4 CTB Regs
68 IS Reg 2(1) IS Regs definition of 'partner'
JSA Reg 1(3) JSA Regs definition of 'partner'
FC Reg 2(1) FC Regs definition of 'partner'
DWA Reg 2(1) DWA Regs definition of 'partner'
ETU Rule 2(1) ETU Scheme definition of 'partner'
HB Reg 2(1) HB Regs definition

of 'partner'
CTB Reg 2(1) CTB Regs
definition of 'partner'
All s137(1) SSCBA 1992
definition of 'married couple'
and 'unmarried couple'
69 **HB** Sch 5 para 24 HB Regs
CTB Sch 5 para 24 CTB Regs
70 para 34429 AOG
HB/CTB para C2.12.ii.a and b
GM
71 **FC** Sch 3 para 4 FC Regs
DWA Sch 4 para 4 DWA Regs
ETU Sch 5 para 4 ETU Scheme
72 **IS** Reg 2(1) IS Regs definition of
'relative'
JSA Reg 1(3) JSA Regs definition
of 'relative'
FC Reg 2(1) definition of 'close
relative' and Sch 3 para 4 FC
Regs
DWA Reg 2(1) definition of
'close relative' and Sch 4 para 4
DWA Regs
ETU Rule 2(1) definition of 'close
relative' and Sch 5 para 4 ETU
Scheme
HB Reg 2(1) HB Regs definition
of 'relative'
CTB This is not defined for CTB
but presumably the same
definition will apply
73 CSB/209/1986; CSB/1149/1986;
R(SB) 22/87
74 **IS** Sch 10 para 10 IS Regs
JSA Sch 8 para 15 JSA Regs
FC Sch 3 para 11 FC Regs
DWA Sch 4 para 11 DWA Regs
ETU Sch 5 para 11 ETU Scheme
HB Sch 5 para 11 HB Regs
CTB Sch 5 para 11 CTB Regs
75 CIS/494/1990
76 **IS** Sch 10 para 8(a) IS Regs
JSA Sch 8 para 13(a) JSA Regs
FC Sch 3 para 9(a) FC Regs
DWA Sch 4 para 9(a) DWA Regs
ETU Sch 5 para 9(a) ETU
Scheme
HB Sch 5 para 9(a) HB Regs
CTB Sch 5 para 9(a) CTB Regs
77 **IS/JSA** para 34375 AOG
FC/DWA para 53271 AOG
78 **IS** Sch 10 para 6 IS Regs
JSA Sch 8 para 11 JSA Regs
FC Sch 3 para 6 FC Regs

DWA Sch 4 para 6 DWA Regs
ETU Sch 5 para 6 ETU Scheme
HB Sch 5 para 7 HB Regs
CTB Sch 5 para 7 CTB Regs
79 **FC** Sch 3 para 7 FC Regs
DWA Sch 4 para 7 DWA Regs
ETU Sch 5 para 7 ETU Scheme
80 R(SB) 4/85
81 CFC/15/1990
82 **IS** Sch 10 para 19 IS Regs
JSA Sch 8 para 24 JSA Regs
FC Sch 3 para 20 FC Regs
DWA Sch 4 para 20 DWA Regs
ETU Sch 5 para 20 ETU Scheme
HB Sch 5 para 20 HB Regs
CTB Sch 5 para 20 CTB Regs
83 **IS** Sch 10 para 23A IS Regs
JSA Sch 8 paras 28 and 29 JSA
Regs
FC Sch 3 para 24A FC Regs
DWA Sch 4 para 24A DWA Regs
ETU Sch 5 para 25 ETU Scheme
HB Sch 3 para 39A HB Regs
CTB Sch 5 para 30A CTB Regs
84 **IS** Sch 10 para 15 IS Regs
JSA Sch 8 para 20 JSA Regs
FC Sch 3 para 16 FC Regs
DWA Sch 4 para 16 DWA Regs
ETU Sch 5 para 16 ETU Scheme
HB Sch 5 para 16 HB Regs
CTB Sch 5 para 16 CTB Regs
All CIS/7330/1995
85 **IS** Sch 10 para 11 IS Regs
JSA Sch 8 para 16 JSA Regs
FC Sch 3 para 12 FC Regs
DWA Sch 4 para 12 DWA Regs
ETU Sch 5 para 12 ETU Scheme
HB Sch 5 para 12 HB Regs
CTB Sch 5 para 12 CTB Regs
86 **IS** Reg 41(2) IS Regs
JSA Reg 104(2) JSA Regs
FC Reg 25(2) FC Regs
DWA Reg 28(2) DWA Regs
ETU Rule 34(2) ETU Scheme
HB Reg 34(2) HB Regs
CTB Reg 25(2) CTB Regs
87 **IS** Sch 10 para 5 IS Regs
JSA Sch 8 para 10 JSA Regs
FC Sch 3 para 5 FC Regs
DWA Sch 4 para 5 DWA Regs
ETU Sch 5 para 5 ETU Scheme
HB Sch 5 para 6 HB Regs
CTB Sch 5 para 6 CTB Regs
88 CIS/635/1994

89 **IS** Sch 10 para 13 IS Regs
JSA Sch 8 para 18 JSA Regs
FC Sch 3 para 14 FC Regs
DWA Sch 4 para 14 DWA Regs
ETU Sch 5 para 14 ETU Scheme
HB Sch 5 para 14 HB Regs
CTB Sch 5 para 14 CTB Regs
90 **IS** Sch 10 para 14 IS Regs
JSA Sch 8 para 19 JSA Regs
FC Sch 3 para 15 FC Regs
DWA Sch 4 para 15 DWA Regs
ETU Sch 5 para 15 ETU Scheme
HB Sch 5 para 15 HB Regs
CTB Sch 5 para 15 CTB Regs
91 **IS** Sch 10 para 16 IS Regs
JSA Sch 8 para 21 JSA Regs
FC Sch 3 para 17 FC Regs
DWA Sch 4 para 17 DWA Regs
ETU Sch 5 para 17 ETU Scheme
HB Sch 5 para 17 HB Regs
CTB Sch 5 para 17 CTB Regs
92 **IS** Sch 10 para 23 IS Regs
JSA Sch 8 para 28 JSA Regs
FC Sch 3 para 24 FC Regs
DWA Sch 4 para 24 DWA Regs
ETU Sch 5 para 24 ETU Scheme
HB Sch 5 para 30 HB Regs
CTB Sch 5 para 30 CTB Regs
93 **IS** Sch 10 para 24 IS Regs
JSA Sch 8 para 30 JSA Regs
FC Sch 3 para 25 FC Regs
DWA Sch 4 para 25 DWA Regs
ETU Sch 5 para 26 ETU Scheme
HB Sch 5 para 31 HB Regs
CTB Sch 5 para 31 CTB Regs
94 **IS** Sch 10 para 11 IS Regs
JSA Sch 8 para 16 JSA Regs
FC Sch 3 para 12 FC Regs
DWA Sch 4 para 12 DWA Regs
ETU Sch 5 para 12 ETU Scheme
HB Sch 5 para 12 HB Regs
CTB Sch 5 para 12 CTB Regs
95 **IS** Sch 10 para 12 IS Regs
JSA Sch 8 para 17 JSA Regs
FC Sch 3 para 13 FC Regs
DWA Sch 4 para 13 DWA Regs
ETU Sch 5 para 13 ETU Scheme
HB Sch 5 para 13 HB Regs
CTB Sch 5 para 13 CTB Regs
96 **IS** Sch 10 para 7 IS Regs
JSA Sch 8 para 12 JSA Regs
FC Sch 3 para 8 FC Regs
DWA Sch 4 para 8 DWA Regs

ETU Sch 5 para 8 ETU Scheme
HB Sch 5 para 8 HB Regs
CTB Sch 5 para 8 CTB Regs
97 **IS** Sch 10 para 41 IS Regs
JSA Sch 8 para 39 JSA Regs
FC Sch 3 para 43 FC Regs
DWA Sch 4 para 42 DWA Regs
ETU Sch 5 para 41 ETU Scheme
HB Sch 5 para 38 HB Regs
CTB Sch 5 para 37 CTB Regs
98 **IS** Sch 10 para 36 IS Regs
JSA Sch 8 para 35 JSA Regs
FC Sch 3 para 38 FC Regs
DWA Sch 4 para 37 DWA Regs
ETU Sch 5 para 36 ETU Scheme
HB Sch 5 para 36 HB Regs
CTB Sch 5 para 35 CTB Regs
99 Sch 10 paras 47-49 IS Regs
100 Sch 5 paras 50-51 HB Regs
101 Sch 5 paras 50-51 CTB Regs
102 **FC** Sch 3 paras 50 and 51 FC
Regs
DWA Sch 4 paras 49 and 50
DWA Regs
ETU Sch 5 para 46 and 48 ETU
Scheme
HB Sch 5 paras 49 and 52 HB
Regs
CTB Sch 5 paras 49 and 52 CTB
Regs
103 **IS** Sch 10 para 38 IS Regs
JSA Sch 8 para 36 JSA Regs
FC Sch 3 para 40 FC Regs
DWA Sch 4 para 39 DWA Regs
ETU Sch 5 para 38 ETU Scheme
HB Sch 5 para 39 HB Regs
CTB Sch 5 para 38 CTB Regs
104 **IS** Sch 10 para 39 IS Regs
JSA Sch 8 para 37 JSA Regs
FC Sch 3 para 41 FC Regs
DWA Sch 4 para 40 DWA Regs
ETU Sch 5 para 39 ETU Scheme
HB Sch 5 para 40 HB Regs
CTB Sch 5 para 39 CTB Regs
105 **IS** Sch 10 para 40 IS Regs
JSA Sch 8 para 38 JSA Regs
FC Sch 3 para 42 FC Regs
DWA Sch 4 para 41 DWA Regs
ETU Sch 5 para 40 ETU Scheme
HB Sch 5 para 41 HB Regs
CTB Sch 5 para 40 CTB Regs
106 **FC** Sch 3 para 48 FC Regs
DWA Sch 4 para 47 DWA Regs

107 **IS** Sch 10 para 18 IS Regs
JSA Sch 8 para 23 JSA Regs
FC Sch 3 para 19 FC Regs
DWA Sch 4 para 19 DWA Regs
ETU Sch 5 para 19 ETU Scheme
HB Sch 5 para 19 HB Regs
CTB Sch 5 para 19 CTB Regs

108 **IS** Sch 10 paras 42-43 IS Regs
JSA Sch 8 paras 40 and 41 JSA Regs
FC Sch 3 paras 44-45 FC Regs
DWA Sch 4 paras 43-44 DWA Regs
ETU Sch 5 paras 42 and 43 ETU Scheme
HB Sch 5 paras 43-44 HB Regs
CTB Sch 5 paras 42-43 CTB Regs

109 **IS** Sch 10 para 46 IS Regs
JSA Sch 8 para 44 JSA Regs
FC Sch 3 para 49 FC Regs
DWA Sch 4 para 48 DWA Regs
ETU Sch 5 para 47 ETU Scheme
HB Sch 5 para 48 HB Regs
CTB Sch 5 para 48 CTB Regs

110 **IS** Sch 10 paras 31-33 IS Regs
JSA Sch 8 para 33 JSA Regs
FC Sch 3 paras 33-35 FC Regs
DWA Sch 4 paras 33-35 DWA Regs
ETU Sch 5 para 34 ETU Scheme
HB Sch 5 paras 28, 29 and 42 HB Regs
CTB Sch 5 paras 28, 29 and 41 CTB Regs

111 **IS** Sch 10 para 17 IS Regs
JSA Sch 8 para 22 JSA Regs
FC Sch 3 para 18 FC Regs
DWA Sch 4 para 18 DWA Regs
ETU Sch 5 para 18 ETU Scheme
HB Sch 5 para 18 HB Regs
CTB Sch 5 para 18 CTB Regs

112 **IS** Sch 10 para 29 IS Regs
JSA Sch 8 para 31 JSA Regs
FC Sch 3 para 31 FC Regs
DWA Sch 4 para 31 DWA Regs
ETU Sch 5 para 32 ETU Scheme
HB Sch 5 para 32 HB Regs
CTB Sch 5 para 32 CTB Regs

113 **IS** Sch 10 para 22 IS Regs
JSA Sch 8 para 27 JSA Regs
FC Sch 3 para 23 FC Regs
DWA Sch 4 para 23 DWA Regs
ETU Sch 5 para 23 ETU Scheme
HB Sch 5 para 23 HB Regs
CTB Sch 5 para 23 CTB Regs

114 **IS** para 34454 AOG
FC/DWA para 53471 AOG
HB Reg 73(1) and (3) HB Regs
CTB Reg 63(1) and (3) CTB Regs

115 **IS** Sch 10 para 34 IS Regs
JSA Sch 8 para 34 JSA Regs
FC Sch 3 para 36 FC Regs
DWA Sch 4 para 36 DWA Regs
ETU Sch 5 para 35 ETU Scheme
HB Sch 4 para 38 HB regs
CTB Sch 4 para 40 CTB Regs

116 **IS** Sch 10 para 30 IS Regs
JSA Sch 8 para 32 JSA Regs
FC Sch 3 para 32 FC Regs
DWA Sch 4 para 32 DWA Regs
ETU Sch 5 para 33 ETU Scheme
HB Sch 5 para 33 HB Regs
CTB Sch 5 para 33 CTB Regs

117 **IS** Sch 10 paras 50 and 54 IS Regs
JSA Sch 8 paras 45 and 49 JSA Regs
FC Sch 3 paras 52 and 56 FC Regs
DWA Sch 4 paras 51 and 55 DWA Regs
ETU Sch 5 para 49 ETU Scheme
HB Sch 5 paras 53 and 57 HB Regs
CTB Sch 5 paras 53 and 57 CTB Regs

118 **IS** Sch 10 paras 51, 53 and 55 IS Regs
JSA Sch 8 paras 46, 48 and 50 JSA Regs
FC Sch 3 paras 53, 55 and 57 FC Regs
DWA Sch 4 para 52, 54 and 56 DWA Regs
ETU Sch 5 para 50 ETU Scheme
HB Sch 5 paras 54, 56 and 58 HB Regs
CTB Sch 5 paras 54, 56 and 58 CTB Regs

119 **IS** Sch 10 para 52 IS Regs
JSA Sch 8 para 47 JSA Regs
FC Sch 3 para 54 FC Regs
DWA Sch 4 para 53 DWA Regs
ETU Sch 5 para 51 ETU Scheme
HB Sch 5 para 55 HB Regs
CTB Sch 5 para 55 CTB Regs

120 **IS** Sch 10 para 6(1) IS Regs
JSA Sch 8 para 11(1) JSA Regs
FC Sch 3 para 6(1) FC Regs
DWA Sch 4 para 6(1) DWA Regs

ETU Sch 5 para 6(1) ETU
Scheme
HB Sch 5 para 7(1) HB Regs
CTB Sch 5 para 7(1) CTB Regs
121 **IS** Sch 10 para 21 IS Regs
JSA Sch 8 para 26 JSA Regs
FC Sch 3 para 22 FC Regs
DWA Sch 4 para 22 DWA Regs
ETU Sch 5 para 22 ETU Scheme
HB Sch 5 para 22 HB Regs
CTB Sch 5 para 22 CTB Regs
122 **IS** Sch 10 para 20 IS Regs
JSA Sch 8 para 25 JSA Regs
FC Sch 3 para 21 FC Regs
DWA Sch 4 para 21 DWA Regs
ETU Sch 5 para 21 ETU Scheme
HB Sch 5 para 21 HB Regs
CTB Sch 5 para 21 CTB Regs

5. Notional capital
123 **IS** Reg 51(6) IS Regs
JSA Reg 113(6) JSA Regs
FC Reg 34(6) FC Regs
DWA Reg 37(6) DWA Regs
ETU Rule 40(6) ETU Scheme
HB Reg 43(6) HB Regs
CTB Reg 34(6) CTB Regs
HB Reg 43(6) HB Regs
CTB Reg 34(6) CTB Regs
124 **IS** Reg 51(1) IS Regs
JSA Reg 113(1) JSA Regs
FC Reg 34(1) FC Regs
DWA Reg 37(1) DWA Regs
ETU Rule 40(1) ETU Scheme
HB Reg 43(1) HB Regs
CTB Reg 34(1) CTB Regs
125 CIS/124/1990; CSB/1198/1989
126 R(SB) 9/91
127 CIS/124/1990
128 CIS/40/1989
129 CIS/621/1991
130 CIS/264/1989
131 CIS/7330/1995, para 12(3)
132 R(SB) 38/85
133 para 34817 AOG
134 **IS** Reg 51(1) IS Regs
JSA Reg 113(1) JSA Regs
FC Reg 34(1) FC Regs
DWA Reg 37(1) DWA Regs
ETU Rule 40(1) ETU Scheme
135 R(SB) 12/91
136 CIS/2627/1995
137 CIS/236/1991

138 **IS** Reg 51(7) IS Regs
JSA Reg 113(7) JSA Regs
FC Reg 34(7) FC Regs
DWA Reg 37(7) DWA Regs
ETU Rule 40(7) ETU Scheme
139 CIS/240/1992
140 CIS/634/1992
141 CIS/12403/1996
142 **IS** Reg 51(6) IS Regs
JSA Reg 113(6) JSA Regs
FC Reg 34(6) FC Regs
DWA Reg 37(6) DWA Regs
ETU Rule 40(6) ETU Scheme
HB Reg 43(6) HB Regs
CTB Reg 34(6) CTB Regs
143 CIS/30/1993, but other
commissioners have taken a
different view (*see*, eg, CIS/25/
1990 and CIS/81/1991)
144 **IS** Reg 51(1) IS Regs
JSA Reg 113(1) JSA Regs
FC Reg 34(1) FC Regs
DWA Reg 37(1) DWA Regs
ETU Rule 40(1) ETU Scheme
HB Reg 43(1) HB Regs
CTB Reg 34(1) CTB Regs
All R(IS) 14/93
145 R(IS) 14/93
146 para C2.69 GM
147 para C2.97 GM
148 para C2.92 GM
149 **IS** Reg 51A IS Regs
JSA Reg 114 JSA Regs
FC Reg 34A FC Regs
DWA Reg 38 DWA Regs
ETU Rule 41 ETU Scheme
HB Reg 43A HB Regs
CTB Reg 35 CTB Regs
150 **IS** Reg 51A(1) IS Regs
JSA Reg 114(1) JSA Regs
FC Reg 34A(1) FC Regs
DWA Reg 38(1) DWA Regs
ETU Rule 41(1) ETU Scheme
HB Reg 43A(1) HB Regs
CTB Reg 35(1) CTB Regs
151 s25(1)(c) SSAA 1992
HB Reg 66(2) HB Regs
CTB Reg 57(2) CTB Regs
152 para C2.84 GM
153 R(IS) 9/92
154 R(IS) 1/91; R(IS) 9/92
155 R(IS) 9/92
156 **IS** Reg 51(2) IS Regs
JSA Reg 113(2) JSA Regs
FC Reg 34(2) FC Regs

DWA Reg 37(2) DWA Regs
ETU Rule 40(2) ETU Scheme
HB Reg 43(2) HB Regs
CTB Reg 34(2) CTB Regs

157 CIS/368/1994

158 **IS** Reg 51(3)(a)(ii) and (8) IS
Regs
JSA Reg 113(3)(a)(ii) JSA Regs
FC Reg 34(3)(a) FC Regs
DWA Reg 37(3)(a) DWA Regs
ETU Rule 40(3)(a) ETU Scheme
HB Reg 43(3)(a) and (7) HB Regs
CTB Reg 34(3)(a) and (7) CTB
Regs

159 **IS** Reg 51(8) IS Regs
JSA Reg 113(8) JSA Regs
FC Reg 34(3)(a) FC Regs
DWA Reg 37(3)(a) DWA Regs
ETU Rule 40(3)(a) ETU Scheme
HB Reg 43(7)(b) HB Regs
CTB Reg 34(7) CTB Regs

160 **IS/JSA** para 34866 AOG

161 **IS** Reg 51(3A) IS Regs
JSA Reg 113(3A) JSA Regs
FC Reg 34(3A) FC Regs
DWA Reg 37(3A) DWA Regs
ETU Rule 40(3) ETU Scheme
HB Reg 43(3A) HB Regs
CTB Reg 34(3A) CTB Regs

162 **IS** Reg 51(3)(a)(i) IS Regs
JSA Reg 113(3)(a)(i) JSA Regs

163 **IS** Reg 51(3)(b) IS Regs
JSA Reg 113(3)(b) JSA Regs
FC Reg 34(3)(b) FC Regs
DWA Reg 37(3)(b) DWA Regs
ETU Rule 40(3)(b) ETU Scheme
HB Reg 43(3)(b) HB Regs
CTB Reg 34(3)(b) CTB Regs

164 **IS** Reg 51(4) IS Regs
JSA Reg 113(4) JSA Regs
FC Reg 34(4) FC Regs
DWA Reg 37(4) DWA Regs
ETU Rule 40(4) ETU Scheme

165 **IS** Reg 51(5) IS Regs
JSA Reg 113(5) JSA Regs
FC Reg 34(5) FC Regs
DWA Reg 37(5) DWA Regs
ETU Rule 40(5) ETU Scheme
HB Reg 43(5) HB Regs
CTB Reg 34(5) CTB Regs

166 **IS/JSA** para 34375 AOG; *see also*
R(IS) 13/93
FC/DWA para 53372 AOG

167 paras 34876-77 and 53373 AOG

168 *CAO v Knight* (CA) 9 April 1997

169 **HB** Reg 43(4) HB Regs
CTB Reg 34(4) CTB Regs

6. How capital is valued

170 **IS** Reg 49(a) IS Regs
JSA Reg 111(a) JSA Regs
FC Reg 32(a) FC Regs
DWA Reg 35(a) DWA Regs
ETU Rule 38(a) ETU Scheme
HB Reg 41(a) HB Regs
CTB Reg 32(a) CTB Regs

171 R(SB) 57/83; R(SB) 6/84

172 R(SB) 18/83

173 R(SB) 6/84

174 **IS** Reg 49(a)(i) IS Regs
JSA Reg 111(a)(i) JSA Regs
FC Reg 32(a)(i) FC Regs
DWA Reg 35(a)(i) DWA Regs
ETU Rule 38(a)(i) ETU Scheme
HB Reg 41(a)(i) HB Regs
CTB Reg 32(a)(i) CTB Regs

175 **IS** Reg 49(a)(ii) IS Regs
JSA Reg 111(a)(ii) JSA Regs
FC Reg 32(a)(ii) FC Regs
DWA Reg 35(a)(ii) DWA Regs
ETU Rule 38(a)(ii) ETU Scheme
HB Reg 41(a)(ii) HB Regs
CTB Reg 32(a)(ii) CTB Regs

176 CIS/255/1989

177 R(SB) 27/84

178 R(SB) 2/83; R(SB) 31/83

179 **IS** Reg 49(b) IS Regs
JSA Reg 111(b) JSA Regs
FC Reg 32(b) FC Regs
DWA Reg 35(b) DWA Regs
ETU Rule 38(6) ETU Scheme
HB Reg 41(b) HB Regs
CTB Reg 32(b) CTB Regs

180 **IS/JSA** Part 34 Appendix 3 AOG
FC/DWA Part 53 Appendix 2
AOG
HB/CTB C2: Annex B GM;
Circular A31/98 (July 1998)

181 **IS** Reg 52 IS Regs
JSA Reg 115 JSA Regs
FC Reg 35 FC Regs
DWA Reg 39 DWA Regs
ETU Rule 42 ETU Scheme
HB Reg 44 HB Regs
CTB Reg 36 CTB Regs

182 CIS/15936/1996; CIS/263/1997;
CIS/3283/1997 (joint decision);
CAO v Palfrey and Others (CA),
The Times, 17 February 1995

(upholding CIS/391/1992 and
CIS/417/1992 apparently to be
reported as R(IS) 5/98)
183 CIS/7097/1995; CIS/15936/
1996; CIS/263/1997; CIS/3283/
1997 (joint decision – common
Appendix para 17)
184 The Social Security Amendment
(Capital) Regulations 1998 SI
No.2250
185 CIS/15936/1996; CIS/263/1997;
CIS/3283/1997 (joint decision)
186 **FC/DWA** para 53056 AOG
HB/CTB para 2.42 GM
187 R(IS) 2/93
188 **IS** Reg 49(a) IS Regs
JSA Reg 111(a) JSA Regs
FC Reg 32(a) FC Regs
DWA Reg 35(a) DWA Regs
ETU Rule 38(a) ETU Scheme
HB Reg 41(a) HB Regs
CTB Reg 32(a) CTB Regs
189 R(IS) 18/95
190 R(SB) 18/83; R(IS)
2/90
191 CIS/654/1993
192 **IS/JSA** para 34681 AOG
FC/DWA para 53132 AOG
HB/CTB para C2.34 GM
193 *Peters v CAO* (appendix to R(SB)
3/89)
194 **IS** Reg 50(a) IS Regs
JSA Reg 112(a) JSA Regs
FC Reg 33(a) FC Regs
DWA Reg 36(a) DWA Regs
ETU Rule 39(a) ETU Scheme
HB Reg 42(a) HB Regs
CTB Reg 33(a) CTB Regs
195 **IS** Reg 50(b) IS Regs
JSA Reg 112(b) JSA Regs
FC Reg 33(b) FC Regs
DWA Reg 36(b) DWA Regs
ETU Rule 39(b) ETU Scheme
HB Reg 42(b) HB Regs
CTB Reg 33(b) CTB Regs
196 **IS** Sch 10 para 21 IS Regs
JSA Sch 8 para 26 JSA Regs
FC Sch 3 para 22 FC Regs
DWA Sch 4 para 22 DWA Regs
ETU Sch 5 para 22 ETU Scheme
HB Sch 5 para 22 HB Regs
CTB Sch 5 para 22 CTB Regs

Part 10

Administration of benefits and appeals

Chapter 50

· ·

Claims, backdating and getting paid

This chapter contains:
1. Who should claim (p2:480)
2. How to make a claim (p2:481)
3. When to claim (p2:486)
4. How your claim is dealt with (p2:491)
5. Getting paid (p2:492)
6. Deductions from your income support or jobseeker's allowance (p2:500)
7. Recovery of benefits from compensation payments (p2:508);

This chapter deals with benefits administered by the Benefits Agency. It does not cover housing benefit, council tax benefit, earnings top-up, statutory sick pay, statutory maternity pay, bonuses, the benefits in Chapter 29 or payments from the social fund. For information about claims for these see pp1:530, 1:581, 1:501, 1:26 and 1:96 and Chapters 28, 29, 30 and 31.

You should look at this chapter if you are claiming:
- attendance allowance;
- child benefit;
- disability living allowance;
- disability working allowance;
- family credit;
- guardian's allowance;
- incapacity benefit;
- income support;
- industrial injuries benefits;
- invalid care allowance;
- jobseeker's allowance;
- maternity allowance;
- retirement pension;
- severe disablement allowance;
- widows' benefits.

These benefits are administered by part of the DSS called the Benefits Agency. Most of these are dealt with at your local Benefits Agency office. However, there are exceptions. For example:

- if you live in certain parts of London, your claim is processed by special Benefits Agency offices in Glasgow, Belfast, Ashton-in-Makerfield and elsewhere (although you can still hand deliver your claim to your local office);
- all claims for certain benefits are processed centrally:
  - child benefit is administered in Washington, Tyne and Wear (see Appendix 1);
  - jobseeker's allowance (JSA) is administered by the Employment Service, part of the Department for Education and Employment, on behalf of the DSS – claims are dealt with at local JobCentres and payments are made from a central computer;
  - attendance allowance and disability living allowance claims are administered initially by regional disability centres and then by the Disability Benefits Unit in Blackpool;
  - family credit, disability working allowance and invalid care allowance claims are administered by central units in Preston.

You can find your appropriate local benefit office by looking in the telephone directory for business and service numbers under 'Benefits Agency'. See Appendix 1 for the addresses of the central units. For information about who makes the decisions when you claim see Chapter 53. To find out about challenging a decision, see Chapters 53 and 56.

1. Who should claim

You generally claim benefit for yourself. If you cannot do so, another person can claim on your behalf (eg, an appointee – see below – or your parent if you are a child claiming disability living allowance).

If you are part of a couple, you can sometimes choose which one of you claims income support (IS), income-based JSA, family credit, housing benefit or council tax benefit (see p2:114) for both of you. It is important for you to work out how you would be better off.

If you have children, you can claim child benefit but other people might also be entitled (see p1:238). If you cannot decide who should claim, the Secretary of State can decide for you (see p1:238).

Appointees

The Secretary of State can authorise someone else (eg, a friend or relative) called an 'appointee' to act on your behalf if you cannot claim for yourself – eg, you are mentally ill or suffering from senile dementia.[1] This is not necessary if a court has already appointed someone else to look after your affairs. The appointee takes on all your rights and responsibilities as a claimant. For example, s/he must notify the Benefits Agency of changes in your circumstances. Normally this would only apply from the date the appointment is agreed, but if someone acts on your behalf before becoming your official appointee her/his actions can be validated in retrospect by her/his appointment.[2] Someone can become an appointee by applying in writing to the Benefits Agency. S/he must be over 18.

If you are an appointee for a claimant who dies, you must re-apply for appointee status in order to settle any outstanding benefit matters.[3] An executor under a will can also pursue an outstanding claim or appeal on behalf of a deceased claimant even if the decision was made before the formal grant of probate.[4]

2. How to make a claim

In almost all circumstances, to qualify for a benefit, you must make a claim.[5] There are exceptions to this rule for retirement allowance (see p1:223) and certain retirement pensions which do not have to be claimed if you are already receiving certain other retirement pensions or widows' benefits – see p1:149.[6]

You can get claim forms from your local Benefits Agency office or JobCentre. Some of the Benefits Agency leaflets about benefits (see Appendix 3) contain claim forms at the back. For information about where you should return your claim form, see the chapter in this *Handbook* about the benefit you are claiming. A claim for JSA must be made in person at a JobCentre, unless the Secretary of State tells you otherwise (see p1:353).[7]

You should claim as soon as you think that you might be entitled to a benefit, even if it might take you time to collect all the information required on the form. See p2:486 for further information about your date of claim.

Very occasionally, it may be in your interests to wait for the next calendar year to claim JSA on the basis of a better record of national insurance contributions (see p1:272). It is also in your interests to delay claiming family credit (FC), earnings top-up (ETU) and disability working allowance (DWA) in some circumstances (see pp1:466 and 1:479).

In some limited circumstances your claim can be backdated (see p2:487). The rules are very strict.

Amending or withdrawing your claim

You can **amend** your claim by writing to the local benefit office or JobCentre.[8] If your letter is received before a decision is made, the Secretary of State can treat your claim as amended from the date it was initially made.

You can **withdraw** your claim at any time before a determination is made, for example, where you claimed family credit when you were due to have another child and would be better off claiming once your baby is born. It is treated as withdrawn from the date when the request is received.[9]

Is your claim valid?

You cannot get benefit until you make a valid claim. To be valid, your claim must be in writing and should normally be made on the appropriate Benefits Agency form. For claims for benefits other than IS and JSA, the Secretary of State may decide to treat any letter or other written communication as being a valid claim.[10] Claims for IS and JSA must *always* be made on the appropriate form.

The Government may make it a condition of entitlement to every benefit that you attend an interview with an adviser. This is known as the 'single gateway'. The changes will be piloted in certain areas starting in June 1999, although it will not be compulsory to attend an interview until April 2000. See p2:90 for further information.

Because the decision whether to accept your claim as valid is made by the Secretary of State (see p2:565), you cannot appeal to a tribunal. However, whether a claim has been made (eg, if the Benefits Agency has no record of your letter and suggests that you never wrote it) and, if so, when it was received by the Benefits Agency, are adjudication officer (AO) decisions (see p2:561), so you can appeal to a tribunal.[11]

If your claim is valid, it is referred to an AO to decide if you are entitled to benefit. The Benefits Agency can ask you to provide further information to support your claim or even ask you to attend a medical examination before it makes a decision (see pp2:22 and 2:33). However, this should not prevent a decision being made on your claim (but see p2:581 for the position when the Social Security Act 1998 takes effect).

A valid claim can be backdated for up to three months in certain circumstances (see p2:487).

Extra conditions for income support and jobseeker's allowance

It is your responsibility to:[12]
- complete your claim form fully and correctly; *and*
- to produce information and evidence to verify your claim.

This is known as the **onus of proof rule** or evidence requirement. See pp1:356 and 1:450 for the information you can be asked to provide.

If you do not fill in the form properly or provide all the information and evidence required, the Benefits Agency notifies you that your claim is defective and contacts you to put things right. It might telephone or write to you or, in the case of IS, even visit you to get the information or evidence. But it might simply return your claim form. You should provide the information or evidence or complete the form and return it to your local office within one month of your initial contact (or that of someone contacting the Benefits Agency on your behalf). If you do not, you might lose benefit (see p2:487 for information about when your claim can be backdated).

You are exempt from the onus of proof rule if:[13]

- you could not complete the form or get the information or evidence required because of a physical, mental, learning or communication difficulty. You must also show that it is not reasonably practicable for someone to help you complete the form or get the proof on your behalf; *or*
- the information or evidence required does not exist; *or*
- you could not get the information or evidence required without serious risk of physical or mental harm. You must also show that it is not reasonably practicable to get it in another way; *or*
- you could only get the information or evidence required from a third party and it is not reasonably practicable to get it from her/him; *or*
- the Secretary of State thinks sufficient proof has been provided to show that you are not entitled to IS or JSA – eg, because your capital is too high – so it would be inappropriate to require further proof about your income.

If you are unable to complete your claim form or provide the required information or evidence for one of the reasons listed above, you should give your local office notice of this as soon as possible, ideally by explaining this on the claim form or by ringing or visiting the benefit office or JobCentre as soon as possible. The Benefits Agency says that such notice must be given within one month of the date when you first contacted it. Explain your circumstances fully. You can provide supporting letters, for example, from a social worker or a solicitor. If the Benefits Agency accepts that you are exempt from the onus of proof rule, it can help you to fill in the form or give you longer to complete it or collect evidence or information on your behalf or tell you that you do not have to provide the information after all.

If you are claiming JSA, you are normally required to attend an interview at which a properly completed claim form is handed in. Your claim is then treated as made on the date you first notified your intention to claim (usually when you picked up the form and made the appointment for the interview), or the first date in respect of which your claim is made if this is later.[14] If you fail to attend the interview or hand in a properly completed form you might lose benefit (see p1:354).

Other benefits

For benefits other than IS or JSA if you just write a letter or send the wrong form, the Benefits Agency sends you the appropriate form to fill in. Similarly, if you do not fill in the form properly, it returns it to you. If you get it back to the Benefits Agency correctly filled in within a month, you count as having made a valid claim on the date of your first letter or form.[15] The Secretary of State can extend this one-month period if s/he thinks this is reasonable[16] –

eg, because you were ill. See p2:487 for other situations when your claim can be backdated.

Example

Geraldine was claiming JSA and wrote to the Benefits Agency office to say that her husband had died. She was unaware that she could claim a widow's payment. Two years later, she finds out about widow's payment. She can ask the Secretary of State to treat her letter as being a claim for widow's payment. She should write to her local Benefits Agency office and argue that she should have been given proper advice two years ago.

Providing information to support your claim

The Secretary of State may require you to provide documentation and evidence relevant to your claim and you can be asked for an interview to discuss your circumstances if this is reasonable.[17] You may be able to claim travelling expenses for this.[18] Remember, in the case of IS and JSA, you might not count as having made a valid claim until you provide all the information and evidence required (see p2:482).

To find out what information and evidence you are required to provide, see the chapter in this *Handbook* about the benefit you are claiming.

As well as providing information and evidence, you are also usually required to:

- provide proof of your identity (see below); *and*
- satisfy what is known as the NINO requirement (see p2:485).

Proof of identity

The Benefits Agency might ask you to produce documents or evidence that help to prove your identity. If you are claiming benefit for your partner or an adult dependant (see p1:93) you must prove her/his identity too. You can prove your identity with a passport, a national identity card issued by an EU member state, or a letter issued by the Home Office acknowledging your application for asylum (known as a SAL). However, there are many other things that can help you to prove who you are. Examples include your birth certificate, full driving licence, a travel pass with a photograph, a local council rent card or tenancy agreement or even paid fuel or telephone bills. Remember:

- it is important to tell the Benefits Agency about any other people who can confirm what you have told it – eg, your solicitor or other representative, or a support group or official organisation;
- you should not be refused benefit simply because you do not have any documents, especially where it is unreasonable for you to have or obtain

them. Ask the Benefits Agency to make a decision on your claim and you can then appeal.

In some cases the Benefits Agency may refuse to accept evidence that you are who you say you are. Many travellers and Irish claimants find that the evidence they provide is simply not accepted as genuine – eg, there is suspicion about the validity of birth certificates. Asylum-seekers and Black people may also face hostility and mistrust when claiming. If, for example, you are an asylum-seeker and you have had to use forged papers to flee from persecution, the Benefits Agency might assume you are making a fraudulent claim. Press it to be clear about what is required and why, and complain if you feel any requests for information are unreasonable (see p2:661). You may also wish to approach your local race equality council if you feel that you have suffered racial discrimination.

The NINO requirement

When you claim benefit you must usually satisfy the national insurance number requirement – known as the NINO requirement:[19]

- by providing a national insurance number and information or evidence to show that it is yours; *or*
- by providing evidence or information to enable the Benefits Agency to trace your national insurance number, if you do not know it; *or*
- by applying for a national insurance number if you do not have one and providing enough information and evidence to allow one to be allocated to you.

You are exempt from the NINO requirement if:

- you are under 16 and the benefit is disability living allowance (DLA);[20]
- the benefit is child benefit, guardian's allowance, housing benefit (HB), council tax benefit (CTB), statutory sick pay, statutory maternity pay or social fund payments. However, the Government intends to introduce a NINO requirement for claims for HB and CTB (see p1:532);[21]
- you made your claim before 1 December 1997 and the benefit is disablement benefit, incapacity benefit, IS, maternity allowance, reduced earnings allowance, retirement pension, severe disablement allowance or widows' benefits;[22]
- you made your claim before 9 February 1998 and the benefit is attendance allowance, DLA, DWA, FC or invalid care allowance;[23]
- you made your claim before 5 October 1998 and the benefit is JSA.[24]

If you are claiming a means-tested benefit as a couple (see p2:114), or are claiming extra benefit for an adult dependant with your non-means-tested benefit (see p2:93), your partner or adult dependant must also satisfy the NINO requirement unless you claimed for her/him (or are treated as having done so) before 5 October 1998.[25]

It is an AO (see p2:561) who decides whether you satisfy the NINO requirement.[26] If s/he decides you do not and refuses your claim, you can appeal (see Chapter 56).

3. **When to claim**

You are not usually entitled to benefit for any day before your **date of claim**. See the chapter in this *Handbook* about the benefit you are claiming for information. Remember:
- you might be able to claim in advance if you know you are not entitled now but will be later – eg, you are coming out of hospital (see the chapter in this *Handbook* about the benefit you are claiming);
- your claim might be backdated in certain circumstances (see p2:487);
- if you claim the wrong benefit, your claim can be treated as one for the right benefit (see below).

What if you claim the wrong benefit?

If you have claimed the wrong benefit but are in fact entitled to another benefit, your original claim can sometimes be treated as a claim for the right benefit.[27] This might be a way around the strict rules for backdating benefit (see pp2:487-91). To find out which claims can interchange, see below. See also the section 'What if you claim the wrong benefit' in the chapter about the benefit you should have claimed.

Interchange of claims[28]

Benefit claimed:	May be treated as a claim for:
Incapacity benefit	Severe disablement allowance, maternity allowance
Severe disablement allowance	Incapacity benefit, maternity allowance
Maternity allowance	Incapacity benefit, severe disablement allowance
Widows' benefits	Retirement pension
Retirement pension	Widows' benefits
Income support	Invalid care allowance
Attendance allowance	Disability living allowance
Disability living allowance	Attendance allowance
Disability working allowance	Family credit
Family credit	Disability working allowance

In addition a claim for:

- **child benefit** can be treated as a claim for guardian's allowance, an increase of another benefit for your child (see p2:106) or even maternity allowance for the period since your child's birth and *vice versa;*[29]
- guardian's allowance can be treated as a claim for an increase of another benefit for your child (see p2:106) if you are not entitled to guardian's allowance;[30]
- **attendance allowance (AA)** or **disability living allowance (DLA)** can be treated as a claim for an increase in disablement pension where constant attendance is needed (see p1:217) and *vice versa.*

If you claim a non-means-tested benefit (other than child benefit) but are not entitled to it, your claim may be treated as a claim by someone else for an increase in her/his benefit for you (see p2:106). If you claim an increase of a non-means-tested benefit for a child or adult dependant (see Chapter 36) but are not entitled to it, the claim may be treated as a claim by someone else who is entitled.[31] An increase of incapacity benefit (IB) can be treated as an increase of severe disablement allowance (SDA) and *vice versa.*

The decision whether a claim can interchange is made by the Secretary of State (see p2:565). He does not have to accept your claim for one benefit as a claim for another but usually decides in your favour if the Benefits Agency should have realised from your claim that you had made a mistake. You cannot appeal if this is refused. Your only remedy is to seek a judicial review (see p2:637).

Backdating your claim

There are strict time limits for claiming benefits.[32] However, if you miss the time limit for claiming, your claim can sometimes be backdated for up to three months. If you want your claim to be backdated you must ask for this to happen or it will not be considered.[33]

Remember, claims for:

- some benefits can be backdated automatically (see p2:488);
- some benefits can only be backdated in very limited circumstances (see p2:489);
- AA, DLA[34] and earnings top-up (ETU) can never be backdated;
- if you claim the wrong benefit, your claim can sometimes be treated as a claim for the benefit you should have claimed (see p2:486).

For exceptions to the rules, see the chapter in this *Handbook* about the benefit you are claiming.

If you are prevented from receiving backdated benefit due to an error on the part of the Benefits Agency, you should try to persuade it to meet its moral obligation and make an *ex gratia* payment or extra-statutory payment to you, as compensation (see p2:663). To do this, simply write to your Benefits

Agency office and ask. The intervention of an MP or the Ombudsman (see p2:662) may help in these circumstances.

If you satisfy the conditions for getting benefit it should be paid from your date of claim. If backdating is refused you have a right to appeal (see Chapter 56). Payment should not be held up because you are challenging the decision on backdating.

Benefits that can be backdated automatically

Claims for the following benefits can be backdated for up to three months:[35]

- IB (Chapter 3);
- SDA (Chapter 4);
- industrial injuries benefits (Chapter 11);
- child benefit (Chapter 12);
- guardian's allowance (Chapter 13);
- increase of non-means-tested benefit for a dependant child or adult (Chapter 36);
- retirement pension (Chapter 13);
- widows' benefits (Chapter 7). The time limit can be extended in some cases eg, when you did not know your husband had died (see p1:128);
- maternity allowance (p1:100); *and*
- invalid care allowance (ICA – Chapter 5).

If you want backdated benefit for a period before your actual date of claim (see p2:486) you must show that you would have qualified for the benefit had you claimed at the time. For example, if you want to claim three months' backdated IB, you must show that you have been incapable of work (see p2:14) for the past three months.

If you want your claim to be backdated you must ask for this to happen or it will not be considered.[36] You do not have to show any special reasons for your delay in claiming. If you ask for your claim to be backdated, this should happen automatically.

You may have been entitled to a benefit for more than three months when you claim. In this situation, you can ask for your claim to be backdated the full three months but you cannot get more than this.

Example

Glen is self-employed. He has been off sick for six months but did not realise he could claim IB. He makes a claim and asks for it to be backdated. He qualifies for IB and is paid three months' arrears.

There are exceptions to the rules. If you miss the time limit for claiming disablement benefit for occupational deafness (prescribed disease A10) or occupational asthma (prescribed disease D7) – see p1:209 – or widow's payment (see p1:113), you may lose your right to benefit altogether.

Backdating income support, jobseeker's allowance, family credit and disability working allowance

If you want to claim income support (IS), jobseeker's allowance (JSA), family credit (FC) or disability working allowance (DWA) for a period before your date of claim (see pp1:452, 1:356, 1:465 and 1:479), your claim can be backdated:

- for up to one month if the Secretary of State decides there are good administrative reasons (see below);
- for up to three months if you can show that it was not reasonable to expect you to claim before you did and your delay was for one of the specified reasons on p2:490.

Note: there are exceptions to the rules. See the chapter in this *Handbook* about the benefit you are claiming. If you are claiming backdated IS after you are awarded refugee status the backdating rules do not apply (see p2:216).

If you want your claim to be backdated you must ask for this to happen or it will not be considered.[37]

If you are claiming benefit late, it is important to explain why. Provide evidence or information that backs this up, for example, a copy of the letter from your adviser or information from your employer which misled you (see p2:490). If you have been misled, misinformed or insufficiently informed by an officer of the DSS, explain how and when this happened and where possible, give the name and a description of the officer concerned. Where relevant, you should explain why there is no one else who could help you make your claim.

One month backdating – for good administrative reasons

The Secretary of State can backdate your claim for up to one month, but only if it is 'consistent with the proper administration of benefit' and one of the following applies:[38]

- your claim is late because the office where you are supposed to claim was closed – eg, due to a strike – and there were no other arrangements for claims to be made;
- you could not get to the benefit office or JobCentre due to difficulties with the type of transport you normally use and there was no reasonable alternative;
- there were adverse postal conditions – eg, bad weather or a postal strike;
- you stopped getting another benefit but were not informed before your entitlement ceased so you could not claim IS, JSA, FC or DWA in time;
- you claimed IS or JSA in your own right within one month of separating from your partner;

- you claimed FC within one month of your entitlement to IS or JSA ceasing;
- you claimed DWA within one month of your entitlement to IS, JSA, incapacity benefit or severe disablement allowance ceasing;
- a close relative of yours died in the month before your claim. 'Close relative' in these circumstances means your partner, parent, son, daughter, brother or sister.

Three months backdating – for other specified reasons

Your claim can be backdated for up to three months if you can show that it was not reasonable to expect you to claim earlier than you did for one of the following specified reasons:[39]

- you have learning, language or literacy difficulties *or* are deaf or blind *or* were sick or disabled (but not if you are claiming JSA) *or* were caring for someone who is sick or disabled *or* were dealing with a domestic emergency which affected you *and* it was not 'reasonably practicable' for you to get help to make your claim from anyone else;
- you were given information by an officer of the DSS or the Department for Education and Employment and as a result thought you were not entitled to benefit;
- you were given advice in writing by a CAB or other advice worker, a solicitor or other professional adviser (eg, an accountant), a doctor or a local authority and as a result thought you were not entitled to benefit;
- you or your partner were given written information about your income or capital by your employer or former employer or a bank or building society and as a result you thought you were not entitled to benefit;
- you could not get to the benefit office or JobCentre because of bad weather.

Even if one of these applies, you might be paid less than three months' arrears if you claim because of a new interpretation of the law.[40]

If a person has been formally appointed by a court or the Secretary of State to act on your behalf, it is your **appointee** (see p2:480) not you who must show that it was not reasonable to expect her/him to claim sooner than s/he did for one of the reasons listed above.[41] If someone is informally acting on your behalf, you must show this. You must also show that it was reasonable for you to delegate responsibility for your claim and that you took care to ensure the person helping you did it properly.[42]

Extra backdating after awards of qualifying benefits

If you claim DWA, IB, SDA or ICA your claim may, in some cases, be refused while you are waiting to hear whether you (or in the case of ICA, the person you are caring for) are entitled to a qualifying benefit (see pp1:475, 1:38, 2:24, 1:65 and 1:81). In these circumstances if you make a further claim once the qualifying benefit is awarded, your IB, SDA or ICA are backdated to the date of your original claim or the date on which the qualifying benefit was first payable (whichever is later).[43] You must make your further claim within three months of the date of the Benefits Agency's decision to pay the qualifying benefit

You might not be entitled to IS or JSA currently but would be once you or another member of your family becomes entitled to another benefit. See p2:578 for information about what you must do to get extra backdating.

Note: These rules may change when the Social Security Act 1998 takes effect (see p2:581).

4. **How your claim is dealt with**

Once your claim is accepted as valid it should be referred to an adjucation officer (AO) (see p2:561) for a decision.[44] If you are later asked for additional information or evidence but do not provide it, or you do not attend an interview, your claim still has to be referred to an AO who is not entitled to withhold a decision even if you have not complied with the Secretary of State's request for further evidence.[45] The AO, and the tribunal if you appeal, must make a decision on the available evidence. Obviously, an AO or tribunal is unlikely to decide in your favour if you fail to provide evidence which would help to show you are entitled to benefit. You should make sure that the AO has all the evidence that might be relevant. The stricter rules for claiming jobseeker's allowance (JSA), and income support (IS) (see p2:482 for details of the onus of proof rule), place a greater burden on you as a claimant.

Until your claim is passed to an AO to decide, there is no decision on it against which you can appeal.

Once the AO has made a decision on your claim, if benefit is awarded it is awarded:
- for a set period of 26 weeks if the benefit is family credit (FC), disability working allowance (DWA) or earnings top-up (ETU) (see pp1:468 and 1:482); *or*
- for a set period or for life if the benefit is attendance allowance, disability living allowance or disablement benefit (see pp1:192 and 1:214); *or*
- for a fortnight at a time if the benefit is JSA; *or*
- in all other cases, for as long as you continue to be entitled to benefit.[46]

Your award may be reviewed if your circumstances change or if you cease to satisfy the conditions for entitlement (see pp2:570 and 2:571). If you are claiming FC, ETU or DWA, your award can only be reviewed in limited circumstances (see pp1:468, 1:483 and 1:505).

If you disagree with a decision on your claim, you can seek a review (see Chapter 53). You can also appeal (see Chapter 56). If you are unhappy about how your claim has been dealt with you can make a complaint or even seek compensation (see Chapter 57).

Changes of circumstance after you claim

You may be on benefit for a quite a long time during which your circumstances may change. You must inform the benefit office or JobCentre, in writing, of any change which might affect the amount of or your right to benefit.[47] Keep a copy of the letter you send reporting such changes. The Benefits Agency can accept notification by some other method (ie, by telephone), but this is not always acted on so it is best to do it in writing.

If you fail to report a change and as a result receive too much benefit, the Benefits Agency might take steps to recover the overpayment (see p2:517) or even treat this as fraud (see Chapter 52).

5. **Getting paid**

The Secretary of State decides how benefit is paid to you.[48] Benefit can be paid by girocheque or order book which you can cash at nominated post offices.

Alternatively you can choose to be paid some benefits by direct credit transfer into a bank or other account either four-weekly or quarterly in arrears. It may also be possible to be paid cash in certain circumstances – eg, if you live at an unsafe address.[49]

In some areas there are trial schemes for paying benefit by a Benefit Payment Card. This is like a credit card which you hand in to the post office when you collect your benefit and it connects to a central computer which authorises payment.

How, when and how often your benefit is paid depends on what benefit you have claimed.[50] You are sometimes paid in advance and sometimes in arrears. See the chapter in this *Handbook* about the benefit you are claiming for further information.

Once you have been awarded benefit you must cash the payment within a year of it being due.[51] This period can be extended if you can show good cause for the delay.[52] However, an order book is only valid for three months and a giro for one month. If you do not cash them within this period you have to try to get a replacement.

Who is paid your benefit

Payment is usually made directly to you but there are some circumstances in which payments can be made to other people or organisations on your behalf.

- If you are unable to manage your own money or if you die, your benefit is paid to a person appointed to act on your behalf (see p2:480).[53]
- If it is in the interests of you, your partner or your children, the Secretary of State can pay your benefit to another person.[54] For example, if your partner is refusing to support you, all or part of her/his benefit can be paid to you. If you are neglecting your children even though benefit is being paid for them, it might be paid to another person to help look after them.
- If you are claiming income support (IS) or income-based jobseeker's allowance (JSA) and are getting help with your housing costs (see Chapter 46) these are usually paid direct to your lender on your behalf (see p2:502).
- If you are claiming IS or JSA, and are in certain types of debt, payments can be made to your creditors on your behalf (see p2:501).[55]

Getting more than one benefit

You can claim a combination of benefits. However, there are rules which deal with situations where you are entitled to more than one non-means-tested benefit at a time (see below) or to an increase in your non-means-tested benefit for an adult dependant (see p2:93) while that person is her/himself entitled to benefit. These are known as the 'overlapping benefit' rules. These rules also apply where more than one person is claiming for the same child or adult dependant (see p2:495) and where you are getting child benefit or guardian's allowance as well as an increase in your non-means-tested benefit for your child (see p2:495).

Remember:

- disability living allowance (DLA) care component and attendance allowance (AA) overlap with constant attendance allowance.[56] Otherwise AA, disablement benefit (see p1:215), reduced earnings allowance (see p1:217) and retirement allowance (see p1:223) can be received in addition to any of the other benefits described in this *Handbook* – eg, you may receive incapacity benefit, both components of DLA and disablement benefit all at once;
- you might qualify for IS, income-based JSA, family credit, earnings top-up, disability working allowance, housing benefit or council tax benefit in addition to your non-means-tested benefit, although the non-means-tested benefit is usually taken into account as income (see p2:405).

Earnings replacement benefits

Some benefits are available to compensate you for your inability to work through unemployment, sickness, pregnancy or old age. These are known as 'earnings replacement' benefits. You cannot usually receive more than one of the following 'earnings replacement' benefits at a time.

- Contributory benefits:
  - contribution-based JSA;
  - incapacity benefit;

- maternity allowance;
- retirement pension;
- widow's pension;
- widowed mother's allowance.
- Non-contributory benefits:
  - severe disablement allowance;
  - invalid care allowance.

Where there is an entitlement to more than one of the benefits above the following rules apply:[57]
- a contributory benefit is paid in preference to a non-contributory benefit. However, this is topped up by any balance of a non-contributory benefit due;
- weekly benefits are paid and topped up by any balance of daily benefit (unless the claimant makes an application to receive the daily benefit in full) – see the chapter in this *Handbook* about the benefit you are claiming to see if it is a daily or a weekly benefit;
- the highest rate benefit is paid, or if the rates are the same one benefit is paid.

Other adjustments

If you are getting a **training allowance** paid by a government department or training agency, your earnings replacement benefit is reduced by the amount of the training allowance.[58]

If you are getting **unemployability supplement** under the industrial injuries scheme or war pensions scheme your earnings replacement benefit, other than maternity allowance is reduced by the amount of the unemployability supplement. You cannot usually get more than one **retirement pension** at a time. However, there are special rules if you are a widow or widower entitled to both a Category A (see p1:138) and a Category B retirement pension (see p1:138) and your Category A pension would be paid at a reduced rate because you have not paid enough contributions (see p2:274). In this situation your basic Category A pension is increased by either:[59]
- £39.95 a week; *or*
- the amount of any shortfall up to £66.75 a week;

whichever is less. You are also entitled to an additional pension on your own contribution record and one on your spouse's record up to the maximum additional pension a person could theoretically receive on one contribution record.[60]

Earnings-related additions to non-means-tested benefits

Additional pensions under SERPS (see p1:153) and graduated retirement benefit (see p1:140) do not overlap with non-means-tested benefits. However, if two or more benefits would otherwise be payable with an additional pension and graduated retirement benefit, only the higher or highest total of additional pension and graduated retirement benefit payable in addition to one of those benefits is due.[61]

There are exceptions to this rule if you are a Category B retirement pensioner whose own contribution records would entitle you to a Category A retirement pension or if you are a widow who receives transitional long-term incapacity benefit (IB) (see p1:47).

An age addition paid with IB, severe disablement allowance (SDA) or retirement pension overlaps with another age addition.[62]

Increases to non-means-tested benefits in respect of adult dependants

Only one person may receive an increase of benefit in respect of the same dependant, except when one of you receives an increase because the dependant is someone employed by you to look after your child(ren) and the dependant does not live with you (in this case, both of you can claim). Equally, you may only receive one increase in respect of an adult dependant. If, apart from those rules, more than one increase would be payable, only the higher or highest total is paid.[63] See p2:93 for who can claim increases for dependants.

An increase for an adult dependant also overlaps with any of the benefits listed on pp2:493-494 or training allowances which are payable to that dependant – eg, you are claiming an increase of retirement pension for your partner, but s/he is claiming incapacity benefit in her/his own right.[64] If the increase is less than the benefit payable to your dependant, the increase is not paid. If the increase is greater than the basic benefit, you get the difference. This does not apply if the adult is not residing with you and is employed by you to care for a child.

Child benefit, guardian's allowance and increases to non-means-tested benefits for child dependants

Only one person may receive child benefit or an increase to a non-means-tested benefit for a child dependant for the same child (see pp1:232 and 2:97).

The standard rate of child benefit (see p1:241) does not overlap with any other benefit. However, if you receive the extra £4.80 a week payable for your eldest child (see p1:241), any other benefit or increase paid for the same child, or guardian's allowance, is reduced by £1.45.[65]

You cannot get the lone parent rate of child benefit if, for the same child, you get an increase in widowed mother's allowance, disablement benefit, ICA or retirement pension.[66] Instead you get the standard rate of child benefit for the child. Increases in IB or SDA are reduced by £6.75 a week if you receive the lone parent rate of child benefit for the same child.[67]

All increases for children and child's special allowance overlap with guardian's allowance and industrial death benefit for children and are reduced by the level of guardian's allowance you get for the child.[68]

Lost and missing payments

If you are entitled to benefit, the Secretary of State has a duty to pay you.[69] This duty is only discharged when you cash your giro or order book. If your giro is lost or stolen before you have had a chance to cash it, the Secretary of State has a duty to replace it. This applies even if the giro is later cashed by someone else.[70] The Benefits Agency may make enquiries, but it is for the Benefits Agency to prove you cashed your giro or order book, not for you to prove you did not. The Benefits Agency says your giro or order book should be replaced immediately if you deny you received or cashed it, where there is no evidence otherwise.[71]

Getting a replacement giro or order book

If you lose a giro or order book after you have received it, report the loss immediately to the benefit office or JobCentre by telephone or personal visit and confirm the loss in writing, requesting a replacement at the same time. You should also report the matter to the police, and note the investigating officer's name and number. The Benefits Agency should replace your giro or order book straightaway unless there are good grounds for refusal.[72] It should not delay, for example, to trace a giro or paid order.[73]

If the Benefits Agency refuses to issue a replacement, or takes too long considering your request, you can take legal action to get the benefit due to you. You cannot appeal to a tribunal if a payment goes missing, but you can sue the Secretary of State in the county court.[74] This can take time, so you may wish to claim a crisis loan to tide you over (see p1:667).

Before taking legal action you should write to the local Benefits Agency office requesting it to replace the giro immediately. Explain that court action will be taken if it does not respond. Keep a copy of the letter.

If the Benefits Agency does not replace your giro or order book, you need to begin proceedings in the local county court. The forms to do this are available from the county court. Complete these and return them to the court. You have to pay a court fee, calculated as a percentage of your unpaid giro. The fee is refundable if you win. The Benefits Agency is allowed time to respond to your summons, but you will almost certainly find that the local Benefits Agency office will replace your giro without the need to proceed to a court hearing. Your court fee is repaid separately by the Benefits Agency Solicitors (see Appendix 1 for address), and you should not withdraw the summons until you have received both a replacement giro and your court fee. If the Benefits Agency refuses to pay benefit for a future period covered by a lost order book, you can take court action in the High Court (see p2:637).

Suspension and withholding of payments

The Secretary of State can *suspend* payment of your benefit if:

- **a question has arisen about your entitlement.**[75] In this case, all or part of the benefit due to you is suspended pending a review or appeal of the decision about your entitlement. For example, if you are being paid IS but it is thought that you are in full-time work, your benefit may be suspended while information is gathered about the true situation;

- **you have been getting JSA** and a question has arisen whether you are available for or actively seeking work. Your JSA is suspended until this matter is resolved;[76]

- **it looks as though your award of benefit should be superseded or revised;**[77]

- **you are awarded benefit by a tribunal, commissioner or court but the Benefits Agency wants to appeal against that decision.**[78] If this happens, your award can only be suspended for three months after the adjudication officer (AO) receives the decision while the Benefits Agency considers an appeal to the social security commissioner or courts. If it decides to appeal, it must notify you in writing within the three months. You are then not paid until your case is resolved. If the AO misses the time limit for appealing then the Benefits Agency may still be allowed to appeal (if the AO has 'special reasons' for a late appeal – see p2:615) but the benefit you have been awarded must be paid to you while the appeal is going through;

- **you are due to be paid arrears of a benefit but you may also have been overpaid.**[79] All or part of your arrears may be withheld while the possible overpayment is investigated;

- **the Benefits Agency is appealing (or considering an appeal) to the courts about someone else's claim**, and the issue in the appeal affects your claim.[80] All or part of your benefit can be suspended until the appeal is decided or the time limit for appealing has expired. This rule only applies from 30 June 1998.[81] If your benefit was suspended in this way prior to that date, you should ask the Benefits Agency to start paying your benefit immediately and to give you what has been withheld so far. You should be given what was withheld even if the appeal about someone else's claim has already been decided. Even if the decision was negative, you should be paid up to the date of that decision. If the Benefits Agency refuses to pay, you should seek advice. Where a tribunal, a commissioner or a court has awarded you benefit, the Benefits Agency can only suspend your benefit if it appeals your case (see above).[82]

Your benefit can be *withheld* if:[83]

- **you fail to provide information in support of your claim** within 28 days of being asked;

- **you do not send in sick notes;**

- there are doubts about where you are living;
- you are claiming JSA and **fail to attend the JobCentre** when asked to do so or you **miss a signing on** or fail to provide a postal declaration (see p1:366). You could lose entitlement altogether if you cannot show 'good cause' (see p1:369).

If you later fulfil these requirements you can be paid any benefit that has been withheld, but you must normally apply to the Benefits Agency within 12 months if the payment is not made automatically.[84]

Note: When the Social Security Act 1998 takes effect, the Secretary of State will also be able to withhold making a decision while a test case is pending (see p2:587).

Challenging decisions to withhold or suspend benefit

Even if the Secretary of State may legally suspend benefit in your case, that does not mean that he must do so and he may be willing to continue to pay your benefit, or at least some of it, if you can show that you will suffer hardship otherwise. So, if you receive a letter telling you that your benefit has been suspended, it is always worth writing back explaining how the suspension will affect you and asking the Benefits Agency to reconsider. This is an important letter and it may be wise to get advice (see Appendix 2) before writing.

The decision to suspend or withhold benefit is made by the Secretary of State and you cannot appeal against it to a tribunal. Your only remedy is judicial review (see p2:637). You must negotiate to get your benefit reinstated and/or request an interim payment (see p2:499). You should try to persuade the Secretary of State that it is unreasonable to suspend or withhold payment of your benefit, particularly if hardship is caused.

The Social Security Act 1998

When the Social Security Act takes effect (see p2:582 for the timetable for implementation), the Benefits Agency will also be able to suspend your benefit if you:

- fail to provide information requested by the Benefits Agency.[85] Your claim will be terminated if you do not provide the information within one month (see p2:499);
- fail to submit to a medical examination on two consecutive occasions without 'good cause'.[86] No earlier than one month after your benefit is suspended, the Secretary of State can decide to terminate your claim.[87]

Failure to satisfy the information requirements

If you fall into one of the following categories you can be required to supply information or evidence to enable the Secretary of State to determine whether a decision on your claim should be revised or superseded (see pp2:582 and 2:585):

- a question arises as to whether you are entitled to benefit or whether a decision on your award should be revised or superseded;[88]
- you have requested that a decision on your claim be revised or superseded;
- you have failed to comply with a request for documents, information or facts;
- you are entitled to benefit on the basis of incapacity for work.[89]

To satisfy the information requirement, you must either supply the information or evidence required within one month (in some cases a longer period can be allowed) or satisfy the Secretary of State that it does not exist or you cannot obtain it.[90]

If you fall into the first category above, the Secretary of State can suspend payment of benefit and then request the information or evidence. If you fail to satisfy the information requirement within one month of the request for information being made, your entitlement can be terminated.[91] Entitlement can only be terminated if payment was suspended in full.[92] The termination takes effect from the date payment was suspended (or an earlier date if you cease to be entitled for another reason).[93]

If you fall into one of the other categories, you have one month to satisfy the information requirement. If you do not do so, payment can be suspended.[94] After a further month your entitlement can be terminated.[95]

Interim payments

If payment of your benefit is delayed you may be in urgent need of money. If this is the case, you can ask for an interim payment.

An interim payment can be made where it seems that you are or may be entitled to benefit and where:[96]

- you have claimed it but not in the correct way (eg, you have filled in the wrong form, or filled in the right form incorrectly or incompletely – see p2:482) and you cannot put in a correct claim immediately (eg, because the Benefits Agency office is closed). This is an important provision because it allows for a payment of benefit to be made before the information requirements and other conditions for making a valid claim for benefit are met (see p2:482); *or*
- you have claimed it correctly, but it is not possible for the claim, or for a review or appeal which relates to it, to be dealt with immediately. However, if your claim is being appealed, an interim payment can only be made if the Secretary of State thinks you are entitled to some benefit. This rule might be invalid in a case involving EC law.[97] If you think this applies to you, you should seek advice; *or*

• you have been awarded benefit, but it is not possible to pay you immediately other than by means of an interim payment.

The decision whether or not to award an interim payment is the Secretary of State's and therefore you cannot appeal to a tribunal if you are refused, although it may be possible to apply for judicial review (see p2:637). If you are refused an interim payment, contact your MP and see Chapter 31 to find out if you can get a crisis loan. You could also try using the emergency service (see below).

An interim payment can be deducted from any later payment of benefit and if it is more than your actual entitlement, the overpayment can be recovered.[98] You should be notified of this in advance, unless it is an interim payment of:

• IS made because you have not received child support maintenance (see p2:292). In this case, any overpayment is recovered from the arrears of maintenance rather than your benefit; or

• DLA and you are terminally ill or had an invalid vehicle.

Emergencies

If you have lost all your money or there has been a similar crisis, it is possible to get help at any time. Any local police station should have a contact number for Benefits Agency staff on call outside normal office hours.

If you are unable to contact the Benefits Agency your local social services office may be able to help. The police station should have a contact number.

It is important, if you need money urgently, that you provide as much information you can to support your claim. It may help if you can get an advice agency or third party (such as a health visitor or social worker, doctor or MP) to support you.

---

6. **Deductions from your income support or jobseeker's allowance**

Your income support (IS) and jobseeker's allowance (JSA) are usually paid directly to you but there are some circumstances when money can be deducted and paid to a third party on your behalf. These are known as 'direct payments'. Most 'direct payments are to clear debts but some are to help you budget for current costs. Deductions can be made from IS and income-based JSA (see p2:50). They can also be made from contribution-based JSA but only in limited circumstances (see p2:501)

What deductions can be made

Amounts can be deducted from your IS or income-based JSA to pay for:[99]
* housing costs paid to your lender under the mortgage payment scheme (p2:502);
* other housing costs (p2:503);
* rent arrears (p2:504);
* residential accommodation charges (p2:504);
* hostel payments (p2:504);
* fuel (p2:505);
* water charges (p2:505);
* council tax arrears (p2:505);
* community charge arrears (p2:505);
* fines (p2:506); *and*
* child support maintenance (p2:301).

You may also have deductions made for the recovery of social fund loans (p1:664) and overpayments (p2:525).

Deductions from contribution-based jobseeker's allowance

Deductions can be made from your contribution-based JSA for the payments listed above (other than child support maintenance – see example below) if you have an 'underlying entitlement' to income-based JSA. This means that if you were not entitled to contribution-based JSA, you would be entitled to income-based JSA of at least the same rate (see example below).

Deductions can also be made from contribution-based JSA if you have no underlying entitlement to income-based JSA, but only for community charge arrears, council tax arrears, fines and child support maintenance arrears.

Example 1
Tina is 27 and receives contribution-based JSA of £51.40 a week. She has no other income and no savings. The amount of the income-based JSA she would receive if she was not getting contribution-based JSA would also be £51.40 a week. Deductions can be made from Tina's contribution-based JSA as if she were receiving income-based JSA.

Example 2
George is 42. He receives contribution-based JSA of £51.40 a week. His wife works full-time. Because of this, if George were not getting contribution-based JSA he would not be entitled to income-based JSA. As he has no underlying entitlement to income-based JSA, deductions can only be made from his contribution-based JSA for community charge or council tax arrears, child support maintenance arrears and fines.

When can deductions be made?

Deductions and direct payments to third parties can only be made if you or your partner are liable to make the payments.[100] If there is a doubt whether you or your partner are liable, deductions should only be made if there is evidence that you are liable – for example, the bill is in your name or your partner's name.

Do you have to agree to deductions?

You must consent before direct payments are made for housing costs arrears, rent arrears and service charges for fuel and water; fuel costs (including arrears) and water charges (including arrears) if the total to be deducted for these payments exceeds 25 per cent of your family's applicable amount (ie, allowances and premiums – see p2:318).[101] Any housing costs included in your applicable amount (see Chapter 46) should not be taken into account when calculating the 25 per cent.[102]

The Benefits Agency can make deductions without your agreement if it is made for: community charge or council tax arrears; fines; child support maintenance; current housing costs; current mortgage interest; nursing home charges or hostel charges not included in your housing benefit (HB). Consent is not needed for these deductions even if the total amount deducted exceeds 25 per cent of your applicable amount.[103]

The deductions

Deductions are made at the Benefits Agency office before you receive your regular benefit payment. If you want to have deductions made to help you clear any arrears or debts, ask at the Benefits Agency office dealing with your IS or JSA claim. If you disagree with a decision about deductions, you can appeal (see p2:611).

The mortgage payment scheme

When you first claim IS or income-based JSA you may not receive help with your housing costs (see Chapter 46) and you must meet these costs from other income – eg, a mortgage protection policy. Once you qualify for help with housing costs the amount for mortgage interest or interest on loans for repairs and improvements is usually paid direct to your lender for each complete week that you are on benefit.[104] The only exceptions to this are where your lender is not covered by, or has opted out of, the mortgage payments scheme.[105] The Benefits Agency should tell you if this is the case and you must pay your own mortgage.

Your housing costs are deducted from your total IS or income-based JSA entitlement and you get the balance.[106] You have to make up any difference between what the Benefits Agency pays to your lender and the amount you owe them. This could include such things as mortgage capital, non-dependant deductions or a restriction due to excessive housing costs. If you get incapacity benefit, severe disablement allowance or retirement pension paid on the same giro or order book as your IS, deductions can be made from these benefits too. If you do not have enough benefit to meet the full cost, all but 10 pence of your benefit is paid over and you must pay the rest yourself.[107]

Payments are made four-weekly in arrears[108] even if your payments are due on a calendar month basis, so you may appear to be in arrears even though your full mortgage is being met. You might need to explain this to your lender. If the Benefits Agency deducts your housing costs from your IS or income-based JSA, but fails to pay these to your lender in time and as a result you have to pay interest on arrears that build up or you lose your home, you should seek advice. You might be able to claim compensation.[109]

If you have more than one type of housing cost or more than one loan, deductions for non-dependants (see p2:356) and certain restrictions for excessive housing costs are apportioned using a formula (see p2:507).[110]

If you are in mortgage arrears, no amount towards the arrears can be deducted from your benefit if your lender is covered by the mortgage payments scheme. If you are in this situation, you should seek financial advice. If you are in arrears and your lender is not covered by the mortgage payment scheme, see below.

If you have a mortgage protection policy the amount of mortgage interest paid direct is reduced. The reduction is the amount of income from the insurance policy which is taken into account.[111]

If an overpayment of mortgage interest is paid to your lender see p2:528.

Other housing costs[112]

The IS or income-based JSA for your mortgage interest is usually paid direct to your lender under the mortgage payments scheme (see above). If this applies to you (or would if your lender had not opted out of the scheme) then the deductions under this provision only cover payments for other types of housing costs (see p2:341).[113]

If your current IS or income-based JSA includes money for such housing costs and you are in debt for these costs (excluding payments for ground rent or feu duty unless paid with your service charges or for a tent[114]), deductions can be made from your benefit both to clear the debt and to meet current payments. Deductions are made if it would be 'in the interests' of you or your family to do so.

You only qualify for direct deductions if you owe more than half of the annual total of the relevant housing cost. This condition can be waived if it is in the 'overriding interests' of you or your family that deductions start as soon as possible – eg, repossession of your home is imminent.[115]

In the case of mortgage payments, the adjudication officer must be satisfied there are arrears.[116] You must have paid less than eight weeks' worth of full payments in the last 12 weeks. The amount of mortgage interest taken into account is the amount after deductions for non-dependants (see p2:356).

Rent arrears[117]

If you are in arrears with your rent (including any inclusive water, fuel and service charges) while on benefit, an amount can be deducted from your IS or JSA and paid direct to your landlord.

Rent arrears do not include the amount of any non-dependant deductions (see p1:525), but can cover any water charges or service charges payable with your rent and not met by HB. Fuel charges included in your rent cannot be covered by direct deductions if they change more than twice a year.

To qualify for direct deductions your rent arrears must amount to at least four times your full weekly rent. If you have not paid your full rent for more than eight weeks, direct deductions can be made automatically if your landlord asks the Benefits Agency to make them.[118] If your arrears relate to a shorter period, deductions can only be made if it is in the overriding interests of your family to do so.[119] In either case the adjudication officer must be satisfied that you are in rent arrears. Even if you are, you can ask her/him not to make direct deductions – eg, where you are claiming compensation from your landlord because of the state of repair of your home.[120] Once your arrears are paid off, direct payments can continue for any fuel and water charges inclusive in your rent.[121]

Residential accommodation charges[122]

The amount of IS or income-based JSA you are paid may cover charges for your accommodation if you live in a residential care or nursing home, or local authority residential accommodation (see p2:167).

These charges can be met by direct deductions from your benefit if you have failed to budget for the charges from your benefit and it is in your interest that deductions should be made. Even if these conditions do not apply direct payments can be made if you are in a home run by a voluntary organisation for alcoholics or drug addicts.

Hostel payments[123]

If you (or your partner) live in a hostel *and* you have claimed HB to meet your accommodation costs *and* your payments to the hostel cover fuel, meals, water charges, laundry and/or cleaning of your room, part of your IS or JSA can be paid direct to the hostel for these items. You do not have to be in arrears for this to apply. These costs are all items which cannot be covered by HB (see p1:520) and which you must meet from your IS or JSA. Fuel costs are not paid direct if the charge varies according to actual consumption, unless the charge is altered less than three times a year.

Fuel debts[124]

If you are in debt, an amount can be deducted from your benefit each week and paid over to the fuel board in instalments – usually once a quarter. This is known as 'fuel direct'. In return, the fuel board agrees not to disconnect you. Deductions can be made where:[125]

- the amount you owe is £51.40 or more (including reconnection or disconnection charges if you have been disconnected); *and*
- you continue to need the fuel supply; *and*
- it is in your interest to have deductions made.

An amount is deducted for the fuel you use each week (your 'current consumption') as well as for the arrears you owe. The amount deducted for current consumption is whatever is necessary to meet your current weekly fuel costs. This is adjusted if the cost increases or decreases. Deductions for current consumption can be continued after the debt has been cleared.[126]

Water charges[127]

If you get into debt with charges for water and sewerage, direct deductions might be made – 'debt' includes any disconnection, reconnection and legal charges. If you pay your landlord for water with your rent, deductions are made under the arrangements for rent arrears (see p2:504).[128]

Deductions can be made if you failed to budget and it is in the interests of your family to make deductions.[129] If you get into debt with water charges you should consider making an agreement for direct deductions because the water authority can cut off your water supply if you do not meet your debts and current charges. If you are in debt to two water companies you can only have a deduction for arrears made to one of them at a time. Your debts for water charges should be cleared before your debts for sewerage costs, but the amount paid for current consumption can include both water and sewerage charges.[130]

Council tax and community charge arrears[131]

Deductions for council tax or community charge arrears can be made from IS or JSA if the local authority gets a liability order from a magistrates' court (in Scotland, a summary warrant or decree from a sheriff's court) and applies to the Benefits Agency for recovery to be made in this way. For community charge purposes, if they want to recover arrears from both you and your partner the order must be against both of you. Deductions can be made for arrears and any unpaid costs or penalties imposed. Deductions cannot be made for council tax arrears while community charge deductions are being made.

Fines, costs and compensation orders[132]

Magistrates' courts (any court in Scotland) can apply to the Benefits Agency for a fine, costs or compensation order to be deducted from your IS or JSA. Only one court application can be dealt with at a time – if a second application is made it is not dealt with until the first debt is paid.

Deductions can only be made if you are 18 or over, on IS or JSA, and you have defaulted on payments. Payments continue until the debt is paid off, or your IS or JSA ceases or is too low to cover the repayments.

Child support maintenance

Deductions can be made from an absent parent's IS or income-based JSA as a contribution towards the maintenance of her/his child(ren) – see p2:301.[133]

How much can be deducted?

Deductions are made to pay off the debt, or current weekly costs or both.[134] Deductions are made from your IS and any incapacity benefit, retirement pension or severe disablement allowance paid with it in the same giro or order book. They are also made from your JSA.[135] You must be left with at least 10 pence. Council tax and community charge arrears can be deducted from IS and JSA only.[136]

If deductions are being made from your contribution-based JSA where you do not have an underlying entitlement to income-based JSA (see p2:501) for community charge arrears, council tax arrears or fines, the maximum deduction is one-third of the weekly amount of JSA for a person of your age. If deductions are being made for child support maintenance arrears, see p2:303 for the maximum amounts.

If deductions are being made from your IS, income-based JSA (or contribution-based JSA where you have an underlying entitlement to income-based JSA – see p2:501), maximum deductions are shown below.

Type of arrears	Deduction for arrears	Deduction for ongoing cost
Mortgage direct payments*	Nil	Current weekly cost
Housing costs*	£2.60 each housing debt (maximum of £7.80 payable)	Current weekly cost
Rent arrears	£2.60	Nil (met by HB)
Fuel	£2.60 each fuel debt (maximum of £5.20 payable)	Estimated amount of current consumption

Water charges	£2.60 (adjusted every 26 weeks)	Estimated costs
Council tax	£2.60	Nil (met by council tax benefit)
Community charge	£2.60 (single person) £4.05 (couple)	Not applicable
Fines	Nil	£2.60
Child maintenance	Nil	£5.20
Residential accommodation charges	Nil	The accommodation allowance (for those in local authority homes). All but £14.75 of your IS (for those in private or voluntary homes)
Hostel charges	Nil	Weekly amount assessed by local authority

* If you have more than one type of housing cost and these are not met in full because of a restriction on the amount which can be covered (see p2:354), or a non-dependant deduction (see p2:356) the direct payment to meet current weekly costs is reduced as follows:[137]

Multiply the amount of the restriction and/or deduction by the amount of the item of housing costs to be paid direct and then divide by the amount of total housing costs.

This ensures that such reductions are shared proportionately between different items of housing costs.

More than one debt

For **IS** and **income-based JSA** deductions for arrears can be made for more than one debt. However:

- the maximum amount that can be deducted from your benefit for arrears (excluding community charge arrears) and a contribution towards child maintenance (if you have to make one) is £7.80 a week.[138] The total amount deducted from benefit may be more than £7.80 if you are having deductions made for current costs as well as for arrears. If the total amount of deductions for arrears would exceed £7.80 a week, the deductions are made in a set order of priority (see p2:508);
- if deductions of £5.20 are being made for items of a higher priority than child maintenance (see p2:508), half of the child maintenance deduction is made – ie, £2.60;

- in the case of fuel, rent arrears, water charges and housing costs arrears, if the combined cost of deductions for arrears and current consumption is more than 25 per cent of your total applicable amount (see p2:318) the deductions cannot be made without your consent.[139]

Where there is no underlying entitlement to income-based JSA, the maximum amount that can be deducted in total (for debts) from **contribution-based JSA** for community charge or council tax, fines and child support maintenance arrears is one-third of the age-related amount of contribution-based JSA payable.[140]

Priority between debts

If you have more debts or charges than can be met within the limits for direct payments (see above), they are paid in the following order of priority:[141]
1st housing costs not covered by the mortgage payment scheme (see p2:340)
2nd rent arrears (and related charges)
3rd fuel charges
4th water charges
5th council tax and community charge arrears
6th unpaid fines, costs and compensation orders
7th payments for maintenance of children

If you owe both gas and electricity, the Benefits Agency chooses which one to pay first, depending on your circumstances. If you have arrears for both council tax and community charge, only one application can be dealt with at a time and the earliest debt should be dealt with first.[142]

If you have been overpaid benefit or given a social fund loan, you may have to repay these too by having deductions from your benefit.[143] You should argue that these deductions should take a lower priority.

7. **Recovery of benefits from compensation payments**

If you are seeking compensation from someone (a defendant) through the courts, for example, because you have been unfairly dismissed or because you have suffered a personal injury, you might be awarded damages to compensate you for your loss. However, if, as the result of a defendant's action, you have had to claim benefit, the amount of damages to be awarded is reduced by the amount of benefit you received.

Employment cases

In a wrongful or unfair dismissal case, the claim for loss of earnings is reduced by the amount of jobseeker's allowance (JSA) you received.[144] The Secretary of State is able to recover an equivalent sum from your employer if it is an unfair dismissal case dealt with in an industrial tribunal,[145] but not if there is a settlement, or it is a wrongful dismissal case dealt with by a court.

Personal injury cases

If you are paid compensation in respect of an accident, injury or disease after 6 October 1997, those compensating you can reduce compensation paid to you when you have received benefit in respect of a particular loss for which the compensation is paid. They must then pay money back to the Benefits Agency. It does not matter whether the payment is voluntary, with or without legal proceedings, or by order of a court. A reduction is not made if the compensation is paid for pain and suffering because benefits are not paid for this. You are therefore able to keep all compensation paid for that reason.

Note: The rules in relation to payments made for injury prior to 6 October 1997, but on or after 3 September 1990, or claims in relation to a disease on, or after 1 January 1989 are dealt with under the old scheme. See CPAG's *Rights Guide to Non-Means-Tested Benefits*, 20th edition, 1997/98, pp230-32.

What benefit can be recovered?

What benefit can be recovered depends on what the compensation is for.

Compensation	Recoverable benefits
Loss of earnings	Disability working allowance, disablement benefit, incapacity benefit, IS, invalidity pension, JSA, reduced earnings allowance, severe disablement allowance, sickness benefit, statutory sick pay, unemployment benefit
Cost of care	Attendance allowance, DLA care, disablement benefit paid for constant attendance (see p1:217) or exceptionally severe disablement (see p1:217)
Loss of mobility	mobility allowance, DLA mobility

Before you are paid compensation, those compensating you must apply to the Secretary of State for what is known as a certificate of recoverable benefits.[146] The certificate tells them which benefits you received for the same event. It allows them to deduct the recoverable benefits paid during 'the relevant period' (see below) from your compensation:[147]

Those compensating you become liable to pay the Secretary of State for the total amount of recoverable benefit (see above) 14 days after the certificate is issued.[148] Those compensating you remain liable even if they fail to apply for a certificate.[149]

The '**relevant period**' is usually the period of five years from the date:[150]

- of your accident or injury if you are claiming compensation for an accident or injury; *or*
- you first claimed a recoverable benefit (see p2:509) if you are claiming compensation in respect of a disease.

The relevant period ends if those compensating you make a final payment of compensation, or an agreement is made under which compensation already paid is accepted as being in final payment.[151]

- -

Example
Gary receives a £30,000 compensation payment consisting of £15,000 for loss of earnings, £5,000 for pain and suffering, and £10,000 for the cost of care. By the time the award is made he has received £20,000 of incapacity benefit, and £5,000 DLA care. The award for loss of earnings is reduced to nil, Gary will receive the full award for pain and suffering, but his award for the cost of care is reduced by £5,000. The compensator is liable to pay the DSS recoverable benefits of £25,000, and pays Gary a net award of £10,000 (£5,000 pain and suffering + £5,000 care).

- -

Any compensation reduced by this method is treated as paid to you. Those compensating you must give you a statement showing how the payment has been calculated, even if the recovery of benefits reduce a particular type of compensation to nil. If the recoverable benefit (see p2:509) exceeds the compensation paid to you for a particular loss, those compensating you still have to pay the Benefits Agency the balance.

Exempt payments

Prior to 6 October 1997, compensation payments of under £2,500 were exempt from the rules on recovery of benefits. To date no such figure has been set under the new rules so the recovery rules apply to all claims no matter how small. However, certain compensation payments are exempt.[152] These include:

- payments under the Fatal Accident Act 1996, the Vaccine Damage Act 1979 and the NHS industrial injury scheme;
- payments under the Pneumoconiosis Compensation Scheme and certain payments for loss of hearing;
- criminal injuries compensation;
- contractual sick pay and redundancy payments;

- payments from insurance companies from policies agreed before the accident; *and*
- payments from certain trusts.

Challenging a recovery decision

The Secretary of State may review a certificate of recoverable benefit (see p2:579) if he is satisfied that it was issued in ignorance of, or was based on a mistake as to, a material fact or if there was an error in its preparation, eg, a miscalculation.[153] You and those compensating you can both appeal against the certificate but not until the compensation payment has been made and the benefit paid back to the Benefits Agency. There are only two possible grounds of appeal:[154]

- that the amount, rate, or period of benefit specified on the certificate are wrong; *or*
- that the benefits specified were not paid because of an accident injury or disease.

Appeals are heard by a medical appeal tribunal[155] (see p2:629). Further appeals lie to a commissioner in the usual way (see p2:631).[156]

Other sources of information

Details of the procedures to be followed and other advice can be obtained from: Compensation Recovery Unit, Department of Social Security, Reyrolle Building, Hebburn, Tyne and Wear NE31 1XB (Tel: 0191 489 2266). A guide to the procedures called *Social Security Recovery of Benefits: Procedures for Liaison with Compensation Recovery Unit – A Guide for Companies and Solicitors*, is available free from the DSS (see Appendix 1).

Notes

• •

References are to statutes and regulations as amended up to 8 March 1999. All regulations are (General) Regulations unless otherwise stated. There is a full list of abbreviations in Appendix 13.

1. Who should claim

1 Reg 33 SS(C&P) Regs
2 R(SB) 5/90
3 CIS/642/1994
4 CIS/379/1992

2. How to make a claim

5 s1 SSAA 1992
6 Reg 3 SS(C&P) Regs as amended
7 Reg 4(6)(a) SS(C&P) Regs
8 Reg 5(1) SS(C&P) Regs
9 Reg 5(2) SS(C&P) Regs
10 Reg 4 SS(C&P) Regs
11 R(U) 9/60; R(S) 1/63
12 Reg 4(1A) SS(C&P) Regs
13 Reg 4(1B) SS(C&P) Regs
14 Reg 6(4A) SS(C&P) Regs
15 Reg 4(7) SS(C&P) Regs
16 Reg 4(7) SS(C&P) Regs
17 Reg 8(2) SS(C&P) Regs; reg 23 JSA Regs
18 s180 SSAA 1992
19 s1(1A) and (1B) SSAA 1992; reg 2A IS Regs
20 Reg 1A(1) SS (DLA) Regs
21 Reg 1A SS(GA) Regs; reg 2A HB Regs; reg 2A CTB Regs
22 s1(1A) SSAA 1992 came into effect on 1 December 1997 for these benefits
23 Reg 1A SS(AA) Regs; reg 1A Regs; reg 2A(2) DWA Regs; reg 2A(2) FC Regs; reg 2A(2) SS(ICA) Regs
24 Reg 2A(2) JSA Regs
25 Reg 2A(3) DWA Regs; reg 2A(3) FC Regs; reg 2A(2) SS(IB) Regs; reg 2A(2) IS Regs; reg 2A(3) SS(ICA) Regs; reg 2A(2) JSA Regs; reg 1A SS(MA) Regs; reg 1A(2) SS (WB&RP) Regs; reg 2A(2) SS(SDA) Regs
26 para 5 Memo AOG Vol 2/12

3. When to claim

27 Reg 9(1) and Sch 1 SS(C&P) Regs
28 Sch 1 SS(C&P) Regs
29 Reg 9(2) and (3) SS(C&P) Regs
30 Reg 9(6) SS(C&P) Regs
31 Reg 9(4) and (5) SS(C&P) Regs
32 Reg 19 and Sch 4 SS(C&P) Regs
33 R(SB) 9/84
34 ss65(4), (6) and 76 SSCBA 1992
35 Reg 19(2) and (3) and Sch 4 SS(C&P) Regs
36 R(SB) 9/84
37 R(SB) 9/84
38 Reg 19(6) and (7) SS(C&P) Regs
39 Reg 19(4) and (5) SS(C&P) Regs
40 s68 SSAA 1992
41 R(SB) 17/83; R(IS) 5/91; CIS/812/1992
42 R(P) 2/85
43 Reg 6(16)-(23) SS(C&P) Regs

4. How your claim is dealt with

44 s20(1) SSAA 1992
45 R(SB) 29/83
46 Reg 17 SS(C&P) Regs
47 Reg 32(1) SS(C&P) Regs

5. Getting paid

48 Reg 20 SS(C&P) Regs
49 para 5039 IS Guide (payments volume)
50 Regs 22-26A SS(C&P) Regs
51 Reg 38(1) SS(C&P) Regs
52 Reg 38(2A) SS(C&P) Regs
53 Regs 30 and 33 SS(C&P) Regs
54 Regs 34 SS(C&P) Regs
55 Reg 35 SS(C&P) Regs
56 Reg 6 SS(OB) Regs
57 Reg 4(5) SS(OB) Regs
58 Reg 6 SS(OB) Regs
59 s52(2) SSCBA 1992
60 s16(1), (2) and (6) SSCBA 1992; reg 2 SS(MAP) Regs as amended
61 Reg 4(4) SS(OB) Regs
62 Reg 4(3) SS(OB) Regs

63 Reg 9 SS(OB) Regs
64 Reg 10 SS(OB) Regs
65 Reg 8 SS(OB) Regs
66 Reg 2(4)(a) and (5) CB&SS(FAR) Regs
67 Reg 8 SS(OB) Regs
68 Reg 7 SS(OB) Regs
69 Reg 20 SS(C&P) Regs
70 *Walsh v DSS*, Bromley County Court, 12 February 1990. Not reported – see *Welfare Rights Bulletin 96*
71 para 5 *Missing Payments Guide*, December 1994
72 para 5 *Missing Payments Guide*, December 1994
73 para 8 *Missing Payments Guide*, December 1994
74 R(IS) 7/91
75 Reg 37(1)(a) SS(C&P) Regs
76 Reg 37(1A) SS(C&P) Regs
77 Reg 37(1)(b) SS(C&P) Regs
78 Reg 37(1)(c) SS(C&P) Regs
79 Reg 37B SS(C&P) Regs
80 s21(2) and Sch 6 para 5(1) SSA 1998; reg 37A SS(C&P) Regs
81 In *R v Secretary of State ex parte Sutherland* (QBD) 7 November 1996
82 *R v Secretary of State for Social Security ex parte Mulgrew* (unreported case)
83 Reg 37AA SS(C&P) Regs
84 Reg 37AB SS(C&P) Regs
85 s22 SSA 1998
86 s24 SSA 1998; reg 19(2) SS&CS(D&A) Regs
87 Reg 19(4) SS&CS(D&A) Regs
88 Reg 16(3) SS&CS(D&A) Regs
89 Reg 17(2) SS&CS (D&A) Regs
90 Reg 17(4) SS&CS(D&A) Regs
91 Reg 18(2) SS&CS(D&A) Regs
92 Reg 18(4) SS&CS(D&A) Regs
93 Reg 18(1)(a) SS&CS (D&A) Regs
94 Reg 17(5) SS&CS(D&A) Regs
95 Reg 18(3) SS&CS(D&A) Regs
96 Reg 2 SS(PAOR) Regs
97 *Factortame Ltd and Others v Secretary of State for Transport (No.2)* [1991] 1 AC 603 [1991] 1 All ER 70
98 Regs 3 and 4 SS(PAOR) Regs

6. Deductions from your IS or JSA
99 Regs 34A and 35 SS(C&P) Regs

100 Sch 9 para 2(1) SS(C&P) Regs
101 Sch 9 para 8(2) SS(C&P) Regs
102 Sch 9 para 8(2) SS(C&P) Regs
103 Sch 9 para 8 SS(C&P) Regs
104 Reg 34A and Sch 9A para 2 SS(C&P) Regs
105 Sch 9A paras 8 and 9 SS(C&P) Regs
106 Sch 9A para 3 SS(C&P) Regs
107 Sch 9A paras 3 and 5 SS(C&P) Regs
108 Sch 9A para 6 SS(C&P) Regs
109 *Pazio v Secretary of State for Social Security* (Birmingham County Court, 1996) – see report in *Welfare Rights Bulletins 133*, p14 and *138*, p14
110 Sch 9A para 3 SS(C&P) Regs
111 Sch 9A para 3(4) SS(C&P) Regs
112 Sch 9 para 3 SS(C&P) Regs
113 Sch 9 para 3(5) SS(C&P) Regs
114 Sch 9 para 1 SS(C&P) Regs
115 Sch 9 para 3(4) SS(C&P) Regs
116 CIS/15146/1996
117 Sch 9 para 5 SS(C&P) Regs
118 Sch 9 para 5(1)(c)(i) SS(C&P) Regs
119 Sch 9 para 5(1)(c)(ii) SS(C&P) Regs
120 Sch 9 para 5(6) SS(C&P) Regs; R(IS) 14/95
121 Sch 9 para 5(7) SS(C&P) Regs
122 Sch 9 para 4 SS(C&P) Regs
123 Sch 9 para 4A SS(C&P) Regs
124 Sch 9 para 6 SS(C&P) Regs
125 Sch 9 para 6(1) SS(C&P) Regs
126 Sch 9 para 6(4) SS(C&P) Regs
127 Sch 9 paras 1 and 7 SS(C&P) Regs
128 Sch 9 para 7(1) SS(C&P) Regs
129 Sch 9 para 7(2) SS(C&P) Regs
130 Sch 9 para 7(7) SS(C&P) Regs
131 CC(DIS) Regs; CT(DIS) Regs; CIS/ 11861/1996
132 Regs 1-7 F(DIS) Regs
133 s43 CSA 1991
134 Sch 9 SS(C&P) Regs
135 Sch 9 paras 1 and 2(2) SS(C&P) Regs
136 Reg 2 CC(DIS) Regs; regs 2-3 CT(DIS) Regs
137 Sch 9 para 3(2A) SS(C&P) Regs
138 Sch 9 para 8(1) SS(C&P) Regs
139 Sch 9 paras 5(5), 6(6), 7(8) and 8(2) and (3) SS(C&P) Regs

140 Sch 9 para 8(4) SS(C&P) Regs
141 Sch 9 para 9 SS(C&P) Regs
142 Reg 4 CC(DIS) Regs; reg 8
   CT(DIS) Regs
143 Regs 15 and 16 SS(PAOR) Regs;
   reg 3 SF(RDB) Regs

7. Recovery of benefits from compensation payments

144 *Nabi v British Leyland (UK) Ltd*
   [1980] 1 WLR 529 (CA)
145 EP(RUB&SB) Regs
146 s4 SS(RB)A 1997
147 s8 and Sch 2 SS(RB)A 1997
148 s6(4)SS(RB)A 1997
149 s7 SS(RB)A 1997
150 s3 SS(RB)A 1997
151 s3(4) SS(RB)A 1997
152 s1 and Sch 1 SS(RB)A 1997; reg
   2 SS(RB) Regs
153 s10 SS(RB)A 1997
154 s11 SS(RB)A 1997
155 s12 SS(RB)A 1997
156 s13 SS(RB)A 1997; reg 13
   SS(RB)App Regs

Chapter 51

· ·

Overpayments

This chapter covers all the rules about overpayments of benefit. It contains:

1. 'Ordinary' overpayments (p2:516)
2. Duplication of payments (p2:524)
3. Recovery of 'ordinary' overpayments and duplication of payments (p2:525)
4. Excess benefit credited to bank and other accounts (p2:527)
5. Mortgage interest paid directly to a lender (p2:528)
6. Overpayments of housing benefit (p2:529)
7. Overpayments of council tax benefit (p2:539)
8. The effect of recovery of housing benefit from your landlord (p2:540)

There are a number of ways that you might be paid too much benefit by the Benefits Agency or by a local authority, some of these through no fault of your own. The rules for each type of overpayment spell out if you have to repay it. If you have been overpaid a payment from the social fund (see Chapters 30 and 31) you might have to repay that too.

If the Benefits Agency or local authority say that the overpayment was made due to fraud you might be prosecuted or offered a penalty as an alternative to going to court. See Chapter 52 for further information. You also should seek advice.

Note: If you were paid too much income support (IS) or jobseeker's allowance (JSA), this could mean that you were also paid too much housing benefit and council tax benefit. If you are in this situation, see p2:529.

- If you have been paid too much IS or income-based JSA because other income was paid late, see p2:524 for information about duplication of payments.
- If excess benefit was credited to your bank or other account, see p2:527.
- For IS and income-based JSA, if too much mortgage interest (see p2:343) has been paid direct to your lender, see p2:528.
- If you have been overpaid housing benefit or council tax benefit, see pp2:529 and 2:539.
- For all other overpaid benefits and social fund payments, see p2:516.

1. 'Ordinary' overpayments

The rules covered in this section *do not* apply where:
- you have been paid too much income support (IS) or income-based jobseeker's allowance (JSA) because other income was paid late (see p2:524 for the rules on duplication of payments);
- too much mortgage interest has been paid direct to your lender (for these rules, see p2:528).

This section covers the rules that allow recovery of overpayments of:
- all of the benefits covered in this *Handbook*, other than housing benefit (HB) and council tax benefit (CTB). For HB and CTB, see pp2:529 and 2:539;
- social fund maternity expenses, funeral expenses, cold weather and winter fuel payments (see pp1:626, 1:629, 1:635 and 1:637);
- payments from the discretionary social fund paid after 5 October 1998 (see Chapters 30 and 31).

This type of overpayment is referred to in this *Handbook* as an 'ordinary' overpayment. The rules about recovery of overpayments of payments from the discretionary social fund are generally the same as for other 'ordinary' overpayments. See p2:523 for the differences to the rules.

'Ordinary' overpayments, only have to be repaid if:[1]
- you have misrepresented or failed to disclose a material fact (see pp2:518-21); *and*
- as a result, too much benefit has been paid (see p2:521).

It does not matter if you innocently misrepresented your situation or you failed to tell the local office certain facts because you did not understand how the benefit scheme works. You might still have to repay. The overpayment may be recovered from the person who made the misrepresentation or failed to disclose the material fact, even if this is not the benefit claimant.[2]

If the Benefits Agency thinks an overpayment was made due to fraud, as well as recovering the overpayment it can prosecute you or offer you the option of paying a penalty as an alternative to going to court. You should seek advice before agreeing to pay. See Chapter 52 for further information.

Overpayments made before 6 April 1987

Before 6 April 1987, overpayments of non-means-tested benefits (see p1:4) were not recoverable unless a claimant had failed to use due care and diligence to avoid overpayment. In most cases, overpayments recoverable under the present law would have been recoverable under the old law too, but in some cases the results would have been different. The old law tended to be more favourable to claimants, although sometimes it worked the other way round.

The old law still applies if the overpayment which the Benefits Agency is seeking to recover from you was made before 6 April 1987 even though the law has now changed for overpayments which were made after that date.[3] For further information about the old law, see CPAG's *Rights Guide to Non-Means-Tested Benefits*, 9th edition, 1986/87, p8.

Overpayments made before 24 July 1996

Prior to 24 July 1996, an overpayment could generally only be recovered if the adjudication officer (AO) made a decision to recover it at the same time as s/he reviewed your entitlement to benefit (see below).[4] However, at that time, most decisions about recovering overpayments were made after benefit entitlement had been reviewed. In this circumstance, an overpayment could only be recovered if an appeal was made against the review decision and the AO asked the tribunal to decide whether the overpayment was recoverable. If you think the rules have not been applied correctly in your case, you should seek advice.

When can an overpayment be recovered

If you have been overpaid, an AO must review your entitlement to benefit (see p2:570) and decide the correct amount you should have been paid.[5] Until your entitlement has been reviewed, you cannot be asked to repay an overpayment. You can argue that the decision that you have been overpaid is invalid if your entitlement to benefit has not been reviewed and you should not have to repay.[6] However, it is likely that your entitlement will then be reviewed correctly and benefit may then be recoverable (see p2:497). Pending this review, some or all of your current benefit can be suspended (see p2:497).

If you are 16 or 17 and have been overpaid discretionary JSA to avoid severe hardship (see p1:338), the Secretary of State must 'revoke' your award of JSA (see p1:341) before you can be asked to repay the overpayment.[7]

Whether an overpayment can be recovered then depends on the answer to the following three questions:
- Did you fail to disclose or misrepresent a material fact?
- Did an overpayment result?
- How much is repayable?

For all three, the burden of proving the case lies with the AO.[8]

Note: For JSA, because you claim at one office (ie, the JobCentre), references to the Benefits Agency in this section on overpayments should also be read as references to the Employment Service. If you have given any information to the Benefits Agency *or* Employment Service, you should be able to argue that you have disclosed it to both.

Did you fail to disclose or misrepresent a material fact?

Overpayments can only be recovered if you failed to disclose (see below) or misrepresented (see p2:519) a 'material fact'. If the Benefits Agency have simply come to a different conclusion about the facts than you, you can argue that an overpayment should not be recovered.[9] A **'material fact'** is one which is relevant to how much benefit you should be paid.[10]

Facts	*Conclusions about the facts*
You have arthritis	You are incapable of work
A friend of the opposite sex is sharing your flat	You are living together as husband and wife
You have a bad back	Your mobility is severely restricted most of the time

You have a duty to report your circumstances correctly and to notify the Benefits Agency (and JobCentre in the case of JSA) when they have changed (see p2:569 and the section 'Changes of circumstance' in the relevant benefit chapter of this *Handbook*).

Failure to disclose

Failure to disclose occurs where you do not give the Benefits Agency relevant information – eg, you forget to tell it that you or your partner's working hours or pay have increased. You cannot be said to have failed to disclose something you did not know about unless there is some reason why you should have been aware of it.[11]

- It must be reasonable to have expected you to notify the office of the particular facts. It is irrelevant that you did not personally realise the need to tell the Benefits Agency these facts – the test is whether a reasonable person would have realised that disclosure was required.[12]
- You cannot assume that changes in your social security benefits, paid by one section of the Benefits Agency, are known to the other sections. You should give the section for the benefit you are claiming any information which might affect that benefit.[13] On the other hand, you cannot be expected to understand exactly how the Benefits Agency works so that making a disclosure to the office where your claim is being handled and making a specific reference to your claim is enough because you can then reasonably expect the person receiving the information to pass it on to the right person.[14]
- It is not necessary for you to show that you told the office in writing about your situation. It will do just as well if you give the information over the

telephone, or in an office interview, either verbally or by presenting the relevant documents.[15] However, it is always best to notify the office in writing and to keep a copy of your letter.

- If you filled in a form while giving information, a tribunal should look at what you said on the form, but also consider whether you gave the necessary information in another way.[16] If you fail to fill in a form correctly, but give the relevant information in the wrong place, you have disclosed the facts.[17]
- If you have made a statement in person or over the telephone but the Benefits Agency says there is no record of this, you only have a case to answer once the adjudication officer has shown, 'on the balance of probabilities', that there would be a record of the conversation at the local office if it had taken place. In order to do this, the AO must give a tribunal information on:[18]
  - the instructions which should have applied for recording and attaching information to a claimant's file;
  - whether there were the appropriate administrative arrangements to enable these instructions to be carried out;
  - to what extent *in practice* these instructions are, or are not, carried out.

  Where there is no record of what happened, other than your own statement, the Benefits Agency will not be able to prove that there has been a recoverable overpayment.[19]
- You need not report a change directly to the Benefits Agency if you give the information in another way which might reasonably be expected to reach the relevant local office – eg, you tell the pensions section and ask it to inform the income support section too. However, if you realise or should have realised that the information has not reached the relevant section, you are under an obligation to take further steps to inform it.[20] A short time may elapse before you can reasonably be expected to realise that the original information has not been acted on.[21]
- The Benefits Agency sometimes points to warnings and instructions, for example at the back of your order book, that you should have read.[22] But it should not rely on warnings on forms you were asked to sign without having a proper chance to read.[23]

Misrepresentation

Misrepresentation occurs where you have given the Benefits Agency information which is inaccurate – eg, you gave an incorrect answer to a specific question on the claim form.

- This can be completely innocent[24] – eg, where you meant to declare your partner's earnings but forgot to put these on the claim form.
- You would not be guilty of misrepresentation if you add the phrase 'not to my knowledge' to your statement.[25]

- A written misrepresentation may be qualified by an oral one so that, if you fill in a form incorrectly but explain the situation to an officer when handing in the form, the explanation has to be taken into account when deciding whether what is stated on the form amounts to a misrepresentation. For example, if you say you have no income on the form but ask whether you should have mentioned your occupational pension, you should – depending on the reply – be treated as having mentioned the occupational pension on the form.[26]

- The misrepresentation must relate to your current claim. If you have declared a fact on a previous claim but inadvertently give incorrect information on a later claim, you have misrepresented. The Benefits Agency is not required to check back for you.[27] However, if what you say on your claim form is obviously incorrect and the AO does not check this out, the overpayment is due to Benefits Agency error not your misrepresentation and you do not have to pay it back. For example, if you say you pay ground rent and are a freeholder, the AO should recognise that this must be incorrect and check before paying you benefit.[28]

- If you are incapable of managing your affairs but nevertheless sign a claim form which is incorrectly completed, you cannot later argue that you were not capable of making a true representation of your circumstances to avoid recovery.[29]

Most overpayments arise due to a failure to disclose facts (see p2:518) and it is easier to challenge such a decision than to show that you did not misrepresent anything. Because of this the Benefits Agency relies on general statements which you have signed to argue that a failure to disclose facts can later become a misrepresentation. This can occur in two situations:[30]

- **when you sign the claim form**. Some claim forms end with a statement: 'I declare that the information I have given is correct and complete'. If you gave correct answers but left out relevant information because you were unaware of it, the information is incomplete and you have failed to disclose. You can argue that signing the declaration does not convert this into a misrepresentation as the declaration means 'complete insofar as I have knowledge of the material facts';[31]

- **when you cash a giro or an order book**. Each time you do this you are signing a declaration that you have reported any facts which could affect the amount of your benefit. If you knew a fact but failed to declare it (eg, where you were claiming IS, then start getting incapacity benefit so are not entitled to as much IS but did not tell the IS section your circumstances had changed) you are misrepresenting your circumstances each time you sign the declaration, and the overpayment is recoverable due to *both* your original 'failure to disclose' *and* the later misrepresentation.

However:
- if you did not declare a fact because you were unaware of it, signing the declaration does not amount to a misrepresentation because all you are declaring is that you have correctly disclosed those facts *which were known to you*;[32]
- if you were told by the Benefits Agency that certain facts are irrelevant to your claim, then signing the declaration cannot be a misrepresentation if you fail to disclose those facts.[33]

Did an overpayment result?

Even if you admit that there is information you failed to give the Benefits Agency or that you did misrepresent your circumstances, you can still argue that this was not the cause of the overpayment. If something else caused the overpayment, it should not be recovered. If the Benefits Agency has been given the correct information to decide your claim by someone else, but fails to act on it, you could argue that any overpayment did not arise because of your failure.[34]

How much is repayable?

It is always worth checking how the overpayment has been calculated as you may be asked to repay too much by mistake. Do not be afraid to ask the Benefits Agency for more information if you need it. To calculate the amount of the overpayment, you should do the following:
- determine the dates between which you have been paid too much benefit;
- work out the total amount of benefit you were paid over the period;
- work out the correct amount of benefit you should have received during the period;
- deduct this from the total amount of benefit you were paid.[35]

The Benefits Agency cannot add any interest charges to the amount of the overpayment.

The amount of the overpayment is the difference between what you were paid and what you should have been paid.[36] The Benefits Agency works out what you should have been paid using the information that you originally gave it, plus any facts which you misrepresented or did not disclose.

The AO must consider whether you have also been underpaid IS or income-based JSA (see Chapters 20 and 14) for a past period.[37]
- If your benefit **claim contained enough information** to alert the adjudication officer to your potential need, but s/he did not investigate this fully, you can argue that the underpayment should be offset against the overpayment. It does not matter if the overpayment was for a different period, so long as there was sufficient information to alert the AO to your need for extra benefit.[38]

- If **additional facts are needed** to prove you were underpaid IS or income-based JSA, you cannot offset the underpayment against the overpayment.[39] However, if you have been getting IS or income-based JSA, you can ask the Benefits Agency to review your claim (see p2:570). It could then withhold any arrears owed to you (see p2:575) to reduce the overpayment.[40]

You should claim any other benefits to which you may have been entitled and ask for these to be backdated (see p2:487) so you can repay the overpayment. You should not delay in making the claims or you could lose out.

Example

Bert has been claiming JSA but was working full-time (see p2:5). The Benefits Agency decides he has been overpaid JSA and decides to recover it. Bert is on a low wage and has children, so he should claim family credit and ask for this to be backdated.

If you were overpaid a benefit which overlaps with another benefit you claimed but were not being paid (see p2:493 for the overlapping benefit rules), you should seek a review of that benefit and ask for it to be paid instead (see p2:570).

Example

Kathy has been claiming widow's pension (WP) but has been living with her new partner. She had also been claiming severe disablement allowance (SDA) but this was not being paid because of the overlapping benefit rules. The Benefits Agency decides she has been overpaid WP and that it should be recovered. Kathy should ask the Benefits Agency to review the decision not to pay her SDA and offset any arrears she is paid against the overpayment.

If you were overpaid a benefit, but in fact were entitled to another benefit, check whether the claim for the benefit you were overpaid can be treated as a claim for the other (see p2:486).

Example

Maxine should not have been receiving IS because her partner is in full-time paid work (see p2:6). However, she is caring for her aunt who is disabled and receiving attendance allowance. Maxine should ask the Benefits Agency to treat her claim for IS as a claim for invalid care allowance (ICA) and offset arrears of ICA against the IS she has been overpaid.

If you were overpaid IS, income-based JSA, family credit or disability working allowance because you had too much capital (see p2:442), the overpayment is calculated taking account of the fact that, had you received no benefit, you would have had to use your capital to meet everyday expenses. For each 13-week period, the Benefits Agency assumes that your capital is reduced by the amount of overpaid benefit.[41] This is known as the 'diminishing capital' rule. However, although your capital is treated as reducing for these purposes, if you reclaim benefit your full capital counts (see p2:458).

Challenging an overpayment decision

Whether or not you are the claimant, you can appeal (see p2:611) if you:[42]
* do not agree that you owe the Benefits Agency money;
* disagree that an overpayment can be recovered; *or*
* disagree with the amount to be recovered.

You can appeal if the decision concerns a payment from the *regulated* social fund (see Chapter 30). If you have been overpaid a payment from the *discretionary* social fund, see below.

Do not pay back any of the money until your appeal has been decided, as the Benefits Agency may keep any money you voluntarily repay, even if you later win your case![43] You should write to the Benefits Agency and explain that you do not intend to repay any of the money until your appeal has been decided. If the Benefits Agency is already making deductions from your benefit (see p2:525) you should ask it to stop doing this straightaway.

It is the Secretary of State who decides whether to recover an overpayment. However, this is discretionary, so you can ask him not to do so (see p2:526). See p2:525 for further information about the way overpayments can be recovered.

For the differences for payments from the *discretionary* social fund, see below.

Payments from the discretionary social fund

If, after 5 October 1998, you have been overpaid a payment from the discretionary social fund (see Chapters 30 and 31), it can be recovered under the rules for recovery of 'ordinary' overpayments detailed in this chapter (see pp2:516-24). The Benefits Agency says that it only intends to do this if you were overpaid because you fraudulently claimed another benefit. It should not use these rules to recover a payment where: [44]
* you are given a loan or grant for an item but use the money to buy something else instead; *or*
* one social fund officer (SFO) decides to give you a loan or grant but, for example following a request for a review, another SFO interprets the guidance (see p1:643) differently.

Challenging an overpayment decision

You have a right to request a review of a decision that you have been overpaid, but must do this within 28 days. See pp2:601-606 for further information about internal reviews of social fund decisions. If you do not agree with the review decision, you can seek a further review by a social fund inspector. See pp2:606-608 for further information about social fund inspector reviews.

You should write to the social fund officer and explain that you do not intend to repay any of the money until your review request has been decided. If deductions are already being made from your benefit you should ask for this action to be stopped straightaway.

2. **Duplication of payments**

This section only applies to payments of:
- income support (IS); *and*
- income-based jobseeker's allowance (JSA).

Sometimes you receive too much IS or income-based JSA because money which is owing to you does not arrive on time. When you get your arrears, you must repay the IS or income-based JSA which you would not have received if the other income had been paid on time.[45] This is to prevent a 'duplication of payment'.

The rule applies to any income which affects the amount of your IS or income-based JSA. This includes:
- other social security benefits;
- arrears of child support maintenance paid to you for the period from your application to the date it is assessed by the Child Support Agency (see p2:304);
- benefits paid by other European Union member states.[46]

Even though it was not your fault that the income was paid late, the Secretary of State can make you pay it back. However, as this is discretionary, you could ask him not to do so. See p2:526 for further information about how to do this. See p2:524 to see how the overpayment can be recovered.

Example
Aysha claimed child benefit when her baby was born but it was not paid for several weeks. Her IS continued to be paid at the full rate while she was not actually receiving child benefit. However, if child benefit had been promptly paid, her IS would have been paid at a lower rate. The Benefits Agency recovers overpaid IS from the arrears of child benefit Aysha is owed.

3. Recovery of 'ordinary' overpayments and duplication of payments

If an overpayment of benefit must be repaid, it can be done through deductions from most of the benefits in this *Handbook*. However, no deduction can be made from guardian's allowance, child benefit, housing benefit, or council tax benefit.[47]Remember that recovery is discretionary (see p2:526). Except in the case of income support (IS), income-based jobseeker's allowance (JSA), family credit (FC) and disability working allowance (DWA), deductions can only be made from the benefit of the person who has to repay the overpayment (see p2:516).

For IS, income-based JSA, FC and DWA overpayments, as long as a couple are married or living together as husband and wife (see p2:115), the amount overpaid can be recovered from either partner's IS, income-based JSA, FC or DWA.[48]

If an overpayment of IS or income-based JSA occurred because of a duplication of payment (see p2:524), the Benefits Agency normally deducts any overpaid IS or income-based JSA from the arrears owing to you.[49] However, if it omits to do so you can still be asked to repay even if you have spent the money.

Overpayments can also be recovered from arrears of benefit you are owed, except arrears where the benefit has previously been suspended (see p2:497).[50]

If you are an appointee who misrepresents circumstances, or fails to disclose something, you can argue that it is the claimant who has to repay any overpayment, not you as you are simply acting on her/his behalf.[51]

An overpayment can be recovered from a claimant's estate if s/he dies.[52]

Maximum deductions from benefit

For some benefits, there is a maximum weekly amount that can be deducted.[53] These benefits are:
* IS;
* income-based JSA; *and*
* contribution-based JSA (but only if you would be entitled to income-based JSA at the same rate).

The following are the maximum amounts which can be deducted weekly:
* £10.40 if you have admitted fraud or been found guilty of fraud; *or*
* £7.80 in any other case.

The deduction can be increased by half of any:[54]
- earnings subject to the £5, £10 or £15 disregard (see p2:396); *or*
- charitable income subject to a disregard (see p2:412); *or*
- benefit subject to a disregard (see p2:405).

If you have been overpaid *contribution-based* JSA but are not entitled to *income-based* JSA (see above), the maximum deduction is one-third of the personal allowance for someone of your age (see p2:319).[55] However, this depends on whether you have any other deductions being made from your JSA (see p2:501).

Remember, the above are maximum amounts. The Benefits Agency might be persuaded to deduct less, especially if you have other direct deductions made from your benefit.

If you have been overpaid a **benefit other than IS or income-based JSA**, the rules limiting the maximum payment that can be deducted do not apply. The Benefits Agency usually wants to deduct one-third of your weekly benefit. However, you can argue that your rate of repayment should be less than this.

Other methods of recovery

Benefit may also be recovered by enforcement proceedings in the county courts in England or Wales or the Sheriffs' Courts in Scotland.[56] The Benefits Agency might use these proceedings, for example, if you have gone back to work and are no longer claiming benefit.

Once a decision of an AO, tribunal or commissioner is produced, the court has to enforce it unless you persuade the court to delay enforcement (what is known as a 'stay of execution') while you appeal against the relevant decision. If you are in this situation, you should seek advice.

The Secretary of State's discretion

It is important to note that a tribunal cannot 'write off' part of the overpayment even if there are mitigating circumstances. It can only decide if it is recoverable and, if so, how much is repayable. In a case where you acted in all innocence and hardship is likely to be caused, the best tactic is to apply to the Secretary of State who has the discretion to decide whether or not to recover the overpayment. You can do this by writing to the local office, but it is sometimes more effective to write direct to the Secretary of State at the House of Commons. Although he does not deal with your case personally, it can ensure that local staff take your case seriously if they are asked to investigate by the Secretary of State. In either case you may wish to involve your MP. If you have been underpaid in the past but cannot now get arrears, for example because of the rules on backdating (see p2:487), ask the Secretary of State to reduce the amount to be recovered by this sum if s/he will not write it off altogether.

Recovery 'at common law'

In the drive to recoup money lost through overpayments the Benefits Agency is increasingly trying to use other means to get money back. There has been an increasing number of cases in which the Benefits Agency is claiming to be entitled to recover overpayments of benefit not under the rules described in this chapter, but by relying instead on what it claims are its rights under what is known as the 'common law'.

At 'common law' it is possible for someone to reclaim money through the courts from someone to whom it has been paid as a result of a mistake of fact. If the Benefits Agency does retain its common law rights then it would be entitled to use this procedure to recover overpayments even where there has been no misrepresentation (see p2:519) or failure to disclose (see p2:518) and indeed even if the overpayment was entirely caused by its own mistake rather than yours.

If you are in this situation, you should seek urgent advice. You can argue two things:
- The rules about overpayments are in the Social Security Acts. These rules replaced the 'common law' as far as overpayments of benefit are concerned.
- The Social Security Acts say it is an AO (see p2:561) that must decide whether there has been an overpayment and that you have a right to appeal to a tribunal against the decision – on this basis, a court would have no jurisdiction to decide the point.

If the Benefits Agency threatens to use the 'common law' in your case you should get advice from a solicitor immediately. Tactically the best course may be to apply for judicial review of the decision to proceed in this way (see p2:637). Alternatively, you may simply wish to defend the action in the county court. There are a number of defences to this type of court action which would not be available to you if the Benefits Agency had used the rules described in this chapter. In practice, the Benefits Agency has tended to back down if challenged.

---

4. Excess benefit credited to bank and other accounts

Your benefit can be paid by direct credit transfer into a bank or other account – for example a building society (see p2:492). If you are credited with too much benefit, the excess benefit can be recovered in certain circumstances (see below).[57] This is the case even if the rules for recovery of overpayments do not apply (see pp2:517 and 2:523).

As with 'ordinary' overpayments (see p2:516), an adjudication officer must review your entitlement to benefit (see p2:570) and decide the correct amount you should have been paid.[58] Until your entitlement has been reviewed, you cannot be asked to repay the excess benefit. You can argue that the decision that you have been paid excess benefit is invalid if your entitlement has not been reviewed and you should not have to repay.[59] However, it is likely that your entitlement will then be reviewed correctly and the excess benefit may then be recoverable (see below).

When can excess benefit be recovered?

Excess benefit credited to your bank or other account can only be recovered if:[60]

- you were notified in writing, before you agreed for your benefit to be paid into a bank or other account, that excess benefit could be recovered; *and*
- the Secretary of State has certified that you were paid excess benefit because of the direct credit transfer system itself.

Note: If excess benefit cannot be recovered under the rules described above, it could still be recoverable under the 'ordinary' overpayment rules (see p2:516) or those for recovery of duplication of payments (see p2:524).

5. Mortgage interest paid directly to a lender

This section only applies to payments of:
- income support (IS); *and*
- income-based jobseeker's allowance (JSA).

If you are getting help with your housing costs within your IS or income-based JSA (see Chapter 46) your mortgage interest is usually paid direct to your lender (see p2:502). Any overpayment of mortgage interest which is paid directly to your lender must be sent back to the Benefits Agency by that lender if it arose because:[61]

- you ceased to be entitled to IS or income-based JSA, but only if the Benefits Agency asks for repayment within four weeks of your entitlement ceasing; *or*
- you were entitled to less IS or income-based JSA because there was a reduction in:
  - the amount of your outstanding loan; *or*
  - the standard interest rate (see p2:348); *or*
  - your actual mortgage interest rate;
  but the Benefits Agency did not reduce your mortgage direct payments.

In the latter case your mortgage account should simply be corrected, but where you come off IS or income-based JSA and interest is recovered, you will be in arrears unless you have started to make payments yourself.

In practice, the Benefits Agency often stops sending your lender your ongoing housing costs until they have recovered the overpayment, rather than ask a lender to return what was overpaid. However, the Benefits Agency should not do this if you are put into arrears as a result.[62] If you are put into arrears, you should seek advice immediately to avoid losing your home.

You can appeal to a tribunal (see p2:611) if, for example, you think the rules do not apply to you or if the Benefits Agency has not reviewed your IS or income-based JSA properly (see p2:572) or if you dispute the amount being recovered.[63] If you are not to blame for the overpayment or would suffer hardship, you can also ask the Secretary of State to use her/his discretion not to ask your lender to repay the overpayment.

The Benefits Agency can also recover overpaid mortgage interest under the rules for 'ordinary' overpayments[64] described on pp2:516-524 – eg, where it fails to ask your lender to repay within four weeks of you going off IS or income-based JSA. If it tries to do this, you should make sure that those rules actually apply.

6. **Overpayments of housing benefit**

This section does not apply to:
* benefits covered in this *Handbook* other than housing benefit or council tax benefit; *or*
* payments from the social fund.

The overpayment rules for these are covered on pp2:516-529.

This section covers the rules that allow recovery of overpayments of housing benefit only.

The rules about recovery of overpayments of council tax benefit (CTB) are generally the same as for housing benefit (HB). The references given in this section cover both HB and CTB. See p2:539 for the exceptions to the rules for CTB.

If the information you give a local authority when you claim HB is wrong, or if you do not report a change in your circumstances (see p1:543), you could end up being paid too much HB. It does not matter if you did this innocently. You might still have to repay. You could also be overpaid as a result of an official error or delay that is not your fault.

If you have been overpaid income-support (IS) or income-based jobseeker's allowance (JSA) then you may also have been overpaid HB. This is because your automatic passport to maximum HB (see p1:519) ceases when you are no longer entitled to IS or income-based JSA. If you are in this situation, you should claim HB immediately on the basis that you are not on IS or income-based JSA. You should ask for HB to be backdated.

To see from whom an overpayment can be recovered, see p2:533.

You can seek a review (see Chapter 54) for example, if you:

- do not agree that you owe the local authority money;
- disagree that an overpayment can be recovered;
- disagree with the amount to be recovered;
- do not think the local authority has followed the correct procedures.

Do not pay any of the money back until your review request has been dealt with. If the local authority is already making deductions from your HB (see p2:534) or deductions are being made from your other benefits (see p2:537) you should ask it to stop this straightaway.

If the local authority thinks an overpayment was made due to fraud, as well as recovering the overpayment it can prosecute you or offer you the option of paying a penalty as an alternative to going to court. You should seek advice before agreeing to pay. See Chapter 52 for further information.

What is an overpayment?

An overpayment is an amount of HB which has been paid, and which the local authority later decides that you were not entitled to under the HB rules.[65] Being 'paid' includes payment to you, your landlord or somebody else and also includes HB credited to your local authority rent account (see p1:538).[66]

When can an overpayment be recovered?

An overpayment can only be recovered if the local authority has taken the following five steps. It must:

- decide whether the overpayment is legally recoverable;
- decide whether recovery of the overpayment should be sought, and if so from whom;
- work out how much of the overpayment is repayable and for what period;
- decide how the overpayment should be recovered and at what rate;
- notify you of all the above decisions regarding the overpayment and give you an opportunity to request further information or a review (see pp1:536 and 2:590).

Step one: Is the overpayment legally recoverable?

Overpayments can have many causes, but the general rule is that an overpayment is recoverable.[67] However, certain types of overpayment are not always recoverable (seep2:531). An overpayment may be recoverable even if it was caused by an innocent mistake on your part or was somebody else's fault.

Remember that in most cases, the local authority has the discretion to decide whether or not to recover an overpayment (see p2:535).

For the differences for overpayments of council tax benefit see p2:539.

Overpayments that are always recoverable

There are two types of overpayments which are always recoverable:

- An overpayment which is the result of the local authority overestimating your HB when making an interim payment (see p1:543). When the local authority decides how much HB you should actually get, it is obliged to recover any excess you were paid from future HB payments.[68] However, if you stop getting HB before the local authority decides, this rule does not apply. In this case, the overpayment can only be recovered under the other rules described in this section.
- Where an overpayment of HB that relates to a future payment is credited to your rent account. In this case, the overpayment can be recovered even if it was made as a result of an 'official error' (see below).[69] Where an overpayment of HB caused by an official error has been credited to your account for a *past* period, see below to find out if it is recoverable.

Overpayments that are not always recoverable

Overpayments that do not fall into the two categories above are not recoverable if you can show that the following three conditions are met:[70]

- the overpayment was caused by an official error (see below); *and*
- no 'relevant person' caused the official error to be made (see p2:532); *and*
- no relevant person could be expected to have realised that an overpayment was being made (see p2:533).

An **'official error'** is defined as a mistake, whether in the form of an act or omission, by the appropriate authority or by an officer or person acting for that authority or by an officer of the Department of Social Security or the Department of Employment acting as such'.[71] It therefore includes the following:

- a mistake made by the local authority in calculating your entitlement;
- a failure by the local authority to reduce your HB when you inform it of a change of circumstances;
- a failure by an officer of another department of the local authority, such as a social worker, to pass on details of a change of circumstances, where s/he has promised to do so. This is an official error because the definition does not require the mistake to be made by an officer in the department handling HB. A mistake by any local authority officer will be an official error if it results in an overpayment;
- similar mistakes by somebody carrying out functions relating to HB on behalf of the local authority, for example a private agency to whom work has been contracted out;

- a mistake made by the Benefits Agency in calculating your entitlement to IS or income-based JSA which results in a wrong calculation of your entitlement to HB;
- a failure by the Benefits Agency to pass on information to the local authority. DSS guidance says that this is not an official error,[72] but you should argue that there are procedures for the Benefits Agency to pass information to local authorities and if these are not followed it is an omission by the Benefits Agency and therefore falls within the definition;
- wrong advice given to you by an officer of the local authority, the Benefits Agency or the Employment Service, provided that s/he is acting as an officer at the time (rather than, say, as a friend giving you informal advice).

The list above is not exhaustive. The official error does not have to be the sole cause of the overpayment. An overpayment is 'caused by' an official error if it is one of two or more reasons why the overpayment occurred.[73]

No 'relevant person' caused the official error

An official error does not prevent the overpayment being recoverable if the error was partially or wholly caused by a '**relevant person**'. You are a relevant person if you are:

- the HB claimant; or
- a person acting on the HB claimant's behalf, whether because s/he is unable to deal with her/his affairs or because s/he has asked the authority in writing to deal with you on her/his behalf (see p1:532); or
- a person to whom the payment was made, which would include a different person acting on the HB claimant's behalf or a landlord.

The local authority might say it only needs to show that *any* relevant person caused the official error but it does not have to pursue that person for the overpayment.[74] If the local authority tries to recover an overpayment from you but it was another person who caused the official error, you should argue that the structure of the rules means that recovery must be sought from the person causing the official error. You could also argue that the authority should exercise its discretion to recover from that person instead (see p2:533). See p2:534 for information about who overpayments can be recovered from.

Examples of how you might cause an official error include:

- making a mistake in information given to the local authority which results in it wrongly calculating your benefit;
- failing to disclose a change of circumstances to the local authority (see p2:570). If you fail to do this, even if you told the Benefits Agency about the change, the local authority might say you are contributing to an official error by the Benefits Agency if the Agency fails to pass on the information to the local authority.

No relevant person could be expected to have realised that an overpayment was being made

Even if the official error was not caused by a relevant person, an overpayment is still recoverable if any relevant person (see p2:532) knew, or ought reasonably to have known, that an overpayment had been made. The extent to which you can reasonably be expected to realise that an overpayment is being made to you depends on the extent to which the local authority has advised you about the scheme or your duties and obligations, particularly about your duty to notify changes of circumstances. It depends not on what you know, but on what you could have known at the time of the payment or the notification.

Remember, the local authority must show not just that you could have reasonably been expected to know that you might have been overpaid, but that you *were* overpaid.[75] You should always argue that as a claimant, you cannot be expected to know the intricacies of the HB rules and that, unless it was glaringly obvious that a change of circumstances would reduce your HB, you should be given the benefit of the doubt.

If you or some other 'relevant person' could only have realised that there was an overpayment at some point during the period of the overpayment, the overpayment is only recoverable from that date.

Step two: Should the overpayment be recovered and if so from whom?

Apart from certain interim payments of HB on account (see p1:543), the local authority has a **discretion** whether to recover an overpayment.[76] Some recover all recoverable overpayments and others only recover those caused by claimant error.

Nevertheless, local authorities have a legal duty to exercise their judgement on whether or not to make a recovery on the merits of each and every individual case. While they may have general policy guidelines on how to approach the issue in a consistent manner, these must not be so rigid as to effectively decide the outcome of each case in advance. A policy of always recovering recoverable overpayments could be challenged by judicial review (see p2:596).

If you have been overpaid and this was either not your fault or the result of a genuine mistake or oversight on your part, you should ask the local authority not to recover the overpayment, especially if recovery causes you hardship. If the local authority still insists on proceeding with recovery action, you should ask for a review (see p2:590). The local authority might say that you cannot ask for a review in these circumstances.[77] You should request a review and argue that this is wrong. A decision to recover is known as a 'determination' under the HB rules and is therefore open to review (see p2:590).[78] You can also argue that the housing benefit review board (see p2:592) has the same power to exercise discretion as the local authority.[79]

If the overpayment was caused by someone else, you could suggest that recovery is made from her/him (but where this is your landlord, see p2:540).

You may be asked to repay an irrecoverable overpayment on a voluntary basis. You are under no legal obligation to do so.

Who is the overpayment recoverable from?

An overpayment can be recovered from:[80]

- you (or your partner if you were members of the same household – see p2:115 – both at the time the overpayment was made and while it is being recovered); *or*
- the person to whom the payment was made. This could be your landlord, or someone acting on your behalf; *or*
- from the person who misrepresented or failed to disclose a material fact (see pp2:518-521) where this caused the overpayment. This means that an overpayment could be recovered from your landlord – eg, even where s/he did not actually receive the payment.

In the event of death of the person from whom recovery is being sought, local authorities may consider recovering any outstanding overpayment from that person's estate.[81]

For the differences for overpayments of CTB, see p2:539.

Step three: How much is repayable and for what period?

It is a good idea to check the amount of an overpayment to ensure the local authority has calculated it correctly. Do not be afraid to ask for more information if you need it. The local authority should distinguish between parts of an overpayment that are recoverable and those which are not. To calculate the amount of the overpayment, you should do the following:

- determine the dates between which you have been paid too much benefit;
- identify the period or periods over which the local authority is entitled to recover;
- work out the total amount of HB you were paid over the period(s) during which the local authority can recover;
- work out the correct amount of HB you should have received during the period(s) of recovery. If you have been overpaid HB because you are no longer entitled to IS or income-based JSA (see p1:519) you must make a fresh claim and ask for this to be backdated;[82]
- deduct the HB you should have been paid from what you were paid.[83]

The authority is not allowed to add any interest charges to the amount of the overpayment.[84]

For the differences for overpayments of council tax benefit, see p2:539.

Deductions from the overpayment

Besides any amount of HB which you should have been paid (see p2:534), the local authority must deduct other amounts from the overpayment (this is known as 'offsetting'). These are:

- extra rent paid into your rent account. If you have been getting HB over the overpayment period and, for some reason, have paid more into your rent account than you should have paid according to your original (incorrect) benefit assessment, the extra rent you paid can be deducted from any overpayment made during that period. The local authority might not apply this rule where you paid extra rent to repay rent arrears;[85]
- reductions under the diminishing capital rule (see below).

You are not entitled to have other amounts deducted.

If you were overpaid HB because you had too much capital, the overpayment is calculated taking into account the fact that had you received no HB, you would have used your capital. This is known as the **'diminishing capital rule'**. This only applies in the following circumstances:[86]

- you were overpaid for more than 13 weeks; *and either*
- the overpayment was caused by a misrepresentation of, or a failure to disclose, the amount of your capital (see pp2:518-521 for the meaning of misrepresentation and failure to disclose); *or*
- the overpayment was caused by an error (other than an 'official error' – see p2:531) as to your capital (or that of a member of your family – see pp2:113-114).

For each 13-week period the local authority assumes that your capital is reduced by the amount of overpaid HB.[87] However, although your capital is treated as reducing for these purposes, if you reclaim benefit your full capital counts (see p2:443).

Step four: How should the overpayment be recovered and at what rate?

A local authority can decide how much of a recoverable overpayment it will actually recover. It can ask for the whole amount at once or recover it by instalments. If agreement cannot be reached, there are several different ways in which a local authority can seek to recover an overpayment. When an overpayment is recovered from your landlord, you should take careful note of how that affects your liability to pay rent (see p2:540). Overpayments of HB can be recovered:

- from payments of HB (see p2:536);
- from other benefits (see p2:537);
- for local authority tenants only, by adjusting your rent account (see p2:537);
- through the courts (see p2:538).

You should check that the methods used by the authority and the rates of recovery are consistent between groups of claimants. For example, council tenants should not be required to repay overpayments in a lump sum (ie, the whole overpayment is debited to their account) where private tenants can repay by instalment – eg, by weekly deductions made to their HB. If this is happening, you should ask for a review.

For the differences for overpayments of council tax benefit, see p2:539.

Recovery from payments of HB

A local authority is entitled to recover an overpayment by deducting sums from HB payable to any person from whom an overpayment can be recovered (see p2:534).[88] As well as yourself, this could be your partner or your landlord (see below). Deductions can be made from both future payments of HB and any arrears of HB that are owing.

Recovery from your partner

Where you were overpaid HB while you were a claimant, the local authority may recover an overpayment from payments of HB made to your partner but only if *all* the following conditions are met:[89]

- the overpayment was made to you, rather than to your landlord or someone acting on your behalf;
- you and your partner were living in the same household (see p2:115) *both* at the time of the overpayment *and* when the deduction is made. You must have been living together for the whole period of the overpayment, not just for part of it.

Recovery from a landlord

If you have been overpaid HB, the local authority may recover the overpayment from:

- HB paid to your landlord personally, as a claimant;[90]
- HB paid directly to your landlord on your behalf (if the overpayment was paid to her/him on your behalf).[91] The notification of the overpayment (see p2:538) should make it clear from whom the authority is recovering;
- HB paid directly to your landlord on behalf of claimants other than you (even if the overpayment was paid to her/him on your behalf).[92]

When HB is recovered from a landlord in this way, there are special rules as to how this affects your liability to pay rent (see p2:540).

The rate of recovery

There are no rules limiting the maximum payment that can be deducted. However, you can argue that your rate of repayment should be reasonable. If you are on IS or income-based JSA, you should argue that the weekly maximums for those benefits should apply (see p2:525). You should also ask the local authority to take into account any other debts or financial commitments or health problems you may have.[93] Complain if the rate of recovery is causing you hardship and suggest an amount you think you can afford.

Recovery from other benefits

The local authority can ask the Benefits Agency to recover an overpayment by making deductions from most of the benefits in this *Handbook*. However, deductions cannot be made from child benefit or guardian's allowance. You can argue that deductions to recover an overpayment of HB cannot be made from incapacity benefit.[94] Overpayments of HB cannot be recovered by deductions from CTB (and *vice versa*).[95]

An overpayment can also be recovered from benefits paid to your landlord personally.[96]

Deductions can only be made if:[97]

- a recoverable overpayment has been made as a result of a misrepresentation or failure to disclose (see pp2:518-521) a material fact by you or on your behalf or by or on behalf of some other person to whom HB has been paid; *and*
- the local authority is unable to recover that overpayment from any HB entitlement; *and*
- the person who misrepresented or failed to disclose is receiving enough of at least one of the relevant benefits (see below) to allow deductions to be made.

There are no rules limiting the maximum payment that can be deducted. However, you can argue that your rate of repayment should be reasonable. If you are on IS or income-based JSA, you should argue that the weekly maximums for those benefits should apply (see p2:525). You should make representations to the Benefits Agency if deductions cause hardship.

If deductions stop because you are no longer entitled to a particular benefit, or the amount to which you are entitled is insufficient for deductions to be made, the Benefits Agency notifies the local authority which, once again, becomes responsible for any further recovery action.

Adjustment of a rent account

If you are a local authority tenant, the local authority can recover an overpayment by adding it as a debt to your rent account. If a local authority recovers overpaid HB by adjusting your rent account, the overpayment should be separately identified and you should be informed that the amount being recovered does not represent rent arrears.[98] If the local authority is trying to seek possession of your home on the grounds of rent arrears you should seek advice. It should not be able to say you owe it rent arrears if you have only been overpaid HB. Local authorities are reminded in Benefits

Agency guidance that overpayments of HB in respect of their own tenants are not rent arrears and should not be treated as such.[99]

Note: An overpayment cannot be recovered in this way if you have a private or housing association landlord. However, an overpayment can be recovered from your landlord (see p2:536). If the local authority recovers from your landlord, you might count as being in rent arrears (see pp2:540-542).

Court action

If a local authority cannot use any of the methods of recovery above, and you cannot agree on repayments, it can try to recover the money you owe through the county court (sheriff's court in Scotland) if it thinks you could afford to make repayments. You have six weeks to ask for a review of a decision that an overpayment is recoverable (see p2:590). This should be borne in mind when local authorities are deciding when to start proceedings.

A local authority should not use court proceedings to recover an overpayment if it has not followed the correct procedure (see p2:530). The correct procedure has not been followed if, for example, the local authority has not issued the correct notification (see p2:538).[100]

An authority may use one of two means of recovering through the courts. It can:

- sue you for the debt created by the overpayment.[101] If the correct procedure (see p2:530) has not been followed, you can use this as a defence to the authority's claim.[102] You may also be able to make a compensation claim in certain circumstances (see p2:597). However, you are not allowed to say that you should have received more HB because you must seek a review instead (see p2:590);[103]
- use the special rules to register the overpayment as a debt which can then be recovered using a court procedure.[104] Seek advice if you think the local authority is not entitled to do this.

If the local authority is successful in using court proceedings against you, you may have to pay legal costs and interest as well as the overpayment. Remember that court procedures often require you to take action within a very short period of time. If the local authority is threatening to use court proceedings, seek urgent advice.

Step five: Notification of overpayments

If the local authority decides that a recoverable overpayment has occurred, it must write to the person from whom recovery is being sought – see p2:534 – (within 14 days, if possible) and notify her/him accordingly.[105] This notification must state:[106]

- the fact that there is an overpayment which is legally recoverable;
- the reason why there is a recoverable overpayment;

- the amount of the recoverable overpayment;
- how the amount of the overpayment was calculated;
- the benefit weeks to which the overpayment relates;
- if recovery is to be made from future benefit, how much the deduction will be;
- if recovery is to be made from your landlord by deduction from direct payments of HB of a claimant other than you (if you were overpaid – see p2:536), your identity and the claimant whose HB will be deducted;[107]
- that you have a right to ask for a further written explanation of any of the decisions the local authority has made regarding the overpayment, how you can do this and the time limit for doing so;
- that you have a right to ask the local authority to reconsider any of the decisions it has made regarding the overpayment, how you can do this and the time limit for doing so.

It may also include any other relevant matters.

If you write and ask the local authority for a more detailed written explanation of any of the decisions it has made regarding an overpayment, it must send you this within 14 days or, if this is not reasonably practicable, as soon as possible after that.[108] If your local authority does not give proper notification, you should write and point out that the decision to recover the overpayment is not valid until you are given proper notification. No recovery should be sought until after you have been notified and have had a chance to discuss your case or apply for a review.[109]

7. **Overpayments of council tax benefit**

An overpayment of council tax benefit (CTB) is called 'excess benefit'.[110] The rules about recovery are the same as for housing benefit (HB) (see pp2:529-538), with the following exceptions.

Is the overpayment recoverable?

The criteria for when an overpayment is recoverable are the same as for HB (see pp2:530-533), except that the following categories of overpayments are always recoverable:

- an overpayment of CTB credited to your council tax account that relates to a future period, even if it was made as a result of an 'official error' (see p2:531);[111]
- an overpayment which has arisen because you were paid CTB, but then your council tax liability was reduced because of a disability reduction, discount, transitional relief or charge-capping (see p1:572);[112]

- an overpayment that results from the local authority changing the levels of council tax for the financial year.[113]

The amount of the overpayment

As with all overpayments, the amount overpaid is the difference between what you were actually paid and what you should have received. However, there are two possible variations of what should have been paid – either a reduced amount of main CTB (see p1:571), or a second adult rebate (see p1:571) if you are eligible for this and it would have been higher than the revised amount of main CTB.

When assessing the amount overpaid the local authority should do both calculations (see pp1:574 and 1:579), and can only recover the balance between the higher of the two figures and the amount which you in fact received. It is always worth checking that the second adult rebate calculation has been done and that the correct amount is being recovered.

From whom can recovery be made?

Recovery of a CTB overpayment is always from the CTB claimant or the person to whom benefit was paid – eg, your partner or an appointee. There can be no recovery from any other person, even if s/he caused the overpayment.[114]

CTB is recoverable by the same methods as HB (see pp2:535-538) with the following exceptions:

- the overpayment can be recovered by increasing your outstanding council tax liability;[115]
- the local authority cannot use the special court procedures for recovering the overpayment (see p2:538). If it wishes to recover through the court, it must sue you instead. It may not start proceedings for 21 days after it notifies you of the amount due.[116]

---

8. **The effect of recovery of housing benefit from your landlord**

If you are a private or housing association tenant, an overpayment of housing benefit (HB) recovered from your landlord (see p2:536), could leave you owing your landlord money. This could put you in difficulty, particularly if your tenancy agreement allows your landlord to get possession of your home if you are in arrears of rent.

If you received HB yourself, and then paid your landlord, you are treated as having paid the amount of HB towards your rent.

However, the rules are different if HB was paid directly to your landlord by the local authority. In this case, whether you are put in rent arrears when an overpayment is recorded depends on when the overpayment was made (see below).

Whether HB was paid direct to your landlord or not, s/he may still try to claim that even if you owe no rent, you nevertheless owe a debt under common law, which is probably not correct. If s/he threatens to sue you, seek advice straightaway.

If you are a local authority tenant, these rules do not apply. However, the local authority can recover an overpayment of HB by making deductions from your rent account. To see how these rules might affect you, see p2:540.

Direct payments before 7 April 1997

Where you were overpaid HB before 7 April 1997, and HB was paid direct to your landlord, you are still treated as having paid that amount towards your rent. This is because the local authority is effectively paying your rent for you, and so your obligation towards your landlord is discharged (subject to you paying any difference between your rent and the HB).[117]

What this means is that your landlord cannot say that you have rent arrears of the amount of the overpayment that s/he has had to repay.

Direct payments between 7 April 1997 and 3 November 1997

On 7 April 1997, the Government tried to change the law where HB was paid directly to a landlord.[118] For such payments made after that date, the rule says that you are *not* treated as having paid your rent when:
- you were not entitled to a payment of HB paid to your landlord or to part of such a payment; *and*
- the HB overpayment was recovered in whole or in part from your landlord.

If your landlord tries to rely on this rule to get possession of your home, you should argue that the Government had no power to make it and your landlord cannot rely on it. This is because at the time the rule was made, the Government was only allowed to make rules saying when and how local authorities could make payments to landlords.[119] There was no power to make rules to say how such payments affected the legal rights of you and your landlord.

You might be able to use this argument to prevent your landlord claiming that recovery of the overpayment of HB put you into rent arrears. However, because there is a risk of you losing your home if your landlord were to seek possession, you should seek advice *immediately*. You can try to argue that since the argument could be used against the Government, you should be allowed to use it against your landlord. Anyone in this situation should seek advice *immediately*.[120] If it is right that landlords cannot rely on this rule, you will be in the same position as before 7 April 1997 (see p2:541).

Direct payments after 4 November 1997

Where you were overpaid HB after 4 November 1997 and HB was paid directly to your landlord, the following rules apply:

- Where you are overpaid, and the local authority recovers the overpayment from your landlord by making deductions from direct payments of **other tenants' HB** (see p2:536), the other tenants are treated as having paid the amount of the deduction towards their rent.[121]
- Where you are overpaid, and the local authority recovers the overpayment from your landlord by making deductions from direct payments of **your HB**, you are treated as having paid the amount of the deduction towards your rent but only where your landlord is convicted of an offence or agrees to pay a penalty (see p2:553) in relation to that overpayment.[122]
- If the local authority decides to recover under this rule, it must notify both your landlord and you that you are to be treated as having paid your rent.[123]

In these situations, it is clear that your landlord cannot claim that you are in arrears of rent. It is also much easier to argue that your landlord cannot sue you under common law for a debt (see p2:541).

The law does not make clear what happens in other cases where deductions are made from your HB. If you are in this position, you could try to argue that the rules do not say what happens in your case, and so the same rules apply as before the law was introduced (see p2:541). If this is right, you should be treated as having paid your rent. However, because there is a risk of you losing your home if your landlord were to seek possession, you should seek advice *immediately*.

Notes

References are to statutes and regulations as amended up to 8 March 1999. All regulations are (General) Regulations unless otherwise stated. There is a full list of abbreviations in Appendix 13.

1. **'Ordinary' overpayments**
   1 ss71 and 71ZA SSAA 1992; Sch 6 para 8 SSA 1998
   2 s71(3) SSAA 1992
   3 *Plewa v Chief Adjudication Officer* [1994] 1 WLR 317 (HL) overruling *Secretary of State for Social Security v Tunnicliffe, The Times,* 8 January 1991 (CA)
   4 CIS/451/1995 (following this case s71 SSAA 1992 was amended); note that CSIS/174/1996 decided the opposite.
   5 s71(5) SSAA 1992
   6 s71(5A) SSAA 1992; CSSB/621/1988 and CSB/316/1989; R(SB) 7/91
   7 s71A SSAA 1992
   8 R(SB) 34/83
   9 R(S) 4/86; R(I) 3/75
   10 CSB/1006/1985
   11 R(SB) 54/83
   12 R(SB) 21/82; R(SB) 28/83; R(SB) 54/83; R(A) 1/95
   13 Reg 32(1) SS(C&P) Regs
   14 R(SB) 15/87
   15 CSB/688/1982; R(SB) 12/84; R(SB) 20/84; R(SB) 40/84
   16 R(SB) 18/85
   17 CWSB/2/1985
   18 CSB/347/1983; R(SB) 10/85
   19 R(SB) 33/85; CSB/1195/1984
   20 R(SB) 54/83
   21 CSB/393/1985
   22 R(G) 2/72
   23 R(U) 6/70
   24 *Page v CAO* (CA), *The Times,* 4 July 1991
   25 *Jones/Sharples v CAO* [1994] 1 All ER 225; R(SB) 9/85
   26 R(SB) 18/85
   27 R(SB) 3/90
   28 CIS/222/1991
   29 *Sheriff v CAO, The Times,* 10 May 1995
   30 *Jones/Sharples v CAO* [1994] 1 All ER 225; *Franklin v CAO, The Times,* 29 December 1995; CIS/674/1994; CIS/583/1994
   31 CIS/674/1994
   32 *Franklin v CAO, The Times,* 29 December 1995
   33 CIS/53/1994
   34 CIS/159/1990; CS/11700/1996
   35 **HB** Reg 104(a) HB Regs
   CTB Reg 90(a) CTB Regs
   36 R(SB) 20/84; R(SB) 24/87
   37 Reg 13 SS(PAOR) Regs
   38 R(IS) 5/92
   39 *Commock v CAO* reported as appendix to R(SB) 6/90; CSIS/8/1995
   40 Regs 15 and 16(3) SS(PAOR) Regs
   41 Reg 14 SS(PAOR) Regs
   42 ss22(5), 30, 32(9) and 33 SSAA 1992
   43 CSB/688/1982
   44 paras 8 and 9 Social Fund Bulletin 17/98, 9 September 1998

2. **Duplication of payments**
   45 s74 SSAA 1992
   46 R(SB) 3/91

3. **Recovery of 'ordinary' overpayments and duplication of payments**
   47 Reg 15 SS(PAOR) Regs
   48 Reg 17 SS(PAOR) Regs
   49 s74(2)(b) SSAA 1992
   50 Reg 16(3) SS(PAOR) Regs
   51 CIS/332/1993; CIS/12022/1996 decided the opposite
   52 *Secretary of State for Social Services v Solly* [1974] 3 All ER 922; R(SB) 21/82
   53 Reg 16(4), (4A), (5) and (6) SS(PAOR) Regs
   54 Reg 16(6) SS(PAOR) Regs

51

55 Reg 16(5A) SS(PAOR) Regs
56 s71(10) SSAA 1992

4. Excess benefit credited to bank and other accounts
57 s71(4) and (5) SSAA 1992
58 s71(5) SSAA 1992
59 CSSB/621/1988 and CSB/316/1989; R(SB) 7/91
60 Reg 11 SS(PAOR) Regs

5. Mortgage interest paid directly to a lender
61 Sch 9A para 11 SS(C&P) Regs
62 *R v Secretary of State for Social Security ex parte Golding* (CA), *The Times,* 15 March 1996
63 CIS/5206/1995
64 CIS/5206/1995

6. Overpayments of HB
65 **HB** Reg 98 HB Regs
   CTB Reg 83 CTB Regs
66 **HB** Reg 98 HB Regs
   CTB Reg 83 CTB Regs
67 **HB** Reg 99(1) HB Regs
   CTB Reg 84(1) CTB Regs
68 Reg 91(3) HB Regs
69 Reg 99(4) HB Regs
70 **HB** Reg 99(2) HB Regs
   CTB Reg 84(2) CTB Regs
71 **HB** Reg 99(3) HB Regs
   CTB Reg 84(3) CTB Regs
72 para A7.14 GM
73 *Duggan v Chief Adjudication Officer, The Times,* 13 March 1988, CA
74 *Warwick DC v Freeman* [1994] 27 HLR 616
75 *R v Liverpool City Council ex parte Griffiths* [1990] 22 HLR 312
76 **HB** Reg 100 HB Regs
   CTB Reg 85 CTB Regs
77 para A7.51 GM
78 **HB** Reg 79(2) HB Regs
   CTB Reg 69(2) CTB Regs
   Both *Welfare Rights Bulletin 120,* p9
79 **HB** Reg 83(2) HB Regs; *R v Ellesmere Port and Neston HBRB ex parte Williams,* 15 November 1996, CA
   CTB Reg 72(2) CTB Regs
80 **HB** Reg 101 HB Regs
   CTB Reg 86 CTB Regs

81 paras A7.54-56 GM
82 *R v Wyre Borough Council ex parte Lord*
83 **HB** Reg 104(a) HB Regs
   CTB Reg 90(a) CTB Regs
84 *R v Kensington and Chelsea RBC ex parte Brandt* [1995] 28 HLR 528 at 537, QBD
85 **HB** Reg 104(b) HB Regs; para A7.27 GM
   CTB Reg 90(b) CTB Regs
86 **HB** Reg 103 HB Regs
   CTB Reg 89(1) CTB Regs
87 **HB** Reg 103(1)(a) and (b) HB Regs
   CTB Reg 89(1)(a) and (b) CTB Regs
88 **HB** s75 SSAA 1992; reg 102 HB Regs
   CTB s75 SSAA 1992; reg 87(2)(a) CTB Regs
89 **HB** Reg 101(2) HB Regs
   CTB Reg 86(2) CTB Regs
90 s75(5)(a) SSAA 1992; reg 2(2)(a) HB(RO) Regs
91 s75(5)(b) SSAA 1992; reg 2(3) HB(RO) Regs
92 s75(5)(c) SSAA 1992; reg 2(3) HB(RO) Regs
93 para A7.44 GM
94 Reg 105(1)(a) HB Regs; incapacity benefit is not a benefit payable under the SSA 1975
95 **HB** Reg 105 HB Regs
   CTB Reg 91 CTB Regs
96 Reg 2(4) HB(RO) Regs
97 **HB** Regs 102 and 105 HB Regs
   CTB Regs 87(3) and 91 CTB Regs
98 *R v Haringey LBC ex parte Azad Ayub* [1992] 25 HLR 566, QBD
99 paras A7.40-43 GM
100 *Warwick DC v Freeman* [1994] 27 HLR 616, CA
101 Reg 88 CTB Regs; para A7.38 GM
102 *Warwick DC v Freeman* [1994] 27 HLR 616, CA
103 *Plymouth CC v Gigg,* 16 May 1997, CA
104 s75(7) SSAA 1992
105 **HB** Reg 77(1)(b) HB Regs
    CTB Reg 67(1)(b) CTB Regs

106 **HB** Sch 6 paras 2, 3, 6 and 14
HB Regs; para A7.42 GM
CTB Sch 6 paras 2, 3, 6 and 16
CTB Regs
107 Reg 4(4) HB(RO) Regs
108 **HB** Reg 77(4) and (5) HB Regs
CTB Reg 67(2) and (3) CTB Regs
109 para A7.51 GM

7. Overpayments of CTB

110 Reg 83 CTB Regs
111 Reg 84(5) CTB Regs
112 Regs 83(a) and 84(4) CTB Regs
113 Regs 83(b) and 84(4) CTB Regs
114 Reg 86(1) CTB Regs
115 Reg 87(2)(b) CTB Regs
116 Reg 88 CTB Regs

8. The effect of recovery of HB from your landlord

117 *R v Haringey LBC ex parte Azad Ayub* [1992] 25 HLR 566, QBD
118 Reg 93(2) HB Regs
119 s5(1)(p) SSAA 1992
120 *Wandsworth BC v Winder* [1985] AC 461, HL
121 s75(6) SSAA 1992
122 s75(6) SSAA 1992; reg 3(1) and (2) HB(RO) Regs
123 Reg 3(3) HB(RO) Regs

52

Chapter 52

. . . .

Fraud

This chapter covers the rules about fraud. It contains:
1. What happens if you are investigated or accused of fraud (p2:547)
2. Investigation of claims (p2:547)
3. Prosecution of offences (p2:551)
4. Penalties (p2:553)
5. Formal cautions (p2:555)
6. The effect of fraud investigation on benefit claims (p2:556)
7. Working families tax credit, disabled person's tax credit and fraud (p2:557).

It is not an offence to make mistakes or forget to tell things to the Benefits Agency or local authority, if you have not done so deliberately. However if too much benefit is paid as a result, money may be recoverable (see p2:516). You may commit an offence if you deliberately mislead the Benefits Agency or local authority or if you fail to notify a change of circumstances that you are required to notify. In this chapter 'fraud' refers to such offences.

Where the Benefits Agency or the local authority believe you have committed fraud:
- you may be at risk of being prosecuted (see p2:551);
- you might be given the option of paying a penalty instead of being taken to court (see p2:553);
- for benefits other than housing benefit and council tax benefit you may be given the option of accepting a formal caution (see p2:555).

In each case you should seek urgent advice before taking any action or making any statements.

In their efforts to stop fraud, there is a danger that the Benefits Agency and local authorities will try to prosecute and punish people who have just made mistakes or who do not understand the system.

The best way to avoid misunderstandings is to ensure that the Benefits Agency and local authority always know everything about your circumstances and those of your family (see p2:113 for who counts as your 'family') and any non-dependants living in your household. Tell them everything – even if you are not sure whether they want to know (see p2:492 for more details).

1. What happens if you are investigated or accused of fraud

Your claim may be referred for investigation for a number of reasons:
- someone has informed the Benefits Agency or local authority, that you should not be getting benefit;
- you have put something inconsistent on a form or you have said something suspicious at an interview;
- information has come to light as a result of cross-checks or data-matching carried out by the Benefits Agency or local authorities. Information held can be cross-checked against other information held on Benefits Agency, Contributions Agency and local authority computers (see p2:548);
- the place where you or your partner work may have been 'raided' by fraud investigators or information may have been provided by the employer.

Fraud investigators may be part of a multi-disciplinary team including customs officials, immigration officers or police officers . Such teams carry out raids and roadside checks. They will have wider powers than Benefit Agency or local authority fraud investigators acting alone.

2. Investigation of claims

If the Benefits Agency or local authority discovers something inconsistent in the information it holds, it will often start an investigation into your claim. It does not have to tell you about the inquiries that it is making straightaway, but will normally wait until it has gathered all the information it needs and then ask you to attend an interview to explain matters.

Local authority fraud officers gained powers to carry out fraud investigations from the Social Security Administration (Fraud) Act 1997. Only local authority fraud officers who have a certificate of appointment authorised by the Secretary of State have such powers.[1] Although Benefits Agency and local authority investigators have broadly similar powers there are some small differences in the detail.

Powers to seek information

Local authorities and the Benefits Agency have powers to gather a wide variety of information from other public bodies for the purposes of:
- the prevention, detection, investigation or prosecution of social security offences;

- checking the accuracy of information relating to benefits, contributions or national insurance numbers;
- amending or supplementing such information.

The Benefits Agency can seek information from:
- tax authorities;[2]
- government departments – this provision relates in particular to issues about passports, immigration, emigration, nationality and prisoners;[3]
- the registration service, which is under an additional duty to report particulars of deaths to the Secretary of State for social security purposes;[4]
- local authorities.[5]

Local authorities have no specific powers to seek information from the above bodies themselves but are entitled to any information that the Benefits Agency is holding.[6]

Both local authorities and the Benefits Agency can seek information about redirected post and have undelivered social security post returned to them.[7]

All information gathered is confidential to the bodies concerned with administration of benefit, including private companies contracted to carry out such functions. Unauthorised disclosure of such information is a criminal offence.[8]

The Data Protection Act 1984 restricts the use of material held on computer. The DSS has produced a code of practice for data matching which applies to all information held or sought by the Benefits Agency.[9] If local authorities or the Benefits Agency make a request for information based on either the information seeking provisions above, or investigative powers below, which is inappropriate or unreasonable, the matter can be referred to the Data Protection Registrar for investigation if the information sought is held on computer. The new Data Protection Act 1998, which expands protection to written records, is not yet in force.

Powers of investigation

The Benefits Agency and local authorities have powers to appoint inspectors to look at claims which they think may be wrongful.[10] The inspectors are given wide powers to do the following:[11]
- enter premises where a business operates. This does *not* include your home unless the inspector has some reason to think that a business is operating from there. Local authority investigators must also be satisfied that it is the only premises where the business is operating;
- make inquiries and examine documents about a person the inspector believes to be claiming or receiving benefit;
- interview people in premises that are liable to be inspected;

- require that information or documents are produced by people who are:
  - in buildings which are inspected; *or*
  - are employers or employees; *or*
  - believed by the officer to be claiming or receiving benefit; *or*
  - (local authority inspectors) in possession of documents or information about a person claiming or receiving benefit.[12]

Information sought under these powers must be reasonably required by the investigation officer. Entry must be at a reasonable time and an inspector must produce her/his certificate of appointment. If you obstruct an inspector or refuse to supply information, you may commit an offence.[13]

While the powers of inspectors are wide, they are not police officers. They cannot come into your home without your permission (except where your home is also where you run a business – see above) and they cannot arrest you. In addition, they cannot make you give information or answer questions in such a way as to confess that you or your spouse (not including your partner if you are not married) are guilty of an offence.[14]

Inspectors do not have the power to remove original documents or copy documents. However, they can require access to original documents for inspection.

You cannot be prevented leaving somewhere by a local authority or Benefits Agency fraud inspector. If you are prevented from leaving, you should later get legal advice. You may have grounds to bring an action for false imprisonment. You do not have to answer any questions if you are interviewed (see below), but if you are cautioned (see p2:550) a refusal to answer may be used as evidence to infer guilt in any criminal proceedings.

Inspectors are 'persons charged with the duty of investigating offences or charging offenders' and are therefore bound by codes of practice under the Police and Criminal Evidence Act 1984 in investigating a claim.[15] If the codes are breached, this may restrict the use of evidence that inspectors have obtained.[16] If you think the inspectors have acted unfairly, you should seek advice.

Interviews

During investigations inspectors may carry out fact-finding interviews to gather information. If you are suspected of fraud, officers should carry out a formal interview, known as an interview under caution. These usually happen at the local benefit or local authority's offices. You may not be told why the interview is happening. Failure to inform claimants of the purpose of a fraud interview has occasionally been successfully challenged in the courts as an attempt to mislead suspects into admitting an offence before realising the possibility of prosecution. Although not a breach of the codes of practice it may result in an unfairness, which means that a court may rule that the interview is inadmissible as evidence. The DSS issued guidance to local authority fraud officers suggesting that all letters inviting claimants to interviews under caution, should broadly state why an interview is being held and the possibility of criminal prosecution.[17]

If you think you may be interviewed by fraud officers, seek advice before you go. Legal aid may be available if you go to a solicitor. Try to bring a friend or adviser to the interview to support you and take notes.

Fraud officers sometimes put pressure on claimants to admit to things that are not accurate. It can be very upsetting to be accused of committing an offence, but it is important that you remain calm and listen carefully to the questions you are asked. If you do not understand anything, ask for clarification. Think carefully about the implications of the answers you give.

You should always be **cautioned** before the interview if there are grounds to suspect that you have committed an offence. If the inspector fails to do so the interview may not be admissible in court. If you are interviewed under caution, you may make a written statement if you wish to explain matters.

The recommended form of caution

You do not have to say anything. But it may harm your defence if you do not mention when questioned something which you later rely on in court. Anything you do say may be given in evidence.[18]

If you do not understand the caution, its meaning should be explained to you. If you think you can explain the situation that has arisen, you should probably do so, since if you do not mention it at the interview you are more likely to be disbelieved if you are prosecuted.[19] In addition, if you are able to explain matters, your benefit is less likely to be taken away (see p2:556). Do not confess to something that you did not do, just to finish the interview or to try to prevent your benefit being stopped.

You have an absolute right to get legal advice and you should be reminded of this during the interview. You must be told that you are free to leave at any time.

A formal interview is either taped or someone writes down what you say. You should be asked to read through the notes of the interview afterwards and sign them to agree that they are accurate. It is important that you check them carefully and challenge anything that you think is wrong, since it may be difficult to do so later. If you do not have anyone with you at the interview, try to write down as much as you can remember about what was said shortly afterwards because it may be difficult to remember later.

3. **Prosecution of offences**

There are a number of different offences that you can commit if you mislead an authority. They can broadly be divided into two categories according to the level of penalty and where you are tried. Any fine that you have to pay is in addition to any overpayment that may be found to be recoverable (see Chapter 51). Remember that the figures given are the maximum penalties, in practice they are usually much smaller.

Besides the offences set out below, you can also be charged with offences under the Theft Act 1968: theft, obtaining property by deception and false accounting.[20] These tend to be used only for the most serious offences.

Less serious offences

The maximum penalty for these offences is a £5,000 fine or three months in prison, or both.[21] You commit these offences when you do any of the following:

- make a statement which you know to be false, or give information or documents that you know to be false in some way that is significant.[22] You can commit this offence even if you do not intend to get any benefit as a result;[23]
- fail to tell the Benefits Agency or local authority about a change of circumstances which you know that you have to report (see p2:492), without reasonable excuse;[24]
- make another person or allow another person to withhold a change of circumstances from the Benefits Agency or local authority when you know s/he has to notify them of it, without reasonable excuse.[25]

You do not 'know' something if you are merely careless about whether or not something is true, or if you fail to find out.[26] Reasonable excuse could be anything that might make a reasonable person act as you did, such as wrong advice or some personal circumstance like illness or bereavement. You cannot be convicted of either of the last two offences due to anything you did or failed to do before 1 July 1997.[27]

Advisers and other third parties

Offences can be committed by any person who is required to make statements or notify changes of circumstances, not just the claimant. The offence of knowingly allowing or knowingly causing a claimant to fail to notify a change of circumstances, does not place any additional duty on advisers to notify the Benefits Agency or local authority of a claimant's change of circumstances. In order to bite there must be some sort of implied permission given to the person, under a duty to notify, not to do so.[28] You do not 'allow' somebody to do something unless you are able to stop them doing it. You may also be able to use a defence of reasonable excuse if for example you are under a threat of violence or owe a duty of care or confidentiality to a client. If you are an adviser you should not be liable if you have advised your client fully as to the law and the requirement to notify a change of circumstances. You should do nothing to help facilitate a failure to notify a change of circumstances (eg, help complete a claim or review form which you know is inaccurate). The Government has stated that it does not intend this offence to apply to advisers acting in good faith.[29]

More serious offences

You can be charged with a more serious offence if in addition to committing the acts subject to the lesser offences above you are also:[30]
- acting dishonestly. This means that in committing the offence you do something that most people would consider dishonest and that you must have known this;[31] *and*
- trying to get benefit paid to yourself or some other person.

If you are convicted in a magistrates' court, you can be fined £5,000 or imprisoned for six months. If you are convicted in the Crown Court, the fine is unlimited and you can be imprisoned for up to seven years.

Will you be prosecuted?

Not all cases where there is evidence to justify a prosecution are taken to court. In some cases you may be given the chance to pay a penalty or accept a formal caution instead (see below). In some cases no fraud action is taken at all. The factors that the Benefits Agency and local authorities may take into account include the strength of the evidence, the amount of benefit involved, whether an offence was planned, and your personal circumstances.

There are time limits for prosecutions of the less serious offences set out above. A prosecution must be started by the *later* of the following dates:[32]
- three months from the date the Benefits Agency or local authority thinks that it has enough evidence to prosecute you; *or*
- 12 months from the date you committed the offence.

Prosecutions of the more serious offences may be started at any time.

What to do if you are prosecuted

The most important thing to do is to get advice. You may be entitled to legal aid to have a solicitor or barrister represent you in court. You should check carefully that the Benefits Agency or local authority is able to prove all the parts of the offence you are charged with. Do not plead guilty until you have been able to get advice.

4. Penalties

The Benefits Agency or local authority may offer you the option of agreeing to pay a financial penalty, instead of risking prosecution.

The penalty is 30 per cent of the recoverable overpayment caused by an offence committed since 18 December 1997.[33]

The penalty is added to the overpayment of benefit and is recoverable in the same way as the overpayment[34] (see pp2:525 and 2:535). Guidance from the DSS to local authorities suggests that where an overpayment is being recovered from weekly benefits, deductions to recover the penalty should be instituted once the overpayment is fully recovered.[35]

The option of paying a penalty

You can *only* be offered the option of paying a penalty when three conditions are fulfilled:[36]

- an overpayment has been found to be recoverable from you. The Benefits Agency or local authority must have gone through the process of reviewing your award of benefit and issuing a decision that the overpayment is recoverable (see pp2:517 and 2:530); *and*
- the overpayment was due to an act or omission on your part. This act or omission must have been after 18 December 1997;[37] *and*
- there are grounds for prosecuting you for an offence relating to the overpayment.

You must be issued with a notice which sets out, in broad terms, how the scheme works[38] and gives you information about how you agree to pay a penalty or notify your withdrawal of your agreement.[39] If you are not issued with a proper notice, it may not be possible for the Benefits Agency or local authority to enforce the penalty, just as it cannot recover an overpayment (see pp2:517 and 2:538).

The notice will usually be sent with an invitation to an interview to discuss accepting the penalty. The DSS strongly recommends that the interview is carried out by an officer who was not involved in the interview under caution.[40] The interview will relate only to the offering of a penalty. You will not be able to use it to add to or alter any statement that you made about the alleged offence in an interview under caution. You should not be pressured or coerced into accepting a penalty at the interview. If you are unable to decide whether or not to accept the caution at the interview the Benefits Agency considers it reasonable to allow you five days to make up your mind:[41]

- If you agree to pay a penalty you are immune from prosecution for any offence in relation to the overpayment.[42] Note that this would not stop you being prosecuted in the future if you committed another offence, or in relation to a different overpayment if there was more than one.

- If it is found on review that the overpayment is not recoverable, any penalty that you have paid must be repaid to you.[43] This does not appear to affect the existence of the agreement, so you are still immune from prosecution.

- If the amount of the overpayment is changed on review, the agreement is nullified, so you lose the immunity and any penalty you have paid must be repaid to you, unless you enter into a fresh agreement.[44]

- If you decline to accept the penalty, the Benefits Agency or local authority will consider prosecuting you.

Changing your mind

If you enter into an agreement to pay a penalty, you are entitled to change your mind within 28 days and tell the Benefits Agency or local authority in the way that is specified on the penalty notice.[45] You then lose your immunity, but you do not have to pay the penalty and if you have paid any part of it, it must be refunded.

The legislation does not allow for the period to be extended. However, if you do not get advice, because you are scared of being prosecuted, until after the 28-day period expires, and it turns out that the Benefits Agency or local authority had insufficient grounds to prosecute you, it is possible that you may be able to take court proceedings to set aside the penalty agreement on the grounds of the authority's 'undue influence'.[46] If this applies to you, seek advice.

Should you accept the penalty?

There is a risk that you will be invited to pay a penalty when there is insufficient evidence to prosecute you. If you are offered a penalty, make sure that you are told what evidence the Benefits Agency or local authority has against you. The fraud officer can only recommend that your case is considered for prosecution. The legal department will decide whether to prosecute you if it believes that the case is suitable for prosecution (see p2:551). You will not automatically be prosecuted if you refuse to accept an administrative penalty.

Remember also that 30 per cent of the overpayment may be a substantial amount of money. For minor offences, it may be that the fine imposed on you is less than the penalty. You may prefer to do community service rather than go further into debt. On the other hand, a penalty does not give you a criminal record. You should seek advice and carefully consider your options.

5. **Formal cautions**

On the 1 June 1998, the DSS instituted a system of 'cautioning' for social security offences. This system operates only within the Benefits Agency although a few local authorities have similar systems of their own. The cautioning system is not laid down in regulations but based on guidance modelled on the established guidelines for the police's practice of cautioning.

The system works very similarly to the penalty system above. The DSS tell us that cautions will generally be aimed at less serious frauds where the value of overpayment is low. A formal caution will only be offered when an interview under caution has been carried out, an overpayment has been calculated and the fraud officer believes that there is sufficient evidence to prosecute you for an offence.

You will attend a formal caution interview, where you will be asked to sign a record admitting the offence and accepting the caution. If you accept a caution you will be immune from prosecution for the offence that you have admitted, this may encompass overpayments of more than one benefit.

The caution certificate is sent to Benefits Agency headquarters in Leeds and the caution is recorded on a central database. The record will initially be kept for five years. A properly recorded formal caution may be cited in court if a person is successfully prosecuted for a subsequent offence, it may then become part of a criminal record.

If you refuse to admit the offence and accept a formal caution your case will be considered for prosecution.

Whether to accept a caution

Accepting a formal caution is an admission of guilt. Once you have accepted a caution you cannot change your mind. However, it might be possible to seek a judicial review of the decision to offer a caution.

Although accepting the formal caution will mean that you are immune from prosecution for offences specified on the certificate, you may be prosecuted for related offences not specified, such as a housing benefit overpayment. The formal caution is kept on a database and will be subject to data protection rules. Information about the caution can be disclosed to other bodies in some circumstances; for example, to local authorities for use in housing benefit and council tax benefit matters or to the police for use in criminal investigations.

If you are subsequently found guilty of another offence in court, your formal caution could be cited and may mean that you get a stiffer sentence.

As with penalties, a formal caution may be offered in circumstances where there is insufficient evidence to prosecute you for an offence. You will not necessarily be prosecuted just because you refuse to accept a caution. You should not admit to something that you did not do just to avoid the threat of prosecution. Consider all your options carefully and seek advice.

6. The effect of fraud investigation on benefit claims

Your benefit cannot be stopped wholly because of fraud. However, the Benefits Agency or local authority is entitled to suspend or withhold your benefit if it has a doubt as to whether you are entitled (see p2:497). Note that there will be wider powers for suspension when the new Social Security Act is implemented (see p2:581). You will often have difficulties in getting your benefit restored during an investigation or after you have been prosecuted. The Benefits Agency or local authority should not withhold your benefit indefinitely without making a decision as to whether you are in fact entitled or not. If you think the investigation is taking too long, you should complain (see p2:662). If that brings no results, seek legal advice about forcing them to make a decision.

Being under investigation for fraud can be very distressing. Fraud officers can take your papers away from the section normally dealing with your claim and it can sometimes be difficult to find out what is happening. Fraud officers cannot make decisions on your entitlement, they merely pass on evidence to decision makers. You should not withdraw your claim unless you know that you are not entitled to benefit. Always insist on a proper decision from an adjudication officer or local authority benefit assessor.

The decision as to whether you should be prosecuted is separate from a decision to recover an overpayment (see Chapter 51). Whether you are entitled to benefit, the amount and recoverability of any overpayment are decided by Benefits Agency or local authority benefit assessors without regard to dishonesty of intention. Any decision that they make can be appealed or reviewed in the usual way (see p2:590 for housing benefit/council tax benefit; pp2:570 and 2:611 for other benefits). The fraud investigation department decides whether your actions were fraudulent and whether action to prosecute, award penalties or caution you should be taken. The two processes are independent and have different tests, therefore a decision or appeal relating to your claim should not normally be delayed awaiting the outcome of criminal prosecution, and a court awarded fine will not prevent separate action for overpayment recovery. However, successful prosecution of a fraudulent offence will alter the burden of proof in an overpayment appeal and if a court has awarded compensation to the Benefits Agency or local authority it cannot also recover that amount as an overpayment.[47]

Whatever the result of an investigation or prosecution, the Benefits Agency or local authority may take more time assessing future claims because it checks out your circumstances thoroughly. Again, if it takes too long for it to make a decision, you should complain. You should not be prevented from making a fresh claim during a fraud investigation if your circumstances have changed. You could also apply for interim payments (see p2:499-500) or help from the social fund (see Chapter 31).

7. Working families tax credit, disabled person's tax credit and fraud

From 5 October 1999, family credit and disability working allowance will be replaced by new tax credit schemes, see p1:489. The tax credit schemes will be administered by the Inland Revenue, not the Benefits Agency. At the time this *Handbook* went to print the final details of the new schemes were not available, but from information set out in the Tax Credits Bill, it appears that the local authority and Benefits Agency's powers to investigate fraud and penalise or prosecute fraudsters will not apply to suspected tax credit fraud.

Instead the Inland Revenue will have the same powers to investigate tax credit fraud as it has to investigate underpayment of taxes. The Inland Revenue produces a code of practice (Code of Practice 2: Investigations) which explains your rights and what will happen if the Inland Revenue decides to look into your tax matters. The Inland Revenue can prosecute cases of fraud, but it is more common for financial penalties to be awarded. A penalty cannot be refused although it may be appealed, see below. Agreeing to pay a financial penalty to the Inland Revenue does not provide immunity from prosecution for that offence[48] although it is a factor which may make prosecution less likely.

Where you have fraudulently or negligently failed to provide information or given false information or evidence in relation to a tax credit claim, penalties of up to £3,000 or 100 per cent of the overpayment of tax can be awarded. The Inland Revenue can reduce the amount of the penalty. When setting the penalty, it will consider issues such as the seriousness of the offence, whether you came forward willingly and how co-operative you were during the investigation. Penalties must be determined within six years of the date they are incurred or within three years of the final determination of entitlement to tax credit. Penalties are collected as if they are underpaid tax and in some cases interest is charged on penalties and overpayments caused by fraud or negligence.

Employers and, in some cases, employees who wish to appeal against a decision that a claim is fraudulent or negligent, or a penalty that has been awarded, do so to the General or Special Commissioners under provisions in the Taxes Management Act. Where it is alleged that, in connection with a claim for tax credits, you have fraudulently or negligently:

- made a false statement; *or*
- failed to provide information and evidence required under social security legislation; *or*
- provided incorrect information or evidence required under social security legislation

you can appeal any determination or penalty to a unified appeal tribunal set up by the Social Security Act 1998 (see p2:648).

It is important that you seek advice if you are suspected of fraud or awarded a penalty in connection with tax credits as this is a new area for both the Inland Revenue and social security appeal tribunals to deal with.

Notes

· ·

References are to statutes and regulations as amended up to 8 March 1999. All regulations are (General) Regulations unless otherwise stated. There is a full list of abbreviations in Appendix 13.

2. Investigation of claims
1 s110A(4) and (6) SSAA 1992
2 ss122 and 122A SSAA 1992
3 s122B SSAA 1992
4 ss124 and 125 SSAA 1992
5 ss122D and 122E SSAA 1992
6 s122C SSAA 1992
7 ss158A, 158B, 182A, and 182B SSAA 1992; Housing Benefit Fraud Circular HB/CTB F5/98
8 s123 and Sch 4 SSAA 1992
9 Department of Social Security Code of Practice for Data Matching: October 1998. Available from DSS Public Enquiry Office.
10 ss110(1) and 110A SSAA 1992
11 ss110(2) and 110B(1) SSAA 1992
12 s110B(2) and (7) SSAA 1992
13 s111(1) SSAA 1992
14 ss110(7) and 110B(4) SSAA 1992
15 s67(9) PACE 1984
16 s78(1) PACE 1984
17 Housing Benefit Fraud Circular HB/CTB F5/97
18 Code C para 10.4 PACE 1984
19 s34 Criminal Justice and Public Order Act 1994

3. Prosecution of offences
20 *Osinunga v DPP, The Times*, 26 November 1997, DC
21 s112(2) SSAA 1992
22 s112(1) SSAA 1992
23 *Clear v Smith* [1981] 1 WLR 399, DC
24 s112(1A)(a) SSAA 1992
25 s112(1A)(b) SSAA 1992
26 *Taylor's Central Garages v Roper* [1951] 115 JPR 445
27 s25(5) SSA(F)A 1997; SSA(F)AO No. 1
28 *R v Chainey* [1914] 1 KB 137 at 142, DC.

29 *Hansard*, Commons Standing Committee E, 21 January 1997, cols 316-17
30 s111A(1) SSAA 1992
31 *R v Ghosh* [1982] QB 1053 at 1064D-G, CA
32 s116(2)(b) SSAA 1992

4. Penalties
33 s115A(3) SSAA 1992
34 s115A(4)(a) SSAA 1992
35 para 44(e) and (f) Housing Benefit Fraud Circular F4/98
36 s115A(1) SSAA 1992
37 s25(7) SSA(F)A 1997; Art 2(1)(b) SSA(F)AO No.5
38 s115A(2)(a) SSAA 1992; reg 2(1) SS(PN) Regs
39 s115A(2)(b) SSAA 1992; reg 2(2) SS(PN) Regs
40 para 24 Housing Benefit Fraud Circular F4/98
41 para 48 Housing Benefit Fraud Circular F4/98
42 s115A(4)(b) SSAA 1992
43 s115A(6) SSAA 1992
44 s115A(7) SSAA 1992
45 s115A(5) SSAA 1992
46 *Williams v Bayley* [1866] 1 House of Lords 200 (HL)

6. The effect of fraud investigation on benefit claims
47 CIS/683/1994

7. WFTC, DPTC and fraud
48 HC 18 October 1990, Vol. 177, col 882

Chapter 53

- -

Decisions and reviews

This chapter covers:
1. Decisions (see p2:561)
2. Contacting benefit offices (p2:568)
3. Changes of circumstance after you claim (p2:569)
4. Reviews (p2:570)
5. The 'anti-test case' rule (p2:580)
6. The Social Security Act 1998 (p2:581)

- -

Note: The rules described in this chapter are due to change radically from June 1999 when the Social Security Act 1998 begins to take effect. The new rules are explained on pp:2:581-587. To see when the new rules apply, see p2:582.

- -

Once you have made a valid claim for benefit (see p2:481), a decision on the outcome must be made by an adjudication officer (see p2:561). Some decisions about your claim are made by the Secretary of State (see p2:565) and if you are claiming severe disablement allowance or disablement benefit, some are made by adjudicating medical authorities (see p2:566).

If you disagree with the decision, you can challenge it by seeking a review (see pp2:570-580) or in some cases, by appealing to a tribunal (see Chapter 56). If your circumstances change after a decision is made, you may also be able to seek a review (see p2:570).

This chapter does not cover housing benefit (Chapter 25), council tax benefit (Chapter 27), statutory sick pay (Chapter 2), statutory maternity pay (p1:91) or the benefits in Chapter 29. It also does not cover payments from the *discretionary* social fund (see Chapter 31).

You should look at this chapter if you are claiming any other benefits in this *Handbook*, including payments from the *regulated* social fund (see Chapter 30).

1. Decisions

It is important to know who is making the decision on any particular question in your case because this determines how you can challenge it. Decisions could be made by:

- an adjudication officer (see below);
- an employment officer (see p2:564);
- the Secretary of State (see p2:565);
- an adjudicating medical authority (see p2:566).

Decisions on applications for payments from the discretionary social fund (SF) are made by social fund officers but those for payments from the regulated social fund are made by adjudication officers (AOs). See Chapter 55 for information about challenging a discretionary social fund decision.

The adjudication officer

AOs are civil servants in either the Benefits Agency or in the case of some jobseeker's allowance (JSA) decisions, the Employment Service of the Department for Education and Employment (see below). An AO makes most initial decisions on claims for social security benefits.[1] The exceptions to this rule are:

- decisions which have to be made by the Secretary of State (see p2:565);
- some decisions about JSA which are made by employment officers (see p2:564);
- disablement questions in relation to severe disablement allowance (SDA) and industrial injuries disablement benefit, which are referred to adjudicating medical authorities (AMAs – see p2:566);
- decisions on 'diagnosis' and 'recrudescence' questions for industrial diseases (see pp2:208-210).

The AO may decide the case in your favour, or against you, or (except in the case of claims for attendance allowance (AA), disability living allowance (DLA) and disability working allowance (DWA)) may decide to refer it to a social security appeal tribunal (SSAT –see p2:630).[2] It is uncommon for an AO to refer cases to a tribunal unless an appeal is already pending on your claim, but it is a procedure which is sometimes used when the evidence is contradictory – eg, there is a dispute between you and your former employers over the circumstances of your dismissal from work.

If your claim is for income support (IS), JSA or a social fund maternity expenses payment (see p2:626), the decision about whether you are entitled may depend on an AO elsewhere being consulted on your case. In this situation it is assumed s/he has decided against you and benefit is refused in the meantime.[3]

It is not possible to sue an AO for negligence in the way s/he decides your claim.[4] If a decision is wrong, the only thing you can do is seek a review or appeal against it. But the position is different if you are given wrong advice by an employee of the Benefits Agency or Employment Service. See p2:663 for information about seeking compensation.

Note: AOs are due to be abolished when the Social Security Act 1998 takes effect. Their functions will be carried out by the Secretary of State. See p2:581 for further information.

Adjudication officers and jobseeker's allowance

A special kind of AO makes decisions about whether you satisfy the 'labour market conditions' for JSA (see Chapter 14). These are called Employment Service AOs. There are two types of Employment Service AOs:

- labour market AOs ; *and*
- sector AOs.

Labour market AOs are based in JobCentres. However, most decisions are made by sector AOs who usually work in a central office (sometimes called a 'sector office') which deals with claims from a number of different JobCentres. Any reviews of, or appeals against, labour market AOs' decisions are the responsibility of sector AOs. So, for example, if you and your EO (see p2:564) cannot agree on what should be in your jobseeker's agreement (see p1:315) or your EO thinks you lost your job through misconduct and that you should be sanctioned (see p1:388), your case is referred to an AO in the sector office for a decision.

Examples of decisions made by Benefits Agency and Employment Service AOs

Employment Service	Benefits Agency
Whether a jobseeker's agreement is reasonable	Whether you are incapable of work
Whether you are available for work	Calculation of your earnings
Whether you are actively seeking work	Whether benefit can be 'exported' (see p2:242)
Whether you have left a job	Whether you satisfy the disability conditions for benefit
Whether you have lost your job through misconduct	Whether your claim can be backdated
Whether you have given up or lost your place on a training scheme	Whether you have been overpaid benefit
Whether your refusal or failure to carry out a jobseeker's direction was reasonable	Whether you satisfy the habitual residence test

Delays

You rarely get an immediate decision on your claim because the facts need to be checked and your benefit calculated. However, an AO should decide your claim within 14 days 'so far as is practicable'.[5]

If you have been waiting more than 14 days for a decision, contact the benefit office. First check that your claim has been received. If it has not, let the office have a copy of your claim or fill out a new form and refer them to the claim form you sent earlier. If the Benefits Agency does not accept that you made the claim, you may have to claim again and ask for it to be backdated if possible (see p2:487).

If your claim has been received but not dealt with, ask for an explanation. If you are not satisfied with the explanation for the delay, make a complaint (see Chapter 57). The Benefits Agency has target times for dealing with claims and these are displayed in local offices. See the chapter in this *Handbook* about the benefit you are claiming for the relevant target time.

In addition to taking the steps already described, you should ask the office to make interim payments to you while you wait for a decision (see p2:499). You may be able to claim IS or a crisis loan from the social fund (see Chapters 30 and 31) if you have inadequate resources. The amount of any IS paid to you may be deducted from arrears of social security benefits which you subsequently receive.[6]

Delay in making decisions is a relatively common problem. To remedy this, you can quote the statutory time limit of 14 days and the target times for dealing with claims. You can also threaten to complain to the customer service manager or the Chief Executive of the Benefits Agency (see p2:662) or threaten a complaint to the Ombudsman (see p2:662). In an extreme case it might be possible to make an application for judicial review, but you would need to see a solicitor.

Note: The 14 day time limit for dealing with claims is to be abolished when the Social Security Act 1998 takes effect. However, the Benefits Agency says there will still be target times for dealing with claims.

Notification of decisions

You should be notified in writing of the AO's decision.[7] There are exceptions to this rule. Written notice does not have to be given if:

- you have been awarded benefit for a period immediately after a period when you were getting that benefit at the same rate. However, you must be given written notice if the decision was made after you requested a review; [8]
- for IS and JSA only:[9]
  - the decision is to pay you in cash and it would be impractical to give you a written decision; *or*
  - your benefit is being stopped and you already know why or it is reasonable not to give you a written decision.

You must be informed of your right to appeal to a tribunal or if the decision is about AA, DLA or DWA, your right to seek a review (see p2:570). In addition, in the case of IS and JSA, the written decision should show how your benefit has been worked out.[10] You can ask for a more detailed breakdown.

Sometimes a decision is unclear or difficult to understand or you may simply want to know the reasons for it. You have a right to a written statement of reasons for the decision.[11] However, if the decision is about IS or JSA, you must ask for these within three months of being given the decision in writing.[12]

What if you disagree with an adjudication officer's decision?

If you think an AO's decision is wrong you can:
- seek a review of the decision (see p2:570);
- appeal to a tribunal (see Chapter 56).

If you disagree with a decision about your AA, DLA or DWA, you must ask for a review of the AO's decision before you can appeal (see p2:573).

Employment officers

Some people working in JobCentres – known as 'employment officers' (EOs) – work for the Employment Service. If you are claiming JSA, they are the people you see when you go for your 'new jobseeker interview' (see p1:362), when you sign on each fortnight and when you go for advisory and Restart interviews (see p1:372-373). Their job is to agree with you the steps you are willing to take to get back to work (see p1:308), to keep a check on those steps and to offer practical help and advice with your search.

EOs make some decisions which affect your claim. For example, they are able to issue a jobseeker's direction (see p1:384) if they believe that there are steps you could take to help you find work and you refuse to take those steps of your own free will. They are also required to draw up a jobseeker's agreement which both of you must agree and sign as a condition for getting JSA (see p1:315).

What if you disagree with an employment officer's decision?

You cannot appeal against a decision to issue a jobseeker's direction (see p1:384), but if you are sanctioned by an AO for failing to comply with it (see p1:384) you can appeal against the sanction (see p1:387).

If you cannot reach an agreement with your EO about the terms of your jobseeker's agreement (see p1:315) or whether your jobseeker's agreement should be changed (see p1:320) you can ask for it to be referred to an AO for a decision. See pp1:38 and 1:321 for details of the procedure. If you disagree with the AO's decision, you can appeal (see Chapter 56).

The Secretary of State

Some questions have to be decided by the Secretary of State for Social Security. In practice, such decisions are made by specially authorised officials who are called Secretary of State's representatives.

Decisions on a large number of matters are made at the Secretary of State's discretion. See below for examples of decisions made by the Secretary of State.

Examples of decisions made by the Secretary of State
- Who should be the claimant when a couple are unable to decide.
- Whether:
  - to accept a claim made other than on the approved form;
  - a claim for one benefit can be treated instead of, or in addition to, a claim for another benefit;[13]
  - to demand recovery of an overpayment, and the amount of weekly deductions (subject to the maximum, see p2:525);
  - to suspend benefit pending determination of a question on review or appeal;
  - to take action against people who are liable to maintain claimants (see p2:290);
  - to appoint a person as an appointee (see p2:480);
  - to issue or replace giros and order books and how benefit should be paid;
  - to pay an interim payment;
  - a school or college is a 'recognised educational establishment'.
- The circumstances in which a claim is to be treated as withdrawn.

What if you disagree with a Secretary of State's decision?
You cannot appeal to a tribunal against a Secretary of State's decision. However, if you think a Secretary of State's decision is wrong you can:
- ask him to exercise his discretion to reconsider the decision. You should do this by writing to your local office giving reasons;[14]
- seek advice about whether you can apply for judicial review (see p2:637).

Special procedure
Certain questions are dealt with by a special procedure.[15] These are to do with contributions and a person's employment. Such decisions are now made by the Inland Revenue – eg, whether you:
- are an 'employed earner' for the purposes of paying contributions or entitlement to industrial injuries benefits; *or*
- are liable to pay contributions of a particular class; *or*
- have paid contributions for a particular period; *or*
- are the employee or employer of another person;[16] *or*
- satisfy the conditions for receipt of home responsibility protection.[17]

There is a special procedure for resolving disputes on these questions. At the time this book was published, regulations had not been laid. See CPAG's *Welfare Rights Bulletin* for further details. The DSS tells us the procedure is likely to be as follows.

A decision on your claim may be taken first by an AO (see p2:561) if it appears that there is no dispute. You are notified of the decision, and the reasons for it, and invited to reply if you are dissatisfied. On receipt of you reply, the AO should investigate and give you further explanation if this is needed. If you are still dissatisfied, the AO can refer to the Inland Revenue for a decision. You may appeal to the High Court (In Scotland the Court of Session). Alternatively, you may ask for a review.

When the Social Security Act 1998 comes into force for the benefit in question (see p2:581), the procedure will change. The Secretary of State will refer contribution issues to the Inland Revenue for a decision. The Inland Revenue will give either an initial decision or a formal decision that can be appealed. The Secretary of State can continue to deal with other issues relating to the claim. The Inland Revenue decision on contributions is binding on the Secretary of State.[18] Appeals on most contribution issues will be dealt with by the Tax Appeal Commissioners.[19] Appeals on home responsibilities protection and whether contributions can be credited will be dealt with by unified appeal tribunals (see p2:654).

Appeal tribunals will also be able to refer to the Inland Revenue for decisions on contribution issues which are relevant to a benefit appeal. The Secretary of State may revise (see p2:582) the decision on your claim as a result.[20]

Adjudicating medical authority

An adjudicating medical authority (AMA) is a:[21]
- doctor – known as an 'adjudicating medical practitioner'; *or*
- medical board – consisting of two or more doctors.

Cases involving some prescribed diseases (B6, C15, C17, C18, C22(b), D1, D2, D3, D7, D8, D9, D10, D11 or D12 – see Appendix 8) are determined by specially qualified medical boards.[22]

AMA's only make decisions about SDA (see Chapter 4) and disablement benefit (see p1:215).

The questions dealt with by AMAs are:[23]
- the 'diagnosis' and 'recrudescence' questions relating to industrial diseases. Medical boards deal with references from AOs (see p2:561);
- the 'disablement questions' relating to SDA and disablement benefit (see pp1:61 and 1:215). These are referred to AMAs for their initial decision. The AMA is usually a single doctor. If yours is an industrial disease case or if the

Secretary of State (see p2:56) so directs, the questions are referred to a medical board;
- an application for a review of any decision on the above questions. This is referred to a medical board for its initial decision.[24]

The doctor or board is there to give you a medical examination and is not concerned with other aspects of your case. AMAs do not hold hearings in the same way as tribunals. You have no right of representation before them although, with your consent, the presence of anyone 'likely to assist them' to make the decision can be allowed.[25]

The doctor usually takes a statement of your condition from you, so make sure you are clear in your mind about what your symptoms are. This is particularly important if your condition is fluctuating or if you want to describe an aspect of your condition that the doctor will not be able to see for her/himself. One way of making sure that you give the doctor all the relevant information is to write it down before you go so that you can just hand it to the doctor when you attend the examination (remembering to keep a copy for yourself). However, you should still talk to the doctor about your symptoms because that makes it easier for any uncertainties to be cleared up.

Notification of decisions

You have a right to a written notice of the AMA's decision.[26] This must include:
- a statement of the findings of the AMA; *and*
- if the decision was not unanimous, the reasons why a member disagreed with the decision.

You must be informed of your right to appeal to a medical appeal tribunal (MAT – see p2:629).

What if you disagree with an adjudicating medical authority decision?

If you disagree with an AMA decision you can appeal to an MAT (see p2:629).

Special procedure

The 'diagnosis' and 'recrudescence' questions for industrial diseases (see pp1:208 and 1:210) are decided by a special procedure.

First, an AO (see p2:562) must obtain a medical report, unless a suitable one is already available.[27] Then your case may either be decided by the AO or referred to an AMA for its decision.[28]

If the case is decided by an AO, you may appeal to an AMA. You must appeal by writing to the local benefit office within three months of being sent the decision.[29] The time may be extended in certain circumstances (see p2:645).[30] See pp2:629-630 for the procedure before medical boards.

Note: The time limit for appealing is likely to be reduced to one month when the Social Security Act 1998 takes effect (see p2:581).

2. **Contacting benefit offices**

Writing to the benefit office or JobCentre is nearly always the best way to have your case dealt with. It ensures there is a permanent record of what you said and enables you to cover all the points you want to make clearly. Always put your name, address, the date and your national insurance number at the top of your letter. Always try to make a copy of it. You should also keep all letters and forms sent to you. Such a record may help you or your adviser to work out later whether any decision can be challenged.

The Benefits Agency says it will reply to all letters within 10 working days (seven days if it is a letter of complaint). If you are sent a partial reply you should be told how long it will be before your letter can be fully answered. The person writing to you should give their name and telephone number.

If there is a delay in getting a reply, you can telephone to find out why, but it may be better to write a short reminder and only telephone if you still receive no response.

On occasion, **telephoning your benefit office or JobCentre** may be necessary. If you are a London claimant, try your branch office first. If you have to ring the centre in Belfast, Glasgow or Ashton-in-Makerfield, you are only charged the local rate. If you telephone the office:
- ask for the relevant benefit section;
- be ready to give your surname and national insurance number;
- try to get the name, title and telephone extension number of the person you speak to as this may be useful in the future;
- make a brief note of what is said, together with the date. If the information is important, follow up the telephone call with a letter confirming what the Benefits Agency said so that any misunderstanding can be cleared up. Offices are usually reluctant to write merely to confirm a telephone conversation.

Visiting the benefit office or JobCentre enables you to have a detailed conversation with an officer. Check the opening times first. An appointment can usually be arranged by telephone. You should expect the receptionist to see you within 10 minutes. However, at busy times you may have to wait longer, but this should not be more than 30 minutes. Be prepared to wait longer if you need to see someone else. The receptionist should tell you how long it is likely to take. If you want a private interview, this should be provided. Staff you see wear name badges so you can make a note of their names. Remember:

- to take any documents with you which may be relevant otherwise you may be asked to make a second visit to provide the additional information;
- to follow up any important meeting with a letter confirming the points you or the Benefits Agency have made or ask the office to confirm in writing any advice to you;
- that you can take a friend or relative with you, not only for moral support, but also as a witness to what is said.

If you cannot get to the office (eg, because of your age, health or a disability) an officer may be able to make a **home visit** if your case cannot be dealt with by telephone. Ask for a visit if you need one. If you are refused and are not satisfied with the explanation, ask to speak to a supervisor or the customer services manager.

If you are a London claimant, you can go to your local branch office to discuss your claim. The staff contacts the social security centre in Belfast, Glasgow or Ashton-in-Makerfield if necessary.

3. **Changes of circumstance after you claim**

You may be on benefit for quite a long time, during which your circumstances may change. You must inform the benefit office or JobCentre, in writing, of any change which might affect the amount of or your right to benefit.[31] Keep a copy of the letter you send reporting such changes. The Benefits Agency or JobCentre can accept notification by some other method (ie, by telephone), but this is not always acted on so it is best to do it in writing.

If you are getting benefit and your circumstances change so that you are entitled to more or less benefit, an adjudication officer (AO) can carry out a review (see p2:570). You can seek a review or the AO can decide to do one her/himself.

If you are refused benefit or your entitlement to benefit ends you should make a fresh claim if your circumstances change. You *cannot* seek a review in this situation.[32] If you are appealing against the decision refusing or stopping your benefit, you should make a fresh claim when your circumstances change and appeal if you are still refused. If you do not, you could lose out (see p2:624). This is because if you appeal to a social security appeal tribunal or disability appeal tribunal against a decision refusing benefit or terminating your award on or after 21 May 1998, the tribunal cannot take a change of circumstances into account if it happens after the decision with which you disagree (see p2:624).

To find out when a change of circumstances takes effect, see the chapter in this *Handbook* about the benefit you are claiming.

If you fail to report a change and as a result, you receive too much benefit, the Benefits Agency might take steps to recover the overpayment (see p2:525) or even treat this as fraud (see Chapter 52).

4. Reviews

Any decision affecting entitlement to benefit may be reviewed if certain conditions are met. This can be done even if the decision was made a long time ago. Reviews can be a way around the strict time limit for appealing to a tribunal (see p2:615). Following a review, your benefit could be increased but it could also be decreased or stopped altogether. See below to see what you should consider before seeking a review.

In most cases, there must be grounds for review (see pp2:572-573). In the case of attendance allowance (AA), disability living allowance (DLA) and disability working allowance (DWA), you can ask for a review, simply because you disagree with the decision, if you do so within three months of it being sent to you.

For decisions, other than AA, DLA and DWA, you can choose to appeal instead of seeking a review. See pp2:613-614 before you decide what to do. If you disagree with a decision about AA, DLA or DWA you must seek a review before you can appeal (see p2:573).

You can ask for a review or an AO or the Secretary of State may decide that one is necessary. The person who wants the review is the one who has to show there are grounds.[33] It is best to ask for a review in writing giving the reasons why you think one should take place. Claims for benefit or questions about your entitlement can be treated as requests for review.[34] For AA, DLA and DWA, if you make a claim within three months of being refused benefit, your claim must be treated as a request for a review.[35]

If a review decision does not give you all that you wanted, you can try to appeal against the original decision[36] (but if the original decision was made more than three months ago, see p2:645).

Note: These rules are due to change when the Social Security Act 1998 takes effect. See p2:581 for further information.

The risks of review

Following a review, the original decision may:
- remain the same; *or*
- be changed either to increase or decrease the amount of your benefit or take away your entitlement altogether.

If the review reduces the amount of benefit to which you are entitled it may mean that you have been overpaid. See Chapter 51 for information about overpayments and when they can be recovered.

There are therefore some risks involved in seeking a review particularly if the benefit is AA, DLA or disablement benefit. You should seek advice before you seek a review if you are concerned about what could happen in your case.

People from abroad

If you are a person from abroad whose right to reside is 'subject to any limitation or condition' (see p2:205) and you have been getting severe disablement allowance, AA, DLA, or invalid care allowance since before 5 February 1996 or child benefit since before 10 October 1996, you should not initiate a review of your benefit. If you ask for a review you risk losing your benefit altogether (see p2:206).

Disability living allowance

As well as the risks described above, you should seek advice if you are seeking a review:
- because you have not been awarded one component of DLA (see pp1:160 and 1:169) when you are already in receipt of the other; *or*
- of the rate you have been awarded of one component when you are quite satisfied with the rate you have been awarded of the other.

In these circumstances the AO may consider the component which is not the subject of the review, but s/he does not have to do so.[37]

If you have been awarded one component of DLA for life (see p1:192), the AO can consider the rate of that component, or the length of time for which it has been awarded. However, s/he should not do so, unless you ask for a review on that basis, or 'information is available' to her/him which gives reasonable grounds for believing that entitlement to the component, or entitlement to it at the rate awarded or for that period, ought not to continue.[38]

Review by an adjudication officer

If there are grounds for review (see pp1:572 and 2:573), an AO may review any decision of :
- another AO (other than those on 'diagnosis' or 'recrudescence' questions for industrial diseases – see pp1:208 and 1:210); *or*
- a tribunal; *or*
- a commissioner.

In the case of an AO's decision on AA, DLA and DWA this only applies if it is more than three months since the decision was made. However, you can ask for a review without having to show any grounds at all if you ask for the review within the three months (see p2:573).

If you are applying for a review of a decision about a payment from the regulated social fund (see Chapter 30) you should seek the review within one month of the time limit for claiming the payment (see pp1:628 and 1:634). If you do not, you could lose out (see p2:628). You can ask for a review or an AO can decide to do one her/himself.

If you are getting benefit but you cease to satisfy the conditions of entitlement, the decision awarding you benefit must be reviewed before your benefit can be stopped. This can only be done if one of the grounds for review applies (see below and p2:574).[39] This is also the case even where the amount of benefit to which you are entitled is simply reduced or increased – eg, where you are claiming income support (IS) because you are sick but you then recover and have to claim on the basis that you are a lone parent.

To find out how much benefit you can be paid after a review, see p2:576.

Reviews of benefits

This section applies to all benefits except AA, DLA, DWA (for reviews of these benefits see p2:573).

A decision may only be reviewed if:[40]

- **There was a mistake about the facts of your case or it was made in ignorance of relevant facts.** If a decision is reviewed on this ground, the review decision takes effect from the beginning of the period covered by the original decision.
- The original decision was made by an AO (not a tribunal or commissioner) and was **legally wrong**. This is what is known as an 'error of law' (see p2:632).
- **Your circumstances have changed since the original decision** or it is anticipated that they will do so and this means the decision is no longer correct. For family credit, reviews on this ground are limited. See p1:468 for the changes of circumstance that affect your FC.

A decision can only be reviewed on the basis of a change of circumstance if you are currently entitled to benefit and your situation changes. If you were correctly refused benefit in the past and your circumstances are now different, you must make a fresh claim.[41] See p2:569 if you are appealing the decision to refuse you benefit.

An amendment to the law counts as a change of circumstances, but a decision of a court or commissioner that the law has been wrongly interpreted does not.[42] A new medical opinion is not a change of circumstances,[43] but a medical opinion following an examination might give evidence of such a change.[44] For IS and jobseeker's allowance (JSA), some situations never count as a change of circumstance – ie, the repayment of a student loan, and your absence from a nursing or residential care home for less than a week.[45]

To see when a change of circumstances takes effect, see the chapter in this *Handbook* about the benefit you are claiming.

- The original decision on your claim was based on a **Secretary of State's decision** which has itself now been changed.
- For JSA only, you had been treated as **available for work or actively seeking work** and this has now been reconsidered.

If you are trying to get arrears going back several years, it can be difficult to identify the grounds for review, particularly where the Benefits Agency has destroyed old papers relating to your claim. If you are the one who wants the review to be conducted, the onus is on you to show that there are grounds for review. You cannot simply rely on the Benefits Agency's lack of evidence.[46]

If you **disagree with the review decision** you may appeal to a tribunal (see Chapter 56). You have to persuade the tribunal that there are grounds for review and also that the original decision was wrong.

Reviews of attendance allowance, disability living allowance and disability working allowance

If you want to challenge a decision on a claim for AA, DLA or DWA there are two types of review:

- 'any grounds' reviews where all you have to do is show you disagree with the decision (see below);
- 'any time' reviews where you must show grounds for review (see p2:574).

There can be risks involved in seeking a review. See p2:570 for further information.

'Any grounds' reviews

If you disagree with a decision on your claim, you cannot appeal straight away. Instead you must ask for a review. You do not need to show specific grounds for review, so it is enough that you simply think the decision is wrong.[47] You must write to the AA unit, DLA unit or DWA unit, or your local Disability Benefits Centre if it is a new claim for AA or DLA, within three months of the decision being sent to you.[48] The three-month limit can be extended where your request for a review was delayed in the post by industrial action.

Note: The rules are due to change when the Social Security Act 1998 takes effect. You will only have one month to dispute a decision without having to show grounds (see p2:583).

The review is carried out by a different AO from the one who made the original decision. The AO conducting the review decides what further evidence is needed in order to come to a decision, and how to collect this.

You should consider providing medical evidence from a GP or consultant that supports your case. If you are claiming AA or DLA, evidence or information from your carer or a diary of your walking or care needs over a period may be equally useful.

If you **disagree with this type of review decision** you may appeal to a tribunal (see Chapter 56). It can occasionally be more appropriate to seek another review instead of appealing (see below).

'Any time' reviews

If it is more than three months since a decision has been made, it can only be reviewed if: [49]

- **there was a mistake about the facts of your case or it was made in ignorance of relevant facts** (see p2:572);
- the original decision was made by an AO (not a tribunal or commissioner) and was **legally wrong** (see p2:632);
- **your circumstances have changed since the original decision** or it is anticipated that they will do so and this means the decision is no longer correct (see p2:572). For DWA, reviews on this ground are limited. See p2:483 for the changes of circumstance that affect your DWA;
- the decision was to make an award wholly or partly after the claim was made but on the basis that some condition would be fulfilled in the future and that condition has not been fulfilled; *or*
- in the case of AA and DLA only, the decision was that someone was terminally ill and there has been a change of medical opinion in relation to that.[50]

You can ask for a review or an AO can decide to do one her/himself.

You might have been refused AA, DLA or DWA in the past but did not seek an 'any ground' review (see p2:573). If you then make a fresh claim outside the three-month time limit for an 'any ground' review and qualify, you might be able to show that the earlier refusal was made in ignorance of a relevant fact. You can argue that you would have been awarded benefit initially had the AO known all of the facts.

The Secretary of State can make investigations to get information and evidence to help an AO conduct a review.[51] In the course of these investigations, if the benefit is AA or DLA, you can be required to submit to a medical examination.[52] If you fail to do this more than once part, or all, of your benefit can be withheld unless:

- you show that you had 'good cause'; *or*
- you provide medical evidence which the Secretary of State accepts instead of a medical examination; *or*
- the Secretary of State already has medical evidence which s/he thinks is acceptable.

Failure to submit to a medical examination counts as a relevant change of circumstances (see p2:574) allowing your claim to be reviewed.[53] The Benefits Agency is currently conducting a large scale investigation of existing claims for AA and DLA (see p1:194).

If you **disagree with the review decision** you cannot appeal to a tribunal straightaway. Instead, you must first seek an 'any grounds' review (see p2:573).

What happens if your claim is reviewed?

After an AO carries out a review s/he makes a new decision. If it is a review where you must show grounds for review (see pp2:572 and 2:574), s/he can decide, there are:

- no grounds for a review and to refuse to review; or
- grounds for review and that the original decision was correct; or
- grounds for review and that the original decision should be changed.

If the benefit is AA, DLA or DWA and it is an 'any grounds' review (see p2:573), s/he can decide:

- the original decision was correct; or
- the original decision should be changed.

If a decision is reviewed in your favour, you receive arrears of benefit (but see p2:576 for how far back your arrears can be paid). A possible consequence of a decision *not* being reviewed in your favour is that you may have been overpaid. The AO decides whether or not to recover the overpayment (see p2:517). There is no limit on how far back an overpayment can be recovered.

What if you disagree with a decision following a review?

If you do not get all that you wanted from the review, you can challenge the AO's decision. How this is done depends on the benefit.

If the benefit is **AA, DLA or DWA** you:

- appeal to a disability appeal tribunal (DAT) (see p2:627), if you disagree with a decision on an 'any grounds' review (see p2:573); or
- seek an 'any grounds' review, if you disagree with a review where you must show grounds (see p2:574). If you are still dissatisfied after the 'any grounds' review, you can then appeal to a DAT (see p2:627).

For all **other benefits and payments from the regulated social fund** you can appeal to a social security appeal tribunal (see p2:630) or a medical appeal tribunal (see p2:629).

Where the AO has said there are no grounds for a review (see pp2:572 and 2:574), you must show why there are, as well as give your reasons for disputing the original decision. In an appeal the tribunal must identify which decision is to be reviewed, if relevant, establish whether there are grounds for review and from what date, and then, if you are entitled to benefit, check if the limitations on backdating restrict the arrears which can be paid (see below).[54]

It is possible for a tribunal to review a decision itself if new facts, of which the AO was unaware but which give grounds for review, come to light during the hearing.[55] It is not necessary for it to adjourn the hearing and refer the matter back to an AO, though it may choose to do this instead.

A review can be a quicker and simpler way to challenge a decision with which you disagree than an appeal. It can also be a way of getting round the three-month time limit for appeals (see p2:615). But see p2:580 if you are seeking a review because you think a test case applies to you and p2:613 for help in deciding whether to seek a review or to appeal.

Payment of arrears of benefit on review

If, following a review, the AO agrees to change a decision in your favour, you can usually get arrears of benefit going back up to one month before the date you requested a review, or if you did not request a review, from the date the review took place.[56] There are exceptions to this rule if the benefit is:

- **AA or DLA.** If you claimed AA or DLA and were refused but after an 'any grounds' review (see p2:573) you were awarded benefit, you can get arrears of benefit going back to the date of your original claim.[57] If you asked for a review where you had to show grounds for review (see p2:574) you can get arrears of benefit going back up to one month before the date you requested the review, or if you did not request a review, from the date the review took place. [58]
- **A payment from the regulated social fund** (see Chapter 30). A revised payment can only be made if you ask for a review within one month of the time limit for claiming the payment (see pp1:628, 1:634 and 1:638).[59] If you seek a review outside the one-month limit, a payment can only be made if you satisfy the rules for getting more than one month's backdating (see p2:577).
- **Family credit or DWA.** Payment of arrears is not restricted *unless* the review was because of ignorance of, or a mistake about, the facts (see p2:577) and you were aware of (or it was reasonable to expect you to be aware of) these facts but you failed to tell the Benefits Agency. In this case, you can only get a maximum of one month's arrears from the date you informed the Benefits Agency of the facts.[60]

It is important to make it clear that you want payment for the past period.

You can sometimes get more than one month's backdating (see p2:577). You might get less than one month's backdating if the 'anti-test case' rule applies (see p2:580).

If you were underpaid benefit because of a clear error by the Benefits Agency you could apply for compensation as well as getting arrears owed to you (see p2:663).

More than one month's backdating

In some cases, you can get unlimited arrears going back to your date of claim, or the date of entitlement to another benefit, or the date upon which benefit would have been payable, had information been available or a mistake not occurred. You can get more than one month's backdating if:

- The ground for review was that **the decision was legally wrong** (see p2:572) because the AO overlooked or misinterpreted statute law or caselaw (see pp2:640 and 2:641) when deciding your claim.[61]
- The ground for review was **ignorance of, or mistake about, the facts** (see p2:572) and you can show that the decision is being changed because:[62]
  - there is specific evidence which the AO (or tribunal) who originally decided the claim had, but which they failed to take into account even though it was relevant. This applies even if the evidence does not conclusively prove your entitlement. So long as it raised a strong possibility that you were entitled, it should have been taken into account;[63]
  - there is documentary or other written evidence of your entitlement which the DSS, DHSS or Department of Employment had, but failed to give to the AO (tribunal or commissioner), at the time of the earlier decision;
  - new evidence has come to light which did not exist earlier and could not have been obtained. This only applies if you provide this evidence as soon as possible after it is available to you.
- Your **incapacity benefit (IB)** is reviewed on the basis that you are entitled be paid at the long-term rate because you have become entitled to the highest rate of the care component of DLA, even though you have been incapable of work for less than a year.[64]
- You are claiming **IB or severe disablement allowance (SDA)** and the AO carries out a review on the grounds of ignorance or mistake as to material fact (see p2:572) and decides that you are entitled to benefit because you are exempt from the 'all-work' test (see p2:24).[65]
- The AO certifies in the review decision that the only ground for awarding you benefit on review (or increasing the amount of benefit payable) was either: [66]
  - a decision of the Secretary of State for Social Security on **whether you satisfy the contribution conditions;** *or*
  - a matter relating to the number of days for which you have been entitled (or treated as entitled) to **short-term IB.**
- Your **IS or JSA** is being reviewed to include help with mortgage interest (see p2:345) or interest on a loan for repairs and improvements (see p2:350), but only if the review could not take place sooner because your lender did not supply the Benefits Agency with your mortgage details. In this case, you can get up to eight weeks' arrears.[67]

Extra income support and jobseeker's allowance after an award of a 'qualifying benefit'

You can get more than one month's backdating if you want your IS or JSA to be reviewed because you, or a member of your family, have become entitled to another benefit (known as a 'qualifying benefit') or to an increase in its rate, and arrears of the 'qualifying benefit' are payable for more than one month.[68] See p2:113 for who counts as your family.

This provision helps if you did not get certain premiums paid with your IS or JSA because of delays in assessing your entitlement to a 'qualifying benefit' – eg, where a DLA claim took 18 months to be decided and you have missed out on the severe disability premium for this period. You can only ask for a review if you have claimed IS or JSA. It is therefore important to claim IS or JSA while you are waiting to hear about your claim for a 'qualifying benefit'. If you wait to claim IS or JSA until you hear, you can only get arrears if you satisfy the backdating rules on p2:487.

Currently, it seems you can only get arrears of IS or JSA back to the date you or a member of your family are awarded a 'qualifying benefit', or an increase in its rate, if you were on IS or JSA while you were waiting to hear about it. If you claimed IS or JSA but were refused, you cannot get the decision refusing you IS or JSA revised even though you can now show that you were actually entitled.[69] In this situation, you must make a fresh claim for IS and should do this as soon as possible.

CPAG understands the DSS did not intend the rule to operate in this unfair way and has put an administrative solution into effect. If you claim IS or JSA while waiting to hear about a claim for a 'qualifying benefit':

- the Benefits Agency should check whether you are entitled to IS or JSA on the basis of your present circumstances, regardless of whether you are entitled to a 'qualifying benefit'. If you are, it awards IS or JSA. If you later get a 'qualifying benefit' your IS or JSA is reviewed in the usual way (see p2:571);
- if you do not qualify for IS or JSA until awarded a 'qualifying benefit', the Benefits Agency should wait to make a decision on your IS or JSA claim until the award of 'qualifying benefit' is made. This is what is known as 'stockpiling' your claim.

If you have already been refused IS or JSA but have since been awarded a 'qualifying benefit' you should claim IS or JSA again and ask for this to be backdated. Contact your local benefits office and let it know what happened. If you lose benefit because of the way the rules operated, ask the Benefits Agency for an extra-statutory payment to cover the period before your fresh IS or JSA claim.

Review by the Secretary of State

Questions which are determined at the discretion of the Secretary of State (see p2:565) may be reconsidered by him at any time. There do not have to be specific grounds for review.[70]

Reviews by the Secretary of State are discretionary. If you disagree with a decision, your only remedy is to apply for judicial review (see p2:637).

Review by a medical board

A medical board may review a decision of:
- an AO on the 'diagnosis' and 'recrudescence' questions for industrial diseases (see pp1:208 and 1:210);
- an adjudicating medical practitioner (see p2:566);
- another medical board; or
- a medical appeal tribunal (MAT – see p2:629).

The grounds upon which a decision may be reviewed depend on the type of benefit under consideration and the body which made the original decision.

Any decision may be reviewed if the medical board is satisfied that it **was given in ignorance of, or was based on a mistake, about relevant facts**.[71] For information about this ground (see p2:572) but remember, there is an important limitation. A decision may only be reviewed if there is 'fresh evidence'.[72] That means evidence that could not reasonably have been obtained and produced to the body making the first decision.[73]

Any decision concerning the disablement questions for SDA or disablement benefit (see Chapters 4 and 11) may be reviewed on the ground of **'unforeseen aggravation'** of your disability.[74] 'Unforeseen aggravation' means:
- your condition has deteriorated; or
- you still have a disability at the end of the period for which you have been given an assessment (see p1:215).

A difference of medical opinion does not necessarily mean that there has been a change in your circumstances. Therefore a new medical opinion does not necessarily mean there has been 'unforeseen aggravation'.[75]

If you wish to apply for a review of a decision of an MAT (but not an adjudicating medical practitioner or medical board) on the ground of 'unforeseen aggravation', you must first apply to the tribunal for leave.[76] Write to your local Benefits Agency office.

Any decision of a medical board may be reviewed on the ground that it was **legally wrong**.[77] An adjudicating medical practitioner can review a decision of another adjudicating medical practitioner on this ground.

Payment of arrears of benefit on review

If a medical board reviews a decision, it is necessary for the AO to review her/his decision about the amount of benefit you are to receive. Any increase of disablement benefit or reduced earnings allowance is paid from a maximum of one month before the date of your application for the review or if you did not request a review, from the date the review took place.[78] In the case of a review on the grounds of 'unforeseen aggravation' (see p2:579), the amount of arrears is limited to the period of the new assessment which does not begin more than one month before the date of the application for review.[79]

What if you disagree with a decision?

You may appeal to an MAT (see p2:629) against a decision of a medical board to review or not to review a decision.[80]

5. **The 'anti-test case' rule**

The adjudication officer (AO) must make decisions in accordance with the law. If a court or commissioner has decided a case in one way, the AO must follow that decision in other cases with similar facts. For more information about the cases which the AO must follow, see p2:641. However, there is a rule – known as the 'anti-test case' rule – which says that some court and commissioner decisions should be ignored when AOs are considering a claim or making a review for periods before they were given. This is intended to prevent you from taking advantage of a test case brought against the DSS, but it goes rather wider. If the 'anti-test case' rule applies, you can only get arrears of benefit going back to the date of the decision in the test case.

How the 'anti-test case' rule operates

If a commissioner or court decides that a tribunal (or, in limited circumstances explained below, an AO) in a totally different case (the 'test case') has made an error of law (see p2:613), the AO must decide any part of *your* claim or review which relates to the period *before* the test case decision as if that tribunal decision had been found by the commissioner or court in question not to have been wrong.[81] The 'anti-test-case' rule only applies if the test case is the first authoritative decision on the issue, and not merely a later decision which confirms an earlier decision *and*:[82]

- you make a claim after the date of the test-case decision; *or*

- you seek a review whether before or after the date of the test case decision and this is done on the grounds that the decision in your case was found to be legally wrong by the decision of the commissioner or court in the test case (and not for some other reason – see pp2:572 and 2:573);[83] *or*
- an AO refuses to review an earlier decision, but, on appeal, a tribunal carries out a review based on a decision made by a court or commissioner after the AO's decision.

The test case decision only has to be disregarded for the period before it was made if it found the tribunal to have been wrong, not if it found the tribunal to be right.

The 'anti-test case' rule also applies if the High Court (in Scotland, the Court of Session) has found an AO to have been wrong on an application for judicial review.

You can avoid the 'ant-test case rule' by appealing rather than seeking a review (but see p2:645 if you have missed the time limit for appealing). You can do this even if a review has taken place but has not given you all the arrears you are claiming.[84] This means that in cases where the 'anti-test case' rule might apply, it may be better to appeal first (applying for leave to appeal out of time if necessary – see p2:645) and only ask for a review if you cannot appeal. For further details on reviews and appeals, see p2:613 and Chapter 56.

Note: For information about the way the 'anti-test case' rule will apply when the Social Security Act 1998 takes effect, see p2:587.

6. **The Social Security Act 1998**

As part of its plan to develop a modern, integrated benefit system, the Government is changing the procedures for decision-making, reviews and appeals. This section covers the rules on decision-making and reviews where these are changing. For information about appeals, see p2:648.

Under the new rules, there will no longer be adjudication officers or social fund officers. All decision making powers will be transferred to the Secretary of State.

The present system for reviewing decisions will be replaced with powers to 'revise' or 'supersede' decisions (see pp2:582-585).

When do the new rules take effect?

When the new rules take effect depends on the benefit you are claiming. See the implementation timetable[85] below for further information.

At the time this handbook was written it was not clear what the transitional arrangements would be. See CPAG's *Welfare Rights Bulletin* for updates.

Benefit	Rules take effect
Child support	1 June 1999
Child benefit, guardian's allowance, industrial injuries benefits	5 July 1999
Retirement pension, widows' benefits, IB, SDA and maternity allowance,	6 September 1999
FC, DWA and tax credits	5 October 1999
JSA, DLA, AA, ICA, credits of contributions or earnings, home responsibilities protection, vaccine damage payments	18 October 1999
IS, the social fund and all other purposes	29 November 1999

Notification of Secretary of State decisions

You must be given written notice of a Secretary of State's decision and told of your right of appeal. If the decision notice does not include a statement of reasons, you can request one within one month.[86] The Secretary of State must provide a statement of reasons within 14 days.[87]

Disagreeing with a decision of the Secretary of State

You will be able to appeal to a tribunal against some decisions of the Secretary of State. See p2:612 for further details. In addition, you will be able to ask the Secretary of State to:
* 'revise' a decision (see below); *or*
* 'supersede' a decision (see p2:585).

If you want to seek a 'revision' or appeal against a decision you should not delay. The time limit for these will only be one month (see pp2:583 and 2:586). For information about how an application for a 'revision' could affect your appeal rights and the time limit for appealing, see p2:615.

Revisions

If you disagree with a decision of the Secretary of State, you will be able to seek a 'revision' prior to appealing.[88] This is not compulsory. So if you are appealing about attendance allowance, disability living allowance or disability working allowance, unlike at present, you will be able to appeal straightaway without having to seek a review.

Seeking a revision is simpler and you could receive a decision more quickly. You also get two bites at the cherry because if your application for a revision is turned down, you are given a fresh decision. You can then appeal against the new decision to a tribunal (see p2:650). However, see p2:651 for some important problems you should bear in mind.

If you are uncertain whether your request for a revision is being acted on, you should remember to appeal against the original decision within the time limit (see p2:651). If you ask for a revision *and* appeal, your appeal could lapse if the Secretary of State revises the decision even if you do not get everything you want (see p2:650).

You will not have to ask for a revision in writing although it is always best for you to do so. This will ensure that the Secretary of State understands that you are asking for a decision to be reconsidered, not just seeking an explanation or complaining about the rules.

Example

Stan is awarded income support, but the Benefits Agency says he is not entitled to help with his housing costs. He telephones the benefit office and complains that he has not got enough money to live on. The benefit office takes no action because it thinks Stan is simply letting off steam, not seeking a revision. Stan should have made it clear he wanted a revision. He can still ask for one (or appeal) but only if he is within the time limit (see below and p2:651).

It will be worth following up your request for a revision with the Benefits Agency to ensure your application has been accepted.

When can you seek a revision?

You will be able to ask for a decision to be revised by the Secretary of State or s/he can decide to do this himself.[89] The DSS says you will be able to ask for a revision in the following circumstances:

- On 'any grounds'. You have to ask for a revision within a 'dispute period' of one month[90] (but see p2:584).
- At 'any time':
  - If there was an 'official error'[91] – including situations where the Benefits Agency failed to take into account evidence that you provided or to pass evidence to the person making the decision. If someone outside the DSS or DfEE materially contributed to the error, it does not count as official error;[92]
  - If you misrepresented or failed to disclose facts (see p2:572) and as a result, the decision is more favourable to you than it would have been otherwise.[93] In this case, you will have been overpaid benefit and the Benefits Agency might seek to recover the overpayment (see Chapter 51);

- if a decision has been made that JSA is not payable for any period because a sanction applies;[94]
- you were refused benefit but are now entitled to it because you have been awarded another benefit (a qualifying benefit);[95]
- you were awarded benefit, but are now entitled to it at a higher rate because you were awarded a another benefit (a qualifying benefit).[96]

If a decision is revised, you will be issued with a new decision in writing.[97] If you disagree with the new decision, you will have one month to appeal to a tribunal (see p2:651).[98] You will also be able to seek a revision at 'any time' if the decision is one against which you have no right of appeal (see p2:649).[99]

The Secretary of State will only be able to revise a decision on the basis of your circumstances at the time the decision was made.[100] If your circumstances have changed, you will instead have to ask for the decision to be 'superseded' (see p2:585).

The Secretary of State will not have to consider any issue not 'raised by' your application for a revision.[101] You should therefore ensure you tell him all the points about the decision with which you disagree.

The 'dispute period'

The DSS says you will have to ask for a decision to be revised within one month of being sent the decision. You will only be able to ask for a revision outside this one-month period in limited circumstances and must do so within an absolute time limit of 13 months. You will have to show that it is reasonable to grant your request, that your application has merit and that there are special circumstances which mean that it was not practicable for you to request a revision within a month.[102]

The Secretary of State can ask you for more evidence or information if s/he thinks s/he needs this to consider all the issues raised by your application for revision. You must provide this information within one month (or such longer period as the Secretary of State allows). If you do not do so, your application will be decided on the basis of the information and evidence you have already provided.[103] In some cases, failure to provide the information could lead to payment of your benefit being suspended and your entitlement being terminated (see p2:498).

Payment of arrears of benefit after a revision

The revised decision will take effect from the date on which the original decision with which you disagree took effect – eg, your date of claim. You can get arrears of benefit going back to that date. However, if the Secretary of State considers that the date from which the original decision took effect was wrong, the revised decision can take effect from the correct date.[104]

Supersessions

If you think that a decision is wrong but it is more than one month since it was made, you will be able to ask for a 'supersession' if you can show there are grounds – eg, the decision did not take all the facts into account or there has been a change in your circumstances.[105] You will be able to ask for a decision to be superseded by the Secretary of State or he will be able to do this himself.[106] A request for a revision or a notification of a change in circumstances can be treated as a request for a supersession.[107]

The grounds for a supersession

The DSS says it will be possible for a decision to be superseded on the following grounds:[108]

- there has been, or it is anticipated that there will be, a **relevant change of circumstances** (see p2:572). You can only get a supersession on this ground if you have been awarded some benefit. The following do **not** count as relevant changes of circumstance:[109]
  - repayment of a student loan;
  - absence from a residential care or nursing home (see p2:167) of a person in receipt of IS or JSA who does not have preserved rights;
- the decision was made by the Secretary of State and was **legally wrong** or it was made in **ignorance of relevant facts** or there was a **mistake about the facts** of your case (see p2:572). A decision can only be superseded if you ask for this to happen (or the Secretary of State decides that this is necessary) outside the one-month 'dispute' period for seeking a revision (see p2:584). However, if you failed to disclose or misrepresented the facts, the Secretary of State can revise a decision at any time (see p2:583);
- the decision was made by a tribunal or a commissioner and was made in **ignorance of relevant facts** or there was a **mistake about the facts** of your case (see p2:572);
- you were awarded benefit, but, from a later date than the award began, are entitled to that benefit at a higher rate because you were awarded another benefit (a **'qualifying benefit'**);
- you have been awarded JSA and the Secretary of State subsequently decides that this should not be payable because a sanction applies (see Chapter 18).

The Secretary of State will not have to consider any issue not 'raised by' your application for a supersession.[110] You should therefore ensure you tell him all the points about the decision with which you disagree. The Secretary of State can ask you for more information or evidence in order to allow him to consider all the issues raised by your application for a supersession. If you do not provide the information or evidence within one month (or such longer period as the Secretary of State allows), your application is considered on the basis of what you have already provided.[111] Note that, in some cases, if you do not supply the information or evidence, payment of benefit can be suspended and entitlement terminated (see p2:498).

Note: If you think a decision is wrong because of an 'official error' you will be able to ask for a revision at any time (see p2:583). If you fail to disclose or misrepresent material facts, the Secretary of State will be able to revise a decision at any time (see p2:583).

Payment of arrears of benefit after a decision has been superseded

The arrears of benefit you can be paid after a decision has been superseded depend on the ground for the supersession. The general rule is that, if a decision is superseded, the new decision takes effect from the date it was made or the date the application was made.[112] The exceptions to this are as follows:[113]

- Where there has been, or will be, a **change in your circumstances** and the decision is advantageous to you (see p2:650), arrears will be paid from the date of the change so long as you notify the Secretary of State of the change within one month of it taking place.[114] If you fail to notify the change within the month, you can apply for an extension of time in limited circumstances, but have to do this within 13 months of the date the change occours. The circumstances in which you are allowed an extension of time to report a change of circumstances are the same as those in which a late request for revision can be accepted (see p2:584). You must write explaining your reasons for lateness.[115] However, if the decision is *not* advantageous to you, it always takes effect from the date of the change.[116] This means that if you fail to notify a change of circumstances in time, you will have been overpaid and the Benefits Agency might seek to recover the overpayment (see Chapter 51).

- Where a tribunal or commissioner made the decision in **ignorance of facts** or made a **mistake about the facts**, and as a result the decision was more advantageous to you than it would otherwise have been, the supersession will take effect from the date on which the original decision took effect.[117] In any other case, the new decision takes effect from the date it was made.

- Where you have become entitled to benefit (or entitled at a higher rate) because you have been **awarded a 'qualifying' benefit**, you will be able to get arrears going back to the date you claimed the benefit or at a later date if this is reasonable.[118]

- A decision to apply a sanction to your JSA takes effect from the subsequent benefit week, or subsequent payment.[119]

- A decision to award the long-term rate of IB (see p1:37) because you are entitled to the highest rate of the care component of DLA, takes effect from the date you became entitled to the highest rate of the care component.[120]

- A decision to award IB or SDA on the grounds that you are to be treated as incapable of work because you have a severe condition (see p2:15) takes effect from the date from which you are to be treated as incapable of work.[121]
- If your lender delays supplying information about your loan, a decision to award an amount for housing costs in your IS or income-based JSA can take effect up to eight weeks before the date the decision on your award was superseded (or up to eight weeks before your application for supersession). There are special provisions to deal with the effective date of a new decision following other changes effecting housing costs in your IS or income-based JSA, such as a change in the amount of eligible capital or a change in the standard rate.[122]

You may get less arrears than this if a decision is being superseded as a result of a decision in a test case (see below).

What if a test case decision is pending?

If a test case is pending (see p2:580), the Secretary of State can already suspend payment of your benefit (see p2:497). When the Social Security Act takes effect, s/he will also be able to postpone making a decision.[123] This means you will not be able to appeal until a decision is made in the test case. If you have already appealed to a tribunal, see p2:655.

The DSS says that if you would be entitled to benefit even if the test case were decided against you, the Secretary of State will be able to make a decision. This will be done on the assumption that the test case has been decided in the way that is most unfavourable to you. However, this does mean that you will at least be paid some benefit while you wait for the result of the test case

If the decision on your claim or request for a revision or supersession is postponed, once a decision has been made in the test case, the Secretary of State, the tribunal or the commissioner will then make the decision. If the test case goes in your favour, you will be paid the extra benefit you are owed. However, if a decision has not been postponed the 'anti-test case' rule applies (see p2:580).

Notes

•••

References are to statutes and regulations as amended up to 8 March 1999. All regulations are (General) Regulations unless otherwise stated. There is a full list of abbreviations in Appendix 13.

1. **Decisions**

1 s20 SSAA 1992
2 s21(2) and (3) SSAA 1992
3 Regs 56 and 56A SS(Adj) Regs
4 *Jones v Department of Employment* [1989] QB 1 (CA)
5 s21(1) SSAA 1992
6 s74 SSAA 1992; regs 7-10 SS(PAOR) Regs
7 Regs 18 and 55 SS(Adj) Regs
8 Reg 18(2) SS(Adj) Regs
9 Regs 55(3) and (4) SS(Adj) Regs
10 Reg 55(5) SS(Adj) Regs
11 Reg 18(1) SS(Adj) Regs
12 Reg 55(7) SS(Adj) Regs
13 Reg 9(1) and Sch 1 SS(C&P) Regs
14 Reg 17(2) SS(Adj) Regs
15 s17(1) SSAA 1992
16 s8 SSC(TF)A 1999
17 s17 SSC(TF)A 1999
18 s10A SSA 1998
19 s8(5) SSA 1998
20 s24A SSA 1998
21 Reg 34 SS(Adj) Regs
22 Reg 36(2) SS(Adj) Regs
23 s45 SSCBA 1992; reg 36(1) SS(Adj) Regs
24 s47(1) SSAA 1992; regs 36(1)(a) and 53(1) SS(Adj) Regs
25 Reg 36(9) SS(Adj) Regs
26 Reg 37 SS(Adj) Regs
27 Reg 45 SS(Adj) Regs
28 Reg 46 SS(Adj) Regs
29 Reg 48(2) and Sch 2 SS(Adj) Regs
30 Reg 3(3) SS(Adj) Regs

3. **Changes of circumstance after you claim**

31 Reg 32(1) SS(C&P) Regs
32 Sch 6 para 2 SSA 1998

4. **Reviews**

33 CSB/376/1983; R(I) 1/71; CI/11/1977

34 R(I) 50/56
35 s30 (13) SSAA 1992
36 *CAO v Eggleton & Others* (CA) March 1993
37 ss32(2) and (3) SSAA 1992
38 s32(4) SSAA 1992 ; R(DLA) 1/95
39 Reg 17(4) SS(C&P) Regs; CSIS/ 137/1994(T)
40 ss25(1) , 30(2) , (4) and (5) and 35(1) and (3) SSAA 1992
41 Sch 6 para 2 SSA 1998; CIS/767/ 1994
42 *CAO v McKiernon* (CA) 8 July 1993
43 R(S) 4/86
44 CSIS/137/1994(T); CIS/856/1994
45 Regs 63(5), 63A(6) and 64 SS(Adj) Regs
46 R(IS) 11/92
47 s30(1) SSAA 1992
48 Reg 25(2) SS(Adj) Regs
49 s30(2) SSAA 1992
50 s30(4) SSAA 1992
51 s30(7A) SSAA 1992
52 s57A SSAA 1992; Regs 8C-E SS(AA) Regs and regs 5A-C SS(DLA) Regs
53 Reg 67A SS(Adj) Regs
54 CIS/714/1991
55 s36 SSAA 1992; R(IS) 15/93
56 Regs 59(1), 60(1), 63(1) and 63A(1) SS(Adj) Regs
57 Reg 59(1C)(b) SS(Adj) Regs
58 Reg 59(1C)(a) SS(Adj) Regs
59 Reg 67 SS(Adj) Regs
60 Regs 65 and 66 SS(Adj) Regs
61 Reg 57(3) SS(Adj) Regs
62 Reg 57(2) SS(Adj) Regs
63 *Saker v Secretary of State for Social Services*; R(I) 2/88
64 Reg 59(1A) SS(Adj) Regs
65 Reg 59(1B) SS(Adj) Regs
66 Reg 59(3)(b) SS(Adj) Regs
67 Regs 63(1B) and 63A(1B) SS(Adj) Regs

68 Regs 63(1A) and 63A(1A) SS(Adj) Regs
69 CSIS/80/1995; AM(AOG)66, 17 February 1998
70 Reg 17(3) SS(Adj) Regs
71 s47(1) SSAA 1992; regs 36(1)(a) and 53(1) SS(Adj) Regs
72 Regs 53(1) and 61 SS(Adj) Regs
73 R(I) 16/57; R(P) 3/73
74 s47(4) SSAA 1992; reg 36(1)(a) SS(Adj) Regs
75 R(M) 5/86
76 s47(7) SSAA 1992
77 s47(2) SSAA 1992; reg 36(1)(a) SS(Adj) Regs
78 Reg 60(1) SS(Adj) Regs
79 Reg 62 SS(Adj) Regs
80 s47(9) SSAA 1992; regs 36(1)(a) and 53(3) SS(Adj) Regs

5. The 'anti-test case' rule

81 s69 SSAA 1992; Sch 6 para 6 SSA 1998; reg 58 SS(Adj) Regs; *CAO and Another v Bate* (HL) [1996] 2 All ER 790
82 CFC/2298/1995
83 *CAO and Another v Woods* (CA), unreported, 12 December 1997; CDLA/12045/1996
84 CIS/566/1991; CIS/788/1991
85 Reg 1 SS&CS(D&A) Regs
86 Reg 28(1) SS&CS(D&A) Regs
87 Reg 28(2) SS&CS(D&A) Regs

6. The Social Security Act 1998

88 s9 SSA 1998
89 Reg 3(1) SS&CS(D&A) Regs
90 Reg 3(1)(b) SS&CS(D&A) Regs
91 Reg 3(5)(a) SS&CS(D&A) Regs
92 Reg 1(3) SS&CS(D&A) Regs
93 Reg 3(5)(b) SS&CS (D&A) Regs
94 Reg 3(6) SS&CS(D&A) Regs
95 Reg 3(7) SS&CS(D&A) Regs
96 Reg 3(7) SS&CS(D&A) Regs
97 Reg 28 SS&CS(D&A) Regs
98 s9(5) SSA 1998; reg 31(1) SS&CS(D&A) Regs
99 Reg 3(8) SS&CS(D&A) Regs
100 Reg 3(9) SS&CS(D&A) Regs
101 s9(2) SSA 1998
102 Reg 4 SS&CS(D&A) Regs
103 Reg 3(2) SS&CS(D&A) Regs
104 Reg 5 SS&CS(D&A) Regs
105 s10 SSA 1998; reg 6(2) SS&CS(D&A) Regs
106 Reg 6(2) SS&CS(D&A) Regs
107 Reg 6(5) SS&CS(D&A) Regs
108 Reg 6(2) SS&CS(D&A) Regs
109 Reg 6(6) SS&CS(D&A) Regs
110 s10(2) SSA 1998
111 Reg 6(4) SS&CS(D&A) Regs
112 s10(5) SSA 1998
113 Reg 7 SS&CS(D&A) Regs
114 Reg 7(1)(a) SS&CS(D&A) Regs
115 Reg 8 SS&CS(D&A) Regs
116 Reg 7(2) SS&CS(D&A) Regs
117 Reg 7(5) SS&CS(D&A) Regs
118 Reg 7(7) SS&CS(D&A) Regs
119 Reg 7(8) SS&CS(D&A) Regs
120 Reg 7(10) SS&CS(D&A) Regs
121 Reg 7(11) SS&CS(D&A) Regs
122 Reg 7(13)-(23) SS&CS(D&A) Regs
123 s25 SSA 1998

Chapter 54

∙∙∙

Challenging a housing benefit or council tax benefit decision

This chapter covers how to challenge housing benefit and council tax benefit decisions. It contains:

1. Changes of circumstance after you claim

The local authority can take into account any changes in your circumstances after they have decided your claim for benefit.

If you challenge their decision by asking for a review, the local authority or review board (see p2:592) can take into account any changes in your circumstances after the date of the decision you are challenging.

You do not need to make a fresh claim for benefit.

2. Reviews

A review is the process by which a local authority or a housing benefit review board (see p2:592) looks again at a decision and decides whether it should be altered. Such a review may be in your favour, may reduce the amount of benefit you receive or result in your benefit being stopped.

If you wish to challenge a decision, you can do so only by asking for a review. There are two stages in the review procedure. You must firstly write to the local authority and ask them to look again at their decision. This is known as an internal or first review. If necessary, you can then request a further review by a review board consisting of local councillors.

Internal reviews

The local authority can review any of its own decisions, and those of a review board, at any time if:

- there has been a change of circumstances (see pp1:543-544); *or*
- it is satisfied that the decision was made in ignorance of, or based on a mistake as to, some material fact. In the case of a review board decision (see p2:592), this must be shown by fresh evidence that was not available to the review board (and which could not have been put before the review board at the time); *or*
- in the case of a local authority decision only, it is satisfied that it was based on a mistake as to the law. However, local authorities cannot decide that a regulation is invalid because the Secretary of State exceeded her/his powers in making it.[1]

If a decision is amended on a review initiated by a local authority, this counts as a fresh decision requiring notification in the normal way, so you can ask for yet another review (see below) if the decision is unfavourable to you.[2]

If your housing benefit (HB) has been suspended (see p1:541) and you have failed to provide information the authority has asked you to provide within four weeks then the authority *must* review your entitlement.[3] It may extend the four-week period to 13 weeks if it considers it reasonable to do so. The review is treated as though it was made under the powers set out above, so you have the right to a further review (see p1:592).

Your right to a review

You can also ask for a review of any decision (including a local authority review decision) simply on the ground that you disagree with it. The right to a review also applies to other people affected by the decision (see p1:535).[4] Such an application must be received by the local authority within six weeks of the initial decision being notified to you,[5] although the authority can allow a late application if there are special reasons,[6] these are not defined. The same phrase is used for appeals to the social security commissioners so arguably should be interpreted in the same way (see p2:647). The local authority must tell you of your right to apply for a review every time you are notified of a decision.[7] If it fails to do so, that is a special reason for allowing a late application. An application for an extension of the six-week time limit must be made in writing, and, if it is refused, the local authority's decision is final[8] (although, in an exceptional case, it might be challenged by judicial review – see p2:596).

If you want a written explanation of the reasons for the decision from the local authority (see p1:536) so that you can state your case more effectively, the period between your request reaching the local authority and the explanation being posted to you is ignored when calculating the six-week limit (see 2:591).[9] It is often worth asking the local authority for a written explanation before formally requesting a review, because the law is complicated and you then know the basis on which the decision was taken. However, if the reasons for the decision are clear or your situation is urgent, you should not delay asking for a review. You can ask for a further written explanation at any time.[10]

There is no time limit laid down within which the authority must carry out the review. Some local authorities have a policy of carrying out the review within 14 days of receiving a request for a review.

You must be notified in writing of the outcome of the review. The information given to you following the review must conform to the normal rules about the notification of decisions (see p1:536). It must also inform you of your right to ask for a further review by a review board (see below).[11]

If a decision is altered on review, the revised decision takes effect from the date of the original decision.[12] However, if the review results in an increase in your HB, arrears cannot normally be paid for more than 52 weeks before the date the local authority first received your request for the review. The only exception is where the authority has reversed a decision not to backdate your claim under the 'good cause for a late claim' provisions (see p1:534) – in which case any arrears may be paid for up to 52 weeks before the date your request for backdating was made.[13]

The housing benefit review board

A hearing before a review board is the nearest thing there is to an independent appeal for HB/council tax benefit (CTB) cases. Although review boards are not really independent, they must act as if they are. The review board is made up of local authority councillors.

Applying for a hearing

If you have exercised your right to a review (see p2:591), and remain dissatisfied with the local authority's decision, you can write and ask for a further review. It is this 'further review' that is carried out by a housing benefit review board.

When you apply, you must give your reasons for requesting a further review. These need not be detailed or technical as long as it is clear what it is you disagree with. The request for the further review must reach the local authority within 28 days of the notification of the internal review being posted to you.[14] The review board may extend the deadline if there are special reasons for doing so (see p2:591). An application for an extension of the time limit must be made to the chair of the review board in writing, and, if it is refused, the review board's decision is final (although, in an exceptional case, it might be challenged by judicial review – see p2:596).[15]

The hearing

A hearing before a review board should take place within six weeks of your request reaching the local authority or, if that is not reasonably practicable, as soon as possible after that.[16] Some authorities make claimants wait months for a review board hearing. If this has happened in your case, write and threaten to make a complaint of maladministration to the Ombudsman (see p2:598). However, if you are challenging a decision to restrict your eligible rent (see Chapter 26) and the local authority has asked the rent officer to reconsider your case as a result, the review board may decide to defer your hearing pending the outcome.[17]

You must be given at least ten days' notice of the time of the hearing and the place where it will be held, otherwise you have the right to insist on another date being set.[18] If you have been given adequate notice but would like the hearing to be postponed, or if you wish to withdraw your request for a hearing altogether, you must write to the chair of the review board who decides whether the hearing should still proceed.[19]

The review board consists of at least three local authority councillors (or members of the New Town Corporation, Development Board for Rural Wales or Scottish Special Housing Association), one of whom acts as chair.[20] If there are only two members of the board present when you attend, the hearing can go ahead provided all parties consent.[21] DSS guidance suggests that the board should not consist of anyone who has had a previous involvement in your case.[22] If the issue to be considered by the review board affects your claim for HB and/or CTB and/or community charge benefit (eg, the assessment of your income), the same review board can consider your claim for any combination of all three benefits at the same time, provided everyone concerned in the case agrees.[23]

Procedure at the hearing

The chair of the board decides how the hearing should be conducted.[24] You also have the right to attend the hearing and to present your case, call witnesses and question the local authority's witnesses. You can be accompanied to the hearing or be represented. During the hearing your representative has the same rights as you in presenting your case.[25] The local authority should pay your travelling expenses and those of one other person who accompanies or represents you, also any other person affected – eg, called as a witness.[26] The tactics for presenting a case before the review board are similar to those for social security appeal tribunals (SSATs – see p2:644).

The review board has the right to ask people to give evidence, but it cannot compel anyone to appear before it who does not wish to.[27] If you fail to attend a hearing, the review board can proceed in your absence.[28] If you were unable to attend through circumstances beyond your control, and the review board has given an unfavourable decision, you may be able to have the decision 'set aside' (see p2:595).

Adjournments

If the review board decides to adjourn a hearing and the case is subsequently heard by a board composed of any different members, the second board should hear your whole case again.[29]

The decision

After hearing your case, the review board either confirms or alters the decision of the local authority.[30] If the board is not unanimous, a majority decision is taken. If there is an even number of members, the chair has a second or casting vote if necessary.[31] The chair must record the board's decision and its finding on the facts relevant to your case.[32]

In arriving at its decision, the review board is bound only by the law and not by any local authority or DSS policy. It may exercise any discretion open to the local authority under the regulations.[33] It is bound by decisions on HB/CTB in the High Court, the Court of Appeal, the House of Lords and the European Court of Justice. Decisions in these courts on other benefits or related issues may be persuasive. It is not bound by any of its own previous decisions, nor by any of the decisions made by SSATs or social security commissioners on similar cases and issues in other areas of the social security system, although it can take them into account. However, it should be slow to disagree with a commissioner's decision as commissioners are judges with considerable experience of this sort of law.

A copy of the decision of the review board must be sent to you within seven days of the decision being made or, if that is not practicable, as soon as possible after that. The decision must include the reasons for the decision and the board's findings of fact.[34] These should give a clear explanation of why you have won or lost.[35] If the review board has altered the local authority's decision in any way, the local authority must implement the board's decision with effect from the date the original decision was made.[36]

If the board has awarded additional HB, arrears may only be paid for up to 52 weeks before the date on which the local authority completed its initial review (see p2:591). The only exception is where the review board has overturned a previous local authority decision not to backdate a claim under the 'good cause for a late claim' provisions – in which case any arrears may be paid for up to 52 weeks from the date your claim for backdating is treated as having been made (see p1:534).[37]

A decision of a review board may be subsequently reviewed by a local authority in certain circumstances (see p2:591).

There is no right of appeal from a review board's decision but, if the decision was wrong in law, you can apply for judicial review (see p2:596). Grounds for review can include a review board's failure to explain its decision properly as required by the regulations.

Correcting a decision

Both local authorities and review boards can correct any accidental errors which have occurred in their decisions.[38] An accidental error is a slip of the pen, a misprint, a mathematical error, or the omission of a word, etc. Corrections may be made at any time and take effect as though they were part of the original decision, or record of the decision, being corrected. Every person affected must be informed of the correction. You cannot seek a review against the correction of a decision, but you can ask for a review of the decision itself.[39]

Setting aside a decision

Both local authorities and review boards also have the power to set aside their own decisions if the interests of justice warrant it.[40] 'Setting aside' means deleting the decision as though it had never been made. A new decision is then made.

The law allows a decision to be set aside if it appears just to do so because:[41]

- you, your representative, or some other person affected by the decision, were not sent, or did not receive, a document relating to the matters concerned in that decision, or the document arrived too late;
- in the case of a hearing before a review board, you, your representative, or some other person affected by the decision were not present;
- for some other reason, the interests of justice require it. The same grounds apply to appeal tribunal decisions (see p2:626).

Any person affected by a decision may apply to have that decision set aside.[42] Applications must be in writing and must reach the local authority or review board concerned within 13 weeks of the notification of that decision being posted to the applicant.[43] The 13-week limit cannot be extended but does not include any period before the correction of (or refusal to correct) an accidental error, or the setting aside of a previous decision.[44] The local authority or review board must send copies of an application to set aside a decision to any other persons affected by the decision and give them a reasonable opportunity to comment.[45]

The outcome of an application to have a decision set aside must be notified in writing to every person affected as soon as possible, and this must contain a statement explaining the reasons for meeting or rejecting that request.[46]

If your request to have a decision set aside is rejected, this cannot be challenged through requesting either an internal review or a further review by the review board.[47] But you may still be able to request a review of the original decision itself (see p2:591). through requesting either an internal review or a further review by the review board. In applying the time limits for requesting a review, no account is taken of any period between the date when the notification of the decision, and the notification of the refusal to set it aside, were each posted to you.[48] If you have been denied a fair hearing before the review board and your request to have the board's decision set aside is turned down, you may be able to challenge this by way of a judicial review (see below).

3. **Appealing to the court**

Judicial review is a method of challenging a decision of any form of tribunal, government department or local authority. Applications are to the High Court (in Scotland, the Court of Session), and should be made within three months.

In practice, it is not a procedure that can be used very much in social security cases except in HB and CTB cases against decisions of review boards. That is because there are two major restrictions on the power of the court to intervene. First, the court very seldom intervenes if there is an alternative right of appeal. Secondly, the court can only intervene to correct an error of law. For these purposes, error of law has the same meaning as for appeals to a social security commissioner in income support cases (see p2:632).

Review boards quite often make errors of law (including the failure to make proper findings of fact and give adequate reasons for their decisions). If you consider that one has been made in your case, you should consult a solicitor. Legal aid is available in judicial review cases.

Claims for damages

If a local authority has failed to carry out its obligations under the HB scheme or has failed to carry them out properly – in other words if it is in 'breach of statutory duty' – you may be able to sue for damages if you can show you have suffered financial loss as a result. An authority would be in breach of statutory duty if, for example, it had not determined a claim where it was under a duty to do so or if it had not paid HB to which you were entitled.

However, the Court of Appeal has decided that a landlord cannot sue a local authority for failure to make direct payments (see p1:539) even if s/he has suffered financial loss as a result.[49] The Court said that a landlord would, in these circumstances, simply have to follow the review procedure (see p2:591). The Court made other comments in this case which appear to indicate that *no one* (whether a claimant, landlord or anyone else) could ever sue a local authority for breach of statutory duty. Elsewhere in the judgement it appears to accept that such claims *can* sometimes be brought. You should argue that the case simply related to direct payments and that claims for damages for breach of other statutory duties can be brought. An example is where someone loses her/his home because the authority failed to make a payment on account of HB (see p1:543). If you are in this situation, you should get advice.

Meeting the cost of going to court

Legal aid is available for cases in the Court of Appeal, the High Court and the Court of Session and you should certainly obtain legal advice and representation.

---

4. Complaints

The review procedure enables you to challenge the way that a local authority has applied the law in your case. If you wish to challenge the *manner* in which your claim was dealt with rather than the actual decision itself, you should make use of the local authority's complaints procedure. Where there is no formal procedure, you should begin by writing to the supervisor of the person dealing with your claim, making it clear why you are dissatisfied. Include details of everything that has gone wrong, and make it clear what you expect the council to do about it – eg, sort out the claim within seven days, make a formal apology, compensate you for any loss. If you do not receive a satisfactory reply, you should take the matter up with someone more senior in the department and ultimately the principal officer. Send a copy of the letter to your ward councillor and to the councillor who chairs the council committee responsible for HB/CTB. If this does not produce results, or if the delay is causing you severe hardship, you should consider a complaint to the Ombudsman (see p2:598) or court action.

Local authority offices are the responsibility of a senior officer (the relevant officer's name or title usually appears on its headed notepaper). In turn, those officers are responsible to councillors and you can write to one of your local councillors or the chair of the relevant council committee. Government departments also monitor local authorities so, if all else fails, you can write to the relevant minister – ie, the Secretary of State for Social Security.

The local government Ombudsman

If you have tried to sort out your complaint with the local authority but you are still not satisfied with the outcome, you can apply to the Commissioner for Local Administration (more commonly known as the local government Ombudsman). The Ombudsman can investigate any cases of maladministration by local authorities. The most common type of maladministration dealt with by the Ombudsman is delay in processing claims or applications for review. Failing to properly apply the procedure for dealing with claims is also covered as is failing to give you proper notifications about your entitlement, though in most cases if there is a right of appeal against a decision the best remedy is to use that right.

You may apply to the Ombudsman by writing to the appropriate local office (see Appendix 1). The Ombudsman has extensive powers to look at documents held by the local authority on your claim. You may be interviewed to check any facts. Straightforward cases can be dealt with in about three months. The Ombudsman can recommend financial compensation if you have been unfairly treated or suffered a loss as a result of the maladministration. A complaint may also make the authority review its procedures, which could be of benefit to other claimants.

Notes

References are to statutes and regulations as amended up to 8 March 1999. All regulations are (General) Regulations unless otherwise stated. There is a full list of abbreviations in Appendix 13.

2. **Reviews**

1 Reg 79(1) and (1A) HB Regs; reg 69(1) and (1A) CTB Regs
2 Reg 79(6) HB Regs; reg 69(7) CTB Regs
3 Reg 91A(8) HB Regs; reg 81A(8) CTB Regs
4 Reg 79(2) HB Regs; reg 69(2) CTB Regs
5 Reg 79(2) HB Regs; reg 69(2) CTB Regs
6 Reg 78(3) and (4) HB Regs; reg 68(3) and (4) CTB Regs
7 Sch 6 para 3 HB Regs; Sch 6 para 3 CTB Regs
8 Reg 78(3), (4) and (5) HB Regs; reg 68(3), (4) and (5) CTB Regs
9 Reg 79(4) HB Regs; reg 69(4) CTB Regs
10 Reg 77(4) and (5) HB Regs; reg 67(2) and (3) CTB Regs
11 Reg 79(2) and Sch 6 paras 4 and 5 HB Regs; reg 69(2) and Sch 6 paras 4 and 5 CTB Regs
12 Reg 79(3)(b) HB Regs; reg 69(3)(b) CTB Regs
13 Reg 79(3)(c) and 72(15) HB Regs; reg 69(3)(c) and 62(16) CTB Regs
14 Reg 81(1) and (2) HB Regs; reg 70(1) and (2) CTB Regs
15 Reg 78(3)–(5) HB Regs; reg 68(3)–(5) CTB Regs
16 Reg 82(1) HB Regs; reg 71(1) CTB Regs
17 Reg 82(1A) HB Regs
18 Reg 82(3) HB Regs; regs 70(5) and 71(3) CTB Regs
19 Reg 82(5) HB Regs; reg 71(5) CTB Regs
20 Reg 81(3) and Sch 7 HB Regs; reg 70(3) and Sch 7 CTB Regs
21 Reg 82(7) HB Regs; reg 71(7) CTB Regs
22 paras A6.66 and B6.18 GM

23 Reg 81(4) HB Regs; reg 70(4) CTB Regs
24 Reg 82(2)(a) HB Regs; reg 71(2)(a) CTB Regs
25 Reg 82(2)(c) HB Regs; reg 71(2)(c) CTB Regs
26 Reg 82(9) HB Regs; paras A6.68 and B6.22 GM; reg 71(9) CTB Regs
27 Reg 82(2)(c)(ii) and (d) HB Regs; reg 71(2)(c)(ii) and (d) CTB Regs
28 Reg 82(4) HB Regs; reg 71(4) CTB Regs
29 Reg 82(5) and (6) HB Regs; reg 71(5) and (6) CTB Regs
30 Reg 83(1) HB Regs; paras A6.70 and B6.24 GM; reg 72(1) CTB Regs
31 Reg 82(8) HB Regs; reg 71(8) CTB Regs
32 Reg 83(4) HB Regs; reg 72(4) CTB Regs
33 Reg 83(2) HB Regs; reg 72(2) CTB Regs
34 Reg 83(5) HB Regs; reg 72(5) CTB Regs
35 *R v HBRB of Sefton MBC ex parte Cunningham* [1991] 23 HLR 534, QBD
36 Reg 84 HB Regs; reg 73 CTB Regs
37 Regs 79(3)(c), (5) and 83(3) HB Regs; regs 69(3)(c) and (5) and 72(3) CTB Regs
38 Regs 85(1) and 87(1) HB Regs; regs 74(1) and 76(1) CTB Regs
39 Reg 87(3) HB Regs; reg 76(3) CTB Regs
40 Reg 86(1) HB Regs; paras A6.79–82 and B6.33–6 GM; reg 75(1) CTB Regs
41 Reg 86(1) HB Regs; reg 75(1) CTB Regs
42 Reg 86(1) HB Regs; reg 75(1) CTB Regs

43 Regs 78(2) and 86(2) HB Regs;
regs 68(2) and 75(2) CTB Regs
44 Reg 87(2) HB Regs; reg 76(2)
CTB Regs
45 Reg 86(3) HB Regs; reg 75(3)
CTB Regs
46 Reg 86(4) HB Regs; reg 75(4)
CTB Regs
47 Reg 87(3) HB Regs; reg 76(3)
CTB Regs
48 Regs 78(2) and 87(2) and (3) HB
Regs; regs 68(2) and 76(2) and
(3) CTB Regs

3. **Appealing to the Court**
49 *Haringey LBC v Cotter* [1996] *29
HLR 682*

Chapter 55

Social fund reviews

This chapter covers:
1. Internal reviews (p2:602)
2. Social fund inspector reviews (p2:606)

The social fund (SF) review system only covers decisions relating to community care grants, budgeting loans and crisis loans (see p1:641). Decisions relating to funeral, maternity and winter payments (see p1:626) can be appealed against, in the same way as most other benefits (see p2:611).

There is no right of appeal against community care grant, budgeting loan and crisis loan decisions. There is, instead, a review system, which is divided into two distinct stages:

* first, an internal review is carried out within the Benefits Agency office, which made the decision under review;
* second, an applicant has a right to request a further review of the decision by a social fund inspector (SFI). SFIs are part of an Independent Review Service, based in Birmingham (see Appendix 1), which conducts second-tier reviews independently of the Benefits Agency.

You should always consider asking for a review if you are dissatisfied with a decision. You should be aware, however, that a review decision could be more unfavourable then the original decision (see p2:605 – Tactics) and that the scope for a revision of a budgeting loan decision is very limited (see 1:658).

Note

The new budgeting loan scheme from April 1999 (see p1:658) has resulted in changes to the law and guidance relating to social fund reviews. At the time of writing, the new directions and guidance had not been published. Any corrections or updates to the information in this chapter will be covered in CPAG's *Welfare Rights Bulletin*.

If you request a review of a budgeting loan decision which was made prior to 5 April 1999, it should be dealt with under the old rules (see CPAG's *National Welfare Benefits Handbook*, 1998/99, 28th edition for details). This means you could ask for a discretionary review at any time and argue, for example, that you should have been awarded a community care grant rather than a budgeting loan.

1. **Internal reviews**

Powers of review

The law relating to internal reviews is set out in primary legislation and legally binding Social Fund Directions.[1] All decisions made by social fund officers (SFOs) are subject to review,[2] including:

- the refusal of a community care grant or loan;
- the amount awarded;
- payment to a third party or instalments;
- refusal to determine a repeat application (see p1:644).

When the relevant provisions of the Social Security Act 1998 are implemented, SFOs will be known as 'appropriate officers'. Decisions about the repayment of loans are made by the Secretary of State and are not subject to review, but can still be challenged (see pp1:644-673).

Internal reviews are carried out by reviewing officers, who are SFOs or specially appointed reviewing officers.[3]

A reviewing officer must review a decision if:
- you apply for a review within the time limit (see p2:603 – procedure);[4] *or*
- a decision was based on a mistake about the law, the SF directions or a material fact, or was given in ignorance of a material fact; *or*
- in the case of community care grants and crisis loans only, there has been a change of circumstance since the decision was given; *or*
- in the case of budgeting loans only, there has been a change in the maximum awards set by the district manager (see p1:662) or a change in the person's ability to repay a budgeting loan (see p1:662).[5]

In the last three cases, the reviewing officer can conduct a review at any time, with or without an application.

A reviewing officer may review a decision:
- if you misrepresented or failed to disclose a material fact, in which case any overpayment is recoverable;[6] *or*
- '....in such other circumstances as he thinks fit'.[7]

In both the above cases, the reviewing officer can conduct a review at any time, with or without an application. The second case above offers wide (but discretionary) scope for reviews on any grounds, and at any time (eg, if you have missed the time limit for a mandatory review).

Procedure

Applying for a review

You must apply for a review of a decision by writing to the Benefits Agency within 28 days of the date the decision was issued to you.[8] Your application must include your grounds for requesting a review (see p2:608 – Tactics).[9] If somebody is making an application on your behalf, it must be accompanied by your written authority (unless the person is your appointee – see p2:480).[10]

Late applications can be accepted for 'special reasons'.[11] 'Special reasons' are not defined. They could include reasons why the application is late (eg, ill health, domestic crisis, wrong advice) or any other reasons (eg, you will suffer hardship without a review). The restrictive definition given to the phrase 'special reasons' for late appeals does not apply to the SF. If the Benefits Agency does not accept there are special reasons, get advice. You may have to threaten judicial review if its refusal is unreasonable.

If your application is out of time, you can also ask a reviewing officer to conduct a discretionary review (see p2:602).

The Benefits Agency can ask you to submit further information in connection with your application if reasonably required.[12]

You can withdraw your application in writing at any time.[13]

Review interviews

If a decision is not wholly revised in your favour, you must be given the opportunity to attend an interview.[14] The interview should either be conducted in person, (at the local Benefits Agency office or in your home, for example, you are seriously ill or disabled), or by telephone, if you agree.[15] You have the legal right to be accompanied to an interview by a friend or adviser.[16]

During the interview, you must be given an explanation of the reasons for the review decision and an opportunity to make representations and submit any additional evidence.[17] The reviewing officer must make an accurate written record of the interview, including your representations, which must be agreed and signed by you (you should be sent a copy if the interview was conducted by telephone).[18]

Decisions

You are entitled to a written decision on your application for review, which must include notification of your right to request a further review by an SFI.[19] There are no legal time limits for carrying out reviews and notifying decisions. If there are unreasonable delays, you should complain to the SF manager and if necessary, ask your MP or an advice agency to assist.

How review decisions are made

Community care grants and crisis loans

When carrying out a review relating to a community care grant or bugeting loan a reviewing officer must have regard to all the circumstances of each case and in particular:[20]

- the nature, extent and urgency of the need;
- the existence of resources which could meet the need;
- whether any other person or body could wholly or partly meet the need;
- the local budget (see p1:642);
- the SF directions (see p1:642);
- national and local guidance (see p1:643); *and*
- in the case of crisis loans, the likelihood of re-payment and the time it would take.

The High Court has ruled that need and the priority of an application should be assessed before budgeting considerations are taken into account.[21]

The reviewing officer must also:[22]

- check whether the original decision was legally correct, eg, sustainable on the evidence, based on all relevant considerations and a correct interpretation of the law;
- check that the SFO acted fairly and reasonably and exercised discretion properly;
- check that you were given the opportunity to put your case and that there was no bias;
- take into account all the circumstances which existed at the time of the original decision and any new evidence and relevant changes in circumstances since the decision was made.

The reviewing officer does not have to take into account any issue not raised by the application for review.[23]

The above legal duties establish what should be a thorough and exacting system for review. The practice, however, rarely lives up to the theory. Many reviewing officers do not have the time and training required and there is a tendency for SFO decisions to be confirmed, unless new evidence comes to light.

As with SFO decisions, budget considerations and the guidance or priorities tend to be the major determinants of decision making.

Budgeting loans

When carrying out a review relating to a bugeting loan decision, a reviewing officer must have regard to the same factors as SFOs (see p1:659).[24] This means that like SFOs, they cannot exercise individual discretion and are bound by the factual criteria set out in the SF directions (see p1:659).

The reviewing officer must also take into account:[25]
- the applicant's personal circumstances as they existed at the time of the original decision;
- the material facts confirming the applicant's personal circumstances which existed at the time of the original decision;
- any new evidence supporting the material facts which confirms the applicant's personal circumstances existing at the time the original determination was made and has since been produced;
- any new loan debt the applicant has received;
- the relevant district budget at the time of the review decision.

The reviewing officer does not have to take into account any issue not raised by the application for review.[26]

The above legal duties and restrictions mean that the scope for revision of a decision is extremely limited. In practical terms, unless it emerges that the original decision was based on incorrect information relating to the factual criteria, the decision will merely be confirmed by the reviewing officer (in practice, the computer – see p1:660).

Tactics

- You should always consider requesting a review if you are dissatisfied with a decision. You should bear in mind, however, that you could end up with a less favourable decision if it is determined that you misrepresented or failed to disclose a material fact and must repay a community care grant (see p2:523).
- You should also bear in mind the limited scope for a successful review of a bugeting loan decision (see p1:658). There is little point in requesting a review if the factual criteria were correctly applied in your case unless there is a change in the maximum awards set by the district budget (see Chapter 31 and p1:662). Whether or not your circumstances have changed, you should consider re-applying for a bugeting loan (see p1:645).
- Your application for review must be in writing and you should retain a copy. If your application is late, you should give your special reasons why it should be considered out of time (see p2:603). Alternatively, you could ask the reviewing officer to conduct a discretionary review (see p2:602).
- You should explain, as fully as possible, why you disagree with the SFO's decision. Community care grants are often refused on the grounds that your application was not for one of the purposes for which a community care grant can be given, or because your application was of insufficient priority. You should explain how your application *is* for one of the allowable purposes (see p1:647) and why it should be given high priority. If you are unhappy about the amount awarded, you should explain and justify the reasonableness of the amount you asked for.

- You should weigh up the pros and cons of whether you want a review interview to be conducted in person or by telephone. The telephone may be more convenient but you may be able to get your case across more effectively in person and can take a friend or representative with you. If you attend an interview, you should ask to be interviewed in a private room and complain if one is not offered. Always insist on an interpreter if you are not familiar with English. You should, of course, make sure that all your evidence and representations are recorded.
- Finally, you should be prepared for a negative review decision and to pursue your case by requesting a further review by an SFI (see below).

2. **Social fund inspector reviews**

Powers of review

The law relating to reviews by social fund inspectors (SFIs) is set out in primary legislation and legally binding SFI directions.[27]

All decisions which have been reviewed by a reviewing officer, are subject to further review by an SFI (see below).[28]

The SFIs conduct their reviews independently of the Benefits Agency. They are part of the Independent Review Service for the SF, based in an office in Birmingham (see Appendix 1).

SFIs can:[29]

- confirm the decision of the reviewing officer; *or*
- substitute their own decision; *or*
- refer the case back to an SFO for redetermination.

Procedure

Applying for a further review

You must apply for a further review in writing within 28 days of the date the review decision was issued to you.[30] Your application must include your grounds for requesting a further review (see p2:608 – Tactics).[31] If somebody is applying on your behalf, you must send your written authority (unless the person is your appointee).[32] You should specifically authorise the person to make an application for further review by an SFI on your behalf. You need to do this even if you supplied written authority when you first applied for an internal review.

Late applications can be accepted for 'special reasons' (see p2:603).[33] You must send your applications to the local Benefits Agency office and not directly to the SFI office in Birmingham. The local office sends your application together with all relevant papers to Birmingham. Decisions about late or incomplete applications must be made by the SFI and not the local office. The SFI writes to you direct for further information or evidence.

Process

Reviews are almost always conducted on the basis of written information. You have no right to an oral hearing although an SFI can interview you, if necessary, at a mutually convenient location.

You are sent copies of all the papers which the SFI has about your case before the review takes place. You should look through the papers and send any written comments you have to the SFI on the form provided. It will help your case if you can identify any inconsistencies, judgemental assumptions or incorrect interpretations of the directions in the reviewing officer's decision, which should be set out in full in the papers you receive.

Decisions

You receive a detailed written decision from the SFI. There are long delays (often several weeks) with SFI reviews and you could complain to your MP about these. Crisis loan reviews should be done urgently (see above). If you are unhappy about an SFI decision, get advice. There is no right of appeal, but you can ask an SFI to reconsider her/his decision – eg, because it is unreasonable or wrong in law.[34] You can also apply for a judicial review of the decision in the High Court (see p2:637).

If a case is referred back to the Benefits Agency for another internal review, the SFI should identify the factors which need further consideration. An SFO must re-determine the case and send you a new decision, with a full explanation of how this was reached, taking into account the SFI's comments.[35] If you are dissatisfied with the new decision, you have the right to request a further review by an SFI.

How social fund inspectors' decisions are made

When carrying out a further review, SFIs must take into account the same factors as reviewing officers must, when conducting internal reviews (see p2:602).[36] This means they must exercise individual discretion in community care grant and crisis loan reviews but are bound by the factual criteria in budgeting loan reviews.

The High Court has ruled that it must be clear from the SFI's decision that s/he has taken the Secretary of State's guidance into account.[37] In another case, the Court ruled that the SFI must apply the law at the time of the SFI decision, not the law at the time of the original SFO decision.[38]

SFI decision making tends to be of a much higher standard than reviewing officer decision making. SFIs are more independent and thorough and tend to be less bound by local budgets and guidance.

Tactics

- You should always consider requesting a further review if you are dissatisfied with a reviewing officer decision. SFI decision making is more thorough and independent and your application is more likely to be successful than at the internal review stage. You should bear in mind, however, the points made on p2:601 about the possibility of a less favourable decision and the restricted scope for budgeting loan reviews.
- Your application must be in writing and sent to your local Benefits Agency office. It needs to contain the same sort of information as an application for an internal review (see p2:603).
- If your case is urgent, state this and explain why. There is a special express procedure if you are seeking a review of a crisis loan decision; you can ask the local office to fax the decision and papers to the SFI office rather than rely on a courier.
- If is a good idea to contact the SFI office a few days after submitting your application to make sure they have received it. Local Benefits Agency offices are told to send applications on to Birmingham by courier on the day they are received whenever possible. Complain to the SF manager and, if necessary, your MP if there are delays.
- When you are sent the papers relating to your case by the SFI, you should look through them carefully and make any appropriate comments on the form provided.

Notes

• •

References are to statutes and regulations as amended up to 8 March 1999. All regulations are (General) Regulations unless otherwise stated. There is a full list of abbreviations in Appendix 13.

1. **Internal reviews**
   1 s66 SSAA 1992; s38 SSA 1998; SF Dirs
   2 s66 SSAA 1992; s38 SSA 1998
   3 SF Dir 31
   4 s66(1)(a) SSAA 1992; s38(1)(a) SSA 1998
   5 SF Dir 31
   6 s66(1)(aa) SSAA 1992; s71ZA SSAA 1992; s38(1)(b) SSA 1998
   7 s66(1)(c) SSAA 1992; s38(1)(c) SSA 1998
   8 Reg 2(1)(a) and (2)(a) SF(AR) Regs
   9 Reg 2(4) SF(AR) Regs
   10 Reg 2(6) SF(AR) Regs
   11 Reg 2(3) SF(AR) Regs
   12 Reg 2(5) SF(AR) Regs
   13 SF dir 37
   14 SF dir 33
   15 SF dir 33
   16 SF dir 33
   17 SF dir 34
   18 SF dir 35
   19 SF dir 36
   20 s66 SSAA 1992; s38 SSA 1996
   21 *R v SFI ex parte Taylor*, The Times, 20 January 1998
   22 SF dirs 32 and 39
   23 s66(5A) SSAA 1992; s38 SSA 1996
   24 s66(6)(b) SSAA 1992; s38(7) SSA 1998
   25 SF Dirs 32 and 39
   26 s66(5A) SSAA 1992; s38(6) SSA 1998

2. **Social fund inspector reviews**
   27 s66 SSAA 1992; s38 SSA 1998; SFI Dirs
   28 s66(3) SSAA 1992; s38(3) SSA 1998
   29 s66(4) SSAA 1992; s38(4) SSA 1998
   30 Reg 2(1)(b) and (2)(b) SF(AR) Regs

31 Reg 2(4) SF(AR) Regs
32 Reg 2(6) SF(AR) Regs
33 Reg 2(3) SF(AR) Regs
34 s66(5) SSAA 1992; s38(5) SSA 1998
35 SF Dir 38
36 s66 SSAA 1992; s38 SSA 1998; SFI Dirs 1-4
37 *R v IRS ex parte Connell* (QBD) 3 November 1994
38 *R v SFI ex parte Ledicott* (QBD) 24 May 1995

Chapter 56

. . . .

Appeals

This chapter covers:

. . . .

The rules described in this chapter are due to change radically from June 1999 when the Social Security Act 1998 begins to take effect. In particular, the time limit for appealing is likely to be reduced to one month. The new rules are explained on pp2:648-657. To see when the new rules will apply, see p2:649.

. . . .

If you disagree with a decision about housing benefit (HB), council tax benefit (CTB), earnings top-up or payments from the discretionary social fund you *cannot* appeal to an independent tribunal. Instead you can seek a review. To find out more about challenging:

- an HB or CTB decision, see Chapter 54;
- a decision about a payment from the discretionary social fund, see Chapter 55;
- an earnings top-up decision, see p1:506.

You *can* appeal to an independent tribunal against any decision taken by an adjudication officer (AO) (see p2:561) or adjudicating medical authority (see p2:566). There are currently three types of tribunal (although this is due to change – see p2:627). You appeal to:

- a **disability appeal tribunal (DAT)** if the benefit is disability working allowance (DWA), disability living allowance (DLA) or attendance allowance (AA) (see Chapter 22 and pp1:195 and 1:484) and your appeal concerns a question about your disability; *or*
- a **medical appeal tribunal (MAT)** if the benefit is either industrial injuries benefit or severe disablement allowance and your appeal concerns a question about your disability. You also appeal to an MAT if you are appealing about

what is known as 'recrudescence' (see p1:210) in respect of a prescribed industrial disease (see p1:208); *or*

- a **social security appeal tribunal (SSAT)** if you are appealing against any other decision of an AO. This includes appeals against decisions about social fund payments from the regulated social fund and appeals about whether you are incapable of work (see p2:15).

There are very strict time limits for appealing (see p2:615). For more information about DATs, MATs and SSATs, see p2:627.

If you are appealing about something which could affect the amount of benefit you are paid, for example, your AA, DLA or industrial injuries benefit, you should seek advice before appealing. Because the tribunal will look at your case afresh, there is a risk you could lose benefit.

In some cases, you can seek a review as well as appealing against a decision. See p2:613 before deciding what to do. In the case of AA, DLA and DWA, you must seek a review before you can appeal (see p2:573). If you are claiming jobseeker's allowance (see Chapter 14) you must seek a review of the first decision made about the terms of your jobseeker's agreement (see p1:315) or any variation of it before you can appeal (see p1:320).

1. **Appeal rights**

It is important to know who makes a decision on any particular question in your case because that determines how you challenge it. For Secretary of State decisions, see p2:565. For adjudication officer decisions, see p2:561. For adjudicating medical authority decisions, see p2:566.

It is important to remember that:

- there is a strict time limit for appealing – normally only three months (see p2:165). This will be reduced to one month when the Social Security Act 1998 takes effect (see p2:648);
- you must provide certain information when you appeal (see p2:615);
- you must appeal in writing and normally on the appropriate form. If you do not use the appropriate form, the chair of a tribunal can accept your appeal so long as it is in writing and includes all the information required (see p2:615).[1] There is no guarantee the chair will do this, so use the form wherever possible. The appeal form is contained in leaflet NI246, *How to appeal,* which is available at Benefits Agency offices;
- the completed appeal form (see above) should be sent or delivered to the Benefits Agency office (or JobCentre) that made the decision with which you disagree. The Benefits Agency (or JobCentre) must pass forms or appeal letters to the Independent Tribunal Service (ITS – see p2:620);
- the ITS decides if your appeal is valid, not the Benefits Agency.[2]

If you want the tribunal to deal with your appeal quickly, make this plain on your appeal form, explaining why. You could also telephone the clerk to the tribunal at the ITS to check that your appeal has been received and to ask her/him to deal with the matter quickly.

See p2:631 for advice about how to prepare an appeal.

A tribunal chair may dispose of an appeal without a hearing if s/he is satisfied that the tribunal has no power to hear it (eg, you have appealed to a tribunal about your housing benefit or council tax benefit).[3]

Secretary of State decisions

Decisions made by the **Secretary of State** (see p2:565) *cannot* be appealed. Although you can try to persuade the Secretary of State to change her/his decision, if s/he refuses, your only legal remedy is to apply to the High Court for judicial review (see p2:637).

Adjudication officer decisions

You *can* appeal to an independent appeal tribunal against decisions taken by an **adjudication officer** (AO – see p2:561). You must seek a review of AO decisions about attendance allowance (AA), disability living allowance (DLA) and disability working allowance (DWA) before you can appeal (see p2:573). You can choose to seek a review before you appeal against AO decisions on other benefits and payments from the regulated social fund, but you do not have to do so. See p2:613 before deciding what to do.

The type of tribunal which will deal with your appeal depends on the benefit and the issue with which you disagree. There are currently two types of tribunal that deal with AO decisions:

* disability appeal tribunals (DAT – see p2:627); *and*
* social security appeal tribunals (SSAT – see p2:630).

Note: The system for appeals is due to change when the Social Security Act 1998 takes effect (see p2:648).

Sometimes, an AO refuses to make a decision on your claim. If an AO does this, it effectively prevents you having the right to appeal. However, an AO must make a decision on every valid claim.[4] See p2:482 for what counts as a valid claim. You can then appeal and it is up to the tribunal to decide whether the decision is correct.

Reasons for the adjudication officer's decision

Before appealing against a decision, it is useful to know why it was given. You have a right to a written statement of reasons for an AO's decision. However, if the decision concerns income support (IS) or jobseeker's allowance (JSA), you are not given the reasons for the decision automatically. You must apply for these within three months of being given the decision in writing.[5] Ask for the reasons for the decision as soon as possible so you can appeal within the three-month time limit (see p2:615).

On receiving the statement of reasons, if there are grounds for a review, you may decide it is worth asking for a review of the decision rather than appealing straightaway (but see p2:613). In any case, if you appeal, an AO looks at the decision again and may decide to review the decision (see p2:570).

In the case of AA, DLA and DWA you must seek a review before you can appeal (see p2:573).

Adjudicating medical authority decisions

You *can* appeal to an independent appeal tribunal against any decision taken by an **adjudicating medical authority** (AMA – see p2:566). AMAs make decisions about what are known as 'disability questions' if you are claiming one of the industrial injuries benefits (see Chapter 11) or severe disablement allowance (see Chapter 4). The 'disability questions' are:[6]
- whether you have suffered a 'loss of faculty' (see p1:211) and in the case of industrial injuries benefits, whether the loss of faculty was caused by an industrial accident or disease (see p1:211);
- the extent of your disability, assessed on a percentage basis (see p1:211 and Appendix 7); *and*
- the period to be covered by your assessment (see p1:214).

AMAs also make decisions about what is known as 'recrudescence' (see p1:210) in respect of a prescribed industrial disease (see p1:208).

The type of tribunal that deals with your appeal is a medical appeal tribunal (MAT – see p2:629).

Note: The system for appeals is due to change when the Social Security Act 1998 takes effect (see p2:648).

Reasons for the adjudicating medical authority's decision

Before appealing against a decision, it is useful to know why it was given. You have a right to a written notice of an AMA's decision. This must include a summary of the findings of the AMA and if the decision was not unanimous, the reasons why a member disagreed with the decision.[7]

On receiving the written notice of an AMA's decision, if there are grounds for a review, you may decide it is worth asking for a review of the decision by a medical board (see p2:579) rather than appealing straightaway (but see below).

Review or appeal?

Reviews and appeals are both ways of challenging decisions. If you can opt to seek a review instead of appealing (see p2:570) you need to choose your method of challenge with care. For more information about reviews of decisions, see Chapter 53. Remember: if you disagree with a decision about your AA, DLA or DWA you *must* seek a review before you can appeal (see p2:573).

Note: The rules on reviews are due to change when the Social Security Act 1998 takes effect (see p2:582).

Advantages of applying for a review

The main advantages of applying for a review are that it is simpler than appealing and you could receive a decision more quickly. In some cases, there is no time limit for seeking a review (see p2:572). You also get two bites at the cherry because, if your application for a review is turned down, you can always appeal against the new decision (or the original decision if you are within the time limit – see p2:615).

Disadvantages of applying for a review

There is a major disadvantage of applying for review. In some cases you may not be paid all the arrears of benefit due to you if you seek a review, even if you are successful. See p2:580 for information about the arrears of benefit you can be paid following a review.

In deciding whether you would want to ask for a review or make an appeal, you should take into account all of the factors that might lead to arrears of benefit being limited. These include:
- the length of time since the original decision;
- the type of benefit;
- whether the original decision was simply an administrative error on the part of the Benefits Agency;
- whether the 'anti-test-case' rule (see p2:580) applies to you.

If you think there is a risk that you will not obtain all the arrears you are due you should appeal instead of applying for a review.

Problems in making an appeal

There is not usually any risk attached to making an appeal. However, if you are appealing to a DAT or an MAT and the rate of the benefit you are claiming could go down, you should seek advice before you appeal.

Remember: there are strict time limits for appealing (see below). If your appeal is late, you must get the permission of a tribunal chair before you can appeal (known as leave to appeal – see p2:632) and this is only given in very limited circumstances.

The time limit for appealing

Your appeal, including all the information described on below, must arrive at the relevant Benefits Agency office (see below) within the three months beginning with the date the written decision was sent to you.[8] However, you should send your appeal in earlier if you can.

The time limit for appealing is very strict (but see p2:645 for information about appealing late). It is very important that you provide all the information required (see below) within the time limit. Your appeal is not treated as made until you do.[9] If you do not include all the information on your appeal form, the chair or clerk to the tribunal can make a 'direction' requiring you to provide the information you left out within a certain period of time.[10] The chair or clerk to a tribunal can give you extra time beyond the three-month time limit to provide the information required,[11] but there is no guarantee that s/he will do so. In any case, s/he can only give you a maximum of 14 more days.

If you do not provide the information within the time limit, you have to ask the chair of a tribunal to accept a late appeal (see p2:645). However, it is extremely difficult to get a chair to do this so it is better that you provide all the information in time. If you have sent your appeal form but the chair or clerk only asks for extra information after the time limit has expired, the DSS has said it is their intention that your appeal should be allowed under the late appeal rules (see p2:645).

Note: The time limit for appealing is likely to be reduced to one month when the Social Security Act 1998 takes effect (see p2:651).

How to appeal

You must appeal in writing, preferably using the appropriate appeal form (see p2:611), within three months of being notified of the decision with which you disagree. You should send or deliver your appeal to:

- your local Benefits Agency office if you are appealing to an MAT or SSAT (the JobCentre if you are appealing to an SSAT about your JSA); *or*
- the benefit office which sent you the decision if you are appealing to a DAT. This could be your regional Disability Benefit Centre or the national Attendance Allowance and Disability Living Allowance Unit.

A tribunal chair may allow a late appeal in limited circumstances (see 2:645). For further details about how to make a late appeal, see p2:646.

Information you must provide when you appeal

When you appeal you must provide the following information:[12]

- the name of the benefit you are appealing about – eg, IS or incapacity benefit;

- the date the Benefits Agency sent you the decision with which you disagree. You can find this date on the letter notifying you of the decision;
- a summary of your reasons for saying the decision was wrong. You should not simply say you think the decision was wrong, but explain why.

Examples

'The Benefits Agency says I have been overpaid IS because I failed to disclose that my wife had started working part time, but I wrote to them as soon as she started work and told them what her take-home pay would be.'

'The decision is that I should not get income-based JSA for my son because he left school in June. This decision is wrong because my son decided to stay on at school and do his 'A' levels.'

If you are appealing to an SSAT or DAT, it might also be helpful to include information and evidence which supports your appeal because before the appeal hearing an AO looks at the decision again and might review it (see below).

What happens after you appeal

The Benefits Agency prepare the appeal papers and send a copy to you and a copy to the the local independent tribunal service (ITS) office. You should then receive a questionnaire (called an 'enquiry form') from the clerk of the ITS asking you whether you want an oral hearing (see p2:617) and, if so, when you and your representative (if you have one) are available to attend. You must return the questionnaire within 14 days (the chair or clerk to a tribunal has discretion to increase this period).[13] You are also sent a leaflet containing information about appeals and how to find someone to represent you at the hearing if this would be helpful.

Note: When the Social Security Act 1998 takes effect (see p2:648), your appeal could be struck out if you fail to return the questionnaire (see p2:653).

When you are appealing to an SSAT or DAT an AO looks at the decision you are appealing about again and might change the decision, for example, on the basis of any facts, information or evidence that you provided with your appeal form. However, if you do not get everything you think you are entitled to, your appeal must still go ahead.[14]

A chair can decide your appeal should be heard straightaway if s/he thinks you have no chance of winning – eg, where you have claimed IS but you are aged 15 or where you have claimed family credit but have no children.[15] Before your appeal is heard, you must be given proper notice (see p2:620). You must also be offered the option of an oral hearing (see p2:617).

You might find that your appeal is not dealt with if there is a **test case pending** (see p2:648) which deals with the same issues. Currently, you can insist that your appeal is dealt with but it might then be adjourned (but see p2:625). These rules are due to change when the Social Security Act 1998 takes effect (see p2:655).

Oral or paper hearings

If you want an **'oral hearing'**, you must state this on the questionnaire (see above) or tell the clerk to the tribunal.[16] You are more likely to win your appeal if you attend an oral hearing, particularly where you are going to an MAT (see p2:629) or there is an argument about the facts of your case. The clerk also asks the Benefits Agency if it wants an oral hearing. Even if neither you nor the Benefits Agency want an oral hearing, the chair of the tribunal might decide that one should take place.[17] This could happen if the chair feels an oral hearing is necessary to help the tribunal make its decision.

If neither of you opt for an oral hearing and the chair does not think one is necessary, the tribunal makes its decision by looking at what you said on your appeal form, any evidence or other information you provided to support your appeal, and the Benefits Agency's submission (see p2:618). This is known as a **'paper hearing'**.

You should consider carefully whether to opt for an oral or a paper hearing. You may feel that you would rather not attend an oral hearing, for example, because you are worried about speaking for yourself or would have difficulties getting there. But remember:

- if you attend an oral hearing, you can explain your side of the story to the tribunal and you are more likely to win;
- you can seek advice before you decide what to do;
- you can ask someone to represent you (see Appendix 2). If you take someone with you to an oral hearing your chances of winning are much higher. You can take a friend, relative, adviser or representative with you[18] – you can have more than one person if the chair of the tribunal agrees;[19]
- you, an interpreter (if needed) and any witnesses may be able to get travel expenses paid. You can claim for meals, loss of earnings and childcare costs;[20]
- if you opt for a paper hearing, you should think about what other information and evidence you can get to support your appeal, and send it to the tribunal. You should make sure that everything you want to say in support of your appeal has been put in writing and that there are no other documents which you would like the tribunal to see. You must send this to the clerk to the tribunal within 10 days of being sent the Benefits Agency's submission about your appeal (see p2:618). See pp2:638-645 for information about sorting out the facts and checking the statute law and the case law that applies in your case.

The Benefits Agency's submission

The Benefits Agency prepares a detailed explanation of the reasons for its decision (in the case of SSATs and DATs, this is known as the AO's submission and in the case of MATs, the Secretary of State's submission) and this is sent to you on form AT2 along with a bundle of papers relevant to your appeal. Where your appeal involves a medical issue or one about your disability, a record of all the medical examinations you have had in connection with your claim (or previous claims for the same benefit) are included. The Benefits Agency's submission and the bundle of papers should be sent to you as soon as it is received by the ITS, usually six to eight weeks after you appeal.

If your appeal is to be dealt with at an oral hearing (see p2:617) you are also told when and where the hearing will be. See p2:617 for information about how much notice you must be given.

If your appeal is to be dealt with at a paper hearing (see p2:617), and you want to provide more information or evidence to the tribunal, you must do this within 10 days. If you opted for a paper hearing, but once you have seen the Benefits Agency's submission decide you want an oral hearing after all, you may be able to change your mind. You must tell the clerk to the tribunal before the tribunal makes its decision.

Providing other information

Once you have seen the Benefits Agency's submission, you might want to provide additional information to support your appeal. For example, you might want to get independent medical evidence or provide supporting statements from witnesses. If your appeal is to be dealt with at a paper hearing, you must provide this information within 10 days of being sent the Benefits Agency's submission (see p2:618). Even if you are going to have an oral hearing, it is useful to provide information in advance. See pp2:638-645 for further information about how to prepare an appeal.

Information you must provide

The chair or clerk to the tribunal might issue directions requiring you or the Benefits Agency to provide further information or documents.[21] A chair can require you or the Benefits Agency to provide information or documents that are needed to help the tribunal make its decision. You can also ask the chair to require the Benefits Agency to provide these.

The chair or the clerk can require you to:
- provide information, where your appeal form is incomplete (see p2:615);
- reply to the letter asking you about when you are available for a hearing (see p2:617).

If you are required to provide any information or documents, it is important that you do so. If you do not, the chair can:[22]

- strike out your appeal (see below). This means that your appeal is cancelled;
- decide to hear your appeal straightaway, but only if:
  - you have not explained why you have not provided what has been required; *and*
  - the tribunal has sufficient information to make its decision.

  This might happen, for example, where your appeal was adjourned for you to get evidence, but you have not done so after a considerable period of time. You must still be asked whether you want an oral hearing (see p2:617) and if you do, must be given proper notice (see p2:620).

What if you do not pursue your appeal?

A chair can strike out your appeal for 'want of prosecution' if you do not appear to be pursuing it. This cancels your appeal and it does not go ahead. This might happen where you fail to provide information or documents that you have been required to provide by a chair or clerk (see p2:618) or you fail to tell the clerk when you can attend a hearing (see p2:616).[23]

You must be notified if this is being considered and you must be given a reasonable amount of time to explain why you think your appeal should not be struck out. You do not have to be given notice where your address is not known or cannot be found out easily. If the chair is satisfied with your explanation and decides not to strike out your appeal, s/he might decide to hear your case straightaway (see above), or to give instructions to speed your appeal along.

If a chair strikes out your appeal, you have three months to ask for it to be reinstated.[24] It may be reinstated if you did not receive notice that your appeal might be struck out (see above) unless no notice was sent to you because your address was not known or could not have been found out easily. If the chair refuses to reinstate your appeal, you might be able to make a fresh appeal.[25] See p2:615 for the time limit for appealing and p2:645 for late appeals.

Note: The rules for striking out appeals are due to change when the Social Security Act 1998 takes effect (see p2:653). There will be additional reasons why a chair might strike out your appeal.

Withdrawing an appeal[26]

If you change your mind about appealing, you can withdraw your appeal. You must apply in writing to the clerk to the tribunal. S/he must allow you to withdraw your appeal unless the Benefits Agency has already notified the clerk that it is opposed to this. However, once the appeal tribunal hearing has begun, you can only withdraw your appeal with the consent of the chair and provided the tribunal has not yet made a decision. Once an appeal has been withdrawn it cannot be reinstated, but if you decide that you want to go ahead after all, you could try to make a late appeal against the AO's or AMA's original decision (but see p2:566).[27]

The oral hearing

You must be sent notice of the oral hearing (see p2:617) at least seven days before the hearing is to take place unless you agree to less notice than this. If you have not been given the correct notice, the tribunal can only go ahead if you agree.[28] If you give up your right to notice, for example because you want your appeal to be dealt with quickly and are happy for it to be listed at short notice, the tribunal can go ahead with the hearing even if you are not there.[29]

If the hearing date is inconvenient or you want more time to prepare your case, you can ask for it to be **postponed**. You must apply in writing to the clerk to the tribunal, saying why you want your case to be postponed. You should do this as soon as you decide that you want a postponement.[30] The ITS is very keen to avoid postponements, so you should ring before the hearing is due to take place to check if this has been agreed. If you do not attend and have not asked for a postponement, the tribunal can hear the case without you,[31] and you are less likely to succeed. If you are refused a postponement but do not attend the hearing, the tribunal should consider whether to adjourn.[32] The hearing should not go ahead if you have advised them that you cannot attend and have asked for another hearing date, especially if you have a good reason for not attending.[33] If the tribunal makes a decision in your absence with which you disagree, you can try to appeal to a social security commissioner (see p2:631) or you can ask for the decision to be set aside (but see p2:626).

An appeal is heard in public unless you or your representative request a private hearing, or the chair thinks it should be in private.[34] In practice, it is extremely rare for members of the public to turn up. However, the rule does mean that you could sit in on the case before your own.

The paper hearing

You are not sent notice of a paper hearing (see p2:617). The tribunal makes its decision in your absence and you are then notified of its decision (see p2:625).

2. Tribunal procedures

Tribunals are independent of the Benefits Agency. The standards of tribunals are the responsibility of the President of the Independent Tribunal Service (ITS). The ITS is divided into regions, with a chair for each region who recruits and trains tribunal members. The names and addresses of the President and the regional chairs are given in Appendix 1.

The President issues circulars to guide tribunals on how they should conduct themselves. Copies of the circulars can be obtained by contacting one of the ITS offices listed in Appendix 1.

Each region has a panel of **chairs** and **tribunal members**. The people who hear your appeal are drawn from this panel. The chair of a tribunal is always a lawyer. S/he makes a note of what is said by you, your representative, the adjudication officer (AO) and any witnesses.

The chair has to record the tribunal's decision, and a statement of its findings on the relevant facts of the case and the reasons for its decision. See p2:625 for information about decisions.

For more information about who is likely to deal with your appeal, see p2:629 for social security appeal tribunals (SSATs), p2:630 for medical appeal tribunals (MATs) and p2:627 for disability appeal tribunals (DATs).

If you have a complaint about a chair or tribunal member, or the way a hearing is conducted, write to your regional chair or the President of the ITS (see Appendix 1 for addresses).

The tribunal's administration is dealt with by clerks who are civil servants assigned to the tribunals by the President. They have purely administrative duties and do not take part in making the tribunal's decision.

Note: The way tribunals are made up and how they are administered are due to change when the Social Security Act 1998 takes effect (see p2:648).

People present at hearings

The tribunal consists of a **chair** and up to two **wing members** – tribunal members who sit on either side of the chair. Wherever possible, at least one member of the tribunal should be the same sex as you.[35] To see who makes up a DAT, an MAT and an SSAT, see pp2:627, 2:629 and 2:630.

The **clerk to the tribunal** is there in an administrative capacity – eg, to pay expenses (see p2:617). The clerk takes no part in making the decision on your appeal and should not express any views on the case.

The **presenting officer** represents the Benefits Agency. S/he is seldom the person who made the decision you are appealing about. S/he explains the reasons for the decision, but is not there to defend it at all costs. S/he may provide information which helps your case.[36]

If your appeal is about whether you are incapable of work, a **medical assessor** is also present at the hearing. S/he is a doctor who is there in an advisory capacity. S/he advises the tribunal on medical issues but should take no part in making the decision on your appeal.

Procedure at an oral hearing

The procedure for all tribunals is broadly similar. When the tribunal is ready to hear your case, you are taken in with the presenting officer (see above). There are no strict rules of procedure.

The chair should start by introducing the members of the tribunal and everyone else who is present. The presenting officer is then usually asked to summarise the Benefits Agency's written submission (see p2:618) and you are asked to explain your reasons for disagreeing with it. Alternatively, you may be asked to explain your position first. You can call any witnesses and can ask questions of the presenting officer, and the tribunal members ask questions of you both.

The tribunal considers all the facts, evidence, law (see p2:640) and caselaw (see p2:641) before it makes a decision. If you think there are mistakes in the tribunal papers, point them out.

Appeals about disability or incapacity for work

You should tell the tribunal how your disability or incapacity affects you at work or in your daily life at home. You should be completely straightforward with the tribunal, neither diminishing nor exaggerating your symptoms. If you feel better on some days than others, explain in what ways and give them an idea as to whether they are seeing you on a good day or a bad day.

The tribunal listens to you and asks you questions. It considers all of the medical reports and other documents in the tribunal papers (see p2:616) and other evidence relevant to your case. It tries to draw out the evidence about your disabilities, perhaps with the help of questioning from the doctor or consultant members. This may confirm the opinions expressed in medical reports with which you disagree, or it may tend to support your view. The tribunal should not feel restricted to merely accepting the medical evidence about you given in written reports.[37]

You are not given a physical examination, nor is there any 'walking test' for the disability living allowance (DLA) mobility component.[38] However, the tribunal may take its visual observation of you into account. It should not attach undue weight to its observations of your walking ability.[39]

A chair can adjourn the hearing (see p2:624) and refer you to a doctor for a medical examination and report where s/he thinks that the appeal cannot be properly decided unless there is such an examination and report.[40] Where this happens the chair should ensure that the report is obtained promptly. The written decision to adjourn for a report should make clear why the tribunal adjourned and what sort of medical evidence is being sought.[41]

Domiciliary tribunals

The ITS tries to ensure there are a sufficient number of accessible tribunal venues to enable claimants to get into the buildings where their cases will be heard. Nevertheless, you may want to appeal but feel unable to get to a hearing. It is, therefore, not impossible for the hearing to be held in your own home. This is known as a 'domiciliary hearing'.

However, the ITS does seek to limit the number of such hearings.[42] Any domiciliary hearing presumably costs quite a lot of their time and expense, and, since one of the members of the tribunal may well be themselves disabled, that member may not be able to get into your home. Therefore, although it is possible for a regional or full-time chair to decide that a case requires a domiciliary hearing there is often a preliminary hearing to consider whether it is really necessary. It may be felt that the appeal could go ahead if further information was obtained, even if you were still unable to attend. This could be because someone who knows you could attend and give evidence about your condition, or you or someone who knows you could send in written or recorded evidence, or a report could be sought from a medical adviser. You could also be asked to give fuller details of why you are appealing. The ITS can also arrange for an ambulance to bring you to and from the normal tribunal venue if that is feasible.

What period can the tribunal consider?

When a tribunal hears your appeal, it considers whether the decision with which you disagree was correct when it was made. However, if your circumstances change after the decision the tribunal can take this into account in some circumstances. This is what is known as looking 'down to the date of the hearing'. The tribunal should look down to the date of the hearing if your appeal was made to:[43]

- an MAT (see p2:629); *or*
- an SSAT (see p2:630) or a DAT (see p2:627) before 21 May 1998.

This means that even if the tribunal thinks a decision was right at the time it was made, it can still decide you are entitled to benefit from a later date.

> *Example*
> An AMA decides that Joel's disablement in respect of occupational asthma (D7) is 10 per cent and he appeals. By the time his appeal is heard by an MAT, his condition has worsened considerably. The MAT decides that the AMA's decision was correct. However, it assesses his disablement as 20 per cent as from the date of the hearing.

A tribunal *cannot* look 'down to the date of the hearing' (see above) if your appeal was made to an SSAT (see p2:630) or a DAT (see p2:627) on or after 21

May 1998.[44] However, any evidence you get after the decision with which you disagree could still be relevant to your appeal.[45]

Note: When the Social Security Act 1998 takes effect (see p2:648), no tribunals dealing with appeals made after 21 May 1998 will be able to look down to the date of the hearing (see above).

Repeat claims

If you are appealing to an SSAT or a DAT on or after 21 May 1998 (or any tribunal after the Social Security Act 1998 takes effect – see above), it is important as a *general* rule for you to consider making a fresh claim (or seeking a review) every time your circumstances change, and appeal if you are unhappy with the subsequent decision (but see below). This is particularly so where your appeal is about:

- whether you are incapable of work (see p2:14) or qualify for attendance allowance or DLA and your condition has worsened;
- whether you satisfy the 'habitual residence test' (see p2:234); *or*
- how much capital or income you have and this changes.

If you wait until the tribunal makes its decision and this goes against you, you could lose out. You could only get arrears going back to the date your circumstances changed if you make a fresh claim (or seek a review) and ask for benefit to be backdated. See pp2:488 and 2:489 for how far your benefit can be backdated.

> #### Example
> Ravi has been getting incapacity benefit (IB) for some time. An AO decides he is fit for work and stops his IB. He appeals. While awaiting his appeal hearing, his health deteriorates, he makes a fresh claim and is awarded IB. When the tribunal hears his appeal against the original decision it upholds the AO's decision. However, because Ravi made a fresh claim when his circumstances changed, he has not lost out.

Where you make a fresh claim (or seek a review – p2:570) and have appealed, you should ask for all of the appeals to be heard together by the same tribunal.[46]

In some cases, it might not be a good idea to appeal after making a fresh claim (or seeking a review). If you are in any doubt about what to do, you should seek advice.

Adjournments

Your case may be adjourned unfinished to be heard on another day because, for instance, more evidence is required. Failure to adjourn to allow you to get relevant evidence is an error of law (see p2:632) and you can appeal to the commissioner to get the decision overturned (see p2:631).[47] A tribunal might adjourn your case if there is a test case pending which deals with the same issues as your appeal.[48] If this happens, you should ask them to hear your appeal based on the law as it currently stands, if this is in your interests, rather than waiting for the result of the test case. The rules are due to change when the Social Security Act 1998 takes effect (see p2:648).

If your appeal is adjourned a new tribunal must rehear your case from the beginning unless it has the same members as before or, in the case of an SSAT only, you agree to it being heard by two members of the previous tribunal without the third.[49]

You can appeal against a decision to adjourn your appeal though it is often quicker to press for a fresh hearing.[50]

The decision

If the tribunal is unable to come to a unanimous decision, it makes a majority decision. Usually you are told of the tribunal's decision at the hearing and you are given a decision notice confirming it. The decision notice includes a summary of the tribunal's reasons for its decision. If it is not given at the hearing or you opted for a paper hearing (see p2:617), the decision notice is sent to you later by the clerk. You must also be informed of:[51]

- your right to request a 'full decision' (see below);
- the conditions for appealing to the commissioner (see p2:631).

A decision can be corrected or set aside (see p2:626).

The full decision

If you lose your appeal and want to appeal to the commissioner (see p2:631) you must generally have what is known as a '**full decision**' (but see p2:632).[52] You should ask for one as soon as possible after the tribunal makes its decision.

A chair might decide to give you a 'full decision' at the hearing or to send one to you later on.[53] If not, you have a right to request one. The chair **must** provide a full decision if you ask for it within 21 days of being sent or given the decision notice (see above). If you mistakenly ask the chair of the tribunal for permission to appeal to the commissioner (see p2:632) instead of a full decision, s/he should treat this as a request for a full decision.[54]

If you ask after the 21-day time-limit has expired, the chair might agree to provide a full decision but there is no guarantee of this. If the chair fails to provide a full decision, whether or not you ask for it in time (see above), you should see p2:632 and seek advice.

A full decision must include the tribunal's reasons for its decision and relevant findings of fact. This must be a legible record of the evidence.[55] If the decision is not unanimous, the full decision must give the reasons why a tribunal member disagreed.[56]

The Benefits Agency can also ask for a full decision. If this happens, it means the Benefits Agency is considering appealing to the commissioner.

There are now guidelines for the way MATs should record and explain their decisions (see p2:632).

After the hearing

If you have won your appeal, the Benefits Agency ought to carry out the tribunal's decision straightaway. It can do this on the basis of the decision notice (see above). However, it has three months in which to appeal against the tribunal's decision to a social security commissioner (see p2:631). If considering an appeal, you will not be paid while it decides what to do. If the Benefits Agency decides to appeal, you are not paid until the commissioner hears the case.[57] See p2:497 for details of what the Benefits Agency must do before it can suspend your benefit. If you are left without any money, you might be able to apply for an interim payment (see p2:499), or get a crisis loan (see p1:667).

What if you disagree with the tribunal's decision?

A tribunal's decision is final. However:
- if the written decision contains an accidental error this can be **corrected** by the tribunal.[58]
- it can be **reviewed** in the normal way – eg, where your circumstances have changed since the decision was made or new facts have come to light (see pp2:570-575). However, where the tribunal made a mistake about the law you must appeal to a social security commissioner (see below);
- you or the Benefits Agency can **appeal to a social security commissioner** (see p2:631). Remember: if you want to appeal to a social security commissioner, you must generally have a copy of the full decision of the tribunal (but see p2:625). You should ask for this within 21 days of being sent or given the decision notice (see p2:625);
- a decision can be **set aside**, which means the decision is cancelled and your appeal is heard again. A tribunal can only do this if it thinks it is *just* and:[59]
  - you, your representative or the presenting officer (see p2:621) did not receive the appeal papers or other relevant documents, or did not receive them in sufficient time before the hearing; *or*
  - you, your representative or the presenting officer (see p2:621) were not present at the hearing. However, if you or the presenting officer chose not to attend it may not be just to set the decision aside. If you did not ask for an oral hearing (see p2:617) the decision cannot be set aside for this reason unless it would clearly be in the 'interests of justice' (see below); *or*
  - 'the interests of justice so require'. This applies where there has been a 'procedural irregularity'.[60] A failure to produce sufficient evidence at the hearing is not a procedural irregularity.

The Benefits Agency may also ask for a decision to be set aside.

You must apply for the decision to be set aside within three months of the decision being sent to you. A late application is only accepted if there are special reasons. The special reasons do not have to relate to your own personal circumstances or actions. They could include the amount of money involved or how strong your case is. See p2:647 for information about what might count as a special reason. Applications are normally decided without a hearing, so make sure you give a full explanation of your reasons when you apply.[61] You cannot appeal against a refusal to set aside, but you may be able to apply for judicial review (see p2:637). You could also try to appeal to the commissioner (see p2:631) against the tribunal's original decision. The time limit for seeking leave to appeal to the commissioner (see p2:632) runs from the date you were sent the tribunal's refusal to set aside.[62]

If a decision is wrongly set aside, any subsequent rehearing by a tribunal is invalid. The second tribunal could thus refuse to rehear the case if there was no power to set aside the previous decision.[63]

Note: The rules on when tribunal decisions can be set aside are due to change when the Social Security Act 1998 takes effect (see p2:656).

3. **The different tribunals**

This section tells you about the different tribunals. For:
- disability appeal tribunals (DATs), see below;
- medical appeal tribunals (MATs), see p2:629;
- social security appeal tribunals (SSATs), see p2:630.

Disability appeal tribunals

DATs hear appeals against adjudication officer (AO) decisions (see p2:561) about whether you satisfy the disability conditions for disability working allowance (DWA), disability living allowance (DLA) and attendance allowance (AA) (see Chapters 10 and 22) and if so, for what period. They also hear appeals about the rate at which DLA and AA should be paid to you. If your appeal is about other aspects of your entitlement to these benefits, for example, about whether you meet the residence conditions, then it is heard by an SSAT (see p2:648).

See p2:638 for advice about preparing a case and finding advice or representation.

Note: The time limit for appealing is due to be reduced to one month when the Social Security Act 1998 takes effect (see p2:651).

What the disability appeal tribunal can consider

In practice, most difficulties arise where a tribunal fails to consider whether you qualify for one of the components of DLA when there is clear evidence before them that they should do so.[64] However, you may be appealing about not being awarded one component of DLA (see Chapter 10) when you are already in receipt of the other. Or you may be appealing against the rate of one component of DLA when you are quite satisfied with the rate you receive of the other. In these circumstances the tribunal *does not have to* consider the component which is not the subject of your appeal.[65]

In addition, if you have been awarded a component of DLA for life (see p2:192), then the tribunal *should not* consider the rate of that component, or the length of time for which it has been awarded, unless either your appeal is expressly about one of those questions, or information is available to the tribunal which gives it reasonable grounds for believing that entitlement to the component, or entitlement to it at the rate awarded or for that period, ought not to continue.[66]

Example

Gina has a serious accident. She is awarded the higher rate of DLA mobility (see p1:160) because of walking difficulties, but is only awarded the lowest rate DLA care (see p1:170). She can challenge the decision on DLA care by seeking a review, then appealing. If her award of DLA mobility is for life (see p1:192), then the tribunal should not remove it unless there is information available that gives the tribunal reasonable grounds for thinking that Gina is not entitled to it at the higher rate, or at all, or for such a period. However, it is important for Gina to remember that the tribunal might take the medical evidence available and the discussions about her disabilities that take place during the hearing into account.

If Gina's award of DLA mobility is for a limited period only, the tribunal *can* reconsider the DLA mobility award, although it may choose not to do so.

Who can appeal

You can appeal to a DAT if you are the benefit claimant. If you have an appointee (see p2:480), s/he can appeal on your behalf.

You can appeal to a DAT if you are acting on behalf of someone claiming AA or DLA (even if this is without her/his knowledge) and you are appealing about whether or not s/he is terminally ill (see p1:180).[67]

The tribunal members

A DAT always consists of three people. The tribunal cannot proceed if any one of the three members is absent.[68] There is a **chair** who is a lawyer, a **doctor** who is a GP, and **someone experienced in dealing with the needs of**

disabled people, either in a professional or voluntary capacity or because s/he is disabled.[69]

No one may act as a tribunal member on a case where s/he would be affected by the outcome, or where s/he has already been involved in the case in some capacity.[70] This means that your own GP or any Benefits Agency doctor who has examined you cannot be the medical member. However, this member may also work as an adjudicating medical practitioner in connection with severe disablement allowance (SDA) and industrial injuries benefits.[71]

Medical appeal tribunals

MATs hear all appeals by claimants against decisions of adjudicating medical authorities (AMAs) about your industrial injuries benefit or SDA. This includes decisions made by medical boards (see p2:566).[72] See p2:566 for information about the decisions made by AMAs. MATs also deal with appeals concerning recovery of benefits from compensation payments (see p2:508).

If you want to appeal about other aspects of your claim for an industrial injuries benefit or SDA, for example, whether you suffered an industrial accident or were overpaid, you appeal to an SSAT. See p2:630 for information about SSATs.

See p2:638 for advice about preparing a case and finding advice or representation.

Note: The time limit for appealing is due to be reduced to one month when the Social Security Act 1998 takes effect (see p2:651).

Who can appeal

You can appeal to an MAT if you are the benefit claimant. If you have an appointee (see p2:480), s/he can appeal on your behalf.

References on behalf of the Secretary of State

If the Secretary of State considers that the decision an AMA (see p2:566) has made is wrong, s/he can ask the AO to refer the case to a MAT.[73] Such a reference is usually made because the Secretary of State thinks that the AMA was too generous. However, references are sometimes made if your benefit award is thought to be too low, or because it is believed that the AMA made an error of law. The procedure for a reference is the same as on an appeal.

The tribunal members

An MAT always consists of three people. The tribunal cannot proceed if any member is absent.[74] There is a **chair**, who is a lawyer and two **consultants**. Neither is necessarily an expert in the field of medicine relevant to your case (although the Independent Tribunal Service – see p2:620 – does make efforts to appoint specialists where possible).

Medical examination at the oral hearing

The arrangements for the hearing are similar to those for other tribunals (see p2:622) but hearings take place only where there are facilities for the doctors to examine you. After the main hearing, the medical members often examine you in a separate room in the absence of everyone else, including the chair and usually your representative, although you can have someone with you as a chaperone or to help you if you need assistance undressing. When you are examined, make sure you tell the members of the tribunal if you are in pain or suffering discomfort. It is also a good idea to give the tribunal a full list of any medicines you are taking.

After the hearing and any examination, the tribunal members discuss the evidence and the law by themselves.

Social security appeal tribunals

You can appeal to an SSAT against decisions made by AOs (see p2:561) on all matters except for certain decisions about your disability (if you are claiming DWA, DLA or AA – see p2:627) and certain decisions concerning industrial accidents and diseases (see p2:629). For these you must appeal to a DAT or an MAT (see pp2:627 and 2:629). SSATs deal with appeals against decisions on payments from the regulated social fund (see Chapter 30).

See p2:638 for information about preparing a case and finding advice or representation.

Note: The time limit for appealing is due to be reduced to one month when the Social Security Act 1998 takes effect (see p2:651).

Cases referred by the adjudication officer

Sometimes – particularly where there is a dispute about the facts between a claimant and, say, an employer in a case of dismissal due to alleged misconduct – the AO does not make any decision at all but simply refers the case to a tribunal.[75] In such cases, the procedure is the same as it is on an appeal (see p2:616) except that the bundle of papers does not include a letter of appeal from you.

Appeals about jobseeker's agreements

If you are appealing against an AO's direction to enter into or vary a jobseeker's agreement (see p1:315), the SSAT has power to issue its own directions about what the terms of your jobseeker's agreement should be.[76]

If you have an existing jobseeker's agreement and the SSAT directs how it should be varied, the AO can bring your present agreement (and therefore also your entitlement to JSA) to an end if you do not sign a new agreement which complies with the SSAT's directions within 21 days.[77]

Who can appeal

You can appeal to an SSAT if you are the benefit claimant. If you have an appointee (see p2:480), s/he can appeal on your behalf.

If an 'ordinary' overpayment of a benefit or a duplication of payment of IS or income-based JSA can be recovered from you, you can appeal to an SSAT.[78] This is the case even if you were not the person who claimed the benefit that was overpaid. See p2:516 for further information about ordinary over-payments and p2:524 about duplication of payments.

If an AO decides that you are entitled to statutory sick pay (see Chapter 2) or statutory maternity pay (see p1:91), your employer has the right of appeal to an SSAT.[79]

The tribunal members

An SSAT consists of up to three people. There is a **chair**, who is a lawyer, who sometimes sits with one or two **wing members** (see p2:621). They are supposed to be people who have knowledge or experience of conditions in your area, and who are representative of people living or working there. Your appeal is heard by a chair on her/his own if:

- it is a paper hearing (see p2:617);
- it is an application to set aside a tribunal's decision (see p2:626);
- an accidental error in a tribunal's decision needs to be corrected (see p2:626); or
- the appeal concerns the 'all-work test' (see p2:22).

Your appeal is heard by a three-person tribunal in all other cases with the following exceptions. It can be heard:

- by a chair and one wing member if you agree;[80]
- in the absence of one or both of the wing members even if you do not agree, but only if: [81]
  - you were advised in advance that the law changed on 21 May 1998; and
  - one or both of the wing members cancelled or failed to turn up; and
  - reasonable efforts were made to find replacements.

Where an SSAT consists of only two people, the chair has the casting vote.[82]

4. Appealing to the social security commissioner

Both you and the Benefits Agency have a further right of appeal to a social security commissioner against a decision of a disability appeal tribunal (DAT), medical appeal tribunal (MAT) or social security appeal tribunal (SSAT). This is only the case, however, if the tribunal has made an 'error of law' (see below).[83] Commissioners have only very limited powers to deal with questions of fact. However, if you have new evidence, it might enable you to apply for a review of the tribunal's decision (see p2:570) and you can do that while the appeal is pending.

Error of law

The tribunal made an **error of law** if:[84]
- it got the law wrong or misinterpreted it – eg, it misunderstood the particular benefit rule concerned;
- there is no evidence to support its decision;
- the facts it found are such that, had it acted reasonably, and interpreted the law correctly, it could not have made the decision it did. This argument can be used where the facts are inconsistent with the decision – eg, a tribunal finds that a man and a woman live in separate households, but decides they are living together as husband and wife;
- there is a breach of the rules of natural justice. This is where the procedure followed by the tribunal leads to unfairness (eg, you are not allowed to call witnesses to support you or the tribunal refuses a postponement (see p2:652), even though you cannot attend for a good reason and have told it so), and the result is that you lost without having a chance to put your case properly;[85]
- it does not give proper findings of fact or provide adequate reasons for its decision (see p2:625). The tribunal must not simply say what its decision was. It must put down sufficient reasons so that you can see why, on the evidence, it reached the conclusion it did. It can rely on the summary of the facts given in the Benefits Agency's submission (see p2:618), but only if these are not in dispute and s/he has covered all relevant issues.[86] If you and the Benefits Agency disagree about the facts the tribunal must explain which version it prefers and why.

In the past, claimants often encountered problems with MATs giving wholly inadequate – or sometimes no – reasons for refusing an appeal. In particular, these decisions often failed to state clearly why the tribunal was disagreeing with the medical evidence put forward on behalf of the claimant or with the doctors whose views had formed the basis of previous awards of benefit. This failure made it very difficult to appeal to the commissioners. Claimants who did so often found that they did not succeed. MATs now have guidelines that they must follow.[87]

How to appeal to the commissioner

You must first obtain permission to appeal to the commissioner – known as obtaining '**leave to appeal**'.[88] This means that you have to show that there has possibly been an error of law (see above) and that you have the beginnings of a case. If you wish to appeal, you must generally have the tribunal's full decision but see below.

You should first apply for leave to appeal to the chair of the tribunal.[89] You must do this by writing to the clerk of the tribunal at the regional office within three months of being sent the full decision of the tribunal.[90] You must include a copy of the full decision (see p2:625) with your application for leave to appeal.

If the chair refuses you leave to appeal, you may make a fresh application direct to a commissioner. You must do this within 42 days, beginning on the day after the date on the notification that you were refused leave to appeal by the tribunal chair.[91] You should again include a copy of the full decision with your application for leave to appeal. However, if you do not have the full decision, the commissioner can still give you leave to appeal so long as you can show that the tribunal made an error of law (see p2:632) without it, for example, because sufficient information was given in the decision notice (see p2:625).[92]

If you miss the time limit, you may still apply for leave to appeal. However, your application must be made direct to a commissioner who gives you leave only if there are special reasons for the delay (see p2:647).[93]

What happens when you get leave to appeal?

Once you have been given leave to appeal, you must send what is known as a notice of appeal within six weeks.[94] You are sent a form on which to do this. The time may, again, be extended for special reasons (see p2:647). You may have been told that your notice of application for leave has been treated as a notice of appeal, in which case you do not have to send in another.[95]

The information about how to prepare an appeal on pp2:638-645 also applies to appeals to the commissioner.

The Benefits Agency might agree with you that the tribunal made an error of law (see p2:632). If this happens the commissioner can:[96]
* set aside the tribunal's decision;
* refer your appeal back to be heard by a different tribunal; *and*
* issue a direction to the tribunal who will hear your appeal again. You or the Benefits Agency can ask the commissioner to do this and suggest what the direction should say.

Note: The time limit for appealing to the commissioner is likely to be reduced to one month when the Social Security Act 1998 takes effect (see p2:651).

The written procedure

Adjudication officers (AOs) at the Central Adjudication Services (see Appendix 1 for address) deal with the Benefits Agency's side of the case. A bundle of documents is prepared by that office and sent to the commissioners' office where it is added to any submissions from you. The commissioners' office then sends copies of the bundle, including the AO's submission, to you. You may find that the Benefits Agency supports your appeal and suggests that the commissioner consider referring it back to be heard by a different tribunal (see p2:633).

You are given 30 days in which to reply to the submission of the AO, although the commissioner may extend the time limit.[97] If you have nothing to add and do not want to reply at any stage, tell the commissioners' office. A commissioner has the power to strike out an appeal that appears to have been abandoned, although you can apply for it to be reinstated.[98]

When the commissioner has all the written submissions, if your appeal is not to be referred back to another tribunal (see 2:633), s/he decides whether or not there should be an oral hearing of the appeal. If you ask for an oral hearing, the commissioner will hold one unless s/he feels that the case can be dealt with properly without one.[99] Occasionally, the commissioner decides to hold an oral hearing even if you have not asked for one.

If there is no oral hearing, the commissioner reaches a decision on the basis of written submissions and other documents.

Because of the length of time you usually have to wait before your case is dealt with, you should make a fresh claim for benefit if, for example, your circumstances change and see pp2:623 and 2:624.

Oral hearings

If there is an oral hearing, it will be at the commissioners' offices in London, Edinburgh or Belfast, or at the law courts in Cardiff, Leeds or Liverpool. You are told the date in good time and your fares are paid in advance if you want to attend. At least half a day is set aside for each case. Usually, one commissioner hears your case. However, if there is a 'question of law of special difficulty', the hearing may be before a tribunal of three commissioners,[100] but the procedure is the same.

The hearing is more formal than those before tribunals but the commissioner lets you say everything you want to. Commissioners usually intervene a lot and ask questions so you need to be prepared to argue your case without your script. A full set of commissioners' decisions (see p2:643) and the statute law (see p2:640) are available for your use. The AO is usually represented by a lawyer, so you should consider trying to obtain representation as well.

The commissioner may exclude members of the public if intimate personal or financial circumstances, or matters of public security are involved.[101] This is not usually necessary because it is rare for anyone not involved in the case to attend.

The decision

The decision is always given in writing[102] – often at some length – and it may be a few weeks before it is sent to you.

If the commissioner agrees that an SSAT's or a DAT's decision was wrong, the case is usually sent back to a differently constituted SSAT with directions as to how the tribunal should go about reconsidering the issues.[103] However, if the commissioner feels that the record of the decision of the original tribunal contains all the material facts, or s/he feels that it is expedient to make findings on any extra factual issues necessary to the decisions, the commissioner makes the final decision.[104] It is unusual for a commissioner not to send a case back to a tribunal if there is a dispute about facts not determined by the original tribunal, unless all the evidence points in one direction.[105]

If the commissioner agrees that a MAT's decision was wrong, the case is always sent back to a tribunal.[106] This must be a different tribunal than the one that heard your appeal originally, unless the commissioner says otherwise.[107]

What if you disagree with a commissioner's decision?

A commissioner's decision is final. However:

- a commissioner may correct or set aside her/his decision in the same way as a tribunal (see p2:626);[108]
- it can be **reviewed** in the normal way – eg, where your circumstances have changed since the decision was made or new facts have come to light (see pp2:570-575). However, where the commissioner made a mistake about the law you must appeal to a court (see below);
- you or the Benefits Agency can **appeal to the Court of Appeal** (in Scotland, the Court of Session) – see p2:637.

5. **Appealing to the courts**

Appeals from social security commissioners

You may appeal against a decision of a commissioner to the Court of Appeal (in Scotland, the Court of Session). You can only do this if there has been an error of law (see p2:632) and you must first obtain leave to appeal.[109]

The staff of the Court of Appeal do their best to be helpful, but the procedure in the court is strict, formal and far less flexible than the procedure before a tribunal or a commissioner. The Benefits Agency will certainly be represented by a barrister at the hearing. You should therefore obtain legal advice and apply for legal aid before appealing. If you live in England or

Wales and are unable to get help and have to represent yourself, you should telephone the Civil Appeals Office (part of the Court of Appeal in London) on 0171 936 6409/6916 and ask for a copy of the leaflet, *I want to appeal – what should I do?*, and then follow the instructions in that leaflet.

England and Wales

In England and Wales, the procedure is as follows.

- An application for leave to appeal to the Court of Appeal must first be made to a commissioner, in writing within three months of the date when you were sent the commissioner's decision. The commissioner may extend the time limit for special reasons (see p2:647).[110] If you do not apply to the commissioner within the time limit and the commissioner refuses to extend it, the Court of Appeal (or Court of Session) cannot hear your appeal and you can only proceed by applying to the High Court (in Scotland, the Court of Session) for judicial review of the refusal to grant a late appeal (see p2:637).[111]

- If the commissioner refuses to give you leave to appeal (for reasons other than being outside the time limit), you can apply direct to the Court of Appeal for leave.[112] Your notice of application should be lodged with the Civil Appeals Office within six weeks of being sent notification of the commissioner's refusal.[113] The court may extend the time but you must explain the reasons for your delay and file a sworn statement (called an 'affidavit') in support of an application for an extension of time.[114]

- Generally, the Court of Appeal first considers your application for leave to appeal without an oral hearing. If leave is refused, you may renew your application in open court by writing to the court office but must do this within seven days. Similarly, if leave is granted, the Chief Adjudication Officer or the Secretary of State has seven days in which to ask for an oral hearing.[115]

- If leave to appeal is granted by a commissioner or the Court of Appeal, you must serve a notice of appeal on the relevant parties. There are strict time limits for doing this.[116] The solicitor to the Benefits Agency will accept service at New Court, 48 Carey Street, London WC2A 2LS on behalf of the Chief Adjudication Officer or the Secretary of State (see Appendix 1 for the address).

- If the Court of Appeal refuses you leave to appeal after an oral hearing, you cannot appeal further, nor apply for a judicial review.

You cannot appeal to the Court of Appeal against a commissioner's refusal to grant you leave to appeal against a tribunal's decision, but you can apply to the High Court for judicial review of such a decision.[117]

Scotland

In Scotland the procedures for appealing to the Court of Session are similar but there are a number of crucial differences. In particular, some of the time limits are shorter:

- If the commissioner refuses you leave to appeal to the Court of Session you are only allowed 14 days from the date of notification to lodge a further application for leave to appeal with the Court of Session. This is a very short time limit. In practice, it means that if you want to appeal, you should consult a solicitor at the earliest opportunity and certainly before you apply to the commissioner for leave. If you wait until the commissioner refuses you leave before you seek legal advice it will probably be too late.
- If the commissioner grants you leave to appeal, the six-week time limit runs from the date the commissioner makes the decision, not the date on which it is notified to you.
- The Court of Session hears applications for leave to appeal in open court rather than making the decision simply by reading the papers as in England and Wales. The Benefits Agency often agrees that the application for leave and the appeal itself are heard at the same time.

The Chief Adjudication Officer or the Secretary of State has the same rights of appeal as you.

Applying for judicial review

Occasionally it is possible to challenge decisions with which you disagree by going to court for a judicial review. To do this, you need the services of a solicitor, law centre or legal advice centre.

For example, you can apply for judicial review of a decision made by:

- the Secretary of State (see p2:565) ;*or*
- a tribunal chair refusing to grant you leave to appeal (see p2:632); *or*
- a social security commissioner refusing to grant you leave to appeal (see p2:632); *or*
- a social fund officer or inspector refusing you a payment from the discretionary social fund (see Chapter 31); *or*
- a local authority housing benefit review board (see p2:592) about your claim for housing benefit or council tax benefit (see Chapters 25 and 27).

However, this procedure cannot usually be used if you have an independent right of appeal, such as against the decision of an adjudication officer or a social security appeal tribunal.

If you want to apply for judicial review of a local authority decision, see p2:596.

Meeting the cost of going to court

Legal aid does not cover representation before tribunals or even the commissioners. However, if you are on income support or income-based jobseeker's allowance or have a very low income, the Green Form scheme (in Scotland, the Pink Form scheme) for free legal advice and assistance may cover not only advice but also preparatory work for a hearing, such as obtaining medical reports and writing submissions. If you have a solicitor acting for you in an industrial injury claim against your employer, s/he may have medical and other reports and evidence which you can use for your benefit claim.

If you are not eligible for Green (or Pink) Form advice and assistance, or you want to be represented by a lawyer at a hearing, you are likely to have to pay. If your claim is worth hundreds of pounds, it may be a worthwhile investment. But, remember that many non-lawyer advisers know more about social security law than lawyers and their advice is usually free.

Legal aid *is* available for cases in the Court of Appeal, the High Court and the Court of Session and you should certainly obtain legal advice and representation for these. The legal aid authorities have, in the past, taken the view that an application to a commissioner for leave to appeal to the Court of Appeal cannot be covered by legal aid. However, it is arguable that such an application is a step 'preliminary to' proceedings in the Court of Appeal and is thus work for which legal aid is available.[118]

6. **How to prepare an appeal**

Appeals are taken on all sorts of issues so the advice given here can only be fairly general.

Appeals may concern disputes about facts or disputes about the law or both. You usually need to think about both the facts and the law because they are connected. The law tells you which facts are relevant and the facts tell you which bits of the law you need to consider. Always try, if possible, to link the facts of your case and your arguments to the rules laid down in the benefit regulations (see p2:641).

Sorting out the facts

You are likely to know more than anyone else about the facts of your case. Your key task is to pass your knowledge (and the knowledge of others who know something about the facts) on to the tribunal. A tribunal is a complete re-hearing of your case, so fresh facts and arguments can be put by either side.[119] Remember to:

- check through the appeal papers carefully to work out where there are disagreements between you and the Benefits Agency. This helps you decide what evidence you need to win your case;
- gather evidence to back up what you are saying (see below). If you want to give any evidence or information to the tribunal, send it to the clerk to the tribunal at least five days before your oral hearing. Otherwise the tribunal might decide to adjourn your appeal (see p2:624). The clerk sends a further copy to the adjudication officer or the Secretary of State who might then decide to support your appeal;
- ask any witnesses who support your case to attend the hearing. Both you and the Benefits Agency can ask witnesses to come and give information. Chairs do have the power to refuse to hear witnesses who are not relevant, but they should always be fair to you and generally allow witnesses to speak, even if it looks like they may have nothing useful to say.[120]

Evidence

Evidence consists of what you (and any witnesses) actually say at the hearing and any documents which you produce to support your appeal. Proving your case with additional evidence is useful but not essential.

The presenting officer (see p2:621) puts the Benefits' Agency's case at the tribunal but is rarely the person who actually made the decision in your case. The presenting officer's submissions are not evidence,[121] nor are comments made by another Benefits Agency officer if s/he did not make the decision on your claim.[122]

A tribunal cannot dismiss your verbal evidence without a proper explanation of why it has done so.[123]

The presenting officer can report what other people have said. This is called hearsay evidence. Tribunals can accept hearsay evidence, but they should carefully weigh up its value as proof, given that the person who originally made the statement is not present at the hearing. Most evidence relied on by the Benefits Agency is written and you can point out that you have not had the opportunity of questioning the witnesses. You are not entitled to insist on the presence of any particular witness,[124] but you should argue that the tribunal should not place any weight on the written evidence of, say, an interviewing officer if you are disputing the interview.

Written evidence

Written evidence includes letters of support, medical reports, wage slips, bank statements, birth certificates and anything else which helps to prove the facts. If, for example, the Benefits Agency says that you failed to disclose an increase in your earnings and you have been overpaid, you could explain to the tribunal how and when you told them, but it is even better to produce a copy of the letter which you sent informing them of the change.

Medical evidence

If you are getting medical evidence it is essential that it deals with the points in dispute if that is possible. Sometimes, a doctor might not know much about the effect of a disability on your everyday life, in which case your evidence or that of a friend or relative may well be of more use. Where a medical report is required, there are two ways of obtaining one, apart from simply writing to the doctor yourself. Either a solicitor can obtain one for you or the tribunal can refer you for an examination and obtain a report if the medical issue in your case is one of 'special difficulty'.[125] If the lack of a report is causing you difficulties at a tribunal hearing, you could remind the tribunal of this power to obtain one itself.

You may have problems at the hearing if your opinion about the effect of your illhealth or disabilities is contradicted by evidence from an examining doctor or your own GP. It is well established that your own evidence to the tribunal does not require any corroboration and should be accepted unless there is a strong reason for not doing so.[126] But this does not assist you where there is a conflict of evidence, with you taking one view and the doctor another. The tribunal might say that the evidence of the doctor should be preferred to yours, as you have a direct interest in the outcome of the proceedings and any doctor does not.[127] If relevant, you should point out that the doctor's reports were written after only a limited examination and discussion. If your GP does not know much about your day to day living activities or walking abilities you should say so. You should seek further medical evidence in support of your view in advance of the hearing if you foresee any such conflict of evidence.

Checking the law

The Benefits Agency does not always get the law right and you should emphasise a point that it has overlooked. If you know what the law says, you know what facts you have to prove.

The primary sources of social security law are statute law (see below) and case law decided by commissioners and the courts (see p2:641). It is fairly easy to find both sorts of law once you know what you are looking for. The footnotes in this *Handbook* are intended to point you in the right direction. You should also look carefully at the Benefits Agency's submission (see p2:618), as that refers to the statute law and caselaw which it thinks is relevant. There are also a number of books which can help by explaining the law and referring you to relevant legislation and cases (see Appendix 3).

Statute law

The law consists of Acts of Parliament and regulations. The Acts of Parliament which set out the basic rules of entitlement to the benefits in this *Handbook* are:

- the Social Security Contributions and Benefits Act 1992; *and*
- the Jobseekers Act 1995.

The Acts of Parliament which set out the rules on how the benefit scheme is administered are:
- the Social Security Administration Act 1992; *and*
- the Social Security Act 1998.

The Acts set out the main framework and empower the Secretary of State to make regulations covering the details. These regulations are known as 'statutory instruments'. Appendix 13 contains a list of Acts and regulations.

The best way to look up the relevant statute law is to read one of the annotated volumes of legislation:
- *CPAG's Income Related Benefits: The Legislation*, edited by Mesher and Wood if your appeal relates to income support, income-based jobseeker's allowance, family credit or disability working allowance or payments from the regulated social fund;
- *Medical and Disability Tribunals: The Legislation* edited by Rowland if your appeal relates to severe disablement allowance, disability living allowance, attendance allowance or industrial injuries benefits;
- *CPAG's Non-Means-Tested Benefits: The Legislation*, edited by Bonner *et al* if your appeal relates to the other benefits covered by this *Handbook*.

In these books, the law is set out with a helpful commentary which explains the rules and often explains how they have been interpreted by the commissioners and the courts. Details of these books are in Appendix 3.

In rare cases, the books do not contain all the regulations that are relevant. If so, you can purchase the regulations individually from the Stationery Office. However, the Acts and regulations are amended from time to time and this can lead to difficulties when you are trying to discover the current state of the law or chase up a reference. Unless your appeal is an old one and the law has changed since the relevant time, it is usually much easier to refer to the loose-leaf book, *The Law Relating to Social Security*. This is in 10 volumes – the 'Blue Volumes' or the 'Blue Books'. Most large reference libraries have a copy. In addition, your local Benefits Agency office has a copy which you are allowed to look at free of charge.[128] Make sure that it is up-to-date.

Benefit laws are complicated and the staff who administer benefits are issued with **guidance** manuals and circulars. However, the Benefits Agency and tribunals are only bound by what the law says, not by the guidance. Nevertheless, it is sometime useful to check out the guidance.

Caselaw

When a commissioner or a court decides an appeal, the decision sets what is known as a precedent. An adjudication officer, adjudicating medical authority, social security appeal tribunal, medical appeal tribunal or disability appeal tribunal deciding a similar case must follow that precedent.[129] Unreported decisions (see below) must be followed by appeal tribunals in the same way as reported ones (see below).[130] Sometimes commissioners' decisions conflict. To help you decide which cases to use, see p2:643.

All commissioners' decisions have file numbers. One example is CU/255/1984. The last numbers indicate the year in which the appeal was lodged. The second letter indicates the type of benefit involved in the decision. See below for the full list. An extra 'S' or 'W' after a 'C' denotes a Scottish or Welsh case, as in CWG/3/1978. Some decisions are 'starred' by the commissioner if, for example, they deal with an important issue or with an aspect of benefit law for the first time.

Each year, the most important cases are chosen to be reported by the Chief Commissioner. These are published by the Stationery Office and are called 'reported decisions'. They are given a new number – eg, CU/255/1984 became R(U) 3/86. All reported cases since 1951 begin with an 'R'. Again, the second letter denotes the type of benefit. The last numbers indicate the year in which the case was decided.

Commissioners' decisions references

A	attendance allowance
CR	compensation recovery
DLA	disability living allowance
DWA	disability working allowance
F	child benefit (and family allowance – now abolished)
FC	family credit
FIS	family income supplement
G	general (all benefits not covered in other categories)
I	industrial injuries benefits
IB	incapacity benefit
IS	income support
JSA	jobseeker's allowance
M	mobility allowance
P	retirement pensions
S	severe disablement allowance (and sickness and invalidity benefit – now abolished)
SB	supplementary benefit
SMP	statutory maternity pay
SSP	statutory sick pay
U	unemployment benefit (now abolished)

Getting commissioners' decisions

Individual reported decisions may be purchased from the Stationery Office, as may bound volumes, although all the early ones are out of print. However, each local Benefits Agency office has a set which you are allowed to look at.

Unreported decisions may be purchased from the Office of the Social Security Commissioners (see Appendix 1). Some decisions are available on the internet at http://www.hywels.demon.co.uk/commrs/decns.htm. If an unreported decision is to be used at a tribunal hearing by the Benefits Agency, a copy should be supplied to you. Similarly, if you wish to use one, you should supply copies to everyone, preferably by sending one to the tribunal clerk in advance of the hearing.

Summaries of all reported commissioners' decisions and most 'starred decisions' (see p2:642) are published in CPAG's *Welfare Rights Bulletin*.

It is worth checking the decisions referred to by the Benefits Agency. Sometimes, they rely on part of a decision only and fail to mention another part which is more favourable to you. To find other cases relevant to your own, you can use the footnotes in this guide or any of the books listed in Appendix 3.

Which cases to use

Caselaw can seem less precise than statute law (see p2:640) and frequently cases seem to contradict each other. Very often there are small differences in the facts of the cases which justify the different results. You need to find cases where the facts are similar to yours. If cases appear to be against you, look at the facts of those cases and see whether any differences justify a different decision in your case. This is known as 'distinguishing' cases. One distinction may simply be that what seemed reasonable in the 1950s does not seem fair in the 1990s.[131] It should also be remembered that most appeals before April 1987 were decided when there was a right of appeal to commissioners on questions of fact as well as law so tribunals may not necessarily be erring in law if they take a different view from a commissioner.

Where there is an irreconcilable conflict between two or more cases, a tribunal has to choose which decision to follow. It normally follows a reported decision in preference to an unreported one, and must follow a decision of a Tribunal of Commissioners in preference to a decision of a single commissioner.[132] Decisions of the House of Lords, the Court of Appeal or of the High Court on an application for judicial review (or, in Scotland, the Court of Session) take precedence over all commissioners' decisions.[133]

Commissioners have more freedom and do not have to follow the decision of another single commissioner if satisfied that the earlier decision was wrong.[134] However, a single commissioner must follow a decision of a Tribunal of Commissioners although, if s/he thinks it may be wrong, s/he can ask the Chief Commissioner to appoint another tribunal to reconsider the

56

Chapter 56: Appeals
6. How to prepare an appeal
. . . .

point. A Tribunal of Commissioners does not have to follow the decision of another tribunal but usually does so.[135]

Debates in Parliament

Where the statute law (see p2:640) is ambiguous, the courts – which includes tribunals and commissioners – can look at statements made to Parliament by ministers when the law was first made.[136] It may therefore be worth checking the House of Commons and House of Lords official reports (known as 'Hansard') to see what was said in Parliament when the rules were first introduced. The House of Commons Public Information Office publishes a book called 'PHIL' (Parliamentary Holdings in Libraries in Britain and Ireland) which tells you the nearest library in which you can find *Hansard*. Unfortunately PHIL costs £10 but your local library may have a copy even if it does not have Hansard as well. If you want more detailed help, ring the House of Commons Public Information Office on 0171 219 4272. You can also find *Hansard* on the internet at http://www.parliament.the-stationery-office-office.co.uk/pa/cm/cmhansrd.htm.

Hansard can be a confusing publication. You need the volumes which deal with parliamentary debates and written answers rather than those covering the proceedings of standing committees. Then each volume has two sets of numbering; one for parliamentary debates and one for written answers. There are two columns on each page, each of which has a separate number, so, for example, a single volume may have two columns numbered 609. The best way of finding what you want is to use the comprehensive index which is updated fortnightly. Again, references in the index are to column numbers and those relating to Written Answers are prefixed by the letter 'W'. The ones you may need for your appeal are the ones which relate to parliamentary debates and have no prefixes.

Presenting your case to the tribunal

Each case is different and hearings are informal so there is no set pattern for presenting cases.

It is a good idea to send in any detailed submission and medical reports before the hearing. Some claimants like to use a written submission at the hearing and to read directly from it. However, tribunals usually ask questions so it is necessary to be able to talk about your case without the script.

It is helpful to make it clear at the beginning which bits of the Benefits Agency's submission are in dispute. It is, then, usually best to tell the tribunal about the facts first and to call any witnesses before turning to legal arguments.

It is the tribunal's job to help you to say everything you want by putting you at your ease and asking the right questions. If you forget to say something when it is your turn to speak, do not hesitate to add it at the end of the hearing.

Advice and representation

There are a number of agencies which can advise you about social security matters and can help you prepare your case for the tribunal hearing. Some can also represent you at hearings if you feel that someone else can put your case better than you can yourself. See Appendix 2 for more information.

7. **Late appeals**

If you miss the time limit for lodging an appeal, the chair of the tribunal to which you are appealing or the commissioner (if you are appealing from a tribunal) can still allow the appeal to go ahead in certain circumstances. The rules are different depending on whether you are appealing to a tribunal (see below) or a commissioner (see p2:646) – the rules for making a late appeal to a tribunal are much more strict.

Note: The late appeal rules are due to change when the Social Security Act 1998 takes effect (see p2:651).

Late appeals to tribunals

You need the chair of an appeal tribunal's permission to appeal if you miss the three months' time limit (see p2:615) and this is extremely difficult to get. It is often simpler to ask for a review of the adjudication officer's decision instead of making a late appeal, so long as there are grounds for review and this would give you everything to which you are entitled (see p2:570). However, you often get less arrears of benefit if you seek a review (see p2:576).

The chair of an appeal tribunal can only accept a late appeal if:[137]
- your appeal is likely to succeed; *and*
- it is in the 'interests of justice' to do so (see below).

Even if you meet the two conditions above, a late appeal cannot be accepted if it is more than six years since the decision you want to appeal against was made.[138] It is considered to be in the 'interests of justice' to allow a late appeal if:[139]
- there are special reasons which are 'wholly exceptional' and relate to the history and facts of your case; *and*
- the special reasons are sufficiently strong to give you a reasonable excuse for your delay in appealing; *and*
- the special reasons have existed since your deadline for appealing expired (see p2:615).

In addition to the information you must provide on your appeal form (see p2:615) you must explain the special reasons why your appeal is late (see p2:645).[140] The longer you have delayed in appealing, the more compelling the special reasons have to be. See p2:647 for information about what might count as a special reason.

When deciding if there are special reasons, the chair cannot take account of the fact that:[141]

- a court or a commissioner has interpreted the law in a different way than previously understood and applied;
- you (or your adviser) misunderstood or were unaware of the relevant law, including the time limits for appealing.

You must be notified of the chair's decision as soon as is practicable, and must be sent written reasons for it if you ask for these in writing within three months.[142]

You cannot appeal against the refusal of the chair to accept a late appeal,[143] but you can ask the chair to look at her/his decision again, or you may be able to apply to the High Court for judicial review if the decision is clearly unreasonable (see p2:637).

Note: The six-year absolute time limit for appealing (see p2:615) will be reduced to one year when the Social Security Act 1998 takes effect (see p2:651).

Late appeals to commissioners

If you want to make a late appeal to the commissioner then you need to show that there are special reasons why you should be allowed to do so.

In this context – and in contrast to late appeals to tribunals – potentially anything can count as a special reason as long as it is special enough! In particular, special reasons do not have to relate to why the appeal was late[144] (although they may do so). See below for information about what might count as a special reason.

The decision whether or not to allow a late appeal must be made bearing in mind the merits of the appeal and the consequences for the claimant (and the Benefits Agency). The rules should be interpreted liberally, so you do not suffer unfairly.[145] If a commissioner refuses you permission for a late appeal, you do not have a right of appeal against the decision. However, if you ask her/him to look at it again because there is something which is relevant and which s/he did not consider before, s/he may – but does not have to – do so. The only other possible remedy is judicial review (see p2:637) but this may be difficult because, unlike a tribunal chair, a commissioner does not have to give reasons for her/his decision and almost certainly will not do so.[146]

Special reasons

What may or may not be a special reason cannot be defined in advance. It depends on the circumstances of each case and the commissioner or tribunal chair has to make her or his decision on an individual, case by case basis.

You should stress reasons which are personal to you. Leave to appeal is sometimes refused because the reasons given are general ones – ie, ones which apply in a large number of cases – rather than special ones which apply to you specifically.

There are no hard and fast rules about what should be taken into account but the following are obviously relevant.

The reasons for delay

Where possible, explaining the delay is an important part of any application for a late appeal. Do not be worried if some or all of the delay is your fault – almost any explanation is better than none at all. The worst situation is where you have known of the time limit but simply ignored it, but even then it may be possible to say something favourable. Say if things have been difficult at home or you were confused by the rules or just assumed that the Benefits Agency were the experts and had got it right. You should have special reasons for a late appeal if:

- you made a reasonable mistake in calculating the time limit;
- you did not receive the decision;
- you posted your appeal in time but it went astray in the post;
- a mistake was made by your advisers. It should not make any difference that you might be able to sue your advisers for negligence. Professional advisers are not normally negligent and if yours does make an error then that is special to your case;[147]
- you were ill. Applications based on illness should be supported by medical evidence where possible;
- you were given wrong advice or otherwise misled by the Benefits Agency. Many claimants are discouraged from appealing by Benefits Agency officers who advise them incorrectly that any appeal would be doomed to failure. If you have been badly advised by the Benefits Agency and lose money because you are refused a late appeal you should consider claiming compensation (see Chapter 57).

The length of the delay

The less delay there has been the easier it is to justify it, but even a short delay may be too long unless there is either a good reason for it or some other factor which outweighs it. Time limits are meant to be observed. However, there have been cases where leave has been granted five years[148] and even 20 years out of time.

The merits of your appeal

The more likely your appeal is to succeed, the greater the injustice in refusing to allow an extension of time. A strong case is particularly useful if there has been a very long delay and leave is usually granted where there has been a 'clear error' which would have long-term continuing effects unless corrected.[149]

The amount of money at stake

Even if there has been no clear error, leave may be granted if there is a lot of money at stake.[150]

A decision in a test case

The fact that there has been a decision in a test case which establishes that an earlier decision was incorrect can amount to a special reason at least in some circumstances.[151] In any case, if there are other reasons why a late appeal should be granted (see above) these should be emphasised as well as the decision in the test case. Such appeals often involve large sums of money and (given the test case) a clear error in the decision which is being appealed against. Both of these have been accepted as special reasons in other contexts – usually when it is the Benefits Agency which wishes to appeal late rather than you.

8. **The Social Security Act 1998**

As part of its plan to develop a modern, integrated benefit system, the Government is changing the procedures for decision making, reviews and appeals. This section covers the rules on appeals where these are changing. For information about decision making and reviews see pp2:581-587.

When this handbook was written,the regulations had just been laid before Parliament. This chapter is written on the assumption that they become law. See CPAG's *Welfare Rights Bulletin* for updates.

Under the new rules, there will no longer be adjudication officers (AOs) or social fund officers. All decision making powers will be transferred to the Secretary of State. However, you will be able to appeal against some of his decisions (see p2:649) to a tribunal.

The existing types of tribunal will be unified into one. The administration of appeals will pass to the Secretary of State. The Independent Tribunal Service will be renamed the Appeals Service in 1999. When the Social Security Act 1998 is fully implemented, the Appeals Service will consist of:
- an executive Agency headed by a Chief Executive who will be responsible for the administration of appeals; *and*

- the independent panel of members which will be appointed by the Lord Chancellor and headed by the President.

The present system for reviewing decisions will be replaced with powers to 'revise' or 'supersede' decisions (see pp2:582-585). If you disagree with a Secretary of State decision, you will be able to seek a 'revision' (see p2:582) prior to appealing. This is not compulsory. So if you are appealing about attendance allowance, disability living allowance or disability working allowance, unlike at present, you will be able to appeal straightaway without having to seek a review.

If you want to seek a 'revision' or appeal against a decision you should not delay. The time limit for these is one month (see pp2:584 and 2:651). For information about how an application for a 'revision' could affect your appeal rights and the time limit for appealing, see p2:650.

When do the new rules take effect?

When the new rules take effect depends on the benefit you are claiming. See the implementation timetable[152] below for further information. At the time this *Handbook* was written, it was not clear what the transitional arrangements would be. See CPAG's *Welfare Rights Bulletin* for updates.

Benefit	*Rules take effect*
Child support	1 June 1999
Child benefit, guardian's allowance, industrial injuries benefits	5 July 1999
Retirement pension, widows' benefits, IB, SDA (this is intended to cover all 'incapacity for work decisions'), maternity allowance,	6 September 1999
FC, DWA and tax credits	5 October 1999
JSA, DLA, AA, ICA, credits of contributions or earnings home responsibilities protection, vaccine damage payments	18 October 1999
IS and the social fund and all other purposes	29 November 1999

Appeal rights

You will be able to appeal to a tribunal against some decisions of the Secretary of State.[153] The types of decision which can be appealed are the types currently made by AOs (see p2:561).[154] You can appeal against an original decision or a decision made after an application for a revision or a supersession (see pp5:582 and 2:585). In addition, you will be able to appeal against some decisions about your national insurance contributions.

You must be given a written notice of any decision against which you can appeal, including information on your right of appeal and your right to request a statement of reasons.[155] If the written notice does not include a statement of reasons you can request one within one month.[156] The Secretary of State must provide the statement of reasons within 14 days of your request.[157]

Revisions and appeals

You may wish to seek a revision (see pp2:582) before you appeal. Seeking a revision will be simpler and you could receive a decision more quickly. You also get two bites at the cherry because, if your application for a revision is turned down, you can always appeal against the new decision (or the original decision if you are still within the time limit). You do not have to seek a revision and can appeal straightaway. However, if the Secretary of State agrees that the decision is wrong, he might revise it anyway and your appeal could lapse (see below).

Example

Lindsey fails the 'all-work' test (see p2:22) and her incapacity benefit ceases. She asks the Benefits Agency to revise the decision to stop her benefit because her GP has told her to refrain from work. The Benefits Agency considers the new medical evidence but refuses to revise its decision. Lindsey can appeal against the new decision.

There are some important problems you must bear in mind:

- The time limit for appealing (one month – see p2:651) will continue to run while the Secretary of State considers your application for a revision of the original decision. However, when the Secretary of State makes his decision, you can appeal against it.
- Your appeal will lapse if the Secretary of State revises the original decision after you appeal, even if you do not get everything you want.[158] This could happen if you seek a revision, or if the Secretary of State decides one is needed himself. If your appeal lapses, you must make a fresh appeal. Your appeal will only lapse where the new decision is more advantageous to you than the original decision,[159] that is, the decision:
  - awards you benefit at a higher rate or for a longer period;
  - lifts a refusal or disqualification of benefit or a JSA sanction either in whole or in part;
  - reverses a decision to pay benefit to a third party;
  - means you gain financially from the revised decision;
  - says an overpayment of benefit is not recoverable or that less should be recovered.[160]

If the new decision is not more advantageous to you, your appeal against the original decision will have to go ahead. Your appeal is against the revised decision.[161] You have one month from the date the decision is sent to you to make further representations.[162] At the end of that period (or earlier if you agree in writing), the appeal proceeds unless the Secretary of State revises the decision again in a more advantageous way.[163]

Time limit for appealing

The time limit for appealing is to be reduced to one month.[164] If a statement of reasons is requested, you have a further 14 days from the end of that month within which to appeal.[165] If the Secretary of State revises, refuses to revise or supersedes a decision (see pp2:582 and 2:585) the one-month time limit will run from the date you are sent the new decision.[166]

If you miss the time limit, you will be able to:
- make a late appeal in limited circumstances (see below). However, you will not be able to appeal outside of an absolute time limit;
- make a late application for a revision in limited circumstances (see p2:582).

If neither is possible, you will still be able to ask for a supersession if you can show there are grounds (see p2:585).

Late appeals

If you appeal outside the time limit (see p2:651) a late appeal can be allowed in limited circumstances. No appeal can be allowed outside the absolute time limit. This is one year from the date your time limit for appeal (see p2:651) expired.[167] You must write explaining your reasons for lateness and making it clear which decision you are appealing against.[168] A decision to allow a late appeal must be considered by a legally qualified panel member.

A late appeal can only be allowed if the appeal has reasonable prospects of success and it is 'in the interests of justice' for it to be allowed late.[169] It can only be in the interests of justice to allow a late appeal if it was not practicable for you to appeal in time because of one of the following special circumstances:[170]
- you, your spouse or a dependant has died or suffered serious illness;
- you are not resident in the UK;
- normal postal services were disrupted; or
- there are other special circumstances which are 'wholly exceptional'.

The longer you have delayed appealing, the more compelling the circumstances need to be.[171] When deciding if it is in the 'interests of justice' to allow your application, the panel member cannot take account of the fact that:
- a court or commissioner has interpreted the law in a different way than previously understood and applied;
- you (or your adviser) misunderstood or were unaware of the relevant law, including the time limits for appealing.[172] You must be sent a written summary of the panel member's decision as soon as practicable.[173] You

cannot appeal against the refusal to allow your late appeal[174] but you can ask the panel member to look at it again or you may be able to apply to the High Court for judicial review if the decision is clearly unreasonable.

How to appeal

An appeal must be in writing, normally on the appropriate form. Even if you do not use the correct form, the Secretary of State (as opposed to the chair of the tribunal) will be able to accept your appeal, so long as it contains all the information required, including:

- your arguments for saying the decision was wrong; *and*
- enough details about the decision with which you disagree for it to be identified.

The appeal must be signed by you or, if you have provided written authority, by your representative.[175]

If your appeal does not contain sufficient information, the DSS says the Secretary of State will be able to ask for this and give you an extra 14 days to provide it.[176] If you fail to do so, your appeal will be forwarded to the Appeals Service. A legally qualified panel member decides if it has been made properly and can therefore be accepted.[177] Up to the time a decision is made, any further details you send must be passed to the Appeals Service for consideration.[178]

If the appellant dies, the Secretary of State may appoint some other person to proceed with the appeal. A grant of probate or letter of administration to the appeal has no effect.[179]

Oral and paper hearings

As currently, you will have to opt for an oral hearing (see p2:617). It is important that you reply to the letter asking whether you want an oral hearing within 14 days. If you do not do so, your appeal may be struck out (see p2:653).[180] You will be given at least 14 days' notice of the oral hearing[181] (unless you waive your right to this).

Postponements and adjournments

Clerks to the tribunal and legally qualified panel members will be able to **postpone** hearings if you request this in writing, stating the reasons.[182] If you are refused a postponement, you will be given written notice and your request and the refusal will be put to a tribunal.[183] Clerks and chairs can postpone an oral hearing even if this is not requested.[184]

Even if an oral hearing is under way, it can to be adjourned if you or the DSS wants this to happen, or if the tribunal itself thinks this is the best course.[185] If the hearing which has been adjourned is heard by a differently constituted tribunal, there must be a complete rehearing of the case.[186]

When can a chair strike out your appeal?

Your appeal may be struck out for one of the following reasons:[187]
- if it is 'misconceived', ie, if it is 'frivolous or vexatious' or 'obviously unsustainable and has no prospect of success';[188]
- if you did not have a right to appeal against the decision (see p2:649) or the tribunal does not have what is known as 'jurisdiction' to deal with it and you have been informed that it might be struck out:
  - for want of prosecution, including where you have not appealed within the absolute time limit;
  - if you fail to comply with a direction given to you by the chair or clerk to the tribunal, for example, a request to provide information to support your appeal. This could include where you fail to reply to the letter asking you if you want an oral or paper hearing within 14 days. You must be told that a failure to comply could lead to the appeal being struck out.

Procedure for striking out

If your appeal is being struck out for any reason other than that it is 'misconceived', this can be done by a clerk to the tribunal. You can apply for your appeal to be reinstated.

If your appeal is considered to be misconceived, however, it can only be struck out by a legally qualified panel member. The panel member must give you warning of the intention to strike out and tell you the reasons for this. Within 14 days of the notice being sent, you must tell the tribunal clerk in writing whether you wish the question to be considered as a preliminary issue at an oral hearing or whether you are happy for the tribunal to consider the question on the papers. If the issue is to be considered on the papers, you must provide written reasons why your appeal is not misconceived.[189] If you fail to respond within the 14 days, your appeal may be struck out. If the appeal tribunal decides that your appeal should not be struck out, it refers the appeal to the Secretary of State, giving reasons why it is not misconceived. The Secretary of State can either revise or supersede the decision or refer it to a tribunal for a decision.[190]

Reinstating appeals

If your appeal is struck out, you may be able to get it reinstated. You have to ask for this to happen within one month of it being struck out. A legally qualified panel member can reinstate the appeal if:[191]
- you have provided further information and there are reasonable grounds for reinstatement;
- s/he is satisfied that you did not receive warning that your appeal might be struck out;
- it is not an appeal which is out of the tribunal's jurisdiction;

- it should not have been struck out for failure to comply with a direction or for want of prosecution; *or*
- it is not in the interests of justice for the appeal to be struck out.

Withdrawal of an appeal

You or your representative (if you have one) can withdraw your appeal either at an oral hearing or, at any time before your appeal is decided, by giving notice in writing.[192]

Tribunal procedures

There will no longer be a range of different types of tribunal to hear different sorts of appeals. Appeals formerly heard by disability appeal tribunals (see p2:627), medical appeal tribunals (see p2:629), social security appeal tribunals (see p2:630), vaccine damage tribunals and child support appeal tribunals will be heard by a 'unified' tribunal.

The tribunal members

Tribunals will be made up of one, two or three members.[193] The people who hear your appeal will be drawn from a panel of doctors, lawyers, people with an experience of disability and people with financial expertise (eg, accountants).[194] One member of the tribunal must be legally qualified. The type of tribunal appropriate to hear a particular type of appeal will be set out in the rules.[195] These are as follows:

- A three-member tribunal will hear disability living allowance and attendance allowance (see Chapter 10) appeals (a lawyer, a doctor and a person with experience of disability).[196]
- A two-member tribunal (a lawyer and a doctor) will hear appeals about:[197]
  - whether you are incapable of work (see p2:15) (at the time of writing it was not clear whether this will apply only to incapacity benefit and severe disablement allowance);
  - whether you have an industrial disease and the extent of your disablement (see p1:216);
  - whether you are disabled for the purpose of your claim for disability working allowance (see Chapter 22), industrial injuries benefits (see Chapter 11) or severe disablement allowance(see Chapter 4);
  - recovery of benefits from personal injuries compensation (see p2:508);
- A two-member tribunal (a lawyer and a financial expert) will hear appeals involving difficult financial issues, such as profit and loss accounts, balance sheets and the accounts of trust funds. Only complex cases will be dealt with in this way.
- A one-member tribunal (a lawyer) will hear all other appeals.

Where a tribunal has more than one member, the chair will have the casting vote.[198]

If the tribunal feels that your appeal involves a particularly difficult point, it can ask another member of the panel (see above) – known as an 'expert' – to assist.[199] The expert can either be asked to attend at the hearing and give evidence or provide a written report. Any written report should be sent to every party to the proceedings. The expert will not be able to take part in making the decision.

Ensure your appeal is heard by the right tribunal by providing information on your appeal form (see p2:652). The Government has said that you will be able to make representations if you think your appeal is to be heard by an inappropriately constituted tribunal, but there is no guarantee that these will be taken into account unless you can show that the rules about composition of tribunals have not been correctly applied.

Note: Some appeals are already being heard by one- and two-member tribunals. See p2:654 for further information.

Procedure at an oral hearing

Tribunals will not be obliged to consider issues that are 'not raised by' your appeal.[200] It is not yet clear what this means. You should certainly argue that an issue should be considered if:
- it is in the appeal papers;
- it was raised in subsequent representations;
- the evidence before the tribunal should lead it to believe that it is relevant to your appeal.

Tribunals cannot look 'down to the date of the hearing' (see p2:623) if you appealed to a disability appeal tribunal (see p2:627) or a social security appeal tribunal (see p2:630) on or after 21 May 1998. This rule will apply to tribunals (see p2:629) when the Social Security Act 1998 takes effect (see p2:648).

Tribunals cannot carry out physical examinations unless the case related to the assessment of disablement for severe disablement allowance and industrial injuries benefits.[201]

If a test case decision is pending

If a test case is pending (see p2:581), the Secretary of State will be able to suspend payment of your benefit or even postpone making a decision about your claim (see p2:587).[202] This means you will not be able to appeal until a decision is made about the test case.

But what happens if you have already appealed? Where a decision is pending in a test case against a commissioner or court decision and you have appealed to a tribunal or commissioner in a 'look alike' case, the Secretary of State will be able to serve notice requiring the tribunal or commissioner in your appeal:[203]

- not to make a decision in your appeal and refer the case back to him (s/he could then postpone making a decision – see p2:587);
- postpone making a decision until the test case is decided; *or*
- decide your appeal as if the test case had been decided in the way most unfavourable to you, but only if this is in your interests. If this happens, and the test case goes in your favour, the Secretary of State will have to make a new decision superseding (see p2:585) the decision of the tribunal or commissioner in the light of the decision in the test case.[204]

If the decision on your claim or appeal has been postponed, once a decision has been made in the test case, the Secretary of State, the tribunal or the commissioner will then make the decision.

The tribunal's decision

As under the current rules, the DSS says that the tribunal will have to give you a decision notice confirming its decision (see p2:656). You will be able to ask for a copy of the reasons for the tribunal's decision (see p2:656), but have to do this within one month.[205] You can apply for a statement of reasons outside this time limit in the same limited circumstances in which late appeals can be allowed (see p2:651) except that if your application was delayed by other special circumstances these do not have to be 'wholly exceptional'. There is an absolute time limit of three months.[206] A record of tribunal proceedings (sufficient to indicate the evidence taken) is kept by the tribunal clerk for six months. You can ask for a copy within that period.[207]

Setting aside the tribunal's decision

Tribunals can currently set aside a tribunal's decision where it appears it would be just to do so and there has been some procedural difficulty (see p2:626). This will still be the case.[208] However, there will be a further situation when a tribunal's decision can be set aside.

If you seek the permission of a tribunal chair to appeal to the Commissioner (see p2:633) the tribunal chair:

- *may* set aside the tribunal decision if s/he thinks that the tribunal made an 'error of law' (see p2:632);[209]
- *must* set aside the tribunal decision if you and the Benefits Agency agree that the tribunal made an 'error of law' (see p2:632).[210] Commissioners already have the discretion to do this in similar circumstances when applications for leave to appeal are made directly to them (see p2:633).

Your appeal will then be referred back to be heard by another tribunal.

Appealing to the commissioner

You will still be able to appeal to a commissioner if a tribunal has made an error of law (see p2:632 for a definition and pp2:632-635 for further information). However, the time limit for seeking leave to appeal (see p2:632) is reduced to one month starting on the date you are sent the written statement of reasons for the tribunal decision. Outside this time limit, an application for leave can be considered if a legally qualified panel member thinks there are special reasons for doing so.[211] There is an absolute time limit of one year from the date the one-month limit expired.

If you want someone to help you with your appeal you should therefore seek advice *immediately*. If you send further representations in after the time limit has expired, these must be taken into account if a decision on your application has not yet been made.[212] Where the Secretary of State applies for leave you are sent a copy of the application and have a month in which to make representations.[213]

Note: If you and the Benefits Agency agree that the tribunal made an error of law (see p2:622), commissioners already have the discretion to refer your appeal back to be heard by another tribunal (see p2:635).

Notes

• •

References are to statutes and regulations as amended up to 8 March 1999. All regulations are (General) Regulations unless otherwise stated. There is a full list of abbreviations in Appendix 13.

1. **Appeal rights**
   1 Reg 3(5A) SS(Adj) Regs
   2 para 1003, Code of Appeals Procedure
   3 Reg 3(7) SS(Adj) Regs
   4 R(SB) 29/83; R(SB) 12/89; CIS/807/1992
   5 **IS & JSA** Reg 55(7) SS(Adj) Regs **Other benefits** Reg 18 SS(Adj) Regs
   6 s45 SSAA 1992
   7 Reg 37 SS(Adj) Regs
   8 Reg 3 and Sch 2 SS(Adj) Regs; CIS/550/1993
   9 Reg 3(6C) SS(Adj) Regs
   10 Reg 3(6) and (6B) SS(Adj) Regs
   11 Reg 3(6A) SS(Adj) Regs
   12 Reg 3(5) SS(Adj) Regs
   13 **SSATs** Reg 22(1A) SS(Adj) Regs **DATs** Reg 29(1A) SS(Adj) Regs **MATs** Reg 38(1A) SS(Adj) Regs
   14 **SSATs** s29 SSAA 1992 **DATs** s32(7) SSAA 1992
   15 Reg 4(2B) SS(Adj) Regs
   16 **SSATs** Reg 22(1) SS(Adj) Regs **DATs** Reg 29(1) SS(Adj) Regs **MATs** Reg 38(1A/SS(Adj) Regs
   17 **SSATs** Reg 22(1C) SS(Adj) Regs **DATs** Reg 29(1C) SS(Adj) Regs **MATs** Reg 38(1C) SS(Adj) Regs
   18 Reg 2(1)(b) SS(Adj) Regs
   19 para 38(1) *Social Security Appeal Tribunals: A guide to procedure*, TSO
   20 Sch 2 para 7 SSAA 1992
   21 Reg 2(1)(aa) and (ab) SS(Adj) Regs
   22 Regs 4(2A) and 7 SS(Adj) Regs
   23 Reg 7 SS(Adj) Regs
   24 Reg 7(3) SS(Adj) Regs
   25 R(IS) 5/94
   26 Reg 6(2) and (2A) SS(Adj) Regs
   27 R(IS) 5/94
   28 Reg 4(2) SS(Adj) Regs
   29 Reg 4(3A) SS(Adj) Regs
   30 Reg 5(1) SS(Adj) Regs
   31 Reg 4(3) SS(Adj) Regs
   32 CDLA/3680/1997
   33 CIS/566/1991; CS/99/1993
   34 Reg 4(4) SS(Adj) Regs

2. **Tribunal procedures**
   35 s41 SSAA 1992
   36 para 05328 AOG
   37 CM/527/1992
   38 s55(2) SSAA 1992
   39 CDLA/21/1994 qualified by CM/2/1994
   40 s55(1) SSAA 1992; reg 30 SS(Adj) Regs
   41 ITS President's Circular No.1 para 9, June 1997
   42 ITS President's Circular No.4, June 1997
   43 CS/12054/1996, CIB/14430/1996 and CIS/12015/1996(T)
   44 **SSATs** s22(8) SSAA 1992 **DATs** s33(7) SSAA 1992 **Both** Sch 6 para 3 SSA 1998
   45 President's Circular No.15, July 1998
   46 R(SB) 4/85
   47 CIS/643A/1992
   48 President's Circulars No.1 and No.9, June 1997
   49 **SSATs** Reg 22(3) SS(Adj) Regs **MATs** Reg 38(2) SS(Adj) Regs **DATs** Reg 29(3) SS(Adj) Regs
   50 CSIS/118/1990; CSIS/110/1991
   51 **SSATs** Reg 23(3) SS(Adj) Regs **MATs** Reg 38(5) SS(Adj) Regs **DATs** Reg 29(6) SS(Adj) Regs
   52 **SSATs** Reg 24(1)(b) SS(Adj) Regs **MATs** Reg 39(1)(b) SS(Adj) Regs **DATs** Reg 32(1)(b) SS(Adj) Regs
   53 **SSATs** Reg 23(3A) SS(Adj) Regs **MATs** Reg 38(5A) SS(Adj) Regs **DATs** Reg 29(6A) SS(Adj) Regs
   54 CIS/3299/1997; CDLA/5793/1997
   55 CDLA/16902/1996

56 **SSATs** Reg 23(3D) SS(Adj) Regs
MATs Reg 38(5D) SS(Adj) Regs
DATs Reg 29(6D) SS(Adj) Regs
57 Reg 37 SS(C&P) Regs
58 Reg 9 SS(Adj) Regs
59 Reg 10 SS(Adj) Regs
60 R(SB) 4/90
61 CSB/172/1990
62 Reg 11 SS(Adj) Regs
63 CI/79/1990; CIS/373/1994

3. **The different tribunals**
64 CSDLA/180/1994
65 s33(4) and (5) SSAA 1992
66 s33(6) SSAA 1992; CDLA/5793/1997
67 Reg 28 SS(Adj) Regs
68 Reg 29(2) SS(Adj) Regs
69 s42(3) and (4) SSAA 1992
70 Reg 31 SS(Adj) Regs
71 CDLA/224/1994
72 s46(2) SSAA 1992; reg 49 SS(Adj) Regs
73 s46(3) SSAA 1992; regs 46(2) and 60(2) SS(Adj) Regs
74 Reg 38(2) SS(Adj) Regs
75 s21(2) SSAA 1992
76 s11(4) JSA 1995
77 s11(5) JSA 1995; reg 43 JSA Regs
78 ss22(5) and 32(9) SSAA 1992
79 s22(1)(a) SSAA 1992
80 Regs 22(2) SS(Adj) Regs
81 President's Circular No.14, May 1998
82 Reg 23(1) SS(Adj) Regs

4. **Appealing to the social security commissioner**
83 s23 SSAA 1992
84 R(A) 1/72; R(SB) 11/83
85 CS/1939/1995
86 R(IS) 4/93
87 *Kitchen & Evans v Secretary of State, The Times,* 14 September 1993, CM/140/1992 (affirming CM/205/1998)
88 s23(9) SSAA 1992
89 Reg 24(1) SS(Adj) Regs; reg 3(1) SSCP Regs
90 Regs 3(3) and 24 and Sch 2 para 7 SS(Adj) Regs
91 Reg 3(1) and (3) SSCP Regs; CIS/550/1993
92 CIS/3299/1997; CIB/4189/1997; CDLA/5793/1997

93 Reg 3(2) and (5) SSCP Regs; CIS/500/1993
94 Reg 7(1) SSCP Regs
95 Reg 5(2) SSCP Regs
96 ss23(6A) and 48(4A) SSAA 1992; Sch 6 para 4 SSA 1998; Chief Commissioner's Practice Memorandum, 11 August 1998
97 Regs 10, 11 and 12 SSCP Regs
98 Reg 27(3) and (4) SSCP Regs
99 Reg 15 SSCP Regs
100 s57 SSAA 1992
101 Reg 17(4) SSCP Regs
102 Reg 22(2) SSCP Regs
103 ss23(7)(b) and 34(4) SSAA 1992
104 ss23(7)(a) and 34(4) SSAA 1992
105 *Innes v CAO* (CA) (unreported), 19 November 1986
106 s48(5) SSAA 1992
107 s48(6) SSAA 1992
108 Regs 24 and 25 SSCP Regs

5. **Appealing to the courts**
109 ss 24 and 34(5) SSAA 1992
110 Regs 27(2) and 31(1) SSCP Regs
111 *White v CAO* [1986] 2 All ER 905 (CA), also reported as an appendix to R(S) 8/85
112 s24(2)(b) SSAA 1992
113 RSC 0.59 r.21(3)
114 RSC 0.3 r.5 and 0.59 r.14(2)
115 RSC 0.59 r.14(2), (2A) and (2B)
116 RSC 0.59 r.21(2) and r.4(3)
117 *Bland v CSBO* [1983] 1 WLR 262 (CA), also reported as R(SB) 12/83
118 ss2(4)(a) and 15(1) LAA 1988

6. **How to prepare an appeal**
119 s36 SSAA 1992; R(SB) 1/82; R(FIS) 1/82
120 R(SB) 6/82
121 R(SB) 10/86
122 R(IS) 6/91
123 R(SB) 33/85; R(SB) 12/89
124 R(SB) 1/81
125 s53 SSAA 1992
126 R(SB) 33/85
127 CDLA/148/1994, CDLA/692/1994 and CDLA/8462/1995
128 s123(2) SSCBA 1992
129 R(I) 12/75
130 R(SB) 22/86

131 *Nancollas v Insurance Officer*
[1985] 1 All ER 833 (CA), also
reported as an appendix to R(I)
7/85
132 R(I) 12/75
133 *CSBO v Leary* reported as an
appendix to R(SB) 6/85; *see
generally* CS/140/1991
134 R(G) 3/62; R(U) 4/88
135 R(U) 4/88
136 *Pepper v Hart* [1992] 3 WLR 1032

7. **Late appeals**

137 Reg 3(3) and (3A) SS(Adj) Regs
138 Reg 3(3E) SS(Adj) Regs
139 Reg 3(3B) and (3C) SS(Adj) Regs
140 Reg 3(5) SS(Adj) Regs
141 Reg 3(3D) SS(Adj) Regs
142 Reg 3(8) and (9) SS(Adj) Regs
143 R(SB) 24/82
144 R(M) 1/87
145 *R v Home Secretary ex parte
Mehta* applied to social security
law by R(M) 1/87 and R(I) 5/91
146 *R v Social Security Commissioner
ex parte Akbar, The Times*, 6
November 1991
147 But see R(U) 6/68. This will not
count as a 'special reason' if you
are appealing to a tribunal rather
than a commissioner.
148 R(S) 2/84
149 R(M) 1/87; R(I) 5/91
150 R(M) 1/87
151 CIS/147/1995

8. **The Social Security Act 1998**

152 Reg 1 SS&CS(D&A) Regs
153 s12 SSA 1998
154 Schs 2 and 3 SSA 1998
155 Reg 28 SS&CS(D&A) Regs
156 Reg 28(1)(b) SS&CS(D&A) Regs
157 Reg 28(2) SS&CS(D&A) Regs
158 s9(6) SSAA 1998
159 Reg 30(1) SS&CS(D&A) Regs
160 Reg 30(2) SS&CS(D&A) Regs
161 Reg 30(3) SS&CS(D&A) Regs
162 Reg 30(4) SS&CS(D&A) Regs
163 Reg 30(5) SS&CS(D&A) Regs
164 Reg 31(1) SS&CS(D&A) Regs
165 Reg 31(1)(b) SS&CS(D&A) Regs
166 Reg 31(1) SS&CS(D&A) Regs
167 Reg 32(1) SS&CS(D&A) Regs
168 Reg 32(2) SS&CS(D&A) Regs
169 Reg 32(4) SS&CS(D&A) Regs

170 Reg 32(5)and(6) SS&CS(D&A)
Regs
171 Reg 32(7) SS&CS(D&A) Regs
172 Reg 32(8) SS&CS(D&A) Regs
173 Reg 32(10) and (11)
SS&CS(D&A) Regs
174 Reg 32(9) SS&CS(D&A) Regs
175 Reg 33(1)(a) SS&CS(D&A) Regs
176 Reg 33(3)–(7) SS&CS(D&A) Regs
177 Reg 33(8) SS&CS(D&A) Regs
178 Reg 33(9) SS&CS(D&A) Regs
179 Reg 34 SS&CS(D&A) Regs
180 Reg 39 SS&CS(D&A) Regs
181 Reg 49(2) SS&CS(D&A) Regs
182 Reg 51(1) SS&CS(D&A) Regs
183 Reg 51(2) SS&CS(D&A) Regs
184 Reg 51(3) SS&CS(D&A) Regs
185 Reg 51(4) SS&CS(D&A) Regs
186 Reg 51(5) SS&CS(D&A) Regs
187 Sch 5 para 2 SSA 1998; reg 46
SS&CS(D&A) Regs
188 Reg 1 (3) SS&CS(D&A) Regs
189 Reg 48(1) SS&CS(D&A) Regs
190 Reg 48(5) SS&CS(D&A) Regs
191 Reg 47 SS&CS(D&A) Regs
192 Reg 40 SS&CS(D&A) Regs
193 s7(2) SSA 1998
194 s6(2) SSA 1998
195 s7(6) SSA 1998
196 Reg 36(6) SS&CS(D&A) Regs
197 Reg 36(2) SS&CS(D&A) Regs
198 s7(3) SSA 1998
199 Reg 50 SS&CS(D&A) Regs; s7(4)
and (5) SSA 1998
200 s12(8)(a) SSA 1998
201 Reg 52 SS&CS(D&A) Regs
202 s25 SSA 1998
203 s26 SSA 1998
204 s26(5) SSA 1998
205 Reg 53(4) SS&CS(D&A) Regs
206 Reg 54(1) SS&CS(D&A) Regs
207 Reg 55 SS&CS(D&A) Regs
208 Reg 57 SS&CS(D&A) Regs
209 s13(2) SSA 1998
210 s13(3) SSA 1998
211 Reg 58(5) SS&CS(D&A) Regs
212 Reg 58(4) SS&CS(D&A) Regs
213 Reg 58(2) and (3) SS&CS(D&A)
Regs

Chapter 57

• •

Complaints

This chapter covers:
1. Complaining to the Benefits Agency (p2:662)
2. Complaining to your MP (p2:662)
3. Compensation payments (p2:663)

The procedures for review and appeal (see Chapters 53 and 56) allow you to challenge decisions about your entitlement to benefit (including the refusal of benefit). If you want to make a complaint simply about the way in which your benefit claim was handled there are other procedures you can follow. The things you might want to complain about could include:
- delay in dealing with your claim;
- poor administration in the benefit office (eg, they keep losing your papers, or you can never get through on the telephone);
- poor or negligent advice from Benefits Agency or local authority staff;
- the behaviour of members of staff. Most Benefits Agency and local authority staff do a good job and try to be helpful, but you should certainly complain about staff rudeness or sexist or racist remarks.

This chapter covers complaints to the Benefits Agency. If you want to complain to a local authority about how your housing benefit or council tax benefit claim was handled or to seek compensation, see p2:597.

You should ask your local office for any written information on the standards and level of service which you can expect. As part of the 'Citizen's Charter' initiative, the Benefits Agency has produced a 'customer charter'. This sets out standards of service which cover matters such as the prompt and accurate payment of your benefits. There are specific targets set for processing your claim – eg, child benefit claims should normally be decided within 10 working days and claims for severe disablement allowance (SDA) within 36 working days. You can get a copy of the customer charter from your local office or from the customer service branch of the Benefits Agency at the address above. If you have to complain, it may help you if you can show that the Benefits Agency has failed to meet its published standards in your case (see p2:644)

The Benefits Agency produces a leaflet, *Tell us your comments and complaints*, which explains your rights and contains a form which you can use to explain your complaint. It is available from local Benefits Agency offices and on the Internet (see Appendix 3 for address). You might also wish to seek compensation (see p2:663).

Whenever you write to the Benefits Agency, you should be sure to quote your national insurance number and, if you are not writing to the office which is handling your claim, the name and address of that office.

1. Complaining to the Benefits Agency

If you want to complain about how the Benefits Agency has dealt with your individual case, as a first step you should speak to the supervisor. If you are still dissatisfied, you can contact the customer services manager of your benefit office. S/he investigates your complaint and should respond within seven days. If this does not solve the problem you should write to the manager of your district office with details of the complaint. Keep a copy of your letter. If you are still unhappy, you can ask the Benefits Agency for an independent review of your complaint. You may also wish to write a letter for the personal attention of the Chief Executive of the Benefits Agency (for address, see Appendix 1).

If you want to complain about a general issue or policy you can do so in the way described above. You can also take the matter up with your local Customer Council or other body that liases between local agencies and the Benefits Agency.

2. Complaining to your MP

If you are not satisfied with the reply from the officers to whom you have written, the next step is to take up the matter with your MP.

Most MPs have 'surgeries' in their areas where they meet constituents to discuss problems. You can get the details from your local library or citizens advice bureau. You can either go to the surgery or write to your MP with details of your complaint.

Your MP will probably want to write to the benefit authorities for an explanation of what has happened. If you or s/he are not satisfied with the reply, the next stage is to complain to the Ombudsman, via your MP.

The Parliamentary Commissioner for Administration (commonly called the 'Parliamentary Ombudsman' – see Appendix 1) investigates complaints made by MPs against government departments. The Ombudsman's office sends you a leaflet providing further information. Many of the complaints are about benefits. If s/he investigates your case, your MP is sent a full report. If the Ombudsman finds you were badly treated, s/he will recommend an apology and possibly compensation.

3. **Compensation payments**

You should expect prompt, courteous and efficient service from Benefits Agency staff dealing with your claim. If you are dissatisfied with the way your claim has been administered you can seek compensation.

The Benefits Agency sometimes pays compensation if you can show that you have lost out through its error or delay and the loss cannot be made good by a review or an appeal (see Chapters 53 and 56). For instance, if you failed to claim guardian's allowance because you were misled by the Benefits Agency, you could not have the benefit backdated for more than six months. You could, therefore, claim compensation.

The Benefits Agency uses a circular, *Financial Redress for Maladministration*, to help it decide when and how much compensation should be paid. The circular is available from the Stationery Office (see Appendix 1).

Benefits Agency errors

Sometimes the Benefits Agency makes mistakes about the amount of your benefit. Also, you might be given incorrect advice or information by the Benefits Agency which means you do not claim in time. Where possible it corrects the mistake by carrying out a review and awarding you the correct benefit (see p2:570) or by backdating your claim (see p2:487).

If the procedures for review or backdating do not apply or do not properly compensate you for the effects of the mistake that has occurred, you may claim compensation (known as an *ex gratia* payment). You should ask for a payment equal to the money you have lost, but you could also ask for additional amounts to cover interest on arrears, extra expenses you had to pay out, and to compensate you for any hardship or distress suffered because of the mistake. Payments are discretionary, so you should stress the Benefits Agency error and the fact that you have suffered as a consequence of official negligence, in order to ensure payment. If your loss was as a clear result of incorrect advice or negligence on the part of the Benefits Agency, you may be able to bring a court action for damages. You need the help of an advice agency or solicitor to do this.

Delays by the Benefits Agency

Benefits Agency offices have target times for dealing with claims, but they are not always able to meet these. If there is a long delay (eg, in assessing your entitlement or paying you benefit) you are entitled to compensation if:

- a significant reason for the delay was Benefits Agency error; *and*
- the amount of benefit involved was more than £100; *and*
- the delay in payment was more than a set length of time (known as a 'delay indicator' – see below); *and*
- any compensation would be £10 or more.

Delay indicator	Benefit
1 month	DWA
2 months	IS and widows' payments
3 months	JSA, SF maternity expenses payments, community care grants and budgeting loans
4 months	Child benefit, ICB, widow's pension and widowed mother's allowance
5 months	Maternity allowance and SF funeral expenses payments
6 months	FC and DWA
7 months (2 if claimed under the special rules – see p000)	AA and DLA
8 months	Retirement pension
9 months	ICA & SDA
1 year	Industrial injuries disablement benefit

You are not automatically awarded compensation although the Benefits Agency should automatically consider whether it should be paid where you are owed arrears of benefit. However, you should still write to your local Benefits Agency office and ask. If you do not get a sympathetic response you could ask your MP to write on your behalf, or to take up your case with the Social Security Minister.

If you want to seek compensation from a local authority, see p2:597.

Notes

. . . .

References are to statutes and regulations as amended up to 8 March 1999. All regulations are (General) Regulations unless otherwise stated. There is a full list of abbreviations in Appendix 13.

1 *Hansard*, 4 May 1993; paras 137-140 'Financial Redress for Maladministration'

Appendices

Appendix 1

Useful addresses

The President of the Independent Tribunal Service and regional chairs

The President
HH Judge Michael Harris
The President's Office
4th Floor, Whittington House
19-30 Alfred Place
London WC1E 7LW
Tel: 0171 814 6500

The President (Northern Ireland)
Mr CG MacLynn
6th Floor, Cleaver House
3 Donegal Square North
Belfast BT1 5GA
Tel: 01232 539900

Social Security Appeal Tribunals

Acting National Chair
Mr D Turrell
The President's Office
4th Floor, Whittington House
19-30 Alfred Place
London WC1E 7LW
Tel: 0171 814 6500

Regional Chairs
North East
Mr JW Tinnion
3rd Floor, York House
York Place
Leeds LS1 2ED
Tel: 0113 245 1246

Midlands
Mr R Martin
3rd Floor, Auchinleck House
Broad Street
Birmingham B15 1DL
Tel: 0121 643 6464

South East
Mr RG Smithson
ITS, Copthal House
9 The Pavement, Grove Road
Sutton, Surrey SM1 1DA
Tel: 0181 710 2908

North West
Mr RS Sim
36 Dale Street
Liverpool L2 5UZ
Tel: 0151 236 4334

Wales and South West
Mr CB Stephens
Oxford House
Hills Street, The Hayes
Cardiff CF1 2DR
Tel: 01222 378071

Scotland
Mrs LT Parker
Wellington House
134-36 Wellington Street
Glasgow G2 2XL
Tel: 0141 353 1441

Offices of the Social Security Commissioners

England and Wales
Harp House, 83 Farringdon Street
London EC4A 4DH

Address for administration:
5th Floor, Newspapers House
8-16 Great New Street
London EC4A 3BN
Tel: 0171 353 5145

Scotland
23 Melville Street
Edinburgh EH3 7PW
Tel: 0131 225 2201

Northern Ireland
Lancashire House
5 Linenhall Street
Belfast BT2 8AA
Tel: 01232 332344

Benefits Agency Chief Executive
Mr P Mathison
Quarry House, Quarry Hill
Leeds LS2 7UA
Tel: 0113 232 4000

Employment Service Chief Executive
Mr Leigh Lewis
Level 6, Caxton House, Tothill Street
London SW1H 9NA
Tel: 0171 273 3000

Under 18 Support Team (UEST)
Rockingham House
123 West Street
Sheffield S1 4ER
Tel: 0114 259 6001

Compensation Recovery Unit
DSS
Reyrolle Building
Hebburn
Tyne and Wear NE31 1XB

DSS Solicitor
New Court
48 Carey Street
London WC2A 2LS
Tel: 0171 962 8000

Disability Working Allowance Unit
Diadem House
2 The Pavilion
Preston PR2 2GN
Tel: 01772 883300

Earnings Top-up Help Line
Room 306
Norcross
Blackpool FY5 3TA
Tel: 0345 114422

Family Credit Unit
Government Buildings
Cop Lane
Preston PR1 0SA
Tel: 01253 500050

Independent Review Service for the Social Fund
Centre City Podium, 5 Hill Street
Birmingham B5 4UB
Tel: 0121 606 2100

Central Adjudication Services
Quarry House, Quarry Hill
Leeds LS2 7UA
Tel: 0113 232 4000

Chief Adjudication Officer
Mr E Hazelwood
Quarry House, Quarry Hill
Leeds LS2 7UA
Tel: 0113 232 4000

The Pricing Prescription Authority
Sandyford House, Osborne Road
Jesmond
Newcastle upon Tyne NE2 1DB
Tel: 0191 213 5000

Health Service Ombudsman
Millbank Tower
London SW1P 4QP
Tel: 0171 217 4051

Local Government Ombudsman
England
21 Queen Anne's Gate
London SW1H 9BU
Tel: 0171 915 3210

Scotland
23 Walker Street
Edinburgh EH3 7HX
Tel: 0131 225 5300

Wales
Derwen House, Court Road
Bridgend CF31 1BN
Tel: 01656 661325

Northern Ireland
Progressive House
33 Wellington Place
Belfast BT1 6HN
Tel: 01232 233821

The Parliamentary Ombudsman
Office of the Parliamentary
Commissioner
Millbank Tower, Millbank
London SW1P 4QP
Tel: 0171 217 4163

Appendix 2

Getting information and advice

Independent advice and representation

It is sometimes difficult for unsupported individuals to get a positive response from the Benefits Agency. You may be taken more seriously if it is clear you have taken advice about your entitlement or have an adviser assisting you.

If you want advice or help with a benefit problem, the following agencies may be able to assist. (If you cannot find any of these agencies in the telephone book, your local library should have details.)

- Citizens Advice Bureaux (CABx) and other local advice centres provide information and advice about benefits and may be able to represent you.
- Law Centres can often help in a similar way to CABx/advice centres.
- Local authority welfare rights workers provide a service in many areas and some arrange advice sessions and take-up campaigns locally.
- Local organisations for particular groups of claimants may offer help. For instance, there are Unemployed Centres, pensioners groups and centres for people with disabilities.
- Claimants Unions give advice in some areas. For details of your nearest group contact your local Council for Voluntary Services (CVS).
- Some social workers and probation officers (but not all) help with benefit problems, especially if they are already working with you on another problem.
- Solicitors can give free legal advice under the green form scheme (pink form in Scotland). This does not cover the cost of representation at an appeal hearing but can cover the cost of preparing written submissions and obtaining evidence such as medical reports. However, solicitors do not always have a good working knowledge of the benefit rules and you may need to shop around until you find one who does.
- Refugee Council, 3 Bondway, London SW8 1SJ tel: 0171 820 3038.
- Joint Council for the Welfare of Immigrants (JCWI), 115 Old Street, London EC1V 9JR tel: 0171 251 8706.

Unfortunately, CPAG is unable to deal with enquiries directly from members of the public, but if you are an adviser you can phone the advice line from 2.00pm to 4.00 pm, Monday to Friday on 0171 833 4627. This is a special phone line; do not ring the main CPAG number. Alternatively, you can write to us at the Citizens' Rights Office, CPAG, 94 White Lion St, London N1 9PF. We can take up a limited number of test cases including appeals to the Social Security Commissioners or courts.

Advice from the Benefits Agency

You can obtain free telephone advice on benefits on the following numbers. These are for general advice and not specific queries on individual claims.

- **Enquiry line for people with disabilities** 0800 882 200 (in Northern Ireland 0800 220 674), (minicom: 0800 243 355)
- **Disability Working Allowance Helpline** 01772 883 300 (this is not a freephone line)
- **Family Credit Helpline** 01253 500 050 (this is not a freephone line)

If English is not your first language, ask your local Benefits Agency office to arrange for advice in your own language.

Finding help on the Internet

Some information about benefits and a selection of leaflets is available on the Benefits Agency website at: http://www.dss.gov.uk

The RightsNet website at www.rightsnet.org.uk carries details of new legislation and policies affecting social security benefits. It also has links to other useful sites.

Most Acts and Regulations can be found on the central government information website at www.open.gov.uk

Appendix 3

Books, leaflets and periodicals

Many of the books listed here will be in your local public library. Stationery Office books are available from Stationery Office bookshops and also from many others. They may be ordered by post, telephone or fax from The Publications Centre, PO Box 276, London SW8 5DT (tel: 0171 873 9090 fax: 0171 873 8200; general enquiries tel: 0171 873 0011 fax: 0171 873 8247). They also have a website for further information at www.hmso.gov.uk.

1. Textbooks

Compensation for Industrial Injury by R Lewis (Professional Books, 1987). An excellent study of industrial injury benefits.

The Law of Social Security by AI Ogus, EM Barendt and N Wikely (Butterworths). Academic textbook on social security law.

Tolley's National Insurance Contributions 1994-95 (Tolley Publishing Company). A useful book on contributions.

2. Case law and legislation

Social Security Case Law - Digest of Commissioners' Decisions by D Neligan (Stationery Office, looseleaf in two vols). Summaries of commissioners' decisions grouped by subject. Also on the CAS website at www.cas.gov.uk

The Law Relating to Child Support (Stationery Office, looseleaf).

The Law Relating to Social Security (Stationery Office, looseleaf, 11 vols). All the legislation but without any comment. Known as the 'Blue Book'. Vols 6, 7, 8 and 11 deal with means-tested benefits.

CPAG's Income Related Benefits: The Legislation (Mesher) updated by P Wood (Sweet & Maxwell). The most useful legislation with a detailed commentary. 1999/2000 edn available from CPAG September 1999, £61 (prov) with December Supplement incl p&p - if you are a CPAG member. Reduced to £56 per set if ordered from CPAG before 30 July 1999.

Non-Means Tested Benefits: The Legislation by D Bonner et al (Sweet & Maxwell). The legislation with a detailed commentary. 1999/2000 edition available from CPAG September 1999, £61 (prov) with December Supplement incl p&p - if you are a CPAG member. Reduced to £56 per set if ordered from CPAG before 30 July 1999.

CPAG's Housing Benefit and Council Tax Benefit Legislation by L Findlay, R Poynter, P Stagg, and M Ward (CPAG). Contains legislation with a detailed commentary. 1999/2000 edn available from autumn 1999, priced £58 with Supplement incl p&p from CPAG. Reduced to £51 per set if ordered before 30 July 1999. The 11th edition (1998/1999) is still available at £48 per set.

Medical and Disability Appeal Tribunals: The Legislation by M Rowland (Sweet & Maxwell). The 3rd edition main volume (1998) of legislation with commentary is available from CPAG, priced £36 incl p&p - if you are a CPAG member. A Supplement to the 3rd edition is published in autumn 1999, priced £17.

Child Support: The Legislation by E Jacobs and G Douglas (Sweet & Maxwell). The 4th edition of legislation with commentary is available from CPAG from September 1999, priced £44 (prov) incl p&p - if you are a CPAG member. Reduced to £41 if ordered from CPAG before 30 July 1999.

The Social Fund: Law and Practice by T Buck (Sweet & Maxwell). Includes legislation, guidance and commentary. The 2nd edition is available from CPAG from December 1999 priced £46 (prov) incl p&p - if you are a CPAG member. Reduced to £42 if ordered from CPAG before 30 July 1999.

Social Fund Directions are available on the IRS website at www.irssf.demon.co.uk/ssdir.htm

3. Official guidance

Adjudication Officers' Guide (Stationery Office, looseleaf, 13 vols). Vols 4-8 deal with means-tested benefits. Supplementary guidance notes are issued internally – eg, Memo AOG Vol 3/77. Also available on the CAS website at www.cas.gov.uk. (The Central Adjudication Service will be wound down from November 1999 as the decision making and appeal changes are phased in. Therefore, Adjudication Officers' Guidance will no longer be in this format.)

Benefits Agency Guide, IS for 16/17-year-olds, (Stationery Office, amended February 1996).

Charging for Residential Accommodation Guide (Department of Health, one vol).

Child Support Adjudication Guide (Stationery Office, looseleaf).

Child Support Guide (Child Support Agency, looseleaf eight vols).

Field Officers' Guide (Child Support Agency, looseleaf).

Handbook for Delegated Medical Practitioners (Stationery Office, 1988).

Housing Benefit and Council Tax Benefit Guidance Manual (Stationery Office, looseleaf).

Industrial Injuries Handbook for Adjudicating Medical Authorities (Stationery Office, looseleaf).

Income Support Guide (Stationery Office, looseleaf, 8 vols). Procedural guide issued to Benefits Agency staff.

Notes on the Diagnosis of Prescribed Diseases (except pneumoconiosis and related occupational diseases and occupational deafness) (Stationery Office, 1991).

The Social Fund Guide (Stationery Office, looseleaf 2 vols).

The Social Fund Cold Weather Payments Handbook (Stationery Office, looseleaf).

The Social Fund Maternity and Funeral Payments Guide (Stationery Office, looseleaf).

4. Tribunal handbooks

Medical Appeal Tribunals: A Guide to Procedure
(Stationery Office, 1987).

Social Security Appeal Tribunals: A Guide to Procedure
(Stationery Office).

5. Leaflets
The Benefits Agency and DSS publish many leaflets which cover particular benefits or particular groups of claimants or contributors. They are free from your local Benefits Agency office, or on Freephone 0800 666 555, or from your local DSS office. If you want to order larger numbers of leaflets, or receive information about new leaflets, you can join the Benefits Agency Publicity Register by contacting the Benefits Agency, 3rd Floor South, 1 Trevelyan Square, Leeds LS1 6EB, tel. 0645 540 000 (local rate). The DSS also has a Leaflets Unit at Block 4, Government Buildings, Honeypot Lane, Stanmore, Middlesex HA7 1AY. Free leaflets on HB/CTB are available from the relevant department of your local council.
A selection of leaflets is available on the Benefits Agency Website at http://www.dss.gov.uk

6. Periodicals
CPAG's Welfare Rights Bulletin is published every two months by CPAG. It covers developments in social security law and updates this *Handbook* between editions. The annual subscription is £23 but it is sent automatically to CPAG Rights and Comprehensive Members. For subscription and membership details contact CPAG.

Articles on social security can also be found in *Legal Action* (Legal Action Group, monthly magazine) and the *Journal of Social Security Law* (Sweet & Maxwell, quarterly).

7. Other publications – general
Child Support Handbook
£12.95 (June 1999) (£3.50 for claimants)

Council Tax Handbook
£9.95 (1997)

Debt Advice Handbook
£12.95 (4th edn, late 1999)

A Guide to Money Advice in Scotland
£14.95 (1997)

Migration and Social Security Handbook
£15.95 (3rd edn, late 1999)

Fuel Rights Handbook
£10.95 (March 1999)

Guide to Housing Benefit and Council Tax Benefit
£16.95 (summer 1999)

Rights Guide for Home Owners
£9.95 (1998)

Disability Rights Handbook
£11.50 (May 1999)

NHA (formerly CHAR) Benefits Guide
£10.45 (May 1999)

Youthaid's Guide to Training and Benefits for Young People
£7.99 (Spring 1999)

Unemployment and Training Rights Handbook
£9.99 (May 1999)

New Deal Handbook
£7.99 (Spring 1999)

Immigration and Nationality Law Handbook
(JCWI) £16.95

For CPAG publications and most of those in Sections 2 and 7 contact:
CPAG, 94 White Lion St, London N1 9PF. Prices include p&p.

Appendix 4

Disabilities which may make a person incapable of work

Schedule to the Social Security (Incapacity for Work) (General) Regulations 1995

Part 1. Physical disabilities

(1) Activity		(2) Descriptor	(3) Points
1. Walking on level ground with a walking stick or other aid if such aid is normally used.	1(a)	Cannot walk at all.	15
	(b)	Cannot walk more than a few steps without stopping or severe discomfort.	15
	(c)	Cannot walk more than 50 metres without stopping or severe discomfort.	15
	(d)	Cannot walk more than 200 metres without stopping or severe discomfort.	7
	(e)	Cannot walk more than 400 metres without stopping or severe discomfort.	3
	(f)	Cannot walk more than 800 metres without stopping or severe discomfort.	0
	(g)	No walking problem.	0
2. Walking up and down stairs.	2(a)	Cannot walk up and down one stair.	15
	(b)	Cannot walk up and down a flight of 12 stairs.	15
	(c)	Cannot walk up and down a flight of 12 stairs without holding on and taking a rest.	7
	(d)	Cannot walk up and down a flight of 12 stairs without holding on.	3
	(e)	Can only walk up and down a flight of 12 stairs if he goes sideways or one step at a time.	3
	(f)	No problem in walking up and down stairs.	0

(1) Activity		(2) Descriptor	(3) Points
3. Sitting in an upright chair with a back, but no arms.	3(a)	Cannot sit comfortably.	15
	(b)	Cannot sit comfortably for more than 10 minutes without having to move from the chair because the degree of discomfort makes it impossible to continue sitting.	15
	(c)	Cannot sit comfortably for more than 30 minutes without having to move from the chair because the degree of discomfort makes it impossible to continue sitting.	7
	(d)	Cannot sit comfortably for more than 1 hour without having to move from the chair because the degree of discomfort makes it impossible to continue sitting.	3
	(e)	Cannot sit comfortably for more than 2 hours without having to move from the chair because the degree of discomfort makes it impossible to continue sitting.	0
	(f)	No problem with sitting.	0
4. Standing without the support of another person or the use of an aid except a walking stick.	4(a)	Cannot stand unassisted.	15
	(b)	Cannot stand for more than a minute before needing to sit down.	15
	(c)	Cannot stand for more than 10 minutes before needing to sit down	15
	(d)	Cannot stand for more than 30 minutes before needing to sit down.	7
	(e)	Cannot stand for more than 10 minutes before needing to move around.	7
	(f)	Cannot stand for more than 30 minutes before needing to move around.	3
	(g)	No problem standing.	0
5. Rising from sitting in an upright chair with a back but no arms without the help of another person.	5(a)	Cannot rise from sitting to standing.	15
	(b)	Cannot rise from sitting to standing without holding on to something.	7
	(c)	Sometimes cannot rise from sitting to standing without holding on to something.	3
	(d)	No problem with rising from sitting to standing.	0
6. Bending and kneeling.	6(a)	Cannot bend to touch his knees and straighten up again.	15
	(b)	Cannot either bend or kneel, or bend and kneel as if to pick up a piece of paper from the floor and straighten up again.	15
	(c)	Sometimes cannot either bend or kneel, or bend and kneel as if to pick up a piece of paper from the floor and straighten up again.	3

(1) Activity		(2) Descriptor	(3) Points
	(d)	No problem with bending or kneeling.	0
7. Manual dexterity.	7(a)	Cannot turn the pages of a book with either hand.	15
	(b)	Cannot turn a sink tap or the control knobs on a cooker with either hand.	15
	(c)	Cannot pick up a coin which is 2.5cm or less in diameter with either hand.	15
	(d)	Cannot use a pen or pencil.	15
	(e)	Cannot tie a bow in laces or string.	10
	(f)	Cannot turn a sink tap or the control knobs on a cooker with one hand but can with the other.	6
	(g)	Cannot pick up a coin which is 2.5cm or less in diameter with one hand but can with the other.	6
	(h)	No problem with manual dexterity.	0
8. Lifting and carrying by the use of the upper body and arms (excluding all other activities specified in Part I of this Schedule)	8(a)	Cannot pick up a paper-back book with either hand.	15
	(b)	Cannot pick up and carry a 0.5 litre carton of milk with either hand.	15
	(c)	Cannot pick up and pour from a full saucepan or kettle of 1.7 litre capacity with either hand.	15
	(d)	Cannot pick up and carry a 2.5 kilogramme bag of potatoes with either hand.	8
	(e)	Cannot pick up and carry a 0.5 litre carton of milk with one hand, but can with the other.	6
	(f)	Cannot pick up and carry a 2.5 kilogramme bag of potatoes with one hand, but can with the other.	0
	(g)	No problem with lifting and carrying.	0
9. Reaching.	9(a)	Cannot raise either arm as if to put something in the top pocket of a coat or jacket	15
	(b)	Cannot raise either arm to his head as if to put on a hat.	15
	(c)	Cannot put either arm behind back as if to put on a coat or jacket.	15
	(d)	Cannot raise either arm above his head as if to reach for something.	15
	(e)	Cannot raise one arm to his head as if to put on a hat, but can with the other.	6
	(f)	Cannot raise one arm above his head as if to reach for something, but can with the other.	0
	(g)	No problem with reaching.	0
10. Speech.	10(a)	Cannot speak.	15
	(b)	Speech cannot be understood by family or friends.	15

(1) Activity	(2) Descriptor	(3) Points
	(c) Speech cannot be understood by strangers.	15
	(d) Strangers have great difficulty understanding speech.	10
	(e) Strangers have some difficulty understanding speech.	8
	(f) No problems with speech.	0
11. Hearing with a hearing aid or other aid if normally worn.	11(a) Cannot hear sounds at all.	15
	(b) Cannot hear well enough to follow a television programme with the volume turned up.	15
	(c) Cannot hear well enough to understand someone talking in a loud voice in a quiet room.	15
	(d) Cannot hear well enough to understand someone talking in a normal voice in a quiet room.	10
	(e) Cannot hear well enough to understand someone talking in a normal voice on a busy street.	8
	(f) No problem with hearing.	0
12. Vision in normal daylight or bright electric light with glasses or other aid to vision if such aid is normally worn.	12(a) Cannot tell light from dark.	15
	(b) Cannot see the shape of furniture in the room.	15
	(c) Cannot see well enough to read 16 point print at a distance greater than 20 centimetres.	15
	(d) Cannot see well enough to recognise a friend across the room at a distance of at least 5 metres.	12
	(e) Cannot see well enough to recognise a friend across the road at a distance of at least 15 metres.	8
	(f) No problems with vision.	0
13. Continence. (other than enuresis (bed wetting))	13(a) No voluntary control over bowels.	15
	(b) No voluntary control over bladder.	15
	(c) Loses control of bowels at least once a week.	15
	(d) Loses control of bowels at least once a month.	15
	(e) Loses control of bowels occasionally.	9
	(f) Loses control of bladder at least once a month.	3
	(g) Loses control of bladder occasionally.	0
	(h) No problem with continence.	0
14. Remaining conscious without having epileptic or similar seizures during waking moments.	14(a) Has an involuntary episode of lost or altered consciousness at least once a day.	15
	(b) Has an involuntary episode of lost or altered consciousness at least once a week.	15

(1) Activity	(2) Descriptor	(3) Points
	(c) Has an involuntary episode of lost or altered consciousness at least once a month.	15
	(d) Has had an involuntary episode of lost or altered consciousness at least twice in the 6 months before the day in respect to which it falls to be determined whether he is incapable of work for the purposes of entitlement to any benefit, allowance or advantage.	12
	(e) Has an involuntary episode of lost or altered consciousness once in the 6 months before the day in respect to which it falls to be determined whether he is incapable of work for the purposes of entitlement to any benefit, allowance or advantage.	8
	(f) Has had an involuntary episode of lost or altered consciousness once in the 3 years before the day in respect to which it falls to be determined whether he is incapable of work for the purposes of entitlement to any benefit, allowance or advantage.	0
	(g) Has no problems with consciousness.	0

Part II. Mental disabilities

(1) Activity	(2) Descriptor	(3) Points
15. Completion of tasks.	15(a) Cannot answer the telephone and reliably take a message.	2
	(b) Often sits for hours doing nothing.	2
	(c) Cannot concentrate to read a magazine article or follow a radio or television programme.	1
	(d) Cannot use a telephone book or other directory to find a number.	1
	(e) Mental condition prevents him from undertaking leisure activities previously enjoyed.	1
	(f) Overlooks or forgets the risk posed by domestic appliances or other common hazards due to poor concentration.	1
	(g) Agitation, confusion or forgetfulness has resulted in potentially dangerous accidents in the 3 months before the day in respect to which it falls to be determined whether he is incapable of work for the purposes of	1

(1) Activity		(2) Descriptor	(3) Points
		entitlement to any benefit, allowance or advantage.	
	(h)	Concentration can only be sustained by prompting.	1
16. Daily living.	16(a)	Needs encouragement to get up and dress.	2
	(b)	Needs alcohol before midday.	2
	(c)	Is frequently distressed at some time of the day due to fluctuation of mood.	1
	(d)	Does not care about his appearance and living conditions.	1
	(e)	Sleep problems interfere with his daytime activities.	1
17. Coping with pressure.	17(a)	Mental stress was a factor in making him stop work.	2
	(b)	Frequently feels scared or panicky for no obvious reason.	2
	(c)	Avoids carrying out routine activities because he is convinced they will prove too tiring or stressful.	1
	(d)	Is unable to cope with changes in daily routine.	1
	(e)	Frequently finds there are so many things to do that he gives up because of fatigue, apathy or disinterest.	1
	(f)	Is scared or anxious that work would bring back or worsen his illness.	1
18. Interaction with other people.	18(a)	Cannot look after himself without help from others.	2
	(b)	Gets upset by ordinary events and it results in disruptive behavioural problems.	2
	(c)	Mental problems impair ability to communicate with other people.	2
	(d)	Gets irritated by things that would not have bothered him before he became ill.	1
	(e)	Prefers to be left alone for 6 hours or more each day.	1
	(f)	Is too frightened to go out alone.	1

Appendix 5

Statutory maternity pay and maternity allowance

If your baby is expected during the week which begins on Sunday	your 'qualifying week' begins on Sunday +	and the earliest week for which you can get SMP or MA begins on Sunday++
7.3.99	22.11.98	20.12.98
14.3.99	29.11.98	27.12.98
21.3.99	6.12.98	3.1.99
28.3.99	13.12.98	10.1.99
4.4.99	20.12.98	17.1.99
11.4.99	27.12.98	24.1.99
18.4.99	3.1.99	31.1.99
25.4.99	10.1.99	7.2.99
2.5.99	17.1.99	14.2.99
9.5.99	24.1.99	21.2.99
16.5.99	31.1.99	28.2.99
23.5.99	7.2.99	7.3.99
30.5.99	14.2.99	14.3.99
6.6.99	21.2.99	21.3.99
13.6.99	28.2.99	28.3.99
20.6.99	7.3.99	4.4.99
27.6.99	14.3.99	11.4.99
4.7.99	21.3.99	18.4.99
11.7.99	28.3.99	25.4.99
18.7.99	4.4.99	2.5.99
25.7.99	11.4.99	9.5.99
1.8..99	18.4.99	16.5.99
8.8.99	25.4.99	23.5.99
15.8.99	2.5.99	30.5.99
22.8.99	9.5.99	6.6.99
29.8.99	16.5.99	13.6.99
5.9.99	23.5.99	20.6.99
12.9.99	30.5.99	27.6.99
19.9.99	6.6.99	4.7.99
26.9.99	13.6.99	11.7.99
3.10.99	20.6.99	18.7.99

10.10.99	27.6.99	25.7.99
17.10.99	4.7.99	1.8..99
24.10.99	11.7.99	8.8.99
31.10.99	18.7.99	15.8.99
7.11.99	25.7.99	22.8.99
14.11.99	1.8..99	29.8.99
21.11.99	8.8.99	5.9.99
21.11.99	15.8.99	12.9.99
28.11.99	22.8.99	19.9.99
5.12.99	29.8.99	26.9.99
12.12.99	5.9.99	3.10.99
19.12.99	12.9.99	10.10.99
26.12.99	19.9.99	17.10.99
2.1.00	26.9.99	24.10.99
9.1.00	3.10.99	31.10.99
16.1.00	10.10.99	7.11.99
23.1.00	17.10.99	14.11.99
30.1.00	24.10.99	21.11.99
6.2.00	31.10.99	21.11.99
13.2.00	7.11.99	28.11.99
20.2.00	14.11.99	5.12.99
27.2.00	21.11.99	12.12.99
5.3.00	21.11.99	19.12.99
12.3.00	28.11.99	26.12.99
19.3.00	5.12.99	2.1.00
26.3.00	12.12.99	9.1.00
2.4.00	19.12.99	16.1.00
9.4.00	26.12.99	23.1.00
16.4.00	2.1.00	30.1.00
23.4.00	9.1.00	6.2.00
30.4.00	16.1.00	13.2.00
7.5.00	23.1.00	20.2.00
14.5.00	30.1.00	27.2.00

+ This is the 15th week before the baby is due. See Chapter 6 for more information.
++ This is the 11th week before the baby is due (unless your baby is born earlier. See Chapter 6 for a possible exception).

Appendix 6

Pensionable age for women aged between 40 and 45 on 6 April 1995

Date of birth	Pensionable Age (in Years/Months)	Date Pensionable Age Reached
06.04.50 - 05.05.50	60.1 - 60.0	06.05.2010
06.05.50 - 05.06.50	60.2 - 60.1	06.07.2010
06.06.50 - 05.07.50	60.3 - 60.2	06.09.2010
06.07.50 - 05.08.50	60.4 - 60.3	06.11.2010
06.08.50 - 05.09.50	60.5 - 60.4	06.01.2011
06.09.50 - 05.10.50	60.6 - 60.5	06.03.2011
06.10.50 - 05.11.50	60.7 - 60.6	06.05.2011
06.11.50 - 05.12.50	60.8 - 60.7	06.07.2011
06.12.50 - 05.01.51	60.9 - 60.8	06.09.2011
06.01.51 - 05.02.51	60.10 - 60.9	06.11.2011
06.02.51 - 05.03.51	60.11 - 60.10	06.01.2012
06.03.51 - 05.04.51	61.0 - 60.11	06.03.2012
06.04.51 - 05.05.51	61.1 - 61.0	06.05.2012
06.05.51 - 05.06.51	61.2 - 61.1	06.07.2012
06.06.51 - 05.07.51	61.3 - 61.2	06.09.2012
06.07.51 - 05.08.51	61.4 - 61.3	06.11.2012
06.08.51 - 05.09.51	61.5 - 61.4	06.01.2013
06.09.51 - 05.10.51	61.6 - 61.5	06.03.2013
06.10.51 - 05.11.51	61.7 - 61.6	06.05.2013
06.11.51 - 05.12.51	61.8 - 61.7	06.07.2013
06.12.51 - 05.01.52	61.9 - 61.8	06.09.2013
06.01.52 - 05.02.52	61.10 - 61.9	06.11.2013
06.02.52 - 05.03.52	61.11 - 61.10	06.01.2014
06.03.52 - 05.04.52	62.0 - 61.11	06.03.2014
06.04.52 - 05.05.52	62.1 - 62.0	06.05.2014
06.05.52 - 05.06.52	62.2 - 62.1	06.07.2014
06.06.52 - 05.07.52	62.3 - 62.2	06.09.2014
06.07.52 - 05.08.52	62.4 - 62.3	06.11.2014
06.08.52 - 05.09.52	62.5 - 62.4	06.01.2015
06.09.52 - 05.10.52	62.6 - 62.5	06.03.2015
06.10.52 - 05.11.52	62.7 - 62.6	06.05.2015
06.11.52 - 05.12.52	62.8 - 62.7	06.07.2015

Date of birth	Pensionable Age (in Years/Months)	Date Pensionable Age Reached
06.12.52 - 05.01.53	62.9 - 62.8	06.09.2015
06.01.53 - 05.02.53	62.10 - 62.9	06.11.2015
06.02.53 - 05.03.53	62.11 - 62.10	06.01.2016
06.03.53 - 05.04.53	63.0 - 62.11	06.03.2016
06.04.53 - 05.05.53	63.1 - 63.0	06.05.2016
06.05.53 - 05.06.53	63.2 - 63.1	06.07.2016
06.06.53 - 05.07.53	63.3 - 63.2	06.09.2016
06.07.53 - 05.08.53	63.4 - 63.3	06.11.2016
06.08.53 - 05.09.53	63.5 - 63.4	06.01.2017
06.09.53 - 05.10.53	63.6 - 63.5	06.03.2017
06.10.53 - 05.11.53	63.7 - 63.6	06.05.2017
06.11.53 - 05.12.53	63.8 - 63.7	06.07.2017
06.12.53 - 05.01.54	63.9 - 63.8	06.09.2017
06.01.54 - 05.02.54	63.10 - 63.9	06.11.2017
06.02.54 - 05.03.54	63.11 - 63.10	06.01.2018
06.03.54 - 05.04.54	64.0 - 63.11	06.03.2018
06.04.54 - 05.05.54	64.1 - 64.0	06.05.2018
06.05.54 - 05.06.54	64.2 - 64.1	06.07.2018
06.06.54 - 05.07.54	64.3 - 64.2	06.09.2018
06.07.54 - 05.08.54	64.4 - 64.3	06.11.2018
06.08.54 - 05.09.54	64.5 - 64.4	06.01.2019
06.09.54 - 05.10.54	64.6 - 64.5	06.03.2019
06.10.54 - 05.11.54	64.7 - 64.6	06.05.2019
06.11.54 - 05.12.54	64.8 - 64.7	06.07.2019
06.12.54 - 05.01.55	64.9 - 64.8	06.09.2019
06.01.55 - 05.02.55	64.10 - 64.9	06.11.2019
06.02.55 - 05.03.55	64.11 - 64.10	06.01.2020
06.03.55 - 05.04.55	65.0 - 64.11	06.03.2020
06.04.55	65.0	06.04.2020

Appendix 7

Prescribed degrees of disablement

1. Schedule 2 to the Social Security (General Benefit) Regulations 1982

Description of injury	Degree of disablement %
1 Loss of both hands or amputation at higher sites	100
2 Loss of a hand and a foot	100
3 Double amputation through leg or thigh, or amputation through leg or thigh on one side and loss of other foot	100
4 Loss of sight to such an extent as to render the claimant unable to perform any work for which eyesight is essential	100
5 Very severe facial disfiguration	100
6 Absolute deafness	100
7 Forequarter or hindquarter amputation	100

Amputation cases – upper limbs (either arm)

Description of injury	Degree of disablement %
8 Amputation through shoulder joint	90
9 Amputation below shoulder with stump less than 20.5 cms from tip of acromion	80
10 Amputation from 20.5 cms from tip of acromion to less than 11.5 cms below tip of olecranon	70

Description of injury	Degree of disablement %
11 Loss of a hand or of the thumb and 4 fingers of 1 hand or amputation from 11.5 cms below tip of olecranon	60
12 Loss of thumb	30
13 Loss of thumb and its metacarpal bone	40
14 Loss of 4 fingers of 1 hand	50
15 Loss of 3 fingers of 1 hand	30
16 Loss of 2 fingers of 1 hand	20
17 Loss of terminal phalanx of thumb	20

Amputation cases – lower limbs

Description of injury	Degree of disablement %
18 Amputation of both feet resulting in end-bearing stumps	90
19 Amputation through both feet proximal to the metatarso-phalangeal joint	80
20 Loss of all toes of both feet through the metatarso-phalangeal joint	40
21 Loss of all toes of both feet proximal to the proximal inter-phalangeal joint	30
22 Loss of all toes of both feet distal to the proximal inter-phalangeal joint	20
23 Amputation at hip	90

Description of injury	Degree of disablement %
24 Amputation below hip with stump not exceeding 13 cms in length measured from tip of great trochanter	80
25 Amputation below hip and above knee with stump exceeding 13 cms in length measured from tip of great trochanter, or at knee not resulting in end-bearing stump	70
26 Amputation at knee resulting in end-bearing stump or below knee with stump not exceeding 9 cms	60
27 Amputation below knee with stump exceeding 9 cms but not exceeding 13 cms	50
28 Amputation below knee with stump exceeding 13 cms	40
29 Amputation of 1 foot resulting in end-bearing stump	30
30 Amputation through 1 foot proximal to the metatarso-phalangeal joint	30
31 Loss of all toes of 1 foot through the metatarso-phalangeal joint	20

Other injuries

Description of injury	Degree of disablement %
32 Loss of 1 eye, without complications, the other being normal	40
33 Loss of vision of 1 eye, without complications or disfigurement of the eyeball, the other being normal	30

Loss of fingers of right or left hand
Index finger:

Description of injury	Degree of disablement %
34 Whole	14

Description of injury	Degree of disablement %
35 2 phalanges	11
36 1 phalanx	9
37 Guillotine amputation of tip without loss of bone	5
Middle finger:	
38 Whole	12
39 2 phalanges	9
40 1 phalanx	7
41 Guillotine amputation of tip without loss of bone	4
Ring or little finger:	
42 Whole	7
43 2 phalanges	6
44 1 phalanx	5
45 Guillotine amputation of tip without loss of bone	2

Loss of toes of right or left foot:
Great toe:

Description of injury	Degree of disablement %
46 Through metatarso-phalangeal joint	14
47 Part, with some loss of bone	3
Any other toe:	
48 Through metatarso-phalangeal joint	3
49 Part, with some loss of bone	1
2 toes of 1 foot, excluding great toe:	
50 Through metatarso-phalangeal joint	5
51 Part, with some loss of bone	2
3 toes of 1 foot, excluding great toe:	
52 Through metatarso-phalangeal joint	6
53 Part, with some loss of bone	3
4 toes of 1 foot, excluding great toe:	
54 Through metatarso-phalangeal joint	9
55 Part, with some loss of bone	3

The degree of disablement due to occupational deafness is assessed using tables and a formula to be found in regulation 34 of and Schedule 3 to the Social Security (Industrial Injuries) (Prescribed Diseases) Regulations 1985 as amended.

Appendix 8

. . . .

Prescribed industrial diseases

Part I of Schedule 1 to the Social Security (Industrial Injuries) (Prescribed Diseases) Regulations 1985 as amended

Prescribed disease or injury	*Occupation*
A Conditions due to physical agents	**Any occupation involving:**
A1 Inflammation, ulceration or malignant disease of the skin or subcutaneous tissues or of the bones, or blood dyscrasia, or cataract, due to electro-magnetic radiations (other than radiant heat) or to ionising particles	Exposure to electro-magnetic radiations (other than radiant heat), or to ionising particles.
A2 Heat cataract	Frequent or prolonged exposure to rays from molten or red-hot material.
A3 Dysbarism, including decompression sickness, barotrauma and osteonecrosis	Subjection to compressed or rarified air or from molten or red-hot material.
A4 Cramp of the hand or forearm due to repetitive movements	Prolonged periods of handwriting, typing or other repetitive movements of the fingers, hand or arm.
A5 Subcutaneous cellulitis of the hand (Beat hand)	Manual labour causing severe or prolonged friction or pressure on the hand.
A6 Bursitis or subcutaneous cellulitis arising at or about the knee due to severe or prolonged external friction or pressure at or about the knee (Beat knee)	Manual labour causing severe or prolonged external friction or pressure at or about the knee
A7 Bursitis or subcutaneous cellulitis arising at or about the elbow due to severe or prolonged external friction or pressure at or about the elbow (Beat elbow)	Manual labour causing severe or prolonged external friction or pressure at or about the elbow
A8 Traumatic inflammation of the tendons	Manual labour, or frequent or repeated

Prescribed disease or injury	*Occupation*
of the hand or forearm, or of the associated tendon sheaths	movements of the hand or wrist.

A9 Miner's nystagmus

Work in or about a mine.

A10 Sensorineural hearing loss amounting to at least 50dB in each ear, being the average of hearing losses at 1, 2 and 3 kHz frequencies, and being due in the case of at least one ear to occupational noise (occupational deafness)

(a) The use of powered (but not hand-powered) grinding tools on metal (other than sheet metal or plate metal) or work wholly or mainly in the immediate vicinity of those tools whilst they are being so used; *or*

(b) the use of pneumatic percussive tools on metal, or work wholly or mainly in the immediate vicinity of those tools whilst they are being used; *or*

(c) the use of pneumatic percussive tools for drilling rock in quarries or underground or in mining coal or in sinking shafts or for tunnelling in civil engineering works, or work wholly or mainly in the immediate vicinity of those tools whilst they are being used; *or*

(ca) the use of pneumatic percussive tools on stone in quarry works, or work wholly or mainly in the immediate vicinity of those tools whilst they are being so used; *or*

(d) work wholly or mainly in the immediate vicinity of plant (excluding power press plant) engaged in the forging (including drop-stamping) of metal by means of closed or open dies or drop hammers; *or*

(e) work in textile manufacturing where the work is undertaken wholly or mainly in rooms or sheds in which there are machines engaged in weaving man-made or natural (including mineral) fibres or in the high speed false twisting of fibres; *or*

(f) the use of, or work wholly or mainly in the immediate vicinity of, machines engaged in cutting, shaping or cleaning metal nails; *or*

(g) the use of, or work wholly or mainly in the immediate vicinity of, plasma spray guns engaged in the deposition of metal; *or*

(h) the use of, or work wholly or mainly in the immediate vicinity of, any of the following machines engaged in the working of wood or material composed partly of wood, that is to say: multi-cutter moulding

Prescribed disease or injury

Occupation

machines, planing machines, automatic or semi-automatic lathes, multiple cross-cut machines, automatic shaping machines, double-end tenoning machines, vertical spindle moulding machines (including high-speed routing machines), edge banding machines, bandsawing machines with a blade width of not less than 75 mm and circular sawing machines in the operation of which the blade is moved towards the material being cut; *or*

(i) the use of chain saws in forestry.

(j) air arc gouging or work wholly or mainly in the immediate vicinity of air arc gouging; *or*

(k) the use of band saws, circular saws or cutting discs for cutting metal in the metal founding or forging industries, or work wholly or mainly in the immediate vicinity of those tools whilst they are being so used; *or*

(l) the use of circular saws for cutting products in the manufacture of steel, or work wholly or mainly in the immediate vicinity of those tools whilst they are being so used; *or*

(m) the use of burners or torches for cutting or dressing steel based products, or work wholly or mainly in the immediate vicinity of those tools whilst they are being so used; *or*

(n) work wholly or mainly in the immediate vicinity of skid transfer banks; *or*

(o) work wholly or mainly in the immediate vicinity of knock out and shake out grids in foundries; *or*

(p) mechanical bobbin cleaning or work wholly or mainly in the immediate vicinity of mechanical bobbin cleaning;

(q) the use of, or work wholly or mainly in the immediate vicinity of, vibrating metal moulding boxes in the concrete products industry; *or*

(r) the use of, or work wholly or mainly in the immediate vicinity of, high pressure jets of water or a mixture of water and abrasive material in the water jetting industry (including work under water); *or*

(s) work in ships' engine rooms; *or*

Prescribed disease or injury

Occupation

(t) the use of circular saws for cutting concrete masonry blocks during manufacture, or work wholly or mainly in the immediate vicinity of those tools whilst they are being so used; *or*

(u) burning stone in quarries by jet channelling processes, or work wholly or mainly in the immediate vicinity of such processes; *or*

(v) work on gas turbines in connection with –

i) performance testing on test bed;

ii) installation testing or replacement engines in aircraft;

iii) acceptance testing of Armed Service fixed wing combat planes; *or*

(w) the use of, or work wholly or mainly in the immediate vicinity of –

i) machines for automatic moulding, automatic blow moulding or automatic glass pressing and forming machines used in the manufacture of glass containers or hollow ware;

ii) spinning machines using compressed air to produce glass wool or mineral wool;

iii) continuous glass toughening furnaces

A11 Episodic blanching, occurring throughout the year, affecting the middle or proximal phalanges or in the case of a thumb the proximal phalanx, of:
(a) in the case of a person with 5 fingers (including thumb) on one hand, any 3 of those fingers; *or*
(b) in the case of a person with only 4 such any 2 of those fingers; or
(c) in the case of a person with less than 4 such fingers, any one of those fingers, or, as the case may be, the one remaining finger (Vibration White Finger)

(a) The use of hand-held chain saws in forestry; *or*

(b) the use of hand-held rotary tools in grinding or in the sanding or polishing of metal, or the holding of material being ground, or metal being sanded or polished by rotary tools; *or*

(c) the use of hand-held percussive metal-working tools, or the holding of metal being worked upon by percussive tools, in riveting, caulking, chipping, hammering, fettling or swaging; *or*

(d) the use of hand-held powered percussive drills or hand-held powered percussive hammers in mining, quarrying, demolition, or on roads or footpaths, including road construction; *or*

(e) the holding of material being worked upon by pounding machines in shoe manufacture.

A12 Carpal tunnel syndrome

The use of hand-held powered tools whose internal parts vibrate so as to transmit that

Prescribed disease or injury   *Occupation*

                                                  vibration to the hand, but excluding those
                                                  which are solely powered by hand.

B Conditions due to biological agents

B1 Anthrax   Contact with animals infected with
                              anthrax or the handling (including the
                              loading or unloading or transport) of
                              animal products or residues.

B2 Glanders   Contact with equine animals or their
                              carcases

B3 Infection by leptospira   *(a)* Work in places which are, or are
                              liable to be, infested by rats, field mice or
                              voles, or other small mammals; *or*
                                   (b) work at dog kennels or the care or
                              handling of dogs; *or*
                                   (c) contact with bovine animals or pigs
                              or their meat products

B4 Ankylostomiasis   Work in or about a mine

B5 Tuberculosis   Contact with a source of tuberculous
                              infection

B6 Extrinsic allergic alveolitis   Exposure to moulds or fungal spores or
(including farmer's lung)   heterologous proteins by reason of
                              employment in:
                                   (a) agriculture, horticulture, forestry,
                              cultivation of edible fungi or malt-working; *or*
                                   (b) loading or unloading or handling in
                              storage mouldy vegetable matter or edible
                              fungi; *or*
                                   (c) caring for or handling birds; *or*
                                   (d) handling bagasse

B7 Infection by organisms of the genus   Contact with:
brucella   *(a)* animals infected by brucella, or
                              their carcasses or parts thereof, or their
                              untreated products; *or*
                                   (b) laboratory specimens or vaccines of,
                              or containing, brucella

B8 Viral hepatitis   Close and frequent contact with:
                                   (a) human blood or human blood
                              products; *or*
                                   (b) a source or viral hepatitis

B9 Infection by *Streptococcus suis*   Contact with pigs infected by
                              Streptococcus suis, or with the carcases,
                              products or residues of pigs so infected

B10 (a) Avian chlamydiosis   Contact with birds infected with
                              chlamydia psittaci, or with the remains or
                              untreated products of such birds

B10 (b) Ovine chlamydiosis   Contact with sheep infected with
                              chlamydia psittaci, or with the remains or
                              untreated products of such sheep

Prescribed disease or injury	*Occupation*
B11 Q fever	Contact with animals, their remains or their untreated products
B12 Orf	Contact with sheep, goats or with the carcases of sheep or goats
B13 Hydatidosis	Contact with dogs

C Conditions due to chemical agents

C1 Poisoning by lead or a compound of lead	The use or handling of, or exposure to the fumes, dust or vapour of, lead or a compound of lead, or a substance containing lead
C2 Poisoning by manganese or a compound of manganese	The use or handling of, or exposure to the fumes, dust or vapour of, manganese or a compound of manganese, or a substance containing manganese
C3 Poisoning by phosphorus or an inorganic compound of phosphorus or poisoning due to the anti-cholinesterase or pseudo anti-cholinesterase action of organic phosphorus compounds	The use or handling of, or exposure to the fumes, dust or vapour of, phosphorus or a compound of phosphorus, or a substance containing phosphorus
C4 Poisoning by arsenic or a compound of arsenic	The use or handling of, or exposure to the fumes, dust or vapour of, arsenic or a compound of arsenic, or a substance containing arsenic
C5 Poisoning by mercury or a compound of mercury	The use or handling of, or exposure to the fumes, dust or vapour of, mercury or a compound of mercury, or a substance containing mercury
C6 Poisoning by carbon bisulphide	The use or handling of, or exposure to the fumes or vapour of, carbon bisulphide, or a substance containing carbon bisulphide
C7 Poisoning by benzene or a homologue of benzene	The use or handling of, or exposure to the fumes of, or vapour containing benzene or any of its homologues
C8 Poisoning by a nitro- or amino- or chloro-derivative of benzene or of a homologue of benzene, or poisoning by nitrochlorbenzene	The use or handling of, or exposure to the fumes of, or vapour containing, a nitro- or amino- or chloro-derivative of benzene, or of a homologue of benzene, or nitrochlorbenzene
C9 Poisoning by dinitrophenol or a homologue of dinitrophenol or by substituted dinitrophenols or by the salts of such substances	The use or handling of, or exposure to the fumes of, or vapour containing, dinitrophenol or a homologue or substituted dinitrophenols or the salts of such substances
C10 Poisoning by tetrachloroethane	The use or handling of, or exposure to the fumes of, or vapour containing, tetrachloroethane

Prescribed disease or injury	Occupation
C11 Poisoning by diethylene dioxide (dioxan)	The use or handling of, or exposure to the fumes of, or vapour containing, diethylene dioxide (dioxan)
C12 Poisoning by methyl bromide	The use or handling of, or exposure to the fumes of, or vapour containing methyl bromide
C13 Poisoning by chlorinated naphthalene	The use or handling of, or exposure to the fumes of, or dust or vapour containing, chlorinated naphthalene
C14 Poisoning by nickel carbonyl	Exposure to nickel carbonyl gas
C15 Poisoning by oxides of nitrogen	Exposure to oxides of nitrogen
C16 Poisoning by Gonioma kamassi (African boxwood)	The manipulation of Gonioma kamassi or any process in or incidental to the manufacture of articles therefrom
C17 Poisoning by beryllium or a compound of beryllium	The use or handling of, or exposure to the fumes, dust or vapour of, beryllium or a compound of beryllium, or a substance containing beryllium
C18 Poisoning by cadmium	Exposure to cadmium dust or fumes
C19 Poisoning by acrylamide monomer	The use or handling of, or exposure to, acrylamide monomer
C20 Dystrophy of the cornea (including ulceration of the corneal surface) of the eye	*(a)* The use or handling of, or exposure to, arsenic, tar, pitch, bitumen, mineral oil (including paraffin), soot or any compound, product or residue of any of these substances, except quinone or hydroquinone; *or* *(b)* exposure to quinone or hydroquinone during their manufacture
C21 (a) Localised new growth of the skin, papillomatous or keratotic (b) squamous-celled carcinoma of the skin	The use or handing of, or exposure to, arsenic, tar, pitch, bitumen, mineral oil (including paraffin), soot or any compound, product or residue of any of these substances, except quinone or hydroquinone
C22 (a) Carcinoma of the mucous membrane of the nose or associated air sinuses (b) primary carcinoma of a bronchus or of a lung	Work in a factory where nickel is produced by decomposition of a gaseous nickel compound which necessitates working in or about a building or buildings where that process or any other industrial process ancillary or incidental thereto is carried on

Prescribed disease or injury

Occupation

C23 Primary neoplasm (including papilloma carcinoma-in-situ and invasive carcinoma) of the epithelial lining of the urinary tract (renal pelvis, ureter, bladder and urethra)

(a) Work in a building in which any of the following substances is produced for commercial purposes:

(i) alpha-naphthylamine, beta-naphthylamine or methylene-bis-orthochloroaniline

(ii) diphenyl substituted by at least one nitro or primary amino group or by at least one nitro and primary (including benzidine);

(iii) any of the substances mentioned in sub-paragraph (ii) above if further ring substituted by halogeno, methyl or ethoxy groups, but not by other groups;

(iv) the salts of any of the substances entioned in sub-paragraphs (i) to (iii);

(v) auramine or magenta; *or*

(b) the use or handling of any of the substances mentioned in sub-paragraph (a) (i) to (iv), or work in such a process in which any such substance is used, handled or liberated; *or*

(c) the maintenance or cleaning of any plant or machinery used in any such process as is mentioned in sub-paragraph (b), or the cleaning of clothing used in any such building as is mentioned in sub-paragraph (a) if such clothing is cleansed within the works of which the building forms a part or in a laundry maintained and used solely in connection with such works; *or*

(d) exposure to coal tar pitch volatiles produced in aluminium smelting involving the Soderberg process (that is to say the method of producing aluminium by electrolysis in which the anode consists of a paste of petroleum coke and mineral oil which is baked in situ).

C24 *(a)* Angiosarcoma of the liver

(a) Work in or about machinery or apparatus used for the polymerization of vinyl chloride monomer, a process which, for the purposes of this provision, comprises all operations up to and including the drying of the slurry produced by the polymerisation and the packaging of the dried product; *or*

(b) Osteolysis of the terminal phalanges of the fingers

(b) work in a building or structure in which any part of that process takes place.

(c) Non-cirrhotic portal fibrosis

Prescribed disease or injury	*Occupation*
C25 Occupational vitiligo	The use or handling of, or exposure to, para-tertiary-butylphenol, para-tertiary-butylcatechol, para-amyl-phenol, hydroquinone or the monobenzyl or monobutyl ether of hydroquinone
C26 Damage to the liver or kidneys due to exposure to carbon tetrachloride	The use of or handling of, or exposure to the fumes of, or vapour containing carbon tetrachloride
C27 Damage to the liver or kidneys due to exposure to trichlormethane (chloroform)	The use of or handling of, or exposure to the fumes of, or vapour containing trichlormethane (chloroform)
C28 Central nervous system dysfunction and associated gastro-intestinal disorders due to exposure to chloromethane (methyl chloride)	The use of or handling of, or exposure to the fumes of, or vapour containing chloromethane (methyl chloride)
C29 Peripheral neuropathy due to exposure to n-hexane or methyl n-butyl ketone	The use of or handling of, or exposure to the fumes of, or vapour containing, n-hexane or methyl n-butyl ketone
C30 Chrome dermatitis, or ulceration of the mucous membranes or the epidermis, resulting from exposure to chromic acid, chromates or bi-chromates	The use or handling of, or exposure to, chromic acid, chromates or bi-chromates.

D Miscellaneous conditions

D1 Pneumoconiosis	*[Occupations specified in reg 2(b) of, and Part II of Schedule 1 to, the Social Security (Industrial Injuries) (Prescribed Diseases) Regulations 1985 which are too numerous to set out here. They are all occupations involving exposure to dust, such as mining, quarrying, sand blasting, grinding, making china or earthenware, boiler-sealing and other work involving the use of stone, asbestos, etc.]*
D2 Byssinosis	Work in any room where any process up to and including the weaving process is performed in a factory in which the spinning or manipulation of raw or waste cotton or of flax, or the weaving of cotton or flax, is carried on
D3 Diffuse mesothelioma (primary neoplasm of the mesothelium of the pleura or of the pericardium or of the peritoneum)	Exposure to asbestos, asbestos dust or any admixture of asbestos at a level above that commonly found in the environment at large.

D4 Allergic rhinitis which is due to exposure to any of the following agents:
   (a) isocyanates
   (b) platinum salts
	Exposure to any of the agents set out in column 1 of this paragraph

Prescribed disease or injury   Occupation

(c) fumes or dusts arising from the
manufacture, transport or use of hardening
agents (including epoxy resin curing
agents) based on phthalic anhydride,
tetrachlorophthalic anhydride, trimellitic
anhydride or triethylenetetramine

(d) fumes arising from the use of rosin
as a soldering flux

(e) proteolytic enzymes

(f) animals including insects and other
anthropods used for the purposes of
research or education or in laboratories

(g) dusts arising from the sowing,
cultivation, harvesting, drying, handling,
milling, transport or storage of barley,
oats, rye, wheat or maize, or the handling,
milling, transport or storage of meal or
flour made therefrom

(h) antibiotics

(i) cimetidine

(j) wood dust

(k) ispaghula

(l) castor bean dust

(m) ipecacuanha

(n) azodice-bonamide

(o) animals including insects and other
anthropods or their larval forms, used for
the purposes of pest control or fruit
cultivation, or the larval forms of animals
used for the purposes of research,
education or in laboratories;

(p) glutaraldehyde;

(q) persulphate salts or henna;

(r) crustaceans or fish or products
arising from these in the food processing
industry;

(s) reactive dyes;

(t) soya bean;

(u) tea dust;

(v) green coffee bean dust;

(w) fumes from stainless steel welding;

D5 Non-infective dermatitis of external   Exposure to dust, liquid or vapour or any
origin excluding dermatitis due to ionising other external agent except chromic acid,
particles or electro-magnetic   chromates or bi-chromates capable of
radiant heat)   irritating the skin (including friction or
                                             heat but excluding excluding ionising
                                             particles or electromagnetic radiations
                                             other than radiant heat)

Prescribed disease or injury

D6 Carcinoma of the nasal cavity or associated air sinuses (nasal carcinoma)

Occupation

(a) Attendance for work in or about a building where wooden goods are

(b) attendance for work in a building used for the manufacture of footwear or components of footwear made wholly or partly of leather or fibre board; or

(c) attendance for work at a place used wholly or mainly for the repair of footwear made wholly or partly of leather or fibre board

D7 Asthma which is due to exposure to any of the following agents:

Exposure to any of the agents set out in column 1 of this paragraph

(a) isocyanates

(b) platinum salts

(c) fumes or dusts arising from the manufacture, transport or use of hardening agents (including epoxy resin curing agents) based on phthalic anhydride, tetrachlorophthalic anhydride, trimellitic anhydride or triethylenetetramine

(d) fumes arising from the use of rosin as a soldering flux

(e) proteolytic enzymes

(f) animals including insects and other anthropods used for the purposes of research or education or in laboratories

(g) dusts arising from the sowing, cultivation, harvesting, drying, handling, milling, transport or storage of barley, oats, rye, wheat or maize, or the handling, milling, transport or storage of meal or flour made therefrom

(h) antibiotics

(i) cimetidine

(j) wood dust

(k) ispaghula

(l) castor bean dust

(m) ipecacuanha

(n) azodicarbonamide

(o) animals including insects and other anthropods or their larval forms, used for the purposes of pest control or fruit cultivation, or the larval forms of animals used for the purposes of research, education or in laboratories;

(p) glutaraldehyde;

(q) persulphate salts or henna;

Prescribed disease or injury   *Occupation*

    (r) crustaceans or fish or products
arising from these in the food processing
industry;

    (s) reactive dyes;

    (t) soya bean;

    (u) tea dust;

    (v) green coffee bean dust;

    (w) fumes from stainless steel welding;

    (x) any other sensitising agent
(occupational asthma)

D8 Primary carcinoma of the lung where
there is accompanying evidence of
one or both of the following:

    (a) asbestosis;

    (b) unilateral or bilateral diffuse
pleural thickening extending to a thickness
of 5mm or more at any point within the
area affected as measured by a plain chest
radiograph (not being a computerised
tomography scan or other form of
imaging) which –

    i) in the case of unilateral diffuse pleural
thickening, covers 50% or more of the
area of the chest wall of the lung
affected; or

    ii) in the case of bilateral diffuse pleural
thickening, covers 25% or more of the
combined area of the chest wall of
both lungs.

    (a) The working or handling of asbestos;
or any admixture of asbestos; or

    (b) the manufacture or repair of
asbestos textiles or other articles containing
or composed of asbestos; or

    (c) the cleaning of any machinery or
plant used in any of the foregoing
operations and of any chambers, fixtures
and appliances for the collection of
asbestos dust; or

    (d) substantial exposure to the dust
arising from any of the foregoing
operations

D9 Unilateral or bilateral diffuse pleural
thickening extending to a thickness of
5mm or more at any point within the
area affected as measured by a plain chest
radiograph (not being a computerised
tomography scan or other form of
imaging) which –

    i) in the case of unilateral diffuse
pleural thickening, covers 50% or
more of the area of the chest wall of
the lung affected; or

    ii) in the case of bilateral diffuse pleural
thickening, covers 25% or more of the
combined area of the chest wall of
both lungs.

    (a) the working or handling of asbestos
or any admixture of asbestos; or

    (b) the manufacture or repair of
asbestos textile or other articles containing
or composed of asbestos; or

    (c) the cleaning of any machinery or
plant used in any of the foregoing
and appliances for the collection of
asbestos dust; or

    (d) substantial exposure to the dust
arising from any of the foregoing
operations

Prescribed disease or injury	*Occupation*
D10 Primary carcinoma of the lung	*(a)* work underground in a tin mine; or
	(b) exposure to bis(chloromethyl) ether produced during the manufacture of chloromethyl methyl ether; *or*
	(c) exposure to zinc chromate, calcium chromate or strontium chromate in their pure forms.
D11 Primary carcinoma of the lung where there is accompanying evidence of silicosis	Exposure to silica dust in the course of –
	(a) the manufacture of glass or pottery;
	(b) tunnelling in or quarrying sandstone or granite;
	(c) mining metal ores;
	(d) slate quarrying or the manufacture of artefacts from slate;
	(e) mining clay;
	(f) using silicous materials as abrasives;
	(g) cutting stone;
	(h) stone masonry; *or*
	(i) work in a foundry
D12 Except in the circumstances specified in regulation 2(d),	Exposure to coal dust by reason of working underground in a coal mine for a period of, or periods amounting in the aggregate to, at least 20 years (whether before or after 5 July 1948) and any such period or periods of incapacity while engaged in such an occupation
(a) chronic bronchitis; *or*	
(b) emphysema; or	
(c) both,	
where there is accompanying evidence of a forced expiratory volume in one second (measured from the position of maximum inspiration with the claimant making maximum effort) of –	
(i) at least one litre below the mean value predicted in accordance with Lung Function: Assessment and Application in Medicine, by JE Cotes, 5th Edition 1994 published at Oxford by Blackwell Scientific Publications Limited (ISBN 0-632-03926-9) for a person of the claimant's age, height and sex; *or*	
(ii) less than one litre.	

Appendix 9

Upper and lower earnings limits

Year	Lower earnings limit £	Upper earnings limit £
1975-76	11.00	69.00
1976-77	13.00	95.00
1977-78	15.00	105.00
1978-79	17.50	120.00
1979-80	19.50	135.00
1980-81	23.00	165.00
1981-82	27.00	200.00
1982-83	29.50	220.00
1983-84	32.50	235.00
1984-85	34.00	250.00
1985-86	35.50	265.00
1986-87	38.00	285.00
1987-88	39.00	295.00
1988-89	41.00	305.00
1989-90	43.00	325.00
1990-91	46.00	350.00
1991-92	52.00	390.00
1992-93	54.00	405.00
1993-94	56.00	420.00
1994-95	57.00	430.00
1995-96	58.00	440.00
1996-97	61.00	455.00
1997-98	62.00	465.00
1998-99	64.00	485.00
1999-2000	66.00	500.00

Appendix 10

· ·

The 'Helping you back to work' form (ES2)

The 'Helping You Back To Work' form will be used by your employment officer to draw up your jobseeker's agreement and to determine whether you satisfy the labour market conditions. These rules are covered in Chapter 15. The following provides some guidance as to why the questions on the form are asked and how they may be relevant to your claim for JSA.

1. Surname

2. Other names

3. Title Mr Mrs Miss Ms Other title

4. National Insurance (NI) number

Get this from payslips or papers from the Inland Revenue. Or get in touch with your Social Security office.

Do not delay your claim if you do not have a national insurance or have lost it.

5. Are you able to work?

No   Yes

6. Are you willing to work?

No   Yes

If you are not *willing* and *able* to work, your availability for work will be in doubt. You may be claiming JSA because you have been refused incapacity benefit (IB) or because the Benefits Agency has stopped paying IB or income support to you because you have failed the 'all work test'. If you have failed the all work test you are treated as being capable of work for JSA. If you are appealing against the decision that you are capable of working, the fact that you are claiming JSA should not be used against you. If you are not appealing, the fact that you have failed the all work test should be accepted by the employment officer (EO) as evidence that you are capable of work for JSA –

even if you have a physical or mental condition which may restrict the work you can do.

7. Are you looking only for a temporary or casual job?

This might be because you are starting another job soon, have been laid off, have been placed on short-time.

No

Yes   Please tell us why. And tell us how long you want the temporary or casual job to last.

You can get JSA if you are only looking for temporary work, but you must be looking for temporary work for an 'acceptable reason' (Employment Service Guidance) – for example while you are waiting to start another job, self employment, training or education (ie, you may be a student who is entitled to claim during vacations). You must be able to show that you have reasonable prospects of obtaining temporary work. If temporary jobs are not available in the location or in the type of work you are prepared to accept, your availability may be in doubt. You may be wanting temporary or casual work because you are working short time or laid off from your usual job. If you are on an 'approved' employment related full-time course (for people aged 25 or over), you will be required to be available for casual work during vacations.

8. What is your usual job?

If you do not have a usual job, write None.

If you have a usual occupation you may be allowed a permitted period for up to 13 weeks. The type of work you did before you became unemployed may be relevant to whether you have the skills and experience for the type of work you are looking for now.

9. What types of job are you looking for?

Please do not write Any. We need to know as much as possible about the work you are looking for. If you are not sure about the type of work you could do, or the type of work available, please ask us at your interview.

You will be asked to put down specific job titles, for example the Employment Service Guidance states that 'welding or labouring' would need further explanation. You must normally have the necessary skills, qualifications and experience (if they are required) for the type of work you are looking for, or your availability may be in doubt (unless your lack of experience, etc, is not seen as a barrier to getting the work). If you are given a permitted period you can restrict your jobsearch to your usual occupation. If you do not have a permitted period, you will be expected to consider jobs outside your usual occupation (if you have one) unless you can show that you have a reasonable prospect of finding work. As a general rule, the longer you remain unemployed, the fewer restrictions you are expected to place on the work you are looking for. If you place restrictions and there is a doubt about your availability you should be asked to sign the statement on page 15 of the form.

10. Do you have a disability or health problem which affects your day-to-day activities?

No   Yes

Have you ever had one?

No   Yes

11. Do you have a disability or health problem which affects the work you do?

No   Yes   Please tell us how it affects the work you can do.

If you have a disability or a health problem the EO will consider whether you are capable of doing the work of the type that you are looking for. If you have recently failed the 'all work test' and have been refused IB or income support (IS) or had IB or IS stopped you should be treated as capable of work for the purposes of JSA. You can place *any* restrictions on your availability (type of work, hours you work, location, etc which are related to your physical/mental condition so long as the restrictions are reasonable in the light of your condition – you do not have to show that you have a reasonable prospect of finding work. If you have any medical problems which may affect the work you can do it is important that you tell the Employment Service at the beginning of your claim. You can place restrictions on the rate of pay you are prepared to accept after the first six months of your claim if the restriction is related to your health problem or disability and you can also restrict the pay to at least the level of the minimum wage.

If your medical condition restricts your availability for work you may be referred to a disability employment adviser (DEA). This is not compulsory (unless you are issued a jobseeker's direction) but if you refuse to see a DEA when your EO advises it you may raise doubts about your availability for work.

If you have a health problem or disability you will generally have priority access to training schemes and employment programmes.

The information you give in Qs 10 and 11 may be relevant to deciding what steps are reasonable for you to take to actively seek work (see Qs 23 and 24 below).

12. Please tell us about any qualifications and work experience you have which will help you get a job.

We mean qualifications like degrees, GCSEs, O, A or AS levels, City and Guilds, NVQs, SVQs or GNVQs, National Diplomas. And work experience that may help you get the type of work you are looking for. For example joinery, building, foreign languages, computing, typing.

This information will be used to check whether you have the qualifications or experience required for the type of work you are looking for. Your answers may be relevant to deciding whether you should have a permitted period and its length. You may be expected to broaden your jobsearch (at the end of the permitted period if you have one) to include jobs for which you may have the relevant skills.

13. Please tell us about any abilities and interests which may help you get a job.

They could be things you do every day, outside interests or hobbies. You may, for example, be good at making things, organising, selling things, figures. Or you may have a good eye for detail, be very practical, be understanding and patient, be able to take care of people, be able to work as part of a team.

This information will be used when deciding on the type of work that you may be able to do, particularly at the end of a permitted period when you are expected to broaden your jobsearch. You may have a skill or interest but is it something you would like to use in a job or pursue as a career? When you answer this question, bear in mind that your answers may be used by the Employment Service to identify jobs you are expected to be available for. Your answers may be used to identify training. Be realistic about what you are willing to do.

14. Do you have a written summary of your skills, abilities and experience? This is sometimes called a CV.

No   Yes   Please bring this to your interview.

If you have a CV this will be kept with your records. It is not necessary that you have one or that you give a copy to the EO. Preparing (or updating a CV) can be counted as a step to actively seek work.

15. Can you start work as soon as you find a job?

No   Please tell us the reason. And tell us how soon after finding a job you could start work.

Yes

You must be able to start work immediately or

– at 24 hours notice if you provide a service.

– at 48 hours notice if you do voluntary work or look after a child or adult.

You must be able to start work immediately unless you come within one of the categories of people who can have 24 hours', 48 hours' or up to one week's notice (ie, people working part time) . If you cannot start work within the required timescale you may not be available for work. If you are a carer, you may be able to place restrictions on the hours you work, but you may also be asked to provide details of the care arrangements you would have in place when you are working.

16. What is the lowest wage you are willing to accept?

£   every hour/week/month/year

Tell us the amount before tax, National Insurance or anything else has been taken off. Do not include bonuses or overtime. If the amount you put does not give you a good chance of finding work, your allowance may be affected. You can discuss this at your interview.

It is important that you do not price yourself out of the labour market. You cannot be required to work for pay below the minimum wage – see p1:420. In addition you can restrict the rate of pay you are prepared to accept in the following circumstances:

1) during a permitted period (if you are given one), to the rate of pay in your usual occupation;
2) if you have a physical or mental condition and the restriction is reasonable in the light of your condition (ie, to meet the cost of a disability);
3) if you can show that you have a reasonable prospect of getting a job for the wage you require.

You cannot place any restrictions on pay after you have been unemployed for six months or more (unless the restriction is due to a physical or mental condition - subject to the minimum wage). At the end of a permitted period you may be expected to work at a lower wage than for your usual occupation, unless you have a reasonable prospect of finding work at the rate of pay you are willing to accept.

If the rate of pay is considered too high, the EO should tell you this at the interview. Your EO may not accept an answer such as 'the going rate for the job' – s/he may want you to be more specific. If you are notified of a job vacancy, the rate of pay is not of itself sufficient reason to refuse to apply for it.

17. Are you doing any education or training.

No   Yes

If you answer yes you will be asked to complete a 'student questionnaire' (form ES 567S). You will not get benefit if you are a student and your course is 'full time' (except for certain students during the summer vacation or people aged 25 and over who are attending a full-time 'approved' course). If your course is part-time, your answers to the student questionnaire will also be used to decide whether you are available for work.

18. Do you want to limit the days and hours you are available for work?

No   Please go to question 20 on the next page.

Yes

To qualify for JSA you must generally be willing and able to work at least 40 hours a week *and* be willing to work for less than 40 hours a week if required. There are, however, exceptions to this general rule:

1) subject to conditions you may be able to restrict the hours you are willing to work to at least 40 a week (ie, so that you are not required to work for less than 40);
2) you can restrict the maximum hours you are willing to work to less than 40 if the restriction is because you have a physical or mental condition or because you are a carer;
3) you are a short-time worker.

It is important that you answer this question carefully. You do not have to be available to work every day and/or at any time. The days and times that you are available to work will be set out in your jobseeker's agreement (see below). If you answer 'No', it may be difficult to then refuse a job on the grounds that the hours are unsuitable. Note that there are new rules about the number of hours you can be required to work –see p1:420.

19. What days and hours are you available for work?

	Earliest start time		Latest finish time		Most hours I can work	
Monday	am	pm	am	pm	☐
Tuesday	am	pm	am	pm	☐
Wednesday	am	pm	am	pm	☐
Thursday	am	pm	am	pm	☐
Friday	am	pm	am	pm	☐

Saturday am   pm   am   pm   ☐

Sunday am   pm   am   pm   ☐

Most hours I can work each week   ☐

You must be available for at least 40 hours a week – except in special circumstances. For example, if you have a health problem or disability, are looking after a child or adult.

Example

The **earliest** you can start in the morning is 7 am. The **latest** you can finish in the evening is 6 pm. But the **most hours** you could work between these times might be 8 hours.

You do not have to be available to work every day of the week, but if you do state a preferred pattern of working, the hours and days you are prepared to work must give you a reasonable prospect of getting a job (unless the pattern is due to a physical or mental condition). Your pattern of work (or 'pattern of availability') will be compared to that for jobs of the type, location and rate of pay you are looking for. The pattern will be recorded in your jobseeker's agreement.

You may want to be flexible on the days you work (ie, you may be willing to work any day of the week) but subject to a maximum of 40 hours for the week. It is important that you are realistic about the days and hours that you are prepared to work or you could be expected to apply for jobs which you do not consider suitable.

20. What town or areas are you looking for work in?

Please be specific. Do not put *Anywhere* unless you are willing to work anywhere. We need to know how far you are willing to travel to work.

You may want to define the areas in which you are prepared to work by name and/or stating the maximum daily travelling distance or time. In most cases, it is not reasonable to expect you to travel for more than one hour in each direction by public transport to get to work (refer to travelling time and good cause). You may be expected to travel for longer if you would not otherwise have a reasonable prospect of getting the work you are looking for. You do not have to move to find work, but it may be easier to place restrictions on the type of job you are looking for if you are prepared to move (ie, you are more likely to have a reasonable prospect of getting a job).

The EO will most likely refer to the information about local and national jobs stored on the Labour Market System (LMS). If you say you are prepared to move, remember that the LMS is connected to every JobCentre – your EO could notify you of a vacancy in the area you say you are willing to move to.

21. What vehicles are you licensed to drive?

None

Car

Public service vehicle (PSV) or Passenger carrying vehicle (PCV)

Motorbike

Heavy or large goods vehicle (HGV or LGV) Class

Other

This is relevant if it is connected to the type of work you are looking for. EOs are advised to check that you have the relevant licence for the type of work you are looking for.

22. Do you own your own transport?

No   Yes

You must have your own transport if it is required for the job you are looking for. If you do not have your own transport, the EO will consider the implications this has on you being able to get to work in the areas you are looking for work (see Q20), and whether it prevents you having a reasonable prospect of finding work because of your restrictions on the type of work you are looking for.

Your efforts to find work

23. Please tell us how you are going to look for work.

To find work I will

Contact employers to see if they have any vacancies.

Visit or phone the JobCentre to find and apply for jobs.

Look in newspapers to find and apply for jobs.

Register with employment agencies – other than the JobCentre.

Ask family, friends and people I have worked with before about possible jobs.

At your interview we will talk about your plans and what should be in your Jobseeker's Agreement. If you are not sure how you are going to look for work, we can talk about it at your interview.

A qualifying condition for JSA is that you taking steps to 'actively seek work'. The type and number of steps you are expected to take will vary from week to week – what is reasonable will depend on your circumstances. The steps you are expected to take will be recorded in your jobseeker's agreement and you will be asked about the steps you have taken when you sign on. Again, be realistic – do not promise more than you can achieve. The steps suggested in Q23 are not exhaustive – other steps may be appropriate or more reasonable in your case. Do not overestimate what you will be able to do to find work. In some circumstances you can be treated as actively seeking work (eg, when you are dealing with a domestic emergency).

24. Please tell us about any thing else you will do to find work and improve your chances of finding work.

> For example making a list of possible employers, making a written record of your skills, abilities and experience, finding out about other jobs you could do.

You may be required to take steps that not only help you to find work but which also improve your chances of being employed (ie, improve your 'employability'). You may be required to do more to find work at the end of your permitted period (if you have one) or the longer you remain unemployed. The steps you agree to take to find work should be set out in your jobseeker's agreement.

25. Please tell us if you need information about any of these things.

> Preparing a written summary of your skills, abilities and experience. This is sometimes called a CV.
>
> Writing letters to employers.
>
> Filling in application forms.
>
> Doing well at interviews.
>
> Talking to employers on the phone.
>
> Benefits for people in work, for example Family Credit.
>
> Advice on starting a small business.
>
> Advice on managing your job search if you have a health problem or disability.
>
> Use the box below to tell us about any other help you need to find work or improve your chances of finding work.

It is not compulsory to do any of these (unless you have been issued with a jobseeker's direction), but a willingness to pursue any of these will help you to satisfy the availability and actively seeking work requirements. You may be asked to consider these things at the end of a permitted period and/or at review interviews. An unreasonable refusal may create a doubt about your availability. If you need help with these activities, you may be referred to an ES adviser or an employment programme or training scheme.

Your declaration

I declare that to the best of my knowledge the information I have given on this form is true and complete.

I have read and understood the notes on this form.

26. Please sign and date this form

Signature   Date

27. Please tick this box if someone filled in this form for you   ☐

Appendix 11

Jobseeker's Agreement

Jobseeker's allowance will usually only be paid if you have entered into a
jobseeker's agreement. Until you have agreed the contents of the jobseeker's
agreement with your employment officer, your claim will not be passed to the
Benefits Agency.

Jobseeker's Allowance — *Jobseeker's* Agreement

0213/1

Jobseeker's Agreement

This Jobseeker's Agreement sets out
- when I can work
- the types of job I am willing to do
- what I am going to do to find work and increase my chances of finding work.

I, or an Employment Service adviser, can ask for it to be changed at any time. If we cannot agree about changing the Agreement, an independent adjudication officer will be asked to look at it.
If I am not satisfied with their decision, I can have it looked at by another adjudication officer. If I am still not satisfied, I can appeal to an independent tribunal.

Availability for work

I understand I must
- be available for work
- *(unless the limitation is for health reasons)* have a reasonable chance of getting work if I limit
  - the kind of work I am willing to do
  - the rate of pay I will accept
  - where I am willing to work
  - the hours I am willing to work
- be capable of work.

Permitted period

* I know I can limit myself to accepting work in my usual job and at my usual wages from   /   /   to   /   /
After this I will be interviewed about broadening my availability and job search.

Actively seeking work

I understand that I must actively seek work. I will be asked regularly to show what I have done to find work. I have been advised to keep a record of what I do to find work.

Jobseeker's Allowance

I understand my allowance may be affected if I
- do not do enough to find work
- am not available for work
- reduce my chances of getting work, or
- becomes incapable of work.

If this happens, I will be told and my case may be sent to an independent adjudication officer for a decision.
If I am not satisfied with the decision, I can appeal to an independent tribunal.
I understand that this is general information and not a full statement of the law.

* The adviser has read this Agreement to me.

Jobseeker's signature		Adviser's signature	

Date	/ /	Date	/ /

		Adviser's name	

		Telephone number	

(* Please delete as appropriate)

		TAM date	/ /

Name

The types of job I am looking for

SOC

I am willing and able to start work

◯ immediately   ◯ within 48 hours   ◯ Other

◯ within 24 hours   ◯ after giving a weeks notice

I want to limit the days and hours I am available for work

◯ No

◯ Yes

I am available for work these days and these hours

	Earliest start time	Latest finish time	Most hours I can work
Monday			
Tuesday			
Wednesday			
Thursday			
Friday			
Saturday			
Sunday			

Most hours I can work each week

Other agreed restrictions on my availability and/or agreed restrictions on types of work

NI number		Claim file/cycle	

What I will do to identify and apply for jobs

○ Write to at least ___ employers a week

○ Phone at least ___ employers a week

○ Visit at least ___ employers a week

○ Contact the Jobcentre at least ___ times a week

○ Ask family, friends and people I have worked with before

○ Look in these newspapers and trade papers

How often I will look

Other activities including any steps to improve my chances of finding a job

Our commitment to you

Jobseeker's Charter
If you are out of work and looking for a job, we want to offer you the best possible service.
Our Jobseeker's Charter sets out the standards of service we aim to provide. It also tells you how to complain if you are not satisfied. You can get a copy of the Charter from your Jobcentre.

What you can expect from us
You can expect us to
- wear a name badge and give our name when we answer the phone or write
- be polite, considerate, open and honest
- respect your privacy. In most cases we can provide a private room for sensitive interviews
- apologise if we get things wrong, explain what happened and put things right promptly
- deliver our services fairly and to the same high standards regardless of race, sex, disability or religion.

Your views
We regularly ask people what they think of our service and we publish the results. We welcome your comments at any time. If you want to comment or complain, ask for a copy of our leaflet.

Jobs
The vacancies we display should be up to date and available. We will not display vacancies which discriminate unlawfully because of race, sex, disability or religion. We encourage people of all ages to apply for the vacancies we display.

Information
We will give you advice about employment opportunities, training and setting up your own business.

Health problems and disabilities
If you have a health problem or disability which affects the type of work you can do we will tell you about the special help available.

Interviews
You will be asked to attend the office regularly. Each time we will
- talk about your search for work
- make sure your Agreement is up to date
- see what other help we can give you.

If possible you will be seen by the same person or someone from the same team.

Jobseeker's Allowance
If you are entitled to Jobseeker's Allowance we will aim to get the right money to you on time.

Other benefits
We will give you information about other benefits you may be entitled to.
You may get benefit even when you start work, for example, Family Credit.

More about our services
You will find more information about our services in the leaflet *Just the job*.

Appendix 12

Employment Service decisions

Some Employment Service decisions are made by front-line adjudication officers based in JobCentres (see Chapter 17). Most of the decisions concerning the labour market conditions are made by adjudication officers (AOs) based in sector offices.

Decisions to be made in JobCentres

- Refusal to enter into a jobseeker's direction
- Failure to attend an Employment Service interview
- Failure to provide a signed declaration
- Neglecting to avail of a place on a training scheme or employment programme*
- Failure to attend a training scheme or employment programme*
- Refusal of a place on a training scheme or employment programme*
- Failure to accept a place on a training scheme or employment programme*
- Giving up a place on a training scheme or employment programme*
- Failure to apply for a place on a training scheme or employment programme*
- Failure/refusal to apply for a place on a training scheme or employment programme*

* Unless connected with the New Deal for 18–24-year-olds, when the case will usually be passed to the sector AO.

Decisions to be made by sector adjudication officers

- Leaving employment voluntarily
- Losing employment through misconduct
- Whether a proposed jobseeker's agreement is reasonable
- Proposed variation of a jobseeker's agreement
- Termination of a jobseeker's agreement because of failure to comply with an AO's direction to vary the terms of the agreement
- Availability for work
- Availability because of absence from home
- Availability – studying for 16 hours or less

- Availability – not available within time limits
- Availability – restrictions on hours
- Availability – restriction on type of work
- Not regarded as available – studying for more than 16 hours
- Not regarded as available – prisoner on temporary release
- Not regarded as available – in receipt of maternity allowance
- Actively seeking employment
- Refusal of employment
- Neglect to avail of employment
- Loss of place on a training scheme through misconduct (except for 16/17-year-olds with a severe hardship direction. This is a Secretary of State's decision)
- Loss of a place on an employment programme through misconduct
- Refusal or failure to carry out a jobseeker's direction
- Discharge from HM forces

Decisions to be taken in regional adjudication offices

- Involvement in a stoppage of work due to a trade dispute
- Withdrawal of labour in connection with a trade dispute

Decision making and appeals

When the new 'decision making and appeals' (DMA) process is implemented from 18 October 1999, new titles will be given to adjudication officers at all levels as follows:

Existing adjudication terminology	*DMA terminology*
Sector adjudication officer (SAO)	Sector decision maker (SDM)
Sector adjudication manager (SAM)	DMA business manager (DBM)
Regional adjudication manager (RAM)	DMA regional manager (DRM) or
adjudication manager for Wales/	DMA manager for Wales/
Scotland	Scotland
Sector adjudication office	DMA sector office (DSO)
Regional adjudication team/office	DMA regional team/section/
	office (DRT)
Adjudication officers	Decision makers
Adjudication technical support manager	DMA technical support
(previously deputy RAM)	manager (DTSM)

Appendix 13

Abbreviations used in the notes

AC	Appeal Cases	IRS	Independent Review Service for the Social Fund
All ER	All England Reports		
Art(s)	Article(s)		
CA	Court of Appeal	JPR	Justice of the Peace Reports
CAO	Chief Adjudication Officer		
		para(s)	paragraph(s)
CMLR	Common Market Law Reports	QB	Queen's Bench Reports
CSBO	Chief Supplementary Benefit Officer	QBD	Queen's Bench Division
DC	Divisional Court	r	rule
ECJ	European Court of Justice	reg(s)	regulation(s)
ECR	European Court Reports	RSC	Rules of the Supreme Court
FLR	Family Law Reports		
HBRB	Housing Benefit Review Board	s(s)	Section(s)
		SBAT	Supplementary Benefit Appeal Tribunal
HC	High Court		
HL	House of Lords	SBC	Supplementary Benefits Commission
HLR	Housing Law Reports		
ICR	Industrial Cases Reports	Sch(s)	Schedule(s)
		SLT	Scots Law Times
		WLR	Weekly Law Reports

Acts of Parliament

AIA 1996	Asylum and Immigration Act 1996
CA 1989	Children Act 1989
CSA 1991	Child Support Act 1991
ECA 1972	European Communities Act 1972
ERA 1996	Employment Rights Act 1996
HSS&SSA Act 1983	Health and Social Services and Social Security Adjudication Act 1983
IA 1978	Interpretation Act 1978
ICTA 1988	Income and Corporation Taxes Act 1988
JSA 1995	Jobseekers Act 1995
LAA 1988	Legal Aid Act 1988
LGFA 1992	Local Government Finance Act 1992
MCA 1973	Matrimonial Causes Act 1973

NAA 1948	National Assistance Act 1948
NHSA 1977	National Health Service Act 1977
NHSCCA 1990	National Health Service and Community Care Act 1990
NHS(S)A 1978	National Health Service (Scotland) Act 1978
NIA 1965	National Insurance Act 1965
PA 1995	Pensions Act 1995
PACE 1984	Police and Criminal Evidence Act 1984
PSA 1993	Pension Schemes Act 1993
RHA 1984	Registered Homes Act 1984
SS(IFW)A 1994	Social Security (Incapacity for Work) Act 1994
SSA 1975	Social Security Act 1975
SSA 1979	Social Security Act 1979
SSA 1986	Social Security Act 1986
SSA 1990	Social Security Act 1990
SSA 1998	Social Security Act 1998
SSAA 1992	Social Security Administration Act 1992
SSA(F)A 1997	Social Security Administration (Fraud) Act 1997
SSC(TF)A 1999	Social Security Contributions (Transfer of Functions etc) Act 1999
SSCBA 1992	Social Security Contributions and Benefits Act 1992
SSPA 1975	Social Security Pensions Act 1975
SS(RB)A 1997	Social Security (Recovery of Benefits) Act 1997

European law

Secondary legislation is made under the Treaty of Rome 1957, the Single European Act and the Maastricht Treaty in the form of Regulations (EEC Reg) and Directives (EC Dir).

Regulations

Each set of regulations has a statutory instrument (SI) number and a date. You ask for them by giving their date and number.

CB Regs	The Child Benefit (General) Regulations 1976 No.965
CB(Amdt) Regs	The Child Benefit (General) Amendment Regulations 1987 No.35
CB(RPA) Regs	The Child Benefit (Residence and Persons Abroad) Regulations 1976 No.963
CB&SS(FAR) Regs	The Child Benefit and Social Security (Fixing and Adjustment of Rates) Regulations 1976 No.1267
CB&SS(FAR) Amdt Regs	The Child Benefit and Social Security (Fixing and Adjustment of Rates) (Amendment) Regulations 1998 No.1581
CC(DIS) Regs	The Community Charge (Deductions from Income Support) Regulations 1990 No.107
CS(AIAMA) Regs	The Child Support (Arrears, Interest and Adjustment of Maintenance Assessments) Regulations 1992 No.1816

CS(C&E) Regs	The Child Support (Collection and Enforcement) Regulations 1992 No.1989
CS(CEOFM) Regs	The Child Support (Collection and Enforcement of Other Forms of Maintenance) Regulations 1992 No.2643
CS(IED) Regs	The Child Support (Information, Evidence and Disclosure) Regulations 1992 No.1812
CS(MA) Regs	The Child Support (Miscellaneous Amendments) Regulations 1996 No.1945
CS(MAP) Regs	The Child Support (Maintenance Assessment Procedure) Regulations 1992 No.1813
CS(MASC) Regs	The Child Support (Maintenance Assessments and Special Cases) Regulations 1992 No.1815
CSAT(P) Regs	The Child Support Appeal Tribunals (Procedure) Regulations 1992 No.2641
CT(DD)O	The Council Tax (Discount Disregards) Order 1992 No.548
CT(DIS) Regs	The Council Tax (Deductions from Income Support) Regulations 1993 No.494
CTB Regs	The Council Tax Benefit (General) Regulations 1992 No.1814
CTB Amdt Regs	The Council Tax Benefit (General) (Amendment) Regulations 1997 No.1841
DWA Regs	The Disability Working Allowance (General) Regulations 1991 No.2887
DWA&IS Regs	The Disability Working Allowance and Income Support (General) Amendment Regulations 1995 No.482
EP(RUB&SB) Regs	The Employment Protection (Recoupment of Unemployment Benefit and Supplementary Benefit) Regulations 1977 No.674
F(DIS) Regs	The Fines (Deductions from Income Support) Regulations 1992 No.2182
FC Regs	The Family Credit (General) Regulations 1987 No.1973
HB Regs	The Housing Benefit (General) Regulations 1987 No.1971
HB(Amdt) Regs	The Housing Benefit (General) Amendment Regulations 1995 No.1644
HB(Amdt) Regs 1996	The Housing Benefit (General) Amendment Regulations 1996 No.965
HB(Amdt 2) Regs	The Housing Benefit (General) Amendment (No.2) Regulations 1997 No.1974
HB(ILA) Regs	The Housing Benefit (Information from Landlords and Agents) Regulations 1997 No.2436
HB(RO) Regs	The Housing Benefit (Recovery of Overpayments) Regulations 1997 No.2435
HB&CTB(Amdt) Regs	The Housing Benefit and Council Tax Benefit (General) Amendment Regulations 1997 No.852

I(EEA)O	Immigration (European Economic Area) Order 1994 No.1895
IRB&JSA(PA) Amdt Regs	The Income-related Benefits & Jobseeker's Allowance (Personal Allowances for Children and Young Persons) (Amendment) Regulations 1996 No.2545
IRBS(Amdt 2) Regs	The Income-related Benefits Schemes (Miscellaneous Amendments) (No.2) Regulations 1995 No.1339
IRBS&SF(MA) Regs	The Income-related Benefits Schemes and Social Fund (Miscellaneous Amendments) Regulations 1996 No.1944
IS Regs	The Income Support (General) Regulations 1987 No.1967
IS(AT) Regs	The Income Support (General) Amendment and Transitional Regulations 1995 No.2287
IS(JSACA) Regs	The Income Support (General) (Jobseeker's Allowance Consequential Amendments) Regulations 1996 No.206
IT(E) No.13 Regs	The Income Tax (Employment) (No.13) Regulations 1982 No.66
JSA Regs	The Jobseeker's Allowance Regulations 1996 No.207
JSA(TP) Regs	The Jobseeker's Allowance (Transitional Provisions) Regulations 1996 No.2657 (as amended)
MA(VSB) Regs	The Mobility Allowance (Vehicle Scheme Beneficiaries) Regulations 1997 No. 1229
NA(AR) Regs	The National Assistance (Assessment and Resources) Regulations 1992 No.2977
NHS(CDA) Regs	The National Health Service (Charges for Drugs and Appliances) Regulations 1980 No.1503
NHS(DC) Regs	The National Health Service (Dental Charges) Regulations 1989 No.394
NHS(GOS) Regs	The National Health Service (General Ophthalmic Services) Regulations 1986 No.975
NHS(OCP) Regs	The National Health Service (Optical Charges and Payments) Regulations 1997 No.818
NHS(TERC) Regs	The National Health Service (Travelling Expenses and Remission of Charges) Regulations 1988 No.551
RA(RPORE) Regs	The Residential Accommodation (Relevant Premises, Ordinary Residence and Exemptions) Regulations 1993 No.477
RCH Regs	The Residential Care Homes Regulations 1984 No.1345
RO(AF)O	The Rent Officers (Additional Functions) Order 1995 No.1642
RO(HBF)O	The Rent Officers (Housing Benefit Functions) Order 1997 No.1984
SF(App) Regs	The Social Fund (Applications) Regulations 1988 No.524
SF(AR) Regs	The Social Fund (Application for Review) Regulations 1988 No.34

SF(Misc) Regs	The Social Fund (Miscellaneous Provisions) Regulations 1990 No.1788
SF(RDB) Regs	The Social Fund (Recovery by Deductions from Benefits) Regulations 1988 No.35
SFCWP Regs	The Social Fund Cold Weather Payments (General) Regulations 1988 No.1724
SFM&FE Regs	The Social Fund Maternity and Funeral Expenses (General) Regulations 1987 No.481
SFWFP	The Social Fund Winter Fuel Payment Regulations 1998 No.19
SMP Regs	The Statutory Maternity Pay (General) Regulations 1986 No.1960
SMP(ME) Regs	The Statutory Maternity Pay (Medical Evidence) Regulations 1987 No.235
SMP(PAM) Regs	The Statutory Maternity Pay (Persons Abroad and Mariners) Regulations 1987 No.418
SS(AA) Regs	The Social Security (Attendance Allowance) Regulations 1991 No.2740
SS(Adj) Regs	The Social Security (Adjudication) Regulations 1995 No.1801
SS(BTWB) Regs	The Social Security (Back to Work Bonus) Regulations 1996 No.193
SS(BTWB) (No.2) Regs	The Social Security (Back to Work Bonus) (No.2) Regulations 1996 No.2570
SS(C1CCP)O	The Social Security (Class 1 Contributions – Contracted-out Percentages) Order 1992 No.795
SS(CMB) Regs	The Social Security (Child Maintenance Bonus) Regulations 1996 No.3195
SS(C&P) Regs	The Social Security (Claims and Payments) Regulations 1987 No.1968
SS(CatE) Regs	The Social Security (Categorisation of Earners) Regulations 1978 No.1689
SS(CE) Regs	The Social Security (Computation of Earnings) Regulations 1996 No.2745
SS(Con) Regs	The Social Security (Contributions) Regulations 1979 No.591 (as amended)
SS(Con) Amdt 4 Regs	The Social Security (Contributions) Amendment (No.4) Regulations 1992 No.668
SS(Cr) Regs	The Social Security (Credits) Regulations 1975 No.556
SS(DLA) Regs	The Social Security (Disability Living Allowance) Regulations 1991 No.2890
SS(EEEIIP) Regs	The Social Security (Employed Earners' Employment for Industrial Injuries Purposes) Regulations 1975 No.467
SS(EF) Regs	The Social Security (Earnings Factor) Regulations 1979 No.676
SS(EoFCoEF) Regs	The Social Security (Effect of Family Credit on Earnings Factors) Regulations 1995 No.2559

SS(GA) Regs	The Social Security (Guardian's Allowance) Regulations 1975 No.515
SS(GB) Regs	The Social Security (General Benefits) Regulations 1982 No.1408
SS(GRB) No.2 Regs	The Social Security (Graduated Retirement Benefit) (No.2) Regulations 1978 No.393
SS(HIP) Regs	The Social Security (Hospital In-Patients) Regulations 1975 No.555
SS(IB) Regs	The Social Security (Incapacity Benefit) Regulations 1994 No.2946
SS(IB)(CTAS) Regs	The Social Security (Incapacity Benefit) (Consequential and Transitional Amendments and Savings) Regulations 1995 No.829
SS(IB)T Regs	The Social Security (Incapacity Benefit) (Transitional) Regulations 1995 No.310
SS(IB-ID) Regs	The Social Security (Incapacity Benefit – Increases for Dependants) Reuglations 1994 No.2945
SS(ICA) Regs	The Social Security (Invalid Care Allowance) Regulations 1976 No.409
SS(IFW) Regs	The Social Security (Incapacity for Work) (General) Regulations 1995 No.311
SS(II&D)MP Regs	The Social Security (Industrial Injuries and Diseases) Miscellaneous Provisions Regulations 1986 No.1561
SS(IIPD) Regs	The Social Security (Industrial Injuries) (Prescribed Diseases) Regulations 1985 No.967
SS(IIRE) Regs	The Social Security (Industrial Injuries) (Regular Employment) Regulations 1990 No.256
SS(IoM)O	The Social Security (Isle of Man) Order 1977 No.2150
SS(J&G)O	The Social Security (Jersey and Guernsey) Order 1992 No.1735
SS(MA) Regs	The Social Security (Miscellaneous Amendments) Regulations 1998 No.563
SS(MAP) Regs	The Social Security (Maximum Additional Pension) Regulations 1978 No.949
SS(MatA) Regs	The Social Security (Maternity Allowance) Regulations 1987 No.416
SS(ME) Regs	The Social Security (Medical Evidence) Regulations 1976 No.615
SS(NIRA) Regs	The Social Security (Northern Ireland Reciprocal Arrangements) Regulations 1976 No.1003
SS(OB) Regs	The Social Security (Overlapping Benefits) Regulations 1979 No.597
SS(PAOR) Regs	The Social Security (Payments on account, Overpayments and Recovery) Regulations 1988 No.664
SS(PFA)MA Regs	The Social Security (Persons from Abroad) Miscellaneous Amendments Regulations 1996 No.30

SS(PN) Regs	The Social Security (Penalty Notices) Regulations 1997 No.2813
SS(RB) Regs	The Social Security (Recovery of Benefits) Regulations 1997 No.2205
SS(RB)App Regs	The Social Security (Recovery of Benefits) (Appeals) Regulations 1997 No.2237
SS(SDA) Regs	The Social Security (Severe Disablement Allowance) Regulations 1984 No.1303
SS(STB)(T) Regs	The Social Security (Short-Term Benefits) (Transitional) Regulations 1974 No.2192
SS(WB&RP) Regs	The Social Security (Widow's Benefit and Retirement Pensions) Regulations 1979 No.642
SS(WBRP&OB) (T) Regs	The Social Security (Widow's Benefit, Retirement Pensions and Other Benefits) (Transitional) Regulations 1979 No.643
SS&CS(D&A) Regs	The Social Security and Child Support (Decisions and Appeals) Regulations 1999 Draft
SSA(F)AO No.1	The Social Security Administration (Fraud) Act 1997 (Commencement No.1) Order 1997 No.1577
SSA(F)AO No.5	The Social Security Administration (Fraud) Act 1997 (Commencement No.5) Order 1997 No.2766
SSB(Dep) Regs	The Social Security Benefit (Dependency) Regulations 1977 No.343
SSB(MW&WSP) Regs	The Social Security (Benefit) (Married Women and Widows' Special Provisions) Regulations 1974 No.2010
SSB(PA) Regs	The Social Security Benefit (Persons Abroad) Regulations 1975 No.563
SSB(PRT) Regs	The Social Security Benefit (Persons Residing Together) Regulations 1977 No.956
SSBU(No.2)O 1991	The Social Security Benefits Up-rating (No.2) Order 1991 No.2910
SSBUO 1999	The Social Security Benefits Up-rating Order 1999 No.264
SSCP Regs	The Social Security Commissioners Procedure Regulations 1987 No.214
SSFA(PM) Regs	The Social Security and Family Allowances (Polygamous Marriages) Regulations 1975 No.561
SSP(HR) Regs	The Social Security Pensions (Home Responsibilities) Regulations 1994 No.704
SSP Regs	The Statutory Sick Pay (General) Regulations 1982 No.894
SSP(MAPA) Regs	The Statutory Sick Pay (Mariners, Airmen and Persons Abroad) Regulations 1982 No.1349
SSREFO	The Social Security Revaluation of Earnings Factor Order 1997 No.1117
WF Regs	The Welfare Foods Regulations 1996 No.1434

Rules

ETU Scheme	The Earnings Top-up Scheme 1996
ETU(A&P) Rules	The Earnings Top-up (Applications and Payments) Rules 1996
ETU(A) Rules	The Earnings Top-up (Assessment) Rules 1996

Other information

See Appendix 3 for fuller details of the following publications.

Advice Notes	Social Fund Inspectors' Advice Notes.
AOG	The *Adjudication Officers' Guide*.
CSAG	The *Child Support Adjudication Guide*.
CSRCG	The *Child Support Requirement to Co-operate Guide*.
CWPH	The *Social Fund Cold Weather Payments Handbook*.

Employment Service Guidance

ESG – I vol	Interventions volume
ESG – LOA vol	Local Office Adjudication volume
ESG – IP vol	Interviewing Policy volume
ESG – PK vol	Product Knowledge volume
ESG – 16/17 vol	16/17-year-olds
ESG – NJI vol	New Jobseeker's Interview volume

GM	The *Housing Benefit and Council Tax Benefit Guidance Manual*.
HC Handbook	*IS for Homeless Customers, Hostels, Residential Care and Nursing Homes*.
IS Guide	This is a largely procedural guide to the implementation of income support, which is issued to adjudication officers/DSS staff.
SF Dir/SFI Dir	Direction(s) on the discretionary social fund. They are printed in the *Social Fund Guide* and Mesher Wood.
SFG	The *Social Fund Guide*. The latest edition issued in February 1999, was made available too late for references to be included in this *Handbook*. It is available from Corporate Document Services, Savile House, Trinity Arcade, Leeds LS1 6QW.

References like CIS/142/1990 and R(SB) 3/89 are references to commissioners' decisions (see p2:642).

Index

Because the Handbook is divided into separate sections covering the different benefits, many entries in the index have several references, each to a different section. Where this occurs, we use the following abbreviations to show which benefit each reference relates to:

(AA)	Attendance allowance	(C-JSA)	Contribution-based jobseeker's allowance
(CTB)	Council tax benefit		
(DLA)	Disability living allowance	(I-JSA)	Income-based jobseeker's allowance
(DPTC)	Disabled person's tax credit		
(DWA)	Disability working allowance	(JSA)	Jobseeker's allowance
(ETU)	Earnings top-up	(MA)	Maternity allowance
(FC)	Family credit	(SDA)	Severe disablement allowance
(HB)	Housing benefit	(SF)	Social fund
(IB)	Incapacity benefit	(SMP)	Statutory maternity pay
(ICA)	Invalid care allowance	(SSP)	Statutory sick pay
(IS)	Income support	(WFTC)	Working families tax credit

Entries against the bold headings direct you to the general information on the subject, or where the subject is covered most fully. Sub-entries are listed alphabetically and direct you to specific aspects of the subject.

change of circumstances 1:263
claiming for others 1:259
claims 1:259, 261
complaints 1:263
date of claim 1:260
delays 1:263
effect of stay in hospital 2:163
entitlement to other benefits 1:264
fraud 1:263
hospital inpatient 2:163
imprisonment 1:258
increases for dependants 2:110
information to support claim 1:260
interchange of claims 2:487
late claims 1:262
missing parent 1:257
overlapping benefits 2:495
overpayments 1:263
payment 1:262
payment abroad 2:243
persons from abroad 2:233
prisoners 2:184
qualifying children 1:256
reviews – changes under Social Security
    Act 1998 2:582
tax 1:264
treated as entitled to child benefit 1:256
treatment as income
    (FC/DWA/ETU/HB/CTB) 2:407
    (IS/I-JSA) 2:405
who can claim 1:255
who should claim 1:260
guidance
DLA mobility component 1:166
guided learning
definition 2:135

H

habitual residence test
definition 2:235
(IS) 2:234
persons from abroad
    (IS) 2:208
refugees 2:216
repeated benefit claims 2:237
halls of residence
(HB) 2:144
hardship
avoiding student rent deduction
    (HB) 2:146
crisis loans 1:340
rent restrictions
    (HB) 1:560
see also: severe hardship
hardship payments 1:425–24
16/17-year-olds 1:344
definition of hardship
    (JSA) 1:428

duration of C-JSA 1:279
entitlement to other benefits 1:435
hardship statement 1:434
jobseeker's agreement referred to AO
    (JSA) 1:319
when payments can be made 1:429
who can claim 1:426
health and safety
working hours 1:420
health benefits 1:613
16/17-year-olds 2:153
capital 1:622
low-income certificates 1:623
requirements 1:622
health care equipment 1:624
helping you back to work form
(JSA) 1:359
higher pensioner premium
earnings disregards 2:400
(IS/I-JSA/HB/CTB) 2:327
New Deal education and training option
    discretionary fund 2:65
qualifying benefits
    (IS/I-JSA/HB/CTB) 2:325, 328
qualifying for DWA 1:476
temporary absence from GB
    (IS) 2:245
hire purchase agreement
(HB) 1:511
to buy home
    (HB/I-JSA) 2:341
holiday pay
crisis loans for unpaid holidays 1:672
on leaving work
    (HB/CTB) 2:395
    (IS/I-JSA) 2:393
treatment as capital 2:447
treatment as earnings
    means-tested benefits 2:388
    non-means-tested benefits 2:368
holidays
actively seeking work rule
    (JSA) 1:311, 313
available for work rule
    (JSA) 1:306, 314
for carer
    (ICA) 1:88
holiday abroad
    (JSA) 1:306, 311, 314
New Deal subsidised employment
    option 2:58
treated as full-time work 2:10
while on New deal for 18/24-year-olds
    2:56
home
treatment as capital 2:448
treatment of relative's home 2:450

ORDER FORM: for more copies of this or other CPAG handbooks

- **WELFARE BENEFITS HANDBOOK**, 1999/2000 edn

April 1999   1 901698 16 5   £20.00
                                                                                    (2 vols)

(£5.00 the set for individual benefits claimants – direct from CPAG)

- **CHILD SUPPORT HANDBOOK**, 1999/2000 edn

Fully revised and updated annually to tell you all you need to know about the child support scheme.

'The definitive guide' – THE ADVISER
'It is difficult to recommend this book too highly' – FAMILY LAW

June 1999   1 901698 17 3   £12.95

(£3.50 for benefit claimants – direct from CPAG)

- **FUEL RIGHTS HANDBOOK**, 11th edn

This standard practical guide to the rights of gas and electricity consumers is essential for any adviser helping clients cope with fuel bills, debt and related problems with fuel supply.

'The presence of the Fuel Right Handbook on an adviser's bookshelf is imperative...buy this book' – ROOF

April 1999   1 901698 11 4   £10.95

- **RIGHTS GUIDE FOR HOME OWNERS**, 12th edn

The most up-to-date and reliable guide to the financial rights of home owners. It includes coverage of housing law in England, Wales and Scotland, as well as social security issues.

'Explains very lucidly what someone having trouble repaying the mortgage can do' – THE GUARDIAN

November 1998   Publ.CPAG/Shelter   1 901698 12 2   £9.95

- -

ORDER FORM – payment with order

_____ Welfare Benefits Handbook @ £20.00 (2 vols)   £ _____

_____ Child Support Handbook (June 1999) @ £12.95 each   £ _____

_____ Fuel Rights Handbook @ £10.95 each   £ _____

_____ Rights Guide for Home Owners @ £9.95 each   £ _____

PRICES INCLUDE POSTAGE & PACKING   Total: £ _____

CPAG's Welfare Benefits CD-ROM: please send me a free trial disk (Oct 1999) – YES / NO

I enclose a cheque/PO for £_____ payable to CPAG

Name _____

Organisation (if relevant) _____ Tel no _____

Address _____

_____ Postcode _____

Return this form to CPAG, 94 White Lion Street, London N1 9PF, or DX 36608 FINSBURY